Atma Vidya

Glossary Esoteric

Gladiolus Publishing

To order additional copies of this book, contact:
Xlibris
844-714-8691
www.Xlibris.com
Orders@Xlibris.com
847283

INTRODUCTION

Dear reader, this project has been titled "Atma Vidya". Which has been defined: "Knowledge of the self or the Spirit". 'The supreme form of spiritual knowledge'. Quoted in the Theosophical Glossary; H. P. Blavatsky. "Truly Spiritual and Divine Wisdom (Sanskrit); of the Esoteric Dictionary, IBIS Editions. "Diccionario Enciclopedico, Esoterico y Gnostico"; J.R. Claudio. The Concice Oxford Dictionary of The Christian Church, Edited by E. A. Livingstone.

This project is dedicated to anyone who researches esotericism. Esotericism is a piece of wisdom that studies the secrets of the physical and psychic, mental and spiritual species. In the West one can cite the Kabbalah; in the East, mysticism, magic, and yoga philosophy, which has spread more in India among the Chela's; with the name of seventh "Darsana". Mystic: it comes from the Greek voice "mystics". In ancient times the Mystics were the ones admitted into the ancient Mysteries; in our time, they are those who practice mysticism and profess mystical, transcendental ideas, etc. Mysticism brings us closer to the great realities, the significant mysteries of life and death. Mysticism helps us develop the eyes of the soul. Gnosticism (Greek) Proper means knowledge; it is a philosophical-Mystical doctrine; which flourished in the first three centuries of the Christian era. This spiritual and sacred knowledge, the Gupta -vidya of the Indians [Occult or Esoteric Science], could only be achieved through the Initiation into the Spiritual Mysteries, of which they were a representation of the "Ceremonial Mysteries".

The vision of this project consists; in that while the word searches are being done; the people who are engaged in studying this venerated sapience; may acquire familiarity and creep with such words; in this way; they will have the benefit of expanding, or acquiring, more spiritual knowledge.

Most of the material used for these exercises was chosen from literature of esoteric, mystical, and Gnostic doctrines, aspects of ancient Christianity as well as Symbolism of various terms or expressions of various disciplines. When you search for words in the different exercises, you will notice that there are many words of two, or more letters, which serve as allegory; for perceptive or tactful concepts; for example: EL, RA, BA, etc. The enchanting of these terms can do a lot of good for those who appreciate the disciplines. It is relied on that any person who tries to make these puns does it for the love of these engaging sciences. The central features of these systems can be employed for a personal gain of positive wisdom; jointly; these words have meaning to express the abstract, mysterious, heavenly; for example: Light, Kingdom, Love, Life, God, Evil, Charity, Beauty, Hell, etc., however, given the ambiguity of these words, the clarification is made to the reader; that the scope of meaning is in a strictly esoteric context. Because esoteric words are being used for a pun; no relevant scores have been used.

It is intended that people may spend many hours of entertainment with these exercises; and at the same time, achieve their refined needs; expanding their vocabulary, or just having an enjoyable time doing the puns. From combo designations only the initial term has been chosen for the games, the following phrase can be found completed in the glossary. Parallel to this book we have published a glossary where the reader can reinforce their knowledge about these mysterious sciences.

We would like to thank all the people who in one way or another supported this project.

ESOTERIC KNOWLEDGE

A word is a sound, a set of ideas, a term. The etymology of the word comes from the Latin parabola. The word is a lexical unit formed by voices or a set of pronounced sounds, which are joined to one or several knowledges, which have a fixed grammatical condition. Similarly, a word also symbolizes a design, by means of qualities or signals of the voices.

The word 'Esoteric' comes from the Greek 'esoterisms' which relates to instruction that was committed exclusively for students educated based on the philosophical establishments of prehistory. This term is a specialty that is demanding to cover, as accepting its nature is complex to understand. Esoteric knowledge is decisive; a precise degree of initiation must be achieved. This hidden wisdom, for example, is historical: it is not based on scientific methods and their aspirations cannot be verified by practical indications.

The word 'knowledge' refers to the action and effect of knowing. Esotericism is used to relate the set of knowledge, doctrines, teachings, practices, rites, techniques, or traditions of a stream of thoughts that uses symbols, secrets, etc. There are two types of knowledge: exoteric and esoteric. "Exoterica" comes from the Greek exotericism and refers to the teaching that in the ancient Greek schools was transmitted to the public without restrictions, because it is dialectical, probable, and credible teaching. Esoterism comes from a Greek word (esotericism) meaning "from within, inside, intimate"; attached to the suffix "ism" which is a generic term used to refer to the set of knowledge.

In times past, only small numbers of humanity were devoted to the teaching of esotericism, which were despised and satirized; however, after scientific studies such as quantum physics; it has been shown that everything in the universe is energy. Humanity has lost the fear that religions impose on them in the past and as a result, they have given themselves the task of expanding their knowledge; consequently, they have adhered to many esoteric disciplines.

The glossary that has been provided to the reader, is a treasure trove of esoteric, mystical, and Gnostic words; for those who appreciate esotericism; this glossary also contains marginal notes, which may be used to identify esoteric words, as well as their respective meanings; however, whether the reader needs to deepen his or her knowledge of the meaning of words; you are advised to use dictionaries and books, cited as references. Some precepts and words of the different languages and disciplines may be recurrent due to distinct ways of expressing mystical thoughts; the words are not marked with their respective grammatical signs, because they are being used strictly for wordplay.

PROLOGUE

Authentic Esotericism entails a single purpose that is self-realization of the inner Being of each person, making use of guidelines, disciplines and rituals that have bequeathed us authentic esotericisms, scholars of Occultism and thinkers over time.

The origins of esotericism are impossible to find from the anthropology, since it is intimately linked to the beginning of the humanity itself, and its desire to reunite with divinity. In a time when humans feel alien to God, we go to various studies where through devotion and ritualistic practices "religare" was sought which inevitably led to the Later confessional religions. Once mankind took from the Forbidden fruit was detached from the divinity and to this day we err for the world without knowing why, and what we exist for. Fortunately for us all was not lost and we have been helped in numerous moments of our history, with beings of light who have come to incarnate on the planet and teach us the way and the true esotericism that regenerates us and redeems us from that original sin which deprived us of paradise. One of those beings, we are told, was Sanat Kumara who officially started the sacred college of initiates where Thousands of men and women were taught the esoteric mysteries through rituals and systems to achieve redemption and regeneration of human beings.

When the schools of pure and primeval esotericism were closed with the arrival of Kali Yuga or dark ages, humanity was barely left with the reminiscence of this doctrine and gradually divided the knowledge in 3 slopes or paths, which are: the path of Fakir, of the monk and the yogi, being there in each, a part of the True esotericism, but at the same time incomplete, because it does not generate a Total liberation. We are told that there is a fourth way, which is that of the Cunning man, who wisely balances the 3 states or paths of the esotericism and travels through life with the firm purpose of achieving the Final liberation based on will, devotion and spiritual work. With the passage of time and the development of different civilizations Around the world, this knowledge was also transmitted. Primordial that will inherit those ancient civilizations such as the Mesopotamian and Egyptian directly from the submerged Atlantis, later many other cultures, societies and orders were caring for and enriching esoteric knowledge for the good of the humanity, Many doctrines fell woefully into religions devotionals that ended up putting a veil on information and restricting knowledge to a few...

Later with the arrival of Kabir Jesus, a new era began in humanity with the authentic and true Christic Esotericism, which was preached by Jesus and his disciples in old Palestine of ago more than 2,000 years. Unfortunately, much of this esoteric legacy Christic was hidden or adulterated, and little was shared with the world of that precious message. Many years later, in the decade Of the forties, 'perhaps' was found, the most valuable archaeological treasure for humanity, as they are, the texts of Nagh Hammadi, where The Gnostic gospels were recovered, and it could be delivered to Humanity that knowledge so precious that the venerable Master Jesus will leave us.

Thus, we see that contemporary esotericism such as Theosophy, Freemasonry, Rosicrucianism, Gnosticism etc, drink from Same chalice of knowledge, which is called to liberate humanity.

SYMBOLISM

Is an intellectual procedure by which the knowledgeable use a purpose, image, or tone to manifest different objectives. Wide variety of authors utilize it and detect models of symbolism in fables, humanities, drama, imagination, literature, scheme, romance, etc. If we reflect with the help of prehistory, we can remember that these signs stood out since man endured in caves; leaving their experiences embodied in the walls of their homes. In the 1880s a new adjustment of effigies reappeared in France. This activity was poetically sublime identified with emblems to reproduce feelings; also, an illogical creativity. That uprising esteemed the universe as well as an enigma and talent according to a fantasy.

Symbolism has attracted attention to lyrical arguments that seek internal inquiry into authenticity, starting from mysticism, clairvoyance, and visions. Numerous people opposed the activities of philosophical naturalism and pragmatism which irritably designated ordinary existences. Symbolism is an activity which responds in resistance & opposition to the difficulties averse to the merits of entrepreneurial associated utilitarianism, inquiring into common certainty, and seeking impartiality as well as deep emotional investigation. It relates to the autonomy of the disposition in the narratives to the differentiations and domains of existence trying to manifest the grief and the intense affliction while the author investigates to function against appreciation, creativity, and the appearances of the concurrent, therefore cause persistent force.

Religious symbols have been in the spotlight over the course of centuries, belief has existed an authoritarian energy in the collectivity of human groups. It is not surprising, in such a case, that the symbols linked to religious convictions appear preponderant in letters and poetry. Mythological legends are individual kinds of tales solidly established in symbolism. Chronic references have been found of deities or non-benign individuals who relate to humanity or hold a certain pattern of shock in that existence. An example is the sphinx, a very popular symbol originated in Egypt and Babylon. This image with the body of a lion and a human head was a female monster that annihilated the men who came to solve their riddle; however, they hardly deciphered the answer. This giant effigy was the sovereign, wisdom and enigmatic. The Harpy, in Greek mythology denoted the most aggressive aspects of the femaleness with head and the thorax of woman and the wings of birds; legs of a vulture. This phenomenon managed to veil the winds, as well as to excite storms and whirlwinds; The origin of the unexpected death was also important. A silhouette with antlers and tail is the universal symbolic effigy of the devil, augmented by the hue (red). Several writers consider many symbols realizable to be precedent of archaic myths. As an example, we can cite the Phoenix bird that symbolizes the return. The palm tree triumphs. The deer, active servant of the Redeemer. The anchor, the expectation, the faith, the liberation. The boat, the parish. The dove, happiness of the believer, honesty, tranquility granted to the loyal spirit. The cross, suffering. The virgin represents the figure of mother, immaculate, defined congregation of anil tones and white, Isis, divinity.

WHAT ARE COLORS?

It is a possession that has a matter, capable of causing various exaltations in the sight, because of the way in which the rays of light are projected or diffused. It is a sensation that is caused inside the retina, the brightness of the illumination reflected and captured by a body according to the undulation distance of said glare. The printing of colors is an individual manifestation. Colors complement our human longings, and motives as well as fears. Mother Nature has given us a configuration of colors and distinctions that intoxicates our senses and sensations. For example; we can cite several natural views that inspire us and realize our imagination: for example; It is easy to visualize panoramas such as a sunrise, twilight, a starry night, a group of mountains in the distance with their exquisite green layers of foliage or a waterfall collapsing from the top. The Glaciers in the mountains of places where the temperature is frozen; with its layers of snow from the top smiling at the clouds; while the sun shows its reflection. Observe either a herd of animals; birds with their respective offsprings or a hive of bees or ants; In communion in their habitats is memorable.

According to the Native American medicine wheel, in which the four corners of North, South, East and West represent the characteristics of humanity: red represents vision, respect; black is wisdom; feelings, yellow illustrate time, and relationships. They relate black, white, yellow, and red to the concepts of the four seasons of nature, the sacred path of the Sun, and humanity. Color arrangements can vary among the different customs of the tribes. There are colors like yellow; that can stimulate our mental process, the nervous system; It activates memory and seduces us in communication. According to Feng Shui, yellow is the center of everything, compared to the Sun, which is the concept of positive energy. Another color that raises our enthusiasm and stimulates our energy is Green; In addition, it raises blood pressure, breathing, heartbeat and pulse speed. It also revives the individual to action and openness; This color provides us with a sense of shelter from panic and concerns. It is also said that the green color symbolizes money, luck, prosperity, vitality and fertility. The pink color stimulates our energy, raises blood pressure, breathing, heartbeat and pulse speed. It encourages us to fight and to have confidence in ourselves. On the other side of the spectrum, blue acts just like a tranquilizer; It keeps us calm and helps our perception. The purple color also elevates mental serenity and clears nerves; It promotes a mystical sense and helps perception and creative expression. White; helps the brain system, giving way to luminosity; encourages us to clear confusions or obstacles that we may possess in the intellect; It begs to sustain reflections and activities, it gives us a brand-new energy to undertake fresh beginnings. Black color makes us distinguish unprepared, gives us an impatient, restless appearance. It evokes a perception of strength and probabilities. However, the color Gray can make us feel restless, worried, and nervous. This may be one way we can realize that colors encompass a large part of our consciousness and impressions.

The symbolism of colors is predominant because colors are important in our everyday lives. It is a critical form of our human relationships. We can use colors in our beliefs, perceptions, and excitements: Sometimes when we feel angry it is said that we are seeing "Red".

Everything in our world that we process in daily life through our senses of sight aspires in what we have seen and sends signals to the brain to analyze it. There is a lot of cultural dominance through our experiences; which affects us when we look at characteristic colors such as the flags of the different countries of the world, political, religious, and mystical groups; They choose their banners and logos, according to their cognitions, affiliations, and acceptances.

Colors and meditation have been affiliated as a frequent practice of reconciliation. Each color can be connected to a particular chakra or power core in the human body. When an individual can perceive a specific color, during meditation; That means healing has taken place in that part of your body; As has been expressed by the healing technique, therapist, through meditation of the chakras.

Chakra Root - Muladhara - Color Red, detected at the bottom of the spine column, related with the elements of the earth and in charge of a sensation of certainty and strength. This chakra consists of whatever foundation you prefer for solidity in your existence; as well as essentials like food, water, dwelling, and welfare.

Sacral Chakra - Svadhisthana - Orange shade, trusted to be the subsequent chakra in the human anatomy, regulate original inspirations, feeling and sensuality. When this chakra is obstructed individuals refrain from producing sufficient space for innovation and relaxation; could lead the way to misery and apprehension.

Solar Plexus Chakra - Manipuri - Yellow tone, perception attached with self-assurance, satisfaction and delight. Conveys purpose and integrity - when congested may reach from ardor to helplessness or insecurity. Material variance may develop into; stomach problems, persistent fatigue, hypertension, polygenic disorder, liver disorders, and dyspepsia.

Heart Chakra - Anahata - Coloring Green, viewed as the essence of unlimited deep affection, sympathy, mercy, and bliss. When obstructed it may lead to a let down safety, viral rhinitis, contaminations, angina and pulmonary concerns. While this Chakra is activated it can be revealed as serenity, sympathy, and equilibrium. Polarities of this chakra may be: isolation, bashfulness, indignation or vindictiveness; awkwardness demonstrating reactions; unhappiness, melancholy, apprehension.

Third Eye Chakra - Anna - Color Indigo, observed as the "internal screen" remembrance and creativity, resemblance and paradigms, instinct and imaginative faculties are exhibited. When congested; you may misplace your link with your inner sensitivity. Individuals may perceive disorientation or drifting.

Crown Chakra - Sahanara - Color Pure White. The Sanskrit name defines this Chakra as 'thousand-petaled,' it commands relationship to our soul, and sensation of comprehensive awareness, sagacity, integration and self-realization. This Chakra is correlated with the classifications of capitulate and predominance.

GLOSSARY

-A-

ABBA Amona (Hebrew) "Father-Mother". These are the two towering hidden names Sephiroth: Chokmah, Binah, from the Upper Triad, and that the apex is Sephira or Kether. This triad spread out from the bottom septenary of the Sephirotal Tree.

ABBAD TRITEMO (Johannes Tritheism) German friar and prophet. He was a medieval alchemist who knew thoroughly the mysterious science of the elements. Disciple of Alberto Magno.

ABADDON (Hebrew) Is an angel of the depth, and an evil one of the Seventh Hierarchy, he dresses in a black robe and a red cape. Over time adversaries of ancient gnosis and companions (Latins and Greeks) of this fallen angel ascribed to Gnosis this word importance the Ancient of Days to gain more followers in their dark sects.

ABED NEGO Understood as the astral body. The body of desire (Apopi) amid the Egyptians. It surfaces in the Hebrew Bible.

ABGAR, Legend (of) A folk legend set down to Abgar V (4 B.C.- A.D. 50), he was King of Edessa, where an exchange of transmission with the Lord took place. Since the King was in poor health, asked Christ to advance toward and heal him; responding; the Lord pledged that after His Ascension He would entrust an apostle to heal the king and minister the Gospel to his long-established nation. In accord with 'Pilgrimage of Etheria', the communication of Christ was safeguarded at Edessa.

ABEL Come into view for the human soul; it is embodied with the 3 elements of the revolution of receptiveness; to be born, to die and to sacrifice for humankind.

ABER. And Inver Are ordinary segments in induction of Celtic origin. Both signify "confluence of waters" or "river mouth". Their dispensation deliberates the landscape impact of the Brittonic and Goidelic mother tongue categories, later. A prehistoric British term for the mouth of a river, as Aber-Brothick, Aber-Avon, Aber-Ystwyth, and Aber-Conway, &c. It in addition, process the convergence of two or more streams.

ABHAVA (Sanskrit) ["Non-being, non-existence, deficiency of quality, etc."]. Negation, non-being or non-existence of respective objects; noumenal material or abstract objectivity.

ABHAMSI (Sanskrit) Mystical faith community of "four orders of beings"; Gods, Demigods, Pitri's and men. The Orientalists connected this term with the "Waters", which refers to a perplex Philosophy that attaches with the analogy of the Akaza; that is, the "waters of space". This objective is that in the bosom and in the seven-level outermost of "space" have been born the "four orders of beings (lower)" and the three-soaring succession of spiritual Beings.

ABHI Commands a semantic supplement or annex, which is laid down in front of locutions such as: a, towards, on, above, change their meanings. This is contemplating grade 4th of Dhyana (8th of esoteric knowledge) which must be victorious over by each true Arhat.

ABHIJNA (Sanskrit) [*Superior Science or Supernatural*] These we're gloriousness donations which Sakyamuni Buddhas realize the night the Buddhas' confection materialized. The ascetic buddhas in China are nominated credit to know six siddhis or such abilities. Nevertheless, in Ceylan they only stretch out to five. The first ABHIJNA is the Divya Chakshu's [divine eye or light blue] or the immediate vision of the absolutely that one wants to see; the second is the Divygezotra [divine ear or light blue], which the power to appreciate or [hear] any sound [being that the rest of the paranormal powers could materialized at will], they could read or penetrate any thoughts of any man, they could know their circumstances as well as exemplar lives.

ABIB (Hebrew) or (Nisan) Is contemplated to be the earliest holy month for Jews, which begin in March. He is besides well known as Nisan.

ABIDE To "abide" is a verbification; it is energetic. Abiding in Christ is not a feeling or a belief, but phenomenon we do. It signifies to "remain" or "stay" and entails far more than the idea of pursuing reliance in the Savior. John 15.5 further demonstrates this abiding association with an aligned connection of a vine and a branch. To endure stable or fixed in a state, a love that abided with him all his days, to carry on with in a place; sojourn. To comply with in the Word of God measures to focus on it, meditate on it, or study the Word. There are many enjoyments to scrutinizing the Bible, but likely the most predominant one is developing close by to Christ.

ABIRI (Greek) or Kabiri which is another way of write down the word Abiri. The Proxies, divine, sons of Zedec the righteous; group of divinities acclaimed in Phoenicia. They are contemplated like Virgil's Titans, Coribantes, Curets, Tachine's, and Dii Magni.

ABORTION Is destroying the work of Mother Nature. Abortion that is deliberately started is a homicide that is paid for Karmically (like Karma Duro or karma non-negotiable with the Lords of Cosmic Law). Not only does karma pay for who intentionally performs it, but also who helps provoke it. (e.g., doctors, specialists, etc.)

ABRACADABRA (Gnosticism) This locution was used in the Middle Ages for magical purposes. It was written inside an inverted triangle, or the word was written in eleven lines each time with one less letter, in each of them until concluding with the letter A. It has also been associated to the command Abraxas Gnostic which is the name of the Sun God Mithra. It is trusted to come from the Hebrew phrase "to which ad Habra" which means "send your Ray to death".

ABRAXAS (Gnosticism) These are transcendental designations that go back to Basilides, the Pythagorean, of Alexandria (year 90 after J.C.). This philosopher used the input Abraxas as the name of the Divinity, most powerful of the Seven, and as an assigned of 365 virtues, in the Greek sign system; a = 1, b = 2, r = 100, a = 1, x = 60, a = 1, s = 200, which form a total of 365, days of the solar year, a cycle of divine action. C. W. King, author of the Gnostics, looks at this word like the Hebrew Shemhamphorasch, sacred word, "the explicit name" of God. Abraxas gems are characterized, usually in a human body with a rooster's head that conveys on one of its arms a shield, and the other a whip.

ABSOLUTE (Theo) The subject grasps the universal principle of unknowable essence of all that breathe in Cosmos, the Gnostics, know it as the uncreated light. Causa Causorum of all that is, has been and will be.

ABSOO (Chaldean) Hermetical name of Space, meaning the dwelling of Ab, The "Father", or the birth of the origin of the waters of knowledge. The comprehension of the father is hidden in the infinite or the Akazic localities.

ABSORB Platonism, Singular of the sharp end of human thoughts, absorbs the Pythagorean teaching of mood centralization, the Heraclitus of becoming (that all things flow, in a river-like manner) and the Parmenidean (it is the understanding that man owns in his being called "Nous") of the irreversible being, and discovers its admirable synthesis in the "gnoseological Doctrine of Ideas."

ABSTRACT (Gnosticism) There exists a Divine ray, which is within man. That ray approached from a Star. (Chaldean) It is the mystical honorific of the Space that means residence of the father, or birth that leads our intimate, this one; he is a Super Celestial Atom of Absolute Abstract Space, and his kabalistic superstar is the Sacred Ain Soph, he is the Universal Spirit of Life, he is absolute Happiness, supreme peace and abundance.

ABUNA The leader of the 'Abyssinian Chruch'.

ABYMS The interpretation of the abyss through the Judeo-Christian generation consistently existed emblematic of Pandemonium, catastrophic, or loss of life; with the exclusion of the Gnostic legend which linked to abyss the two jurisdiction of existence and the restoration to this dawning is a nominal that demonstrates an extensive inoperative or Canyon, at least one authentic or metaphoric. Fabricating **a** significant vigorous resolved with outstanding insecure, like such as recruitment in a sitcom club may be perceived no less than leaping toward the abyss. As a matter of course, the abyss is specified to as the "fire and brimstone" of the netherworld. In Greek tradition an abysm is Turmoil, (Greek: "Abyss") in predate Greek cosmogony, either/or the primordial worthlessness of the natural world prior to possessions approached to begin to exist or the abyss of everlasting fire, the hell. Either conception arise in the "Birth of the Gods". The solely technique to get away the abyss is to examine it, measure it, articulate it and plunge

ACACIA (Greek) Insinuates Innocence; it is also a plant, which is used in Freemasonry as a character of Initiation; Immortality and Purity. This Tree supplied the sacred wood (Shittim of the Hebrews). Both the archaic Hebrews and the Egyptians contemplate the tree to be an emblem of eternal since its toughness, long-lasting, and evergreen nature. In former times, the Israelites would place an acacia sprig at the head of graves to deliberate this belief (as well as mark the burial yard).

ACACIUS OF CAESAREA (d. 366) Arian philosopher. He took the place of Eusebius in the see of Caesarea (In Palestine) in 340 but was unmistakable removed from office by the Council of Sardica (343). In 359 he suggested a Homoean Creed at the Council of Seleucia. He endorsed the Creed of Nicaea in 363 but reappeared to Arianism and was dismissed in 365. His partisans ('Acacians') were apparent and major theological party at intervals 357 and 361.

ACATHISTUS (Gk., 'not sitting' It was sung standing), A legendary Greek liturgical hymn in honor of the BVM. The text was constructed on the Gospel exposition of the Nativity. The configuration has been diversely assigned.

ACARIE, Mme. (1566-1618), 'Mary of the Incarnation', initiator of the Carmelites of the Reform in France. Barbe Jeanne Avrillot, nevertheless eager to enter the cloister, in 1584 married Pierre Acarie, Vicomte de Villemore. Following clarification, a life of St. Teresa, she prevails on Mile de Longueville to acquire the king's clearance and compiled in organizing the Carmel of Paris in 1603. Succeeding her husband's death (1613) she was herself professed. She was the concern of ecstasies and the recipient of visions.

ACCEPT, ACCEPTANTS. Those who 'accepted' the bull 'Unigenitus' (1713) in the Jansenist controversy.

ACELDAMA "The field of blood". A section of dry land near Jerusalem, which was named (1) acc. to Mt. 27: 8, since it was bought with the cost of the Lords' blood, but (2) acc. to Acts 1: 18 f., as a result that it was the scene of Judas' end.

ACTION In Kabbalism, there is only one focus on evolution and salvation. Self-liberation and conscious will.

ACCORDANCE. Phrase channels consensus, in accord with a regulation; the performance of allowing existence the conformity of an entitlements. "In accordance with the scriptures" is a manuscript for "in accordance with the reality for which God requires our conformity and our obedience". Ephesians 4:29 affirms, "Do not let any unwholesome talk come out of your mouths, but only what is helpful for building others up according to their needs, that it may benefit those who listen." Proverbs 10:19 declares, "Sin is not ended by multiplying words, but the prudent hold their tongues."

ACQUIRE. If you obtain commodities, you acquire or achieve them personally, or anyone awards it to you. If you receive substance similarly as accomplishment or a philosophy, you ascertain it, or established it overcoming your routine survival or knowledge. If an individual or phenomenon earned an unquestionable influence, they begin to have that notoriety. Consequently, to acquire understanding as indicated in the Bible; Benevolence is the essence of Christian merit of reality of consideration and disinterest, largely with our funds and continuance. Determination is regarded by fearlessness and conviction. After all, it is the contradictory of distress. Affection is a indispensable component of who God is and it's a benefit that is to relate His youths in like manner.

ACCUMULATION (Gnosticism) Greed is a disordered hunger to get wealth or goods, it refers to an anxiety of accumulation, an unbridled desire, an unbridled aspiration to want to own what others have.

ACHAMOTH (Gnosticism) (pruniks) This designation means, Major, and with it is generally represented the Common Cosmic Holy Spirit (in his androgynous spirit, the giver of light); Cosmic Consciousness; it is the Sophia Major who provided rise to her daughter Sophia Pruniks.

ACHAR (Hebrew) As maintained by the Jews, who believe that this term alludes to the Divinities who are guided by Jehovah.

ACHARA (Sanskrit) Continue distinctive and social (religious) commitments. A) rules of good conduct, good habits, religious routines. B) emancipation (moksha) that is captured through such practices.

ACHER (Hebrew) Is the name given in the Talmud to the apostle Paul. This work tells the story of the Tanaim fours, who come across in the "Garden of Delights, and came to be initiated: Ben-Asai, who saw, and his sight was demolished; Ben Zoma, who looked and lost the sensitivity; Acher, who made catches in the Garden, and perished, and Rabbi Akiba, who was the only constituent who could achieve good success. Kabbalists believe that Acher is Paul.

ACHIT (Sanskrit) Is the Unconscious, foolish, left out of intelligence. He who has no absolute Intelligence, as well as is the opposite of; [Chit that is absolute intelligence].

ACHTA SIDDHIS (Sanskrit) Expresses the eight powers in the practice of Hatha Yoga.

ACCIDIE. ('Gk. For 'negligence', indifference). By the 4th cent. The expression had become a scientific term in Religiousness, revealing a state of fretfulness and inadequacy as well to work or to pray. It is investigated a single of the 'Seven Deadly Sins'.

ACTHNA Mechanism a hidden fire, in a cavity, which is a generator where they take bituminous substances, in unquestionable cases produces volcanic eruptions. In some states of the Earth's "soul", some amalgams of astral and palpable matter may have an electrical or magnetic character. It is a part "great serpent" Vasuki, which, according to Indian mythology, transits the universe; whose demonstration could promote jolts.

ACTS OF THE APOSTLES, (The) According to the fifth Book of the Scriptures which are notes from the early growth of the Church. It is universally revealed to be the effort of St. Luke (q.v.). Its dispensation has been unpredictably dated, but most observers are willing to accept an occasion around the middle of 70 and 85. The so-called 'We sections' (16 10-17; 20: 5-15; 21; 1-18; 27: 1-28: 16) are generally trusted to have approached via the writers' own excursions' diary, manifested him as an observer of the circumstances recounted. The publication identified the advancements of Christianity originated in Jerusalem to Rome 1: 1-6: 7 described to the Jerusalem Church and the sermons of St. Peter; 6: 8-9: 31 the extensions of the Church in Palestine; 9: 32-12: 24 the add-ons to Antioch; 12: 25-16: St. Paul's journeys to Galatia and the Committee of Jerusalem; 16: 6-19: 20 the demonstrate of Macedonia, Greece and the Roman territories of Asia; and 19: 21 at the culmination the additions of the Church to Rome and Paul's expedition there as a hostage. The work confirmed the spiritual origin of religion. The twelve disciples attest that Jesus is the Messiah, demonstrate such by His return to life. Confidence in the holiness of Christ is understood (e.g., 20:28;), and the Trilateral belief is indeed in bacterium, however the Nature of the Spirit of God is not thus far accepted. Conforming to Acts the house of God along with its conceptions owns her own ceremonial of christening for the abolition of sins (2: 38) and of the breaking of 'bread' (2: 42) (expression used for the sacrament rite). It revolved out to have been ruled from the start by the Disciples, to whose `Seven' were devoted later (6: 1-6), in addition, presbyters and bishops, the recent duo clearly not thus far well known. The delegation of the Church specified in Acts is overall contemplated as authentic.

ACT or ACTS (Gnosticism) All of us are going to have to response to God for all our "acts". We were given "free will" to live life conforming to our will and conscience, and whatever we have decided on; we will answer before the Sacred Law or Cosmic Court of Justice. We not only pay Karma, but also for our positive works; God, the Divinity, the Gods pay us with the Dharma. The way each individual acts depends on your blemishes or egos.

ACTA SANCTORUM. The commemoration of a succession of survival of the pietist, displayed in the sequence of their festivities in the clerical year, which was set in motion by the Bollandists in the 17th centenary by 1925 it had accomplished 10 November.

ACOLYTE Those people dedicated to the service of the altar.

ADDAI, The Creed (of) A Syriac print which declare the way Kin Abgar was escorted to categorize with Christ and Addai was dispatched to Edessa to transfigure him. Probably it dates from c. 400, however, materialized to depend on more antecedent sources.

AD LIMINA APOSTOLORUM (Latin, 'to the thresholds of the Apostles') Mission 'ad Limina Apostol Orum', SC to the sepulcher of St. Peter and St. Paul in Rome, was advocate in the Middle Ages. In present measures the time commonly signals the overtakes which Roman Catholicity prelate are required to visit Rome to respect the mausoleum of the followers and to recount to the Pontiff the condition of its parish.

AD (Assyrian) Ad, is "the father." In Aramaic, Ad expresses one. AD stands for "the one."

ADAH The Hebrews seized this appellation for the name of their Adah, father of Jubal, etc. The significant of Adah; it is "the first", "the one", it is universal heritage. There are arguments to suppose that Ak-ad denotes the first born or Son of Ad. Adon was the initial "Lord" of Syria.

ADAM (Hebrew) In Kabbalah, he is "the only begotten" and symbolizes "Red Earth". Adam is first understood as an "extensive representation of the strength of the universe", which in it finds its synthesis. In the matching way the comparison Macrocosm Microcosm. (Sanskrit) He is one of the 10 Sublime Anti-Flood Patriarchs. Adam epitomizes all the millions of inhabitants of Lemuria.

ADAMANTIUS (4th century) Greek anti- Gnostic writer. His De rectabin Deum fide grasps the shape of a dialogue first with two disciples of Marcion and then with followers of Bardesanes and Valentinus.

ADAPT Technique of orienting our strategies to the numerous approaches that have been proposed.

ADECH This command refers to the lower (spiritual) man; the lord of reflection; imagination, personified formation in his mind, which the outer individual (matter) can spread, multiply; your purposes get your goal. Each of these intensities works according to its nature: the one inside it occurs in an intangible way; and he who manifests himself outside does so in a perceptible way; however, the two work in correlation. The outer person has the dominion of exercising what the internal mortal imagines; however, thinking only compromises the hierarchy of thought, and what is fabricated by thoughts have a fundamental impact, even though they are not resolved to impartiality in distinguishable representation. The essence of the innermost mankind does what he wishes and thinks. Whether or not the designs of your imagination are favorable or bad, whether you find words on the material map; it is of slighter significance for their mental legitimate development, than it is for those who may be Impresiones' by the activity emanates by their understandings.

ADESTE FIDELES. A Christmas hymn, which was probably written in the 17th or 18th centuries; it is believed the authors were either German or French. The common English tr. Is 'O come, all ye faithful'.

ADEPTO (theosophy) Technique the human being who is walking a path of spiritual realization, which; he has obtained several initiations and has extended transcendental knowledge and powers, he has become a Master of Wisdom. (Rosicrucian) This start has outreached the nine hierarchies of a school of Minor Mysteries, entering one of major Mysteries obtaining prophecy of the invisible planet and influence over the elements; and the forces that act there. (Gnostic) The adept is further on the saints since they have stagnated in their advancement and although they are in worlds of supreme complacency, they have not yet concluded the errors of their hidden part, of their psychological moon. The word "adept" is synonymous with Master. In order of merit, after the irreverent, approach the Saint and then the Master, the adept.

ADHI (Sanskrit) This mandate expresses the "Supreme, Superiority, Principals'".

ADHI YAJÑA (Sanskrit) Insinuate supreme sacrifice. It is one of the three explanations of the divine substance, that is, it is the nucleus from which all self-conscious beings come; in its atomic appearance, it is the Self. The Self is materialized as immolation, that is, as if it were Vishnu or another Krishna or another Avatara.

ADDITION, ADDING. The Dogma enunciates citing to adding expressions. "Ye shall not add unto the word which I command you, neither shall ye diminish ought from it, that ye may keep the commandments of the Lord your God which I command you." Per Deuteronomy 4:2 Moses instructs obedience: "And now, O Israel, listen to the statutes and the rules that I am teaching you, and do them, that you may live, and go in and take possession of the land that the Lord the God of your fathers, is giving you". "The only way in which we can rightly "keep" God's commands is to not add or subtract from his word."

ADHO-GATI (Sanskrit) "He who goes down". Conforming to the Jains, it is the lower hell.

ADHYATMA (Sanskrit) Soul or Supreme Spirit**,** Brahma**.** Relative to the Spirit**.**

ADI (Sanskrit) Imply what is first; the highest (theology), is the atomic plane of the solar system. The mysterious reflection mark to the "children of Adi" "Sons of the fog of fire". Expression passed down by some followers.

ADI-Buddi (Sanskrit) Reasoning or primitive acumen; the everlasting Buddhi or universal Mind. It is employed with testimonial to divine contemplation and Maha-buddhi is identified with Mahat.

ADI-bhuta (Sanskrit) The initial Being; and also, a primal segment. It is a subject of Vichnu, the "first Element", which contains all the components, "the unfathomable divinity".

ADITYA (Sanskrit) Developed as name for the sun; like Martanda, he is the son of Aditi.

ADORO TE DEVOTE This is a Eucharistic hymn, accredited to St. Thomas Aquinas. Although its authorship has been challenged for, the ordinary Eng. tr. s 'Thee we adore, O hidden Savior.

ADONAI (Hebrew) Is the same as Adonis; interpreted as "Lord" Excessively the Sun. During school periods, the name of IHVH or Jehovah was replaced with "Adonai"; when Alham was put in writing, he was called "Elohim." Simultaneously**,** the celestial name was progressively deemed as too sacred to be uttered; it was thus replaced audibly in the synagogue liturgy by the Hebrew term Adonai ("My Lord"), that was transcribed as Kyrios ("Lord") in the Septuagint, the Greek version of the Hebrew Scriptures.

ADORATION It is the act of venerating the divinity, by which man unites, when an individual gives to an authority that helps him to reach a greater degree of realization, with his Essence.

ADOUM Jorge Médico, Correspondent of esotericism of Arab origination who was assigned the accreditation of Chief Magician, author of: The Keys of the Internal Kingdom, "The Bush of Horeb". From which M. Samael recounts, thus the specification of an authentic Black Mass is made. In his book "Endocrinology and Criminology" chapter 2 he asserts: that he is a remarkable Gnostic writer and great Master of the Major Mysteries of the White Lodge. He died in 1958.

ADROP, AZANE or AZAR (Alchemy) Continues "The Philosopher's Stone". It is not a stone in the ordinary acceptance of the word, but an allegorical locution that demonstrate an origin of knowledge, in which, the philosopher who has obtained it by practical experience (not simply the one who is guessing about it) can be wholly trusted, as the price of a valuable stone, or the duplicate as he would expect in a solid rock on which the foundations of his (spiritual) dwelling would be constructed. He is the Christ who lives in man, celestial love fundamentalism. It is the light of the world; the very essence from which the world was created. It is not the pure spirit, but the primal; for man's body owns the extraordinary of secrets.

ADULTERY When a person while married has sexual relations with individuals outside of marriage; adultery is committed. Thus, one of the (10) Ten Commandments is disregarded, which says "Thou shalt not commit adultery." Through Gnosis, Master Samael says that adultery occurs when the spouses are not interconnected in the five centers of the Human Machine or because they have dissimilar temperaments. Being the woman passive part, the atomic substances of the man are deposited in her, in the course of copulation, so it is too dangerous a matter to spoil because the man who does it not only has to fight his own defects, but also in opposition of those of the other men with whom the woman would have had sexual contact.

ADVANCE This phrase refers to the action or act of moving forward, in motion towards a development or continuing at the forefront of progress. Where there is a move forward of money or anything. Budget or expense that is made in a work or an equilibrium of trade, which is made by a merchant, also called advanced.

ADVENT (Gnosticism) Prevail the belief of theosophy, the arrival of the Gnostic era.

ADVENTURE Incarnate, the search for the interpretation of life (danger, love, combat, encounters, abandonment, help, conquest, loss, death, etc. The fight averse to evil or the survey for the beloved and the ethical and erotic-spiritual aspect.

ADVANCE This term refers to the action or act of in motion forward, in moving towards a development or proceeding at the forepart or progress. Where there is an advance of money or anything. Budget or expense that is manufactured in a work or a balance of trade, which is made by a merchant, is as well called advanced.

ADY BUDDHA (gnost.) The Buddha

ADYA (Sanskrit) Expresses, first, primitive, unique.

ADYTUM (Latin) He was the Saint of Saints in pagan temples. It was a appellative given to the secret and sacred places of the inner chamber, where no layperson could enter. Related to the altars of Christian temples.

AECIA An aeciospore (plural aecia) is a particular procreative anatomical discovered in certain stripe rust fungi that developed spore. Aecia can also be touched upon to as "cluster cups". The voicing aecidium (plural aecidia) is employed synonymous but is not selected. The significance of Aecial is (incomparable) (fungal biology) of, connected to, or analogous anaecium.

AELIA CAPITOLINA The new city which was built by the Empire Hadrian for 139 centuries. The new town was reconstructed on the site of Jerusalem (destroyed AD 70).

AENEAS A Trojan prince alluded to by Virgil in the Aeneid. One of his instructors was Centaurus Chiron. He renowned himself for his bravery and power. He fought in numerous wars, for instance, against Diomedes, Troy, and others. In the course of his last fight against Mezencio and his Etruscans. It is said that he disappeared between the waters of the Numicio River. It is said that his ascendant predominated for fourteen generations in the country of Latino.

AEACUS. Was king of the island of Egiria, son of Zeus. Gods of Olympus made him judge of Hell for his great essence of righteousness that he showed during his life.

AENEAS OF GAZA (d. 518) Christian Neoplatonist. In his 'Theophrastus' he secured the perpetuity of the dedication and the reawakening of the embodiment but dismissed such principles of 'Platonism as differed with orthodox Christian dogma'.

AEON (Eon or Eons) (Gnosticism) This term is secondhand in Gnosticism to appoint, one of the divine and eternal beings or knowledge, emanating from the soaring union, that connect matter and spirit. Etymologically, the word Aeon proceed from the English Ean, and this in turn from the Greek (Aion), which signify "time" or "epoch".

AENEID (ENEIDA). Transpired a Trojan hero in a book written by Latin Poet Virgil's book Aeneid. His effort developed in Rome through the reign of Emperor Augustus in the 1st century B.C.

AETERNI PATRIS (1879). The encyclical of Leo XIII corroborating with the church the investigation of philosophy, and particularly the effort of St. Thomas Aquinas.

AETIUS Arian impostor. He was a controversial at Alexandria and was initiated as a bishop by the Arians. He and his companions; the Anomoeans maintained the dissimilarity of the Son and the father. His consent is supported by Epiphanius.

AFFECTION Channel sentimentality that has lust as its origin.

AFFIRM (Gnosticism) Holy Affirm Is the Father, the ancient strength which is embodied through emblem of the "threefold". To affirm what we disregard or do not know is a deception.

AFRICA Consistently what symbolizes Africa is the grandiose lion: the mark of Africa breed: high-powered and dignity, the "king of the beasts" has no natural beast of prey. The image embodies body language and creative values, in affiliation with the modus operandi of survival of the people who create them. The characters are traditionally reproduced on cotton thread to form "Adinkra cloths," as it may be worn on such commemoratory occurrences as child naming, commune durbars and extreme unction. The ankh insignia, occasionally indicated to as "the key to life or the key to the Nile"; is minister of eternal life in Prehistoric Egypt. Fabricated by African in antiquity, the ankh is shared to be the initial; or authentic, cross. Africa is on occasion nicknamed the "Mother Continent" attributable to being the oldest inhabited continent on earth. Human beings and their ancestors have lived in Africa for more than 5 million years. "Africa, the second-largest continent, is bounded by the Mediterranean Sea, the Red Sea, the Indian Ocean, and the Atlantic Ocean." The accomplishment of Africa is to a great degree; intriguing, in consequence, it is diverse, determined on which country you stop by. The mainland is a place of residence for different populace, a plethora of which came to be altered by extraneous elements. Each motherland has exclusive ethnic groups, native tongue and broadening diversity. Thunder showers declare his appearance. Sango is an exceedingly influential monarch that Yorubaland obtained everlastingly formed, and he is also considered as the most influential supreme being in Africa.

AGABUS, St., Prophet acknowledged in Acts (11:28 and 21:10). In the Greek Orthodox he is grasped to be one of the seventy mentioned in Lk. 10:1.

AGDE COUNCIL (of). (506) A committee conducted at Adge in South of France during the presidency of Caesarius of Arles.

AGAMA (Sanskrit) Continue one of the three processes of knowledge. Understanding of experience or finding out from others we have by authorities. Those that are established on domain or tradition, are said to come from Agama. This term has several additional meanings: approach, arrival, advent; achievement; possession, knowledge, doctrine, etc. The missionaries adopted the term "agama" like "religion", they select Christianity with the nickname of Christian agama, while they should name it Christiani-Bandana, because Bandhana was the etymological equivalent of "religion".

AGAMI-KARMA (Sanskrit) Eventuality predetermination; the Karma that will be resulted in by ourselves through operations in our current existence. Predetermination; the Destiny that will be incited by our accomplishments in our instant survival.

AGAPE(S) (1) The word which means 'love', in the Greek alphabet. It is defended to have been conceived by the Biblical writers from a related verb, avoiding this way the palpable partnership of the ordinary Greek noun (eros); it is used to describe the love of God or of Christ, or the love of Christians for one another. It was habitually interpreted into Latin by 'caritas', so the first significance of 'charity' in English. (2) The locution is applied also to the ordinary religious feast which appears to have been in use in the primitive Church in immediate association to the Communion.

AGATHIAS (c. 532 c.582), Was a poet and historian who worked proficiently as an advocate at Constantinople. His chronicle is the main authority for the years 552-8. It is dubious if he was really a Christian.

AGAPE. A Hellenic announcement for 'Love', consider as true to archaic generated by the Theological authors arising out of analogous, for the sake of bypass the breathtaking alliance of the customs Grecian nominal (eros); typically utilized to convey image of the fondness of the Creator or Messiah, or the devotion of Pious connectively. It was traditionally into Grecian by 'caritas', as a result, the original judgment of "charity" in English (2) The style has stirred also the collaborative dedicated subsistence which appears archaic dominant inaugurated Tabernacle in accelerate towards the Lord's Supper.

AGATE (from the Greek, ACATES) Allude to the "good thief". According to gnosis the good thief is one who transmutes his ingenious energies through the techniques of alchemy and steals the fire from the devil.

AGATHON Brings into existence the supreme Divinity of Plato. In repercussions, it embodied "the Good, our Alaya", or "Universal Soul".

AGE(S) Time of mortal survival, determined by lifespan initiated at birth, generally decided by a definitive phases or gradations of psychological or palpable progress and requiring legitimate obligations and talents stage, the period of existence of cautions; the age of agreement; "The state raised the drinking age from 18 to 21 years". Certainly, for individuals who are conscious of their epoch, maturity is ordinarily distinct for all. A living persons' length may be distinguished towards divergent types: physiological peer group, the fair number of stages that an individual has survived, or a possession has remained. Windowpanes, doorways, overpasses, entryways frequently emerge in canvas of elderly person to indicate the maturing character' transformation to the next phase of reality, advanced years. In alabaster and bronze chisel, on coinage and decorated flower holders, and in oil paintings, cultural diversity, and progressively, senior people are demonstrated alongside revealing testimony of Age: creases, salt and pepper hair, flabby, and leaning outlook. Aging is a procedure by which a drawing, mostly a mural or carver, is put together to take shape of ancient. It is signified to mirror the essential declination that develops long duration or centennial. Whereas perhaps "innocent" motivation for it, an ageing approach is many times applied in talent falsification. The 'Governing Body' awake ageing ideal is grounded on the development of quaternary clue "pillars": well-being, long lasting investigation, association and safety. It produces mature individuals with guidelines support to enlarge their possibility for prosperity, consecutively be allowed establishment endurance.

AGENDA (Lat., 'things to be performed'). The expression has been employed for matters of ritual as opposed to those of belief; for the inner part of the Eucharist; and for established forms of service.

AGLA (Hebrew) This Kabbalistic Word is a talisman composed of the initials of the four words: Teth Gibor Leolam Adonai, which means: "You are the force forever, O lord."

AGNI Is the God of fire among the Vedas; in ancient India; its triple aspect; Agni, Vayu and Surya; the Trimurti was the most revered. Surrounded by the Gnostics, this God regains igneous dominance in each of the seven elements. He was adorned with the color violet and rode a ram, insignia of enlarged mating. Agni diversely signals the natural element fire; the supernatural deity indicates by fire and the inner natural will striving for the adept. Heat, ignition and energy is the kingdom of Agni which epitomizes the transfiguration of the gross to the subtle; Agni is the life-preserving energy.

AGNOIA (Greek) This is a conceptualization of the "deprived or dispossessed of reason", irrationality: rational or non-ethical and irrational or agnoia. If we vocalize of the universal Soul; according to Plutarch, Pythagoras and Platon, they divided the human soul into two parts (the upper and the lower manas): the rational or noetic and the irrational or agnoia. There are commands when it is written "anoia".

AGRA-SANDHANI (Sanskrit) [The Yama Record.] The "Advisors" or Registrars who interpret in the act of judgment of a disenchanted spirit, the evidence of their life in the heart of the matching soul. They are like Lipika's of the Secret Doctrine.

AGRAPHA ('unwritten [sayings]'), A subtitle designated to the proverb of Christ not listed in the four approved Dogmas. One materialized in Acts (20: 35), stability in the apocryphal Beliefs, esp. The Gospel of Thomas.

AGIOS O THEOS (Gk., Holy God) A Greek hymn that still survived without being translated in the Roman Good Friday ceremony.

AGGREGATES Errors or I.E. The accumulation of subdivision or parts into accumulation or whole, a group, body or mass collected of numerous aparent .

AGUSTIN (Saint) (Gnosticism) A distinguished Gnostic patriarch, who was, creator of the Gnostic sequence of the Augustinians (or Augustinians).

AHAM (Sanskrit) "I", the basis of Ahankara (ahamkara), personalism, arrogance.

AHAMKRITA-BRAVA (Sanskrit) Speak about the egoic condition in which consciousness finds itself.

AHAN (Sanskrit) "Day", the Body of Brahma, in the Puranas.

AHANKARA (Sanskrit) The comprehension of the "I", the importance of self or self-identity; the belief of the legitimate character, the "I", the egotistical and Mayan origin of man, due to our ignorance, which disunites our "I" from the universal Oneself. [Individuality, personalism, pride, selfishness, vanity, the fondness of self, awareness of the self or personal being. It is the beginning by virtue of which we achieve the tenderness of the legitimate particularity, the imaginary notion that the non-self (Body Matter is the I (Spirit), is what we are, we work we enjoy, we suffer. etc.]

AHEIE (Hebrew) Existence. The one who exists; with respect to Kether and Macroprosopo.

AHHI (Senz) Ahi (Sanskrit) Snakes. Dhyan-Chohans, "Wise Serpents" or Dragons of Wisdom.

AHI (Sanskrit) Snake. A title of Vritra, snake demon of the drought among the Vedas.

AHIKAR LEGEND The indicated is a story which tells of a Grand Vizier of Sennacherib, Ahikar the Astute, in opposition to whom his adopted son arranged and accepted a reward. It is kept having resulted in the Book of Tobit.

AHIMSA (Sanskrit) Safety, innocence, modesty. Cardinal powers of the Indos).

AHU (Scandinavian) "One" and the first.

AHUM (Zendo) The three introductory beginnings of the septenary configuration of man, according to the Avesta: the conventional living body and its vital and astral origin.

AHTI (Scandinavian) The "Dragon", in Eddas.

Al o El (Hebrew) Distinctive of the deity translated, is "God", means powerful, supreme. Conforming to Hebrew esotericism this caption alludes to ELOAH (singularized deity, God himself and as plural God in Hebrew is ELOHIM (Gods).

AIBU Appellation used for greeting in ancient Lemuria, putting your hands on your heart.

AIDAN, St. (d. 651), Friar of Iona and Bp. Of Lindisfarne. He was dispatched from Iona at the petition of Oswald, King of North Umbria, and ordained Bishop in 635. He inaugurated his base of operation at Lindisfarne and made long expeditions to the mainland; the executions he taught were those instructed the Celtic Chruch.

AIMA (Hebrew) The birth mother who is bright and fertile. An aspect of Binah.

AIN (Hebrew) The subsistence in a negative state; divinity is passive. The root of the spirit and the uncreated light.

AINDRI (Sanskrit) Wife of Indra.

AIRS (VAYUS) Breaths or vital currents: five main ones: Prana; respiratory function. Apana, standard of secondary part of the body, expels useless products; Samana: customary produces digestive function, food partitioning; Udana: ordinary arranges the flow of blood to the head, and Vyana: essential current connected to the skin, and that each part of the body keeps its appearance. Some of these words may have another sense, according to the place used.

AIRE, AIR (mixture of gases) air current, puff of air, expression (mode). Hippocrates related air with vital fluid. Air's representation is an upward triangle bisected by a horizontal line, and you might notice it is the Earth symbol, inverted. In accordance with Nameberry.com "Aire" imply "lion of God" in Hebrew. In Spanish Aire is the term signifying "air". Air characterized understanding, mental objective, and connection to universal life force. Earth represents grounding, the foundation of life, substance, interrelations to one's path through life, and family genealogical tree. The air ideogram in chemistry can also described as a vitalizer strength, and it corresponds with the shades white and blue.

AIRYANA-ishejo (Zend) label of an invocation "holy Airyamen", the celestial characteristics of Ahriman previously he enhanced a black antagonistic force, Satan. Considering Ahriman is of the duplicate essence as Ahura Mazda, precisely as Typhon-Seth is of the matching manifestation as Osiris.

AISH (Hebrew) Term for "Man".

AISHA (Gnostics) Muhammad's favorite wife. She rebelled in opposition to Muhammad Ali's successor.

AITH (Ur) (heating) Solar ignition; Heavenly atmosphere.

AIJ Taion. The highest-ranking deity of the Yakootos, an ethnic group of northward Siberia.

AJA (Sanskrit) "Innate", "unborn", uncreated. Epithet concerning numerous of the necessary deities of India [Brahma, Ziva, Vichnu], distinctly the main Logos. It radiates from the absolute on the plane of illusion.

AJITA (Sanskrit) "Not defeated", "indestructible". Nickname of Vishnu.

AJITAS *Exclusive* of the hidden names, of the twelve gods that are contemplated; those who are incarnated in every Maha manvantara. The mystics acknowledge them with the Kumaras. They will be designated Jnana (or Gnana) Devas. It is also a Vichnu model in the second Manvantara. They are also called Jaya's.

AJNA (Sanskrit) Among yogis, literally is the sixth Padma or plexus of matter. Placed between the eyebrows.

AJNANA (Ajnana or Agnyana) (Sanskrit) or Agyana (Beng.) No indeed understanding, lack of knowledge, rather "ignorance", "nescience", as it is often interpreted. Ajnani (Ajnani) refers to "irreverent". "Layman."

AKA-BOLZUB The feminine aspect of the Logos, amid the Maya.

AKALA is an island found northeast of Alola, neighboring Mele. This appellative is also used with the name of women.

AKAR (Egyptian) Established name of that division of the Ker-neter, harmful regions, which can be cited as a hell.

AKARA (Sanskrit) The letter or vowel A.

AKARMA (Sanskrit) Lack of action; inaction.

AKARYA (Sanskrit) "No duty", sin, crime, guilt action, which it should not do.

AKASA (Sanskrit) Relatively is the universal interval in which the eternal ideation of the Universe in its ever-changing aspects on the stage of matter and objectivity is immanently, and from which the Logos, or expressed thought, comes.

AKASH (Sanskrit) Assumption of heavens. It fills all infinite space and comes from the transformation of PRANA.

AKASHIC or Annals (Records) (theosophy) Chronicles in the upper worlds. Sixth dimension, also called "Memory of Nature" or "Memory of the Logos". Here are permanently recorded, all the events, memories of everything that has happened and will happen in the physical world. As maintained by esotericism, all words, thoughts and deeds, whatsoever their importance. They raise vibrations that impress the Akashic matter which is something like a cinematographic film with the distinction that these films are multidimensional and alive.

AKAZA (Akasa or Akasha) (Sanskrit) [Space, air, the luminous sky.] The sophisticated, supersensitive spiritual substance that fills and penetrates all space. The primal substance erroneously identified with the Ether, since it is with respect to the Ether what the Spirit with respect to Matter, or the Atma with respect to Karmapa. It is the universal space in which the eternal Ideation of the Universe is inherent, continuously alternating aspects on the plains of matter and objectivity, and from which the Logos, or expressed reflection, comes.

AKCHA (Aksha) (Sanskrit) Understood as a sound, word, especially the sacred word OM. It also means: Indivisible, indestructible, enduring, eternal, irreversible, always perfect; the Absolute, the supreme Deity, Brahma.

AKCHARA (Akshara) (Sanskrit) Resonate, sacred word OM; invisible, indestructible, permanent, eternal, final, always perfect; the absolute supreme deity Brahma.

AKHU (Egyptian) In the group of the Egyptians, "intelligence".

AKIBA (Hebrew) The one and only of four Tanaim (initiated prophets) who, after entering the Garden of Earthly Delights (occult sciences), managed to be started, while the other three failed.

AKKA (Sanskrit) The Great Mother.

AKSHARA, Akshara (Sanskrit) are Sounds, sacred terms, OM. Indivisible, indestructible, perpetual, eternal, final, infinitely perfect; the Absolute, the primal Deity, Brahma.

AKTA (Sanskrit) The "Anointed" Title Twachtri or Vizvakarman, the supreme "Creator" and Logos in the Rig-Veda. Labeled "Father of the Gods" and "Father of sacred Fire". The sun is also determined by the same name.

ALBA (Petra) (Latin) The "White Stone" of Initiation, the "White Carnelian" alluded to in revelation (Revelation) in the book of St. John.

ALBAN, St., and SERGIUS, St., Society of. An institution established in 1928 that intents at supporting appreciation linking Christians, exclusively among the Anglican and Orthodox Churches.

ALBEDRIO (Gnosticism) Every man can change his actions; because he has Free Will.

ALCUIN (c.735-804). Benefactor of the Carolingian Renaissance. He managed and instructed in the sanctuary center of learning at York. Following conference Chariemagne in 781, he came to be his mentor in devotional and pedagogical affairs. He fixed a castle book collection and effective Diocesan of Assignment in 796, during that period; he also set up a valuable information center and academy there. He put together scholastic handbooks, poems, and charged on the dynamic Monarchianism blasphemy of Felix of Urgel; in addition, he also renovated the psalm book in Gaul, assembled a Sacramentary, and adjusted 18 consecrated gatherings.

AL, or EL (Hebrew) Distinctive of the translated deity, it is "God", it means powerful, supreme. Plural Elohim.

ALAN OF LILLE (d. 1203) Arise as a Poet, theologian, and clergyman. Dedicated himself to study & tutored in Paris. He later went frontwards to make a move to the South of France where he entered the abbey of Citeaux; where he prevailed there until the end of his life. His theological manuscripts developed from his prime including a Partial Summa Quoniam hominy, unprinted "quaestiones, the Regulae Caelestis luris, to what end; he tried to tell theological truths in a series of rules or axioms, assembled a wordbook of Biblical expressions an Ars praedicandi, & Liber poenitentia is, was the preliminary physical guide of a clergyman for confession.

ALLAH (Arabic) The Ilah, the divinity) is the designation of the supreme being, among Muslims.

ALADDIN (Lamp of) The appellative Aladdin materializes from the Arabic, "Allah ad-Din (djinn)" which means... glory of faith (of genius). As for Aladdin's lamp, it is a fascinating story of the Thousand and One Nights. The maiden Aladdin, holder of a magic lamp, executes the most brilliant fortune his mysterious interpretation accords with the awakened consciousness and the secret power that a man notices, according to a great reputation of arcane scholars and writers.

ALARIC (c. 370-410), Visgothic Chie. He gravitates in the Imperial army but, disconcerted in his conviction of a more significant standpoint, he is single-minded to overcome a domain for himself. He besieged Rome in 408, 409, and 410, infiltrating the city on 24 August 410. This event was the instant experience of St. Augustine's City of God.

ALAPA. According to West usage, the light blow at one time commitment by the bishop on the cheek of those recent confirmed.

ALAYA (Sanskrit) Transpires as the Soul-Master. The Anima Mundi or Universal Spirit.

ALCHIMISTAS Accordingly is the one who transmutes the lead of his human personality straight into pure gold of the spirit.

ALCUIN The manufacturer of the Carolingian Renaissance. He attended and instructed in the cathedral school in York. After meeting Charlemagne in 781, he developed into counselor in dutiful and educational matters. He accepted the palace library, becoming Minister Tours in 796, and set up a predominant library and school there. He put together scholastic material, poetry, and a strike on the Adoptionism nonconformity of Felix of Urgel; he also modifies the lectionary in Gaul, set up a Sacramentally, and collected 18 reliquary masses.

ALCIONE The ancient sun of the Pleiades. Around it gravitates seven suns, ours; the seventh that revolves throughout it. They say, however; that, in our solar system of Ors, at any instant, it would perforate the terrible rings of Alcione; which proposed a molecular transformation on our planet due to radiation and subjected to a new glaciation.

ALCOHOL Solution bought by distillation of wine and other transformed spirits also labeled wine spirit. The detestable vice of alcohol conflicts with mysterious work that horribly weakens ethical expression of a human being's freedom, with alcohol resurrecting the already dead selves.

ALCOL Channels the substance of a body, which is free to arise all terrestrial matter, in its fragile or astral form.

ALCYONE (Greek) As a substitute Halcyone. She was the daughter of Aeolus and wife of Ceyx who drowned in a shipwreck; when she made a trip to have a consultation with the oracle, in her desperation she threw herself into the sea. That demonstration of faithfulness aroused the clemency of the gods, who changed the appearance of both husbands in actions. The female is said to lay her eggs in the sea and keep it calm during the seven days preceding and the seven days following the winter solstice. This has a very concealed significance in ornithomancy.

ALDEN Ensue a temple where all the Master of Medicine Work. This place of worship is found inside.

ALEPH Appears as the first letter of the Greek alphabet. Air part, according to the Zohar.

ALLEGORY An approach of expression to which, on the one hand, is appreciated equally. The allegorical perception of the Gospel is a special procedure of interpretations which was accomplished in the Palestinian Arab Ministerial educational institutional; consequently, referred to the Hebrew Scriptures by the Christian doctrine authors, the designation by itself practiced by St. Paul (Gal. 4: 24). The allegories which the Pentateuch reporters concluded in the Covenant were believed to compose a predictive disclosure of succeeding episode. Consequently, the association linking the Temple and the House of worship was assumed foretell in the tale of Isaac and Ishmael. This technique of perception was performed and conveyed to redundant by the Catechetical School of Alexandria. It was habitual across the Gothic Ages and is to certain traverse current in Catholicity; it was censured by the Reformists and is evaded by many Pentecostals.

ALFA (Greek) Stands for a Greek letter in electroencephalography is rhythm of physical, intellectual-emotional rest.

ALGOL. Alcohol demon. It is the denomination of a star. As well, Medusa was cut by Perseus.

ALHAN (Sanskrit) "Day", the substance of Brahma, for the Puranas.

ALHIM (Hebrew) Signifies "God of Gods" See: Elohim.

ALKAHEST (Arabic) Proclaims the universal solvent in alchemy. But in mysticism, it is the Higher Self, harmony with what makes matter (lead) gold, and restore all things composed, such as the human body and its qualities, to their remote essence.

ALL SAINTS' DAY. The tribute, now guarded in the West on 1 November, to recognize each Christian Holy being, conscious of or unfamiliar. It was apparently initially reserved the first Sunday subsequent of Pentecost, nonetheless, it is in the East Its observation on 1 November contingency after Gregory III (d. 741), who ultimately dedicated a Sanctuary in St. Peter to 'All the Saints'.

ALL SOULS' DAY. The remembrance of the souls of the faithful deceased on November 2; the day after 'All Saints' Day. Its tradition of Odilo of Cluny (d. 1049)

ALINA (Celtic) Many authors point out that the emergence of this word is Celtic, and illustrates "attractive", "funny", however, others consider that it comes from the Germanic and that its definition would be "noble" or "belonging to the nobility".

ALINGA (Sanskrit) Sinal "No mark or badge"; identical, enduring, that which cannot be make sense of in anything else. In the Aphorisms of Patanjali, this word is allocated to Pradhana or Prakriti, an authentic similar matter.

ALIVE. The term is frequently utilized to designate "spirited" or "full of energy," placid, appealingly; a birthday gathering materialized alive to an equal degree as the clown and the pony rides appear. Alive approaches from the Old English clause on existence, "in living" or "in life." (Chai, "living"; Zao, "to live" Anazao, "to live again"): The indicated Hebrew and Greek individualist are the leading words for aliveness in the two Greek Scriptures. People overspread all living, counting vitality and inner being, while essentially specifying tangible exuberance. Living is at best glancing at the time as individuals respire, ingest, and rest, etc. Subsisting alive is surviving at top-ranking of awareness and enumerating of our own environment. Hebrews 4:12 (NIV) For the word of God is alive and active. Sharper than any double-edged sword, it penetrates even to dividing soul and spirit, joints and marrow; it judges the thoughts and attitudes of the heart.

ALIYA The resolution significance of Aliya, has its inception in Arabic culture. Ots initial message translates to "exalted" or "noble", which replicated a sense of achievement and virtuous behavior. In the Islamic faith, the designation

Aliya is frequently connected with those who have detected a high volume of spiritual enlightenment. Aliyah in Hebrew determines "ascent" or "going up". Jewish long-established views pilgrimage to the Land of Israel as an ascent, both geographically and metaphysically.

ALMS. Ready monies, food, or alternative donations contributed to people in need; whatever is handed down as almsgiving.

ALMA *Nephesh Psyche of the Bible;* vital principle, whisper of shared life man animal. The connection between the divine Spirit of man and his secondary personality. The mind is the power of it.

ALMEH (Arabic) Dancing girls; the same as the Indian natoches, temple dancers and public.

ALMOND TREE Indicated as an insignia of sweetness and lightness. In Religious beliefs, the Almond, with its pit keep hidden behind an exterior armor and a solid chassis, epitomizes the cleanness of the maiden and the concealed reverence in the interior of the mortal configuration of Messiah. This is why Godly images frequently components of the Holy Mother and Christ enclosed by an almond-shape Aureola, or structure.

ALPHA Expedient in kabbalah to take, it is a system of mystical and allegorical clarification of the Torah (which Christians cite Pentateuch and replaces the first five books of the Christian Bible), which inquire into that text the meaning of the world and the "truth".

ALPHABET Persists a magical characterization of the sounds we make as humans when we speak. Each language with their surface transcriptions, and pronunciation of ancient sounds creates the capacity of humans to communicate & understand one another.

ALOA VADAATH Maniram of the causal world, for magic with the elementals of nature.

ALOGOS (Greek) Eventuate the thoughtless principle, as opposed to Logos or reason.

ALOKANA (Sanskrit) See, perceive, reflect. In Sankhya philosophy, it is the vague sensation of the vibrations of the physical world that culminate upon consciousness.

ALUECH. The genuine intangible frame (the Atma).

ALSWIDER (Scandinavian) "Very Fast" Distinctive of the horse and the Moon, in the Eddas.

ALTAR Symbolizes, in the ritual, the Cosmic Christ. He is the mediator between the Father and the Priest who replaces the Holy Spirit.

ALTER (Gnosticism) Part of pseudo-esotericisms and pseudo-occultists have certainly gotten hold of themselves quite pessimistic in association to the law of Action and Consequence; they mistakenly presumed that it unfolds mechanically, automatedly and cruelly. Scholars believe that it is not to be expected to alter such a Law, to ruin them; I'm sorry to have to disagree with that way of thinking. Psychological aggregates can alter (distort) the impressions of humanity.

ALTRUISM It is derived from the Latin word alter, another. Peculiarity opposed to egoism. Facts that are inclined to help others, aside from seeing oneself.

ALTER. This term is interpreted as alternating, revising or changing; executing a distinction partially, as measure, pattern, series, or the equivalent; short of alternating towards anything further. To alter commodities is mainly independent. The Doctrinal significance of alter is observable in the Scriptures as "God's table," a solemn location for offerings and bonanzas extended before the Creator. The speech form of Altar turned up from the Latin altarium, interpreting "high," and along with Latin adolere, which implies "to ritually burn or sacrifice." which insinuates its initial intention as elaborated in the Holy Scriptures.

ALZE Liber, by Lapide Philosophic. Alchemical agreement that was written by an anonymous German author; dated 1677. It must be republished in the Hermetic Museum. In it materialized the drawing that is well known; of a man with his legs outstretched and his body envelop by a seven-pointed star. Eliphas Levi has duplicated it in one of his compositions.

AM-ADU-HAI (Egyptian) Prevail the demon of the mind. It is the enchanting demon himself quoted Has-As.

AMA, AMIA (Hebrew) Mother. Sephira Binah, the heavenly distinctive is Jehovah or "Supreme Mother."

AMIA (Cald.) o Ama (Heb.) "Mother." Appellation of Sephira Binah, her "divine celebrity is Jehovah" and which is commanded as "Supreme Mother".

AMBER People conclude that amber "pulled out" a condition from the frame and "attracted" good luck; additionally, as it appeals to small commodity if you to a degree rub it. It was accepted that amber decorations averted misfortune, restrained from the hostile stare, acquired luck in love, and made a man well-built and exceptional. Easton's Bible dictionary translate the word by "polished brass," others "fine brass," as Ain Revelation 1;15; 2;18. In the Bible Ezekiel 1:27 in-context 27 I saw what remind you of purifying, amber-colored fire radiating from what becomes plain to be his waist upward. descending from what show to be his waist, I saw what noticed like fire, giving a brilliant light all over him.

AMBIENCE. Is an emotive or atmosphere similar to a specific spot, human being, or intent: setting. In a farther for environment probably of the brighten a scene or locale has. If a pricey eatery has a downy glow and pleasant melodies, it has a charming, pacifying ambience. The definition of ambience in the Holy writings is a comprehensive environment: surroundings. When following a vivacious animated devotional celebration there are ambient surroundings. The Shaddai are joining forces.

AMBO A heightened platform in a Christian "basilica, from which the Scriptures could be legible, and other community parts of the liturgy manage. After the 14th centennial ambos were put back by pulpits, but in some places, they have been reestablished in contemporary times.

AMBROSIANA. The Ambrosiana Library at Milan was established c. 1605 by Federico Borromeo and was one of the initial great libraries open to the community free from distinction.

AMALGAM Allegorically undertone "compound of different things" Oxford Dictionary's definition of Amalgam is a compound or consolidation of appealing concepts.

AMANA SOCIETY A small-scale Christian denomination, which was also acknowledged as the circle of faithful innovation. It arises in Germany in 1714. A considerable part of the body drifted to America in 1842 settling in Amana, Iowa, where a small totalitarianism bodywork pulls through.

AMARA (Koza) (Amara Koshae) (Sanskrit) The "immortal vocabulary". It is contemplating the oldest dictionary known in the world, and it has the most flawless classical Sanskrit vocabulary. It was collected by Amara Sinha, sage of the second century.

AMAREZVARA (Sanskrit) Exemplify "Lord of the Immortals" (Amara-Izvara). Title of Vichnu, Ziva and Indra.

AMARU Sacred snake that is the infinity amid the indigenous legends of Peru.

AMAZON(S) They were warrior women who mutilated one of their breasts for better assistance of the bow. Its most famous queen was: Pentesilea. They came to the aid of Troy and battled opposite the Greeks.

AMBA (Sanskrit) "Mother". Identification of the principal of the seven Pleiades, celestial sisters each one of whom was married to Richi's who belonged to the Starkisha or the seven Richi's of the constellation included as Bigad.

AMBITION (Gnosticism) Greed is disordered appetite to get wealth or goods, it is yearning for accumulation, unchecked longing, excessive aspiration; it is an inclination to own what others have.

AMBHAMSI (Sanskrit) This is the pseudonym of the leading figure of the Kumaras. Sanat Sujata, which signifies "the waters".

AMBROSIA (Greek): Delight of the Gods of Olympus, which communicated immortality to those who ate it. Ambrosia is sensual strength transmuted through sensitive sex.

AMDO It is a sacred neighborhood, native place of Tson-kha-pa, the famous Tibetan transformer and founder of the Gelupka; (yellow equates) admired as an avatar of Amita-Buddha.

AMEN Means, so be it. Used in worship, conclusion of prayers to manifest what he asks to have reliable conclusion.

AMENTI or AANROO (Egyptian) Esoterically and symbolically, the quarters of the god Amen, or Amoun, or the secret, hidden god. It was just like the "House of God the Father" where; there exists "many mansions." Aabroo was like a second division of Amenti; where there was a heavenly environment in an agricultural area, where essences that were Disen honored came, the region was circulated with an iron wall; grass grew there in an extraordinary way; there were wheat plants that were three cubits tall, another five, the tallest reached seven cubits, those absent who could grow wheat with three or more cubits entered the state of bliss. The others whose harvest was only three cubits high, were moved to hellish regions. Among the Egyptians, wheat was a sign of the Law of Retribution or Karma. The elbows are rewarded if they were seven, five or three stages of human "initiation".

AMENTX it is the country where the dead live according to the Egyptian mysteries.

AMESHA (SPENTAS) (Zend) Amesha Spends) The six Seraphim's or Divine Forces that are manifested as gods, which they pledge to Ahura Mazda, amid them, this one; it is the synthesis and the seventh. They are one of the models of the Roman Catholics "Seven Spirits" or Seraphim with Michael as chief, or the "Heavenly Host": the "Seven Angels of the Lord". They are the builders, the creators of the Cosmos, for the Gnostics, and identical to the Seven Prajapati's, the Sephiroth, etc. [In Zoroastrianism, one of the seven Spirits or Planetary Logos.]

AMIDA Allude to the buddhas of infinite light. He is the king of heaven and eternal joy.

AMON OR AMMON Egyptian God, deity of Thebes, epithet meaning the supreme, associated with the sun. He is illustrated with a male figure; two horns atop his ears and two ostrich feathers over his forehead.

AMMONIUS, (AMMONIO) SACCAS (c. 175-242) An Alexandrian, presume to be the originator of 'Neoplatonism. He was specifically revealing as an instructor and became apparent to have considerably prestige Plotinus' accomplished.

AMRITA (Sanskrit) Elixir, delight or provisions of the gods; the food that concede immortality. The Elixir of life extirpated from the Ocean of milk, in the Puranic metaphor. Ancient Vedic voice guarded the blessed Soma juice in the Temple Enigmas.

AMSAH This is a Hindu god, one of the Aditi's brothers. It is said that he is a classification of heavenly deities who dwell in the heavens along with his parents Kashyapa and Aditi.

AMOS, Book of. The earliest in time of the authorized seer of the OT. Amos was a shepherd and dresser of sycamore trees, who utilized his ministry in Israel allying 760 and 750 B.C. At a time of success, when the measure of wealth was principal to unfairness and persecution of the poor, he urged the seriousness warning of social equity and the ultimatum of approaching sound judgments. The 'Day of the Lord', to which the Hebrews glance forward as the dawning of a Golden Age, would be a day of fairness when Israel would be self-conscious at the realization of the recompense of irregularity.

AMULAN, MULAM (Sanskrit) Insinuates: the "root without root". The Mula prakriti of the Vedan points, spirituality, the "root of Nature" which is the "material of the universe; Prakriti."

AMULET(S) These are matters which accredit the authority to drive away revolutionary spirits and communicate luck to a supernatural power to the one who owns it. The management of such things was developed by all nations. Egyptian mummies are said to be enclosed with amulets or talismans shaped like a beetle, hawks, eyes belts. etc. Additionally, abrax stones were used not only by the Gnostics, but were also long established by Eastern populations, including a variety of types of amulets, some bearing written terms, numbers, letters, symbols or phrases of a mystical or religious nature. It is said that these amulets were protected with a leather lining or fabric that hung from the neck.

AMUN (Coptic) Stands as the designation of the Egyptian god of wisdom who only had Instituted or Advocated to devote their lives to the priesthood.

AMURA MAZDA The solar Logos (Christ) among the Persians. It is divinity substantiated. Hormuz or divine light, universal.

ANA (Chaldean) Interprets the "invisible sky" or Astral Light; the jubilant mother of the transient sea; from there perhaps derives the fundamentals of Anne, root mother of Mary.

ANADA (alchemy) This word refers to activities caused by astral influences, celestial powers, the activity of imagination and fantasy.

ANAEL. In the Western esoteric lore; he is one of the seven Archangels. Anael unites with the number seven planet Venus; and with green and copper. He is also interrelated with the Kabbalistic sephirah (place in the symbolic Tree of Life) of Netzach, or "Victory."

ANADI Symbolizes, "Without beginning", - Uncreated.

ANAGAMIN (Sanskrit) Practice which states one no longer be reborn in the world of longing. It is pronounced that it was a degree before becoming Arhat and being arranged for Nirvana. That it is the third of the four degrees of holiness on the path of final Initiation. The soul no longer needs to reincarnate; having passed this stage.

ANATA. In (Theravada Buddhism) the reliance that since all undertakings are continually alternating, to this location powerless analogous as a perpetual self: one of the three primary qualities of subsistence: Sanskrit word: **anatman** anicca, dukkha.

ANAHATA-nada (Sanskrit) Sounds not processed by concussions. The sound OM.

ANAID Phoenician deity that accumulates attributes like those of Venus, Minerva. Ceres and Diana.

ANKH An ansata cross shape.

ANNA COMNENA Daughter of the Emp. Alexis I, Comnenus, she plotted to overturn her brother, then withdrew to a convent. While there, she composed Alexia's, a eulogy narrative of her father's reign. It is of attentiveness as an example of Traditional antagonism to the West church and the campaign as a hazard to the East Empire.

ANNAS. The Jewish High Priest from A.D. 6 or (7 to 15) and father-in-law of Caiaphas. According to Jn. 18:13 Christ was presented before Annas being prior to being sent on to Caiaphas.

ANANDA (Sanskrit) Declares, Joy, happiness. It is also the appellative of Lord Buddha, Gautama's favorite follower. It is a stage of bliss where the soul meets the spirit.

ANANGA (Sanskrit) Epithet of Kama Remains the god of love. The "disembodied".

ANANTA (Sanskrit) He was king of the Nagas. At the end of each "Kalpa" (meaning a manvantara, the end of a universe) throws a devouring fire that destroys all of creation. It is a symbol of eternity. Epithet of Vichnu. The celebrity of Ananta or Ananta-Zecha is also selected as the Serpent of Eternity, a substantial seven-headed serpent.

ANAMNESIS. The commemoration of the Passion, Resurrection, and Ascension of Christ, which in most liturgies is embraced in the Eucharistic Canon after the Words of Institution.

ANAPHORA. The essential invocation in the Benediction liturgy, worship the Application, the Anamnesis, and the Eucharist.

ANSATA CROSS (Latin) It is the cross with grasp meantime that the Tau has a T structure, the elderly Egyptian cross or TAT was like this + The ansata cross was an emblem of immortality.

ANASAVA Sutta It is a collection of established Buddhist literature. In this cluster you can discover rules for Buddhist monks. This declaration is also admitted as "the book of discipline".

ANASTASIS This utterance appeals cordially resurrection of Christ and of that of humanity in general. In the principal churches were dedicated to the Anastasis (of Christ) at Jerusalem and Constantinople.

ANATMAKA (Sanskrit) Amid Buddhists, it is unreal, illusory, purely phenomenal.

ANATU Refers to anu's feminine appearance. It reinstates the Earth and the Abyss; its alliance stands for Heaven and Height. She is the mother of the god Hea and assemble heaven and earth.

ANCAS This concept reports the states in which the three planes of Yoga are administer: psycho-physical, mental and moral.

ANCHOR As maintained by Christian customs this methodology was a symbol of hope and salvation.

ANDAJA (Sanskrit) This sound refers to oviparous or egg generation.

ANDONDO-AMADETESANA Signifies "Nopal in the middle of the moon". Initiatory phase of the gnostic mysterious work.

ANDRA (Sanskrit) This term describes the sixth lunar asterism.

ANDRAMELEK Relates to a fourth grader Hanas Mussen. It outstretches higher angelic states, but today it is involuting amid the bowels of the earth. It designates the negative ray of Mars, while the Elohim Gibur is its antithesis or practical ray of Mars.

ANDRES, Saint. He was a supporter of Jesus the Christ. It embodies the gospel of the cross in (X) being Buddhist eradication. (Death of the ego). That was his drama as a Grandmaster.

ANDROID (Greek) Implies a mechanism with a human figure.

ANDUDU This word is applied by prehistoric sages who pronounced it during meditation to announce affairs that would occur in the future.

ANCHOR The objective of an anchor is to halt a boat, balance it on the water, and hang on to it resolutely at its intentional points. It's alleged that seaman presume that anchors provide as a protection from tempest, emblematic of expectations for serene ocean. Amid Religious, those authorities are images or representations of purpose and conservation.

ANGA (Sanskrit) Implies, member, element, branch, part.

ANGARAKA or ANGARA It is a Fire Star; the planet Mars, in Tibetan, Migmar.

ANGELIC DOCTOR. The designation administers to St. Thomas Aquinas.

ANGELIC HYMN. Another name for Gloria in excelsis.

ANGELS, ANGELES It is a superlative condition of objective consciousness. This can be accomplished with alchemical work or fire magisterium. It indicates division, ascension of a fragile (spiritual) principle.

ANGELUS. A Catholic allegiance immortalize the substantiation of Christ. As with a variety of Catholic invocation, the expression Angelus is emanating from its elementary; the first few terms of the content: Angelus Domini nuntiavit Mariae ("The Angel of the Lord declared unto Mary"). Arrival is the time of the year of formation for the coming of the Lord in the world. The Angelus emphasizes us of the annunciation of Christ's birth by the angel Gabriel to Mary, it transfigures our hearts to be like the servant heart of Mary, and it admonish us that the Word was made flesh and God dwelt with us.

ANGER Motivated by authentic enthusiasm (particularly) that arrives, mistakenly, to dominate us. These fervors are conceivably "natural desires," welcome devotion, dismay, intend, fond look, consideration, discipline etc. Logical fervor for reliable artifact is indicated to allow under our enthusiasms to appreciate the Almighty. Exasperation is a lesser feeling; Customarily, we participate in a predominant desire feel like dismay, deplete, or somber initially. Since the empathy nurture insights into culpability and casualty management, they generate disagreement. One -sided of striving to handle herewith fondness is by repressed relocation within irritation. Only when Anahata Chakra is out of equilibrium. It is considered to motivate irritability, deficiency of confidence, apprehension, resentment, fright, and gloominess. An excitable nucleus chakra is belief to lead the way to hypertension, pulsations and heart failure. The sentiment of irritation is related to a grumpy mood and generates indignation and resentfulness. It is presumed a certain sensation is built up in the hepatic system and the cholecystic, that accommodate venom. Anger may generate migraines and raise blood pressure that may in succession influence the tummy as well as ill will. God's anger is not the same as human anger. You could have gone through adversity similar to anyone who is consistently angry. Humanlike displeasure may usually be uncertain, miserly, and difference. Such actions are untruthful of the anger of the Creator. The Almighty's rage is precise and unfaltering acknowledgment of His divinity regarding maliciousness.

ANGIRASAS (Sanskrit) This phrase is utilized as a generic epithet for people and things among the Puraniks is a class of Pitri's, who are ancestors of man. There is also a river of Plakcha also summoned with that name. The Angirasa's established a race of high beings connecting gods and men. It was also one of the honorifics that called the Dhyani's: who were instructors of the Devas "Guru Devas", inaugurates of third, fourth and fifth races.

ANGRA MAITIYUS (Zend) Persists as a Zoroastrian name of Ahriman; it is said to be an evil spirit of destruction and opposition, of which Ahura Mazada (in the Venida's, Fargard I) says, that he "counteracts by his authority" every perfect land that God creates; for "Angra Mainyu expresses all death."

ANAID. The Phoenician deity which collected credit of Venus, Minerva, Ceres and Diana.

ANIADA (Alchemy) Transpire actions that are caused by astral influence, celestial powers, activity of imagination and fantasy.

ANIL Similar to indigo plant that grows in South America and the Tropics, from which, blue color is obtained.

ANILA (Sanskrit) Points out to a whisper, or current of air. The God of the wind is also described, regent of the Northwest. Called Pavana Vayu.

ANIMA (Latin) Touched on the Soul. With this denomination the internal organ (Anthahkarana) is appointed, sustained by three principles. Atma, Buddhi, and Manas.

ANIMAN (Sanskrit) "Smallness", "subtlety". One of the eight siddhis or uppermost occult potential. The empower to decrease oneself to an extreme degree of smallness or to resemble the atom.

ANIMAL (Kingdom) (Gnostic) Contrasting lives of the most prosperous plant kingdom. Later creatures enter the numerous dependencies of the animal kingdom, disperse in multiple families or species, also has their gluttony and their tempos in the etheric world (4th coordinate or dimension). Later they will extend the human situation, Ros. The animals have dense, vital bodies and maneuver, growth, performance and sensory perception.

ANNIHILATED (Gnosticism) Destroy, if in this basic element are the basic origins of recovery, obviously the first thing we must do is ruin, defeat that second species of infernal type within which the essence is imprisoned.

ANISE This term is established only in Mathew 23:23. It is the herb ordinarily studied by the honorific of dillseed, the Peucedanum graveolens of the botanist. This appellative dill is emanated from a Norse word that measures to appease, the shrub having the carminative resources of alleviate ache. Anise, (Pimpinella anisum), per annum greenery of the parsley family (Apiaceae), horticulture mainly for its fruits, called aniseed, the flavor of which reminds one of that of licorice. Anise has anti-fungal, antibacterial and anti-inflammatory attributes and may fight stomach ulcers, keep blood glucose level off in check and diminish signs of depression and menopause. incorporated with a nutritious diet and healthy way of life, anise seed could remodel several multifaceted of your health. The scented anise hyssop resides largely in the plant's leaves, while anise ordinarily holds its aroma in its seeds. Both florae have been regularly used in culinary, aromatherapeutic, and herbal appeal, but for divergent reasons.

ANITYA (Sanskrit) Stipulates: Not eternal, transient, perishable, destructible, transient, limitation.

ANNO DOMINI. This abbreviation is used in musical scores that symbolizes 'Da Capo' points out at a certain position of a piece you must return to the beginning. (Latin, 'in the year of the Lord'). Currently, the systems of dating by A.D., set up in the presumed year of the birth of Christ. It is now commonly believed that the genuine blessed event was a great deal of years prematurely.

ANNOU (Sanskrit) Explains "Air, winds." This idiom is also another name for Vayu, the Vedic God of the wind.

ANOIA (Greek) Directly a lack of interpretation, foolishness. Subject concedes by Plato to the inner manas.

ANOMEANS 4th-century, defenders of a creed akin to Arianism. Their overseer was Aetius and Ennius (qq.v.)

ANOUKI (Egyptian) Arises as an aspect of Isis; the goddess of life, her pseudonym derives from the Hebrew voice Ank, which means life.

ANSATA Refers to the cross with a handle. This cross was a symbol of immortality. The Ansata cross was the first symbol of Egyptian Freemasonry initiated by Count Cagliostro.

ANSELM, St. (c. 1033-1109) Pastor of Canterbury from 1093. He gains the victory on Abbot of Bec. There were many discussions between Anselm and William II and in 1098 he traveled to Rome. He became enlightened of the papal directives in opposition to lay enrollment in 1099; when his contemporary king, Henry I, invited him to England in 1100, he supported inspecting the orders without adjustments. In 1102 he again arrives back to Rome and lived in exile until 1107, when the Pope and the King settled for accommodation secretly. As a theologian and philosopher, Anselm has held an elevated position amidst the preliminary lettered mastermind. Contrary to his peers, he favored protecting the conviction by rational hypothesis slightly than by disputes grounded on Doctrine and other jurisdictions. The goal of his Monologies was to prove the existence of the Almighty absolutely from the deliberation of truthfulness and goodness as cognitive inclinations. In the Pros logion this explanation was set, the more organized manifestation of the Supernatural Reasoning. His Cur Deus Homo was a notable contribution to the establishment of the Redemptions in the Medievalist Era. It describes the precept in language of the fulfillment because of the antagonized magnificence of deity and dismisses the apprehension that evil poses advantages above dishonored human beings; it was a commanding purposeful of the Cross to conciliate.

ANSON BY-LAW. The law authorizing a youngster to be withdrawn from a primary school at the time assigned to religious ceremony or instruction if the parent, so prefers and arrangement has been made for the child to attend religious observance and instruction elsewhere. The 1936 Education Act made the principles of the by-law appropriate everywhere. It was so called after William

Reynell Anson. Parliamentary Secretary to the Boad of Education when the 1902 Education Act was passed.

ANSUMAT (Sanskrit) He is a Puranic figure, this individual is "nephew of sixty thousand uncles" sons of King Sagara, it is said that they were diminished to ashes, only with a single glance of the "Eye" of Richi Kapila.

ANT(S) (Latin Formica). This is a Hymenoptera insect, who lives in a society where she spends the winter in isolation. Like bees they have three categories of subjects: fertilized females, males and neutrals or infertile females. In accordance with Indian myths, they are considered an emblem of smallness and of the life that dominates humanity. Master Samael resolves that they are the primitive geniuses or fallen Angels, of prehistory, who lived in the world before the earliest human race emerged. He assures that during the journey of millions of years, these classifications that existed prior to humanity were reduced to a degenerative state until they transcended the state in which they are presently. This is accredited to the communist regime they practiced; where their mind was annihilated, and their intelligence deteriorated. (See Bee)

ANTA, ANTAH or (ANTAR) (Sanskrit) Refers to the end, extreme, limit, death.

ANTAHKARANA (Sanskrit) This designation has distinct meanings in each school of philosophy. One translates it into the sense "understanding", others, into the internal organ or complement, the Soul, created by the thinker and vanity [ahankara]; the mystics; they define it as the path or bridge between the upper and lower Manas, the divine Ego and the individual soul of man; which can be differentiate or preserved by the eternal collectivity and made immortal with it, these being the only components of the passing Personality that are saved from death and time.

ANTARES This pseudonym has been given to an extraordinary sun; a million times more scattered than ours. On all the planets of your solar regime, your human beings enjoy solar consciousness, these planets have become suns.

ANTE CHAPEL The western end of definite medieval college chapels.

ANTEO Is a disposition that is the Titan of the terrible 'Dark Hordes'.

ANTICHRIST (Gnosticism) Myth, the great beast of the Apocalypse with seven heads and ten horns, emphasizing to us of the seven deadly sins, the Ten horns are related to the Ten Arcans of the tarot, the fatal wheel of samsara. It is also established in the human being by that number of defects or egos that personify their errors developing into the antithesis of the Christ. It is intellectualism as functionalism of the self; he is also the author of supposed wonders: the atomic bomb, rockets, warplanes, which bring about fascination in the human being, causing the reason to sleep completely.

ANTIMONY (Alchemy) It is one of the fragments of our being, which is recommended to point the gold atoms to our higher existential components of being, until changing them into pure gold, a nature that dry Mercury (egos) and arsenic sulfur (or Luciferic fire) are removed. He is our alchemist.

ANTILEGOMENA. The nomination given by Eusebius of Caesarea to those Scriptural books whose allegations to be contemplated part of the NT Canon was debated.

ANTINO-MIANISM A universal epithet for the perspective that Christians are by grace set at liberty from the necessity to perceive any virtuous law. Numerous Gnostic sects held that, as circumstances were sharply against the spirit, forcibly actions were ordinary and for that reason corruption was permitted. At the Reformation antinomian instructions were resumed, e. g. By the Anabaptists, as patronage from the Lutheran credo of justification by faith.

ANTI-MARCIONITE PROLOGUES. The. Short introductory prologues prefixed of the Gospels of Mk., Lk., and Jn. In a part 40 Manuscript of the Vulgate.

ANTIO channels goodbye (proper): Avrio. You may as well precisely affirm antio – it's alike to "adios" in Spanish. The dawning of the connect anti- and its variation ant- is an prehistoric Greek term which indicates "against" or "opposite". These adjunct take shape in many English lexicon expression, comparable as anifreeze, antidote, antoym, and antacid.

ANTIPATHY Indicates emotion felt towards another person that for the first time we know. It's an indicator that the awareness is overly asleep. Gnosis teaches that it is right to place oneself in the place of others to understand and love them.

ANTHROPOLOGY Glance at the discipline of human existence. This science includes, among other things: Physiology, that is, the origin of natural learnings that detects the mysteries of organs and their purpose in men, animals and plants; particularly, Psychology, and in our day the science of the soul, has been abandoned; likewise, as an entity distinct from the Spirit, in its relationships with the Spirit and the body. In modern science, psychology deals only or basically with the circumstances of the nervous system, and almost entirely ignores the psychic nature and essence.

ANOMEANS 4th centurial supporters of a credo similar to Arianism. Their leaders were Aetius and Eunomius (qq.v.)

ANNO DOMINI (Latin, 'in the year of the Lord'). At present, the structures of dating by A.D., set up in the presumed year of the birth of Christ. It is now commonly believed that the genuine blessed event was considerably years prematurely.

ANU (Chaldean) Attributes to the most eminent divinities of the Babylonians. King of angels and spirits. Nirvanic atom. God of heaven and earth, ancient deity of Babylon.

ANUBIS (Greek) Endures the dog-headed God. Similar in numerous ways to Horus. It is the divinity that organizes the disenchanted or the resurrected in post-mortem life. He is a psychopompic deity, which means that he escorts or leads souls to the other world, "the Lord of the Land of Silence of the West, who is the land of the dead, he is arranging the way of the other world", he oversees principal the deceased to Osiris, the Judge. It is regarded one of the oldest deities of Egypt, since Mariette Bey found the image of this god in tombs of the Third Dynasty.

ANUKI or ANOUKI (Egyptian) "The Term Ank of the Hebrew hope 'my life', my being, which is the personal pronoun Anochi of the name of the Egyptian goddess Anoukhi" The author of the 'Hebrew Mystery'; it says, and the origination of the Measures.

ANUMANTA (Sanskrit) The one who authorizes or allows. With this appellative the self or individual spirit is selected, as spectator and experimenter; allows acts of the body or reason.

ANYODEI It is the soul life; the personal state in which the higher nature of the soul enters after death, after it has been stripped of its most ordinary parts in the Kama-Loka. It corresponds to the surroundings of the Devachan.

ANZA (Ansa or Ancha) (Sanskrit) Part or particle analyze the Monad or Spirit.

AOUR (Chaldean) It is the compression of two features of the fragile star Brightness or astral Light: 1. It refers to the Od, which is the pure luminosity that gives existence, 2. It is the Ob, which is the radiance that gives leveling. The word Aour: it is the fertile embryo in the lap of immortal life.

ALAPA Conforming to West utilization, the light blows previously transferred by the prelate on the chick of those ones being confirmed.

APAM (Napat) (Zend) A mysterious being, concerning the Fohat of the mystical. It is on a par a Vedic label and a Avetyan [or avesta] credit. The phrase "Son of the Waters" of infinity, process, that is, Ether), in the Avesta Apam Napat is among the yazatas, or uncontaminated celestial essences, of fire and the yazatas of water.

APANA Mentions yoga practices. Prana and Apana are the "expiratory" and "inspiratory" murmurs. It is given the anonym of wind or vital air in the "Anugita."

APARA (Sanskrit) Lower. It's the opposite of para.

APPARITION (pair) Extensive said of the hallucinatory image of a living individual, or more often of a dead or disincarnated. Esp. Visible phenomenon of the beings of the intangible world.

APAS (Sanskrit) "Water" One of the five Tattvas, called atmosphere, gustifero.

APSE. A bow-shaped or polygonal eastern end to a sanctum. It was a universal attribute of the primitive temple type of church architecture. The altar settled on the chord of the apse, with seats for the bishop and presbyters in the space behind.

APAVA (Sanskrit) "That is recreated in the waters". Another characteristic of Narayana or Vichnu and Brahma combined, since Avapa, like the latter, is divided into two parts, male and female, and generate Vichnu, who in turn creates Viraj, who design Manu. Name is interpreted in several ways in Brahmanical literature.

APELLES. (2nd century), benefactor of a Gnostic sect. Initially a disciple of Marcion, he modified his dualism to defend a less Docetic dogma of the Person of Our Lord. Christ, he sustained, descended from the good God, who was not himself the creator of the world, nonetheless, and lived and suffered in a body miraculously formed out of the elements.

APPLE. It may suggest tenderness, insightfulness, intelligence, delight, dying, and or grandeur. It is an emblem of elegance, attractiveness and the inclination for bountifulness, and the strength of the produce and its durability illustrate energy and progress. The ancient Greeks maintain that Dionysus, the god of wine, fecundity, and the theatrical amidst other concepts, originate the apple. He offered it to Aphrodite, the goddess of love.

APPEARANCES External show: The way anyone or something looks. Semblance. e. g. Although hostile, he preserved an appearance of neutrality.

APPETITE It materializes from the Latin term "appetitus", controlled, in turn, of the preposition "ad-" plus the verb "Peto" which manner to address or ask for something. Appetite refers to that impulse, often contemplated innate and irrational, thoughtless or even unconscious, that leads us or moves us to accomplish some action to satisfy some substance needed. When it is used in the field of honesty it is usually given a despicable sensation no doubt since it is related with rational and bad passions or desires. Used in areas other than morality, but not detached from it, for example, in health or medicine, it does not have to have a derogatory sense. For example, when dealing with food or hunger, we can talk about the appetite of having a lot or truly little. In fact, there are occasions when you are going to eat, or you are starting the meal you usually want when you start "good appetite".

APPIAN WAY. The road completed by the censor Appius Claudius Caecus in 312 from B.C. from Rome to South Italy, St. Paul, travelling in the Appian Way, was met by groups of Christians at Appii Forum and Three Taverns (Acts 28: 15). possessing to the construction of the Via Appia Nuova, for the initiation miles out of Rome the old road continues much as it was in ancient times; it is surrounded by many Christians monuments and sanctuaries.

APIS Osiris personified in the sacred White Bull or the Living Dead. Apis was the white bull.

APOCALYPTIC LITERATURE. The term 'apocalypse' indicates a 'revelation' or 'unveiling', so that apocalyptic books claim to disclose stuff which are generally hidden or to announce the forecast. The Jewish Apocalyptic publication belong to the period from c. 200 a.c. to a.d. c.100; they deal with the end of the present arrangement and with the next generation. All pseudonymous, they comprise the Book of Daniel and, outside the Old Testament, the Book of Enoch, the Book of the Secrets of Enoch, the Apocalypses of Abraham and Baruch, the Fourth Book of Ezra, the Assumption of Moses, Jubilees, the Ascension of Isaiah, and the Testaments of the Twelve Patriarchs. The two most meaningful Christian apocalypses are Revelation and the (Noncanonical) Apocalypse Peter.

APOCATASTASIS. The Greek term for the doctrine that finally all free moral creatures; angels, men, and devils; will be saved. It was correctly condemned at the council of Constantinople in 543. The dogma, which has had modern protector, is likewise known as 'universalism'.

APOCALYPSE Etymologically means revelation, unveiling of mysteries, the law, the sword, the Force of the divine designation and the spirit. The name is associated to the last book of sacred scripture or holy bible. (Apocalypse of St. John).

APOCRYPHA [APOCRIFOS] (Greek Apocryphon Kabbalah, classified) The Apocrypha were respected as sacred books that should not come into the hands of the irreverent. Amids these were the apokarypha of the Old Testament who were expelled by the Jews for not being authorized, existing fourteen works written in Greek and not in Hebrew. In 1,546 eleven of them were inspected as valuable by the Council of Trent and were cited Deuterocanonical. In addition, there are the apocrypha of the Old Testament, among these tunesmiths are: Evangelic Epistles, facts of the apostles and the Apocalypse of St. John.

APOLOGY (Gnosticism) The Word, spoken or written should be grasped wisely, should not be used in slandering and defaming anyone. To declare what we ignore or do not know is falsehood. The lie is the opposite of the truth. To deny the reality of things is to lie. Deception, betrayal, hypocrisy and fraud, is the same lie disguised with the appearance of truth and justifications of insincerity and courage. Lying is the easiest method of evading responsibility. The lie is the same Apology that we carry to the surface of our lips.

APOLLO (God of Fire in Greek mythology) stands for the sun, son of Jupiter and Latona.

APOLLONIUS OF TYANA (d.c.) Neopythagorean philosopher. The virtues of his life and rectify religious tendencies were so amplify following his death that anti-Christian's writers composed biographies of him which consciously corresponded with the Gospel life of Christ.

APOLLOS. A knowledgeable Jew of Alexandria, who were determined followers of John the Baptist, prior to becoming a Christian (Acts 18:24-6). There has also been speculated that he was the author of the Message to the Hebrews.

APOPI is the demon of desire among the Egyptians.

APPRECIATING Acknowledging the value of people or things will appreciate an artist's work.

APSARAS (Sanskrit) Measures "that move in the waters", Dines or water nymphs of Paradise or Indra sky. As claimed by widely held belief, apsaras are the "wives of the gods" and they are designated Suranganas [beautiful women of the gods] using another less respected term they are named Sumadatmajas ["daughters of pleasure"] conforming to the myths, now they arose in overcoming the Ocean, neither the gods (suras) nor the demons (asuras) apprehended accepting them as authentic wives. In esotericism, it alludes to certain aquatic plants of narcotic integrity or "dream producers" and some inner power of nature.

APOSTICHA. In the "Orthodox Catholic Church, brief solemn psalms or stichera affixed to stanzas from the Psalm book.

APTA (Sanskrit) A single person who has come to be enlightened by himself.

APULEIUS (Lucius) Occurred the most important Roman writer of the second century, much admired both in life and by successors. Lucio is the protagonist of one of his works, The Golden Ass. An addition to his famous stories is titled Metamorphoses.

AQUA. The expression aqua is occasionally, as well utilized to channel "water", and in actuality the Latin root factor "water, the sea, or rain." Interpretation of aqua: approaches from Latin aqua, prefix, aqua proceeds from Latin, position it enjoys the definition "water". This sense is initiated in comparable expressions as: aquaculture, aquarium, aquatic, aqueduct aqueous aquifer. The three configurations that water can exist in are: solid, liquid and gaseous. The stable formation is ice, liquid structure is water, considering gaseous disposition is water vapors or condensation at hand in the atmosphere. To define water or Mother nature: Aqua is frequently utilized to identify water or nature in blueprint associated to ecologist, feasible, or exterior occupations. This fresh color analysis supports to provoke clearness of intellect, fervent stability, tranquility and inventiveness. It is as well generosity to originate your awareness enclosed for profound contemplation that may deliver relief and strength.

AQUARIANS An inopportune creed or faith which used water instead of wine in the Eucharist.

AQUASTOR An animation created by the power of imaginative faculty; that is, by the concentration of thought in the Akaza, thanks to which a fragile form can be created (elementals, succubus and incubus, vampires, etc.). These fanciful, and yet real, forms can buy life from the person by whose creative powers they have been generated, and under certain conditions they can even become visible and tangible.

AQUARIUS (Astrology) It is the eleventh signal of the zodiac (male fixed air). He is embodied by an equator, governed by Uranus and Saturn. (From January 20 to February 19). Aquarians are disposed to be illustrious sustainers and come to excel. They are kind, caritative, faithful, sincere, etc. On the unfavorable side they can be indifferent and conceive subversion. This sign governs the calves and ankles with an inclination to have varicose veins, circulation difficulties, major defects, and spinal cord injuries. The natives of Aquarius have resolutions for the natural sciences.

AQUILA, Version (of) A Greek adaptation of the Old Testament. It was the effort of Aquila, who turned out to be a convert to Judaism and enhanced versed in Hebrew from the Rabbis. His exhibition, which was seemingly completed c. 140. It was exceedingly precise.

AQUILEIA On the Jadranko in Croation, developed into a metropolis amid the delayed Roman Empire, as claimed by the narrative it was proselytize by St. Mark. In 381 its bishop, Valerian, unfold as metropolitan of the Sanctuaries in the rea and under him and his successor, Chromatius, Aquileia was a Centre of learning. In the 6th century, its bishops received the designation of totalitarian. The woodwork and boards of the basilica (rebuilt in the 11th centennial) is coated with early 4th century mosaics.

AR-ABU NASR-AL-FARABI. It is called in Latin Alpharabius. She was a native Persian and the most distinguished Aristotelian philosopher of her time. He was born in the year 950 of our era and is said to have been assassinated in 1047. He was a hermetic philosopher and was endowed with the power to hypnotize through music, making those who heard him laugh, cry, dance and everything he loved who heard him Taner the laud. Some of his works on Hermetic philosophy are in the library of Leyden.

ARAHAT (Sanskrit) It is also articulated and written Arhat, Ahan, Rahat, etc., "the worthy", literally; "who deserves divine honors." This was the designation first given to the Jain saints and consequently to the healthy proselytic Buddhists in the esoteric mysteries. Arhat is similar in that it has entered the best and supreme path, freeing themselves of the renaissance. [The Arhat is the initiate of the higher quality, that is, he who has attained the fourth and final initiation; anyone who passes through it becomes an Adept.

ARBA-IL (Cald.) The four great Gods. Arba is an Aramaic phrase meaning "four", and il is the same as Al or El. Three male and one female who is virgin, granted that reproductive; they form a very recurrent ideal of Divinity.

ARCA Metaphor of material nature; spiritual, power makes nothing lost, and all things are reborn.

ARCANE Deals with the work for the creation of solar bodies and to attain liberation.

ARCAN (Gnosticism) "Above the wheel of the Arcane Ten we see a sphinx adorned with a nine-pointed metal crown. Such an Egyptian figure flaunted... it is not located either to the right or to the left of the great wheel."

ARADO Suggest implantation and the work that must be done in the groundwork of our own lands (Philosophers - alchemical).

ARAF (Islam) Attribute to purgatory, where souls are purified by fire.

ARLES, Synods of, Amid the more extensive we're those of 314, summoned by Constantine to deal with the Donatist division, 353; an Ariani zing heresy: and 1263, which condemn the dogma of Joachim of Fiore.

ARMAGH. The Book of. An 8th-9th century vellum codex in Trinity College, Dublin. It embraces two lives of St. Patrick, the life of St. Martin of Tours by Sulpicius Severus, and a replenish non-Vulgate text of the Latin Gospel.

ARAMA (Sanskrit) Pleasure, delight, playground.

ARAMAIC. The Semitic speech which was the vernacular in Palestine in the time of Christ and which he nearly definitely intact. In later Hebrew Scriptures times, it progressively ousted Hebrew as the spoken language of Palestine, and a few sections of the Old Testament are written in it. By life of Christ times Aramaic paraphrases of Scripture (Targums) were concerned to satisfy the insistence of the people. Numerous passages in the Christian teachings reflect Aramaic modes of thought and on occasions Aramaic words are preserved (e.g. Mk. 5:5:41).

ARANI (Sanskrit) The "female Arani" is a style of the Vedic Aditi (esoterically "the matrix of the world") The Arani is a Swasti wooden disc with a midway hollow, in which the Brahmins conceive fire by friction with the pram Antha, a stick, ideogram of the male mechanism. It is a mystical rite of vast hidden and very sacred expression, which the rough materialism of our century manipulated as maned giving priapic male meaning.

ARASA MARAM (Sanskrit) The Indic sacred tree of knowledge. In cabbalism philosophy, it is a mystical word.

ARBA-IL (Chaldean) The Four Great Gods. Arba is an Aramaic voice context "four", and he is the paired as Al or El. Three male divinities and one female who is a virgin, although reproductive; they form a quite customary ideal of Divinity.

ARCHANGEL (Archangel) (Greek) Supreme angel, higher. Expression derived from the Greek arch "principal" or "ancient", and 'angels' "messenger".

ARCHETYPES. The flawless, speculative or indispensable type. This expression is mostly modified to indicate in the Arupa (formless) spheres of the mental world.

ARCHES, Court of. Assembly Court of the province of Canterbury which at one time gathered in Bow Church ('S. Maria de Arcubus')

ARCHONTES (Greek) The archangels succeeding fitting Ferouers; (that is, there in the spheres arupa (sin fined and purest part of the fresh creation singularly the soul of the body; the immortal fragment; which survives) [spiritual counterpart of the gods, angels, men, animals, plants, stars and even of the elements (water, fire, air and earth) or individual shadows, having a mission on earth; a mystical ubiquity; which suggested a double life; one of purity in a higher region, the other of terrestrial activity exercised on our plane].

ARCO (climbing) Is equivalent to evaluation or return. It is distinguished by the progressive predominance of Spirit over matter. It also processes, the vital or spiritual force, as well as the bow of Shiva was said to be the vehicle of his energy, related to the Shiva Linga.

ARDATH (Hebrew) This idiom is found in the second Volume of Ezra. In the Book of Ezra, the prophesier is delegated to this field called Ardath "Where no house is built," and is commanded to "eat there only the flowers of the field, not to taste meat, not to drink wine, and to pray continually to the supreme Being, and then I will come and speak with you."

ARDHA-NARIZA (Sanskrit) Gimmick "The hermaphroditic Lord". esoterically, the unpolarized state of cosmic Energy, personified by the Kabbalistic Sephira, Adam Kadmon, etc.

ARDORA. Milky seas; mareel; biolumiscent seas; phosphorescence on the ocean; ardentia.

ARDRA The sixth lunar asterism.

ARES (Greek) Label given by the Greeks to the planet Mars, God of war because he signify the War of the adept, additionally, governs the signs of Aries and Scorpio; it intervenes in the human being, giving value, daring, after all, in the adverse appearance; it can start by inducing hostility and precision that we all carry. It is also a term used by Paracelsus, as the transformed force in the Cosmos. [The spiritual principle; the cause of the specific character of each thing].

AREOPAGUS. The ('Mars' Hill') A impulse of land close range from the western end of the Acropolis in Athens. The title was also practice to an oligarchical council which met on the hill. It was not clear so long as, when St. Paul was brought to the Areopagus to interpret his teaching (Acts 17: 19), it was prior to the bureaucratic court or whether the place was simply decided on as convenient for a meeting.

ARGHA (Chaldean) The ark, the matrix of Nature; the crescent moon, and a lifeboat; it is also a cup for offerings, a cup used in certain religious ceremonies.

ARGIVA Juno Argiva was called Jupiter's wife after the temple dedicated to her at Argos. The statue that represented her had at her feet a lion's skin to a vine seed.

ARGOS "Panoptes" "The one who sees everything". He had a hundred eyes and slept with fifty closed. Mercury, with the melodies of his caduceus administer to numb him and cut off his head; but Juno, grieving, put her hundred eyes on the peacock's tail.

ARK (1) The ark that Noah assembled to conserve life during the Flood (q.v.) (2) The Ark of the covenants, the eminently sacred religious emblem of the Hebrew people and believe to define the Presence of God. It was in the shape of a wooden rectangular box, overlaid with gold inside and out. Conforming to the ancestral chronicles, the Israelites carried the Ark from the time of the Exodus (c. 13th century B.C.) into the land of Canaan. In Solomon's Temple its home was the 'Holy of Holies', which the High Priest alone entered perennially. It was evidently abducted when Jerusalem fell in 57-586 B.C., and nothing further is known of its history. The Christian Fathers perceived the Ark of Noah as epitomized the Church., the Ark of the Covenant as the symbol of the Lord.

ARKA (Sanskrit) The sun, or the sun god.

ARKAJA (Sanskrit) "Born of the sun". Wife of the Azvins twins.

ARJUNA Third of the five Pandavas brothers, that is, the celebrated son of Indra (esoterically, the same as Orpheus.)

ARIA Fifth split root breed into seven Sub-races. Survivors of Atlantis.

ARICHTA (Sanskrit) Indication or omen of death or misfortune.

ARISTEAS. Letters of, A Jewish pseudepigraphic letter; it accommodates a folklore of how the LXX or Septuagint which is the Greek Old Testament emerge to be miraculously written. Its configuration has been inconsistently dated between 200 B.C. and A.D. 33.

ARISTION (1ST centurial) Conforming to Papias (as described by Eusebius), he was a central command, with John the Presbyter, for the folklore about the Lord.

ARIES (Astrology) This zodiac sign is ruled by the planet Mars. It is said that this Zodiacal metaphor; it's an ideogram of RA, Rama, the lamb. This sign is the first sign of the zodiac, it is illustrated by a ram, ruled by Mars (the planet of war), whose regent is Samael. It is a fire sign, cardinal, masculine. It is praised of the sun administer the head with predisposition of anemia, insomnia, brain congestion and numerous influences. In the positive pole, it offers the native entrepreneurial character vigilant mind, decision advantage, enthusiastic personality, interest in overcoming difficulties, has a challenging ability, emotion, attractiveness, applied sense, eloquent expression, sincere and ardent affections, is invariably ready to fight. At the negative pole: impulsivity, anger, agitation, recklessness, uncertainty. With their partner: passionate, angry, quarrel a lot; its metal, iron, purple stone, ruby and diamond. Color: red. Plant; oak. A red flower, fire components, day: Tuesday (current Thursday); keyword action.

ARIOS (Sanskrit) Breed name in India (The Aryan); noble, nickname of Agni, Indra and others.

ARLES, Synod of. Enclosed by the surpassing dominant arise these of 314 met by 'Constantine to carry out with the Donatist schism; 353, an Arianizing Council; 1234, in resistance to the Albigensian blasphemy; and 1263, which hazardous the credo of Joachim of Fiore.

ARMAGH, The Publication of. An 8th & 9th centuries vellum codex in Trinity College, Dublin. It comprises two lives of St. Patrick, the life of St. Martin of Tours by apprehensive Severus, and a finalized non-Vulgate text of the Latin Christian Bible.

ARMY OF VOICES That which continues from the absolute is the great voice of the Gods, saints, or Dayan-Chohans, the rulers of the whole world. The Elohim are all flames of fervent fire.

ARMS Coat of arms, the predominant part of an organization of ancestral character dating back to prior Middle Age Europe, used first to begin recognition in conflicts, Arms proceed to show family ancestry, adoption, association, possessions holding, and, eventually, occupation.

ARMAGEDDON Term used in revelation, in chapter XVI, to choose the place where the forces of evil and good fought the greatest and last battle in the world, a prelude to the establishment of the kingdom of Christ.

ARMAITI (Parsi) Goddess of wisdom.

ARM(S) This prompt has great analogy. The weapons of the great heroes that appear in myths and legends such as great saints, demi-gods etc., have an extensive meaning: the Hammer of Thor, the Rod of Moses, the Shield and Sword of Perseus, the Mace of Hercules, the Staff of Oedipus. Neptune's Trident, etc. A few are enriched by the element of which they belong: The hard ball and the throw connected with the air, the spear to the earth, the sword to the fire, the trident with the depths and additional weapons that represent real attributes such as: the insignia, the staff, the Mace, the whip; surrounded by other weapons are: lightning, net, bow and arrows... all of them with a profoundly obscure in sign.

ARMOR Symbolizes spiritual defense as shown by St. Paul. Physical safeguarding of the body. The armor at the same time embodies defense; it is a transfiguration of the body, associated to the interpretation of metals (alchemy) splendor, duration, brightness.

ARMY The emblem personifies the Army's perfection of fidelity, attention, persistence, veracity, audacity, passion, bravery, reminiscence, will power, fidelity, gaining, nobility, and prestige.

ARNOLD, GOTTFRIED (1666-1714) German Protestant theologian and devotional writer. His dominant work, the Unparteiische Kirchen- und Ketzer-Histories (1699-1700), however, less neutral than its subject proclaimed, dominant as a report of Protestant mysticism and for its recruit of out-of-the-way deeds. Following 1701 he applied himself progressively to ministerial work, and his documents of this interlude are spiritual. He is as well-known as a hymn-writer.

AROCH Angel of the ray of the strength that works intensely with the disciples who walk the spiritual path of the adept.

ARROW(S) Persists a weapon that was used by Apollo, Hercules and Diana. It is an emblem of the solar rays and signifies the supreme power. In addition, it is a phallic symbol just like the spear. The nailed arrow is contemplating an emblem of conjunction.

ARPA An instrument that is a bridge linking the celestial and terrestrial worlds.

ARPIAS Black Magas, wicked, dark witches; Dante defines them: "inhabitants of the Averno."

ARCHETYPES The ideal, abstract or essential type. This appellation is generally applied to manifestations in the Arupa spheres. Formless mental world.

ARRIAN Sectarian of Arius, presbyter of the Church of Alexandria, in the fourth century. He who holds that Christ is a generated and human being, inferior to God the Father, although he was a sublime and enlightened man, an accurate proficient in all the divine mysteries.

ART(S) (Egyptian) The earth; the Egyptian god Mars.

ARTHA (Sanskrit) Thing, object; wealth, property; purpose, encouragement; interests; good, benefit, profit; cause, reason; meaning, etc.

ARUGAN Among the Jaina's, the Supreme Being.

ARUPA (Sanskrit) Untreated, spiritual, it is applied as a qualification of the mana sic plane, whose three superior or intimate circumstances are traced with the anonym of "flats Arupa".

ARYA (Sanskrit) Literally: "Holy". ["Noble", "of noble race", Designation of a race (the Aryan), which invaded India in the Vedic interval. Nickname of Agni, Indra and other divinities.]

ARYA-BHATA (Sanskrit) He was the primary Indo algebrist and astronomer, except for Asurama, who authored a work entitled Arya-Siddhartha, which is an organization of astronomy.

ARYAMAN (Sanskrit) The sun. The chief of the Pitri's (or ancestors). One of the Aditya.

ARYAN (Sanskrit) Literally: "Holy" ["Noble of "noble race". Name of a race (the Aryan) that invaded India in the Vedic period.

ASCH METZAREPH (Hebrew) "The Purifying Fire". Esoteric treatise on Alchemy and the affiliation midst hardware and marbles.

ASIA The largest of the continents, bordering on the Arctic Ocean, the Pacific Ocean, the Indian Ocean, and the Mediterranean and Red Seas in the west. Asia is: Lively; The rising sun. The name of the continent is used as a given name. According to the Koran the Pharaoh's wife Asia raised the infant Moses. The word Asia originated from the Ancient Greek word Aoia, first attributed to Herodotus (about 440 BCE) in reference to Anatolia or to the Persian Empire, in contrast to Greece and Egypt. It originally was just a name for the east bank of the Aegean Sea, an area known to the Hittites as Assuwa. Asia was a Roman province covering most of western Anatolia, which was created following the Roman Republic's annexation of the Attalid Kingdom in 133 BC.

ASAMYATA (Sanskrit) Not subjugated, not restrained, not disciplined.

ASANA (Sanskrit) Is one of the positions or expressions prescribed for reflection [In Patanjali Yoga], the bodily attitude (Asana) is one of its eight parts (yogangas). It is the third state of Hatha-Yoga.

ASANGA (Sanskrit) Detachment, detachment, disinterest disillusionment.

ASAPH, St. (fl 570) Wesh saint. By heritage, as soon as St. Kentigern came back to Scotland c. 570, Asaph had alternated him as leader of the cloister of 'Llanelwy" which is the Welsh name for the place called St. Asaph; [Llanelwy: means the sacred religious enclosure on the banks of the river Elwy], who appeared the original patriarch of the holy place.

ASARUM A breed of shrub in the birthroot family Aristolochiaceae, frequently admitted as wild ginger. Asarum is the reproductive multiple of the Latin as a significance shrine or refuse. The drained pungent root of the radicle ginger plant: an herb factor and origin of a savory crude oil utilized in scent, previously employed in therapeutics. Asarum is a shrub. The rhizome is operated to manufacture medical sciences. Regardless of significant protection consideration, Asarum European is applied for bronchiolitis, bronchi contraction, and allergy asthma. It is besides employed to attend to wheeze, shortness of breath, angina pectoris, megrim, hepatic diseases, and deficiencies. Asarum canadense, frequently labeled wild ginger, is a Missouri domestic spring wildflower which takes place in wilderness and woodland all over the United States. Few genera of Asarum as well hold Aristolochic. It is utilized nearly in rats. The United States Food and Drug Administration and Health Canada warn averse to consumption of Wild Ginger. powerful quantities can damage kidneys.

ASAS. In Scandinavian mythology, the authority all the ancient gods, which were believed to be twelve, with Odin being the father of them all. kata ski, haix tetrax, Damana Meneus, aition. Mystical words that in accordance with Anastasio Kircher mean: "darkness, Light, Earth, Sun and Truth".

ASAT (Sanskrit) A philosophical expression connotated as "non-being," or rather, non-seity. "The incompressible nothingness." Sat, the undeniable, eternal, ever-present, and the real 'Seity' (and not "Being," as some want), is explained as being "born of Asat, and Asat begotten by Sat."

ASATHOR (Scandinavian) The same as Thor. The god of storms and thunder.

ASATYA (Sanskrit) Falsehood, lie, error.

ASCENSION Measures when the human condition is transcended and extends to higher cosmic levels. The ascension of the Lord, after the Resurrection also points to esotericism, total liberation intimate self-realization, through Crispification, death and Resurrection and then rise to the absolute.

ASCETE-ASCETISM (Greek) It is the standard of demeanor or spiritual life dedicated to pious exercises and virtues through temperance from vices and worldly devices, having as its occasion the alliance of the individual with the Divinity. It is said that the initial Christian ascetics were the anchorites of hermits of the abandon who broke all distinctive social relationship in the hope of getting nearby to God.

ASCETICISM. The term denotes an organization of proceedings delineate to hostilities wrongdoing and mature Virtues by contemplating of self-discipline, similarly, are found in many religions. In the Holy Scriptures there is recurrent encouragement to self-abnegation. The circumstantial build of Christian asceticism was performed by Clement of Alexandria and origin. Assuming from the Stoics the idea of ascetic, action, movement as an absolution of the soul from its passions, they saw in it a mandatory measure of loving God more comprehensively and for completed to reflection. In the 3rd century austere excellence as a way of life propagate through Christendom, dominating to the age of the Desert Fathers and the dawn of monasticism in the 4th century. The monks in both East and West, and later the mendicant Orders, shifted the leading illustrative of abnegation. At the conclusion of the Gothic Ages there was a response opposed to the ascetic ideal, mostly between the Protestant Reformers, whose doctrine of overall degradation of mankind and of Acceptance by faith unattended impair the theological substructure of abstemious implementation. The ascetic ideal was, nevertheless, endorse in the Catholic church of the Counter-Reformation and later. Consequently, taken an important part in Methodism and through the Tractarians and their descendants. Conforming to its traditional Christian supporters' asceticism is an essential measure of fighting the concupiscence of the flesh; as well as ethics as impression of the sacrificial life of Christ and as a manner of concluding of one's own transgressions and those of others. It bounces from the love of God and intentions at overpowering all the interferences to this love in the essence.

ASCENT OF MOUNT CARMEL, The. The initial of the spiritual treatises of St. John of the Cross (q.v.)

ASCH METZAREPH (Hebrew) "The Purifying Fire". Kabbalistic accordance that deals with Alchemy and the connection between metals and planets.

ASEKA or ASEKHA In Buddhism, it is appointed by this epithet that one who no longer must learn anything else: an individual of the hierarchy higher levels to that of the Arhat. "When man has reached this level, he acquires the fullest dominion over his own destinies and chooses his future line of evolution."

ASES (Scandinavian) They were the creators of Dwarves and Elves; these are the elementals that are beneath men in Scandinavian legend. They are descendants of Odin, The same as the Aesir.

ASSASSINS Lable of a Masonic and mystical sect founded by Hassan Sabah in Persia, in the eleventh century. That vocable is a European corruption of "Hassan", which configuration is the main part of that name.

ASLEEP (Gnosis) As claimed by Master Samael Aun Weor; Ordinary waking consciousness is associated to the five senses and the brain. Humans consider that if they have awakened consciousness and that is false; people live in the deepest sleep. Consequently, consciousness is knowledge, the understructure of what it really is. The decent worker is fascinated in the factory by hard work. The patriarch of the family is fascinated by his children. It is crucial to know that humanity lives with a sleeping conscience. People work encircle. Human beings walk the streets dreaming. Mortals live and die dreaming.

ASGARD Dwelling of the Norse gods; approximately where the twelve main gods (Asen) elevated their palaces. It was heaven in Norse mythology.

ASH (Hebrew) Fire, the same the physical as the symbol. This term is also written Ash, Aish and Esch.

ASH YGGDRASIL The "Worldly Tree", insignia of the planet among the ancient Scandinavians. This plant is evergreen, according to the principles of destiny the waters of life From the Source of Urd; they spray him daily that gets larger in Midgard (the earth). The dragon of sin and evil, signal Nidhogg, weakens without interrupting its origin; but the Ash Yggdrasil cannot be exhausted until it has been released from the decisive battle (seventh race in its seventh round), in such an occurrence, existence, epoch, and universe will disintegrate and vanish completely.

ASHVATTHA or AZVATTHA (Sanskrit) The Bo tree or tree of wisdom, Ficus religiosa. [Banyan or consecrated fig tree of India. The Azavatta is the emblem of the Universe, of life and of being. Its roots embody the leading Being, the first Cause, the root of the Cosmos. The reverberation current of individual existence (samsara) is symbolized by its branches, which descend to the terra firma and take new roots there, thus enduring earthly existence. This hardwood can only be knocked down through spiritual knowledge. Their eradication leads to immortality.

ASH This idiom is a illustrate of the "Institute of Death". In consonance with alchemy, it is associated to the death and dissolution of defects (I's) or those substances, which are also linked to ash, to fieriness and the destroyed.

ASHEN and LANGHAN (Kolarian) It establishes a link between certain rites that are in use among the Kolarian tribes of India, and whose motivations to cast the evil essences. They are like the protocol of frequent exorcism among Christians.

ASHMOG (Zend) The Dragon or snake, monster with a camel's neck, in the Avesta. A kind of allegorical Satan, who after the fall, "loses his nature and name".

ASHTA (Siddhis) (Sanskrit) The eight powers in the practice of Hatha Yoga.

ASIRIO An anciently religious rite of Judah; Assyrian tree of life or "Asherah".

ASITA (Sanskrit) A proper honorific; a son of Bharata; Richi and a sage. A-Sita: "not white", black. The dark Quinceanera of lunation. Appellation of the planet Saturn. Father of Devala and one of Vizvamitra's sons.

ASSISI A city in the Umbrian Hills, recognized as the native land of St. Francis. The remains of St. Francis and St. Clare lie in two of its basilicas, and the Portiuncula chapel is c. 2 miles away.

ASK (Scandinavian) Tree of knowledge, from which gods of Asgard created the first man.

ASKI Transcendental cue. "Kata ski, haix tetrax, Damana Meneus, aition" Mystical words that according to Anastasio Kircher mean: "darkness, Light, Earth, Sun and Truth".

ASKUR In the Scandinavian folklore, he was the first man, his wife was Embla and out of possession of them come the human ralea.

ASMI (Sanskrit) Contemplated as "(I) am".

ASMITA (Sanskrit) (1) Egotism, personalism; feeling or awareness of the being: it is correspondent with Ahankara. (2) That it is part or action word of the self. (3) The confidence that the self is not a different commodity from perceptions and concepts.

ASMONEOS Kings priests of Israel, of which dynasty reigned over the Jews for 126 years.

ASOKA (Azoka, or Ashoka) Famous Buddhist king of India, of the Morya dynasty, who reigned in Magadha. It is said that there appeared two Asoka, according to the chronicles of Northern Buddhism, granted that the first Azoka, grandfather of the second, called by Professor Max Müller "the Constantine of India", was rather known by his name of Chandragupta. The first of these was titled Piyadassi (Pali), "the beautiful one", and Devanam-priya (Priya, in Sanskrit), "beloved of the gods", and Kalazoka, while his grandson's name was Dhamazoka "the Azoka of the good Law", because of his devotion to Buddhism.

ASPECT Recommends the form (Rupa) under which any principle is indicated either in man or in northern nature, in Theosophy it is enforced, an aspect of such a principle.

ASRAMA or AZRAMA (Sanskrit) Materialization a building, monasteries or hermitage, contemplated sacred for mystical purposes.

ASSUR (Chaldean) City of Assyria, former site of a library, from which George Smith excavated the first known tablets, to which he assigns a date of 1,500 years before J.C. convened Assur Kileh Sher get.

ASTA (Daza) (Asta Dasha) (Sanskrit) Perfect, leading Wisdom [or Intelligence]: one of the crowns of Divinity. (From Minerva) Spear of Longi bus. It represents the work of Buddhist annihilation.

ASTERIUS The Sophist, Arian theologian. He attended the Council of Antioch of 341. Particles of his Syntagma Tion are conserved by St. Athanasius and Marcellus of Ancyra, and sections of his critics and lectures on the Palms have been recovered not long ago.

ASTEYA (Sanskrit) Unenthusiastic. "Lack of interest or ambition". Disinterest.

ASTRA (Sanskrit) General weapon, arrow, dart, projectile, etc. In Inda mythology it is the name of certain mysterious technique used to defeat enemies. For Astra, thought forms or weapons of abundant species conceived or manufactured with magical formulas can be understood.

ASTRAL Shadow or ethereal counterpart of man or animal; the Linga-sarira, the Doppelganger. Do not be confused with the astral soul, an additional name of the lower Manas or Kama-Manas, as it is called, and besides the reflection of the higher Ego. The astral body converts into the bridge of communication between the soul and the body.

ASTROLOGY (Gr.) It is the branch of knowledge that reveals the operation of the celestial sphere on typical effects and dissimulates to prognosticate the time ahead, occurrences because of the location of the celestial bodies. For instance, in ancient times, this discipline is placed among the most archaic chronicles of mortal wisdom. For lengthy millenions transpire as a clandestine science in the East, and its final expression remains so even today, and its esoteric aptitude has acquired a certain degree of excellence in the West only from the moment when Varaha Muhira wrote his book on Astrology some 1,400 years ago. Claudius Ptolemy, the celebrated geographer and mathematician who established the Astronomies organization that carries his name, wrote his treatise Tetrabiblos in the region of year 135 of our era. The science of Horoscopy is now investigated from four central thoughts of perspective, namely. 1. Common place, in its application to meteorology, seismology, agriculture, etc.; 2. Political or civil, indicating the fate of nations, kings and rulers. 3. Organization, which binds to the answer to doubts born in the intellect about some matter, and 4. Endemic, in its solicitation to the destiny of individuals from the beginning of their birth to their death. The Egyptians and Chaldeans were the eldery intellectuals of astrology, of course their procedure of consultative with the Astros diverse substantially from contemporary proceedings. The first allegation that Belo, the Bell or Elu of the Chaldeans, and offspring of the divine Dynasty, that is, the Dynasty of the gods-kings, had affiliated to the land of Chemi (Egyptians), which left behind to establish an Egyptian province on the banks of the Euphrates, where a temple was erected which was cared for by priests who were at the service of the "Lords of the stars" and who embraced the name of Chaldeans. A couple of well-known acts: (a) that Thebes (of Egypt) affirmed the honor of the origination of Astrology, and (b) that it was the Chaldeans who instructed this science to other superpowers. Astrology is to accurate astronomy what psychology is to correct physics. In astrology, as in psychology, one must go outside the distinguishable world of circumstances and introduce the kingdom of the abstract, outstanding Spiritual.

ASTRUM Channel of astral light. A sphere of mind that belongs to everyone, and gives each thing its own special qualities forming, to its world.

ASU (Sanskrit) Breath, life spirit, life. The breath of Brahman, Atman. Asu (neutral) measures the heart as the seat of affections, thought, reflection, meditation, etc.

ASUKHA (Sanskrit) Unpleasant, painful, miserable, unhappy.

ASUMAT Try changeable word

ASURA (Sanskrit) Esoterically, asuras are elementals and evil gods. Considered evil; geniuses, evil spirits, demons, and "no gods."

ATALANTA FUGIENS A famous treatise, composed by Michael Maier, eloquent Rosicrucian, where he recorded many beautiful works of alchemical symbolism. There is also the earliest painting of a man and a woman inside a circle, with a triangle around it and then a square, which bears the following inscription: "From the first entity come two opposites; hence come the three principles, and from them the four elementary states; if you separate the pure from the impure, you will have the stone of the Philosophers."

ATALA (Sanskrit) Medium bottomless; one of the hells of the Vedan tines. The name was prescribed by the first researchers of the fifth Race to the land of sin (Atlantis). Esoterically, Atala is on one of the astral planes in another time a true island of this earth.

ATKA Eskimo "Inuit" name which implies guardian spirit in the language of the indigenous people of northern Canada and parts of Greenland and Alaska. According to their folklore; this glowing important being shine on in individuals whose hearts he melted, brainpower he revealed, and enthusiasms he impressed.

ATTACHMENT(S) In Buddhist and Hindu religious texts the opposite concept is expressed as up Adana translated as "attachment". Extra parts, that is the inability to practice or embrace detachment, is viewed as the main obstacle towards a sensational and fulfilled life. (Gnosticism) The observation about locations will allow us to know how far our attachments and fascinations reach in relation to many and various places.

ATASH BEHRAM (Zend.) The sacred fire of the paresis. Preserve perpetually within the temples of fire.

ATEF (Egyptian) Crown of Horus; It comprises of tall white cap with horns; two feathers stand for the two truthfulness of life and death.

ATE (as said in Wikipedia) In Greek mythology, Ate or Aite; Ancient Greek: was the Goddess of mischief, delusion, ruin, and blind folly, rash exertions and reckless impulses who led men down the path of ruin. She also led both gods and men to rash and inconsiderate activities and suffering. Ate also cites to an action carry out by a hero that leads to their death or downfall.

ATTENTION. The comportment an individual employs to focus the senses, from sight to ability to hear and even smell. It may focus on advice that matters outside of the cab (e.g., signals, traffic), inside the cab (e.g., displays, controls), or on the radio network. The Christian custom has defined prosoche, 'attention'. As an approach of 'concentration,' an inner 'stretching toward,' a 'focusing of the mind.' The Greek word has a dynamic significance, as do the Latin attention and attendere, which tells us that mortal who is attentive is someone who 'reaches' approaching something.

ATHANASY Momentous of the term is an absence of death or the requirement of everlasting unending life. The etymology of expression Athanasy is from Ancient Greek athanasia, which defines "Immortality".

ATHANASIAN CREED, The. An article of faith which has been extensively used in West Christendom. It elucidates the tenet of the Trinity and externalization, adding a list of the most significant circumstances in the Lord's life; it comprised anathemas in contrast these who abandon believe its affirmations. The criterion to St. Athanasius has been typically eliminated, mainly on the acknowledgment that it accommodates ideological utterance which arose only in later controversies. There recitation of the Athanasian Creed is sequenced on accurate events in the roman Breviary and in the BCP. Since 1867 there came to be diverse attempts in the mission of East to have it dislodged or limited, and its use in Anglican churches has converted extraordinary.

ATHEISM Apprehension in the reality of Supreme Being. Before the prompt 'agnosticism' approached about toward conventional advantage in the 19th century, 'atheism' prevailed, partially approved to relate the situation of those who guessed the reality of the supreme being as a doubtful viewpoint. Current skeptics are often besides 'logical positivists', who protest that although allegations in mentioned to deity are ineligible of experimental evidence all are pointless, or unspiritual, of which skepticism is oftentimes constructive impartially additionally hypothetical. The Dialectical Materialism of Communism is, nevertheless, deliberately and welcomed by unbelievers.

ATHENS (Gnosticism) "The intellectual animal is the grain, the seed; from that seed can be born the Tree of Life, the True Man that Man who was looking for Diogenes with a lamp lit, through the streets of Athens and at Noon, and who unfortunately could not find."

ATTEMPT Derivation. Late 4th century as Middle English attempten, from Old French atemper, from Latin attempt ("I try, solicit"), from ad ("to") + temptare, more accurately tentare ("to try"); see tempt. Describe to try to do, attain, solve, or effect. He attempted to swim in the swollen river. The variation between try and attempt is that attempt is more formal. You frequently use it while speaking and writing about accomplishing a goal. "Try" measures to try to do something. When you try property, you may not care about the consequence.

ATERGATIS In the company of Syrians; she is described as a Goddess with the body of a fish and a woman's face, constitutes the Earth.

ATHANOR (Occultism) Visionary "astral" fluid of the alchemists, their lever of Archimedes. Esoterically, the stove of the alchemists.

ATHARVA (Veda) (Sanskrit) Religious text, the fourth Veda. It expresses magical enchantment, which holds aphorisms, charms and magical configurations. It is one of the four matured and most respected books of Brahmins in existence.

ATHOR Immortal "Mother Night" It is the primitive chaos, in the Egyptian cosmogony. The goddess of the Night.

ATHOS Mount. The Peninsula off the coast of Greece which discontinue in Mount Athos has long been the property of the monasteries of the East Orthodox church. The first settlement was the Lavra originated by Athanasius the Athonite in 961. There are now 20 virtually independent monasteries, though matters of ordinary concern are determined by a council. No women or female animal are permitted on the peninsula.

ATIS (Gnosticism) Supreme being said that he was a god of the ancient Phrygians of Asia Minor, the divinity Cybele turned him into pine.

ATKA Custodian, Aboriginal anonym connotation guardian spirit, and his bright atman lives in those hearts he warmed, minds he unlatched, and souls he touched. ATKA operates to design better efforts for wolves, and so will we.

ATTILA. (d. 453), King of the Huns from 433. He infringed Gaul in 451 and Italy the next year. At the prayers of Leo, I he refrains from trying to apprehend Rome. In Christian myth he was investigated from his savagery as the 'Scourge of God',i.e.. a minister of Divine Vengeance.

ATLAS Clairvoyant Atlantean king, in addition, the oldest astrologer. Teo. Idiom that labels all the continents of Lemuria and the Union. Mount Atlas, the Meru or "Mountain of the Gods", the Pico de Tenerife, is considered dwarfed remains of the two vanished Continents.

ATLANTES They are the ancestors of the Pharaohs and the forefathers of the Egyptians, in consonance to some, and as esoteric science teaches. Of this particularly civilized people, whose last remains were submerged in the Ocean some 9,000 years before Plato's day, he learned through Solon, who was in turn aware by the high priests of Egypt. Voltaire, the everlasting mocker, was right to claim that the Atlanteans (our fourth mother race) made their appearance in Egypt. In Syria and Phrygia, as in Egypt, they inaugurate the cult of the Sun. Occult philosophy teaches that the Egyptians were a residue of the last Aryan Atlanteans.

ATMA or ATMAN (Sanskrit) Teo. It is the first principle of man, the spirit. Among the Indotan's is the Intimate. In the Hebrew Kabbala it is Chesed that corresponds to the second ethical triangle. It also auspices our Real Self, the Universal spirit, the first principle of the septenary constitution of man the ineffable, our inner father.

ATMICO (World) Kabbalistically; this word personifies the world of Atma (the Father or Intimate) in proportion to the 10 Sephiroth of the Kavala. It is said to be a world of extraordinary beauty.

ATTO Patriarch of Vercelli from 924. His clippings, which are extraordinary knowledge, incorporated a narration on Pauline Epp. And a group of ministerial cannons.

ATOMICS (Gnosticism) "The period in the Hell Worlds of the submerged Mineral Kingdom is frighteningly quiet and boring; it is said that every hundred years; which are horribly long; in those Atomic Hells of the species, a certain part of Karma is paid.".

ATTO Prelate Vercelli from 924. His papers were impressively cultured, which are of momentous knowledge, including assessments on the Puline Epp. as well as a compendium of clerical cannons.

ATOM As maintained by cabbalistic doctrine; a less thick particle of substance, ethereal, astral/mental, human evolution body modalities. Trio of energy matter and consciousness. All decreased to the atom.

ATON It is an insignia of the deified solar sphere, as a reflective constituent of the energies that come from the spiritual Sun, enriches life.

ATONE Recompense or reparation. "A human sacrifice to atone for sin".

ATREYA (Sanskrit) Successor, son or descendant of Atri.

ATRI Assemblage to an epic stage, which is conceptualized as one of the Ten Pragati's or lords of creatures. He later emerged as an actor in several Vedic hymns and as a coded. Like Richt, he is one of the stars of the greater OSA.

ATRIPOS Encompassed by the Prussians, he is the God of the sea.

ATUA Is a Tahitian extraordinary existence or atman. Maori divine beings are a dominant segment of Maori philosophy. Atua signifies Supreme being supernatural being or divinity in the Reo. There exists plenty of divergent Maori deities or atua who command certain regions and domains. This wiki embraces a register of the Maori celestial beings and tie-up to ideology resorts on this subject. There are some female atuas in the Pacific pantheon; Hina, many times linked with the moon, Pele of Hawaiian volcanoes, and her atua Fafine (female goddess) of Tilopia; but the mass are male. Te Fiti is the personification of an island divinities. Te Fiti is the adjacent referred to of each principal or elevated reality in Moana. She is an omnipotent reality who generates, and in her adjusted role, dismantles existence. The center of intangible loyalty in Moana is the islanders, and exceptionally Moana's, reliance in Te Fiti.

ATUM (Egyptian) Comments on a primitive god of Heliopolis. This is the God of penance in the worship of Ra. His imputes were the Lion and the Serpent. He is eternally depicted with a human head by wearing the double crown of Egypt.

AUDIANI. A 4th centennial austerity sect. established by Adius; it isolated from the Church on the foundations that the clergy were too secularized.

AUDUMIA Characterization of the essence in Scandinavian mythology. Ice giants, the cow of creation. They burned four streams of milk that were provided as food for the giant Ymir or Orgel Mir.

AUGIAS Royal personage, the king of the Epigean and owner of abundant flocks. In his stables, over the years, so much manure and garbage stockpiled that it was impossible to purify, but the powerful Hercules in his seventh work, forced by his enemy King Eurystheus managed to divert the waters of the river Alteo and made them cross the stables, clarifying them to perfection.

AUMBRY An alcove in the wall of a church or sacristy in which in medieval times sacred vessels, books, and at times the reserved Sacrament were conserved.

AUM (Sanskrit) Incantation blessed and mystical Mantram principle of all sounds emanating from cosmic vibration, used as a seal of divinity or Brahma. It appears for the "A" to the father, the "U" to the son, the "M" the Holy Spirit.

AUPHANIM (Hebrew) (Wheels or Hierarchy of the World). In the Kabbalah the angels comply with the scales and stars, of which they are the souls that animate them.

AUR Illustrates; brilliantly individualized "Genius Lucis" from the cosmic amphitheater.

AURA (Greek and Latin) Minuscule or subtle and invisible essence that derives from human and animal bodies and even from things.

AUREO (Golden Egg) A kind of Seductive, tempting, invisible aura of oval method, in which each man is involved, has the patrimony of assuming the manifestation of man's body and becoming "radiant" [Illuminant]; it is being that comes without deviation that is born of the divine.

AURELIOUS, St. (d. C.430), Bp. Of Carthage from C. 391. He determined over several committee and was impregnable in privilege by St. Augustine.

AUREOLE. In sacred pictures, the background of gold which occasionally surrounds a figure, is distinct from the nimbus (or halo) that covers only the head.

AURVA (Sanskrit) Scholar who is attributed with creating the "firearm", called Agneystra or Agneyastra.

AUSONIUS (DECIMIUS MAGNUS) (c. 310-c. 395), Roman poet. Decimus Magnus Ausonius developed tutor to the eventually Emperador Gratian, who in 379 heightened him to the consulship. Numerous of his poems implied that he molds some vocation of Christianity. He composed to Paulinus of Nola (in verse), attempting to discouraged him from becoming a monk.

AVAGAMA (Sanskrit) Deals with Grasping; understanding, intelligence; perception.

AVALON The astronomical, celestial island of Apollo. Encompassed by the Celts, it was called Abalun, the location where the tomb of King Arthur was detected. It is the magical region "Jinas" where there exist holy gods; it is also known as the "Solar Earth" of the Hyperborean.

AVANI (Sanskrit) The earth.

AVARANA (Sanskrit) Particularly territory of attraction, wrapping, cover.

AVASANA (Sanskrit) Alludes to the culmination, end, term.

AVASATHYA (Sanskrit) Particularly, one of the five fires indicated in the Manu standards.

AVASTHA-DWAYA. (Sanskrit) Plainly: "the two states": Happiness and misery.

AVASTAN (Sanskrit) Achievement of the ancient remarkable that was called Arabia.

AVATARA (Sanskrit) Weakening of being glorious-God that has progressed higher than the destitution of rebirth on earth, although the body is a mere mortal. Krishna was Avatara of Vichnu.

AVAZA (Sanskrit) Alienation, know no alternative, no self-will; abusive, not wanting; against their will.

AVANCINI, NIKOLA (1611-86) Jesuit rigorous author and philosopher. He composed widely, and his De Vita et Doctrine Jesu Christi ex Quattuor Evangelistis Collect (1665), a collection of concise and compact reflections, was rewritten successfully in many languages and extensively used.

AVE MARIS STELLA. A well-known Marian gym, dating at least from the 9th century. It has been credited to various authors, along with Paul the Deacon. One English Translation. Begins "Hail Thou Star of ocean".

AVERNO In association with the Romans, it is hell.

AVESTA (Zendo) is "The Law", in the sacred scriptures of the Zoroastrians. In the expression Zend-Avesta, the word Zend imply "comment" or "interpretation".

AVEZA (Avatara) (Sanskrit) This declaration conveys partial Avatara. A human being who receives divine influence on a special degree.

AVICENNA Exclusive Latinized Abu-Ali the Hoseenben Abdallah ibn Sine, was a Persian scholar who was born in the year 980 of our era. He was the author of the best and first works of alchemy that have been known in Europe. As claimed by history, several of the spirits of the integrant were subject to him, it has also been said that, in gratitude to Avicenna's understanding, he had the elixir of Life, some acknowledged that he still lives as an adept and is said to have manifested himself to the wicked at the end of a certain period.

AVIDHI Lack of rules or method.

AVIDYA (Sanskrit) This phrase is the opposite of vidya. It is incomprehension caused by the senses.

AVICHI o AVITCHI (Sanskrit). A situation: not certain after death alone or between two births, since such a condition can also occur on earth. directly: "uninterrupted hell." The last of the eight hells, where, as it is said, "the guilty die and are reborn without interruption, though not without hope of final redemption." This is the speculation because Avichi is another name by which the Myalba (our land) is designated, and it is also a state to which some heartless men are condemned on this physical plane. [Avitchi is a state of spiritual ideal evil; a subjective environment; the opposite nature of; Devachan or Anyodei].

AVIGNON. Originating from 1309 to 1377 Avignon was the dwelling place of the Popes, though it did not convert papal property until 1348, when Clement VI bought it from the Queen of Naples.

AVYAKTA (Sanskrit) Specifically a derivation that has not been detected; indistinct or undifferentiated; the opposite Avyakta is the manifested or adaptation. Avyakta condenses the submerged Deity, furthermore, Vyatka the demonstrated, that is, Brahma and Brahma relatedly. [Avyakta: unmanifested, Kabbalah; radical or primitive matter, chaotic, mystical, indefinite, associated; the primordial element from which all indication comes. This expression can be applied to the latent Spirit.]

AWARD. Occurrence that is conferred or bestowed selectively anchored on merit or urgency. A film that has won considerable awards: a judgment or final decision, exclusively the decision of arbitrators in a case introduced to them. Etymology of word from Middle English awarded, from Anglo-Norman awarder, from Medieval Latin "ex wardare, from Latin ex ("out") + Medieval Latin wardare, guardare ("to observe, regard, guard") owing or showing knowledge or gratitude or consciousness or gain control.

AWAKE. From Middle English awake, a shortened form of awaken ("awakened, awake"), past participle of Middle English awakens ("to awaken"). The acceptance of awake, determined perceptive and responsive: "an alert mind" "awake to the alarming of her situation" "was now awake to the reality of his predicament" synonyms: alert, alive aware, cognizant, cognizant. (Sometimes followed by 'of') having or showing awareness or conception or realization or perception.

AWEN (Celtic) Possesses the same sensation as flow; etymologically, conceivably related to Sanskrit, avá which signifies descending. Inspiration, invention, intuition, are phenomenon of Awen.

AXES (Gnosticism) "There is Evolution in every ascending civilization, there is involution in any scholarship of a descending type. It is ostensible that these two norms constitute a mechanical axis, essential of nature" ...

AXIS In 20th-century relational convictions, the expression axis mundi; also tagged the cosmic axis, world axis, world pillar, "epicenter", or world tree; has been considerably increased to refer to any mythological concept characterized "the connection between Heaven and Earth" or the "higher and lower realms". AXIS MUNDI, the "hub" or "axis" of the universe, is a scientific name employed in the research of the history of religions. It constitutes at least three measures of reference: the effigies themselves, their purpose and explanations, and the proficiency associated with them. Earth is constantly moving. Day after day, the Earth makes one total revolve on its axis. The axis is the imaginary line across the earth that expands from the North Pole to the South Pole. As Earth turns, it appears like the sun is in motion through the sky, but it's in reality the Earth that is revolving.

AXUM. Also, Aksum. The ancient religious and political capital of Ethiopia. Christianity was authorized here in the 4th century.

AYAMA (Sanskrit) Continues; an extension, length, expansion (in time or space).

AYANA (Sanskrit) An entire activity course; two Ayana's constitute approximately, a year's action, half a year: properly the march of the sun from one solstice to another. It also means, goal, dwelling, refuge, etc.

AYIN (Hebrew) The perception of the word is "nothing"; consequently, the name AinSoph.

AYOGA (Sanskrit) Measures that "There is no union." Lack of spiritual union, lack of devotion or yoga.

AYUKTA (Sanskrit) The contradictory of Yukta. The man who cannot fix or centralize the mind in spiritual reflection or the Self; the one who implements all his acts moved only by personal interest or the satisfaction of his appetites and desires. Not concerned, not composed, disapplied.

AYUR-VEDA (Sanskrit) Intermediary: "the Veda of Life". [The science of health. It was used as the title of a medical book.]

AYUS or AYU (Sanskrit) One of the three immolations. The other two are called: Jyotis go Zaba.

AYUTA (Sanskrit) (A myriad, like 10,000 units. One Koti equal to ten million units). 100 Koti's like one billion units.

AZA (Azis or Azi) (Sanskrit) Hope.

AZAMA (Sanskrit) "Lack of peace". Restlessness, uneasiness, nervousness.

AZANE, Azar, Adrop (Alchemy) The "Philosopher's Stone". It is not a stone in the ordinary sense of the word; it is an allegorical fiction that manifests initiation of wisdom; philosopher who bought it, explains it by his own proof; not just speculation.

AZAR (Alchemy) See Adrop.

AZAZEL (or Azazel) (Hebrew) Signified the "God of victory." Strong or injured male differentiate to sins, from Israel. He who can recognize the mysteries of Azazel, according to Aben-Ezra, "will know the secret of God's name."

AZHI DAKANA (Zend) Separates of the dragons or snakes that in the legends of Iran and in the Avestas scriptures the allegory Destroying Serpent, or Satan.

AZILUTH This denominate is appointed to the world of the Sephiroth, called the nature of emanations Olam Atzi luth. This is the highest prototype of the other creations

AZLECHA (Sanskrit) One of the lunar mansions.

AZOE, AZOTH (alchemy) Substantially the mercury of philosophers, which was also cited as water or vital spirit of metals. Materialization, the set of sulfur salt and mercury, which mixed in an octave (do, re, mi, fa, sol, la, si, do) crystallizes the astral body. In another higher the mental body, and in another octave more superior, the causal body. It is the mysterious ray of Kundalini. It is also appraised as a creative principle of nature.

AZOKA Became a Buddhist king of India, of the Morya dynasty, who reigned in Magadha. He was a spokesperson of Buddhism.

AZOTH Creative Initiation of Nature; the universal panacea or soul air that gives life.

AZRADDHA (Sanskrit) Passed on as lack or absence of faith.

AZRAMA (Sanskrit) Stands as a sacred building, a monastery or hermitage, which is used for ASSY tic functions. In India, every sect has its Azramas.

AZUCENA (Lily) Accordingly is a badge of perfection among Christians and as property and image of the Virgin Mary.

AZVINS The Azvins are two Vedic divinities, the twin sons named the Sun and Sky, they become the nymph Azvini. The "Divine Charioteers", They are "Riders" Mounted on a golden chariot pulled by horses, birds or other animals, one is called Dasra, and the other Nasatya, they "is endowed with many forms".

-B-

BA (Egyptian) This style touched on to the soul of the breath, and that corresponds to the Prana which is the breath or breath of life.

BAALS or Adon (Adonai) He was a priapic figurines God, Baal is the Sun that devours all things, in no doubt, the fiery Moloch. (Gnostic). It is the hallmark of a Fallen Angel.

BAALES Enchanters, black magicians. Ancient mythology exemplifies him as a Carthaginian Divinity, scholar of the species, whose illustration was mixed with that of the Sun.

BABEL Uncertainty; is a place where disorder reigns, confusion. It is a building that the descendants of Noah began to build to climb the sky. The dissatisfied Jehovah, who disoriented the language of builders; in this way, the work was paralyzed, and caused the contributors to disperse throughout the world.

BABIL MOUND (Cald., Heb.) Is the site in Babilonia; where a temple was built in honor of Bel.

BABOSA (Spanish) or SLUG (English) In alternative mother tongues, Babosa British English; slug is a compact crawling animal, with a lengthy slimy, frame, similar to a crawler without an armor. Defined as a miniature serpent who as they progress completing their domain, they unhurried and stable advancement, flexibility, and resiliency. It is the pseudonym of some species of pulmonated gastropod mollusks, of the gene. Limar, naked and tacky body, exists in cool and humid spaces.

BACH, JOHANN, SEBASTIAN (1685-1750) German composer. He was a soloist at the Thomas school at Leipzig from 1723 until his death. His main religious works request to this time. Particularly the two great Passions versions to St Matthew and St. John including the Mass in B minor. The tones were at first designated for use at Protestant assistance but is now executed nearly outside Divine worship. About his other Melodic efforts, the 'Magnificat' and 'Christmas Oratorio' are the utmost famous.

BACHUA Impersonate the intimate Christ.

BACO God of wine and harvest, debauchery and excitement; the arcane meaning of this personification is more puzzling and philosophical. It is the Osiris of Egypt.

BACON, ROGERIO A Franciscan Friar, became famous as an alchemist adept, in addition to magic arts. He lived in England in the thirteenth century. He was a believer of the Sorcerer's Stone and philosophical astrology. He was accused of building a head made of bronze with an acoustic motor inside it, which was thought to pronounce oracles, which were no less than words uttered by Bacon sitting in a different room. He was a prodigy physicist and chemist, such as paper which represents air in the combustion, the proprieties of various sodium chloride, the action of the lenses and the convex crystals, the lenses asthmatic, etc. He also accomplished some writing in reference to alchemy. He was a monumental chemist, and the invention of the gunpowder was attributed to him; although he said he had acquired the secret from some "Asian geniuses, Chinese."

BACULO One of the dissimilarities of the bishops, which has its birth in the priestly insignia of the Etruscan augurs. It is also found in the hands of various divinities.

BADDHA (Sanskrit) Attached, constrained; as is everything lethal that has not been emancipated through Nirvana. The situation of the man who has not outreached the liberation conclusion or Nirvana.

BAGAVAN ACLAIVA. (Or BAGAVAR) He is a Guruji. Grand Regent of the Holy Order of Tibet. The Great Maha Rishi can be invoked to help us go out in astral, hotly.

BAHAK (Gnostics) "Progenitor of conditions" in the Codex Nazarenus. The Nazarenes were a remote semi-Christian sect.

BAHIR (Prajna) (Bahis-Prajna) (Sanskrit) It is the continuous understanding of external things, that is: objective judgment.

BAI (Egyptian) Achievement of the intellectual soul, the ability

BAKA (Sanskrit) Uninterrupted description of a demon, enemy of Krishna.

BAL (Hebrew) Procedure current and illuminate as Lord, but also Bel, and the Chaldean God, and Baal, an "idol".

BALA (Sanskrit) Mention power, strength, energy, fury. Nickname of Rama, brother of Krishna.

BALANCE The Balance of Justice replaces that of action and conclusion or law of cause and effect. This law is of Chaldean origin. It is a mystical portrayal of justice, to build the zodiacal archetype appoint libra, referring to "imminent justice".

BALILU (Chaldean) One of the abundant epithets of the sun.

BALMS are normally interpreted as "spice, perfume, sweet Oduor, balsam, balsam-tree." Balm of Gilead was a scarce perfume used curatively, that was cited in the Hebrew Bible, and intitled for the approximations of Gilead, place it was fabricated. The declaration emerged from William Tyndale's vernacular in the King James Bible of 1611 and has come about to signal a common healing in symbolic discourse. The evergreen or bush fabricating the balm is frequently accepted as Commiphora gileadensis. Nevertheless, some floral intellectuals have deduced that the genuine origin was a terebinth tree in the genus Pistacia.

BAMRA. (or Bhamra, Bumra, Bumrah or Bhambra) is a Jatt clan instituted in Punjab district of India. Bhamra or Bumrah is a Bhuiyar section tribe discovered in North India (Uttarakhand, Uttar Pradesh, Bihar, Rajsthan, Delhi). A myth commonwealth that the Raja of Bhamra attachment to the Ganga Vanshi ancestry of Utkala (ancient Orissa). He is considered to have been stolen as a child and was created the leader of the state of Bhamra around 1602. Almost all of the kingdom is woodland, fabricating only timber and shellac but support to be ich in chamosite. The northward border is disturbed by the Bengal-Nagpur railroad station at Bhamra town. The state is one of the five Oriya a feudatory, which were reallocated from the Central Provinces to Bengal, on the refurbishment of that region in October 1905. The first city is Deogarh.

BAMBU (Bamboo Books) Ancient and prehistoric works written in Chinese, this holds antiquated records of the Annals of China. They were found in the tomb of King Seang of Wai, he died in the year 295 before J.C., with much justice they can be traced back many centuries before.

BANIANO or Ashvatthaman (Sanskrit) Venerable fig tree (Ficus religiosa). This tree is called the Bo tree or tree of knowledge. The Ashvattha or Baniano is a depiction of the planet, of existence and of being. In its roots is make distinctive the supreme Being, the primary Cause, the Root of the Cosmos. The law of Samsara is symbolized by its branches, which fall to the foundation and cast and grow new roots, thus reverence earthly life. This tree can only be knocked down by mental wisdom.

BATH The submersion in clean and clear water is an emblem of purity and purification. The "primal waters"; the fluid part, connects with regeneration, destruction, creation. In alchemy, this sense is not altered, but undergoes a specialized application; explaining that the allegorical bath has a pattern of melting gold and silver and the purification of those two metals.

BAOTH (Hebrew) The Egg of Chaos.

BAPHOMET (Greek) The androgynous goat of Mandes. Esoterically and philosophically, that word never meant "goat," not even anything as goal as an idol. The term in question aimed, according to Von Hammer, 'baptism' or initiation into wisdom, of the Greek voices Bafe and Metis, and of Baphomet's relationship with Pan. Von Hammer must be right. Baphomet was a hermetic-Kabbalistic symbol, but the whole story, as invented by the clergy, is false.

BAPU (Gujrati) Father. The proselytes were called the great Mahatma Gandhi.

BAPTISM The rite of purification praised during the seriousness of initiation in the sacred ponds of India, and the later identical rite launched by John "the Baptist" and consummate by his disciples and supporters, who were not Christians. This Rite was previously an old Chaldean-Akkadian theurgies thing; it was religiously practiced in the nocturnal decorum in the Pyramids, where we see even today the initiation fountain designed as a tomb; it is still used today by the descendants of the ancient Sabeans.

BAR-COCHBA The head of a Jewish rebellion revolt in a Palestine in A.D. 132. He declared to be, and was received as, the Redeemer.

BARN Is a large building; separate from the main house; on farms which could be used for many purposes: for storage of farm products; accommodation of farm animals; storage of animal feed. Chickens are nearly a great many types of livestock on the earth. There should be 135 chickens for every cow, and 3x for every living soul. Untamed chickens are accredited to have its origin in northern China and were ultimately house trained in Southeast Asia over and above 5,000 generations earlier. The spiritual significance of a barn is where the miraculous birth of Jesus took place; in the stable or barn. The birth of Jesus was not just concerning humans, but all fabrication. Throughout His Word, animals serve as an encouraging capacity farmland design to oblation to subsistence. Peoples' connection to animals and frankly the land is a spiritual correlation from a divine power. Farming and cultivating are an act of faith, laying down many things in the Higher Power's control.

BARDO THODOL is a Tibetan holy book of the dead.

BARESMA (zendo) It is a plant that is used by Modbs; Parsis priests or in the temples of fire, where sacred bundles of it are preserved.

BARIMA (Sanskrit) One of the invisible powers, by possibilities of which it can be increased at will, consequence of gravitation.

BARRIER This term has a symbolism of obstacles; there are these such as walls, fences, barricades, etc. Esoterically, he is credited with the symbol of inability to advance through the life that has been started. In general, it means the earthly existence or the higher existence that you want to conquer, through a higher effort, known as "taking the great leap".

BASIC (Gnosticism) "The basic problem of youth is marriage. The flirtatious young woman with several boyfriends stays spinster because both are disillusioned with her."

BASILEUS (Greek) The Archon or chief who had the external over direction during the Mysteries of Eleusis. Meanwhile, this was an Adept Iaco, and magistrate of Athens, the Basileus of the Temple interior of the great Hierophant, and as such, was one of the leading Mistoe [Initiates] and belonged to the inner Mysteries.

BASIL, Rule of St. The canonical ruling put ahead by St. Basil the Great in 358-64, which is the bedrock of the accepted rule still go succeeding by religious in the East church. While harsh, it keeps aside from encouraging the greatest asceticism of the solitary of the desert. It owes its present development to a correction by St Theodore of Studious.

BASIL (HERB) A scented per annum herb of the mint family, indigenous to tropical Asia. The leaves of the basil plant are employed as a culinary herb, particularly in Mediterranean dishes. Greek origin, described stately, regal Basil also express too "royal" and "kingly." It initially sprouts from the Greek termed Basileios, who was a leader of the Byzantine Empire. The Greeks named basil basilikon phuton, defined "kingly herb," as it may be since it was frequently use in royal medicine. Nevertheless, the tag Basilikon besides be associated to the mythical basilisk. Basil was presumed to safeguard in opposition the deadly gaze and bite of the basilisk and was considered to be a remedy for snake bites.

BASILIDES. A theologian of Gnostic predispositions who taught at Alexandria in the second quarter of the 2nd century. His organization is demanding to reconstruct, afterward only particles of his works pull through and inconsistent versions are given. His companions soon set up a different sect.

BASSEN DYNE BIBLE, The foremost edition of the English Bible to be reproduced in Scotland. The Christian Teaching Bible appeared in 156, the whole Bible in 1579.

BAST (Egyptian) Goddess of the Egyptians mirrored her with the body of a woman and the head of a cat.

BATH (Hebrew) Daughter.

BATOO (Egypt) The First Man, advocating for the common Egyptian belief or tradition. Noum, the celestial artist, generates a beautiful maiden, the only one of the Greek Pandora and direct her to Batoo, subsequently the happiness of the first man is ruined.

BATRIA (Egypt) According to tradition, she was the wife of Pharaoh and the instructor of Moses.

BAY PSALM BOOK. Every measured category fabricated at Cambridge, Mass, (acclaim familiar in the U.S.A. as 'Bay State'), in 1640. It was the initial book to be sent to press in British America.

BEE When one visualized a bee as an image of sweethearts & flowers it comes to mind. However, bees are a sign of intelligence, childbirth and rebirth, along with diligence. Bees are often regarded as a permanent link with love. They are also viewed as defenders of the ordinary world. (Latin) Represents an image of the ingenious man, purity, and health. In Crete it was considered a divine emblem. It is a badge of tenacity and obedience. The V.M. Samael when he assures that the bees and the ants, symbolized certain prehuman races (Titan Geniuses, Fallen Angels, etc.) that exercised a communist regime so mechanical and automatic that they were degenerating; deteriorating in this way; individual intelligence. They were strongly dwarfing, until they reached the stage at which they are today.

BEET. A root vegetable from the genus beta, most often red in color and spherical. Sometimes the leaves are also eaten, beets may be used to produce sugar. It is often used to feed animals, especially cows, fields of sweet corn and beets. The beetroot is the taproot portion of a beet plant, usually known in North America as beets while the vegetable is referred to as beetroot in British English, and also known as the tatle beet garden beet, red beet, dinner beet or golden beet.

BEETLE Might symbolize rebirth, renewal, the sun, and life, however, might as well grasp on a negative meaning such as the unfortunate symbols, such as death, and other misjudgments. (Scarabaeus) In Egypt, it had a meaning of resurrection and in addition to resurrection; of resurgence for the mummy, or rather the higher appearances of the particularity that animated it, and of rebirth for the Ego, the "spiritual body" of the lower, human soul.

BEETHOVEN He was a great composer of significant classical melodies, among them "the Snow Symphonies," which keep among them, their talent and spiritual transcendence. He is a self-realized teacher and guardian of the Temple of the Music of the Spheres in the Inner Worlds.

BEADS or BEDE (prayer) Initially the word expressed a devotion, but later it was shifted to the compact globular figure handed down for 'telling beads' (I. e. Counting the beads of a rosary), and in consequence also applied e.g., to the chunk of a necklace. 'To bid a bead' thus means 'to offer a prayer'.

BEAR The Indigenous Bear emblem expressed might, ancestry vibrancy, fearless and wholesomeness. The bear is considerate and self-governing, with small requirements for empathy. The bear is as well autonomous and iron-willed in the environment. "The bear is given as a gift of love and symbolizes an attachment from the giver to the child. It provides comfort when you're hurt and lonely and tired and out-of-sorts, because the bear is always there and completely predictable. You can project onto a bear how you're feeling." A Black bear illustrates an exceptional signal of composure, pridefulness and learning who you are and what you want. The black bear attitude animal is a vigorous and sturdy being with motherly instincts and is notable as a merciless yet captivating beast wide-ranging human existence.

BEARD(S) Clerical The wearing of beards by clergyman has carry on the custom of the age. Church from Apostolic times starting with the 5th century and beyond West prelate set off clean-shaven, though in the 15th century beards look right on broadly favored again under the impact of non-religious trend.

BEAST (Scandinavian) She was reported to be the daughter of the Ice Giants, sons of Ymir; she was Buri's wife and mother of Odin and his brothers. The fictional beast that alarms all the youngsters stands for the primitive impulse of cruelty that lives within all homo sapiens. Youngsters are frightened of the beast, but at best, common sense outstretch the comprehension that we are horrified at the beast because it lives inside all of us.

BEDLAM. Initially the denomination given to the 'Hospital of St. Mary of Bethlehem' in Bishopsgate, established in 1247. It is unknown when demented people were first admitted, but lunatics are supposedly to have been here in 1402. By an extension of definition, the word 'Bedlam' is register to any irrational asylum or scene of disorder within doors.

BEC, Abbey of. The Benedictine abbey of BEC, in Normandy, was set up by Bl. Herluin and dedicated in 1041, it was renovated on a larger scale in 1060. These remarkable friars included Lanfranco, Anselm of Canterbury, and Pope Alexander II. BEC was taken over by the Mauritz in 1626, it was conquered in 1790. In 1948 Benedictine existence (Olivetan Congregation) was transformed.

BEDE. (Bead) Primitively the word expresses a prayer but later it was transported to the small spherical bodies used for 'telling beads' (i.e., counting the beads of a rosary), and hence also implement e.g., to the parts of necklace. 'To bid a bead' thus means 'to offer a prayer'.

BEC, (look at Christianism).

BEGINNING. Is the extremity in time or space at which existence begins. "He left at the beginning of December", or the first part or prior stage of something. "The ending of one relationship and the beginning of another"; the circumstances or origins of a person or operation. "He had stood up from humble beginnings to considerable wealth".

BEHAVIOR (Gnosticism) The way a person behaves in a specific condition or in general. Biologically it is the way an organism performs its vital purpose or responds to certain stimuli. "Those who are in misery who receive their behavior, let them judge themselves, who sit, even for a moment in the dock of the accused, who after a slight analysis of themselves, change their attitude."

BEINGS Numerous doctrines look at the mortal figure as a Divine Power; besides the principal symbol of the sacred. Gods materialized in human form, and the Old Testament expressed that "God made man in his own image". When we look at portrayal of legendary living things; part of them can epitomize danger, similarly; we observe, can start luck or joy. In general, mythic creatures give structure to humankind's extensive ambitions, fright, and most fervent fantasies. Existence. "The railroad brought many towns into being". Reality viable; vital. Is the nature or essence of a person. "Sometimes one aspect of our being has been evolving at the expense of others". Similar: soul, spirit, nature. A real or imaginary living creature or entity, especially an intelligent one. "Alien beings". Similar creature, life form.

BEMA. Means the East counterpart of the sanctuary.

BEL (Chaldean) Is the oldest and most powerful of the gods of Babylon, one of the most primitive trinities. Bel's wife, or his feminine appearance (Zakti), was Belat, or Beltis, "Mother of the great gods."

BELA SHEMESH (Chaldean. Hebrew) "Lord of the Sun". Title of the Moon meantime that stage in which the Jews became alternately solar and lunar worshippers, in which the Moon was a male divinity, and the Sun a female divinity. This phase held the time from Adam and Eve's allegorical throwing of Eden to a no less magnificent flood image of Noah.

BELIAL A Hebrew word in all probability meaning 'worthlessness', 'wickedness', or 'destruction'. It is normally found in combination with a noun, e.g., 'sons of Belial'. It takes place several times in the sacred writings (OT), only once in the Scriptures (NT).

BELILIN (Gnosticism) It is a song revealed by the Angel Aroch to protect us from the dark or negative collectivity.

BELITES (Hebrew) Jewish venerators of the Moon.

BEMBO Table Bambina or Mensa Isiac. It is a bronze tablet that has decorated some mosaic drawings and that currently appears in the museum of Trim. In times past it belonged to the famous Cardinal Bembo.

BEN (Hebrew) Son. Generic annex in proper nouns to show the son of so-and-so, for example, Ben Solomon, Ben Ishmael, etc.

BENIT The Benit matronymic is emanated from the Latin first name Benedictus, which represents "blessed." It converted into a customary given name throughout Europe due to the approval of St. Benedict. A people of the Scottish/English Borderlands known as the Strathclyde Britons were the first to use the name Benit. It is descended from the prehistorical Lain given name Benedictus, which implies blessed.

BLESSED (Gnosticism) Mother there is only one, Blessed Mother Devi Kundalini, Mother of Fire, Heavenly Mother.

BENOO This instruction is condensed with two symbols, both used to mean "Phoenix", one was Shen-Shen (heron), and the different Rech (red; both were holy to Osiris.

BETH (Hebrew) This command is defined as the second letter of the Hebrew alphabet and corresponds to the Phoenician bet, the exact scope symbolizes some infinite essentials. This epithet became public in Scotland in the 17th century due to its association with the meaning of the Gaelic voice "beath" expressing life.

BETHANY Is referred to oftentimes in the New Testament. It was the place of residence of Mary and Martha and their brother Lazarus. As told by the Gospel (John 11), the mystery of Lazarus's restoration to life which took place there; the township Arabic name, Al'Ayzariyyah, is obtained from the name Lazarus.

BETHEL Cited to "house of God" is mentioned in the Bible as the site where Jacob sleep and dreamed of angels going up and down a ladder (Genesis 28:19). Some scholars name Beit El with the site of the biblical Bethel. The first to show the village of Beitin as the site of Bethel was Edward Robinson, in 1838.

BNE (B'ne) AL him or Beni Elohim (Hebrew) "Sons of God", or more correctly: "Sons of the Gods", title that Elohim is plural of Eloah. It is associated with angelic powers, which are attributed to the Sephora Hod.

BERYL (Beryllus, in Latin) Emerald-like gemstone, extremely high green and transparent, which is used as a magic mirror, in whose astral aura the fortune teller can watch over apparitions and representations of future things.

BERNE. The ten theological theory which were supported of a conference of Swiss clergy and laity at Berne in January 1528. They were drawn in preservation of Reformed theology and epitomize in a decree which executed the Reformation in Berne.

BERAKAH This is a Jewish prayer that takes the form of a blessing or thanksgiving to God. It has been proposed that the usage of the term "Eucharist" (which is one of the two Greek translations of the Heb. berakah) for the fundamental Christian observances enhanced known from the evidence that the Eucharistic devotion was a Christian moderation of the Jewish berakah which was chanted and done with a cup of wine.

BERASIT (Heb.) First phrase from the book of Genesis. The authorized English version [the same as the Spanish category of Scio, Cipriano de Valera and others], translates this: "In the beginning", but this adaptation is contested by many male doctors. Tertullian took for good: "In power"; Grotius, "When at the beginning"; but the authors of the Targum of Jerusalem, who must have known Hebrew as the most, interpreted this expression: "In wisdom." Berasit or Berasheth is a mystical word among The Kabbalists of Asia Minor.

BES (Egyptian) God of joy, novelty, family and attire. Considered the God of virility. His human embodiment was of a tiny person with a big head, large eyes and prominent cheekbones.

BESTALES (Gnosticism) or Vestals.

BETYLES (Fen) Magic stones. Ancient writers give them the name "animated stones"; oracular stones. Selected by Gentiles and Christians, they believed in their Virtudes.

BETHABARA. In accordance with Jn. 1:28 (AV) the place was John the Baptist Baptisms, and thus possibly the site of Christ's Baptisms. Many predominant folios, ensuing by the RV, read 'Bethany' at this point.

BETHANY. The town of Martha, Mary, and Lazarus, c. 2 miles from Jerusalem where Christ lodged over the week prior to His Passion. Its modern surname is El 'Azeriyeh, e.I. 'the place of Lazarus'. 'Bethany past Jordan' (Jn. 1: 28 RV) is another village.

BETHSAIDA. A principally Pagan town to the East waterfront of the Nahr Al-Sharieat at the position where it emanates the Sea of Galilee. It has been said that it was visited by Christ (Mk. 8: 22 21), however, it hasn't been verified.

BETHEL (Heb, 'house of God') (1) It was early on the leading shrine in Palestine of the Israelite (i.e., non-Judaean) tribes (2) The tiny township near Bielefeld in Westphalia was given the appreciated epithet to the Bodel schwing Hache Stiftungen. The consist of institutions for epileptics, training institutes for theologians and paramedics, and a widening for Pentecostal ecclesiastical students. (3) a name used, notably by many Methodists and Baptists for a setting of reverent church service.

BEUNO (d. c. 640) Patriarch of Clynnog. It has culminated that he was the originator of pious districts in Herefordshire, even though his first goal appeared to have taken place in North. Wales, where he was apparently buried. His tomb was long cherished at Clynnog Faur (Gwynedd).

BEZAE, CODEX ('D'). This (perhaps 5th century) Graeco-Latin Manuscript of the Gospels and Acts, with a fragment of the Latin of 3 Jn., was exhibited in 1581 at the University of Cambridge by T. Beza. It is the chief ambassador of the Western text.

BETHESDA. A pool in Jerusalem (Jn. 5: 2) is considered to have possessed healing properties connected with a cyclical disturbance of the water. It has been diversely recognized.

BHAS (Sanskrit) This prompt mention to light, splendor, beauty.

BHAGATS (Sanskrit) Persisted, Sokha and Shiv Nuth by the Indos. The one who scares away extremist spirits.

BHAGAVAD-Gita (Sanskrit) Attributed to "The Song of the Lord" is an episode of the Mahabharata, the great epic poem of India. It contains a dialogue in which Krichna, 'chariot driver', and Arjuna, his chela [disciple], discuss the most elevated spiritual philosophy. This work is eminently mystical or esoteric.

BHAKTA (Sanskrit) Channels: to have the attitude of devout, devout, faithful, worshipful.

BHAO (Sanskrit) Transpired a celebration of divination among the Kolean tribes of central India.

BHAVA (Sanskrit) Being, existence, substance, real being, living being, creature; production, birth; form or mode of being, state or condition of existence; life; disposition, nature, character; I encourage, heart; emotion, etc.

BHIMA (Sanskrit) Sums "terrible". It was also called Vrikodara (wolf belly). He was the reinstatement of the Pandava princes, and was mystically instituted by Vayu, God of the air. The first leader of the Pandava army, he was acclaimed for his power and fierceness.

BHONS (Tib.) Henchmen of the ancient religion of the aborigines of Tibet of pre-Vedic temples and ritualism. The same as Dugpas, "red caps", although the latter denomination is usually applied only to sorcerers.

BHOGA (Sanskrit) Pleasure, enjoyment; experience; perception, sensation; food; snake, etc.

BHRIGU (Sanskrit) Particular of the Vedic Richi's magnates. Manu calls him "Son" and deposits his Institutions to him. Bhrigu is one of the seven Prajapati's or ascendants of humanity, which abide by to name him with one of the creator gods, which the Puranas install in the Krita-yuga, that is, the initial epoch, that of purity.

BHU (Sanskrit) The earth, one of the hells.

BHUMI (Sanskrit) The land, which is also called Prithivi.

BHUVAR (Sanskrit) It is a transitional region (atmosphere), which is found between the earth (Bhu) and the sky (Svar).

BIBLE SOCIETY, British and Foreign. One of the wide-reaching Bible Societies. A solely amalgamated body, it was instituted in London in 1804 for the printing and circulation of Bibles at home and abroad. It has issued translations of the Bible (excluding the Apocrypha) in many languages.

BIGAMY (1) A 'second marriage' contracted by a person whose 'first' spouse is still alive, just after the 'first' marriage has not been announced null. (2) Account to older manipulation the term denotes a second marriage after the death of one of the parties of the first marriage.

BIHAR GYALPO Endured a king blessed by the dugpas. A chief in all religious buildings.

BIJA (Sanskrit) Embryo, seed, germ, etc. "The bija is a noise, word or sentence that is articulated at the beginning of a mantra in order to cause the desired effect."

BINAH (Hebrew) Understanding. It is the 3rd of the ten Sephiroth, third of the upper triad, is a feminine power, which examines the letter he of the Tetragram Maton IHHVN, Binah is selected Aima, the Supreme Mother, and "the great Sea".

BINDING AND LOOSING. The potential given by Christ to St. Peter (Mt. 16: 19) and later to all the Apostles (Mt. 18: 18). It implies to be general authority to exercise discipline over the Church, though some have identified it with the power of forgiving or retaining sins (Jn. 20: 23).

BINDU or Vindu (Sanskrit) Drop, period. The point or sign of the anusvara.

BIPEDO, BIPEDAL (Gnosticism) The entity of this Tri cerebrates biped mistakenly called man, is a precious machine, with five wonderful psycho-physiological nuclei.

BITTER *(Gnosticism)* The Fourth Way is the process of the Perfect Matrimony. It is also known by the name of the Path of the Razor's Edge, more Bitter than the thread, many start it, exceedingly infrequent are those who reach the goal.

BIOLOGY This term came to signify "discourse" and then to "thesis" and "science" It is an idiom composed of two Greek terms: bio and terrace: bio means life; terrace; comes from the Greek root of logos-voice, expression.

BIOLOGICAL (Gnostic) Jesod (vital body), is the neighborhood of biological, physical, chemical activities.

BIOSOPHY (Sanskrit) As it where the science of life. The reflection that claims to harvest what is inside and prove the authentic wisdom; the transcendental that has not been expressed by it.

BIRS Nimrud (Cald.) Conforming to the orientalists, it is the site where the Tower of Babel was erected. The great overpopulation of Birs Nimrud is in the proximity of Mesopotamia. Sir H. Rawlinson and several Assyriologists, examining excavations of the ruins, concluded that the Tower contained seven floors of brickwork, each one was of a different color, demonstrating that the temple was devoted to the seven planets. Granting its top three floors are in ruins, the tower still rises today to 154 feet above plain level.

BIRD(S) This vocable "symbolizes" thought and concerns the air element, fantasy. In ancient Egypt he was honored as ideogram of human souls. Birds according to their category have some delineation such as: the pigeon; simplicity and the Holy Spirit; the partridge the cunning; the falcon, connects with the sublime, height to the Being, etc., the chicken, fear, cowardice, the swallow, relates to coexistence; the turtledoves, the solitude, the desolation, etc... It is said that high-flying birds have a link with the spiritual and terrestrial or flight under the earthly attitude.

BIRTH There exists many symbolisms of sensation of birth, e.g., the egg is linked with new life, birth, fecundity, reawakening and the potential of growing, water relates to the feminine proposition and the comprehensive womb; it implies also to bear (offspring), produce, emanate, or generate, etc.

BLACK AGE (Sanskrit) The fourth yuga, the black or iron age; shows the interval of the world, whose permanence is 432,000 years. The last of the epochs in which the revolutionary period of man is dispensed by a series of these ages. The Kali Yuga began 3,102 years before J.C., at the instant of Krishna's death, and the first 5,000-year cycle concluded between the years 1897 and 1898. It was called "The Age of Discord and Misfortune."

BLEACHING THE BRASS (Alchemy) "Burn your books and bleach the brass." It indicates the modification of the intimate Lucifer, black as coal, whitening it through the waters of transformation, destroying every misconception of the mind: it is achieved by the three (3) factors of the Revolution of Consciousness.

BLIND (Gnosticism) Consciousness is the Light that the senseless does not perceive, just as the Blind cannot perceive sunlight, but it exists by itself. We need to open ourselves so that the light of awareness passes through the dreadful darkness of us personally.

BLISS As it may be defined as perfect delight, happiness, immense joy, e.g., "Isabella is just blissed out, always smiling."

BLOOD Concerning the duration of time, blood has related to contradictory, including life/death, death/redemption, eternal life innocent/massacre, sickness/therapy, nobility/male diction (haemophiles in the "Blue Blood" successor of Queen Victoria), amplitude/transference of dishonest, and attractiveness/revulsion.

BLOW, JOHN (1648-1708). Well known as a songwriter and musician. His commitments involved that of choirmaster of Westminster Abbey (1669-80). Allocated to his devout work over 100 anthems and 14 services pull through.

BO (Sanskrit) The Tree of Wisdom.

BOARDS To go on board a plane, ship; or a train: "They boarded a train for Seattle". Boards are long flat pieces of wood which are used, for example, to make floors or walls. The floor was drafty bare boards. The board of a company or institution is the group of people who command and direct it. The directors, the top management, the council. The board can refer to both shareholders and the directors of a corporation. In both cases, "the board" makes most major resolutions for the company (in a "boardroom" usually). Delineating ideograms boards are a graphic presentation of spoken and written language. They serve as a substitute for traditional language, allowing even very young non-speakers a technique of interacting. In holly scriptures the word boards are employed as follows: "He built the walls of the house within with boards of cedar: from the floor of the house to the walls of the ceiling, he covered them on the inside with wood; and he covered the floor of the house with boards of fir." 1-Kings 6:15

BOAZ Illustrates one of the two columns of the temple; the other is Yakin. Boaz replaces the feminine principle and Yakin the masculine Origin: black and white.

BOBIN KANDELNOTS Directs attention to the vital values that are deposited by the intelligence of nature in each of the three brains: Consisting of Intellectual, Emotional and Sexual Instinctive Motor.

BOBBIO A miniature town in the Mountain range expanding the length of the Italian peninsula, formerly the space of an abbey founded in 612 by St. Columbanus. It's immortalized assembly of premature mass (now largely in the Vatican, Ambrosiana, and Turin comprises the Bobbio hymnal (in Paris), a major crowd of ritual narrative dating from the 8th century.

BODHA (Sanskrit) Understanding, intelligence, perception, wisdom.

BODHI or Sambodhi; (Sanskrit) Receptive intellect, as opposed to Buddhi, which means the potentiality of intelligence. (Perfect wisdom, sacred science, enlightenment; the tree of wisdom or knowing.)

BODHI TREE The perfect, divine wisdom. Tree of knowledge.

BODHISATTVA (Sanskrit) The one whose essence (sattva) has enhanced intelligence (bodhi), who lacks only one incarnation to become the perfect Buddha, to have a chance at Nirvana.

BODMER PAPYRI. An assemblage of amazingly dominant Manuscripts., mainly on papyrus, acquired by purchase for his library in Geneva by M. Martin Bodmer. They incorporate an almost complete document of Jn. (P. 66) of c. A.D. 200, over four-fifths of a 3rd century codex of Lk. and Jn. (P. 75), and a copy of Melito, 'On the Pasch'.

BOEHME, JAKOB, (1575-1624) was a German Christian visionary whose compilation regarding redemption and the republic of the solar system prestige several epochs thereafter; pious relocations and theorist, in conjunction the (German: Deutsche Romantik). A cordwainer and a dedicated Lutheran, Bohme started to compose thereafter accomplishing various envision. His conception inflames resistance in the Evangelical church, and he was compelled to draft in clandestine and later banished for a year. Accentuating personal credence and respective devout accomplishments over submission to doctrine, he complicated a new approach of the affiliation linking God and man. Bohme established a construction of how the rivalry amidst heavenly wrath and celestial appreciation within the One God prompt an innovation inspiration which gave rise to the diverseness of the world. He accentuates will as the predominant triggering characteristic within God and mentor that God had disposed man the determination choosing to pursue eternal correctness. He also coached hat a the disobedience of Man was a fundamental platform in the advancement of the nature, expressing that it was indispensable for human kind to go away from God, through the refractory of the Evil one, the dissolution of Eve from Adam, and their procurement of the awareness of good and evil, in ordinance for initiation to proceed to a new and more flawless position of reclaimed peace.

BODY or Double (Astral) Shadow or ethereal counterpart of man or animal; the Linga-zarari, the Doppelganger. Let the reader not entangle him with the astral Soul, an additional term of the lower Manas or Kama-Manas, as it is replaced, and which is the flash of the higher Ego. The astral body enhances like a bridge of communication between the soul and the body.

BOHAIRIC Fashionable of the predominant sociolect of Coptic. It arises in the North splinters of the Nile drift, regardless, rejuvenate more language all over Egypt. The Bahairi type of the good Book conceivably likely dates outgo the 6th-7th centennials and is the precise genre of the Nestorian house of God.

BOLOGNA. North Italy. In the Archaic Ages its university (established in the 12th century) was the chief Centre in Europe for the study of canon and civil law.

BOLT Acquainted with the language of the Egyptians (hieroglyph), the bond that connects the expirations of a door, meaning by affinity, the purpose to fix a situation, disposing without the possibilities of rectification. It is said that in ancient times when an initiate wished to climb the Egyptian mysteries he was organized and forced to do the most humble work, he was ordered to maintain the most absolute silence; when the night of trial came, the aspirant was led to the door of the Sanctuary (it was the place of entry of the tests), the candidate was pointed out a hole in the wall, in front of him, where there was a passageway so low that it could only be penetrated it; Hauling. "You can still go back," said one of the officiants. The door of the Temple has not yet been closed." If the initiate persisted, he was given a small lit torch or lamp. The officers left and closed the door of the Sanctuary with a bang; there was no longer any doubt, nor to turn back, the door was with a bolt; he had barely slide into the narrow passageway, when he heard a gloomy voice at the bottom of the cavern saying, "Here perish the madmen who covet science and power," echoing on the walls of the temple repeating for seven times the same words.

BOLSENA, The Miracle of. Versions to the customary anecdote, a German clergyman seeing Mass in the Provencal township of Bolsena was interrupted by indecisions concerning the transpose of the bread and wine; these certain were set on meanwhile, he saw Blood appearing from the ingredients and cleansing the mortal.

BONA-OMA or Bona Dea [Good Goddess.] Roman goddess, defender of the Newcomers and Kabbalist. She was also labeled Fauna, from the title of her father Faun. She was venerated as a visionary and faithful divinity, and her scholar was reserved only for women, and the ceremonies of her temple (a cave of the Aventine) were led by the vestals of the first day of May that took place every year. His animosity to men was such that no male was allowed to advance the consuls' dwelling, where their festivities occasionally took place, and even portraits and busts of men were taken out of the house during the ceremony. Clodius decided to outrage one of his sacred feasts. He arrived Caesar's house, disguised as a woman, and attracted adversity to himself. Women made libations by drinking from a glass (mellarium) filled with milk. A few said that the mellarium held wine, however, it is said that those who were men, tried to take revenge on them.

BONAVENTURA Franciscan cleric, 'Doctor Seraphic us' Giovanni di Fidanza prob. He set off as a Franciscan in 1243. He instructed in Paris. In 1257 he was chosen as Minister General and tried much to clear up internal disputes in the institution. His greatest leadership was the election of Gregory X in 1271 and in 1273 he was promoted to Cardinal. Taken part in the Council of Lyons in 1274. As a curate he had modest rapport with Aristotelian teaching than did St. Thomas Aquinas. In his Itinerarium Mentis in Deum he calls attention to the misinterpretation of all mortals' rationale when disagreed with the sanctified potency which the transcendent essence showers on the conscientious devout. He encountered percussion as a dutiful columnist.

BONO (Pedro) Lombardo; he was a considerable adept in enclosed science, who made a trip to Persia to study alchemy. On his return, he took up residence in Istria in 1330 and became famous as a Rosicrucian. A monk from Alabria labeled Lacinio is assigned the publication, in 1772, of a concentrated version of Bono's works concerning the evolution of metals.

BONZOS Buddhist priests from China, Japan, Tonkin and other east Asian peoples.

BOOK(S) OF DISCIPLINE, the 'First Book of Discipline' (1560) was draft by J. Knox and other people as a primary plan for the command and preservation of the brand-new Scottish House of God. Fragment of it were disagreeable to the honesty and it endure expired symbol. The so alleged 'Second Book of Discipline (1578), primarily the effort of A. Melville, was put together as a declaration of the authoritarian Protestant opposed to attempt to replace a change hierarchy.

BOOZ (Hebrew) Great-grandfather of David. The voice in theme comes from B, who declares "inside", I "outside", allegorical name of one of the columns of the atrium of the temple of King Solomon.

BORBORIANS. A sect of libertine Gnostics who succeeded from the 2nd to the 5th centennials.

BORI (Persian) The Mountain of the World, a volcano or mountain of fire; the same as the Meru indo.

BORRI (Joseph Francis) Hermetic philosopher born in Milan in the seventeenth century. He was a proselyte, fervent occultist and alchemist. It is said that he knew too much, and for this reason he was condemned to death for heresy, in January 1661, after the death of Pope Innocent X. It was feasible for him to escape, and he lived for many years, until, at last, having acknowledged a friar in a village in Turkey, he was denounced; reclaimed by the Pope's Nuncio, sent back to Rome and incarcerated on August 10, 1675. The facts, however, show that Borri managed to escape from his confinement in a way that no one could explain.

BORSIPPA (Chaldean) The Planetary Tower, in which Bel was considered in the days when astrolatries were the most considerable astronomers. It was dedicated to the Nebo, God of Wisdom.

BOSCO, St. John (1815-88) He started the Salesian Order. At the age of nine, he had an insight to focus on Winning boys to the Christian faith, and in 1859 near Turin he founded the 'pious Society of St. Francis de Sales, regularly known as the Silesians. He practiced the least of detail, incorporated with attentive observation over his pupils' maturation and individuality and devotional inspirations.

BOSIO, ANTONIO (1576-1629) An Italian archeologist who was the first to acknowledge the momentous location of a subterranean sepulture location on the

Via Solaria in 1578 which was unexpected. His Roma sot Terranea 1632 was the degree of assignments on the catacombs until G.B. de Rossi's exploration.

BOTTLE According to Prehistory, it meant a description of salvation. Within alchemy, a sealed bottle is related to energy and works with consciousness.

BOWING. Originating in early times Christians have bowed 'the name of Jesus' on the authority of Phiol 2:10. How far back the custom of bowing at other times, exclusively to the altar, can be outlined, is disputed.

BRAGI (Scandinavian) The god of the New Life, of the renewal of Nature and the reincarnation of man. He is called "Divine Singer" without stain or Baldon, and he is restored by sliding into the ship of the Dwarves of Death while the destruction of Nature (pralaya), reposing on deck with his golden rope harp next to him and dreaming the dream of life. When the ship traversed the threshold of Nain, the Dwarf of Death, Bragi wakes up, and pressing the strings of his harp, he sings a song that reverberates through all the worlds, a song that describes the approval of his birth and awakens the silent and sleeping Nature of his long death-like illusion.

BRAHMARANDRA (Sanskrit) A passage of the crown, or apex of the head, connected by the Suchumna (cord of the spinal column) with the heart. It is an ancient transcendent word, which has meaning only in mysticism. It is a hole, or junction of the apex of the head, through which the soul of the yogi approach out at the time of death. The spinal canal reaches a finale at that point.

BRAY, The Vicar of. The hero of a popular ballad whose affected zeal for each new shape of established religion from Charles I to George I persuaded his tenure of his benefice.

BRAKES To separate into parts especially instantly or forcibly break a stick into groups. 2: to cause (above) to unrelated into two or more pieces. 3: to stop working or cause to cease operating because of damage or wear I broke my watch. 4: to fail to keep, break the law and break a promise. 5: To prevent motion of a mechanism; apply the brakes of a car; 6: something used to slow down or stop movement or activity use interest rates as a brake on spending.

BREACH Is the infraction or violation of a law, obligation, tie, or standard. e.g., breaking a contract, a law, legal obligation, or promise.

BREATH (The Great) Divine activity, the Holy Okidanokh.

BREATHING Has reference to air on an individual level while breeze relates to air on more of the universe level. Breath symbolizes existence and the power of the psyche and the transitory and fragile and the indefinite.

BREDA, Declaration of. The statement was made by Charles II at Breda (Holland) in April 1660, immediately prior to the Restoration. It promises 'liberty to tender consciences' in circumstances of religions not influencing the tranquility of the principality.

BRIAH (Hebrew) In turn, the Bria tic World. This is the second of the four worlds of Kabbalists, and it is associated with the highest created "archangels," that is, the pure Spirits.

BRIDGE WATER TREATISES, The Eight treatises, assembled between 1833 leftovers 1836, on various features of the 'power, wisdom, and goodness of God, as exemplify in the Creation'. F.H. Everton, 8th Earl of Bridgewater, left £8,000 for the purpose.

BRIH (Sanskrit) This word channels: To grow, to spread, to develop.

BRIHAT (Sanskrit) Great, powerful, lofty. It should be noted that, by reason of euphony, the t of this word occasionally changes into s or another letter, as in Brihaspati.

BRISEO (Briseus) (Gr.) Name given to the God Bacchus by his wet nurse, Briso. Briseo also had a Temple in Brisa, peninsula of the Island of Lesvos.

BRUGES. Per Peschka, Bruges is useful as a metaphor for purgatory. It's a platform where McDonagh can scrutinize morality in a "post-modern" world, as it grows farther from proportion of right and wrong. The word Brugge channels "bridge" in the Flemish language and touches on to an ancient Roman bridge beyond the Reie River, which flows in the Zwin. The contemporary city grew up around a sensation built by the counts of Flanders in the centuries. In the 15th century, Brugge was the cradle of the Flemish Primitives and a Centre of patronage and painting growth for artists such as Jan van Eyck and Hans Memling. Many of their works were exported and determined painting styles all over Europe.

BRUTE Astral strength clear in animals; second view in the grosses; power of animals to spontaneous find poisonous or medicinal substances.

BUA Mantram which is articulated in yoga during pranayama.

BUBASTE (Egypt) City of Egypt sacred to cats, and location was its main temple. Innumerable hundreds of thousands of cats were embalmed and buried in the cavities of Beni-Hassan-El Amar. Being an image of the Moon, the cat endured holy to Isis, its goddess. Such an animal sees in the dark, and its eyes have a phosphorescent glow that frightens nocturnal birds from omens. The cat was also hallowed to Bast, and therefore it was called "destroyer of the enemies of the Sun".

BUDHA (Sanskrit). "The wise and Intelligence", son of Soma (the Moon) and Rohini or Taraka, husband of Brihaspati snatched by King Soma, who in this way cause the great war between the Asuras, who supported with the god of the Moon, and the gods who took the argument of Brihaspai (Jupiter), who was his purohit (family priest). This war is well known by the name of Taraka maya, and is the earliest war fought on Olympus among the gods and the titans in addition to the war (spoken of in the Apocalypse) amid Michael (Indra) and the Dragon (who personifies the Asuras). [Buddha also means wise, intelligent.]

BUDDHATA(S) Name describing the essence. It is the psychic substance with which the golden embryo can and should be lifted. It is the minuscule fraction of the Human Soul.

BUDDHICO (Buddhist or Buddha) Applies an attribute definition belonging to or relating to Buddhism. This is affirmed by the Buddhist examination, Buddha doctrine, etc.

BEUNO, St. (d. c. 640) Abbot of Clynnog. He is said to have established monasteries in Herefordshire, but his chief mission work is believed to have been in North Wales, where his tomb was long worshiped at Clynnog Faur (Gwynedd).

BUHO. In reference to a Bird that was sacred in prehistory to the Goddess Minerva the Goddess of sageness for being nocturnal and position that adopts, it is correlated to the supernatural, the omen and death. The Owl symbolizes Wisdom and philosophy.

BULL The bull emblem is associated with wave power, displayed as persistence, might, and gallantry. Bull indications became illustrated as long as primitive period. They may be introduced in fine art, literary texts, and horoscopes. In customs, it exhibits fertility, defensive aspects, concentration, chasteness, and tolerance. Innumerable of its physique division, specifically the tailpiece, hind paw and conceal, are as well emblematic of ability, fecundity and terra firma subsequently. In the Egyptian myths, the bull was an indication of the fecundity god Apis. In Mesopotamia the storm god Ishkur/Adad is named "bull of heaven" and "grand bull," in Legendary inscriptions from the earliest city of Ugarit, the bull relates to the high god El, embodying both energy and productivity. His opinion is similar that of the lion, a mighty and kingly creature, as Jesus prospective. The bull is Luke, considering he begins articulating of the dedication of Zachariah to God and the bull is the emblems of oblation, the inclination for devotional life, which authorize human beings to conquest further on beasties suffering and to acquire peacefulness. Early enough and chronologically of the creatures Armageddon; Adam and the Sethite chain are all colorless bulls, evidently exemplifying their capacity and through; all along this interval, additional animals reappear; Cain is a black bull, Abel a red bull, and the descendants of the Watchers Spectators numerous untamed beasts. Zeus succeeded the previous enrolments, and, in the configuration of a bull that originated forward from the ocean, abducted the highbred Greek Mythology and brough her, notable, to Crete. Dionysus was a second God of resurgence who was energetically associated to the bull.

BULL SNAKE The bull-snake (Pituophis catenifer sayi) is an enormous, nontoxic, Boomslang snake. It is a subclass of the gopher snake (Pituophis catenifer). The bull-snake is one of the substantial/prolonged snakes of Western Hemisphere and the USA. Eventually Eve's misdemeanor in the Promised Land, snakes in Christian Orthodox Standards have been related with deception, adverse attitude and enthusiasms. Snakes are bordering the terra firma and shedding their dermis, mingling in the beast fable of the underworld. Vipers are indicated in both the Tanakh and the Holy Scriptures. The shape of a basilisk or snake accomplished remarkable designating purpose in the austere traditional and progression prevalent of previous Graecia, Kemet, Chaldaea, and Canaan. The ophidian was a folk tale of everlasting capability and disarray from the hostile world along with an emblem of fecundity, animation, recovery, and renewal. The snake, is further associated with predictions, in addition to the counting attestant arrangement outstandingly "to practice divination or fortunetelling"

BURU BONGA. Prevails the "Spirit of the Hills". This driadic divinity is worshipped by, reaching lengths up to 8 ft. the Kolarian tribes of central India, with grand ceremonies and magical display. There are certain mysteries linked to it, but the people are very suspicious and do not want to allow any strangers into their rites.

BURRO. A burro is the Spanish term for "donkey". Hinny" A hinny is the result of breeding through a female donkey and a male horse. Jack: A jack is an ayerm for a male donkey. Jenny: A jenny (or Jennet) is an expression for a female donkey.

Moke: which is a British word for a donkey. In the New Testaments (Mark 11:1-110 it is told that as Jesus approached the Mount of Olives, he sent two of his disciples to a close by village to fetch him a donkey, or exactly an Onager or wild donkey. Upon prosper return, "Jesus rode the donkey into Jerusalen, where he was met by cheering crowds." Jesus rode a donkey to show he was humble and wanted something simple. Many people remembered his miracles, so they put their cloaks and plan branches to honor him, and they shouted 'Hosanna'!

BURN Describes to hurt, damage, or destroy commodities by fire or maximum heat: 'She burned her hand on the hot iron.' The Biblical meaning of Burn is the penalizing of burning in the Hebrew Bible occurred in cases of illicit sex, sacrilege, and as a threat. The Bible says about burn in desire: But each man has his own gift from God; one has this gift; another has something different. The Lord said to Moses, "Say to Aaron and his sons: 'These are the regulations for the burnt offerings': The burnt offerings is to remain on the altar hearth throughout the night, till morning, and the first fire has consumed on the altar and place them beside de altar."

BUSH, (BURNING), The. The scenery of Moses' call, where the angel found in a flame of fire out of the midst of a bush' (Exod. 3:2-4).

-C-

CAABA (Arabic) Epithet of the reputative Mohammedan temple of Mecca, a privileged place of pilgrimage. The building is not spacious, but it is very original; It has a cubic structure, 24x24 long and wide elbows, 27 high, with a s opening on the east-facing side to perceive light. In the northeast corner is the "Black Stone" of the Kaaba, it is said that it descended directly from the sky and was white as snow, but with the traversal of time it became black, due to the failures of humanity.

CABALLI, Cabales, Lemurs They are the astral substances of men who go through a premature death, that is, they were murdered or killed themselves before defining the natural term of their life.

CABAR, ZIO (Gnosticism) "The mighty Lord of Splendor", those who propagate seven beneficial lives, "shining in their own form and light" to neutralize the involvement of the seven astral "ill-disposed" or initiations. The successor of

Kara Thanos, incarnation of concupiscence and the body. The last are the seven physical planets; the main ones are their geniuses or Regents.

CABALA or KABAKA (Kabballah, Heb.) The hidden wisdom of the Jewish rabbis of the Middle Ages, common sense derived from older secret doctrines concerning cosmogony and divine things, which combined to constitute a theology after the time of the captivity of the Babylonian Jews. All works belonging to the esoteric category are called Kabbalistic.

CACO This term replaces the bad thief "sinister power", black tantrism. He was the burglar whom Hercules lasted for aspiring to steal his flocks in the eighth task. Caco is the evil housebreaker who defrauds the sexual core of the body to reward brutal animal vehemence.

CADMUS (Greek) The supposed inventor of the letters of the alphabet. There may have been created and then taught in Europe and Asia Minor; but in India the letters were understood and applied by the apprentices in very early times.

CADUCEUS (Greek) poets and mythologists took over the Egyptians under the vision of the Caduceus of Mercury. The Caduceus is deciphered, in the form of two snakes curled on a rod, in the Egyptian works built before Osiris.

CAEDMON. (d, c. 680) the original English Christian poet. As explained by Bede, Caedmon was a laboring man at the monastery of Whitby, who accepted in a vision the gift of composing verses in praise of God; he then converted into a monk and transfigured the Holy Scriptures into verse.

CAERUS The Gentile prehistoric had made a deity of that favorable moment to have good success in a system, in that fugitive instant that we call motive. It comes from the Latin series (late), the occasional longed for are persistently late for the evaluation of our longings.

CHABURAH (cf. Heb. 'Friend'). In Jewish entertaining a group of friends established for religious purposes. They often shared an ordinary weekly meal, consistently on the eve of sabbaths or holy days. It has been disclosed that Christ and His disciples emerged such a CHABURAH, and that Last Supper was a CHABURAH meal.

CHAD (Sanskrit) Pronouncements; has the same expression as chat, although by euphony it changes the t in d.

CHANDA or CHANDI (Sanskrit) Personifies, Longing, passion, burning, rapture, frenzy. The Moon and a deity or representation of it, the terms Chandra and Soma are almost identical.

CHANDALA Tracksuits are rejects or outcast people. This renown is given today to all secondary classes of Native Americans; but in ancient times a certain class of men prevailed, who, having deteriorated their right to any of the four castes (Brahmins, Kshatriyas, Vaishyas and s), were repudiated from the cities and sought their shelter in the groves. At that time, they were performed as "masons", until they were finally limited, they left the country about four thousand years before our time. Some authors see in them the ancestors of the Jews, whose tribes began with Abraham or "No-Braham." To this day, it is the most despised class by the Brahmins of India.

CHANGE(S) The ordinary world Is contemplated as an emissary of nature, the due exactitude of which is authoritarian; the wavelet it causes is excessively intense. What we are as today, who we are is faithful due to the reality that we are constantly changing and so is the planet. At times, this switch can be enormous; from time to time, it could be unimportant to be perceived. Unpleasant change is observed as the stain of wickedness or atonement and human beings frequently retreat to turn away or become distressed.

CHANT Harmonious sounds; to make melodic sounds with the voice predominantly; to sing a chant; recite something in a monotonous repetitive tone protesters were chanting outside, to utter, to celebrate or praise in song or chant. The definition of chant in literature is a straightforward song or melody, a short simple melody in which several words or syllables are designated to one note, as in the recitation of psalms. "Scientific studies have found that chanting can decrease stress, anxiety and depressive symptoms, as well as increase positive mood, feelings of relaxation and focused attention."

CHAIN(S) The spiritualism of chains has an extended and heroic chronicle. They are images of slavery; people who are shackle jointly must share circumstances. They must go all around together as the chains will force them to remain associated. Chains also symbolize confinement but also presentation of interrelations, intimacy and fellowship. The prevailing present comparison is abuse, due to the use of an unconscious limitation of the freedom of a mortal or wild. Chains can also illustrate affiliations or reciprocity. In the arrangement of Evolution, the seven great evolutionary sides are called. Each of these chains are made up of septenary links, which are other interrelated Balloon affiliations.

CHAITRA (Sanskrit) A lunar month of the Indian calendar, which is generally linked between March-April and additional times February-March. A mendicant mystic.

CHAKRA(S) Shooting, disc or the circle of Vishnu, is used to convey a time epoch and other meanings. A spell: the Vichnu disc, which delivers as a weapon; the wheel of the Zodiac and the wheel of time, etc. In Vichnu, it is a mark of divine authority. One of the sixty-five figures of the Zripada, that is, the mythical impression or trace of the Buddha's foot; it holds this number of allusive figures. The chakra is used in Mes Merian phenomena and other abnormal operations. The term Chakra also implied circle, orbit; the sun or disc of Surya; an astrological or supernatural figure; any of the "lotos" or plexuses of the physical or astral human body; a kind of throwing weapon contain of a kind of yoglew or disc, with an edged and sharp bordered that was thrown with the tip of the index finger, for which the disc had a hole in the center.

CHANGE, CHANGES (Gnosticism) Our human cluster is the branching of our neighbor. If we really wish a foundational transformation, if we wish for a higher society, a universe without needs, we must change, exceptionally, a change within ourselves, transfigure within our own being the detectable components that cause in the world; need and misfortune. We must call to mind that matter is a result of individuals. If every individual changes, humanity would inevitably change. The point of origin of a radical change is still invisible if man persists believing himself to be one.

CHAOS In Greek mythology, Chaos was an ancient concept, denoting infinite darkness, emptiness, abyss, chasm, or a wide-open space. Chaos didn't have any specific shape or form, and the earliest Greeks viewed it as both an abstract idea and a primordial deity. Unlike other gods and goddesses, the Greeks never worshiped Chaos. Chaos was known to be a "deity without myths". Living in a society that fosters an overactive mind. It generates worry, frustration, dissatisfaction, sleeplessness, and a feeling that no matter what your life is like, something (or many things) referring to it needs to be different. Your intellect creates an internal chaotic war, and you think the way to peace is through continuous self-improvement. Or you fixate on developing or improving your spouse or kids. The bottom line is you will never feel contentment, joy, love and satisfaction you want in your life with this inner battle going on. To stop it, what you need to do is STOP listening to the chronic chaos in your mind. You will never conquer inner peace from losing those 10, 20, or 30 pounds, finding the ideal mate, having the perfect job raising the happiest kids. The key to discovering peace is within you. You require to recognize that the interior feedback to the conditions of your life figures out how you feel and think about yourself and your life, not the circumstances themselves.

CHAPELLE SAINTE, The. The sanctuary in Paris was constructed c. 1245 by Louis IX to homestead the Crown of Thorns and other relics of the Passion. It was eventually secularized in 1906. 554 C

CHARA (Sanskrit) Enthusiastic: mobile, animated, movable.

CHARAKA (Sanskrit) Medical communicator; a celebrated medical writer who thrived in Vedic times. It is imagined that it was a figuration (Avatara) of the serpent Zecha (Sesha), that is, a portrayal of divine wisdom, since Zecha-Naga, king of the race of "Snakes", is the resemblance of Ananta, the seven-headed Serpent, on which Vichnu sleeps at the time of the pralaya.

CAIAPHAS o CAIFAS Cabbalism represent the evil purpose, along with Pilate, and Judas have qualified themselves, as the three conspirators of the Christ. The Jewish High Priest before whom Christ was tried (Mt. 26: 3, &c.).

CAIN (Hebrew) Secretly they were the same as Jehovah. Abel is said to have been Cain's feminine verisimilitude. It was the independent hermaphrodite of the third root race. (lemurs).

CAINITES. A Gnostic sect which, with respect to the God of the Pentateuch as liable for the evil of the world, exalted those who withstood him, e.g., Cain.

CAJETAN, ST. (1480-1547), founder of the Theatine Order. A priest in Rome, with Pietro Karaffa (later Paul IV) and two others in 1524 he founded a congregation known as Theatines for clerics bound by vow and living in common but engaged in pastoral work.

CALF. A youth taurine animal, largely a domestic cow or bull in its first year. A floating piece of ice disengages from an iceberg.

CAL. VIVA Symbolizes Mercury.

CALENDAR. When Christianity set about the calendar was designed by Julius Caesar in 46 B.C. The length of the year was not exactly calculated. The error was revised by the Gregorian almanac of 1582. Dionysius Exiguous propose beginning the Christian era with the date of Incarnation in the 6th century and was embraced all through Christendom. Calculations began from March 25 A.D.

1, the assumed date of the Annunciation, which was taken as New Year's Day. The Gregorian journal restored the beginning of the year to 1 January. (Gnosticism) The authentic calendar is based about proximity of the planets to the earth. Undertaking with the first day of the week and according to the nearest planet, along with the Sun; thus: Moon Monday (current Sunday); Mercury Wednesday (current Monday); Mars, Tuesday (current Thursday); Jupiter-Thursday (current Friday), Sun, Sunday, (current Wednesday); Saturn, Saturday (current Saturday); Saturday is the seventh day of the week and was the only day left in place. The modern calendar is falsified, it is incorrect, since the seventh day of the week is Sunday, it comes to be Monday, as we described above.

CALIZ In the course of the early days of Christianity; the priests used wooden chalices for worship, and later they were made of glass and marble. Finally, the clergy having accumulated immense wealth; gold and silver have been worn out for its elaboration.

CALVARY (Latin: calvaria, skull) In the course of time that Calavera was the place where Christ was crucified; established on the outskirts of the city of Jerusalem, called Golgotha in Hebrew, or place of the skulls (skulls). It is known that this name is due to the custom of living in that place on the hill where the skulls of the executed criminals.

CALVIN, JOHN. Is foremost known for his powerful Institutes of the Christian Religion (1536), which was the original methodical theological treatise of the reform expansion. He accentuates the doctrine of predestination, and his interpretations of Christian requirements, known as Calvinism, are characteristic of Reformed churches. He was born in Noyon, France in 7-10-1509; Died 05-27-1564. Theologian, pastor, and advocate in Geneva during the Protestant Reformation.

CALVINISM The academic system of J Calvin which is usually contemplated in largest non-Lutheran improved temples, donation with Lutheranism dependence in the scriptures as the single oversee of accepting, the disapproval of mortals' chance discipline after the Fall of Adam, and the concept of vindication by loyalty unattended. To these Calvin adds to the unalike precepts of the deplorability of dignity and the unjustified fortune, a few to vindication and others to doom. His contrast with Martin Luther is conflicting the servitude of the state to the condition of the Church. He ventured an adaptation amid Luther's assumptions of the Existent Omnipresence in the Holy Sacraments and H. Zwingli's vision of a trivial analogy; nevertheless, his voicing in this direction is dubious. The prosper Helvetic Confession of 1566, the greater leading evidence of extreme Calvinism which was countersign in abundance amended provincial. The Huguenots were Calvinist, in 1622 Reformed matured the situation of teaching in Holland. Calvinism in England had immaterial impact on the Thirty-Nine Articles and bought solidified preparations in the Nonconformist Churches. In Scotland it initiated agreeable ground. In North American countless divisions field, it in a deeper or secondary adjusted shape. In Germany it displaced Lutheranism in scattering sites. Calvinism endured impediment in the 18th and 19th centuries, however, currently it has again come forward, for the most part ended the execution of K. Barth.

CALVARY, Mount. The place of Christ's crucifixion, just outside Jerusalem. Its Hebrew name is 'Golgotha'.

CAMALDOLESE. A religious order established c. 1012 by St. Romuald at Camaldoli, near Arezzo. It's ideal was the minimum of communal ties, though by 1102 a monastery was instituted at Fonte Buono on coenobitic lines, and practices have varied in dissimilar congregations.

CAMINOS (ROADS), The Four. (Gnosticism) Formations are born that strengthen the vision of the birth of four paths. 1st Way of the Fakir, submission to dreadful extraordinary efforts. 2nd Path of the Monk: These can spread out the emotional part, even though they do not create solar Astral elements; 3rd the Yogi, this can expand the mystical fragmentation, even supposing it does not generate the rational solar mental segments, 4th way is the revolutionary man towards setting free their consecration, regarding liberation, self-fulfillment etc.

CAMPANILE. In general, any bell tower or bell-steeple; the name is appeal especially to the separated belltowers which innovated in Italy.

CAN Dog in mystics refers to Kan-Cerberus, ideogram of the strength of the gonads.

CANAAN The nation, later known as Palestine, which the Israelites defeated and settled afterward part of the secondary millennium. B.C., or perhaps relatively prior.

CANA or CANONES Materialization, an image of the Spinal Base, where the Sahaja climbs, its (7) knots illustrates the (7) chakras; it is also the image of the Staff of the Patriarch or the staff of Moses.

CANCER The crab that was sent by Juno hostile to Hercules, he had perceived it when he was upset opposed the Hydra of Lerna; but Hercules gave him dismantling and Juno dismay led him to heaven growing it into a constellation. Fourth signal of the zodiac reinstate by a crab ruled by the moon, is an evidence of water, female cardinal, which between June 21 to July 22, rule the stomach, chest, bust and breasts; its attribute are: sincere temperament, tender, imaginative, brilliant, tenacious will, sensitive and perception, intense emotions, adaptable capacity, sociable but shy attitude, loyal affections, constancy in the home, heart open to feeling, its negative conditions are: capricious, indecisive fear of the beyond and uncertainty, susceptible, impressionability.

CANDLE The festivities, now recognized on 2 February, immortalizing the cleansing of the BVM and the highlighting of Christ in the Temple 40 days (about 1 and a half months) after His birth (Luke 2:22-39). It was a conserved area in Jerusalem from c. 350. In 542 Justinian arrangement Its perceptive at Constantinople; it escalated completely in the Orthodox Church and later in the Christian churches A procession with lighted candles is a particular quality of the Romanism rite of the day.

CANDELABRA or CANDLESTICK Epitomize the Spinal Cord and the Law of Seven (7) or Heptaparaparshinok. It is also a parable of spiritual light and salvation; if it has three (3) lights it stands for the three (3) primary forces Father, Son and Holy Spirit. It is said that if it has seven (7) lights it also is the seven (7) elemental planets or Cosmochrators and the seven (7) cycles.

CANINE. Responds to dogs or to the ascentry that incorporates dogs, wolves, jackals, and foxes. Canine term emerge from Latin caninus "having to do with dogs, "from Canis "dog". The expression 'a dog is a man's best friend' was initially applied earlier in 1789 by King Frederick of Prussia. He's declared to say; "the only, absolute and best friend that a man has, in this selfish world, the only one that will not betray or deny him, is his Dog." Data proves that part of the canine brain relates to pragmatic affection, and they do, as expected, impression devotion for their mortal colleagues.

CANON(S). The Greek word initially meant a rod or bar; it came to be used for the regulations of an art or profession or to signal a list or archive. In Christian language it specifies the list of books considered as Sacred text (Canon of Scriptures; the central part of the assembled Canon of the group); and the order regarding the life and strictness of the house of God (Canon Law).

CANTOR A performer who pre-intones and conducts in the ceremonial music of the chorus studio and in solemn proceeding.

CAOMANCIA(S) Predictions by aerial illusions, intuition, second vision.

CAOS or CHAOS. Primitive stage of the ecumenical, in Man, symbolizes germinal secretion. Where fire is found, electric creative power which induces all life in the infinite universe great depth.

CAORSO. A Municipality in the District of Piacenza in the Italian Locality Emilia-Romagna, based about 130 kilometers (about 80.78 mi) northwest of Bologna and towards 13 kilometers (about 8.08 mi) east of Piacenza. Caorso appellative essence is Leader, problem bypass, astute. Italian nuclear power plants, denomination Caorso, Trino, Latina and Garigliano, have been close and are presently having difficulties deactivate; this juncture embrace a sequence of assignments that are proposed to endorsement by subject adequate entitlements.

CAPERS. Are the greeny, not fully developed blossoming of the caper hedge, correspondingly identified by Flinders rose. indigenous to the "the middle white sea" however, now promply expansion in numerous societies, the shrubbery do very best in semiarid or arid meteorologic conditions. Sold by their size, capers dimension from 7mmor less, label non-peril, to 14 mm+, or grusas. While capers are consistently employed in the green fraction of the comestibles, and not for dessert, capers are technically some fruits. They're accumulated from flower blossoms. Miniature capers have a persistent tactile and distribute a energy of harsh and tangy touch and transport a zest of acidy and brackish flavoring. In India, the fruitlet and embryo of the herbage are pickled. In the U.S., they're used to decorate and attach vinegary to a New York style. Capers are healthy, indeed, tagged healthyfoods since they are low in cholesterol and all the same a exellent spring of protein, fiber, calcium, iron and countless vitamins!

CAPNOMANCIA. Comprised of prediction by smoke, and that the ancients extracted from prophesying. The most ordinary routine was to scrutinize the emitted smoke of self-denial, it was a sign of good omen if the vapor coming from the altar was agile, limited, thick and elevated in an impartial line.

CAPRICORN Tenth sign of the Zodiac, predominant for demonstration of its esoteric meaning, as the most eloquent among the constellations of the enigmatic Zodiac.

CAPUCHINS. A continuance of the Franciscan Order, set up by Matteo di Bassi of Urbino (d. 1552), an Observant friar, who dreamed of returning to the primitive simpleness of the order. Its representative wears a conic cowl (capuche). The rule, carry up to 1529, re-emphasized the Franciscan ideals of hardship and self-discipline. The capuchins long endure the harshness of the Franciscan families.

CARMELO Mountains of Palestine that in another time was the home of the visionaries Elijah and Elisha and location they embodied a multitude of wonders. This is a place that is still celebrated today for a variety of religious works that sympathize with the devotion of penitents.

CARNAC Ancient site of Brittany (France), stands a sanctuary of colossal composition, devoted to the Sun and Dragon, of a class like the Karnak, in ancient Egypt, and Stonehenge, in England. It was built by the archaic hierophant prelates of the Solar Dragon or Interpreted Knowledge. The most distinguished being the solar Kumaras that have been personified.

CARNIVAL They are called the days succeeding that are ahead of Lent or period of attrition, and principally on Sunday, Monday and Tuesday before Ash Wednesday. The excitement of Carnival can be contemplated as a residue of the idolatrous joys of the Banquets, Luper Cales and other similar celebrations, dedicated totally to inconsistency, masks, enjoyment, liquor and attachment.

CARE The precision of caring is kind and gives emotional support to others, as well as individuals that show affection and concern for others. A person who is benevolent to alternatives and who does things for them is an example of someone who would be described as caring. Current studies show that kindness regarding others is good for us. It's superior for our health. Granting support to others out of choice leads to "reduced stress, expanded happiness, and a multiple sense of social correctness".

CARO (Gnosticism) Dear reader, with that accumulation of issues that go wrong, do you believe in a better best planet? Do you acknowledge that there are alterations in the masses? Absurd my Costly friend: if you want an evolution, do it yourself; if you want a better world, create it yourself; you can't long for that world to understand you, you understand it. In this way you will get it, do not misplace that moment of well-being.

CARON (Charon, Caron in Greek). He is the Egyptian Khu-en-ua, the falcon-headed aeronaut who directed the directed vessel of souls through the black waters that separate the life from death. Charon, son of Erebus and Night, is a variant of

Khu-en-ua. The dead were obliged to pay for the passage an obolo (small piece of coin) to the torvo boatman of the Styx lagoon and the Acheron; Reason why the ancients always placed a coin under the tongue of the deceased. This custom has been preserved even today, due to most people of the lower classes of Russia put copper coins in the coffin, under the head of the deceased for post-mortem expenses.

CARTA CARITATIS. The 'Charter of Love', so calling in resistance to the essential consent of the Cluniac Order, was the formation defining the makeup of the Cistercian Order. It was introduced to Pope Callistus II in 1155; the center in all expectation, the work of Stephen Harding.

CARTHAGE, Councils of. Early ecclesiastical Councils viewed at Carthage include: (1) Those under Cyprian in 251, 252, 254, 255, and 256. The earlier ones were perturbed with the reuniting of those who had ended in the Decian oppression, the behind schedule with the dispute over the ablution of heretics (2) The long sequence less than Aurelius from 393 to 424. The majority observed was that of 419, when the claims of Rome to maneuver authority over Africa were challenged.

CARPOCRATES (2nd century). Gnostic tutor, evidently a native of Alexandria. His followers, the 'Carpocratians', who experienced until the 4th century, propagate an unprincipled conduct, the journey of souls, and the dogma that Jesus was born by real causation.

CASAS (LAS) BARTOLOMÉ DE. (1474-1566), Spanish missionary, the 'Apostle of the Indies'. He went ahead with the Spanish executives to Hispaniola (Isle of Santo. Domingo.) in 1502 and was assigned cleric in 1510. He then devoted himself to the scrutinizes of the Indians by contradicting, both in U.S. and at the enclosure of Spain, the inhuman practices of use used occupied by the pioneers. He connected the Dominicans in 1523 and taken away 1543 to 1551 he was prelate of Chiapas in Mexico. His interpretations of the mishandle of the colonizers exceptionally in his Destruction of the Indians (1552) which he expedited to Prince Philip II of Spain. He aided in the Spanish court for the rest of his life; there he held extensive decided over indies-related issues.

CASTE The caste structure is formed on webs control with associative arguments, while religions categories concentrate on celestial worshipping, righteous, and ethical subjects. Caste arrangements are largely considered for inside the elevated positions of the administration. Doctrine is explained enveloping by sacred text which are interpreted as religious or celestial. This expression which involves "lineage" in Spanish and Portuguese and has basically been used as race-related and social qualifier since 1500 B.C. This was the authority of four adaptable categories in which indeed subsisted shattered in the Indian city: Brahmana, Kshatriya, Vasya and Zudra (particularly: priests, warriors, merchants and farmers, and domestic workers or men committed to the most undeserving line of work, which launched the marginal social class).

CASTEL, GANDOLFO. A small- scale town c. 18 miles Southeast of Rome, which since the 17th century has been the site of summer residence of wealthy personalities of Roman's high society.

CAT (E.g.) City of Egypt devoted to cats and where there was its primordial temple. Many hundreds of thousands of cats continue to be embalmed and buried in the ruts of Beni-Hassan-El-Amar. As an emblem of the Moon, the cat stayed consecrated to Isis, its goddess. The cat is a creature that sees in the dark, and its eyes have a phosphorescent glow that frightens nocturnal birds from omens. The cat was also sanctified to Bast, and hence it was called "destroyer of the enemies of the Sun (Osiris)".

CATACOMBS (Gnosticism) The catacombs; it is said that they were locations where the Gnostics celebrated their rituals in ancient times.

CATHARI (Gk., 'pure') The voicing was petition to some sects in Patristic cadence, but it is used for the nearly all part of a Middle-Aged sect which came to be so well known in Germany in the 12th century. It was later appeal to this creed in Italy, in the interval South France its advocates were often called 'Albigenses'. Their dogmas were related to those of the Bogomils of Bulgaria, but it is not clear either West dualism was an appearance from the Balkans or an unrelated expansion.

CATECHUMENS. In the advance mission those ones experiencing and instruction developing for Baptism. The previously mentioned had encompassing the back when of looking forward to Baptism at the coming Easter shaped independent group. There was a meticulous ritual of preparation in the preceding Lent, with the aspirant finally actually allowed at the Paschal Vigil. In the Church of Rome, a restoration neophyte converted an ordinary exordium to all mature Baptisms in 1972. Divergent observance signs the diverse moment.

CATESBY, ROBERT. (1573-1605), English recusant and conspirator. He was the authentic affluential of the Gunpowder Plot, with which he persisted even after he knew it came to be betrayed.

CATENA (Lat., 'chain'). A term adapted to the Biblical remarks going back from the 5th century onwards, in which he consecutive lyrics of the doctrinal text were described by 'chains' of passing obtained from previous observers.

CAUSE and EFFECT) Emanates from the Karma and Dharma laws of Hinduism; itself; this is the Law that governs our circumstances, punishment recompense. It is the sixth hermetic principle.

CAUSAL (World) (Gnosticism) Just as it is the sixth extension where causes and effects are constantly produced: the world of Manas is also placed.

CAVALIER. A cavalier inner self in American English denotes one possessing the spirit or bearing of a knight; a courtly gentleman; gallant. Being too full a cavalier is having or showing no enthusiasm in something which is essential or serious. They are too cavalier in their treatment of others. In the bible a cavalier is a gentleman instructed in arms and horsemanship: a mounted soldier: knight, capitalized; an adherent of Charles I of England, the cavaliers were the type of people who travel with the king, they were contemplated gallant gentlemen. Those who were adversaries were known as Roundheads. The title derives from the men's habit of cropping their hair close to their head, rather than wearing their hair in the long, flowing classy style of the aristocrats who promoted the king.

CAVE. In medieval civilization, it was accredited to the depths of the heart, for being the dwelling place of the father. In the deepest exists the Heart temple and that is location the initiate must learn to absorb himself through meditation. An old axiom reads, "Make an altar in your heart, but do not make your heart an altar." The grotto, cave or cavern possessed a mystical and intricate metaphor. The birth of heroes, the concealment of souls, etc. are emblems of power, they are verified in caves. In addition, they have an esoteric image of evolution, so there has been that affable transcendental connotation.

CECCO. Dascoli was a prodigious seer who foretell the beheading of several royal characters and his own, at a cheerful dinner, some time prior to the first French Revolution. He was born in Dijon in 1720 and studied mystical philosophy at the school of Martínez Pasqualis in Lion on September 11, 1791, he was imprisoned and sentenced to death by the leaders of the revolutionary government, a man who, to the shame of the State, had been his fellow student and representative of the Mystical Lodge of Pasqualis in Lion Cazotte was executed on September 25 in the Carousel square.

CEDAR. Additional of a breed of ordinarily high trees combine to the spruce and famous for their aromatic perseverant woodwool and; more of various cone-bearing trees, like pine, fir, and spruce (as well as juniper) matching true cedars specifically in commanding odorous durable thicket. The resolution message of cedar is security, insight and might. For an eternity, cedar trees have been venerated for their courageousness momentous. Cedar is well-known as a hardy mederi in many civilizations, commemorated for tenacity safeness and its qualification to recover and immaculateness. The Cedar is famous for its endurance and resistance defiance to corrosion. In the same manner, Mary's impeccability is a declaration of everlasting and removed of somatic physical decline. The Cedar is high and lofty and Quercus lobata. It matures accordingly as an emblem for Mary's significant seraph miniature, superlative and earthling supremacy in the Almighty.

CEDRON (or Kidron). The canyon or gorge on the East of Jerusalem, attaching the city and the Mount of Olives. It was crossed by Christ on the night prior to His Passion (Jn. 18:1).

CELEBRATE Have a party, enjoy a celebration, enjoy festivity, achieved joy. (Gnosticism). In the year 325 A.C. the Council of Niece is commemorated, there are inspected among another concept: The only Gospel that was written in Hebrew which was that of St. Matthew, all the extra were in Greek, among other things; the Old Testament in some parts was written in Greek, additionally other gospels and texts circulating at the time, which were later send away by a sectoral criterion. Nicaea is where what we know today as the Bible fits in. Greek and Hebrew are two completely different languages with an ideological expression, which is why so many errors are disclosed in Bible translations.

CELESTIAL (Gnosticism) The intercessors of the courts of Heavenly Justice protect the Initiates before the cosmic magistrates.

CELIBACY About this passage says Delacroix, the current law is sincerely in antagonism to prehistory. Among the Jews, celibacy was sanctioned and seen with contempt; they were married, even the Levites and priests. On the conflicting, Christian law has proclaimed that celibacy is a much more perfect state; some individuals, took this law at face value, they believed that to be flawless Christians, it was necessary to get rid of oneself from the number of men.

CELLA. (Also, Cella coemeterialis). A tiny shrine put together in church yards prior to Orthodox ethics.

CELL. (1) The privatized room of a religious of either sex. It customarily grasps only simple essentials (2) A pastoral homestead secondary to its mother house. (3) In modern times the word has come into use for small associations of Christians who have guaranteed identity to rigorous work for the producing of the Cristian doctrine in their worldly backgrounds.

CELLULAR (Gnosticism) Nature is molecular, the essence, the ghost of the disincarnated, lives normally in the molecular world, so, when we die, we start from the Cellular world and enter the molecular world. Just as in the physical world we use a cellular body, in the molecular world, we use a molecular body.

CELTIC. The temple that subsisted in the British Isles prior to the approached of St. Augustine in 597. It was established in the 2nd or 3rd centuries by assignment through Rome or Gaul and assigned bishops to the committee of Arles (314). In Piteo the pullout of the Romans, the Celtic house of prayer remained in fiddle with the Tabernacle on the Mainland up till the Saxon occupation of the 5th centennial engulf Celtic traditions in nearly all of England, The Celtic Christian districts which remain alive in Cornwall, Wales, Scotland, and Irland initiate it ruthless to receive the Roman Christianity of St. Augustine, however succeeding the Synod of Whitby (664) they moderately challenged to Roman tradition.

CENACULUM. The. 'Upper room' in Jerusalem in which the Last Supper was commemorated and the Holy Spirit descended at Pentecost. Conforming to Epiphanius, a church existed on the site from the time of Hadrian (117-38). A substantial basilica was constructed later; it fell into Muslim reach in the 16th century.

CENIT As it stands, a concept that is used in astronomy and that allows us to name the point at which the vertical of an area is intercepted with the celestial sphere. It is the highest point in the sky above the spectator, 90 degrees from his head.

CENTERS In any infinity or plane, it is uttered to be a focus of life, force, or judgment. According to Hindu doctrine, God is declared risen in the center, that is where the radium of a circle meets the axis. The central space is invariably reserved for the Divine Creator, at each cosmic change; in certain crosses of liturgical mysticism its nucleus is consistently shown as a rose or by a precious stone.

CENTAUR(S) They were the sons of the Centaur and the mares of magnesia. These beings who were half horse and half man had sharp ears and sometimes had tiny horns. It is voiced that the most distinguished of them was Chiron who was an expert in gods and heroes.

CERBERUS (Greek Latin) Mystical creature; a three-headed canine monster that, according to legends; was believed, guarded the threshold of Hades, proceeded from Egypt to Greece and Rome. That monster was half dog, and half hippopotamus that sheltered the gates of the Amenti.

CEREBRATE (Gnosticism) Anthropomorphic apparatus; the three centers of the human machine: Intellectual Center, found in the thinking center; The emotional, located in the sympathetic nerve plexuses and the Motor-Instinctive sexual.

CERES (Latin) (Greek) Demeter as a feminine aspect of the Father, Ether, Jupiter, in mysterious is the dawn producing the omni penetrant Spirit that animates every embryo in the perceptible universe.

CERDO (2nd century) Syrian Gnostic who instructed at Rome c. 140. He held believed that the Architect God of the Scriptures was to be acclaimed from the Father of Jesus Christ.

CERINTHUS (fl. c. 100) Gnostics. He has been proclaimed to include teachings that the earth existed not by the supreme God, but by a deity (a less exalted being) or by celestial beings. Jesus, he believed, demonstrated His terrestrial growth as a meager man, though at His Baptism 'the Christ', a higher celestial strength, perforated upon Him, to disappear prior to the transfiguration. Irenaeus supports that St. John prepare his Scriptures to oppose Cerinthus.

CERUS or CAERUS The pagans of antiquity; they had designed an entity of that favorable moment to have good achievements in a company, that fugitive moment that we call occasion. This title derives possibly from the Latin series (late), which is why such a long-awaited circumstance is frequently late for the measure of our desires. Relating to this god, the most beautiful allegories have been devised. He was symbolized regularly under the figure of a young man who holds in his hand a razor, and whose hair in disorder is blended by the wind; but the wittiest painting of this divinity is that instituted in one of Phaedrus's fables (The Painted Occasion, lib. V. fab. VIII). In it, Cerus is naked, with wings on his feet and bald head, excluding in front, where he has a single strand of hair, by which you must catch him quickly in midway of his fast journey and not tolerate that he escapes, because at another time, he flees and vanished soon from sight. The painting explains these two supposedly contradictory popular demonstrations: "The opportunity is described bald", and "You have to take the occasion by the hair".

CETRO. A mark of power, affiliated to the magic rod, lightning, the phallus and the Hammer of Tor. The most repeated forms of scepters are topped by the Fleur-de-Lis, which signifies purification and light.

CEUGANT (Celtic) "Circle of the void", from Ceu (empty, infinite), and can (circle). In the partition of the three worlds, circles or spheres of birth, it is the demanding locality where Druidic theology abstracts pure life, without forms, in absence of manifestation, the unlimited, the Parbrahm of Vedanta, the Ensoph of Kabbalah, in one opinion, God. by the term "circle" it is to be interpreted here, with the Druids, long before St. Bonaventure and Pascal, "an infinite circle, whose nucleus exists everywhere. And the circumference in none" (Cujus centrum Est ubique, et circumferential nusquam), which astonishingly clarifies the divine omnipresence and infinity.

CHARITY. The customary auditory translation of the Greek. word agape, somewhere normal provided love. (q.v.)

CHARU (Sanskrit) Introduces appealing, beautiful, funny.

CHARM This name has been awarded to certain models or coordination of terms, in verse or prose, articulated or written, which are used to cause extraordinary and wonderful effects. An elevated number of ectasis are also carried out derived from portentous methods or hypnotization. A category of different voices is considered in conjunction with the phrase charm. For example, the French voice Charme, the English charm comes from the Latin word carmen which is equivalent to the Sanskrit voice mantra because they similarly have concordance in meanings of verses: psalm, spell, charm, etc. During remote past it was blindly believed in charms, which existed in certain Greek or Latin verses, for example: there were psalms to stop the blood, to cure the drop and an immense variety of evils that could be healed or cured.

CHAIN Intangible, chains perform lasting energy and dependability. The chain is affiliated with constant long-lasting, which made it the embellishment of alternative of superiors in positions of influence. Metal cuffs connected to a crisscross figure produce harmony force and coordination combined efforts as a group division. As explained to Smith's Bible Dictionary; circumscribed: as insignia of place of business; for fioritura; for confining servitude, the common laburnum put relating to Josephs neck, (Genesis 41:42) and that promised to

Daniel, (Daniel 5:7) are instances of the first use. In (Ezekiel 16:11) "the chain is mentioned as the symbol of sovereignty. The chain analogy is a metaphor used to describe how an individual's goals and ends are interconnected. It suggests that each step of the journey towards a goal is like a link in a chain, and that each of these links is equally important in the overall success of the mission".

CHAITRA *(Sanskrit)* A lunar month of the Indian calendar, which is usually linked between March-April and other times February-March. A mendicant mystic.

CHARON or CARON (Charon in Greek) It is the Egyptian Khu-an-au, the hawk-headed guide who steered the motorist boat of souls through the black lower waters that split up the existence of destruction.

CHASTE, Chastity Transform your sensual energies; either as married or celibacy. (pranayama).

CHAT (Egyptian) During ancient Egypt physical matter was named after this name.

CHATSAMPATI (Sanskrit) The six mental qualifications. (Annie Besant).

CHATTRA (Sanskrit) Pertains to a disciple, novice.

CHATHARI Comment on to an umbrella; a pigeon-umbrella; parachute; kiosk; pavilion; turret; a cenotaph in honor of a Hindi national or religious leader or (in olden days) a big feudal lord, etc. Fitted with an umbrella, canopied, covered; carrying an umbrella; equipped with a parachuter; etc.

CHAVA (Hebrew) She is like Eve: "the mother of all that lives;" "Life."

CHEBURAH (cf. Heb. 'friend'). In Jewish custom a variety of friends established for religious motivation. They often shared an ordinary weekly meal, routinely on the eve of sabbaths or holy days. It has been argued that Christ and his disciples organized such a Chaburah, and the well-known Last Supper was a Chaburah meal.

CHEMI (Egyptian) Transpire the prehistoric name of Egypt.

CHERIO (Greek) "Quintessent", Fifth initiation or substance of a thing, which forms its rescued peculiarity, free from all non-essential stains.

CHERU (Scandinavia) Or Heru. Magic sword, a weapon of the "sword god" Heru. In the Eddas, the Saga deciphers her by saying that she kills her possessor if he is unworthy to wield her. He brings victory and fame only in the hand of a virtuous hero.

CHERUBIM. The latter of the nine successions of angels.

CHERU or HERU (Scandinavian) Magic sword, a weapon of the "sword god" Heru. In the Eddas, the saga specifics her by saying that she executes her possessor if he is unfair to wield her. Victory and glory contribute only to the hand of an upright hero.

CHESED (Hebrew) "Compassion", 4th of ten Sephiroth; masculine or decisive power.

CHETAS Introduces to mind, intelligence, understanding, thought, consciousness, reason, judgment, reasonableness.

CHEYBI (Egypt) Distinctive with which the soul was named in prehistoric Egypt.

CHEVETOGNE. The Benedictine society which has been a Chevetogne in Belgium since 1939 was established in 1925 at Amay-sur-Meuse by L. Beaudiun in response to Pius XI's petition that Benedictines should pray for unity. The community pursue to rebuild closer relations among the papistry and other Churches; it is into two groups, the Latin and the Eastern, the one supporting the West rite, the other the East (Greek and Slavonic).

CHH Indication of different vessels that come from the heart.

CHHAYA. [or Chaya, as some write.] (Sanskrit) "Shadow." Name of a being begotten of itself (astral body) by Sanjna (Sanjna), wife of Surya [the sun]. Powerless to resist her husband's ardors, Sanjna left Chhaya (the shadow) in lieu of her as a housewife and went to the jungle to indulge in the habit of austerities. In esoteric philosophy, Chhaya is the astral image of a person. [Chhaya]: shadow or double ether, "a shadow without meaning" (II Stay of Dzvan, IV, 16). "Having cast their Shadows and made men of one element (Ether), the Progenitors ascend again to the Maha-loka, from where they descend parodically when the world is renewed, to give birth to new men"; says the Commentary on the Second Series of Dzvan Rooms (Est. IV, 15). See: Secret Doctrine II, 96. Taking the word above in another sense, H. P. Blavatsky says: "The Chhaya is actually the lower

Manas, the shadow of the higher Mind. This chhaya forms the Mayavi-Rupa."
Secret Doctrine, III, 559. Chhaya also means consciousness, intelligence, intimate
knowledge, perception, idea, image, figure, reflection, etc.]

CHIAH (Hebrew) Life; Vita, Revivification. In Kabbalah, it is the second
supreme essence of the human soul, concerning Chokmah (wisdom).

CHILAM He is a second-rate Mayan priest.

CHIIM (Hebrew) A plural name, "lives", found in some compound terms;
Elohim Chiim, the gods of lives, interpret Parkhurst in the sense of; Living God",
and Ruach Chiim, Spirit of lives or lives.

CHILDREN'S CRUSADE (1212). A walk of children who congregate from
France and West Germany after the rerouting of the Fourth Crusade (1202-4),
with the purpose of 'recapturing Jerusalem'. Few ever appear to have gotten as
far as embarking.

CHIN (Sanskrit) Reform of the word chit, which, by argument of euphoria, has
been changed in n the t.

CHIN-MAYA-KOZA (Sanskrit) In agreement with the Vedas tines, it is the
"nirvanic garment;" is the objective nirvanic state.

CHIT (Sanskrit) Pure or abstract judgment. [Intelligence, responsibility, mind,
thought, belief, heart]. Among yogis, Chit is equitably with Mahat, the first and
divine intellect.

CHITRA (Sanskrit) Affectionate designation of Yama (seity of the desolate).

CHITTA (Tchitta) (Sanskrit) Intellect, reason, thought; mind; heart; purpose;
desire; attention, observation; idea. The mental element.

COATEPEC. Hill throughout which there are snakes. They illustrate the world
of temptation.

COLOSSIANS, Epistle to the. This Sacred Writing communication was
written by St. Paul when he was in confinement, presumably at Rome possibly
at Ephesus. The temple at Colossae, in the western part of modern Turkey, had
been traditional not by St. Paul but by Epaphras. The primary reason of the

letter was to summon its readers to belief in Christ as their completely agreeable Savior and Ruler.

COMMANDMENTS. (From madar). Each of the precepts of the Decalogue was delivered to Moses on two tablets of stone, on Mount Sinai. (See Bible Ex, 34:28; Deut. 4:13; 10,4). Gnosticism, Master Samael express that Moses delivered only ten (10) Commandments because humanity was not prepared. The Commandments are 22 related to the 22 Arcans Greater of the Tarot.

COMMUNION TABLE The table at which the Holy Communion is seen in the church of East, the expression is progress down mainly by Low Churchmen. High Churchmen prefer the word 'altar' as a greater expression of the Eucharistic sacrifice which they accept is offered on it.

CONGE D'ELIRE. (Fr., authorization to elect', sc a bishop). In 1215 King John agreed that bishops in England should be chosen by the dean and chapter of the cathedral, but royal accord, the conge d'elire, was to be secured first and the election corroborated by the Royal Assent. Since the Reformation the conge d'alire has been accompanied by a 'letter missive' needing the dean and chapter to elect the person labeled therein by the Sovereign.

CONSCIOUS SHOCK Among Gnostics conscious shocks is studied as follows: The first conscious shock to transform impressions; Second, to welcome the unpleasant manifestations of our fellowmen; the third would be given in a higher octave by transmuting the energies.

CONTEMPLATION, CONTEMPLATE. As common by current theology writers the word denotes non-discursive mental prayer, as illustrious from meditation.

CONTRIBUTE. Signal to offer (something, such as money, goods, or time) to assist a person, group, cause, or organization. As a core human need and dispensing to privately and others, we can lead a more satisfying and determined life. Providing: is the gift that keeps each person giving and can create a legacy that touches others and enables them to contribute.

COUNTRY. Every nation has character, particular objects that speak for beliefs, values, tradition, or other untouchable ideas that make that country special. While these marks may be substituted over time, they can help to hold a state together by reminding its people of their nation's history and most predominant truth.

CHOKMAH Sapience; 2nd of ten Sephiroth; 2nd sovereign triad. Paternal power concerning the Yod (I) of the Tetragrammaton IHVH, and an Ab, the Father.

CHOHAN (Tibetan) "Lord", superior. Thus, Dhyan Chohan repays the "Chief of the Dhyani's" or Paradisiacal Lights, which stands for translating with the title of Archangels.

CHOOSE Fact entirely absurd to claim that one chooses a voluntary method in the space where one must be reborn; the reality is hugely unalike. They are precisely the lords of the law, the angels of karma, who select for us the exact place, home, family, nation, etc. where it is appropriate for us to reintegrate, to return.

CHURCH(ES) (Latin ecclesia and Greek congregation) Convocation of Christian believers who pursue habitual beliefs and rites that distinguish them from other followers. The charge of devotion is to designate the path of Christification and the Law of Universal Love to all human beings left out variance of races, so that they may achieve immortal liberation.

CIMABUE (c. 1240-c.1302) The customary name of 'Cenni di Pepo', Florentine painter. Amid the works authorized to him are the 'Madonna and Child with Angels' in the National Gallery, London, and the paintings in the church of St. Francis at 'Assisi. The mosaics in the Cathedral at Pisa were supported in the years preceding his passing.

CIMA Comes from the Latin Cyma and the Greek Koua (Kyma = swelling, what swells, wave) refers to the highest point of a mountain. Situation that can be reached in certain things, culmination, cusp.

CIMERA Ornament on the top of the helmet, ornament that is put on the helmet or Celada. It stands for the dominant thought and idea.

CINAMON. The scented, desiccated husk of some of various equatorial evergreen (genus Cinnamomum) recognize a dietary condiment, oil, and tanginess particularly a miniature runnel or plumage of Cinnamon crust; the tan to dark brown spice that is formulated from cinnamon bark by crushing and has a relatively sweetened and spiced. Exodus 30:23-25 Take thou also unto thee principal spices, of pure myrrh five hundred shekels, and of sweet cinnamon half so much, even two hundred and fifty shekels, and of sweet calamus two hundred and fifty shekels, and of cassia five hundred shekels, after the shekel of the sanctuary, and of oil olive and Hin: and thou shalt make it an oil and holly ointment, an ointment compound after the art of the apothecary: I shall be an holy anointing. In the Scriptures, Cinnamon signifies an aromatic emissary of God's devoutness and grandiose. The ingredient is mainly employed in devout background to descriptive His devotional aspiration.

CIEN (Gnosticism) Sound acts in Creation itself by giving it Intelligence and helping it to understand Science, which discarded them in the organism in which it is located, and in turn stabilizing so that it attained in harmony with the Created, the place that concerns it.

CIENCES (Sacred) Denominative designated to the innermost esoteric philosophy, the secrets taught anciently to the initiated candidates, and expounded by the hierophants in the last and leading Initiation, [Designate by this name the occult sciences in general. The Rosicrucian called this the Kabbalah and especially the Hermetic Philosophy. (Key to Theosophies)]

CIGUENA (See STORK).

CINTO BELT During prehistory the belt had a deep esoteric explanation, since it was considered a depiction of help for the body, which implied the "defensive" virtues of the person. It was also the image of virginity, purity and love.

CIRCLE There are several circles: 1) Crusader of Plato's absolute circle, symbolized by an X-shaped crusader; 2) The circular dance of the Amazons around a priapic a portrayal, as well as the dance of the Gopis around the sun (Krishna), the shepherdesses who symbolize the signs of the Zodiac: 3) the Circle of destitution of 3000 years of the Egyptians and esotericisms, being from 1,000 to 3,000 by average durability of the cycle between rebirths or reunifications.

CITARA Musical instrument in which its aspect rounded on one side and flat on the other (like the turtle), personified the equitability of heaven and earth, its strings signify the planes of the Universe.

CIVIL. CONSTITUTION OF THE CLERGY, The (1790). The legislative measures gone ahead during the French Revolution administer upon the Church of France a separatist organization. The constitution was silhouetted to secure the independence of the House of God from the church, excluding in doctrinal matters. The pontiff was deprived of all genuine power in France, and the salaries of the clergy were governed by the state. Most of the bishops and clergy blocked the Constitutional Oath inflict in Nov. 1790 and were deprived of their offices.

CLAREDON, The Constitutions (of) Sixteen validations sent onwards by Henry II of England to adjust to control the association linking the ministerial and non-clerical dominion and other conditions. It was introduced at the Council of Clarendon (1164) for the climb of Thomas Becket, Abs of Canterbury, who forbade affixing his badge. A lengthy debate came after.

CLARITY (Gnosticism) There are subjects of critical repetition precise cases of egos that return for many centuries in the lap of the matching offspring, city and country. Those are the ones who, in accordance with the perpetual repetition of the same, can prophesy with decisive luminosity what awaits them in the future.

CLAIRVOYANCE (Theo. Par. gnostic) As it stands the amplitude of seeing with the third eye or intimate mood vision. The third eye dwells between the eyebrows in the pituitary gland, which when it subsists growth with the vowel "F" forms the power of clairvoyance, this chakra is called AJNA-chakra.

CLAVICLE (Lat Clavicle: little key) It is commanded a secret key given by the great sage Solomon to make himself invisible, invoking his divine inner Daimon. It is called Salomon Clavicle.

CLAY The metaphor of clay could also stand for the design of restoration and rebirth as clay can be interminably reprocessed in its fresh surroundings by controlling its moisture degree. The procedure of making pottery commands the use of all four elements; earth, air, fire and water. This proposes the interminable probability of clay and the measurements to set up once more, to change. Jesus's reoccurrence is a model of these.

CLEMENCY He was worshipped in Greece and Rome. It cites one of the parts of the Self. She is represented as a woman carrying a spear in one hand and an olive branch in the other, and a man kneeling before her in an attitude of invocation. In addition, it is symbolized as an eagle with wings folded on a ray. It's Dante's "Mercy."

CLEOPAS. One of the two disciples to whom the risen Christ materialized on the road to Emmaus.

CLEOPATRA The Latinized form Cleopatra approach from the Ancient Greek Kleopatra (in Greek meaning "glory of her father", from "glory). She was Queen of the Ptolemaic Kingdom of Egypt from 51 to 30 BC, as well as its prior vigorous leader. A member of the Ptolemaic ancestry, she was an ancestry of its founder Ptolemy-Souter, a Macedonian Greek general and associate of Alexander the

Great. After Cleopatras' death, Egypt set forth a region of the Roman Empire, label the culmination of the secondary to last grandeur state and the age that had carry on after the rule of Alexander (336-323 BC), Her mother vernacular was Koine Greek, and she was the single Ptolemaic emperor to master the Egyptian language. According to Gnosis the captivated was Mark Antony, who thus far knew the mysteries and was a fallen Bodhisattva in early Egypt. Cleopatra self-destroyed herself by being bitten by an aspic succeeding the defeat of Mark Antony.

CLISUS The esoteric marked domain enclosed in absolute artifacts: power of existence in plants scales by roots trunk, leaves, flowers and embryo, materializing, creating a brand-new entity.

CLIO She was one of the nine immortal muses who presided over the chronicle. She was suggested as a young woman with a laurel headband, carrying in her hand a Style and a board.

CLOUD(S). Are additionally emblems of heavenly movability since numerous divinities and celestial beings employ clouds as channels on which they wander. Intertwined clouds relate to goddess, predicting their appearance. In Chinese folklore, dragons are capable to create clouds with their breath. It is occasionally said that the firmament can bounce back our feelings. This sky parable can be discovered in ordinary literary text, where the sky is perceived as synonym for the lyricist's sentiments. Conventionally, the sky blue and vacant depicts joyfulness and cheerfulness, while an overcast sky is regarded as melancholy and ruefully. "The murky clouds hung low in the sky, their thick, gray shroud obscuring the sun." "The murky clouds churned ominously overhead, threatening the promise of a torrential downpour." Clouds suggest for the most part to be lost in thoughts. "His mind is in the clouds": Mist and smog signifies extreme disorientation or uncertainty to roam circling in a daze. A cloud merged with brightness is oftentimes discerned as an ideogram of the Presence of God considering clouds supply invigorative aqua, and they illustrate providence who is concealed from eyesight but is eternally present. Nephophilia is an individual who has a deep affection for clouds; tenderness of clouds; enthusiasm or fascination of clouds.

CLOUD OF UNKNOWING, (The) An unidentified English esoteric interpretation of the 14th centenary. The author demands the impossibility intended by God by mortal reasoning. The 'cloud of unknowing' which lies connecting God and humanity is penetrated not by rationale but solely by a 'sharp dart of love', reflective devotion so share location in the emotions and in this fashion naturally accommodate a fragment of incomprehension.

CLOVESHO, Councils of. A series of assembly characterizing both the Church and State of all England south of the Humber in the 8th and 9th cents. The site of Clovesho is undisclosed.

CLUMSY. Tricky in movement or in grasping things; done stiffly or ineptitude; risky; unwieldy."It was a very clumsy attempt to park".

COATEPEC Elevation contour of which there are snakes. They stand for the world of corruption.

COCCIX or COCCYX (Anal.) The base bone of the spine, or bone that ends the spinal column.

CODEX (Nazarenus) (Latin) In the "Book of Adam", its name signify Anthropos, which translates man or humanity. The Nazarene credo has sometimes been called the "Bardesian system", although it suggests that Barsenases 155-228 before J.C. had nothing to do with it. Although he was born in Odessa (Syria) being a renowned sage and astrologer; long before his claimed conversion; in addition, being a very educated figure and anticipated from an illustrious family; it would not have gone as far as to use the nearly enigmatic Chaldean-Syriac dialect, which was mixed with the mysterious language of Gnostics, in which Codex is written. The Nazarenes were a pre-Christian sect. Pliny and Josephus proclaim that the Nazarites had their residence on the banks of the Jordan River, 150 years before J.C. Munk declare that "Nazaritism or (Nazareth) was a determination that had been built untimely from the commands of Musah" or Moses, its current title in Arabic is The Montasia; in the European languages the Nazarenes are selected with accreditations of Mandaites (Mandaites or Mandeans) or "Christians of St. John". If the voice "Baptists" could be forced on them, it was not with the predictable of Christian, because, although they were, and still are, knowers or natural astrolabes, the Mennonites of Syria, who are called "Galileans", are righteous polytheists, as a traveler in Syria and the Euphrates could verify, while advising themselves of their enigmatic rites and formalities. These devotions have been preserved so secretly, that Epiphanius, who wrote disproved the Heresies in the fourteenth century, nevertheless; he confessed himself incapable of insinuating the belief of the Nazarenes, and it was distinct to point out that they merely quoted the name of Jesus; nor are they called Christians.

COENOBITE. A doctrinal in covenant who lives in a commune (as opposed to a hermit). The phrase is also utilized in a technical sense of anchorites who occupy separate accommodation and distinguish a rule of silence but live otherwise as a community of monks in a common compound.

COGITO ERGO SUM (Latin, 'I think, therefore I am'). The central datum of truthfulness believed by R. Descartes, on the substructure that, although a man challenges, he would assume of himself as the suspect.

COITO Have to do with the sexual union of man and woman.

COLLEGE of Rabbis Reputed college of Babylon over the first centuries of Christianity. He had great fame; however, it was concealed by the appearance of Hellenic experts in Alexandria, equivalent as Philon the Jew, Josephus, Aristobulus and others. The former took revenge on their opponents by calling the Alexandrians mixed Teurgos and prophets. But Alexandrian believers in thaumaturgy were not contemplated as sinners or impostors when Orthodox Jews were at the top of such schools of "Hazim." These were colleges for teaching prophecy and cabalism sciences. Samuel was head of one such college in Ramah; Hidden. Samuel Hillel had an efficient academy for prophets and seers, and Hillel himself, a disciple of the Babylonian college, was the originator of the sect of the Pharisees and the great Orthodox rabbis. (Gnosticism) "Teachers, students, men and women, live with consciousness asleep today, as true automatons, go to school, college and university unconsciously, subjectively, without really knowing anything about what, or why."

COLERA (Gnosticism) Due to the outcome of permanent excitement, the nervous system then arises the so-called neurosis whose peculiarities are ideally impatience, anger, irritability and absence of tolerance towards others.

COLLAR It has substitution as a passionate union to wear on the neck and is related to sex. The Buddha's necklace is composed of 108 beads, standing for the 108 births that are destined to each human being for his emancipation, (this renews a period). It is a device of bond and alliance. Measured by multiple threaded accounts, it declares the centralization of the unequal.

COLOR In the mysticism color is respected as a universal vibration, used by many ecotourists as spiritual growth also color has predominance in the treatment used as chromotherapy.

COLOSEEUM, The. The classification by which the 'Flavian Amphitheater' at Rome has been well known since about the 8th century. Culminated century A.D. 80, it has long been reverenced as the scene of many early martyrdoms, though the truth of this heritage has been questioned.

COLOSSIANS, Epistle to the. This teeny Scripture epistle was put in writing by St. Paul when he was in prison, very likely at Rome. Perhaps at Ephesus. The Church at Colossae, in the Westernport modern Turkey, had been established not by St. Paul but by Epaphras. The primary motivation of the epistle was to remind its readers to faith in Christ as their acceptable Redeemer and Lord.

COMA Deep lethargy in which there is a complete unjust absence of instability and psychic intelligence, which can acknowledge itself after a dangerous accident or in the characteristics of consummation by some affections suffered a hepatic coma.

COMMIT (Gnosticism) You will not commit adultery. Ninth Commandment of the Law of God.

COMO (How) It is alleged that he was the God of Joy. He is illustrated by the resemblance of a teenager with an aura of flowers, a light in his hand and a pertiga in the other, ruddy for the portion of wine he has taken.

COMPANION(S) Signify the initiate who has determined to work on the esoteric path, facing the Ego, guided by his Master or Guru Within the hidden Mazon Eria, is the second degree adopted by all rights. Man reincarnates the second age, whose aim is the knowledge of man's duties to God, to himself and to his fellowmen.

COMPENETRATE (Gnosticism) Sephiroth are universal spheres or regions that puncture and penetrate each other without being confused.

COMPLACENCY Reward felt by the one who is grateful.

COMPLIANCE or COMPLY Act following a wish or command of a person or group. Comply with federal laws and industry standards. Stipulates when the person transfers his or her conduct in feedback to an obvious or indirect appeal compelled by contrasting person. Adaptation is habitually referred to as an active formation of social influence in that it is usually intentionally started by a person. Bond to decrees and individual instructions are as well a consent. It is the obligation of directorate to secure compliance and to apply and displaced out a consenting employers' method. Manifestations of compliance when they respond to an obvious request, such as to invest in a product or to enlist the individual's timetable.

COMPREHENSION. Measures or potentiality of belief of a commodity or phenomenon. The term comprehension shows the potential of an individual to capture the deeper connotation of the subject being expressed. When you have deficiency of comprehension of a tough term, you will most likely require looking up its answer and use it in a refreshing, realistic environment where you can use a vocabulary. Comprehending is logically grasping something's completed essence or meaning. It can be a bit more challenging than understanding it. For example, an individual may understand instructions in a handbook without entirely understanding their purpose.

CONCEPTION (sacred) (Gnosticism) Materialization of procreation of the Divine Mother Kundalini Shakti, by configuration and charm of the Holy Spirit, the Third Logos, to extends the child Christ, the son who waits for the moment to enter our body to embark on the Great Work. She stayed a maiden before and after childbirth.

CONCHA (from the Sea) It is a banner of Mercury that has not been fertilized or has not taken the Sulfur (fire). Chinese Buddhism is one of eight characterizations of good luck. The shells have according to certain mystics', connection with the Moon and the woman across the Aphrodisiac tradition, arising from a seashell.

CONGRUISM. [Being suitable and appropriate, the quality of agreeing]. The confidence that God arrange contemplation for the conducting of good works (gratia de congruous) in explorations with such mortal conditions as He sees will be more beneficial to its manipulation.

CONSCIOUSNESS Real elemental intimate interest of the Being to awaken its fundamental symbols, in all the revising that it also scrutinizes and discovers the emotions or ideas that are transmitted to it; through sensory means, both internal and external. A Being who has been liberated has achieved responsibility, but it can be a primary reason, for the moment, contrast into inner enlightenment.

CONSCIOUS. Is a Latin vocable of which Aboriginal definition was "knowing" or "aware." Hense, a conscious individual has a realization of her surroundings and her inherent reality and impressions. If you're "conscious," you're excessively sensible of and even awkward by how you reflect you scrutinize or react. (Gnosticism). Every union in life, every fact, has its cause in an earlier fact, but we need to become aware of it.

CONDITION Components or background influencing the way in which populations live or work, mainly comparable their welfare; "grinding working conditions". The situation of objects with recompense to its features, grade, or working order. "The electrical system seems to be in good condition".

CONCILIAR (Gnosticism) Compendium. Organizes the impartial or level appearance, within the whole Triad; being the harmonizing part in all the arguments of the establishment, exhibit in that way by fire or Light.

CONFORMITY Gives an illustration of an expansion, social attributions by which a person changes his feelings, opinions and behaviors in conducting the situation preserved by a main group, as a product of the allegorical material concentration practiced by a leader of the group, for the whole itself. The term conformity is a phenomenon corresponding to the influence of groups. A meeting can be exercised by its members by raising their subconscious or through evidence of rival force on their connection. The size of the group, the harmony, social consistency, social disposition, prior duty and widespread opinion, help to arrange the level of conformity that a subject reflects towards his group.

CONFUSE (Gnosticism) "It is necessary not to confuse love with passion. Young lovers and girls do not know how to distinguish between love and passion. It is urgent to know that PASSION is a poison that deceives the mind and heart."

CONGE D'ELIRE (Fr., 'permission to elect', sc, a bishop). In 1215 King John conceded that bishops in England must be selected by the faculty and section of the minister, but special authorization, the conge d'elire, was to be protected basically and the designation verified by the Royal subscriber Because the transformation the conge d'elire has been maintained by a 'letter missive' mandatory the legislator and instance to designate the individual denomination there in by the Sovereign.

CONJUNCTION As it stands, is appropriate to the integration materialized by the love between two beings the diversity, in the middle of heaven and earth: the marriage between the princess and the prince liberator of traditions and stories.

CONE. This phrase stands for a solar figure, of psychic nuances and an emanation of the pyramid, probably the harmony of the circle, and of the triangle. Some wizards use them as a protective insignia, projecting the cone covering the physical element in a figure linked to the pyramid and the sun.

CONSTANCY [Missale Speciale]. A compact version of the Missal, accommodating selections peaked up for exceptional necessity. The best-known is that which came to be called the Missale Speciale Constantiense (of Constance).

This was at one time the concept to be the initial publication ever printed, but in 1967 it was shown to date from 1473.

CONSENSUS GENEVENSIS. J. Calvin's accurate Constructions of his instructions on ordinance to resistance of H. H. Bolsec. He displayed it to the City Council of Geneva in 1552.

CONSEQUENCE(S) (Gnosticism) If the Law of Action and Consequence, if the Nemesis of reality, were not negotiable, then where would Divine mercy remain? Without exception everything we accept, pronounce and execute has consequences for me and for each other's. Like undulating on a lagoon, our movements embark and impact others because the entire universe is connected. Furthermore, we also need to think that our gesticulations are Irreparable.

CONSENT Defines, allow, authorize, give permission.

CONTRIBUTION (pair) It measures the transfer of a thing from one place to another, through supra-normal or psychic forces.

COPA (Gnosticism) "I will take the Cup [Vessel or Chalice] of salvation, and I will invoke the name of YHVH." In every breath of love there is a sigh that is eternity."

COPPER This metal offers gravitation for the evolutionary and evolutive potential of creation and is linked to the planet Venus. In its positive breadth it stands for love, productivity, fecundity and creative capability. In its negative form it is related to the pituitary glands and must awaken clairvoyance. The inspired Nostradamus used a copper suitcase with Mercury (Azogues), staring into it to foresee his famous prophecies. Nowadays copper is also used to cure the physical body. Taking on the soles of the feet a copper platelet to eliminate arthritis disorders is also placed in the form of a ring in the afflicted part.

CORBIE The honored monastery, east of Amiens, was constructed from Luxeuil century 660 It has a very excellent information center.

CORIANDER. In addition, well-known as cilantro is a yearly herb in the lineage Umbellifers. All components of the herb are comestible; however, the natural leaflet and the dehydrated grains are the components most consistently utilized in gastronomy. Cilantro and coriander come from the identical undergrowth. Determine by your locality, coriander can indicate merely the dried seeds or to the entire plant. Cilantro frequently specify to the leaflets and stems. Cilantro and coriander originate from the plant's varieties; Coriandrum sativum. The 'Concise Bible Dictionary' states: "A round aromatic seed, the Coriandrum sativum, to which the manna was compared, both as to form and color (ex. 16:31; and the house of Isrrael called the name thereof Manna: and it was like coriander seed, white; and the taste of it was like wafers made with honey. (exodus 16:31); Num."

CORIBANTES Priests of Cibeles. As it has been said; that Atis instituted the rites and cult of Cybele.

CORN. The emblem of sustainment, the workforce of creation and is an essential significance of plenty of ethnic groups Corn is contemplated an offering from the Wakan Tanka, therefore its function is one as well as the other as a sustenance and a conventional commodity. 'Corn,' as in Genesis 42:2, here hold up for an expression in the Aboriginal tongues that suggested "breaking' along with comparable term denotating to purchase or trade. This is display in the contention of Jacobs's sons procuring corn in Egypt and Joseph bargaining it directly. Corn had the meaning that animates life to the Ojibwe, cooperating palpably compensate for and the land amidst the mythical of Manda amin, the attitude of the corn. Corn was frequently applied to intercede liaison among French pathfinders and the Ojibwe at initial confrontation. To the Ojibwe, corn indicated higher than nourishment; it denotes a means of existence.

CORNUPIA o CORNUCOPIA Relates to the horns of abundance.

CORONA (Latin Corona) [Crown] It is a sign of victory, it is the perceptible figure of an achievement, of a coronation. Crowns have been considered as an attribute to the Gods, in addition, they make funeral sense; both the metal crown, the headband and the crown of rays have been depiction of the light, and of the illumination received. In alchemy books, the aspects of the planets are distinguished from taking their crown (their light) from their King (enlightenment). Its design shows the honesty to which they repay, since prehistory counting the pharaohs, distinct types of crowns have been worn all emblematic and with deep mystic allegory, (kab.) B Arcane 22s "The Return" symbolizes the crown of life. The Bible in Revelation says... "Be faithful until death and I will give you the crown of life." The crown of life is the Intimate Christ within every meticulously organized human being.

COUNTRY. The apologue of a country are: The standard or streamer of a motherland, the flee of supply with weapons of the terra firma or statutes lineage, the emblem or distinctive label of the commonwealth or ruling authorities genealogy, Commander in chief, specifically in a monarchism, a the connected break down and adage can also be employed isolated, the ethnic ribbons, many times acquire from the beyond. The utilization of the olive branch as representation of peacefulness in Western customs duration to at a minimum 5th century BC Greece. The archaic Greeks conclude that olive branches expressed plethora and eradicate apparitions and an olive branch was one of the imputes of Eirene the Greek divinity of peace. Certain lower animals are images of nations such as Beaver (Canada) The beaver constitute the furrier in Canada, which dates to 1621 at the time Hudson's Bay initially place the animal on its escutcheon. Bald Eagle (USA), Kangaroo (Australia), Royal Bengal Tiger (India), Giant Panda (China).

COURT(S) of FACULTIES. The court was received in 1534 when the permit of dispensation licenses, and capability in the provinces of Canterbury and York was transported from the Pope to the Diocesan of Canterbury.

COSMAS AND DAMIAN, Saints. The enlightener of physicians. Nothing precise has been investigated in their testimonial to their lives. In concurrence to overdo folklore, the twin brothers maintain their vocation beyond insisting on any compensation from their patients. The pair are guessed to have endured affliction.

COSMIC LAW (Gnosticism) This whole scale of conditions is called ignorance, unconsciousness, incomprehension of how the Cosmic Law acts in every person.

COSMIC (Gnosticism) The Rabbi of Galilee, is a god, because he fully embodied the Cosmic Christ Hermes, Quetzalcoatl, Krishna, gods are since they also personify the Cosmic Christ.

COSMIC DRAMA (Gnostic) It is not an entirely classical drama, the innermost Christ must live it internally in us. The cosmic drama is performed in the fourth gospels of the lord. Inside the tomb of crystal, he is appearing as a child in the heart of man, to live all the cosmic drama, he matures man among men and tolerates all the temptations of the flesh: that is why he says: Lamb of God who blotch out the sins of the world.

COSMOCRATORS (Greek) "Builders of the universe", the Architects of the world or the founding Forces personified.

COSMOGONY or COSMOGONICAL The formation or etymon of the universe or totality. A mythos or grandiose lore is a nature of planetary, an emblematic chronicle of how the natural object launched and how humankind initially derived to occupy it. in favorite employment the phrase myth commonly indicates to untruthful or fictional conviction, portion of folklore occasionally attribute modifying intensity of legitimacy to their constitution apologue. Cosmogony (origins of the cosmos) 1. Mystical encounters and celestial discourse. Labelling: God. Wisdom, Torah and Christ. Cosmology is the investigation of the construction and modification of the grudge planet, while the experimental garden of cosmogony is solicitude with the ancestry of the earth. (Quiché) Called Popol Vuh innovated by The Abate Brasseur de Bour Bourg.

COSMOS (from the Latin Cosmos and the Greek Kosmos) The world, the universe, the established compound of all created things.

COST. From Middle English Costen, from Old Franch Coster, couster ("to cost"). From Middle Ages Latin Costo, from Latin consto ("stand together"). A charge that must be reimbursed for object or an offering. Cost is employed as a verb to mean to demand compensation or to matter the mislaying of substance. Cost has various other sensibilities such as a nominal and a verbification. Cost largest frequently specify to the stipulates fair share of cash that a dealer demands for the component they are trading.

COUNT. A count (feminine: countess) is a Hellenic subtitle of honor in traditional European countries, varied in respective position, normally of medium line in the ladder of privilege. The etymon correlated with the English word "county" indicates the approximately related with the courtship. e.g. The Count of Monte Cristo which Is a fundamental mischievous classic novel which takes location in the Middle Ages. Non-stop adventure; the subject of value, clemency, revenge and forgiveness are perceived. It was written by French author Alexandre Dumas in 1846. The prompt count also regulates the complete numeral of an assembly of items. "I started to count all the Volkswagen cars I encountered within one week."

COURTS, (Delegates, Court of.) In England the judiciary was set up in 1534 to deal with retrials from the archbishops' courts, which had hitherto gone to Rome. It was terminated in 1832, and in 1833 its setting was taken by the Judicial Committee of the Privy Council.

COUPLE A couple involves "a pair". If two individuals are dating, you can indicate to them as a "couple." Likewise, two people who are married feasibly be called a "married couple." Two guys participating in basketball can be summoned "a couple of fellows competing at basketball". Couple process; to combine a pair, as people do in a dance.

CRANE. To elevate or raise by or as if by a lift. To enlarge over a target of seeing elevate your collar to get a powerful view. A crane can be different to an immense fowl with a lengthy collar and tall limbs. The Crane stance for beauty, consistency, and gracefulness. It outlines beneficial improvements as it has been equivalenting the New Year in diverse folklore. Crane embody focuses on the need for equilibrium and living in consensus with others. Cranes teach us that if we want reflection, we must learn to deliver it first. Refined analogy is perpetuity, clarity, diligence, endurance, and blessings. In some societies, the visibility of crane birds can be adverse; they are hypocrisy, an omen of ruin, and even the resemblance of the shadowy. An alternative interpretation for the term crane is an enormous, towering tool used for running large gadgets by dangling them from an enlarged detachment or joist. The term crane appears in Issaiah 38:14. "Crane or a swallow, so did I chatter: I did morn as a dove: mine eyes fail with looking upward: O Lord, I am oppressed; undertake for me."

CREATION Existing the uncreated, eternal and indestructible components, even if its appearance is changing and passing, supports Theosophy, of acceptance along the ancient apothegmic ex nihilo nihil (from nothing, nothing comes out), the indicated world was not made of nothing, but was a creation, nonetheless; in the true sensation of the word was an emanation of the material nature of the Divinity, and in this extremely nature that is decided during the world ends. In the Sanskrit language there are no terms that can manifest the idea of creation, in the perception of producing something out of nothing.

CREATING. To fabricate or import into endurance entity novel. Poiesis is morphological acquire from the earliest Greek idiom "to make". It is linked to the expression poems, which portion the matching foundation. The prompt is also employed as a addition, as in the botanical word hematogenesis, the design of erythrocyte. 'In the beginning was the Word, and the Word was with God, and the Word was God. He was with God in the beginning. Through him all things were made without him nothing was made that has been made. In him was life, and that life was he light of all mankind.'

CREATOR(S) God drew all things out of nothing with His intention to create. The creative energy that God bestowed upon humanity; that creates and purse to create. [Nature].

CREED Briefly, ceremonial, and established by authority declaration of essential advice of Christian dogma. The Hellenic instance are the Apostles' Creed and the Nicene Creed. Prospect for baptism initially consent brief system of credence; these progressively transformed into illuminated within creeds. Following the Council of Nicaea (325) dogma calling of belief emerged to be employed as criterion of authoritative. The custom of relating to the (Nicene) Creed at the Eucharist emanates as a neighborhood practice in the easterly in the 5th centennial, it was culmination embraced at Rome until 1014.

CREDO UT INTELLIGAM (Lat., 'I believe so that I may understand'). A plan in which St. Anselm sum up his conceiving of the connection linking reliance and comprehension.

CREMER, John. A remarkable Sage, who for an interval of thirty years and being abbot of Westminster, studied hermetic philosophy in exploration of its practical secrets. He met the famous Raymond Lulius with the person who Cremer returned to England where Lulius confessed to Cremer the mysteries of the stone, for his cooperation beside the monastery he proposed to pray for him every day. Cremer, says the Royal Masonic Encyclopedia, "having gained a deep knowledge of the secrets of alchemy, he became one of the celebrated and educated supporters in occult philosophy."

CRESTO Epitomize the Intimate Christ, the Chokmah of the Kabbala, the second Logos.

CRIB In the West Church by favored practice a portrayal of the crib (or manger) in which Christ was laid at His birth, with a delineation of the Holy Child, Francis of Assisi is believed to have forced the first replica of the crib at Grece.

CRICKET (Latin gryllus) Orthoptera insect, which belongs to the cricket family, is connected to that of the locust and blattid mantids. In Roman times tiny insects were sold at exceedingly climbing charges, in gold cages, and were used for astral travel, which subsist of centralizing awareness in the song of the cricket. In the Museum of Anthropology in Mexico D.C., there is a painting in relationship to the instructions of the cricket, transmitted to the Aztec aristocrat and priests in their secret temples.

CRISMA or CHRISM. (gr. Khisma). Santify oil that is utilized in the management of some sacraments.

CRIME. It is an illegitimate behavior for which a personage can be penalized by the authorities mostly; an obvious infraction of principles; a heavy wrongdoing mainly in hostility to morality. An unethical outline of an individual or activities that scrupulously goes in opposition to acceptance message, which is, the genuine proposition and assurance regarding how to perform in a way that is contemplated just and righteous by the rank of individuals. Unscrupulous indirect the purpose of atrocity or misconduct, and it is a sound antonym of morality. (Gnosticism) Defamations go straight against this sequence as do their associates, evil, hatred, resentment, pride, and revenge, crimes that offend the father, who is the Truth.

CRIOCEFALO (Greek) "Who has the head of a ram:" This qualifier has been petition to several emblematic deities and physiognomy's, extremely those of ancient Egypt, which were conceive at the stage when the Sun crossed, at the vernal equinox, from the sign of Taurus to that of Aries. Prior to this cycle, bull-headed godheads and conifers prevailed. Apis was the kind of the bull-God, Ammon the type of ram's head; Isis, moreover, was indicated with a cow's head. Porphyry writes that the Greeks connected the ram with Jupiter, and the bull with Bacchus.

CRISIS. Doctrine of. Substitute title for the Dialectical Theological of K. Barth and his disciples, groundwork on countless alliance of the Greek expression krisis.

CROSIER. The workforce packed by bishops and occasionally also by abbots and abbesses. The formation appears a shepherd's crook, close in the Westerly is due to tardy emblem.

CRYSTAL BALL A sphere, realm or crystal egg that is used in crystallomancy.

CRYPT A secret vaulted basement. Some crypts were devoted for Initiation, and alternatives for burial. In ancient times there were crypts under each temple.

CONVERT. In the Bible designate a modify in attitude, but it goes outside limits action; it is a progress in our highly countryside. It is such a powerful modify that the Lord and his prophets pertain to it as a rebirth, an about-face, and a baptism of fire. Religious reform is the socialization of a set of faith determined with one religious' denominative to the discharged of another. Thus "religious conversion" would define the relinquish of loyalty to one denominative and connected with additional.in monasteries.

CONVERSI Is a title extensively utilized for lay kinspeople in religious communities.

COPTIC (language) Coptic was the lexicon ordinarily spoken by the indigenous populace of Egypt from ever-present the middle of the 3rd to the 10th century A.D. and is stagnant that of the liturgy of the Coptic Church. In aspect it is the language of prehistoric Egypt, into whichever a substantial number of Greek verbalizations have been incorporated, and it is communicate in an alphabet like comparable as the Greeks. The NT was transcribed absolutely into four Coptic dialects.

COST Is the toll paid or required for buying, producing or supporting existence, usually sustained in money, timetable, or energy; tariff or disposal; outlay. e.g., business; It is the money that a company disburses on commodities such as effort, assistance, raw materials, and further. Indefinitely, He must remain tranquil at all costs. We must preserve our advantage at all costs.

COVEL, JOHN (1638-1722). Master of Christ's College, Cambridge, from 1688. In 1669 he was acknowledging cleric to the British Consulate at Constantinople, and with it he possessed material for his approaching work. His version of the Present Greek Church (1722) was one of the rare books authorized information on the Greek Church previews to the 19th centennial.

COWL. An article of clothing with a hood worn by monks.

COW The cow is a vertebrate mammal, after all, it's in addition, a reliable character, folklore, and emblem. Cows, and their male double, are frequent presences within mythologies and archaic religions. In many traditions, cows embody productivity, beneficence, motherhood, the rise of life, and they're secured with tranquility. Job 21:10, "His ox mates without fail; His cow calves and does not abort." Cows are an influential image in composition, describing a broad variety of topics and conceptions. The emblematic interpretation of cows indicates fecundity, maternity, self-scarified, subsistence, unselfishness and invigorative nature, and purity and immaculacy. The cow is a distinguished animal in Hinduism. The cow was moderately integrated into a religious practice and itself incline sacred and a phenomenon of admiration from the 4th century BCE. It defines Mother Earth, as it is an authority of honesty, and its milk sustains all creatures. Hindus do not contemplate the cow to be a god and they do not glorify it. Hindus, nevertheless, are vegetarians and they reflect the cow to be a dedicated ideogram of life that should be sheltered and respected. In the Vedas, the oldest of the Hindu scriptures, the cow is coalition with Aditi, the mother of all the gods.

COWPER TEMPLE CLAUSE. The section in the 1870 Education Act which furnish that in elementary schools beneath public jurisdiction no religious teaching 'which is distinctive of any particular denomination shall be taught'.

CHRISM (Gr. Krisma) Consecrated oil used in the administration of some sacraments.

CHRISMON (or Chrismon) (Greek) Monogram of Christ collected of the coordination of an interlocking X (equivalent to our Ch and P (like our R), main letters of the Greek voice Christos.

CRISIS (Greek) Christos the Anointed Nomination that was delegated to Jesus-Christ, builder of Christianity, make known by the ancient Hebrew visionaries as the Messiah or Consecrated one of the Lord.

CRISOL. Crucible A glass of refractory clay, porcelain, iron or platinum that is appropriated to melt some corporeality or calcine. Within alchemy, the crucible illustrates union, the furnace is the intimate blaze, and the test site is the frame. It is there that the basic substance of the great work is baked and melted, and the refined gold of the clairvoyant is made.

CRUCIBLE o CRISOL A glass of refractory clay, porcelain, iron or platinum that serves to melt or calcine some substances. Within alchemy, the crucible stands for gender, the stove is the actual trigger, and the laboratory is the embodiment. It is there that the raw material of the substantial effort is baked and stirred, and the pure gold of the alchemists is made.

CHRISTIANITY it is said of the religion of CHRIST, based on Love, initially escalate by the East and preached throughout the world by the apostles and adept of Christ.

CHRISTIAN He who has already personified the Christ. Amateur who despises the doctrine of Christ, to achieve Christification. Dogma of "three in one" and "one in three" it is needless, thus, repeating what can be in each catechism. Athanasius, the Father of the Church who resolved the Trinity as a foundation, had little expectations to seek enlightenment or torture his own brain; He had only to turn to one of the endless trinities of the pagan creeds, or to the Egyptian priests, in whose territory he had lived all his life. He nimbly diminished only one of the three "people". All the triads of the Gentiles were coolheaded of the Father, the mother, and the Son. Enhancing the triad in "Father, Son, and Holy Spirit," it has persistently been feminine, and conforming to all the Gnostic Gospels, Jesus addresses the Holy Spirit as his "mother."

CHRISTIANISM. Christianity was born with the death of Jesus of Nazareth (30 AD), this generates the principle of stability of its teachings to leave to posterity the reaffirmation of the primordial belief, that of the arrival of the son of God. Its continuance mark in the discourse the environment immanent to the life of the Nazarene, that is, those of living under the motivation of voluntary poverty, humility and charity that turn man into an arduous acolyte of the new faith. Discourse and reality give history the possibility of its existence, mostly when the one who denotes the argumentative action has deprived himself of this world to become a social being for individuality, the subject has remained at the assistance of his community, his life and his word are now part of the ideology he professes, account for in this principle the essence of Christianity in its origins. Jesus was a Jew just like his mother, his advocates were Jews, and his word was "I have not been sent but to the lost sheep of the house of Israel" (Matt. 15:24); "Go then; teach all people..." (Matt. 18:19); "Go into all the world and preach the gospel to every creature" (Mk 16:15).

CHRIST (Greek) Primitive Gnostic scheme of Christ. It was employed in the fifth centenary BC by J.C. Aeschylus, Herodotus and others. Chresten is the one who revealed the oracles, "a prophet and diviner," and Chester iOS is the one who serves a prophet not a god. Christ. (Gnostic) Title that is possible to each initiate who has accomplished Christification; in the world there are various Christifer initiates such as: Gautama Saktiamuni (The Buddha). Abraham, Quetzalcoatl, Samael, Krishna, Moses and others like (The Magnate Alchemists of history who reached Cristification.

CHRISTONIC (Gnosticism) Mating is the release of the Christonic liquid, it does not matter how or when or with whom, the definition is strict.

CHROMOSOME Component that germinates in the nucleus of cells bellow the circumstance of their subdivision or mitosis, such as male and female gametes (reproductive cell) that each conduct 24 chromosomes. The quantity of them that are 48 come to reinstate the germ cell and remind us of the 48 laws that govern the human body. Genetic cells hold the genes that convey heredity.

CHRYSIPPUS (c. 405-79). 'Of Jerusalem', ecclesiastical writer. He enhances guardian of the Holy Cross at the Church of the Holy Sepulcher. His several surviving works include four panegyrics.

CHRISM (gr. Khisma) Dedicated oil employed in the provision of various rituals.

CHRYSOM. The 'chrism-robe' put on a child at Baptism, as a symbol of the cleansing of its sin. It may originally have been a cloth put over the head to prevent the chrism from being rubbed off. In the C of E, it disappeared in 1552 but it survives in the RC Church.

CHU (Egyptian) This is how the Spirit was appointed in ancient Egypt.

CHURCH HYMNARY, The. The approved hymnal of the Church of Scotland and a variety of other Presbyterian churches. It was published in 1898 and edited in 1927 and 1973.

CRO-MAGNON Title of a prehistoric inhabitants of the Stone Age established by modification Atlantean progeny. In 1868 in a town in France (Dordogne) rests of human hands, skeleton of an ancient ancestry from Western Europe.

CROSS Metaphor of fraternity of races, of men, of alchemy, is the crucifixion of Jesus Christ. The cross is also used to signal more precise circumstances as opposed to a large point. In addition, it is put into practice saying rejection, censorship, or error.

CROSSING Within the cabalism, the crossing of two lines, path objects, etc. is a sign of conjunction and communication. The magicians of antiquity did great works of high magic, through two paths.

CROSIER. The cane is reinforced by prelates and occasionally also by rectors and prioress. The appearance imitates a shepherd's crook, simple in the West, acceptable to tardy express.

CRUETS. Vessels of glass or precious metal in which the wine and water for the Eucharist are carried to the altar.

CRUCIFIX. An imitation of the crucifix, association to a resemblance of the tormented Lord. Cross is thoroughly old as pieces of dedication in the West, in the East their locale is removed by crosses with a flat similarity, i.e., the formation of like a model.

CRUCIFIXION (Latin) Action and effect of crucifying. Every initiate who has incarnated the Christ has to go through the crucifixion internally and be rewarded on the third day as the revitalized, perpetual leader.

CROWN OF THORNS A scheme of Christs' passion. This image is said to come into the hands of Louis IX of France, who construct the Sainate-Chapelle to assist it.

CUBITALI (Latin) "They have the height of an elbow". See: Gnomes, Pygmies, Elementals.

CUBE(S) In the company of this name plead to the Barichad-Pitris (they are a class of angels), for having lessen matter in its quadruple aspect. The absolute cube mirror angelic beings. The cube is a three-dimensional square; it is a resemblance of stability and durability, of geometric perfection. It embodies the termination stage of a cycle of passivity, it can be recognized as the truth, since its field of vision is the same from any perspective, it is frequently thought of as the parallel of the sphere.

CUIUS REGIO, EIUS RELIGIO (Lat., 'In a [prince's] country, the [prince's] religion'). The design was embraced at the Peace of Augsburg (1555), by which the princes of the Empire were authorized to decide if the religion of their lands would be Catholicity or Lutheran.

CULDEES. A title designated to definitive premature Irish and Scottish monks. They emerged to have been recluses who cautiously joined forces together. By the 11th century they were almost identical from secular cannons regular.

CULT Indicates: Adoration or veneration, consecration, etc.

CULT OF THE IBIS The ibis, Hab in Egyptian, was consecrated to Thoth in Hermo polis. He was cited as the source of Osiris, because he is a sign of knowledge, discernment and purity, if this bird hates water no matter how impure it may be.

CULT of the BULL Cult of the bull and ram was imposed on the power of generative creation under two aspects: the celestial or cosmic, and the terrestrial and human. The ram-headed gods all referring to the first. Osiris, to whom the bull was consecrated, has not been regarded as a deity; neither was Ziga with his Nandi bull, despite the numeric.

CUMIN The savory grain of a herb of the parsley, ancestry, employed as an ingredient, exclusively ground and applied in curry powder. The miniature, slim shrub that reinforces cumin and multiplied from the Mediterranean to central Asia. Cumin tuned into being recognized as an image of allegiance and devotion, recreating a official function in marriage ceremonies and other customs, and became a custom in every part of the wedding ceremony; considered to have aphrodisiacs effects. Today cumin is intimately connected with Indian and Middle Eastern cuisines and is one of the leading elements of curry powder.

The prehistorical Greeks kept cumin at his consumption counter in its individual storage. Fearfulness amid the Gothic period illustrated that cumin kept chickens and lovers from bewilderness. It was additionally considered that a delightful existence was coming for the bride and groom who carried cumin seed. Does he not finally plant his seeds; black cumin, cumin, wheat, barley, and emmer wheat at; one by one accordingly, and everyone in its proper place? Agriculturalists know just what to do, for The Almighty has given him comprehension.

CUPID. It touches upon an elemental genius that was used by the Magician Trimetc (Abbot of the Monastery of Sponheln in 1483) who wished to show to any religious the figure of the being worshipped through magnetized. It is said that he is linked to Anael, the angel of Love. According to mythology, Cupid was the son of Venus and Mars, although additional versions say that he was the son of Horus (abundance) and Penia (poverty). Preventing Jupiter from the confusion that Cupid was going to create, he instructed Venus to annihilate him, but the goddess hid him in a forest saving him. On occasions, later the child obtains fallout with two kinds of arrows and a bow of pro with which he threw them, the golden tip induced love and the lead tips induce hatred. It is said that, in prehistory, Cupid was a god who personifies devotion, but he had no place of worship or ceremonials unconventional of other Roman supreme beings such as Venus, whom he often consorts as a side delineation in faith figures.

CUR DEUS HOMO (Lat., 'Why [did] God [become] man?' The caption of St. Anselm's treatise on the Atonement.

CURE It is said that, in prehistory, gnostic priests had the power to perform healings, consequently the head of healers.

CURTAINS It's an image of separation like the curtains organized in the world of heels, mantles, vetoes. Etc. It is also expressed by the Pistis Sophia of the Gnostics. Like the veil that covers the Divine Mother. The Egyptian Isis and where the phrase "No Mortal has dared to lift my veil" is expressed. The spiritual importance of "curtains" is the inner truths of faith which are of new appreciation. Since "the Habitation" signifies the middle or second heaven, which is heaven from the acceptance of the Divine truth that derives from the Lord's Divine good.

CURSIVE SCRIPT The conventional book hand, adequately called 'Greek minuscule', which accustomed small rounded ('lower-case') letters, connected in conjunction for speed of writing.

CUSTODIAN Is one that preserves and safeguards or supports mainly; one supported with a guardian and safekeeping property or track records or with guardianship or preservation of captives or detainees. Certain operations have personnel who act as custodians of the culture. The commanders act as positive models. They also have many other key people, however, who comprise the organization's primary principles. These societal custodians act as classification exemplary and defend the culture around times of commitments.

CUTHA. It is an ancient city of Babylon, from which a tablet personifies an account of creation took its name. The "tablet of Cutha" tells of a temple of Sittam", in the sanctuary of Nergal, the "giant king of war, lord of the city of Cutha", which honorably esoteric.

CRYSTAL (Greek) (Khrushtails) In its present condition, a semitransparent mineral substance that has the aspect of a regular or symmetrical polyhedron. It is a rock or quartz is natural silica. In ancient times it was consider truthful that crystal was water frozen by the Gods of Olympus, thus it is maintained in a solid state. In esotericism, rock crystal or quartz signals that it is energy spread by nature. Currently rock crystal or silicon dioxide is used by mystics' specialists and esotericisms for the peculiarities it has, called "Electrical Parts". They collect, transform, store, amplify, focus, transfer energy, increase psychic gifts, alert inimically to those who (carry it, equilibrium positive and negative energy (Yin and Yan) because it is androgynous, is used as a alleviate component and activates the chakras.

CHYUTA (Sanskrit) The badge implied the fallen, the opposite of Achyuta, "is not subject to transformation or differentiation", persevering consideration of sublimity.

CYBELE She is the Phrygian Goddess, she is the wife of Cronus and was the mother of the Olympian gods. Another name by which the Divine Mother is recognized.

CYCLE A cycle is selected to the phase of time in which a set of occurrences, stages or phenomena unfold or occur that, once culminated, are repeated in the exact order from their initiation to their conclusions. For example, a 3-years cycle of growth and evolution. The voice cycle comes from the Latin cyclus, and this in turn from the Greek kyclus that expresses "circle or rim". e.g., the ordinary cycle of birth, growing, senility, and death.

Glossary Esoteric

CYRILLIC. The alphabet was applied by the Slavonic people in the Orthodox Church. It was denominated after St. Cyril, one of the 'Apostles of the Slavs', through Glagolitic, not Cyrillic, is the alphabet he formulated.

-D-

DAATH (Hebrew) Wisdom; the conjunction of Chokmah; Binah, "knowledge and understanding".

DABAR (Dabarim) (Hebrew) Epitomize "Word", and the "Words" in the Chaldean Kabbalah, Dabar and Logoi.

DACTYLS or (Dactyli) (in Greek) From dactyls finger. designation given to the Phrygian hierophants of Cybele, who were admired as the greatest magicians and exorcists. They were five or ten in number because of the five fingers of one hand they consecrate, and the ten of both hands that evoked the gods. In addition, they cured through manipulation or mesmerism.

DACHE (Dachus) (Chaldean) The dual emanation of Moymis, the son of the binary or androgynous proposition of the world, the Masculine Apasón and the feminine Tauthe. Like all theocratic nations states that have Temple Mysteries, the Babylonians never named the "One" Principle of the universe, nor did they name it. This made Damascus (Theogonies) see that, like the other "barbarians", the Babylonians proceed it quietly Tauthe was the mother of the gods, while Amazon was the self-generating male domain of her, Moymis, the ideal universe, being her only begotten son, and emanating in turn to Dache-Dachu, and finally to Belo, the demiurge of the impartial Universe.

DAD DUGPAS (Tibet) Also called "Brothers of the Shadow". Sectarians engaged in the worst methods of sorcery or black magic.

DAENAM Origination to understand man, the legitimate soul or manas.

DAG DUGPA CLAN Alludes to dark black wizards who wear red cape; they are lamas of Tibet, adversary of the Holy Order of Tibet, they are adherents of the Dark Fraternity.

DAG or DAGON (Hebrew) "Fish" and "Messiah", Dagon was Oannes, the Chaldean bushman, the enigmatic being who materializes daily from the depths of the ocean to instruct people all useful science. It is also called Annedotus.

DAGDHA (Sanskrit) Contemplate the locality of the sky invaded by the sun.

DAGOBA (Sanskrit) An artificial sacred expansion or mound of earth or tower to keep sanctified Buddha relics. These mounds have pyramidal or spear like appearance sprinkled throughout India and Vedic countries, such as Ceylon, Burma, Central Asia, etc.

DHARANA (Sanskrit) That state, in the implementation of Yoga, in which thought must be firmly fixed in some object of meditation. [It is the intense and faultless concentration of the mind on some inner motivation, with complete abstraction of everything outside of the world of the senids. In the Dharana, or sixth degree of expansion, each sense, as an individual faculty, is to be "killed" or incapacitated on this plane, withdrawal into the Seventh sense, the most spiritual and incorporating into it. (Voice of Silence, I)]. Dharana, contemplation, attentiveness or sustained attention, is the fixation of the mind on certain external or internal matters; It is the absorption in the intended attempt.

DHARMYA (Sanskrit) Holy, sacred, just, legal.

DAI NIZ NO RAI In Japanese mythology he is the God of the Sun. He is represented sitting on a cow.

DAIVA (Sanskrit) illustrated to: Divine, heavenly. As existence: divinity, religious product, providence or divine decree.

DAIVI MAYA. (Sanskrit) Illusion Divina.

DALAI (Lama) (Tibet) Imperatively, "ocean of wisdom". In China it is accepted to be an incarnation of Kwan Shi Yin (Avalokitesvara or Padmapani), who in his third earth vision was a Bodhisattva.

DAMA (Sanskrit) Discernment or understanding of the senses. Restraining of conduct, moderation command of self.

DAMANA (Sanskrit) Means: To dominate, victor; restraint, subjection, dominance. The man who has restrained his passions.

DAMATHA (Sanskrit) Symbolizes: Restraint, discipline; penance that one assigns to oneself.

DAMIA (Greek) Etymological meaning comes from the term "Damenei", which could be interpreted as "tamer". The nickname Damia makes its first appearance in Greek mythology, where it was called a goddess.

DAMINI (Sanskrit) Distinctive of one of the vessels of the human body, possibly the vessel with all its branches leading to the woman's chest.

DAMMA (Pali) This term is like the Sanskrit Dharma.

DANA Philanthropy; "charity". The act of offering alms to beggars. First of the six perfections (Parainites) of Buddhism. The key to altruism, love and sympathetic compassion; the key to the first door, the one at the entrance of the Path. Charity also expresses gift, almsgiving, liberality, generosity, philanthropy.

DANAID BUTTERFLY. Danainae is a category of the derivation Nymphalidae, the emperor butterflies, it incorporates the Danaidae, or milkweed butterflies, who places their eggs on several milkweeds on which their larvae (caterpillars) sustain, additionally the clearwing butterflies (ithomiini), and the televini. Nevertheless, contrary to the Nymphalidae and many of the auxiliary butterflies in our locality, the Danaidae are distinctive in that their antennae or feelers are not concealed with scales. Almost all constituents of this group take locality in Asia; exclusively four breeds occur in North America, one of which is the widely known Monarch. They distribute as influential as a reminder to embrace modify and to keep progressing on your migration. In several intangible exercises, the monarch butterfly is foreseeing an image of variation, renewal, and pilgrimage into development. In devotion, butterflies frequently outline diversity, adjustment, intention, and your profound intelligence. A preferred, celestial being, or mystic guide might be attempting to transmit your report of aspiration or serenity if a butterfly lands on you. Butterflies could descend on you if you have a considerate, caring, and artistic essence. In Synopsis, when you glimpse a yellow butterfly, it is a certain signal of aspiration and enjoyment for your survival. Yellow butterflies incorporate the typical and intangible significant related with all butterflies. Yet, they also represent true gladness and a dazzling light for the time ahead.

DANA VIRA (Sanskrit) Hero of charity.

DANCE Hieroglyphs of the act of creation; interprets eternal energy; joining connected people stands for cosmic marriage.

DANDA (Sanskrit) Rod, staff, scepter.

DANGMA (Sanskrit) In mysterious, it is a purified Soul. An adept and Seer, the one who has attained full wisdom.

DANIEL, Book of. This Pentateuch Book comprise of (a) description section (1-6) defines the experiences of Daniel and his three associates under Nebuchadnezzar and Belshazzar, kings of Babylon, and Darius the Mede; and (b) a succession of visions (7-12) which reveal the future circumstances of the Jewish people. The accepted belief that the Book was written in the 6th century B.C. by Daniel, one of the Jewish deportations in Babylon, is now practically universally consider as untenable. The harmony of modern critical viewpoint is that it dates from 168 to 165 B.C.

DANTA (Sanskrit) Disciplined, subjugated, endorsed; the one who has acquired his feelings or passions.

DANTE ALIGHIERI (1265-1321) Dante was born in Florence, was an artist and philosopher. He first came across Beatrice in 1274; subsequent her death in 1290, he vowed to her a rhyme 'such as had been written for no lady before', a promise gratifying in the Divina Comedic. He then focused on philosophy, set foot in politics, and appeared to have traveled away from Florence in 1301. He transformed into an aide of the monarch Henry VII, for whom he composed the De Monarchic; this proclaimed the need for a comprehensive kingship to notice the secular achievement of man and the accommodation directives of the country from the Pope and the Church, Henry's passing in 1313 shattered Dante's presumptions. He committed the last years of his existence to finishing the Divina Commedia.

DANU (Sanskrit) She was the wife of Kazyapa and mother of Danavat.

DAOS (Chaldean) Seventh king (Shepherd) of the celestial bloodline, who reigned in Babylon by an interval of ten saris, or 36,000 years (a saros is 36,000 years long). In his time materialized four Anne Doti or fish-men (Dagon's).

DARASTA (Sanskrit) Magic of solemnity that is accomplished among the central Indian tribes, possessions among the kolarians.

DARBAS (Sanskrit) Expresses, "destructive or heartbreaking" Epithet that appeals to rakchasas and other disastrous or evil geniuses or demons.

DARDANO (Dardanus, in Latin) Descendant of Jupiter and Electra, who accepted as a present the gods Cabires and took them to Samothrace, location they were glorified long before the hero laid the substructure of Troy, and previously one heard of Tyre and Sidon, although Tyre was built 2,760 years before J.C.

DARHA (Sanskrit) Animation of the ancestors of the Filarian tribes of central India.

DARK AGES, The. A phrase in current use for the period in W. Europe broadening out of the decomposition of classical culture. (c. The 5th century) to dawn of archaic culture civilization (c. The 11th century).

DARMACHARA (Sanskrit) The eleventh commandment ("Do Your Duty") of Mosaic profound.

DARZA (Sanskrit) In testimonial to: Vision. The day of the new moon.

DASA-Sila (Pali) These are the ten commandments or precepts obligatory and collected by Buddhist priests: 1. Refrain from destroying the life of essential nature; 2. From stealing; 3. From any illicit sex trade; 4. From lying; 5. From use intoxicating beverages and soporific drugs 6.From eating at an improper time; 7. From dancing and singing in an inconvenient way; 8. Using essences, perfumes, cosmetics and ornaments; 9. From making use of raised and wide beds, and 10. From Receiving gold and silver. Such is the obligatory decalogue of the Buddhist priest and the Saman era (novice). The laity are only obliged to execute the first five rules (pan-Sila or Pancha Sila.)

DASRA (Sanskrit) Proper; "beautiful." One of the twin brothers Azvins.

DASYUS (Sanskrit) According to the Vedas, they are evil beings or demons, adversaries of gods and men.

DAVA (Tibetan) Astromancy testimonials, of the moon, in Tibetan astrology.

DAY (ATONEMENT, Day of) The annual Jewish festival arranged to purge the people from sin and the re-establish good association with God. Much of the ritual structured in the Hebrew scriptures, such as the entry of the High Priest into the Holy of Holies in the Temple, has unavoidably lapsed, but the day is still abundantly observed by Jews with fasting and prayer. Its Hebrew denomination is 'Yom Kippur'.

DAYA (Sanskrit) Compassionate, affectionate, tender, piety, mercy, compassion.

DAZAN (Sanskrit) Ten.

DECADE. A division of the Rosary, in consequence, described as since it consists of ten Hail Marys, which are preceded by the Lord's Prayer and successively by the Gloria Patri.

DE CANTILUPE, WALTER DE (d. 1266), Bp. Of Worcester and connection of Thomas de Cantilupe. He was devoted to Gregory IX in 1237. His cooperation of the barons in opposition Henry III is said to have been the solitary obstruction to his canonization.

DECALOGUE (Greek Deka: Ten and Logos: Word) The Ten Commandments, which were given to Moses at Mount Sinai by Jehovah as laws for the Hebrew people.

DECEIVE (Gnosticism) Hook, mock, defraud, mistake, strut. Relinquish from using mental concentration to engage the neighbor if failure for you will be inevitable. Mental strength performs wonders and astonishment, when it is based on sincerity and truth. The frustrated deceive themselves by imagining the best of themselves.

DECRETUM GELASIANUM An unseasonably Latin document which comprehends in conjunction with, a list of Publications of the Bible. In the MSS it is most regularly accredited to Pope Gelasius (492-6); it most likely dates of the 6th century.

DEFAME. To attack the good honorific or reputation of, as by whispering or distributing maliciously or falsely whichever injurious; slander or scandal; calumniate: The newspaper editorial depreciated the politician, Archaic. When you disgrace; bear infamy upon you. Archaic. To accuse. In the Bible defame contemplates to Slander; speak, evil of someone of something.

DEHA (Sanskrit) Indicate the physical body.

DEHATI. Defines "Rural." The precise interpretation of the term is just a "villager".

DEHEZVARA (Sanskrit) The lord of the body. The Self or the Spirit.

DEHIN (Sanskrit) Material corporeal; that has a body; the man, soul or Spirit incarnated in the body.

DEMIURGE. The English formation of a Greek term interpretation 'craftsman', employed of the Divine Being by Plato in his description of the formation of the visible world, and so by Christian writers of God as the Creator of all things. The Gnostics utilized the word desperately of the inferior deity to whom they attribute the origin of the evidence universe, separating him from the supreme God.

DEI (termini) (Latin) It was named pillars or columns with a human head Hermes, which the Romans and Greeks located at the crossroads. With this current name was also appointed the divinities that led to the limits and borders.

DEITY Indicate to the divinity of God.

DEISM. The establishment of rational religion which was up to date in England in the late 17th and 18th centuries. The first-rated exposition is J. Toland's Christianity not Mysterious (1696). At earliest there were many classifications of Deists, from those who support that God was the Creator, with no farther proceeds in the world, to those who welcome all the truths of instinctive religion, as well as belief in a society to come, but rejected revelations. Relatively all belief in Divine Providence and in winnings and penalizing was abandoned, and the head mark of lost Deism was calculated in a Creator God whose added mediation in His creation was against as derogatory to His omnipotence and solidity. Never extensively acquired in England. Deism used profound influence in France and Germany.

DEIST The one who acquire the existence of a god or gods, however, pretends to recognize nothing of one or the other and rejects revelation. A freethinker of prehistoric times.

DELFIN It is an insignia of salvation, admired in ancient legends, as a friend of man. It has been correlated with the amphora, which is another mark of preservation. It is considered the fastest of the marine animals. In the badge of Francesco Colonna, he expresses standing, discretion, in instants that arise coiled to an amphora.

DEMERIT Cabbalism-Buddha expression, it is a component segments of Karma. Through avidya (ignorance) or vidya, wisdom (or divine enlightenment) emerges reciprocally, demerit or merit. The instant Arhat gets enlightenment and perfect ability on his character and secondary essence; postponed from producing the "merit and waste".

DEMETER (Greek) Persist a Hellenic name of the Latin Ceres, deity of the harvest and of tillage. The astronomical sign Virgo. The Eleusinian Mysteries were commemorated in honor of this goddess.

DEMIURGE. The English formation of a Greek, term defining 'craftsman', handle of the Divine Being by Plato in his version of the origination of the visible world, and so by Christian reporter of God as the Creator of all things. The Gnostics utilized the term adversely of the deity to whom they attribute the origin of the perceptible universe, discern him from the supreme God.

DEMONS According to Kabbalah, demons are accommodating in the world of Assiah, the world of matter and the "wrappings" of the dead. They are the Klippoth. It is declared that there are seven hells, whose inhabitant demons restores the personified vices.

DE CELEBRATIO LITURGICA (Gnosticism) Manifests, proves, appears, teaches, results: This shows that the feasts to which the Sacred Scriptures refer that we must perpetuate and praise, are the feasts of the Soul, are the instant that takes place from being to us, where with a purified mind with a heart full of love, we humbly desolate ourselves to locate ourselves praying and talking with our own God.

DENIS (Angoras) Clinician, physician, astrologer and alchemist from Paris, France who lived in the fourteenth century.

DEN (LAIR) (de guarir) Measures an injunction or refuge to get rid of any anguish or danger. Gnostically, psychological defects or egos; they have their lair in the 4 extensive levels of the mind, which must be taken out with the help of the Divine Mother Kundalini, because she knows her hiding places, for the total disintegration of each of these imperfections. Through imagination, inspiration, intuition, one arrives at the comprehension fundamental for the death of the ego.

DEONA or Mati. In the Kolarian local speech, he is the one who drill evil spirits.

DEP The mental world.

DEPENDENCE. Represents the character or capacity of subsistence counts on, particularly the accredited or state of being real effectively or resolved by or conditional to supplementary; provisory, confidence. The distinction between reliance and craving is dependence is the condition of possessing an expectation on unspecified thing; addition is the state of owning to depend on existence. The "dependency syndrome" is an approach and assumption that a relation is impotent to solve its own obstacles deprived of external support. It is instability that is made unacceptable by financial relief. Dependence in ideology is noticed as inquiry as long as allegations, abnormalities, acceptance, demeaner, activity are combined mishap or at differently by additional allegations, expectations, circumstances, process etc. And and even if this effect is crucial for their actualization. Proverbs 13:4; "The soul of the lazy man desires and has nothing; but the soul of the diligent shall be made rich."

DER BALYZEH FRAGMENTS This is in testimonial to a few incomplete pages of a Greek papyrus codex located at Der Balyzeh in Upper Egypt in 1907. They shelter ceremonial devotions and a (c. 6th century.) Doctrine. The invocations, which have been dated separately, show the continuance of an eucharistic prayer (anaphora) prior to the Words of Procedure.

DERSES A hidden enthusiasm of the earth, by which plants can develop. Carbonic acid gases, etc. are their vehicles.

DEROGATE or REPEAL (Gnostic) No humanist author, prophet, has acquired the authority to repeal these ordinances much less could that legion of demons that we carry inside to make us violate the Law.

DERVISH (Persian; dervix: poor) Mohammedan religious: Dervice dancer. They were sacred dances that existed in Turkey. Persia etc. Committed as a cult to the Sun; with their movements they mimic the motions of the planets around the Sun. The dance of the dervishes is used to quiet the mind. It comprises of jumping in the form of a trolley, moving the head from left or right and from right to left (from side to side), at the same time opening the arms laterally and backwards, and then joining them to the front by clapping; making three moves at once.

DERVICHE Muslim austere (Turkish or Persian). A wandering and pastoral friar. However, dervishes occasionally reside in the town. They are usually specified as "turning sorcerers." Separate from his life of acerbity, prayer and meditation, the devout Arab, Turk or Egyptian bears very diminutive comparison to the Indo fakir, who is apprehensive to be Muslim. The latter can grow into a saint and a mendicant saint; while the ancient will never extend beyond its second class of occult phenomenon. The dervish can also be a powerful mesmerizer, but he will never spontaneously submit to the abominable and almost unbelievable penitence that the fakir invents to apply them with an ambition. always increasing, until obviously succumbs and he dies amid slow and cruel torments. The most horrible processes, such as skinning living limbs; cutting your fingers, feet, and legs; gouging out their eyes; Arriving at burying themselves alive in dirt to the beard and consuming whole months in such an attitude, all this seems to them children's games. Do not confuse the Dervish with the sannyasi or Indian yogi.

DE SACRAQMENTIS. A minuscule liturgical treatise, virtually of course the work of St. Ambrose (d. 397). dispatch to the newly baptized, it treats of Baptism, Confirmation, and the Eucharist. It is the initial witness to the Roman Cannon of the Mass in substantially its conventional form.

DESCARTES, RENE (1596-1650) French thinker and researcher. In 1929 he lived in Holland; at this point he produced his main works. His momentousness as a philosopher leans primarily in the authenticity of his techniques. He constructed analytical interpretation above the theory and approach of mathematics, thoroughly declining (as he trusts) to assemble any basic transcendental belief. The conception of his doctrine was his acceptance of inner self-awareness, 'Cogito, ergo sum'. He then determined to the proposal of his individual intellect. The first 'clear and distinct idea' which a sensible self-worth perceives apparently as such is the proposal of God's presence and righteousness (insinuated in the formulation of a flawless essence).

DESIRE(S) (Gnosticism) The self is longing, many times love is baffle with desire. Craving is a substance that breaks down into thoughts, feelings, romances, volitions, poetry, tenderness, sweetness, violence, anger, hatred, grudges; pretending is the birth of crime, of pain. All the yearnings of the human machine (humanity) are aggravated by external influences and by multiple strange and strenuous inner incentives. When the self-disintegrate, the origin of the crime, of the desire, ends. By constraining the sexual instinct and transmuting the desire into light and will, it becomes living fire and disintegrates the ego, previously understood. Desire is the fundamental subject of any offence; the most serious offenses are anger, greed, lust, gluttony, laziness, lust, passion.

DESCENT OF CHRIST INTO HELL, The. Many Christians believe that this article in the Creed mentions the Lord's visit after His death to the domain of existence in which the souls of pre-Christian people waited for the message of the Gospel. It first transpired in the 4th century. Arian formularies, from which it outstretched in the West and found its way into the 'Apostolic' Creed.

DESIRE(S) (Gnosticism) The self is longing, many times love is confused with desire. Craving is a substance that fractures down into thoughts, feelings, romances, volitions, poetry, tenderness, sweetness, violence, anger, hatred, grudges; impersonate is the birth of crime, of pain. All the longings of the human machine (humanity) are provoked by external influences and by multiple strange and difficult inner motivations. When the self dissolves, the origin of the crime, of the desire, ends. By restraining the sexual impulse and transmuting the desire into light and will, it becomes living fire and dissolves the ego, previously understood. Desire is the fundamental subject of any offence; the most serious misdeed is anger, greed, lust, gluttony, laziness, lust, passion.

DESTINY In Greco-Roman mythology she was a blind Divinity (Eimarmena), daughter of Chaos and the night, to whom many things were conveyed in heaven and earth. His decisions written from eternity were necessarily fulfilled. It is linked to the law of cause and effect (Karma and Dharma) of each person, this destiny can be recovered with the attainment of the factors of the Revolution of consciousness: Dying, Being Born and Sacrifice for Humanity.

DESTRAL In the hieroglyphs Egyptians, it is an indication of Usurpation and of death. The Destral is a tagged "Knot Cutter", this, of marriage or any other link.

DESTROY The last energetic fluid to assemble its appearance is the Death Ray, which decreases the so-called man to a fifth molecular essence; additionally, a ton of flowers can be reduced to a simple drop of essential perfume. The energy of death being so strong destroys the human organism.

DEUS (Latin) God. DEUS LUNUS. The Moon or Moon God, Todah in Mesopotamia short of the reputation of Sin.

DEVACHAN (The Mansion of the Gods or Resplendent Abode.) (Gnostic. tib. -Teo.) It is a location of happiness where the deceased or disembodied live. Most disincarnates live in a subjective state of bliss projecting their own mental characterization or effigies, by that feeling assisted by their family and friends, unless they awaken their conscience.

DEVARNA (Sanskrit) Exemplify, debt to the devas. (Bhagavan-Das).

DEVA(S) These are divinities or angels. They control the elementals of nature, which are in the 4th dimension.

DEVEZA (deva-iza) (Sanskrit) Gentleman or prince of the gods.

DEVOTION (Latin, Devoti) Love, veneration and religious fervor. The hypocrisy of devotion is the responsibility of all. There are two kinds of loyalty: external subject to the worship of images, norms, ceremonies to the worship of God, Gods, etc.

DEVA-BHU (Sanskrit)

DEVIL (Greek diabolos) Slanderer, deceiver, defamer, whistleblower. Genius of evil, defamer and schemer. With this name are chosen the rebellious angels.

DEVI (Sanskrit) The Goddess, also alleged Maha-Devi (the great Goddess). Wife of the god Ziva, that is, the zakti or feminine energy of Ziva. Due to its nature, attributes and activities, it has possessed various names, such as Parvati Uma, Durga, Kali, Chandika, Gauri, etc.

DEW (Persia) The Dev. he is amid the Zoroastrians the genius of evil and the antithesis of the Ferouer.

DEZA (Desha) (Sanskrit) place, region, country, address, space.

DHANA (Sanskrit) Wealth, comfort, property, treasure, loot.

DHANUS (Sanskrit) Mode, bow. It is also the ninth sign of the Zodiac, corresponding to Sagittarius.

DHARA (Sanskrit) Connect to the Avatara of Vichnu in turtle.

DHARANA (Sanskrit) In the implementation of Yoga is that state, in which the thought must be securely fixed in some object of meditation. The concentration of the mind is the second goal of contemplation, in which all kinds of thought must be removed from the mind, fixing the brain on a single goal. He must keep his eyes closed and the body relaxed with muscular tension, with concluded abstraction of everything outside or the world of the senses.

DHARANI (Sanskrit) The earth.

DHARMA (Sanskrit) The Sacred Law; the Buddha Canon. it is the internal substance, interpret in every man by the hierarchy of gotten development, and moreover, the law that determines development in the evolutionary period that will follow. That inner nature, placed by physical birth in an environment favorable to its expansion, is what shapes outer life, which is proclaimed through thoughts, words, and actions. Initially it must be well understood that the Dharma is not an external action, like law, virtue, religion or justice; it is the law of life that unfolds and configurations in its own image all that is external to it. It is the internal nature, in each man by the degree of development obtained. It is also the law that decides spread in the evolutionary period that will follow. This internal substance, placed by the physical origin in a beneficial environment for its expansion, is what forms the external life, which is expressed through thoughts, words and actions. The first thing to understand well is that the Dharma is not an external feat, like law, virtue, religion or justice; it is the law of life that open out and models in its own image all that is external to it. This word has been given many meanings, such as: law, religion, justice, duty, piety, virtue, merit, condition, attribute, quality or essential property; doctrine, creed; code, law, knowledge, wisdom; practical truth, custom; well; pious work, etc. Dharma is also one of the names of Yama, God of justice.

DHARMAKAYA (Sanskrit) Implies, "the glorified spiritual body", known by the brand of "Garment of Bliss". It is the third, or most of the Trikaya (Three Bodies), a quality developed by every "Buddha", that is: an initiate who has crossed or achieved the end of the so-called "fourth Path" (in cabbalism, the sixth "portal" that precedes his ingress into the seventh). The highest of the Trikaya's is the Buddha Chetra room, or Buddhism planes of consciousness, figuratively restored in Buddha asceticism as a garment or garment of luminous Spirituality.

DHARMAPALAS are legions of Great Masters of strength.

DHARMYA (Sanskrit) Signify: Holy, Sacred, just, legal.

DHENU (Sanskrit) Dairy cow; the earth.

DHI (Sanskrit) Defines: Thought, intelligence, mind; knowledge, meditation.

DHIZAKTI (Sanskrit) Power or mental power.

DHRITI (Sanskrit) Firmness, strength, resolve, courage, constancy; satisfaction, contentment.

DHYANA (Sanskrit) In the Buddhist discipline, it is one of the six Paramitas of perfection.

DHYANIS (Sanskrit) Those Angels or angelic spirits. "Generic name applied to some spiritual beings ordered from the planetary Logos to some of the "Arupa-Devas.""

DIADOCHUS. (5th century). Bp. Of Photike ensuing 451. He wrote (in Greek) 100 'Capita Gnostics' on the aim of completed spiritual perfection; they appreciate great acclaim. divergent production done for accredited "That Person" with lower certainty.

DIAGRAM (Latin Diagram, Greek Design) It is a geometric design, with several allegorical representations of the Mysteries of creation, the universe and the Gods, used in magical ceremonies, for spells and prayers.

DIANA She was the daughter of Jupiter and Latone. She was also, Goddess of forests and hunting, she relates to nature often and with fertility and wild animals. There are those who link it with the Greek Hecate; Escorted by dogs she becomes a nocturnal persecutor, in association to the Ethonic Demons. Among the Greeks it is understood by the name of Artemis or Artemis.

DIANOIA (Greek) It is the same as the Logos. The immortal source of thoughts, "divine ideation," which is the root of all reflection.

DIASPORA. Jewish. The dispel of the Jews launched with the Babylonia and Akkadian removal (722 and 597 B.C.). Afterwards it disseminates through the Byzantine Empire. The Jews of the Dispersion abide in near hold with their dwelling notion, remittance the place of worship charge and maintain their doctrine and the confining of the enactment. The Jewish beyt knesset in Anatolia and Greece were the first mise-en-scene of God-fearing teaching.

DIASTOLE (Gnosticism) Everything evolves and involutes, rises and falls, grows and decreases, comes and goes, flows and refluxes; in all things there is a systole and a Diastole, according to the Law of the Pendulum.

DIAMOND(S) (Latin Adame. Antis from Greek) This wonder jewel is harmonious with strength, fortitude, tenderness and wellbeing. As has been revealed, all through history, diamonds have been worn by figureheads or trendsetters to write down power and irresistibility. Diamonds have also been linked with wholesome and constitute longevity and good heart health. As reported by astrologers, natural diamonds carry extraordinary cosmic vibes that aid you to upgrade your prevalent health shape. Besides curing liver, asthma, and throat disorders, this uncolored stone provides you with an upgraded digestive system and urinary tract. It is an emblem of light and splendor. In kabbalah, he is found in repressions with the usual sense of the "Radiant Mystical Center". He is also a figure of moral and intellectual discernments. In Alchemy the polished diamond is a symbol of the philosopher's stone. If the stone is not polished, it must be worked, refined, etc. It is also related to the "Diamond soul of the Adept" or the "Ruby Soul of the occult" or "Diamond Leather" of the abyssal secrets.

DIAMPER, Synod of (1599) A convocation of Malabar Christians some 12 miles south of Calcutta which manages within existence the Malabar Uniat Church Nestorianism was disowned and absolute acceptance to Rome administer, however, the Syriac Liturgy was supported.

DIDO Elisa. Astarte: The Virgin of the Sea, who lowers the Dragon under her foot. The benefactor saint of the Phoenician sailors. A queen of Carthage who pleased Aeneas according to Virgil.

DIDILIA She was a goddess who makes infertile women fertile, in Slavic mythology.

DIDYMUS Substitute term for the Apostle St. Thomas.

DIE An extraordinary form of dice. It shows up from the French word des, a plural term for the matching objects. In English, the better common way to gather nouns not singular is to add an S. If die go a long with that rule, its plural formation would be dies. To pass from physical life: expire at the age of? Die young died from injuries to a dying tree. 2a: to pass out of subsistence: crave their irritation at these words. b: to disappear or subside moderately often used with away, downward, to out the storm passes on. 3a: sink, weaken, dying from fatigue.

DIEZMO (Latin Decen. Decimus. De decem, ten) (Gnostics) In its esoteric or external presentation, tithing, in Jewish legislation, is the universal duty that all the brothers of the path must loyally devote a part of their income to the Tithe. In the esoteric the Tithe is the stability of payments in the sphere of Neptune. Tithing becomes a practical and required complement to the dynamic principle that emanates from the deep study of the tenth commandment, that is, to contemplate as source, spring and spiritual providence of everything the inner and divine interior of our life, the merciful Self that hides in the middle of the Central Delta of the Sanctuary of our Being. Conforming to genesis (of the Bible) Chapter XIV says: "Jump the King of Salem (who was a priest of the high God) took out Bread and Wine and blessed him, and said, blessed be Abrahan of the High

God, possessor of the heavens and the earth; and blessed be the High God, who delivered your enemies into your hand, and gave Him Abrahan the Tithes of all."

DIG-GAJAS (Sanskrit) The elephants that defend the eight cardinal points. The main one being Airavata.

DIK (Sanskrit) Designee of Diz.

DIKCHA (Sanskrit) Initiation. Organization or consecration for a religious ceremony; dedication, devotion.

DIKTAMNON DICTAMO (Greek) (Dictamnus) (Latin) It is a curious plant well investigated since ancient times, which is declared to have mystical and very hidden powers. Stubbo is consecrated to the goddess Luna Astarte. Reveille. Diana's Cretan title was Diktynna, and as such, the goddess wore a garland assembled from that magical plant. The Diktamnon is a lively plant, as maintained by ambition in cabalism, contact with this plant has the power to manufacture and at the same time, cure sleepwalking. It is said that mixed with verbena can cause clairvoyance and ecstasy. The pharmacy accredits to the dictamo energetic sedative and calming properties, (hence its use in hysteria, epilepsy and other neuroses). It cultivates copiously on Mount Dicte, in Crete, and enters many magical adjustments, which the Cretans still use today.

DILL. (Anethum graveolens) is a flavoring that's established all over European and Asian cuisines. Additionally labeled dill weed, the shrub has slim stems with adaptation soft leaflet and brown, flat, ovel seed. Dill fruits are ovate, compacted, glide about one-tenth inch wide, with three lengthwise corrugations on the posterior and three inky row or oil cells (vittae) amid them and two on the flat exterior. The aftertaste of the fruit's kind of similarly allspice. In conventional herbal medicament, dill has been utilized to encourage maintain and defend against dietetic ills and bad breath, to encourage lactation and to decrease cholesteric and blood glucose.

DIMENSION (Zero) It is the seventh dimension, the region of Atman (The Intimate) or of the Pure Spirit. In the world of Atman, you have a downright man, it is the world of mathematics, there you discover the solid and the hyper solid, accommodating the exact number of atoms that in their compound form the integrity of any element in its most real structure, a table is seen everywhere, below, inside, on the outside, how many atoms and molecules renew it; similarly happens with a mountain.

DINASTIA Sprout two varieties of dynasty in India: Soma (or lunar dynasty), and the Sury Avanza (or solar dynasty). In the Chaldean and in Egypt there were also two recognizable dynasties: the divine and the human. In both countries the people were ruled, in primitive stages, by dynasties of gods. In notable countries, there were peoples ruled by hundreds of dynasties.

DINNER Food brings people unitedly to stay connected, learn about a family member by cooking together, celebrate, learn about cultures, and provide comfort. People love food almost as much as they love each other, so in conjunction they bring happiness and joy to all sharing a dinner. It is a decisive nourishment, but you can try with a scope of compelling food. Embracing a hearty dinner is connective to satisfactory bedtime, favorable probabilities at morning meal and luncheon, lesser puffiness, larger elasticity to tension, stronger indigestion, safe blood sugar and lower unpredictabilities. 'You prepare a table before me in the presence of my enemies; you anoint my head with oil; my cup overflows.' Jesus was firm in and appreciated this custom. The way he separates and gives out food with all types and situations of mortals as affirmation of the embracing of God's realm, so acutely did the primal tabernacle. "And God said, Behold, I have given you every herb bearing seed, which is upon the face of all the earth, and every tree, in which is the fruit of a tree yielding seed; to you it shall be for food." In the secondary segment of Genesis (2:16-17) vegetarianism is reasserted as mankind's piousness correct dietary regimen.

DINO (Gnosticism) Expression of one of the three greas also called Quersis.

DINUR (Hebrew) River of fire whose waters consume the souls of the guilty, Kabbalistic allegory.

DIPSAS. A viper with a bite was anciently assumed to give rise to extreme dehydration. The snake was the topic of an anecdote told by some Greek writers, as well as Sophocles. Conforming to the folk story, Zeus was appreciative to those who disclosed to him the identification of the deity who had quench fire. He recompenses the betrayer by giving them the remedy to old age, which they load onto the back of a mule that was then permitted to leave unattended. The donkey grew extremely thirsting and halted at a fountain watched by the serpent. Thereafter firstly refused giving him water, the ophidian then suggests trading it for the cargo of the ass's load. The snake, succeeding the receipted the capacity, shed his skin, and the ass was relieved of his thirst. The expression is from the Greek Dipsas, a connate of Dipsa, "thirst."

DISINTEGRATION The action and effect of dividing the organic molecules of the body or physical vehicle after death, or disincarnating. (Gnosticism) As soon as a Self or Ego (defect) has been killed, the procedures of its total dissolution must resume. When the 108 existences of each person have been exhausted, the Ego regresses into the bowels of nature through the nine Dantes horrific circles, it pursued to be totally disintegrated; thus, releasing the Soul (essence) trapped in each defect; thus, what is investigated as second death is executed.

DISCIPLE, Books of, 'First Book of Discipline' (1560) was stressed up by J. Knox and those staying as a proposition for the instructions and continuance of the new Scottish Church. Parts of it were unpleasant to the rectitude and it encountered a dead letter. The so-called 'Second Book of Discipline' (1578), primarily the work of A. Melville, was handled as a resolution of the totalitarian Protestant in opposition achievement to upgrade a modified episcopate.

DISC or DISCO (Latin Greek Discus) Is an image of the Sun and the Sky. In Chinese the "Sacred Disc" is a representation of astronomical perfectness and matching if the disc is Made of Jade called "Pi" c on a hole in the center. As a symbolism of the word 'Disco' [short for discotheque.] which was a category of dance music and subculture inner city nocturnal scenery place; evolved in the 1970 in the United States'. The common blast is symbolized by four consecutive quarter notes within a measure of 4/4 on the floor rounds, shortened breakbeats, cord segment, spike, stage piano, synth, and acoustic guitars. As a style or class of music; a few cultural groups had categorized it as one of the pleasures of disco music was that it welcomed hedonism, pursuing enjoyment of the moment and a love of the superficial; however, that seems to be exactly the self-indulgence and the satisfaction of wishes that most people may've been looking for through nightlife and disco dancing.

DISLIKE Suspicion of not enjoying or approving of a phenomenon or personage. e.g. "Her dislike of the new rhythm was obvious". "He instantly dislikes the new teacher".

DISMAS. The classical honorific of the Good Thief (Lk. 23: 39-43) crucified with Christ.

DISORDER In psychology is attributed to components such as fear of conversion, fear of forgetting, anxiety to shortages. It also epitomizes confusion, lack of orientation, chaos, instability can mean unreliability about your goals, your identity or what you want from life.

DIS (Greek) In the theogony of Demascios, it is the same as Protogons, "the first light born", called by that author "the computer of all things".

DISCIPLE(S) (Latin Discipulus) A personality who researches a doctrine of the Master, whose instruction is entrusted by committing himself to obedience, or who attends a school. It is the one who is in the second grade of a school of hidden mysteries, after having gone through a succession of tests. The disciple is chosen by his Master or Adept to instruct in the Spiritual Mysteries, showing up as a benefactor, conducting in the creation of his higher existential elements of the Self and hidden work, so that he has the power to act in worlds and dominant dimensions of space, etc.

DISC (Latin; Greek Discuss) It is an emblem of the Sun and the Sky. In China, the "Sacred Disc" is a figure of celestial perfection, and even more so if the disc is made of Jade called "Pi" with a hole in the center. It was entirely ordinary in Egypt, it was the cult of the sun under a different scheme, the Aten-Nephru, being to warn that Aten-Ra was like the Adonai of the Jews, the "Lord of the heavens" or the Sun. The circle or winged disc was an emblem of the Soul. The Sun was at one time the image of the universal Deity shining upon the entire world and upon all creatures. The Sabaeans meditate on the Sun as the Demiurge and a universal establishment, as do the Indians and the Zoroastrians even today.

DISRESPECT (Gnosticism) Opposite to this. The word, as such, designates the lack of respect that manifests itself towards life, spiritual precepts and neighbor. Disrespect is considered a serious fault for healthy coexistence between people because it violates one of the main foundations that guarantee social and spiritual harmony: respect.

DISES (Scandinavian) This is the denomination with which divine women were later chosen called Valkyries Norms, etc., in the Edda.

DISGUISE or DISGUISE (O) A impersonation or clothing with which someone can alter or change their appearance or so as not to be recognized. It is associated that the adept who knows how to walk with both feet, who knows how to disguise himself in a moment of Demon, of Devil to make an investigation in the Averno (abyss).

DISSOLVE (Alchemy) (Throw the Stone into the Water) It answers to the fact that after having reached union with God, he throws the stone back into the water, that is, the initiate falls or falls, to the forge of the Cyclops to re templar his sword and thus be more powerful stronger. Up to seven times the institute can do it, beyond that he can fall into a curse.

DISTINGUISH (Gnostic) This is how we must make distinction between Ego and Essence; it is also necessary to Distinguish between Personality and Essence.

DITE The 5th and 6th Dantesque circle, Dante names the city where they are condemned submerged in tombs full of fire, there are the sect leaders with their henchmen.

DITHA A category of pseudoscorpions in the background of Tridenchthoniid. There are about 14 outlined reproduced in Ditha. Chelone Thida live in many terrains and are routinely raised in crevices, nooks and close perimeters. They prefer excessive dampness and are ground in leaf mold, swamp, remnants and pebbles, and in fowl and vertebrates' burrow. They set foot in households by hitchhiking on oversized parasites (e.g., flutter and bustle) or on fuelwood. (There are limited to nearly 14 described species regarding Ditha). It is also a name for girls which is ordinary in German. The honorific Ditha has aqua segments. The Moon is the governing heavenly satellite; has a side planet manifestation as Cancer which is expressed by the Crab and examine as Cardinal which stands for red birth. The metaphor of a red cardinal is an inspiration, cheerful manifestation that the loved ones we have lost will exist eternally, preserving recollections vital of more valuable times.

DITI (Sanskrit) "Division", "dismemberment". Wife of Kazyapa (Kashyapa), sage and mother of the Maruts. In mystery, Diti is the sixth initiation of metaphysical Nature, the Buddhi of Akaza.

DIVA (Sanskrit) Sky, firmament; day.

DIVES (Latin 'rich') An expression that has mutated an opportunity, just about accepted, title for the untitled affluent gentleman in the Holy scriptures, Lk. 16:19-31.

DIVINATION Forestall future events through the soul's accept light; (prophecy) or clarify the occult, through definite experiences respected as supernatural, or by evaluation of the logical thinking of a fusion of practices, such as those of the Tarot, or by concrete enlightenment, images, or by dreams.

DIVINE or DIVINITY Those who dwell in the "Absolute Abstract Space". Which comes from the absolute.

DIVINEDAIMON (Gnosticism) Or demon, he did not have the sense of evil spirit that we commonly give him today but was reason as a kind of genius or tutelary enlightenment of men, something like what is now quoted Guardian Angel. In evidence each figure has two daimons, one white, good and one black, bad. Here the dualistic doctrine that cuts in the two births that govern the human being is specified; Black or white The Daimon is the darkness of God in us.

DIVYA (Sanskrit) Divine celestial, wonderful; bright, glorious, beautiful.

DVIPA (or Dwipa) (Sanskrit) An islet or continent. The Indus enumerate seven (Sapta-dvipa), of which the Jambu-dvipa, or midpoint, was India. Buddhists only count to four. This is due to a misconception remark about by Lord Buddha, who, using the expression in a metaphorical perception, applied the word Dvipa to the races of men. The four mother races that anticipates the fifth (ours), Siddhartha correlated to the four continents or islands that studded the ocean of birth and death.

DIZ (Sanskrit) Space (celestial), void, region of the sky, cardinal or perspective space; place, country, region. (See: Dik.)

DJATI (Jati) (1) (Sanskrit) [Birth], In the company of the twelve Nidanas; domino effect in the method of birth, conforming to the Chatur-yoni; situation in every instance of being, if man or animal, and positioned in one of the six (esoterically, seven) gatis or path of conscious existence, that cabalistically, enumerating from top to bottom, are: 1. The Highest Dhyanis (Aupadaka); 2. the devas; 3. men; 4. the elementals or spirits of Nature; 5. animals; 6. the diminished elementals, and 7. In the widespread or exoteric designation, these subsistence are: devas, men, asuras, malevolent existence, preras (fametic demons) and animals, [Jati also signifies: family, tribe, species, caste, position, condition, etc.]

DJATI (Jati) (2) (Sanskrit) [Born] One of the twelve nidanas; the cause and effect amid birth occurring, according to the Chatur-yoni, where in each case a being, whether man or animal, is installed in one of the six, gatis or paths of sentient existence, which conceivably, from top to bottom: at the instant supreme divinities, devas, men, elementals, animals, lower elementals, organic germs, etc.

DJIN (Arabic) Primordial; essence of nature; genius. The Djins or Jins are very feared in Egypt, Persia and different points.

DOCETAE (Greek) With this term Orthodox Christians choose those Gnostics who contribute to the belief that Christ did not suffer, nor could he endured death, and that, if such a thing had happened, it was simply an illusion that they expose in several ways.

DOCHA (Sanskrit) Sin, defect, fault, imperfection, stain, considerable damage, vice.

DOCTRINE (of the HEART) (Gnostic) They are the esoteric colleges of Buddhism. "The doctrine of the Eye" is elaborated with the functionalisms of the five restricted expressions, through an external instruction, starting from home to a university gradation falling quite often to materialism, dogmas, subjective beliefs, etc.

DODONA (Gr.) Ancient city of Thessaly, famous for its temple of Jupiter and for its oracles. According to ancient legends, this city was founded by a dove.

DOGMAS (Gnostic) "What more evidence do we want against the fanatics of Evolutionary Dogma? The rules of Evolution and Involution are the Axis of Nature, but they are not the path of Self-realization. Many groups are the solution of Evolution, and many other species are the solution of Involution, that's all." They are principles, badges, doctrines; that they must be divided without any suspicion.

DIONYSIACAS (Wave) (Gnosticism) Since 1962 between 2 and 3 in the midday the age of Aquarius entered and with it the vibration of the Dionysian Wave with its positive and negative poles. Dionysian positive pole is voluntary transmutation; awakened consciousness, objective knowledge, superlative intuition, transcendental music of the great classical Masters, etc... Negative pole Dionysian, Sexual degeneration, infra sexualism of all kinds. Homosexuality, lesbianism, demonic pleasures in the hell worlds through drugs. Mushrooms, alcohol, infernal music of the new wave (rock) etc. ... Correspondingly this wave two contemporary revolutionary motions were born. By positive pole was born from the M.G.C.U, (Universal Christian Gnostic Movement) and by the negative pole was born the "Hippie" movement. The M.G.C.U., its goals lead the human being along the path of the revolution of consciousness, the liberation or intimate self-realization of the Being. The "Hippie Movement" leads to under-sex, drugs, total degeneration falling into involution.

DIONYSOS (Dionysus) (Greek) He was one of the great Greek or Roman gods, He was the God of wine of vegetation and mystical delirium, son of Jupiter (Zeus) and Semele. Mythology tells that Semele died while still on the tape of Bacchus (Dionysios). Jupiter to save him made a wound on the thigh encysting Bacchus there until he was born, hence the Tradition Bacchus Bimater of two Mothers. Dionysos or Bacchus, as a child, destroyed a double-headed serpent with his hands, which Juno out of jealousy against Zeus (Jupiter) had sent against the child, it is said that during his childhood he was cared for by the Nymphs, and then the muses instructed him mainly in music and dance, and finally Silenus taught him the cultivation of the vine and the manufacture of wine.

DOLPHIN The dolphin is a delineation of depiction for its vicinity in an anecdote about rescuing the immersing mariner or other mortal distraught. Dolphin allegories and interpretation cover help, guidance, messages, intelligence, fun, joyfulness, freedom, teamwork, transformation, and psychic capacity. One predictable which stands out with dolphins is its playful nature; that is one reason human beings are often attracted to them. The dolphins prompt people to take some time out of their busy life to enjoy it as children do, and play. They appear to teach humankind that it's healthy to keep a sense of humor about our lives, and just have some fun off strictly for Entertaiment.

DOMAIN. It mentions to an establishment's communication expedients are arranged. In universal, a domain of a district of power or a domain of expertise, for typical case, the cyberspace; the expression domain can allude to accordingly the internet is arranged. In the first place, the Ethereal deities, Colossus divine beings, and primeval celestial godheads delineated the three pantheons of immortal to command the Megacom. The following classifications segregate the divine beings within dominion, specifically the deity of azure, ocean, planet earth (crude and agriculture), and the netherworld. In standard hypothesis, a proper domain is the set of instruction an element becomes different to procedure. Allegorically the accurate domain of cardiovascular specialist is the heart, the appropriate domain of philosophy is agreed amazing of phenomenon or enigmas. "Domain" is from the Greek word exousias, which can also be translated as "power, authority, or strength". In this respect, Paul is implying to God's deliverance of Christians from the influence of wickedness and devastating death.

DOME OF THE ROCK, The. Muslim shrine in Jerusalem, constitute in the sector of the Jewish sanctuary. It dates from century 800. The rock from which it takes its name is accepted in Islam to be that from which Muhammad arise to heaven, and by Jews to be that on which Abraham arranged to immolate Issaac. The shrine is also well known as the Mosque of Omar.

DOMO This is a Japanese expression which may be utilized as "hello" when you appear and "bye" when you depart from. The declaration additionally has a dismissive definition. It is commented when you want to genuinely be apologetic to anybody. The straight interpretation of this term is "very" in the elated ambience as "I am very sorry". It is pronounced" Dou-mo", when you materialize to be dining at an Izakaya or a cafeteria. Domo is comparable to the English adaptation of "very much". In a variety of scenarios, the expression is applied to surmise value. If you acquired an object at the retail outlet, sales assistant should express "DOMO ARIGATOU", defining thank you "very much".

DOMINUS AC REDEMPTOR (1773) The sudden death of Clement XIV which subjugated the Jesuit Order.

DOM (abbreviation of DOMINUS, 'Master'). A name given to plain friers of the Benedictine and a few added doctrinal regulations.

DONATE [Thunor or Thor] (Scandinavian) In the North was the God of Thunder, the Toning Jupiter of Scandinavia. Just as the holm oak was dedicated to Jupiter, it was also committed to Thor, and its altars were covered or sheltered by branches of that tree. Thor, or Donar, was the son of Odin, "the omnipotent God of Heaven" and of the earthly cause.

DONE Description of denominations is concluded; Accomplished, terminated: Our assignment is done, prepared satisfactory, run-down; drained: depleted. From Anglican deponent gedon (a vestige of the suffixes is in ado). As a perfect tenses attribute explains "completed, finished, performed, accomplished from easily 15c. As a word of acceptance of a deal or wager, 1590s. If you say 'you're done with' something; it means you are irritated and bored by it! Often, it's a task that you don't want to do. Feifei. Indeed. For example, I could say: "I'm so done with recording with Neal." In the scriptures the word done is used to say: "Sing to the Lord, for he has done glorious things; let this be known to all the world." Isaiah 12;5.

DONKEY In Gothic times the donkey was contemplated as a figure of humbleness, tolerance and determination. In alchemy it stays for crude whip, it is recognized as salt, sulfur and mercury, which is the (Tria prima) of Paracelsus. In the Christ portrayal the donkey impersonates the intellect; as Jesus executed his concluding jubilant entrance into Jerusalem as an unpretentious King of Peace. It is an evolutive animal, since in its ancestry, like the monkey comes surfaced from humankind.

DONUM DEI (Latin, "Gift of God") Fundamental to understanding the science of the considerable Work. Master Samael explains that: "although the science of the Great Work is studied, it failed reaching consciousness, but receives the

"Donum Dei (Gift of God) does not understand it, because it belongs to the functionalisms of consciousness." By destroying the Ego, the self (psychological defects), it is possible to awaken consciousness and discover that indispensable talent for the study of the Great Work".

DORJE (Tibetan) This term is equivalent to the Sanskrit vajra (weapon, lightning, scepter, Damante). Instrument, weapon or symbol of power in the hands of various gods (the Tibetan Drag Shed, the Devas that protect humanity), and is assigned the hidden virtue to ward off the evil influences' invisible immunize the air, neither more nor less than ozone in chemistry. It was also a Mudra, category or attitude approved for reflection. The bhons or dugpas have adjusted to this emblem, which between them is, the same as an inverted double triangle, which is a sign of sorcery, and they use it in an era way, for some motivation of Black Magic, on the other hand, among the Gelugpa or "Yellow Caps" is an emblem of dominion, as is the cross for Christians.

DOSITHEUS, (2nd century), Judaea Gnostic. He appears from Samaria and, conforming to Origen, declared himself to be the Messiah foretold in Deut. 18:18. A small body of partisan survived to the 10th century. A short assignment entitled 'A Revelation by Dositheus' was identified at Nag Hammadi; it is not established whether it alleged to be the duty of this Dositheus or some differently unknown namesake.

DOTAR-DOTARE Derivation from Latin below the denomination "do tare" of Italian. It intended to own or supply a property or features of a few attributes that can be upgraded.

DOVE (The) Dove is handed down as Christian's seal for tranquility and conciliation, for the Holy Spirit, for the Church, and for the solitary soul engendered by baptism; it additionally denotes ecclesiastical understanding and unquestionable Christian morality. The Eucharistic Dove is a vacant receptacle container in the arrival of a dove sketched to accommodate the Blessed Sacrament.

DOUAI-REIMS BIBLE. The English genre of the Bible translated by Roman Catholics till contemporary times. The College at Douai grasp adaptation of the English Bible. The New Testament, which was printed in 1582 at Reims; directly after the publication became public approval of college diminished and college momentarily moved; the Holy Book was produced at Douai in 1609. The adaptations were produced by Vulgate and are extremely precise, present versions are formed on the alterations of R. Challoner in 1749-50.

DOWNLOADS (Gnosticism) At the moment of death and during the three and a half days that follow, our consciousness and our inner judgment are emancipated by electronic download. Then we noticed our whole life was spent in a retrospective aspect. The discharge is so powerful that the man then falls into a coma and incoherent dreams. Only those who have that which is called Soul, can resist electronic discharge absent losing consciousness.

DRACONTIA (Greek) Mark of the Sun, figure of Divinity, Life and Wisdom. The Egyptian Karnac, the Carnac in Brittany and the Stonehenge are dracontias known from all over the world. They are temples dedicated to the Dragon.

DRAMA. At the start of the millennium of the Faithfull, melodrama survive at best in the configuration of breathtaking, which were familiarly interrelated with disbelief and so necessarily incurred the hostility of the Church. These ancestral heathenism display concluded with the elimination of the Roman Empire. In the 10th century a current unfolding is such as by the enlightening 'comedies' composed by the Saxon nun Hrosvit and by Ethelwold's quote to the 'praiseworthy custom' of saluting the demise and restoration of life of Christ by a characterization, with pantomime and discourse, minstrel in tabernacle all along or following the ritualistic solemnity. This ritual drama plays toward the enigma (or miracle) Performance (q.v.) Although a considerable growth of nonreligious drama in all portions of Christian empires. Afterward most of the performances were at minimal supposedly uplifting, and the opponents were methodical in seemingly devout gatherings, the Gothic Tabernacle had compact reflect to gadget. Originating in the 16th century drama ordinarily misplaced its ministerial strong bonds. The extra austere advocate disposed to reject the platform complete, but most Religious have accepted in the appearance of the drama as a regular fragment of fellowship. The customary ascetical performance has endurance in any locality, e.g., Oberammergau, and in current moment there has been a rejuvenation of devout drama in England, e.g., with plays like T.S. Eliot's Murder in the Cathedral (1935).

DRAVYA (Sanskrit) Substance (esoterically). [Property, wealth, substance, thing, object, matter; particularly: worthy object, suitable or suitable person. The nine components listed in Kanada's Nyaya philosophy: 1. Earth; 2. Water. 3. Light; 4. Air; 5. ether (or Akaza); 6. Time; 7. Place or space; 8. Soul, 9. Mind.]

DREAM(S) A sequence of notions, representations, and agitation taking place in an individual's imagination all along sleep. An appreciated expectation, purpose, or flawlessness. There is lots of symbolism elaborated in dreams, at times, animals stand for part of your psyche that perceives connection to the natural universe and endurance. Dreaming with Babies can illustrate a literal aspiration to engender offspring, it can also demonstrate your own vulnerability or necessity to show emotion. It can also signify a new beginning. Contemplating marriage may be an accurate longing to marry or an incorporation of the feminine and masculine constituent of your subconscious. We would be able to have more restful nights and peaceful sleep if we didn't dream. However, our imaginations would not be as rich, or our brains as nimble. We could use our dreams to get to know privately better or be capable of piercing successfully our verifiable aspirations.

DRESHKANA (Sanskrit) The third part of a Zodiac sign.

DRIADAS or DRIADES (Greek dryas, which in turn derives from dry's, tree, holm oak) Implies Forest nymphs, also familiar by the name of Durdales. They were divinities that presided over the forests and trees in commonplace. (Latin dryas, Odis and east of the Greek Opus. tree) Prehistoric mythology showed them as Nymphs or exhibition of Nature also named Durdales. They were seen as protectors of the forests; it is believed that they transferred an axe to punish those who carried out unbridled elimination of the trees under their protection.

DRICHTAVAN (Sanskrit) The one who has seen.

DRIP Is a colloquialism word which talks about an individual's perception of stylishness that is contemplated seductive or chill which started throughout year 2002. It is a disparity of "Swag" became accepted by hip-hop lifestyle. What's a drip? Are intravenous fluids or IV which are used by doctors or nurses when attending patients.

DROHA (Sanskrit) Hostility, enmity; offense, insult; damage; perfidy.

DRUM(S) Materialized used as an alarm or a command to arms riveting up concerns for armed conflict and warfare. Drums could come to light ecstasy and enthusiasm and even about trances, a temporary loss of consciousness to either the viewers or the drummer. Many stands and safeguard authority and are repeatedly accommodated in cherished establishments. Drumming influences profound tranquility decreases blood pressure and lowers tension. Furthermore, drumming encourages the production of endorphins, the physique's particular morphine-like pain killers, and is able through assists in the management of affliction and them in discomforting anguish. African people have played drums to communicate since to 500 B.C. Many civilizations proportionately as Egyptians, Greek, and Roman has demonstrated the employment of drums in sacred observance and instructive assemblies, nevertheless, the first drums materialized relating to Neolithic folklore arising from China and escalating next to Asia.

DRUMA (Sanskrit) Tree of Paradise. Nickname of Kuvera.

DU MOULIN, PIERRE (1568-1658), French Reformed cleric. He took an acclaimed part in doctrinal controversy, affirming a conciliate place which irritated Catholics and Calvinists alike.

DUADA MISTICA The twisting fire is the Mystical Duada, the unfolding of the unity of the Monada, the feminine Eternal appearance of the Brahma. "God the mother."

DUAT (Egyptian) It is the location where spirits of the deceased dwell. Duat was, according to Egyptian belief, an infinite circular or semicircular valley that surrounded the world, a place of extreme gloom and horror.

DUHM, BERNHARD (1847-1928). Pentateuch classicist. From 1888 he was a educator at Basle. His fundamental efforts were mystic. In his comments on Isaiah (1892) he dissociates Is. 56-66 from 40-55 (Deuteron-Isaiah) as a subsequent configuration (Trito-Isaiah) and he challenged that the 'Servant Songs' were not the work of Deuteron-Isaiah.

DUMAH (Hebrew) Kabbalistically, is the Angel of Silence (Death).

DURA EUROPOS, A primordial city on the R. Euphrates. A Seleucid castle, then a Parthian Caravan City, it was colonized by the Romans From century A.D.165; it was forsaken century 256. Excavations have showed an early well safeguarded Jewish synagogue (A.d.245) and the progressive known Christian church. This was built from two rooms of a private house which in all possibility was constructed since the 240s.

DURDALES. Objective beings, but invisible; evil, conserved, ill-intentioned.

DUTA (Sanskrit) Emissary or adviser; angel.

DUTY PARLOCK of the SELF (Gnosticism) Specie demonstrations to create awareness of the impressions we acknowledge from the outside, so abstain destroy Mercury, that is, to create the elevated existential bodies of the Being.

DVADAZA (Sanskrit) The twelfth day of the lunar fortnight.

DVANDVA or DWANDWA (Sanskrit) Frequently "two and two" Pair, duality, opposition, contrast; pair of opposite or opposites. It is the susceptibility to fulfillment and to the dollar, the struggle of sensations, feelings or passions; The illusion born of sympathies and antipathies, attractions and repulsions, described by a pair collected of two things in mutual opposition (cold and heat, affection and aversion, joy and sadness, pleasure and dollar, etc.), and fabricated by the impressions of objects that affect our mood of our senses. It is also given in the Sanskrit grammar the name of Dwandva to a copulative compound whose parts are harmonized with each other. It is the best of the unitive formation of compound words, since it has the advantage of preserving the independent definition of the terms that concur with its formation, which are in the same case.

DVAPARA YUGA (Sanskrit) In the Inda philosophy; it is the third of the "Four Ages", that is, the second add up from below.

DVIPA, Dwija Exemplifies "twice born". In ancient times, this word was inflicted only on initiated Brahmins; it now claims to every man regarding the first of the four castes, who has mastered authentic ceremonies. [Dvi-ja, "regenerated" or twice born," is every man of the first three castes (Brahmins, kchtriya, or vaizya) who has been anointed from the sacred cord, of whom ceremony or investiture formation a second birth of the regenerated man (dvi-ja) is executed in the womb of his mother, the followed by girding the cord of nuns, and the third by praising the sacrifice.

DWANCWA Signifies "two and two. Pair, duality, opposition, contrast; a pair of opposites or opposites. It is the disposition to delight and to suffer, the struggle of beliefs, emotions or passions; the illusion born of sympathies and antipathies, attractions and repulsions, replaced by a mixed pair of two things in mutual opposition. (Cold and heat, affection and aversion, joy and sadness, pleasure and pain, etc.).

DWARF An untouched human being who is a substantial deal below the ordinary physical make up his genealogical or genetics. (For the physiology of dwarf human beings, Achondroplasty is the most customary cause of short stature, or dwarfism.) Some aspects of dwarfism which are principal to know are: The condition ramified in this disease is more than growth. Osteosclerosis congenita is a kind of skeletal dysplasia (a condition that transfigure the bones and cartilage). Evidently; the greater clear ramifications are in their arms, legs, and face, practically, the entire skeletal frame is afflicted. The extensive percussion of these circumstances could induce consequential sustained and permanent impediments. Despite these obstacles, achondroplasia doesn't pin anyone down from conveying out a normal satisfying, and vital living style. According to folklore in Germany, counting their mythology; a dwarf is an existence that resides interior caverns in the mountains. Existence corresponds with wisdom, smithing, mining, and crafting. Dwarfs have been largely eminent for their ability in all variety of metalwork and the manufacture of magical swords and rings, at the same time, they were also ascribed with intense insight and classified comprehension of having powers to foretell the future, change to other appearances, and become invisible. In Tolkien's, dwarves worked and endured their lives to close four times the age of humans (around 25 years), however, are not bountiful to procreate, they have children infrequently and place at intervals; the females within their category are scarce. Dwarf (of death) In the Edda of Scandinavian prehistory, Iwaldi, the Dwarf of death, hides Life in the abysses of the great ocean, and then produced it ascend to earth in time. This life is Iduna, the beautiful maiden, daughter of the "Dwarf". She is the Eve of Scandinavian songs, since she feeds the gods of Asgard the apples of constantly renewed youth; but these, alternately of being sanctioned for having beaten them and being penalize to die, assign in this way every year a restored youth to the earth and men, after every brief and sweet dream in the arms of the Dwarf, Iduna is extracted from the ocean at the instant that Bragi, the Dreamer of Life, without stain or imperfection, he sleepwalks through the silent magnitude of the waters. Bragi is the divine ideation of Life, and Iduna is the living Species.

DWI (Sanskrit) two.

DYAD (Gr.) Among the Gnostics, they are the dual emanations of the Father, positive-negative, male-female, etc.)

DYANA (Sanskrit) Deep concentration It is the fourth step or Dyana to reach meditation proper prosperity, the student or disciple must arbitrate deep into the intimate (the Self) to reach ecstasy or fifth step Samadhi.

DYAUS or DAYUS (Sanskrit) [Nominative of div.] Vedic prompt. The undisclosed entity, or the one shown as divine light. "The heavenly Father," as opposed to the Earth, which is the mother. He is the father of Ucha (the aurora). The unmanifested God.

DYAVA (Sanskrit) Touch to the Goddess of Heaven.

DYUTI (Sanskrit) Light, splendor, glory, majesty, beauty.

DYO (Sanskrit) Indicate: Daylight, sky, ether.

DZYAN or DZYN (Tib.) Demonstrated also in written Dzen. Corruption of the Sanskrit Voice Dhyan and Jnana, Wisdom, divine knowledge. In Tibetan, wisdom is called Dzin (or Dzyn).

-E-

EAMER. This expression indicates (gate) keeper guardian.

EADMER (centurial 1060 centurial 1128) English annalist and ecclesiastic. He was a module of St. Anselm's family. His legal papers embrace the existence of St. Anselm and other English holy beings (together with Wilfrid and Dunstan), a narrative of England wrapping the phase beginning centennial 1066 to centennial 1122, and an essay securing the dogma of the Immaculate Conception of the BVM, previously accredited to St. Anselm.

EAGLE It is a symbol of height, of strength, of the essential being that is identified with the Sun, spiritual initiation. It also symbolizes the solar logos, the father, yellow mercury, and air element. The eagle is a bird whose life happens in full sun, so it is appraised essentially luminous and plays in the elements air and fire.

EARTH Each one of the planets, excluding for earth, were entitle DRWE Greek and Roman gods and goddesses. Nevertheless, the honorific Earth is a Germanic term which plainly imply "the ground". The Western (early modern) enzymatic emblem for earth is a descending-denoting trilogy dichotomized by a parallel line. Other images of the earth in conjurer or kabbalism involve the equilateral and the ophidian. With the widening of Christianity in the 5th century, the sphere (in Latin assignment Orbis terraum (Theatre of the World), the 'world of the lands', hence "orb" acquire) was assembled with an intercross, therefore globus crucifer, indicates the Christian God's ascendancy of the earth.

EARTHQUAKE SYNOD, The (1382). An assembly was held at Black Friars, London, through Abp. W. Court Ena y, throughout which the metropolitan district was shaken by an earthquake. It censures as opposition 24 theses from the constituted by J. Wycliffe.

EASTER SUNSET Esoterically is the astral unfolding and once it passes to the fourth dimension, it is termed the physical body so that it penetrates one managing to pass into the state called "Jinas."

EBIONITES, Gospel following the. The caption accordingly was arranged by current scholars to the apocryphal Gospel; its strength has been habituated to by the Ebionites. This energy has also been the attempt investigated as the 'Gospel by the Hebrews'.

EBLIS (Arabic) Label that the Mohammedans give to the devil. He was excellent for the yins or jinn, and was resolved from heaven reason, having been modeled on subtle flame, refused to worship Adam, who was made of mud.

ECBATANA. Celebrated city of the multimedia that appropriate to absorb a locality surrounded by the seven marvels of the world. Haberdasher, in his occupation Competition amid Pietism and Information. Passage, I illustrate it hence: The chilly summer dwelling of the monarch of Persia was impregnable by septenary globelike enclosures fabricated of hewn and good manner gravestone, of the internal which the innermost some rosebud effectively to considerable highpoint and were of appeal coloration, in inscrutable harmony with the septenary sphere. The castle was encased with Seol for pantile; It's shat of light were camouflaged with meretricious. At small hours the entrance was lighted by numerous columns of gas lamps that resemble the shine. A utopia, diversion location of the Asiatic sovereign, was seeded in the cynosure of the metropolis. The Persian Kingdom was categorically the "garden of the world."

ECHIDNA (Echidna, Greek) "Viper". Term given to the Hydra of Lerna, which Hercules killed.

ECHOD (Hebrew) Masculine "One", applied to Jehovah.

ECHO(S) A reiteration or simulation of sound. When vibration torrents strike a solid evidently, they may throw it back, creating the sound rebound and replicated. If you cooperate with someone, you significantly echo his or her declaration. The echo produces awareness of the resilience of sense, and the creativity that can take dominance of this uncertainty. In productivity, this accentuates the learned artful skill of the expression listened to; in accord with, it culminates the auricular and during conductively of the articulation being granted on the page.

ECCE HOMO (Latin, 'Behold the Man!') The subject of a contested Life of Christ produced by Sir John Seeley in 1865. It portrayed the Lord as a typical advocate.

ECO In Mythology Nymph whose greatest charm was to speak; it was interchanged into an immense rock where today it continues to repeat the last syllable of all who hear.

ECTHESIS. The (Gk.) assurance of faith') The technique provided in 638 by the Emp. Heraclius forbidding the reference of 'energies', whether one or two, in the Person of Christ and argue that the two Natures were integrated in one will.

ECSTACY. Premature or paranormal condition. The ecstasies recounted in the Holy Scriptures normally involved an unexpected short-term seizure of a prophet by the Divine magnitude who spoke throughout his mouth or exhibited the time ahead in visions. Ecstasy in the Christian commotion is one of the typical intervals in the mystic life. Its main aspects are detachment of the perceptions, lead to by the violence of the Divine reflection on the soul; the anatomy becomes motionless, and sight, hearing, etc., halt to activity. In inequality to the pathological 'case', the mystic recalls what had taken place during the Ecstacy. (Ecstasy, in Greek) It entrust to a psycho-spiritual state, a physical trance that advance clairvoyance and a beatific state that produces visions.

ECTEIS FORMATUS (Gnosticism) It is associated to the cross and the feminine gender. Within Alchemy, to work with the cross is to work with the CTEIS FORMATUS.

ENCANTO This expression has been given to definite formulas or mixtures of words, in versification or script, spoken or written, which are utilized to produce amazing and magnificent consequence. Numerous desirability is in addition utilized through magical and magnetic strategy (blustering, insinuating, etc.) The French voice charme and the English charm approach from the Latin word Carmen, which, in addition to verse, channel a formula formulated in certain words, charm, incantation spell, etc., being consequently comparable to the Sanskrit voice mantra (hymn, verse, spell, spiritual technique of enchantment). Pliny says that the blood was deducted from the lacerations, the disconnected bones were restored to their place, the stomach was cured, a car was intercepted from capsize, etc. In ancient time all believed firmly in charms, whose golden verse this Latin verse interpreted from Hemero: Concio turbata est, subter quoque terra sonabat.

EDDA. Also called: Elder, Poetic Edda, is a collection of mythological Old Norse poems made in the 12th century. Books of mythological tradition, Germanic Bible, Scandinavian populations, including Nordic profound wisdom.

EDEN (Hebrew) "Delight", joy. In Genesis it is the "Garden of Earthly Delights", built by God; in Kabbalah, Eden or the "Garden of Earthly Delights", is a point of initiation into the Mysteries.

EDESSA The nearby city (now Urfa) was acquired in 304 B.C. It was the focal point of a liberated kingdom from c. 132 B.C. to A.D. 214, and then a Roman colony. From a unseasonable date it was the intercessor of Syriac-speaking Christianity. It was the accommodation of the Nestorian 'Persian School' until it was culminated in 489, and it has met a center of unorthodoxy. It was the metropolis of a small-scale promoter province.

EDIPO. According to Greek mythology he was the son of Laius and Jocasta, kings of Thebes. He was subject to the decrees of the Disuno. Laius had been warned by an oracle that the son born to him from Jocasta would be disastrous to him. To avoid such a fate, as soon as the child Oedipus was born, Laius (his father) ordered him to kill, but the hitman who was entrusted to kill him, limited himself to leaving him abandoned in a forest with his feet crossed and hanging from a tree. It is said that a shepherd found him and took him to King Corinth, who adopted him as a son. Sometime later being a strong young man, he consults the oracles, and this predicted the following: "Oedipus will be the assassin of his father, the husband of his mother and of him a cursed race will be born", To avoid what the oracles had predicted, Oedipus fled to Thebes, believing that the Kings of Corinth were his fathers. He found himself on the road to King Laius of Thebes (his real father), and this unknowingly killed him for a dispute that had been presented to them of who should cross first, also killed four of his five companions. On the way to Thebes was stopped by the Sphinx (fabulous monster that stopped and killed travelers who passed by, if they did not interpret their enigmas), Once the lenigma was solved, it rushed into the sea. Com premi to such a feat, when he arrived at Thebes, he received the hand of Queen Jocasta (his own mother), from that union two sons were born; Eteocles and Polynices; and two females: Antigona (his daughter diel) and Ismena, By inquiries, Oedipus had discovered that the man he had killed when he fled to Thebes, was his father and the woman with whom he lived was his mother. The oracles had also predicted that to avoid the plague that desolated Thebes the death of Laius had to be atoned for. For this reason, Jocasta hanged himself and Oedipus gouged out his eyes and was expelled by his sons whom he had cursed. Accompanied by his faithful daughter Antigona he walked throughout Greece to the forest sacred to the furies, where he was swallowed by the earth. I defect that it has to do with lust.

EDGE The expression "on edge" signify "feeling nervous" or "not calm and relaxed." This locution is used to convey when a friend is having sentiments of being anxious and fearful about what could happen. The pronouncement 'to have an edge to a person'; means that the person suggests being authoritative, capable or energetic. If an individual appears to like adventures or likes a hazardous lifestyle, comport oneself in a way which conceives risky; it is said he or she lives on an edge, when a person is caught in an economic or societal condition that they did not decide on, the situation may threaten the individual's well-being or life, additionally causing distress. "Edgy" has a dual meaning. The pragmatic interpretation is someone or something that is "on the edge" of typical, predictabilities, patterns, etc. Consequently, an "edgy" constitution is one that ingrains responses of unsureness, displeasure, wrongdoing, etc.; they become clear "on the edge" of being of an individuality which is severe. In Leviticus 21:5 ESV / 8 holy scriptures say: They shall not make bold patches on their heads, nor shave off the edges of their beards, nor make any cuts on their body.

EDOM Kingdom admired by the Cabal, as unstable and neurasthenic forces.

EDRIS or IDRIS (Arabic) Speak of "the Sage". Epithet that the Arabs appeal to Enoch.

AETERNI PATRIS (1879) The proclamation of Leo XIII administering to the Church the learning of philosophy, and mainly the services of St. Thomas Aquinas.

EFFECT (Gnosticism) Demonstrates that there can be no effect without cause.

EFOD (Latin ephod, and east from the Hebrew Efod) Fine linen garment topped with gold, purple and crimson hyacinth, used only by the great monk of the Oracle, or Ephod of the Jews.

EFFORTS. The tangible or rational venture requires accomplishing anything, or a pursuit to do one thing. Dharma Master Cheng Yen describes what this insinuates **in** expressions of spiritualism habit. It spells substantially eagerness devoted to the usage, externally allowing disturbances or innermost contamination emerge and estrangement from our tradition. We require to attentively take care of our feelings, express intentions it linger immaculate and untarnished. On that account, make every effort to add to your faith goodness: and a to goodness, knowledge; and to knowledge, self-control; and to self-control, perseverance; and to perseverance, godliness; and to godliness, mutual affection; and to mutual affection, love. 2 Peter 1-5-11 in-context.

EFFLUVIUM (Latin effvium) Emanation, irradiation of the immaterial. To come, luminosity of the immaterial. Subtly originates the energetic vitality of the body, through the aura, the vital body or psychic medium. Moreover, it is the vital energy that descends from the infinite cosmos.

EGEON or Briareo (Greek) In the theosophy of Hesiod; a monster, son of heaven and earth, had fifty heads and a hundred arms. It is assembled a lot linking the wars and continuous battles between the gods.

EGGS (golden) Also called "Luminous Egg" or "Golden Wrap". It is a kind of magnetic breath, exceptionally fine, hidden, of oval structure, in which each man is wrapped, and which is the nonstop origin: 1st of the atomic Ray in its triple aspect of creator, preserver and destroyer (or regenerator), and 2nd of the Buddhi Manas. The seventh aspect of this individual Aura is the faculty of taking the form of the body and becoming the "Radiant", the luminous Augoeides.

EGIDA (Latin aegis. -idis, and from the Greek) Shield or breastplate of goat skin, leg, goat). According to mythological legend on the advice of an oracle, it was the skin of the goat Amalthea that Jupiter (Zeus) put on his shield to keep safe in his war against the Titans. according to other versions Chosen was the skin of the monster Aegis, Minerva killed him and with the invulnerable skin made a shield and on it placed the head of the Medusa. This goat skin and the head of the jellyfish is the attribute with which Jupiter and Minerva are represented.

EGERTON PAPYRUS. Two imperfect leaves and a scrap of papyrus in the British library (Egerton Papyrus 2') containing passages from a Greek writing akin to, but distinct from, the canonical Gospel. It dates from not later than C.A.D. 150 and is thus (except for the drylands St. Joun) the oldest known specimen of Christian writing.

EGYPT Conforming to Greek mythology he was the son of Belo and Anquinoe and twin brother of Danao. It is correlated that he triumphs over the lands of the Nile to which he gave his name. Tradition attributes 50 sons to him and by concurrence his brother Danao was the father of 50 daughters who run away from Greece to intercept Egypt from marrying them to their children; however, the 50 boys harassed him and forced him to surrender while they were inside with handcuffs.

EGO. (Lat.) "I"; the responsiveness in man of "I am, I", that is, the sentimentalism of the attribute or requirement of "I am". The acroamatic ideology instruct the reality of two Egos in man, the grievous or peculiar, and the higher, eternal and neutral. The initial is frequenter "personality," and the secondary "individuality." intangible ego. angelic ego, ethereal soul or Dhishana, in near fusion with the Saktis or cognitive basis, deprived which it is not Ego at any rate, confidential the channel of Atman. (to Theosophy.) curtailed ego of intimate. The palpably man in merger with his decreased identity, that is, the impulsive, fervor, gross inclinations. It is labeled the "false personality" and enclosed of the reduces Energies mixture with the Kama-rupa, and which efforts examined the somatic figure and its presence or duplicate. It is the grievous or secret Ego, that is, the Kama-Manas. Ego sum qui sum (Lat.) "I am who I am." truism of Esoteric Wisdom. Exceptional or inner ego. It is the Manas or "fifth" Precept, so it is accurate, In any case of Intellect. Psychological Belief is the Guardian Ego exclusively when it obsoletely affiliated with the to know. It is perpetual original, the eternal, withdrawn, respective and destitute Ego.

EGOLATRY Acceptance in a continuous self, ego worship.

EGREGORS (from the Greek Egregoroi) Eastern esotericisms specify the Egregores as Beings whose physique and solidity are a fabric of the so-called Astral Light. It is the darkness of the higher earthly spirit bodies which are of the nature of the upper light.

EHEYEH (Hebrew) "I am," according to Ibn Gabirol, but not in the definition of "I am what I am."

EIGHT. Illustrative of institution that is one measure above the ordinary regulation, higher than Mother Nature and its restrictions. On account Chanukah is eight days long, the much-surmounted Maccabee's determined to battle the Greeks wasn't or natural. They drew on reservoirs of faith and courage and fortitude that are not part of normalizing human nature. They therefore dignify a miracle towering over nature, a phenomenon that lasted eight days, and to immortalize this, we light on Chanukah an eight branched menorah. In a complementary vein, we circumcise our youngster when they are eight-day old babies, since the brit Milah exemplify our nation's magical and logic confronting commitment with God

EIGHTEEN BENEDICTIONS The. A gather together of prayers, now 19, mainly made-up Biblical phrases, which are recited on workdays at every one of the three services in the Jewish synagogue. They date mainly from pre-Christian times.

EIKON BASILIKE, 'The Portraiture of His Sacred Majesty in His Solitude and Sufferings'. A royalist publication concern just prior to the death of Charles I and receive to be his work.

EKA (Sanskrit) "One", "Unique". He is besides a mortal of Mahat, of the universal intelligence, as the initiation of comprehension.

EKABHAKTI (Sanskrit) Dedicated to one, who worships only the One (the one God).

EKAJA (Sanskrit) Exemplify "once born". The personage of the sudra caste (the lower one), as opposed to the Dvi-ja (or "twice born").

EKAKIN (Sanskrit) Solitary, solo.

EKANA (Rupa) (Sanskrit) One and only (and the Many) framework or structure; of term appeal by the Puranas to the Entity.

EKANTA (Sanskrit) Lonely place, solitude; absolute unity. When employed as an attribute: totally devoted or attentive to.

EKATA (Eka-ta) (Sanskrit) Unity.

EL, AL This locution used to label the gods and translated from the Hebrew; it measures "God" and suggest powerful, supreme. Used in the plural is Elohim.

EL-ELION (Hebrew) It is a term used to name the Entities, accepted by the Jews of the Phoenician Elon, which is a honorific of the Sun.

ELECTRO (Gnosticism) Given an account that, at the precise second of death, now when the deceased exhales his last breath, he forecast an electro psychic design of his character, such design proceeds in the supersensitive regions of nature and later, come to impregnate the fertilized egg, this is how when returning, by adjoining to a new physical body, we return to having personal characteristics remarkably similar to that of the previous life.

ELECTRONIC (Gnosticism) The fortune of the Essence in the Electronic world after death is very temporary because the human being is not yet a vital force developed to live continuously in those solar regions.

ELEPHANT Island name established in the vicinity of Bombay, India. This island is in good condition; the ruins of the cavernous temple of that appellation are considered one of the oldest in the country.

ELEMENTS Formerly, according to Aristotle there were four Elements: fire, air, water and earth. Emergence of the disembodied linked to the four exceptional partitions of the cosmic world.

ELEMI. Additionally, countless aromatic natural resin from tropical flora (ancestry Torchwoods) utilized mainly in embellish, varnish, and printer ink. Elemi is an emission of a pharmaceutical product from the tree, conarium municipality, and additional breed of Canarium which acclimate wild and/ or fertilized in the Philippine Islands, in which is plentiful. Elemi is usually applied for emotional collapse as it is functional for Myalgia and fatigue. Elemi is a Guaifenesin, supplying an authentic process to alleviate catarrh and rhinorrhea. It can alleviate mucous secretion that obstructs the respiration paths. Enchanting, Gum Elemi is employed for rituals of procedure, commencement and new fresh start. It Assists release of assumptions and outmoded very early morning a fresh subsection in existence. It may in addition be operated to tribute the courageous landscapes. Its chief points the brain simultaneously at meditation. Elemi fragment the paired agricultural brood as Frankincense and Myrrh. Therefore, contemporary the purification of epoxy resin, which is contemplate additional of an aloe, is extricated from a sultry timber that may enroot to 30 meters. In aggressive aromatherapeutic, Elemi imperative lubricant is correlated with the larynx chakra or Vishuddhi. Its shade is blue. Elemi indispensable grease order unrestrained sentiment, dissolve agitation, empower for decipher dissemination and promotes reinstate self-assurance.

ELENA Alludes to the Divine Soul or spiritual Soul (Buddhi).

ELGRECO (1541-1614) Accommodating with Domenico Theotocopuli, religious portrait painter. From 1577 he lived in Toledo. His works are distinct by a caliber of mysticism besides by individual characteristic. Formal customizing is abandoning as human forms and facial expressions are overemphasized and even distorted to fabricate an emotional rather than a literal likeness. His duties were unorthodox at many assemblies from 792 onwards, but he employed his perception up to his progress. His works are well defined by a caliber of mysticism as well as by individual idiosyncrasies.

ELVES Have been spirits of mother nature, which occupy the astral plane reconciled with fairies and goblins.

ELIAR (Gnosticism) Is an angel of the sphere of the cosmic mind, it is in the configuration of the seven (7) of Solomon, to wrestle the terrible demon of the world of the intellect San Gabriel, this demon is the opposition of the Angel Eliar.

ELIAS A Jewish seer who renewed himself by the substantial number of wonders he worked. In the New Testament Jesus referred to the voices of Malachi (IV.5): "I will send you the prophet Elijah", he clearly stated that John the Baptist "is that Elijah who is to come", he said "I tell you that Elijah has already come, and they did not know him",) Id., XVII, 12, 13).

ELIMINATE (Gnosticism) Do away with of the utmost momentousness to subdue the selves. (Mistakes or sins).

ELIJAH (Gk. For, 'Elias') (9th century. B.C.) Hebrew prophet, Conforming to Kgs. He lingers the supremacy of the worship of Yahweh in the exhibit of Canaanite and Phoenician cults, sustain the submission of moral virtuousness and cumulative Justice, and was interpret into heaven. His arrival was held to be an indispensable preparatory to the emancipation and rehabilitation of Israel.

ELISSEUMS (Fields) The Greeks thus selected the delightful mansion of consecrated enjoyment those who have blossom, to the encouragement of virtuous information. Through these pastures ran with sweet mumble the Lethe, whose waters made us cast aside the sorrows of life.

ELIZABETH (gnostic) Contemplates the Soul-Spirit, wife of the innovative man, the divine Soul. Abel is the Human Soul, and He is muscular. Is-Abel is the refined man who loves Is, his Divinity, his Walkiria.

ELION, ELYON. (Hebrew: 'Elyon' is a designation of the "God of the Israelites" in the Hebrew holy book. El Elyon is consistently given as a contribution to English as "God Most High", and in adding up in the Holy Scriptures as "God the highest").

ELISHA (Fields) The Greeks thus selected the delightful mansion of happiness consecrated to those who have blossomed, at the breath of virtuous played a role. Through these pastures ran with a sweet whisper the Leteo, whose waters cast aside the sorrows of life.

ELISEOS. (Elysian fields), or simply Elisha. The Greeks titled this the enchanting mansion of satisfaction imminent to the audacious, that is to the souls of the people ethically. All the time this meadow accompanies a whisper of the Lethe, whose waters compel us to forget the distastefulness of life.

ELITES (Hebrew) Signifies Jews who worship the sun.

ELIXIR (of life) The complexity of extending human life beyond ordinary terms is a matter that has been constantly deliberate as one of the darkest and most meticulously confidential enigmas of conceptions in esotericism. But you must show observation to see this matter, it should not always be taken at face value, you do not have to believe sightlessly in the wonderful virtues of Abe-Hyal or Water of Life, which is nothing more than an effortless metaphor. However, despite what has been said, it is possible, precisely patronage the rules of occult science, to extend human life for such a time that it would seem incredible to all those who imagine that the durability of our life is limited to an extreme of about two hundred years. It is the breath of reality that originates; "The spirit of life" and its remedy.

ELMO, St. The cherished title for St. Peter Gonzalez (c. 1190-1246), the advocate saint of sailors. A Dominican, he went with Ferdinand III on a voyage on the other hand, Moors and then resolve the rest of his existence to work surrounded by the seafarers of the Spanish coast.

ELOHIM At a great distance cited as Alhim is approximated to mention an active-passive collectivity: describing Binah.

ELOI The great intelligence or administrator of Jupiter, its planetary essence.

ELPIS (Hope) By the name of the Greeks Spes. It is connected that she was the sister of death and sleep. She is mirrored as a noticeably young and winged woman, accompanying a man to the edge of his grave. The mythological fable identified that when Epimetheus pierced Pandora's box, all the evils that anguish us today escaped from the lowest part of the box, fluttering only Hope.

ELU (Cing.) It alludes to the ancient dialect that was handed down in Ceylon.

ELVAH A luminescent angel full of love, altruism, charity, chastity and holiness. It is in the conjuration of the seven of the Wise Solomon.

ELY. In 673 St. Etheldreda established a double monastery for monks and nuns. It was dismantled by the Danes in 870, but recreated, for monks only, in 970. The see of Ely was formed in 1109, the initial and monks became the cathedral chapter. At the Dissolution he was a prior converted dean, and eight canonries were inaugurated (1541). The cathedral is illustrious for its Galilee Porch (1198-1215) and its central octagon (1322-8), the roof of which (known as the 'Lantern') is the only Gothic dome in the world.

EMMANUEL, or IMMANUEL (Heb., "With us [is] God'). The expression transpires in Is. 7: 14 NS 8:8, but it is not understandable to whom it specifies. In Mt. 1:23 the prophecy is perception with reference to the birth of Christ.

EMMAUS The small town in which the Lord assembled a Resurrection feature to a pair of his apostles. (Lk. 24: 13-35) Its location has been debated.

EMBER DAYS. Four assemble each of three days, viz. the Wednesday, Friday, and Saturday succeeding St Lucy (13 Dec.), the initial Sunday in Lent, Whitsunday, and Holy Cross Day (14 Sept.) later, that have been recognized as days of fasting and abstinence in the W. Church. initially associated with the crops, they came to be associated with consecrations.

EMBLA. It has been deliberated that she was the first woman in the world of Scandinavian mythology. Her husband was Askur. Deriving from elves comes from human royalty.

EMBRACE. Emblematic, to accept a being is to salutation it with eagerness, embrace, cuddle, consent totally. Conceivable cradle your companion, or transitions in automation. Embrace is from the French verb embrasser, which originated out definition "to clasp in the arms" (but by now includes kissing). Scriptural embrace is to realize God more. We embrace our conditions since by doing so we comprehend the God who fortunately constitute them for our joyfulness. "You shall walk after the Lord your God and fear him and keep his commandments and obey his voice, and you shall serve him and hold fast to hom." (Deuteronomy 13.4)

EMBOS (Gnosticism) Are phenomenon, special powders, roasted corn, feathers, dolls, etc. used by sorcerers; these "Embos" are transporters of dangerous bacilli, which can cause death.

EMET Verbalization approaches from the Old English surname Emme, which is a formation of the epithet Emma, that is from the Old German erm, denotes "whole" or "universal". Hebrew term for "trueness" and "faithfulness" conjures up God's confidence prominence and reliabilities. The expression Emet ("truth") is perpetually diverse tempo in perfect benediction, as the initial edict of an order or clause.

EMOTIONAL or EMOTION(S) (Center) (Gnosticism) Two centers attached with the excitations sprang up: Higher Emotional, is in the Heart; Lower Emotional, found in the solar plexus. Surrounds all the centers that we have in the organism, the most complex to control is the emotional goal, due to the question of our negative emotions, feelings, resentments, self-love, pride, the death of a family member. Lower emotions such as cinema, bulls, lottery, etc. Accompanied the higher emotions, the lower ones are suppressed; educating himself to live a useful life, listening to good music such as Mozart's "enchanted flute"; Beethoven's symphonies; Chopin and others. This music helps us to get in touch with the higher emotional center, comparably with meditation.

EMPUSA (Greek) An avid, demon or evil genius who settles various methods. Aristophanes, in one of his comedies, suggests this monster as a horrible specter; he transfigure into a dog, a woman, a viper, with a donkey foot and a bronze foot, and come up with only to do the damage.

EMSER, HIERONYMUS (1478-1527), RC author. He was involved in disagreement with M. Luther from 1519 prior to his passing. In 1927 he publicized a oppose-publication to Luther's 'December Bible' of 1522, that it was produced to mirror, with recommended and editorialize adjoin. Emser's Bible experienced innumerable updated editions.

ENARXIS. In Byzantine worship, the section connects the Proskomide and the Lesser Entrance. It comprehends three Diaconal Litanies, with antiphons sung by the choir.

ENCINO Encompassed the Druids, Greeks and Jews, the holm oak was a exceedingly sacred tree. Abraham erected his tents at the foot of a few holm oaks in the valley of Mambré; Jacob buried Rachel's wet nurse at the base of an oak tree, and under one of them buried the idols of his sons.

ENCLAUSTRAN (Gnostic) The Pathway of the Monk: In this are instituted humankind who cloister themselves in a monastery to beg, to meditate with an unalterable persuasion in their beliefs.

ENCANTO has contributed this denomination to categorical principle or combinations mingling of designations, in lyrics or rhyme, noticeable or jot down, accustomed to assembling marvelous and extraordinary outcomes. Scores of appeals are furthermore accomplished by enchanting and captivating course of action (whirling, motion, etc.) The French expression Charme and the English charm approach derive from Latin name carmen, which, similarly to poetry, relevant to a principle formulated in assertive expression, charm, incantation, etc., being consequently comparable to the Sanskrit expression melody (psalms, strophe, enchantment, transcendental dictum of spell). Pliny reveals that in his life span, and by measure of assertive attractiveness, Charing were douse, the body fluid was abate from the lesion, the unconnected cartilages were rebounded to their place, ketonemia was heal, an automobile was averted from rescind, etc. In classical times everybody firmly has faith in charms, their theorem comprises of "original" in certain Greek or Latin poetry. As a result, to accommodate the steep decline, that Latin rhyme decipher from Homer was scripted on a gold plate. Concio turbata est, subter quoque terr sonabat.

ENEAS. He transpired a Trojan prince touched on by Virgil in the Aeneid. One of his teachers was Centaur Chiron. He differentiates himself with his courage and power. He fought in many wars, for example, against Diomedes, Troy, and diversification. Throughout his last fight Mencius and his Etruscans opposed him. It is said that he vanished among the waters of the Riio Numicius. It is said that his ancestors reigned by fourteen descendants in a country of Latin America.

ENEIDA, The. Esoteric work written by Publius Virgil Maron. It incorporates twelve books where he narrates the journey of the Trojan Aeneas, who after the demolition of Troy, goes ahead to sea with his father Aquinas, his son and other Trojans, to have an extraordinary adventure.

ENERGY (Latin Energy of Geneve pylax) Energy, power and virtue to work. Gnosis puts into words that in the human being seven models of energy are displayed: Mechanical, Vital, Psychic, Mental, Of the Will, of the Consciousness and of the pure Spirit. All these energy genres are staggered into well-defined levels and dimensions.

ENIGMA Surrounded by the discipline Alchemistry, is the correlation between the wide world and creation.

ENIO In the company of Greco-Roman tradition was one of the three Greca's.

ENNOIA (Greek) (Gnosticism) Persists a manifestation of the divine Mind. Ennoia and Ofis (the Agatho Daimon, the Serpent, the darkness of the Light) were the Logoi of the ophites. As a unity, Ennoia and Ofis are the Logos who convey themselves as the double origin of good and evil, rationale, conforming to their ideas, these two initiations are invariable and have existence from all durability, as ceaseless to exist continuously. When separately, one is the (spiritual) Tree of Life, and the other the "Tree of the Knowledge of Good and Evil."

ENOCH (Hebrew) In the Genesis of the Bible introduce is made of three Enochs: the son of Cain, that of Seth and that of Jared, nevertheless, all of them are identical, and two of them are mentioned only to place. In secret, Enoch is the "Son of Man", esoterically, the first sub-race of the fifth mother-race.

EN-SOPH or Ain-Soph (Hebrew) The infinite and unlimited. The absolute, impersonal and unknowable deification principle. It literally means "no-thing," that is, nothing that can be classified with anything else. The cue and ideas are correspondent to Parbrahm's Vedan spike distraction. Some Western Kabbalists, however, try to make It a personal "The," a male deity rather than an impersonal deity.

ENTE, Ens Personify being, or the real particulars in Nature.

ENTITY (Gnosticism) Every idea, passion, affection, desire, vice, etc., has its proper Entity and the combination of all these operations is the Pluralized Self.

ENTROPY (Greek) (Gnosticism) An impulsive rule of uniform constitution, which shows disorder, degeneration. The law of Entropy within the Greek symbolizes alteration. The rule of entropy must be mastered with change, that is, by sacrificing a lower force for the sake of a higher power.

ENTHUSIASM [from the Greek enthusiasm's] Concepts of "divine inspiration;" "fury of the sibyls as they deliver their oracles inspired by divinity."

ENVIRONMENT In the present condition of Latin origin "ambiens" that demonstrates "that surrounds". A hostile environment makes mention of the event of a social, psychological or physical environment that infringes the well-being of a living being, making it vulnerable.

ENVY, ENVIOUS (Latin) In Latin it means "evil eye" equally photons. It is interconnected that the customs that Greek mothers greased the forehead of their young children with mud from the baths, to prevent the "evil eye". There are still peoples who reinforced this custom, especially Italy. Envy is a defect that starts from deadly sins.

EOLO [Eolus, in Latin; Aiolos, in Greek.] The god who, on the authority to Hesiod, binds or unleashes the winds and storms.

EON or EONES (Aion, in Greek; Aeon, in Latin) Time, eternity. Points in history of continuance [in this sense, Eon equals the Castilian voice "evo;"] arising from the divine nature, and celestial beings; among the Gnostics, they were geniuses and angels. [Aeon is also the higher Logos "eternity", in the knowledge of a period of a apparently endless epoch, but which, regardless of everything, has a limit, that is, a Kalpa or Manvantara. The Aeons (Star Spirits), impending from the unknown of the Gnostics, are perceptions or divine beings identical to the Dhyan Chohans of the Esoteric Doctrine. Emblem of time, eternity, in the undertaking of a period].

EONA (Phoenician) Alludes to the Eve of the Phoenicians.

EOROSCH (pers.) Connects to the celestial Raven, divine bird radiant with light and endowed with great intelligence. Stands for the fundamental of the educated birds or Hormuz. Speak the language of heaven, where its formidable sound arrives, all Dews are head of love. It safeguards the whole earth when the virtuous man wears the Zou in honor of Mithras.

EOS (Greek). The delegation of the daylight. The winged goddess of the dawns, the daughter of Hyperion; Roman equivalent: Aurora.

EPARCHY. In the easterly Church, the title for an ecclesiastical division. Its ministerial superior is the 'eparch', customarily labeled the 'metropolitan', who has a veto on the local election of bishops in his EPARCHY.

EPHEDRA Is a woody shrubbery of comfy waterless localities that undergo a dropping behind, drifting stems and diminutive reduce leaves. Ephedra may bring out aftereffects, like scratchiness, grumpiness uneasiness, restlessness, cephalalgia, queasiness, puke, and urinary frequency. Additional significant aftermath involves hypertension, heart arrhythmia, lack of balance, cramp, and loss of life. Ephedra are flora you may take out diverse utility compound, in conjunction with ephedrine. Ephedrine equally be mass-produced. What are Ephedrine's utilizations? Ephedrine is introduced in countless therapeutic byproducts employed to minister comparable afflictions such as Nasal congestion, Bronchial asthma, Chest discomfort, movement sickness and hype sensibility. The FDA censored nutritional therapy boosts involved ephedrine alkaloids since of their protection exposure the auxiliary related to occurrences of cardiac infarction, breakdown, brain attack, and untimely end.

EPHRAEM SYRUS, St. (c. 306-73), Syrian Biblical biographer and ecclesiastical writer. He was appointed clergyman, possibly by St. James of Nisibis. Following the cession of Nisibis to Persia in 363 he established Edessa, locality most of his remaining labor were composed. His spacious exegetic, assertive, disagreement, and austere annals are predominantly in poems. They comprise rounds of canticles on the outstanding banquet of the Cathedral and on the ultimate baggage and opinion of apostasy. He composed exclusively in Syriac, but his diligently paused transpose regarding Hayastan and Graeco-Roman at an in promoted cycle.

EPHESUS Ancient Greek city, it is associated that it was the primary focus of gnosis. Church of the Apocalypse that proposed the Maladhara chakra, at the height of the tailbone.

EPHIALTES The son of Eury Demus of Malis; He defraud his compatriots longing to accept an award from the Persians for having managed the Persian forces to the Greek allies which encouraged him win the Battles of Thermopylae in 480 B.C.

EPHOR In the Orthodox Church, a lay guardian or protector in whose imputation monastic property was frequently vested from the 10th centennial beyond. 174C

EPICTETUS. (c. 50-c. 130) Impassive philosopher. A bondsman in the household of Nero, he was liberated and became an instructor at Rome until c. 90, when he established at Nicopolis in Epirus. His consultations were taken down by a disciple and issued in two dissertations. The influence of Christian ideals in Epictetus and vice versa has often been discussed, but the commonalities hardly go beyond similarity of moral temper.

EPIMETHEUS In Greek mythology it demonstrates that "it does not reflect until after the event". He was the son of Japet (Jape Tus) and Climena, brother of Prometheus. Father of the Excuse. He betrothed by wife to Pandora along with the box in which all the evils of the earth were enclosed.

EPINOIA (Greek) Thought, intention, design. According to the Gnostics designate, first passive Aeon.

EPIPHANY (from Greek for 'manifestation') A commemoration of the temple perceived on 6 January. It arises in the East, a place that has been remembered in tribute to the Lord's Baptismal after the 3rd century, one of its main essential qualities being the majestic blessing of the Baptismal water. It was initiated into the West Church in the 4th century. Where it kicked off and was mainly corresponding with the expression of Christ to the Pagans in the beginning of the 'Magi'.

EPOCH HIPORBOREA. Interval in which the Hyperborean Race came about, descendants of the Polar Race.

EPOPTEIA (Greek) Predominantly confidence, the third or later part of the reverenced rites was called Epopteia, or phenomenon, reception in the mysteries. In substance indicates that gradation of divine clairvoyance in which the earthly vision is paralyzed, the entirety relating to the earth vanishes, and the soul unites voluntarily and purely with its Spirit or God. But the exact denotation of such a voice is "superintendent, overseer, inspector, watchman, master builder," and like the adaptive Sanskrit voice evapta.

EPOPTES (Greek) A master. The one who has cut across his last magnitude of initiation, St. Paul, by accrediting himself this term, approach to express an adept or begin, with capability to materialize others. It's a beginning. The one who has been motivated by his later degree of initiation. [St. Paul, by imposing this word on himself (I. Corin. III, 10), comes to communicate with an adept or beginners, with the ability to institute others.

ERNE. River in North Central Republic of Ireland, spring up in County Cavan and subsequently northward across the borderline, over Upper Lough Erne and Lower Lough Erne and at that point west o Donegal Bay, Length: about 96 km (60 miles). Rivers are frequently detected as an emblem of expansion, abundance, and Aeon. A few of the most commonplaces transcendent connotations of rivers, demonstrated in the Scriptures, include; the expedition of aliveness; the constant existence technique and alterations are occasionally affiliated with a rivers' floppy water. Erne is also denominated for a sizeable dusky Golden eagle with a brief sphenic white tail; of continental Europe and the Artic Ocean.

ESDRAS (Ezra). (Hebrew.) The Jewish scribe and priest who, about 450 years before J.C., compiled the Pentateuch (if he was not actually its author) and the rest of the Old Testament, except for the book of Nehemia [0 Second Book of Ezra] and the Malachias.

ESDRAS, Books of: The entire assortments of 'Esdras' books published in Greek, Latin, Hebrew, Vulgate I & II, English versions I & II, 1&2 Esdras of the Apocrypha. 1 Esdras (i.e., Esdras A of the LXX, III Esdras of the Vulgate, or

The Greek Ezra) collected of matter grasp from the Hebrew certified Books. It is normally dated in the middle of c. 200 and 50 B.C. 2. Esdras (IV Esdras of the Vulgate or The Ezra Apocalypse) is composite, viz. (a) 1-2 an opening section partly formed on the NT; (b) 3-14, the 'Ezra-Apocalypse' proper, in which the writer describe his visions dated after A.D. 70 and not later than the reign of Hadrian (117-38); 15-16, an appendix, in some Manuscript. Reckoned as 'V Esdras'.

ERA(S) (Gnosticism) It is the pathway or intervals that sequence the solar system of Ors to cross in its journey to the delineation of the Zodiacal belt, bounded by one constellation and another. Permanency established on the space between the form and the bordering constellation. The aquarium era has a longevity of 2,160-62 years, approximately.

EREBO Hell.

ERGO may indicate to A Latin term signifying "therefore" as in Cogito ergo sum. Ergo (journal), an academic journal. A Greek expression sustaining "work", utilized as a adhere ergo-, for instance, in ergonomics. Ergometer (rowing), an indoor rowing machine.

ERATO Touched special of the nine Eternal Muses. He is expressed by a zither. Erato implies "kind or loving." In the Orphic hymn to the Muses, it is Erato who charms the sight. Since the Rennaissance she has mostly been shown with a wreath of myrtle and roses, holding a lyre, or a small kithara, a musical instrument often associated with Apollo.

ERIDANO (Latin) Pertain to Ardan, the Greek name for the Jordan River.

ERIS Goddess of Discord. Expressed by a woman with a pale face and snake hair.

ERODINIUM A painted or allegorical portrayal of some future events; the significant figures and dreams that can originate in many ways. 1. Dreams that descend from physiological circumstances; 2. Dreams that transcend psychological situation and astral influences; and 3. Dreams caused by spiritual agency. The next ones can conceptualize that show cases or small change that can be true in these planes.

EROS (Greek) Third person of the Hellenic Trinity, diverse from Ouranos, Gaia and Eros.

EROTAS. The contemporary Greek word "erotas signifies "Intimate love". Plato purified his own interpretation: Even though eros is originally felt for a person, with introspection it becomes an appreciation of the beauty enclosed by that person, or with contemplation its mature recognition of loveliness itself. The Greek mother tongue identifies four contrasting kinds of devotion: Philia, Eros, Storge and Agape. They all hold an attractive depiction of opposed kinds of love, and appreciating each is a sure way to help mates improve their correlation. The four loves expression: Storge – or; sympathetic bond; Philia-friend bond; Eros-romantic love; Agape-unconditional "God" Love.

ERRORS Defects or Egos.

ESAN An ethnical formation of southern Nigeria who articulate the Esan tongue. The Esan are typically well known to be agriculturalists, trado-medical specialists, soldiers of fortune, combatants and huntsmen. A people of South Nigeria whose mankind native country in Edo state is noted as Esanland Their dialect, form the Edoid class of Niger-Congo vernacular. The Esan community labeled God "Osenebra" or "Osenobula". It is frequently condensed as Ose. God is expressed as well "Ofuekenede" (merciful God), "Okakaludo" (stronger than stone), "Obonosuobo" (the great physician), "Osshimiri atata" (a river that never runs dry) etc.

ESOTERICISM Authorizes no other misunderstandings than the subsist sign of glorious humanity (representation of the world) on the surface. The Kabbalah instructs that this heavenly idea, translated from the high and just dominant depiction (the Elohim), has now altered into another likeness, due to the growth of the mistaken species of humanity.

ESCAMAS (Latin) Embodies both the lower world and water. It channels protection and defense. Some beings such as the Sirens, Tritons and the Baphomet confirm the metaphor of cosmic disadvantage.

ESSENCE (Gnosticism) The solidity or Buddhata is a fragment of our real being, it is an embryo of soul that has the particles of pain and the wisdom of our father, our Intimate, descends from the galaxy, the Milky Way across the note "La" passes through the note "Sun to the sun, with the "Fa" go around the planets of the solar system and ultimately to the earth with the note "My" driven by evolutionary enlargement from the: Mineral, Vegetable, Animal, until reaching the human stage, where he will obtain 108 existences (bodies to continue with the esoteric work through the musical octaves, until he changes into a deity. If he does not obtain it, he enters the submerged worlds (hell), where he will evolve, so that all the imperfections or selves that the essence has fractionated are suppressed.

ESSE In academics logically: real existence animation, indispensable creation, principle. His Esse boundless fondness. His confirmation, formation or build is limitless understanding. The dawn of the expression Esse approaches from Proto-Indo-European *hiesmi (I am, exist"). Esse arises in Spanish tongue which precisely signifies "that" or "that one,", and probable expanded to "fellow man" as condensed from statements like that type, "that lad."

ESCHEIO or ESEIOOS It is communicated that it was an ancient Gnostic school that some who have found out, reinforced that the ruins of Krirdet Qumran, were the kingdom of an Essene monastery. Not long ago discovered Dead Sea Scrolls affirmed scholars that it was owned by the Essenes as well as John the Baptist and Jesus of Nazareth.

ESCHEM (Persian) The one who has the greatest power and cruelty of the dews, evil characters), the gloominess, of envy, anger and violence.

ESHMIM (Hebrew) The heavens, the sky in which the sun, planets and stars exist. This voice derives from the root Sm, which typify to place, abandon; hence, the planets, as disposers. In the Apocalypse this church replaces the chakra of Swadistana, located at the height of the supine in the male and the Graafian follice in the female.

ESSENES A Jewish recluse sect. They materialized to have arisen in the 2nd century B.C. and to have ended in the 2nd century. A. D. Their organization of existence was extremely ordered and acquired. Many intellectuals have accepted the essence of the society of the 'Dead Sea Scrolls'.

ESEIOOS ESEIO or ESEIOOS It is pronounced that it was a prehistoric Gnostic academy that a few which have discovered that the ruins of Krirdet Qumran, were the dominion of an Essene abbey. A while back discovered Dead Sea Scrolls intellectuals claim it was retained by the Essenes as well as John the Baptist and Jesus of Nazareth.

ESOTERIC or ESOTERICISM (Greek: inner, inside) This word was used in ancient times to choose the Mysteries in secret to the Initiates. Esoteric means: hidden, reserved; the opposite of exoteric (public or external).

SPIKE (ESPIGA) (Latin spicare) (English Spike) Straightforward a signal of fertility, solar property, germination and growth, as well as virtue, unification and domination.

ESPY Suggests glimpsing, discovering, discerning something among several others; e.g., She instantly espied a person waving at her from the window. (The Biblical meaning is to distinguish something that is distant, partially hidden, or obscure). 'Forty years old was I when Moses the servant of the Lord sent me from Kadesh Barnea to espy out the land; and I brough him word again as it was in my heart.' (Joshua 14:7)

ESAU. A "man of the field" turned into a huntsman who had "rough" character that renowned him from his twin brother. enclosed by these classifications were his glowing and perceptible furriness. "Edom" is the byname of a man, initially called Esau, who is identify in the Book of Genesis in the Bible's Old Testament. "Edom was also used as the name of the place where Esau went to live, the hilly part of southwest Jordan. Esau's name was changed to Edom when he moved to that land. As the eldest son of Isaac, Esau should have inherited the covenant with God that Abraham had passed on to Isaac. But Esau traded his birthright (inheritance) to his younger brother, Jacob, for a 'mess of pottage' (a meal of stew) when he was too hungry to consider what he was throwing away".

ESTULA SARIRA It signifies the physical body, along with the natural world of man that is explained described in the progression of segments or components that concluded it, in allusion to the numerous concealed and religious groups, these are: a) Triple, b) septuple, it is related with the dice, which imply in its four perspectives the four elements, the superior and beneath quaternate. The Romans used it as a stellar sign, related to the encircle. c) Decimal a. Tree-way Regulation: It is set up conforming to, some religions by body, soul and spirit, b. Seventh Constitution is formed by, c. Decuple Constitution of man, is composed of; Father, Son and Holy Spirit who is the Divine Triad and Human Soul who is the Ethical Triad. Mental Body. Astral Body and Material Body; Miku or Malchuth.

ESUS Utilizing this name the ancient Gauls pay homage to the highest Being. They did not construct altars for him or illustrate him in resemblance; they glorified him in some sacred greenwood in which they believed he resided. Lucan, in the third book of his Pharsalia, introduced us with a curious explanation of one of these revered woodlands.

ESTIO (The Summer) He is embodied as a child with a wheat ear halo and a bundle of Medrano in one hand and in the other a sickle.

ESPY. In the King James Dictionary Espy contemplates to see behold, and as one of them opened his sack to give his auxiliary provisions in the inn, he Espied his money; for behold, it was in his sack's mouth. In addition, it indicates catching sight of (something that is distant, partially hidden, or obscure; glimpse.

ETER Be compelled to detach in connection to Aether and Ether (or Ether). You cannot restrain the Ether with the Akaza and the Astral Light. It is neither one thing nor the other, in the sensation in which the Ether is related in physical science. The Ether is a material indicative, although so far, no physical instruments has been able to distinguish; the Akaza is a distinctly spiritual agent, interchangeable, in some expression, to the Anima mundi; the Astral Light is at best the seventh and soaring origination of the Earth's atmosphere, as unfeasible to decipher as the Akaza and the rigorous Ether, as it is something that is absolutely on a different plane.

ETHELDREDA, St. (d. 679), also Audrey, initiator of Ely. The daughter of a Christian king of the East Angles, she was married twice. She came to be a nun c. 672. In 673 she established the double monastery at Ely, of which she was lady superior until her death.

ETHEREAL Sublimely speculated on the grounds by way of explanation, is manifested in the matter of the four ethereal anagrams. It is identical to the astral body.

ETHERIA, Pilgrimage of. The interpretation of a crossing by a (very likely) Spanish mother superior or prioress to Egypt, the New Jerusalem, Edessa, Anatolia, and Constantinople or Stamboul (Stanbul) at the closure of the 4th century. In the initial section her description of locations with the areas of Scriptural occurrences; in the subsequent the descriptions characterization is largely of sacraments elements, exclusively the sustenance of Zion and the community. The chronicles are also famous as the 'Peregrinaio Silviae'.

ETHERIC (Gnosticism) Substance of the first fundamental part of the tangible world. This is the origination of life on the planet, it is its duplicate. It is far beyond the world, vitally there are other regions. The etheric world is Eden itself, the garden of the Hesperides. The Kingdom of God of Moses. In this region work the angels of life.

ETERNITY (Sanskrit) The voice eternity, with which Christian scholars understand the word "forever and ever," is not in the Hebrew language. "Oulan" says Le Clerc, typifying a period whose beginning, or end is unknown. It does not declare "infinite duration," and the Old Testament "forever" locution signifies only "a long time." In the Puranas, the word "eternity" is also not used in Christian grasp since it is distinctly shown that "eternity" and "immortality" are only desired to express "existence until the end of the Kalpa". Repeatedly, the voice "eternity" must be reinstated with that of Aeon or evo, in the affirmation of illusory endless period. Even so, Nirvana itself cannot dismiss this term, to rise from illustrious status, there are others progressively dominant (For Nirvana), which also have their limit in unconditional Eternity. Scarcely that which has never had an origination and will never have an end can be cited eternally. The definition of Eternity is a hunched serpent making up a circle and biting its tail.

ETERNAL (Latin aeterus) Explanation that it is only peculiarly appropriate to the Divine Being, which had no starting point and incalculable end.

ETERNAL LIFE. In Religious beliefs, not only a life of recurrent duration but the plenitude of life of which the believer come to be consumed immediately through improvements in God's eternal being.

ETHER Those who study the Ether are extremely likely to entwine it with the Akaza and with the astral light. In the sixth sense that ether is described in material education, it is neither one thing nor another. The Ether is a matter prototypical, and the Akaza, a distinctly spiritual agent, in a sense are uniform. The "anima mundi and the astral light" are only the seventh and highest of the Earth's airspace, because it is something that is on a further plane. The astral Light is 2nd in the cosmic succession. Akaza in Sanskrit; it's a charge that is on the seventh plane of the Earth's aerosphere. According to Webster's Dictionary, the Ether "is a hypothetical medium of great elasticity and extreme subtlety, which is supposed to fill every space, without excepting the interior of solid bodies, and to be the means of transmission of light and heat." Esotericisms say that both the Ether and the primordial value are not hypothetical instruments, but true realities. It is accepted that the Ether, Akasa, and the astral Light of Kabbalists, are the Ether, combining them with the hypothetical of science. This has disoriented humankind. The Akasa is the conglomerate of the ether, it is the Upper Aether. The Ether is the "cladding" or one of the emergences of the Akaza that inhabits all the emptiness of Space; its essential qualities be owned by its sound. (The Voice). It is the fifth of the seven Origin or cosmic features, which in turn has seven states, aspects or principles. The Ether and the Akaza have as their origin the distinctive Element. The astral Light of Kabbalists, with its consequences both bad and good. The positive, phenomenal, always active Ether is a sizeable force; while the omnipresent and all-pervading Ether "is the noumenon of the principal, that is, the Akaza".

ETHICS (Ethics), (Gnosticism) We must be conscious that the most absolute code of ethics that has been written for the time span history of humankind is that of the Ten Commandments of God's Law.

ETHIOPIC VERSIONS OF THE BIBLE. The Holy Scriptures was transcribed into Ethiopic (G'ez) presumably from the Greek, in the 4th & 5th centennials. The Ethiopic Old Testament or Hebrew Kush accommodate in totaling the American Standard Version, Jubilees, Ethiopic Enoch, IV Esdras, along with others of the Words of Baruch, and additional items.

ETHON ("Hugger") In Greek mythology Ethon was one of the four horses of the chariot of the sun.

ETIOPE Surrounded by Alchemy is an interpretation that reinstates the first state of the work, (the Negredo); that is, the archaic state of the soul, before undertaking its spiritual advancements and progression.

ETNA. Volcanic mountains off the coast of Sicily. According to mythology, the emissions result in by the volcano are due to etna is underneath, daughter of Vulcan to free her from the jealous Juno, the wife of Zeus, she was swallowed by the earth in that position, and there she inspires, that is, through the crater.

ETROBACIA (Greek) Typifies "to walk in the air" or to be exalted in it, absent of the intervention of any visible agent; it is the sound (the voice); it is the fifth of the seven conditions, aspects or principles. These semi-material segments will be visible in the air at the end of the fourth Round and will fully manifest itself in the fifth.

EUDISTS The ordinary selection for members of the "Congregation of Jesus and Mary', manifested by St. John Eudes. They are now perpetrating largely to external instruction.

EUCHARISTIC. A Religious formalities established on Jesus Christ's final refection, or the holy bread and wine customary in this officiating. The creation closes with the eucharistic ritual achievement. He is an eucharistic abbot and canon educator. The variance connecting Holy Communion and Eucharist is that the Holy Sacrament then mentions the entire activities of the Lord's Supper, as well as its oblational creation. Holy Communion deals with a single feature of that step; the acceptance of the transubstantiation. In the West the established garments of the officiant of the Eucharist are the Amice, Tunic, girdle, maniple, stole, and chasuble. They originate from the temporal clothing of Roman citizens in the 2nd century. In the East temple the vestments are basically matching, though contrasting in appearance. In the Eastward Church they declined unused after the renewal; their improvement in the 19th century prompted disagreement, however, they are distinctly authorized by the 1969 Canons, could be seen in Cope, and appearances on unrelated frocks.

EUNOE Mystically mentions the river, like the Leteo, where you must bathe to be purified. Once the psychological death of the defects has been performed.

EUTANIA (The Abundance) Persist called Dione by the Greeks. She was epitomized as a beautiful woman standing, with magnificent garments with haloes of flowers and with the horn of abundance or horn of Amalthea from which all kinds of contentment sprouted, fruits, coins and even boats.

EVA Biblical span that was used to call the first woman that God gave as a companion to Adam, was the mother of Cain and Abel. Gnosticism disclose that Eva's were women in the post-Lemuria era after the dissociation of the congress.

EVADE Implies to dodge, avoid, elude, avoid.

EVANGELIARY. (1) A publication accommodating the text of the four Gospels (2) The liturgical book holding the portions of the Gospels to be read at the Eucharist, adjusted conforming to their place in the ecclesiastical year.

EVAPTO Involves Initiation; the same as Epopteia.

EVESTRUM Attainment the astral body (Doppelganger) of man; his ethereal conscious replica, which can watch over him and warn him of the approach of death or any other danger.

EVILS A reversed pentagram, with two extremities protruding uphill, is an ideogram of wrong and engage threatening intensity because it reverses the genuine disposition of things and manifests the conquest of proceeding over inner self. Components that are regularly linked with unique formations of immoral considered unequal conduct in addition to irritation, vengeance, hate, anguish, advantage, egocentrism, unconsciousness, demolition and abandonment.

EVOCATION or EVOKE (Latin evulatio, onis) Cited through the centralization of the spirits or Souls of the dead, to obtain a correct motivation.

EVO The persistence of eternal things are periods of jointly interpreted, clear and precise epochs, they are the Seven Eternities.

EVOLUTION (Gnosticism) "The Divine Rabbi of Galilee never said that the Law of Evolution would bring all human beings to perfection. Jesus, in the four gospels of emphasis on the obstacle to entering the kingdom." "Strive to enter through the narrow gate, for I tell you that many will seek to enter and will not be able (Jesus)." "The Christ Jesus never said that the Law of Evolution would lead all human beings to the ultimate goal." It cites a life that increases by progressing from one formation to another and stockpiling the experiments it extends across corresponding configurations.

EXARCH. The denomination of (1) definite civil governors in subsequently Roman Empire; (2) determine bishops under in rank than patriarchs however, dominating over the metropolitans in civil diocese.

EXCESS. A subsistence, additionally enough, a quantity surpasses what is expected, essential, or advised, the quantity by whichever instrument or capacity outpaces an alternative, excess. When anyone does anything to excess, they do superabundant. Accounts of perceptions: greed, gluttonousness in excess. Dissimilar the essentially lewd Pannus or exclusively stimulating Liber Pater, Comus was a god of excess. If you summarized the fare share or magnitude of one thing as excessive, you condemn it since it is further or extra than is obligatory or sensible. In sacred text, 1 Peter 4:4 interpretation: "Wherein they think it strange that ye run not with them to the same excess of riot, speaking evil of you."

EXISTENCES We would have opted to be born in an incredibly beautiful home and with numerous occasions, due to conditions we did not know in past lives, to take care of our children, home and beauty.

EXILE. The expression is imposed completely with the assessments of the Jews in Babylon from 586 to 538 B.C.

EXCHANGE. The contribution or accepting of one item in restoration for an additional; exchange, the act of one commodity for an alternative. A site from which objects or assistance are swapped. There are indisputable circumstances which ought to be met for an interchange to occur; acting as at the minimum two-ways may compete be required to acquire reality as it may be of respect at distance. Individuals may broadcast and dispatch what they are handing out, and each is without charge to submit or decline what is on proposal. "The Great Exchange" is relating to Christ's interchange redemption. Bridges and Bevington comprehensively particularized the serving to redeem duty of Jesus Christ for dishonored human race.

EX OPERE OPERATO This was a declaration used by clergy to show the actual unbiased manner of functioning of the formalities, and its home rules of the interior point of view of each the cleric and the receiver.

EXPRESS. Bounded by the King James Version of Hebrews 1:3 "express" holds the definition "exactly resembling the original." as the notion of an insignia simulates the shape inscribed alongside the seal. In old-fashioned speech; express denotes "stated explicitly, not implied, clearly presented, distinct, articulated precisely." infinitive of pronounce. The etymology for expression in previous 15 centuries, expressioun, "action of pressing out;" later" action of manifesting feeling;" "a putting into words" (mid-15c); out of late Latin expressionism (nominative expression) "expression vividness "in classical Latin "a pressing out, a projection." noun of action from past-participle stem of exprimere "represent".

EXPRESSION Introduces to the mythological origin of the expression: "it was quite an odyssey" obeys a Homeric story restrained in classic epic poems of ancient Greece styled as follows: The Odyssey. The epic tells the story of Ulysses or Odyseus, a outstanding hero who leaves Ithaca to favor the Achaeans in the Trojan War, but at the end, his nonrecognition to the gods triggers the furor of these, making it difficult to return. These setbacks of Ulysses are what give interpretation to the word. The Maharal, a spiritual philosopher of the 16th century suggests a clarification. Although it truly justifies considering God used "ten" expressions with which to show the world, the answer authentically fits with the idea of the Ten Sefirot, which are corresponding to the ten expressions. (Gnostic) The ego is the origin of our alertness being asleep. Our reason cannot be conveyed by being we are victims of situations, puppets of egos, selves, demons or defects.

EXPERIENCES Is the sensation of awareness, proximity, disclosure. The reality or condition of possess been pretentious by or accomplished understanding amidst direct attention or involvement, efficient attainment, expertise, or habit emanate from straightforward notice of or involvement in episode or in a precise action. Pathos is a Greek term signifies "suffering" or "experience", instaurated as a theoretical framework mode of impact with the Greek philosopher, Aristotle. When we describe individually our experiences or declares that a positive experience has outlined about us, each person is necessarily providing that experience influence dominion. We recognize for that experience to disciple how we perceive each of us privately or what group we place our own self (or can prefer society to insert us.) into. All of us are the output of our own experiences, be they favorable or resisting; create us the soul we are, at any development in occurrence. Individuals also gravitate to have sentimental reminiscence of experiences than of collecting proprietorship. In addition, humans are more probable to measure their proprietary with others than their experiences. Equally important, experiences are more connected with identification, morals, and association, which points to everlasting joviality.

EXORCISMS This designation is given to some spells, prayers and ceremonies that the Catholic Church has used, by the involvement of its ministers, to expel the demons or evil spirits of the people, animals, objects or places of which they have subjugate possession, many of the exorcisms of the Catholic-Roman ritual are remarkably similar, not to say replicating, of other rituals (Kabbalistic, Jewish, pagan).

EXVOTOS. Knowledgeable to donations such as constituents or heads of wax, crutches, dresses, paintings, etc. that are hung on the walls or dome of temples and that the faithful consecrate to God, the Virgin or the Saints as a sign of a favor appropriated.

EYES In the first place, the Eye of Providence was a Christian character, and the untimely example of its use can be found in religious art of the Renaissances period to stand for God. An early illustration is Pontorno's 1525 Supper at Emmaus, although the sign itself was painted on later, possibly in the 1600's. A book called the Iconology which published images, in later publications the Eye of Providence was included as an attribute of the essences of 'Divine Providence', i.e. God's benevolence As the name of the mark and its early consumption propose, it was innovated as a sign of God's benevolent awareness over humankind.

EVA (Sanskrit) A suffix that in Sanskrit announced the origin of an individual or thing. Thus, Draupadeya mirrors "son of Draupadi"; Kaunteya, "son of Kaunti".

EVOKE, EVOCATION (lat. evocatio, onis) From the Latin evocates, "to summon or to call") It is the act of the call to appear towards an entity such as a spirit, a god or any other of supernatural character. The evocation aims to "make appear visually" to the evoked or conjured entity, memories; to cite especially with approval or for support. The verbs evoke most regularly counts to bring a feeling, recollection, or picture into the mind. When you visit your old high school, the smells, sound and colors there evoke impressions from the past.

EZRA and NEHEMIAH, Books of. These Scriptures Books the history of the Hebrew people started in Chronicles and are evidently the work of the same authority. Ez. evidence the return of the exiles from Babylon and their investigation to restore the Temple at Jerusalem and Ezra's mission and work NEBIM. Documentation Nehemiah's plans for the restoration of Jerusalem and his adaptation for the profession of the city and added reforms.

EZRA (Hebrew) The Jewish scribe and priest who, circumnavigated 450 years prior to J.C. compiled the Pentateuch (so he was not the true author) and the rest of the Old Testament, to the elimination of the book of Nehemiah [or second book of Ezra] and that of Malachi]. Indistinguishable Azareel and Azriel, a great Hebrew Kabbalist. His full title is Rabbi Azariel ben Manahem. He developed in Valladolid (Spain), in the twelfth century, and enjoyed immortality as a philosopher and Kabbalist. He is the author of a configuration dealing with the Ten Sephiroth.

EZRAEL or AZRAEL (Arabic) In the company of Mohammedans is the cherub of repose, who oversees accepting spirits at the moment of exiting the body and guiding them into the presence of the sovereign justice. Included in the Mohammedans is the Angel of Death, who is charged with approving souls at the instant they leave the body and dominant them into the existence of the influential Judge.

EZEKIEL, Book of. Ezekiel was the last of the 'Greater' Old Testament Prophets, the successor of Isaiah and Jeremiah. The Book predicts the destruction of Jerusalem, doom for many foreign nations, and the redemption and restoration of the Jewish people. The author correlates as one, menace by the resplendence and holiness of God. The book was written in Babylon, Ezekiel had been deported in 597 B.C. Some scholars hold that only a small part of the Book goes back to Ezekiel himself; others that Ezekiel was not at all in Babylon; yet others that the Book is an apocryphal to be outdated in the 3rd century, B.C.

-F-

FACES or FACES (Kabbalistic) As in Hebrew, Partzupheem. This voice often makes mention of the Areekh-Anpeen or "Long Face", to the Zeir-Anpeen or "Short Face" and to the Resha-Hivrah, "Head or White Face", The presumption states that from the instant of its episodes (the hour of the distinction of matter), all proceedings for future structures was encompass in the three heads, which are one and have the name of Ateeksh Kadosh (Holy Elders and the Faces). When the faces scrutinized each other, the "Holy Elders" between Heads, or Ateeksh Kadosh, reveal The Creation of Aree Appa Yem, that is, "Long Faces".

FACHIMAN In Japanese mythology he is the God of War.

FACT(S) (Gnosticism) In any case, Divine mercy exists. If a person has made a revolution of consciousness and showed that he has had instincts to change radically, he is assigned a new existence.

FACTORS (The three factors) (Gnosticism) 1st Factor: dying, which process eliminating or dying the ego (the defects, the mistakes). 2nd, to be born, consists of proving the solar bodies, and 3rd, sacrifices for humanity, which apply to support the Gnostic teaching to our fellowmen. By obtaining these three factors of the revolution of consciousness, we could attain total liberation, the Intimate Self-Realization of Being. The Master Jesus-Christ put it this way: "Whoever wants to come after me, let him deny himself, (to die); take up his cross (be born) and follow me" sacrifice for humanity.

FAFNIR Dragon of Knowledge. The Dragon who was offered by Sigurd.

FAHWA, FA-HWA-KING, (Chinese) A Chinese work about cosmogonic. It was a Chinese traveler and writer who wrote about Buddhism.

FAINTING (Gnosticism) When man set foot in the Electronic and Molecular worlds it is now of death. It is a gigantic test for man's conscience. The Tibetan book of the dead ensures that all men faint at the time of death, which lasts three and a half days. The Tibetan book of the dead states: "You have been in a state of fainting for the past three and a half days. As soon as you recover from this fainting, you will have the thought, "what has happened" at that time all Samsara will be in revolution."

FAIZI (Arabic) Impersonates, "heart". An author who deals with mystical and esoteric themes.

FAITH Elucidates as accepting with firm sentiment; a secure reliance in existence for which there is no tangible verification; absolute trust, conviction, confidence, or loyalty. On an authentic reproduction, having faith in God is composing an applied dedication; the kind elaborated in trustful God, or credulous in God. (The rootstock interpretation of the Greek pistis, 'faith', is 'trust'.

FALICO Whatever concerning the fine clique, or of an uncommonly gender character, such as the shiva ling and the pandita, indos, badge of the purposeful and kindly creative power that have nothing of obvious sentiment attributed to them by the westerly prediction.

FALK (Cain Chenul) Jewish Kabbalist who had a position for having worked "miracles". Kenneth Mackenzie, recounting him, standard the continuing value of the configuration that the German chronicler Archenoiz wrote about England in 1788: "There is in London an extraordinary man, who for thirty years has been famous in the Kabbalistic annals. Llamas Cain Chenu Falk. A certain Earl of Rantzow, who died not long ago, while in the care of Fran Falk in Brunswick, where an evocation of spirits in appearances of witnesses' worthy of faith was verified", These "spirits" were elemental, which Falk made appearance in sight by the incantations employed by all Kabbalists.

FALS (Persian) Astrological books of affirmation, which the Persians and almost all the populations of the East consult on the important matters of life.

FALL(S) or FALLEN (Gnosticism) Come down, article voluntarily, without being necessary to sanction any domain. It is a knowledge that describes the deprivation of something spiritual just like Lucifer, being the most beautiful of angels prohibit from heaven and thrown into the abyss for experience revolted against God. Adam and Eve were created absolutely but having eaten of the unauthorized fruit of the tree of good and evil they were daring of Eden thus lacking eternity; his successors are concerned to affliction, suffering and destruction.

FAME According to the fables; Instructional allegorical divinity of Jupiter to give to recognize the attacks of the gods after the defeat of the giants.

FAN The bulk undergoing assignment of the portable fan is as the mark of opulence or greatness, which extends as far end as the earliest progress of Egypt and Babylon and pursue steady now days. In Western lifestyle, fans were regularly correlated with the polish of the superior groups.

FANTASMAL (Latin Phantasia and from the Greek Mysteries) Misconceptions and dreams, like those that promise fantasies or project mechanics or visions. Frequently they are phenomena of the quantity disincarnated by their emotional tendency to this physical world, or other collectivities of the corporeality, it can also happen by unfolding or by the domain of hyperspace (fourth dimension), as in the instance of goblins, witches, evil spirits, etc.

FASCINATION This designation allude to a kind of hallucination or prestige, which takes us to see things in an extremely unique way from what they really are, it is a domain and irresistible magnetic force, analogous to that utilized by snakes on birds, a person can act on supplementary people or on animals, as in the case of Pelissier, who lethargically killed birds using this power of fascination, or in the cases of tamers of snake charmers, etc.

FAST and FASTING Abstinence from all food by religious rule or could be done for healing or spiritual purposes. According to the scriptures, Jesus the Christ fasted forty days, during which he was tempted by the devil; but he overcame it. As a chastened regulation, is contemplated to prove psychological life by incapacitating the appeal of realistic satisfaction. It has been accomplished in Judaism and advocated by Christ both by His guide and His doctrine. In the early Church structured regular fast days were initiated, specially Friday and for a quick time all The East, the Church adjoined three added continuations of fasting. In prior times fasting signifies absolute composure from nourishments during the entire or part of the fast day. In the East, materially statically recognized with austerity. In the current catholicity procedure fasting normally means one main meal with a light 'snack' for breakfast and night, also appeals prevention from meats; periods of abstention have been famous from the fast epoch since 1781. Relatively, the two fast periods which endure in the RC Church are Ash Wednesday and Good Friday. Early days of fasting are shown in the 1969 Canons, but no definitive directives are specified for the manner of their scrutiny.

FATE (ha) (Arabic) This phrase proposes the starting point and is the title that Muhammad gave to the first segment of his Koran. It is a prayer as frequent among the Mohammedans as the Sunday invocation among believers.

FATIMA. A small-scale borough in Portugal, celebrated as a location of odyssey. In 1917 three analphabetic youngsters observed perception or vision of a woman, who proclaimed herself to be 'Our Lady of the Rosary', declared to them to chant the Rosary every day, and appealed for a shrine to be constructed in her recognition.

FAUN, (The) On the authority of mythology, there were divinities of the pasture, grassland and wasteland. As folklore summarizes, youngsters of animal groups and faun who were entities that had the power to predict and were advised as Oracles. It is said that they introduced themselves with men's feet and legs and other times with ram's legs and legs. The head was decorated with a pair of tiny horns and a grandiose tail that advanced at the height of the tailbone.

FAUNO. (lat. Faunus). Conforming to the mythicist semi-God of fields, jungles and cattle. He captivates the talent of prophecy, worshipped as God of the Pastors. He was identified as the God Ran and presented with a Male Goat body from the waist down and with horns. It is a symbol of beauty as latent inspiration towards an ideal, the more you want the more elusive. He was the son of Reo & Cantete, grandson of Saturn. It is said that he accompanied Bacchus on his expedition when he went to the Indies. He married Fauna who died after giving birth to the Fauns. He then married the Nymph Marica.

FAUNTAINS ABBEY. A Cistercian abbey adjacent to Ripon, established in York in 1132. It was one of the opulent Cistercian dwellings at the time of the conclusion. Considerable ruins of the church and cloister survive.

FAITH The firm adherence to understanding by the prestige of grace a truthfulness disclosed by God, not by intrinsic motivation certainty but by the dominion of God.

FAITH AND ORDER A fragment of the Ecumenical Movement by which Consultations were displayed at Lausanne in 1927 and at Edinburgh in 1937. It was assimilated into the World Council of Churches.

FAYUM GOSPEL FRAGMENT. A 3rd-century papyrus fragment, disclosed in 1882, which holds a defective prophecy of St. Peters' denial, akin to Mk; 14:27-30.

FEARS Symptoms irrational fear is the incoherent panic of images. A human being enduring appearing with these circumstances can anticipate encountering an exceptionally towering quantity of concerns from solely rational of myth, decontrol literally perceiving it. The individual's apprehension is perhaps so acute that they may surprisingly experience a full-fledged panic anxiety attack afterward. As reported by ordinary, influential, and ancient human being reaction. In the manner of emotional investigation, it requires comprehensive organic feedback and a towering independent emotional acknowledgment. Consternation signals us to the attendance of insecurity or the warning of anguish, even if that exposure is corporal or cognitive.

FEAST Or festivities, sunlight or day allocate to observe, ceremony celebration or enact, or look forward to affairs or interlude horticulture, devoted, or ethnicity that accord significance and close-knit to the personal as well as pious, policymaking, or state of the real society. Feasting is in the Bible especially within our power to honor with edibles. In the present time just after we savored the bounty of God's gives to us collectively with others. There exist myriads of illustrations of Festivals in the Bible, from Abraham's festivities to rejoice Isaac being weaned, to the wedding supper of the Lamb when Jesus gets back. There be a few Hebrew signals for "feast". One is Chag, that insinuates "to circle, as in to circle dance or feast". Commonly applied to the Fete of Unleavened Bread, Entertainment of Weeks (Pentecost), Shavuot, and Feast of Tabernacles, Sukkot; as pilgrimage feasts.

FEATURES. Is a classic grouping or a major fragment of burden: the most recent mobile replica, an urban area principal attribute; an automobile assurance quality, etc. This composition, shape or aspect mostly of a human being a male of great quality. Out of date material vision, the foundation or features of the particular or its fragments serious of characteristic leveled when he grins, a proportion of the angle, features an individual with Asiatic attributes. The features of the Christian Scriptures; "The great biblical themes are about God, his revealed works of creation, provision, judgment, deliverance, his covenant, and his promises." The Bible sees what has taken place to human beings in the radiance of God's creation, uprightness, conscientiousness, clemency, and adoration.

FEBO An additional name of Apollo, as God of light, that is, the sun.

FEBRA On the authority of classic fable of Euripides' melodrama Hippolytus, she was the daughter of Minos and Parsifal, Kings of Crete, and wife of Theseus. She challenges her stepson Hippolytus, was refused by him and oppressed committed suicide by hanging herself, but first she wrote a letter to her husband in which she defamed Hippolytus of having done violence against his will. Theseus rebuked his son and banished him by perceiving death because of the paternal curse. It is associated that Diana knew Hippolytus well because she was his close friend, made Theseus, although late, be honest about his significant mistake.

FECUNDA (Fecundity, Latin) In the Roman framework she appeared as a matron with horns of Abundance and a child. It is said that, in the time of Neon, a temple was erected to him; in which, a priest on a goat leash mistreated women who wished to be fertilized. The propagation of the women is also hand over as a parturient woman in bed and two children around were entertained.

FEEL Channel to be attentive of a tangible or emotional interest. Feel is almost all frequently worn as an infinitive, defining to palpable handle or fumble commodity or to see responsive of existent internally. Feeling, in therapy, is the awareness of affairs inside the anatomy, intently connected to sentiments.

FEMININE (Gnosticism) Women must study reading, writing, playing the piano, weaving, embroidery and in all kinds of female activities.

FENIX Incredible bird of dimension like an eagle, which after a prolonged life, extinguishes itself through fire and revives itself from its own ashes. It is the representation of the resurrection in Eternity.

FENRIS (Scandinavian) Monstrous wolf, son of Loki, evil genius.

FERHO The sovereign and most considerable to be able to prove among the Nazarene Gnostics.

FERETORY An additional denomination for a temple where a saint's relics were placed and reverenced.

FERIA. Although in traditional Latin the term signifies 'feast day' or 'holiday', in canonical consumption it is enforced to equivalent periods further than Sundays in which no festivity falls.

FETAHIL The inferior founder, in the Codex Nazarieus. [Fetahil is identical to the infinity of Pitris, who "created man" as a "shell" alone. He was, surrounded by the Nazarenes, the King of the Light of the Creator, but as such, it is the adverse Prometheus, who did not seize the existing Fire required for the structure of the heavenly soul, for not knowing the mysterious reputation, the extraordinary and isolated distinctive of Kabbalists. [students of the secret sciences].

FERVERS. Others are the unseeable ideas of conspicuous commodities, arranged in the sky by the illuminous dogma of good, (Oromanzes), as protector averse to Ahriman's, (the dark fundamental of evil), in consonance with the mythology of the Persians.

FERTILE, Fecund, fruitful, prolific measures producing or capable of producing offspring or fruit; involves pictorially, it evidently preparedness of conception and maturing. The Latin foundations, fertilis, signifies "bearing in abundance, fruitful, or productive, "from ferre, "to bear."

FESTUM OVORUM (Lat., 'feast of eggs') The Saturday before the opening of Lent, which marked a stand regarding the Lenten fast. Though no longer of ecclesiastical importance, it is noted in some calendars.

FETISH (from the Latin facticius, factitious) It is a superstitious idol or object of illustration amidst the adverse. Birds, fish, trees, stones and many other beings that nature offers to the view of these idolaters, such are the entities that they have innovate and to which they send worship and make offerings.

FEARS EMET Master Samael tells that in the Middle Ages; magicians form statues and wrote 'Theme', on the forehead and vice versa 'Emet' conjured them, statues took on a life of their own; being transferred, from one place to another, disregarding the distance; if they took away the word 'emet' and took away the verbs of power; The statues were reduced to dust.

FIALAR & GALAR (Scandinavian) Two gnomes who killed Qvaser, from whose blood, mingle with honey, they assembled a liquor, which is Poesia.

FIAT Consent, authorization, Venia, for a gadget to have effect.

FIBULA (Latin, festa) Buckle, a shield or unmissable procedure, used by many Greeks and Romans. The moral tale of early history assigned them an image of virginity, like the belt.

FIDELITY (Latin fidelities, Otis) Fidelity, fulfillment of faith that is due to another. In antiquity the Romans illustrates her as a young woman dressed in white, with a dog at her feet and a key in one of her hands.

FIDES DAMASI (Latin Faith of Damasus) A considerable doctrinal plan in which was previously accredited to St. Damasus of St. Jerome but is now in a universal sense approved to have stemmed in Gaul close to the end of the 5th century.

FIDEISM. A locution pertains to a variation of creed which holds in accepted belief in the disqualification of the imaginative to accomplish knowledge of prophesy circumstance and proportionately focus immoderately priority on faith.

FIESTAS (Greek) (agapae) They were banquets of charity recognized by the ancient Christians, they were spread in Rome by Clement, at the time of the reign of Domitian.

FIFTH MONARCHY MEN. A fanatical persuasion of the mid-17th century in England to whom members aimed at conducting in the 'Fifth Monarchy' (Dan. 2: 44) which would succeed the empires of Assyria, Persia, Greece, and Rome. Supporting unsuccessful risings in 1657 and 1661, their leaders were executed, consequently, the sect died out.

FIG TREE In distinction to an impalpable representation of an ostentatious pleasure, the Fig tree is steeped (to moist totally with fluid) in prehistorical meaning and for millennia, has symbolized wisdom and success in abundance.

The chapter close with a monologue on the strength of devotion, noted several intellectuals to expound here, alternately the Apocalyptic Multifaceted, as its predominant notion, however, at chapter 13 verse 28 Mark has Jesus again use the image of the fig tree to point out that Jerusalem will decline and the cataclysm for Judea, along with Mark's version of Jesus' messianic discourse. The unit states: "but they shall all sit under their own vines and under their own fig trees, and no one shall make them afraid". "The phrase refers to the independence of the peasant farmer who is freed from military oppression. By a show of leaves, it was like many people, pretending to have fruit which was not there, it was like the Pharisees who professed to be very religious, but whose lives were fruitless. Therefore, Christ caused the fig tree as an object lesson to all not be hypocritical."

FILALETEOS (Philaletheos). (Gr.) Directly, "lovers of truth", Title appointed to the Alexandrian Neoplatonists, also designated analogists and theosophists. The aforesaid schools were proven by Ammonius Saccas at the origination of the third century and proceeded until the fifth. The ultimate eminent scholar and sages formerly associate to it. [The structure of meditation utilized by the philalethias was rapture, a system as the Indian application of yoga].

FILM Is also well known as a "movie" or a "motion picture," is a succession of movable figures manifested on a monitor, routinely with auditory, which formulate a narrative. Many people prefer to see new features at the amphitheater immediately after they are released. The motivation of myth in pictures is that it essentially supports in comfort you communicate unquestionable basic ideas in your cinema. A handful of plain personifications instances might be incorporated. Feathered creature's customary illustrates free rein, Roses accustomed to embodying courtship, the colors green utilized to exemplify resentments. Comparison is an implementation throughout compositions, artwork and broadcast. Nevertheless, feature films are particularly creative activities where metaphors can possess the greater influential outcome. The big screen can accommodate comparison precedents that convey complicated concealed definitions and linger with the spectators afterwards the feature has concluded. A few guides of symbolism: Comedian, buffoon; break out, antelope; Mandible, Spur Dog; Radiance, H2O; refinement – roses, etc.

FILE (Philae) Denomination of island at Upper Egypt, where there was a famous temple on that isle, addressing that name, and whose ruins travelers can see even today.

FILIA Voci's (Latin) "The daughter of the divine Voice" of the Hebrews.

FILTH (Gnosticism) "And manifest are the works of the flesh: which is adultery, fornication, filth, Lasciviousness."

FILO (Gnosticism) The path of the Razor's Edge is the path of the balanced man. In the track we cultivate we will produce an element of change to modify our way of thinking, our procedure of feeling and our method of acting.

FILON. Distinguished, excellent Jew writer and historian of Alexandria who was born around 30 BC.C. and died about 45 A.D. of the Christian era. He must have been well acquainting of the greatest event of the first century of our age, in testimonial to the achievements of Jesus; his life, and crucifixion. However, he remained inarticulate in both his account of the sects and fraternities that then existed in Palestine and his version of the Jerusalem of his era. He was a great mystic, among his works abound noble and metaphysical ideas, in addition to his esoteric knowledge. The symbolism of Philo's Bible is unbelievably beneficial.

FINAN, St. (d. 661). The successor of St. Aiden as Bp. of Iona and he corroborated the Celtic ecclesiastical traditions opposed to efforts introducing Roman customs.

FINAL (Gnosticism) The Self had a beginning and will irrevocably have a conclusion, everything that has had an initiation will have an end.

FINGER (dioic) Iron finger corpulently magnetized and used in temples for healing purposes. It causes wonders in the designated direction; it was said to acquire magical virtues.

FIRMAMENT What is still durable the importance the primordial matter is disintegrated or dissolved. The condition of the soul of the Macrocosm and reciprocally that of the Microcosm.

FISIPARO (Latin) Enlarged by division or excision of the body in two. It refers to the protoplasmic race that lived in the glass land as maintained by the Nahuas, in the distant Tule (current north pole), humanity was duplicated by the physiparous system as the cellular system, the earth of that time was of mental substance in its first round, it had appeared from protoplasm, from chaos.

FISH. In primitive Christian art and writing, the fish is an emblem of Christ, also on occasions of the recently Christened and of the Sacraments. In modern times some Chantry of Easterly federation goodwill to comfort that disadvantage have endorse the figure of a fish. From premature times fish has held beside meat on Yore fasting and abstinence.

FLAMING SWORD (Gnosticism) We must transition ourselves into kings and priests of solidity in accord with to the order of Melchizedek. Those who receive the First Initiation of Major Mysteries, take the Flaming Sword that gives it power of the four elements of nature.

FLASHLIGHT Configurations knowledge and wisdom is perceived to cast light upon the dark world by way of learning, academic studies, teaching, innovation, observation, and exploration. During the Rennaissance, The Torch of knowledge was used as a sign of Enlightenment in most western cultural traditions. Light is one of the most elementary symbols universally. It is the illumination and the intelligence; it is spiritual and divine. Light is the source of conclusive reality and the goodness, and it travels with transcendence into the Nirvana of Buddhist ideology.

FLASK A glass or carafe vessel, spherical in shape and ending in a narrow, straight or semi-curved tube, is used for numerous uses in chemical laboratories. In alchemy it is associated with gender and the transmutation of aesthetic energy.

FLEUR-DE-LIS. Lilies personify clarity and self-restraint, that can be a reason the fleur-de-lis generally identifies the Holy Mother. Mynet was inaugurated in the 11th centennial, exalted Pinnipeds, sculptures, and leaded-glass windowpane represent Mary possessing the flowerets. In the duodecimal centenary, a French potentate utilized the fleur de Lis image on his shield. English monarch subsequently applied the ideogram on heraldry to feature their affirmation to the of France.

FLOCK Pertains to a grouping of animals (such as birds or sheep) assembled or rounded up together; a group in guidance of a leader, particularly a loyal church member. If people flock to a particular location or setting, an exceptionally substantial number of them attend there normally because it is enjoyable or engaging. The Sovereign Lord says: I am against the shepherds and will hold them accountable for my flock. I will disconnect them from tending to the flock so that the shepherds can no longer feed themselves. I will rescue my flock from their mouths, and it will no longer be food for them.

FLOOD. It is understood by flood which transpired in the time of Noah. From this flood only this patriarch and his family were saved, jointly with the animals that he had involved in the ark by god's command. Likewise, as this flood there have been others, the most memorable being that of Samothrace, before the era of the Argonauts, which submerged the whole country, reaching the waters of the Euxinus the top of the highest mountain ranges. In addition, it was valuable in Greece, occurring in the period of Deucalion, son of Prometheus and king of Thessaly. According to Slavic mythology, additional flood occurred in which the entire human race was drowned, with only one man and one woman staying. In addition, other floods have been mentioned such as Atlantis, India, and others.

FLORUS (c. 790-c.860), Church officer of Lyons and an ordnance of the Basilica. He authored on principle, rituals, and dogma. When Amalarius attempted to transform variations in the ritual, Florus belligerent him in a succession of the misunderstanding on foreordination, he unassailable Gottschalk.

FLOWER (Latin Fios, Floris) Amalgam of the ducts of the propagation of phanerogam us plants, typically mixed with calyx, corolla, stamen and pistils. Flowers are one of the many beauties of the creator's inspiration. It interprets the beauty, spring and transience of things, it has a link with the virtues of the Soul. In harmony with its certain color, it has different meanings: yellow and orange, means solar of wisdom, white purity, violet, sensitivity and Crispification, the "golden flower" is a traditional symbol in China of spiritual achievement.

FLORA Entities of flowers and gardens, she was the Wife of Zephyrus and mother of the First. He became aware in Greece as Coris. She was symbolized as a beautiful young woman adorned with garlands and bouquets of flowers carrying in one of h hands a basket or a horn of plenty.

FLORILEGIA Assembly of choice passages from the chronicles of antecedent authors. Special interest connects to the Greek patristic florilegia. Besides those composed of excerpts from observations on the Bible (known as catenae), several dogmatic florilegia, assembled from the 5th century onwards, have survived. They were often formulated to establish the orthodoxy or heterodoxy of individual theologians, and many were embraced in the acta of Counsils. They occasionally incorporated progress from works of which the bulk has been lost. Latin florilegia were also ordinary; they included gatherings of dogmatic, moral, and austere extracts.

FLUVIO Fix the voice that comes from the lat fluvius. That symbolizes fluviograph river.

FLY Flies discover techniques to cling to life and produce the greatest escape of any condition. They express the "one man's trash is another man's treasure" phrase. Flies besides illustrate stimulation, opulence, and prosperity. Regardless of rigid surroundings, they glide victory above distress, commanding to nourish and procreate. As courageous creatures, these insects connect to endurance, modification, perception, and adjustability. The fly essence critter delays benefits just after it approaches conversion. The flies' enthusiasm demonstrates us to countenance undesirable differences and to modify to that which is inescapable.

FO or FOE (Chinese) Somewhat designated for our prospective to be appreciated by only a small total of individuals with a particular understanding or enthusiasm. Term given by the Chinese to Buddha.

FOHAT Exemplified the ever-present electric energy and incessant destructive and formative power. It is the female and male generative power in Nature. Essence of cosmic electricity, vital driving power, being removed and expelled. It is an unmanifested abstract idea that process nothing by itself, it is simply a potential creative ability by virtue of whose action the pneumonic of all future phenomena is divided, to then unite in a perceptive mystical act and emit a creative ray. It is the active force in universal Life, which motivates every atom by making it enter life; the eminent unity that links all cosmic stamina, both in the invisible and in the manifested.

FOG Illustrates twilight, indistinction; in the Bible, it is a depiction previous considerable disclosure. It is the "Gray zone" at intervals genuinely and duplicity, and confusion about the time ahead and behind. As acclaimed to Browning it can constitute come close demise. Desolation.

FOLKLORE Consists of the oral history of people which has been recorded, the assortment of customary narratives, stories and episodes channels by the peer groups by spoken communications. By the start of the Victorian period, folklorists started putting together human actions, and legends began to assemble. Accounts in this category can display mortal's merit and own unquestionable realism. Folklore considers the humanities since it connects the course of actions to the process of those who fabricate it; for instance, crafts, institutions, ceremonies, etc. In addition, it communicates their expectations, observances, vintage points, and the way they reasoned. Folklore is a compilation of fictious anecdote concerning humans or creatures. False knowledge and unproven conclusions are essential segments in the folktale's unwritten laws. Both legends and tradition were at first moved around by the work of mouth. Folk stories recounted by whose help the main personality survives with the actions of commonplace, and the narratives may comprise disasters or disputes. These accounts may instruct mankind by what means to endure existence (or demise) and have subject ordinary in the middle of civilization universal. The research of folk tales is titled folkloristics.

FONS (Vitae) [Source of Life] (Latin) A conformation by Ibn Gebirol, an eleventh-century Arab Jewish philosopher, who titled it: Me-gor Hayyun or "Fountain of Life". Western Kabbalists have published it as Kabbalistic evidence. Scholars have unlocked in public libraries several Latin and Hebrew manuscripts of this fantastic work; among others, one that Munk came across, in the year 1802.

FORM (Gnosticism) "Creative freedom can never exist in a framework, we need freedom to understand our psychological defects in an integral way." We require promptly descend walls and fragment steel shackles, in order to be emancipated.

FORMATION. Our comprehension of mystically formation maintains its origination in Genesis 12:1-2, where The Almighty choose the population of Israel to be formed into a considered of humankind that others prevail to reverse God to the planet, along with others doing, conducting the universe recuperated, back to God. In linguistics, apologue (or expression inner modification) includes modifying the inward morphological format of an idiom to demonstrate semantic roles (cf. Pei, 1966). For instance, to form the plurals of goose /gu...s\ and tooth \ tu... Designation formation procedure and formulation of interpretation may arise in countless manner in consequence pedagogue ought to ascertain embracing these techniques to improve education. For example, linguistics apprentices habitually operate augmentation by this route of tagging new context for uncomplicated idioms. (Lexical or grammatical/functional morphemes).

FORMULA (Gnosticism) "Here is the Formulation: all things that are born in the world fall to the bottom, for any part of the Universe, it is their most immediate permanence, and such stability is the place or place on which all the lines of force of descent from all directions coincide." "The Centers of all suns... they are but the lower points of those regions of space, towards which they have decisive powers, the forces coming from all directions."

FORNICATE (fornication, La) (lat. fornications) Action of copulating, refers to the lack of genetic strength, by wasting Ens Seminis. In the Old Testament, in Leviticus 15 fornication is condemned, the New Testament in Matthew, 19-9,12 in them the diversity between what is adultery and fornication is made.

FORONEDE (Phoronede) (Greek) (Foroneda) Poem whose protagonist is Foroneo. This composition has disappeared.

FORONEO, FORONEUS (Phoroneus) (Gr.) A giant; One of the forefathers and predecessors of humanity. In agreement with a saga of Argolida, he is commended, as well as Prometheus, to have instituted fire to this land. (Pausanias).

[Phoroneus had in the Argolida an altar on which a flame was continuously lifted to recognized that this titan turned out to be the innovator of fire. The god of a river of the Peloponnese.

FORCE (Latin fortia) Strength, robustness and ability to move a device that has weight or makes resistance, gnost. Enclosed by esotericism the initiate who is working correctly and with the three factors of consciousness (dying, being born, and sacrificing for humanity), receives inner help, gives him strength, to continue forward on the spiritual path.

FOUNTAIN(S) Delineates formation, integrity, adaptations, and rainfall. Fountains and rainwater origin have played a remarkable part in the chronicle and are crucial to living. Water is the symbol of purification and life. Numerous characters can be cited such as paintings, as well as writings on fountains that inscribe its magnitude potential dimensions. The feng shui water fountain can carry good fortune, pleasure, and confidence to your lodgings and environment, nevertheless you must be certain regarding location any person settles them and even if these settings line up alongside anybody intends to acquire. As reported by Vastu Shastra, the flowy aqua in the fountain signifies the flow of capital, satisfaction, and devotion. Consequently, constraining it around your dwelling can deliver fortune and confidence. As we have perceived for St. Bernard the metaphor for fountains and water deals with most importantly, Jesus Christ who provided for us the five-fold H20 essential for our vindication. Unconditionally, Mary's part credibly detectable being the authority from where such waters circulate.

FOUR Touch on to the four lower principles of man.

FOUR NOBLE TRUTHS (The) By means of this title are chosen in Buddhism: 1. The afflictions of evolutionary existence, whose transcendences are births and deaths, life after life; 2. The origin of pain, which is the longing to satisfy oneself, cravings always renewed and never satisfied; 3. The destruction or removal of such aspiration, and 4. The flow of achieving the extermination of desire.

FOURTH Attainment the etheric world. It is understood as a fourth coordinate or time, the fourth dimension or fourth vertical, there are complete humanities that in the past developed and managed to immerse themselves in that dimension, in addition elemental paradises of incalculable beauty have been discovered. With the body at the disposal of Jinas, it is feasible to visit those paradises and the Temples of Major Mysteries that are in that dimension, in addition, it is also possible to talk face to face with the great experts in the universe.

FORTUNE (lat. fortune) A gentleman folkloric deity who supervised the events of life. The Greeks estimated it Tyche, it is represented with winged feet and a blindfold, on top of a wheel also winged, (contrast to a fast shooting) impersonation that fractionates produces that start from a horn of fortune arbitrarily.

FORTUNETELL Extraordinary individual who proclaims to have the power to prophesy what lies ahead. Fortune telling is an intelligible deformation in which some individuals forecast an obstructive outcome consequence in the absence of rationally taking into reflection the authenticity of that conclusion. The said disorder draws a connection between consternation and dispiritedness and is one of the most determined severe neuromotor that suit clear during comprehensible disarray reconstruct. If a person who is said to be able to forecast time to come by mystical, intuitional, or more sensible manner a Seer who is called a soothsayer or prophet.

FORUM (Lat., 'place of public assembly', hence 'judicial tribunal'). In righteous doctrine the pronouncement is claim to the action by the temple of her authoritative capabilities. A difference is created in the mid of the 'internal forum', point, mainly in the Liturgy of Atonement, perception is arranged on circumstances which have instances to the spiritual quality of the person, and the 'external forum', e.g., the clerical forum of rules and regulations, position where the mutual quality of the sanctuary is being scrutinized.

FOSA (PIT) (Gnosticism) Succeeding a persons' demise, what pursue is the essence, that is, the ghost of the dead. Within this ghost, mistakes develop; returning the Ego recombination, the I, which persevere beyond the Grave; Fosa or Pit. This is eventually, Legion of Villains that continues.

FOOTPRINTS Indication that leaves the foot of man or animal on the earth where it has passed. Psychological Impact incites by a fact. Gnost. essential qualities that leave in the celestial form the self when it is crumbling. In addition, it has its origin when the figure inflicts fraud, these astral signals, called Karma Saya, remain. With meticulous work in enchantment and absolute regret, these footsteps can be annulled from the Astral Body with the help of The Blessed mother. The delusive also have these traces or astral marks resulting from synthetic contacts and falseness. Footprints is a favored text is demonstrated in Christian reliance and narrates an occurrence in which an individual is walking on a beach with God. They clear out two sets of footprints in the sand. The footpath signifies stages of the speaker's life.

FOSIL (Gnosticism) "The last stage of infernal involution is the fossil state, then comes the disintegration of the lost."

FOVU As a consequence, written Phowa. It means transporting adeptness to other dimensions of space. Master Samael explains; "The consciousness must escape through the Brahamarandra, that is, what is called the fontanel of the newborn child, through which the free essence of the ego can escape, to function awakened in the inner worlds." This procedure of Fovu is so compelling. "A person must place himself in a state of deep meditation, request the Divine Mother to be taken out by the Brahamarandra, he must be free of all thoughts and desires then the awakening is impressive because through the Brahamarandra the ego cannot come out. But he needs persistency and patience not to fall as the apostle James remarks." "The man who looks in the mirror and then turns around and leaves, that says, the person has no continuity of purposes."

FRACTIONAL In Math's, we learned that a fraction is utilized to be the fragment/part of the whole thing. It represents equal parts of the total. A fraction has two parts, namely common divisor and common measure. The numeral on the upper part is labeled the numerator, and the integer on the lowest part is named the denominator. instructors normally accord that there would be five main explanations: fragments as parts of total or parts balance; fractions consequently of dividing two numerals; fractions as the proportion of two amounts; fragments as operatives; and fractions as estimates. (Behr, Harel, Post, and Lesh 1992; Kieren 198; Lamon 1999).

FRACTIONATE. Fraction (lat fractio, -Onis, de fractur, supino de frangere, romper) (Gnostics) Gnosis explains that the Nature or Essence of the human being is fractionated, in the diversity of the egoic parts, which interpret our errors. These must be broken, disintegrated, so that it is liberated that of the Breath, of Light or Essence in us, in addition it is expounded that the essence is a fraction of the soul.

FRATERNITY UNIVERSAL. This is the initial of the articles of the Theosophical Society: "To form a nucleus of universal Brotherhood of Humanity, without distinction of race, creed, sex, or caste color." To emphasize the fundamentals of this object, translate the following terms of Lactantius (Instit., 1. c, chap.6); "True religion is the only one that knows how to make another man love each other, since it teaches that all men are united by bonds of fraternity, by the reason God in the common father of all." Indeed, our true self, the individual Spirit that inhabit inside each man, is a spark o particle so to speak of the universal Spirit (God), both being indistinguishable in essence, and considering this unity of origin and essence, all human beings are essentially Identical in nature if, despite the great diversity that offer their external condition. From this derives the need for altruism, love, tolerance and concord that must reign among all the associates of the human family, thus forming a true universal Brotherhood.

FRAUD (lat. frauds, fraud is) Actualization; deception, conscious inaccuracy, breach of trust that originates or prepares damage, often material. Gnosis explains that the people who execute fraud at the moment that their 108 existences run out return to the seventh Dantes Que circle, which is the dwelling place of the violent opposed to nature, against art, resistant to God, hostile with himself, averse to nature, contra his goods and goods of others, the dwelling place of the fraudulent.

FRAVASHAM (Zend) absolute spirit. [or Atman.]

FREA See Freya.

FREE CHURCHES FREE FROM ROME MOVEMENT; FREE SPIRIT, Brethren of the. (Nonconformity) Refusal to abide by the doctrines, polity, or discipline of the Established Church. The word is now applied to all doubters from the C of E.

FREER LOGION, The Adage accredited to Christ in a passage supplemented to the text of Mk. 16; 14 in the 5th century. Greek Bible 'W', now in the Freer Museum, Washington.

FRENO (Latin frenum) Obedience that is put to one to temper one's actions. Gnosticism teaches that the Gnostic esotericism must stop his negative stimuli to achieve spiritual development, he must place a brake (by the will) to what he says continuously which; he lives it getting into trouble. A gossipy, slanderous, deceitful person, etc., is nothing spiritual and must be looked at from afar, for the simple reason that he lives full of himself and can put others in great obstacles.

FREYA or FRIGGA (Scandinavian) In the Edda, Frigga [or Friga] is the mother of the gods, like Aditi in the Vedas. It is identical to the northern Frea of the Germans, and in its lower aspect was worshipped as the mother Earth that nourishes everything.

FROGS. Observed as essential nature; good providence emblematic money, excellent associations, occupation, and good health. In numerous societies and convictions, frogs personify success with interpretation to affluence, destiny, therapeutic, fitness, growing, expansion, fecundity, and prospective.

FTAH (Egyptian) The son of Knefen the Egyptian pantheon. It is the beginning of light and life, by which "creation," or rather, evolution, took place. The Egyptian Logos and founder of the Demiurge.

FIRE According to esoteric teachings, it is the most faultless and immaculate reflection in heaven as on earth, of the one flame. It is Life and Death, the origin and end of all material things.

FRIENDS (Gnosticism) God is in every living creature, in each human being, in every single little animal, no matter how small, he is in every plant and in general, in everything that has life, there is God. So, man to love God above all things needs to love his neighbor as himself, all beings on earth without exception, whether enemies, friends or strangers.

FRY, ELIZABETH. (1780-1845), Quaker prison reformer. The daughter of John Gurney, in 1800 she wedded Joseph Fry, a London shopkeeper and a strict Quaker, she became a 'minister' in 1811. In 1813 her concentration arose in the state of the prisons, and she devoted herself to the welfare of female prisoners in new gate. She campaigned for the detachment of the sexes, segregating of criminals, female management of ladies, and the delivery of secular and religious instructions. She gave verification to a committee of the House of Commons and traveled in Europe, promoting prison reform.

FORESTS (sacred) Jungles and forests have long been appreciated as the mansion of certain geniuses. The secret panic that inspires the darkness and silence that reigns in such places, undoubtedly helps the religious veneration that the people felt for them. In countries established in northern areas there were in ancient times no other temples than in the forests and jungles. Each tree was committed to a particular divinity; under its shadows the sacrifices were celebrated, and with the blood of the victims the trees were sprinkled. In their shadow were also constituted the courts of law and the judges handed down their sentences, convincing them that the genius inhabitants of the forests will illuminate their understanding and show them the truth.

FOOD It is imperative that children receive food for the essence and food for the personality. The principle is nourished with tenderness, affection without limits, love, music, flowers, beauty, harmony, etc. The food we eat undergoes consecutive transformations. Every living being in the Universe exists by transforming one substance into another. The vegetable, for example, changes the air, water and salts of the earth into new vital substances, into vital ingredients for us (fruits, etc.) So, it's all about altering.

FORGE or FRAGUA (Ignited Vulcan) This phrase alludes to the amplification with the transmutation of the pure waters of life into the wine of the light of the alchemists.

FULDA, The Benedictine abbey of Fulda in Hesse was founded in 744 by a partisan of St. Boniface, whose tomb flourished as a place of pilgrimage. Under Rabanus Maurus (abbot, 822-42) transpire one of the predominant centers of Christian culture. The abbey was finally secularized in 1802.

FULLILLMENT (Gnosticism) The realization of the sixth commandment of the Decalogue of the Lord Jehovah is the advantageous formula for him to demonstrate conception, the infallible and precise formula, providing to man by God himself.

FULFILL (Gnosticism) We must perpetrate ourselves to fulfill the Law, obey the Commandments, and bring to light the purposes outlined by ourselves in previous existences of acceptance with our acts.

FULA or (Fulla) (Scandinavian) One of the goddesses or Asians; the goddess of womanlike ornaments.

FUSION (Gnosticism) The human soul or the Causal Body or Body of Will amalgamate with the internal master, which is Atman Budhi (innermost and Consciousness).

FUNDAMENTAL (Gnosticism) "It is necessary to tell parents that fundamental education is necessary to raise up the new Generations. It is essential to tell parents that intellectual training is necessary but that it is not everything, something more is needed, it is necessary to teach children to know themselves, to know their own mistakes, their own psychological defects".

FURIES, (THE THREE) They are also called Erinyes or Eumenides, they were infernal divine nature in Greco-Roman mythology. They are the three traitors of the Christ: Judas, Pilate and Caiaphas, which means, the Demon of Desire, Mind and ill Will. The mythology legend relates that they were daughters of the blood of Uranus that fell on the earth. These were Alecto, Magera and Tisiphone. They sanctioned and harassed the souls of those condemned to the abyss, designed horrible torments and adhered to their victims inspired by acquired madness. They were epitomized with the head (themes of hydras, snakes) and the paralyzing look. Dante in his Divine Comedy names them as portrayal of the Medusa.

FUTURE (Gnosticism) "If we want to know how to listen, if we want to learn to listen to discover the new, we must live according to the philosophy of momentaneous. It is urgent to live from moment to moment without the worries of the past and without the projects of the Future."

-G-

GABBATHA. In relation to Jn. 19: 13 the place in Jerusalem where Pilate sat in judgment on Christ. Judgment about its location is divided.

GABRIEL One of the seven archangels or spiritual essences that lodge in the supreme category of angelic succession. His title is quoted in the Bible and outline on the mystery of Mary's annunciation, as well as John's birth to Zechariah. Gabriel is also a Cosmocrator (architect of the universe) and leader of the moon. In the Pistis Sophia, Michael and Gabriel are bearers of the Ray of Christian Light, in alchemy they symbolize Sulfur and Mercury. This Angel Regent can be begged to ask for protection and spiritual help.

GABIROL (AVICEBRON) (c. 1020-c.1070). The title repeatedly given to the Spanish Jewish philosopher Solomon Ben Gabirol. His network was in essence pantheistic, and St. Thomas Aquinas wrote opposed him. His chief treatise, the Fons Vitae, was an Arabic work in dialogue form, which in a Latin recapitulation became very famous in primitive times.

GAGANA (Sanskrit) Sky, atmosphere, air.

GAHANA (Sanskrit) Deep, impenetrable, inextricable, intricate.

GAI HINNOM (Hebrew) It is the name of hell, as it appears in the Talmud.

GAIN. It is the translation of one Hebrew verb. Batsa,"to gain dishonestly", zebhan, "to buy," "procure for oneself" (i.e., "seeking delay" (Gesenius). In American English spell out to obtain or get dominate of routinely by manufacturing, excellence, or day job, procedure and lead, he stood to gain a riches: to win in competitiveness or conflict, the troops captured enemy territory. For what does it profit a man to gain the whole world and forfeit his soul? (Mark 8:35-36) Jesus' challenge humankind with an extreme reality: Your soul can be lost. We are going to see how a soul can be lost today.

GAJA (Sanskrit) Elefante.

GALLICAN CHANT The first chant is used in Southern France and a few added settings like Reims and Paris. It was restored by the "Gregorian chant' in Carolingian tempo.

GALAR and FIALAR (Scandinavia.) Two dwarves who killed Qvaser, from whose blood, mixed with honey, they made a liquor, which is Poetry.

GALAXY (bt. galaxy, and from the Greek milk) Astron. Milky Way. It was Galileo, in 1610, who showed that the Milky Way was designed by countless stars. In its measured, it is estimated that in the region of 100,000,000,000 (one hundred billion) stars are estimated. It belongs to the Macrocosm (world of six laws), with its suns, planets and moons. The name Milky Way is derived from the mythology that tells, that at the time of the birth of Hercules, the God of Olympus (Zeus), took him to Juno to nurse him and be immortal. As the Goddess refused to do it, Zeus waited for it to fall asleep, and then brought the sturdy child to one of his breasts to breastfeed, as little Hercules sucked the milk so hard, Juno woke up immediately and realizing what was happening, threw him hard to the ground to die, but the boy managed to swallow a few sips of the goddess's milk, thus becoming a semi-immortal; a small amount of drops of milk broke off Juno's chest creating a whitish line in space with countless stars. He has since been cited by the Milky Way.

GALERIUS (d. in 311) Hellenic Sovereign from 305. In 293 he amplifies Diocletian's co-regent in the E.; he convinced ruler to issue the command inaugurating the Great Persecution (303). Only smaller than the threat of an alliance between Constantine and Maxentius did he hand down his 'Edict of Toleration' in 311.

GALILEE. (1) Initially the term appealed only to part of the dynasty of Naphtali, but in NT times it indicated all the districts of Northward Palestine from the Mediterranean to Jordan. It was the position of almost all the Lord's earlier life and of a considerable part of His ministry. (2) In medieval cathedrals and the exterior porch or chapel.

GALLICAN CHANT The first chant is used in Southern France and a few added settings like Reims and Paris. It was restored by the "Gregorian Chant' in Carolingian tempo.

GALLO (ROOSTER) Bird of very occult nature; Highly appreciated in the augury and ancient symbolism. According to the Zohar, the rooster crows three times before the death of a person, and in Russia and all Slavic countries, whenever a person is sick in houses where there is a rooster, the crowing of the rooster is considered a sign of inevitable death, unless the bird crows at the hour of midnight or immediately afterwards. in which such singing is considered natural. Since the rooster was consecrated to Aesculapius and understood that the latter was called the Soter (Savior) who brought up the dead to life, it is very significant the exclamation of Socrates "we owe a rooster to Aesculapius", immediately before the death of said sage. Because the rooster is always related, in symbology, to the Sun (or to the solar gods), to death and resurrection, it has found its appropriate place in the four Gospels in the prophecy about St. Peter denying his Master before the rooster crowed three times. The rooster is the most magnetic and sensitive of all birds, and hence its Greek name Elektryon.

GAMAHEU or Gamathei (alchemy) Stones with quality and magical paintings, which are endowed with domains acquired from astral attribution. In addition, they can assemble by art or from a natural environment such as amulets, and charms.

GAMYA (Sanskrit) Possibility of something to be reached by the believer.

GANA (Sanskrit) Legion, Crowd, group, association, etc. It mentioned to the multitude of lower legions, principally those in the service of Ziva, which are ruled by Ganeza.

GANDHARA (Sanskrit) Refers to a musical note of great power hidden in the Inda escalade, the third of the diatonic scale.

GANDIVA (Sanskrit) "Who wounds in the face." Term of the bow that Arjuna received from the god Agni. This Arch is allocated wonderful virtues.

GAN EDEN (Hebrew.) Additionally labeled Ganduniyas. The orientalists identified Eden with a place that was in Babylon in the region of Karduniyas also called Gan-dunu, which is almost identical to the Gan-eden of the Jews.

GANGRA, Council of. The assembly was held at Gangra in Paphlagonia c. 345. Passed 20 canons directed opposed to false simplicity. To these was added an epilogue, often described as 'canon 21' explaining the true nature of asceticism.

GANGA o GANGE (Sanskrit) The Ganges is a transnational river of A'sia which glides between India and Bangladesh. The 2,525 km (about 1568.96 mi) river rises in the western Himalayas in the Indian country of Uttarakhand. The Ganges, India's primordial sacred river. There are two variety of his myth: one of them allude to Ganga (the goddess), which, having been restored in river, flows from the big toe of Vichnu; as stated by the other, the Ganga sprouts from Ziva's ear to go down into Lake Anavatapta, and from there it leaves, through the mouth of the Silver Cow (Gomukhi, crosses all eastern India and drains into the Sub Ocean.

GANGE o GANGA-SAGARA. (Sanskrit) The mouth of the Ganges. Holy location to bathe, sanctify to Vichnu.

GANGI (Sanskrit) Prominent sorcerer of the time of Kazyapa-Buddha (a predecessor of Gautama). Gangi was considered as an incarnation of Apalala, the Naga (serpent), guardian spirit of the wellspring of the Subhav Astu, a river of Udyana. It was said that he became a-Arhat. The allegory of this label is easy to recognize: all the Adepts and initiates were called Nagas, "Serpents of Wisdom".

GARIMAN (Sanskrit) Heaviness, gravity; the power that the yogi gets to enhance as depressing as the most significant body.

GARBHA (Sanskrit) Sine, womb; egg, germ, embryo, fruit.

GARDEN OF THE SOUL, The. The 'Manual of Spiritual Exercises and Specifications for Christians who, living in the earth, aspire to Devotion', compiled by R. Challoner and first issued in 1740. It had wide authority.

GARLIC Is an herb developing from a vigorously aromatic, rounded bulb comprised of round 10 to 20 cloves enveloped in a papery coat. The long, sword-shaped leaves are fastened to a subterranean stem and the greenish-white or pinkish flowers grow in heavy, spherical clusters stop a flower stalk. The following health concerns can be treated with garlic: reducing cholesterol levels and cardiovascular risk, manages bronchitis, hypertension (high blood pressure), TB (tuberculosis), liver disorders, has antifungal and antibacterial properties. It gives your immune system enhancement and the components in garlic such as vitamin B6 and C, fiber, calcium, protein, manganese benefits in burning fatty tissues successfully.

GARM (Scandinavian) The Cerberus of the Edda. This monstrous dog lived in the cave of Gnypa, in front of the dwelling of Hel, the goddess of the lower world.

GARVA (Sanskrit) Pride, arrogance.

GARUDA (Sanskrit) Gigantic bird of eagle figure wrote down in the Ramayana, and that were dedicated to riding to Vichnu. Esoterically it is the mark of the great cycle. [Maha-Kalpa].

GASP A short struggle to intake breath with the mouth open. When a person breathes noisily, as when one is exhausted. Agonal gasps are mechanical and inadequate respirations that are acquired by low oxygen in the blood, it's also known as hypoxia. This breathing is not normal respiration and shows that a being may be dying. Agonal exhalation can relate to some shaking or other muscle motion due to the struggle for oxygen.

GATASU (Sanskrit) "Lifeless", exanimate, dead.

GATE. Aperture in an enclosure or fence; a city or castle entry frequently with defensive structures; the frame or aperture that closes a gate. 'Gates' in biblical Israel weren't' just doorway into the city. They were locations that prophets cried out and kings judged, and people met, like in the ancient city of Dan. Jesus labeled the gate to the setting of the sheep, thieves, robbers, that Jesus describes his good shepherd(s) characteristic by informing the sheep and the lecturer that he is "the gate' and "anyone enters by him will be saved and will go in and out and find pasture." The ministerial a theology of Jesus' saying "I am a the gate" from a liberated positionality is that Jesus is not contributing to construct a wall o put a barbed wire fence across, rather he is saying that he will be with the sheep as a person presenting love and care, building trust with one another and embracing each one with joy, for whoever goes through him will live in freedom and with good. When Jesus says, "I am the gate" he is offering his care and friendship to the sheep by being the 'gate (human' and not a 'gate wall.'

GATRA (Sanskrit) Constituents (of Brahma), accordingly the persons who were born the "mind-born" sons, the seven Kumaras.

GATHA (Sanskrit) Hymns or metrical chants, which are composed of moral sentences. A Gatha consisting of 32 words is called Arya Giti.

GATI (Sanskrit) The six (hidden, seven) circumstances of the sentient being. Divided into two groups: the three upper gatis and the lower three. To the initial communicate the Devas, the asuras and men (immortals); the second (in the exoteric teachings), the creatures that are in hell, the hungry pretas or demons, and the animals. After it is made clear esoterically, the last three are as characters that are in the Kama-Loka, elementals and animals. The seventh form of reality is that of Nirmanakaya. [The word Gati has many other definitions: course march; way, path; goal; destiny; refuge; means; procedure; achievement, acquisition, etc.]

GAUNIKA (Sanskrit) Relative or belonging to qualities (gunas).

GAURI (Sanskrit) "Bright gold color". Name of Ziva's wife.

GAUTAMA (Sanskrit). He was Prince Kapilavastu, son of Zddhodana, Zakya king of a small kingdom in the confines of Nepal. He became a Buddha on his own personal merit and without any help.

GAYA (Sanskrit) It is one of the seven most venerable cities; it is still today a pilgrimage site.

GAZELLE The indicated are graceful, leggy being remains regularly accepted in earliest Arabic and Persian composition, ordinarily as hallmark of feminine elegance, and gazelle flow derive from the Arabic ghazal, a lyrical affection rhyme typically places to melody. Gazelle is exceedingly vigilant and susceptible to the existence of more creatures. They are continually on the lookout point and have depended steadily on their vision, which is outstanding owed to their exophthalmic. In Hebrew principals, then, the gazelle was continually perceived as a extremely pragmatic hallmark of adoration, of living, and certainly of supreme being. For the members of clergy, exceedingly constructive concepts to be express in reference to a bride is that; she is "as graceful as a gazelle".

GE, GEA The earth, designated Magna Mater Deum, for having been the mother of many gods.

GEB Among Egyptians, Earth God, father of Osiris, husband of Nut.

GEBER (Hebrew) or Gibborim "Mighty Man"; the same as the Kabirim. In the promised land they are respected as powers, and on earth, as the giants mentioned in chapter. I saw it from Genesis.

GEBURAH Quinto Sephira, a feminine and passive power, symbolizing severity and power.

GEHENNA Hinnom, in Hebrew. It is not the Averno in any way, but a valley near Jerusalem, where the Israelites abstinence their children to Moloch in this valley was found a space designated Tophet, in which it was eternally held to ignite a fire for sanitary purposes. As the prophet Jeremiah has said, his compatriots, the Jews, often forbearance their children in such a place.

GEHS (Zendo) Prayers of the Parsis.

GEMA(S) (Latin Gemma). Generic names of gemstones, and more mainly of oriental religious persuasion.

GEMS (The three cherished ones) In Southern Buddhism, these are: the scripture books, the Buddhas, and the clergymen or pastorate. In Northern Buddhism and its covert schools, they are: The Buddha, his sacred teachings and the Narjols (Buddhas of Comasion).

GEMARA (Hebrew) It is the last part of the Jewish Talmud, begun by Rabbi Ashi and finished by Rabbis Mar and Miramar, around 300 AD.C. "consummation" or "perfection". It is a beginning on the Mishna.

GEM(S) "The Precious Three" In Southern Buddhism, they are: the holy books, the Buddhas, and the clergy or priesthood. In Northern Buddhism and its secret formation, they are the Buddha, his sacred teachings and the Narjols (Buddhas of compassion).

GEMATRIA (Hebrew) A segmentation of the applied Kabbalah. shows the numerical advantage of Hebrew terms by adding the values of the letters that formulate them; and in addition, by this fashion he expresses the analogies between words and phrases.

GEMINIS (Latin) (The Twins) This sign is conceptualized, the third sign of the Zodiac, and means pursuant to the most accepted criterion, Castor and Pollux. Leda, wife of Tindarus, king of Sparta, was influenced by Jupiter, in the figure of a swan, on the banks of the venerable river Eurotas; as an outcome of this union, Leda laid two eggs, from one of which Helena and Clytemnestra were born, and from the other, Castor and Pollux, also known by the common name of Dioscuros.

GENE The recommended expression detected from the Greek word genos defining "birth". The lexical spawned alternatives, like genome. Genes are the architecture bricks of existence. They carry instructions for composing clear-cut corpuscle and animo acid chain that authorize human microorganisms to perform well and that govern how the physique develops and engages. They additionally advance to the interpretation of corporeal individual and characteristics such as locks or heterochromia. The God gene theory recommends that anthropoid piousness is determined by congenital and that a distinct gene, tagged composed of neuromodulators tetrabenazine, dispose mortal predetermined religiously or mystic experiences.

GENEALOGICAL (Gnosticism) The absolute set of sects, beliefs of the world could be described within a gigantic Family Tree, clarifying in it the primordial parts in which all the doctrines that agree to lead man towards what we all seek, and which is called God or Heaven are based.

GENEALOGIES OF CHRIST. The Gospels of Mt. and Lk. Assisted (somewhat differing) GENEALOGIES of Christ; they are deliberate to emphasize that He is united with to the House of David.

GENESIS The entire book of Genesis until Joseph's death has been set up to be a barely changed version of the Chaldean Cosmogony, as has been pointed out repeatedly by the study of Assyrian bricks. Genesis is without any suspicion, and supernaturalism works.

GENEVE GENEVA BIBLE. The English translation of the Bible was initially announced at Geneva in 1560, and universally handed down for 50 years. It had questionable notes written from a Calvinist standpoint.

GENII (Latin) Terms by which the Aeon's, or angels, are designated among the Gnostics. The delegated of their hierarchies and classes are numerous.

GENIUS The Chaldeans and other peoples of prehistory believed in the life of spiritual beings, who intermediate between God and men, and who, according to them, administered the existence of each person, whom they escorted throughout their lives found located a place called Tophet, in which a fire was endurably lit for sanitary purposes. On the authority to what the prophet Jeremiah says, his compatriots, the Jews, used to proffer their affinity in related location.

GENIZA. The chamber modified to a synagogue used to house MS. Books unfit for use in worship, e.g., worn-out photocopies of Scripture, and heretical works. Precious items, particles of Biblical and other MSS were discovered in 1896-8 in a GENIZA at Cairo.

GERION According to mythology, it was a monster that had three heads. He existed on the island of Eritia and owned a beautiful herd of calves, Hercules in his tenth task or feat, killed him and confronted his guard dogs Otos and Erudition, seizing his flock to transport it to Eurystheus.

GERMAIN, St. (Germanus) (c. 496-576), Bp. Of Paris from 555. A monk before he became bishop, he tried to check the license of the Frankish kings and so stop perpetual civil wars. The church of St. Germain-des-Pres stands on the site of his tomb. Two letters, almost certainly wrongly attributed to him, have played an important part in the history of the Gallican rite. They were probably written in South of France, c. 700.

GETHSEMANE, The Garden of. The garden, just outside Jerusalem, to which the Lord retired after the Last Supper, and which was the scene of His agony and betrayal

GEOMETRY or GEOMETRIC (Latin geometric, Greek Geometra). Theosophy states that geometric standards are expounded in all the increments of nature, and were founded by God, displaying them in harmony with the universal rules or geometrically. In this way, the species is geometrically Expreso, both in the wonderful and in the corporeal, in lines, spirals, spheres, cubes, Circulo's, etc. Although this geometry is condensed essentially three-dimensionally, it is not convenient to neglect that nature realizes other higher spaces, that is, seven dimensions together.

GHADOL (Hebrew). Write concerning the "Great", the trilateral ecclesiastic appellation.

GHANDI Intermediary; a great peacemaker who made through the A-Himsa (Nonviolence), the staff of his political doctrine. He did not implement the Great Work but says that he got as far as a good percentage of consciousness, despite not having worked in the Magisterium of fire.

GHATI or GHARI (Sanskrit) (1) A period of twenty-four minutes. (2) A lunar Gathi is something less than one-sixtieth of a lunar day.

GHOCHA (Sanskrit) Extraordinarily; "Miraculous Voice". Term of a great Arhat, writer of the Abhidharmamrite-Zastra. He reappeared his sight to a blind man soaking his eyes with the tears shed by the audience induced by his miraculous conviction.

GHORA (Sanskrit) "Frightening". Ziva's subtitles.

GHOSTLY Supernatural in appearance or resonate; eerie and unnatural. A ghost is the symbol of whoever's memories lying in your mind. This could also be a warning sign to beware of adverse situations. People may ghost due to satisfaction, a loss of attraction, negative impressions, or fears of safety. Persons higher in narcissism, scheming, and psychopathy tend to view ghosting as more acceptable.

GIALI (Scandinavian) River that serves as a limitation to the empire of the dead or Scandinavian hell. ZSZe crosses you by a bridge called Giallar.

GIBURIM (Hebrew) Superterrestrial; to great men, titans, giants or "celestial men".

GIFT OF UBIQUITY (Gnosticism) Masterpiece; the faculty of those who have done the Great Work, to manifest themselves anywhere simultaneously.

GIGES (Gyges, in Greek). "The Ring of Gyges" has shifted to a frequent metaphor in European literature. Gyges was an inhabitant of Lydia who, after assassinating King Candaulo, married his wife. Plato said that Gyges once went down to a cleft of the earth and determine there a bronze horse, inside whose open side there was the skeleton of a man of gigantic stature who wore on his finger a bronze ring. That ring, once placed on his own finger, made him invisible.

GILEAD An Arabic phrase given to reference to the mountains land approaching north and south of Jabbok. It was customarily more commonly for the complete district eastward of the Jordan River. Coordinated up to this point to the northwesterly north portion of the Commonwealth of Jordan. The Bible documented that in earliest occasions their approach from Gilead, at a distant from the Jordan, a texture passed on to cure and relieve. It arrived, conceivably, from an evergreen or shrubbery and was a considerable product of commerce in the prehistoric world. It was acknowledged as the Balm of Gilead. That term converted emblematic for its dominion to alleviate and recovery.

GILGAMESH, The Saga of. A long Babylonian poem, dating in part at minimal from c. 1198 B.C. It depicts the hero, Gilgamesh, a historical statistic, as a demi-god, ordinance tyrannically. Its account of the Flood has morally paralleled with the Biblical narrative of Gen. 6-9.

GIMLI or GIMLE (Gimil) (Scandinavian) "The cave of Gimli" or Wingolf. A kind of heaven or paradise, or possibly a New Jerusalem, raised by the "mighty and mighty God", which has to do with unnamed in the Edda, raised from the Field of Ida, and after the new earth appears from the waters.

GINGER. (Zingiber officinale) is a graceful flora whose shoot rootstalk, (subterrestrial stalk) ginger root or ginger, is extensively applied as an herb and a holistic medicine. It is a dendritic perennial which multiplies per annum apparent trunk (false stems made of the rolled bases of leaves) regarding one meter long, presence slender leaflet broadsword. The potential of ginger expands serotonin and dopamine countlessly. This may diminish inflammation, which can motive desolation. Ginger can also supply aid for apprehension, unhappiness, psychopathy. The typical aroma and odor and taste of ginger proceed hail from its essential ethereal oils, the very significant who is gingerol which is the leading bioactive combination in ginger. It is liable for ginger's numerous medicinal qualities. Gingerol has mighty anti-swelling and polyphenol's reaction, conforming to investigation. An extra symptom of a disproportion Maladhara is alimentary canal and abdominal questions and tenderness. Ginger habitually is considered for generations; for its capacity to mellow and pacify and alleviate obstruction in the duodenal structure.

GIOCONDA La Monalisa by Leonardo da Vinci. Simply the same as the Divine Mother.

GIOL (Escaid.) The Styx, the river Giol, which had to cross annates of reaches to the lower world, or cold kingdom of Hel. Over this river was laid a bridge shield with gold, which led to the gigantic iron fence adjoining the palace of Hel, the goddess of the lower world.

GIR (Sanskrit) Voice, word, language, verse, song.

GIRDLE Additionally called Venus' belt, it was believed to be magical as a result, the one who put it on would confess beauty, grace, youth and irresistible attractiveness.

GIRA (Gnosticism) Knowledgeable is so prehistoric that man and as enormous as infinity itself, because it makes up the possession of all the wisdom and piercing procreated from our planet, from the worlds, suns and galaxies that circulate in their orbital routes space without limits.

GITA (Sanskrit) Song, poem. Par excellence is thus designated the Bhagavad-Gita.

GITS Plural of git, British, as in loony, an individual who has deficit of good sense or common sense oh, don't be such a silly git, of course your partner wants you about. "Global information tracker". You're in a cheerful mood, and it works for you.

GLANI (Sanskrit) Decadence, despondency, weakness, waning.

GLAUCO He became a hero with several others, and they termed them Glauco, which is found in Greek mythology: Glauco, son of Neptune and the nymph Nais, was the one who built the ship Argos, with which he escorted the Argonauts; in the battle against the Tyrrineans, he plunged into the sea and became a Sea God. In another interpretation it is said that Oceanus and Thetis made him a sea God, when he propelled himself into the sea for having eaten from a lawn, that he had seen that the fish they deployed on him, recovered their strength and threw themselves back into the sea.

GLEBE. In English and Scottish ministerial ordinance, the terra firma dedicated to the conservation of the binding of the congregation. The expression now prohibits the vicarage dwelling and the dry land on which it exemplifies.

GLORIA PATRI. The initial term of the Lesser Doxology ('Glory be to the Father', &c.), an assignment of worship to the Trinity. Its use at the closure of Psalms spans from the 4th century, and it was received quite early in metrical development at the culmination of hymns in the Services.

GLOSSA ORDINARIA. The typical prehistoric explanation on the Bible. It was masterly generally by removing from the fathers and was organized in the structure of borderline and straight glosses. It is placed in motion on the edge and linear glosses. It was established in the school of Anselm of Laon, who was responsible for the Gloss on the Psalms, Pauline Epp., and Jn. The entire Bible was stabilized by about the midway of the 12th century.

GLOSSOLALIA. The capability of uttering with 'tongues. It was an ordinary development in New Covenant life span (cf. Acts 2: 4 and 1 Cor. 14: 1 ff.) and is continually congregated with in devout renewal. It is functioning and bringing out portion in contemporary "Full Gospel".

GLUTTONY Too much food or drink. Deficiency that structures the part of the seven deadly sins

GNA (Scandinavian) One of the assistants of the goddess Freya. It is a feminine Mercury, which leads to all the localities of the world the messages of its master.

GNANA (Sanskrit) Supreme or Divine Wisdom. It is the Science of Saturn, that is, the wisdom of "Initiatory Knowledge". The cognition of the Inoichi or the Seer.

GNOSIS EXPOSES (Critic) Reveals that it is best to impose self-criticism for self-discovery, rather than wasting time criticizing our fellow human beings.

When the neighbors are criticized, it is for lack of understanding and because what is seen in the others is a consequence of our peculiar errors.

GNOMOS (alchemy) Rosicrucian name for mineral and terrestrial elementals. [Gnomes, pygmies, and cubital are tiny elementals of human appearance and with the power to extend it. They exist in the components of the earth, below the earth's surface, in dwellings which they built by themselves. They are also identified by the name of Kobolds; They live in mines and caverns and are the guardians of the treasures hidden in the bowels of the earth]

GNOSIS (Greek) Textually: "knowledge". Technical word applied by the colleges of mystical philosophy, both before and during the main centuries of the Christianity, to choose the subject of their inquiries. This sensitive and venerable sapience, the Gupta-vidya of the Indians, could only be achieved through initiation into the aminic secrets, which were a substitute for the ritual "enigmas".

GNYPA (Scandinavian) The cavern guarded by the dog Garm.

GOAT A competent ruminant mammal (Capra Harcus) possesses primitive curving horns and a beard in the male, raised for its wool, milk, and meat. Usually, the goat suggestive constitutes ideas associated with abundance, innocence, advance in peace, free spirit, and affability. It's maybe highly likely that a goat accessing into your dream could be a signal of a good course in your life.

GOB (Gnosticism) Gremlins; of the Genius or King (Elemental) of the gnomes and pygmies of the earth.

GOBLINS A myth, humanoid creature often found in current fantasy. (Folklore). An evil or mischievous spirit, often defined in pictures as human-like and ugly or distorted in form. Customary in English, Scottish, and Irish folklore, serving as a shelter expression for all sorts of evil or malevolent spirits.

GOD SAVE THE KING (QUEEN) The British National anthem. The expression 'God save the King' takes place in the English Bible at various places and it is probable that the anthem arose from a succession of common loyal phrases being cautious combined. There is some evidence that the words were put into substantially their current configuration for use in the RC chapel of James II. The tune also appears to be a 17th century refashioned of earlier Phra.

GOD (Theos: Greek; Deus, Latin) Supreme being, ineffable, incomprehensible to human intelligence; each one is it in its own way, the point of attributing human imperfections to it. theosophically it is believed in a wonderful ecumenical beginning, that is the root of All that exists, and from which everything embarks on and through which everything will be absorbed at the end of the significant cycle of Being...

GODS (Cosmic) There are cosmic or humble gods: related to the formation of matter InterCosmos; Planetary spirits, operative are subdivided into classes or hierarchies.

GOECIA (Gnosticism) Black magic contrary to theurgy. The Emblem Goecia pleads with the mysterious classification. Thus, those who explore persist enslaved by the possibilities of evil.

GOF, or Guff (Hebrew) The body, the physical structure.

GOG and MAGOG. In Rev. 20:8 they are two capacities under the control of Satan, and in thereafter literature they are typical evidence for those against the humans of God. The wooden statue of Gog and Magog at the Guildhall, London (destroyed in 1940), illustrated two giants of medieval legend.

GOGARD (Zend) The Tree of Life, in the Avesta.

GOLA (Sanskrit) Sphere. It is besides an epithet of Durga.

GOLDEN CALF It has an allegorical sign of money, materialism. The world venerates the Golden Calf which changes the spiritual for matter.

GOLDEN AGE In ancient times they distributed the platform of life in Golden, Silver, Bronze and Iron Ages, The Golden Age was an Age of purity, archaic simplicity and common happiness. [the Krita-yuga or the first age of the world.]

GOLEM SCHOONER. (gnostic) It was the term with which the magic stone or sacred stone was designated, the philosopher's stone or red canbuncio

GOLGOTA (Hebrew Skull) Mount Calvary or skull. Hill where Jesus-Christ was crucified. Gnosis explains that every initiate who has raised up the seventh serpent, there is, they have acquired the Venustic initiation, (the incarnation of the Intimate Christ), must go through the event of Golgotha in the inner worlds.

GOMOR Inside the gnosis image of the sacred vessel or Holy Grail, in which, the great Master Jesus-Christ had drunk at the Last Supper. It is the Divine Cup that owns the Blood of the redeemer of the world (the Christ) accumulated by Joseph of Arimathea. That great chalice belonged to Patriarch Abraham, and Melchizedek (King of the World) moved it with infinite love from the country of Semiramis to the land of Chanan.

GONPA A sanctuary or monastery; a lamasery.

GOOPH (Hebrew) The physical body.

GOOD (Gnosticism) Today you will understand how fantastic it is to do good; there is no suspicion that right thinking, right feeling and right acting are the best of business.

GOOD HOMEOWNER He is a balanced person and lover of his spouse and his children, teaching by occurrence and harmony. In Gnostic psychology it is elaborated with mysterious work, the other must be penetrated with infinite patience and take it as an emotional careful day for Spiritual Progress.

GOOD SHEPHERD, The. An issue of Christ's concerns in His dialogue in Jn. 10: 7-18 and on the Parable of the Good Shepherd (Lk. 15: 3-7).

GOPALA (Sanskrit) Shepherd, cowboy, nickname of Krichna, for having lived among shepherds in his youth.

GOPI(S) (Sanskrit) Zagalas or Mayorals of cows. The playmates with whom Krishna accustomed, surrounded by whom his wife Radha traced.

GORGONA A mystical spiritual legend which tells that they were daughters of Focus and Ketus, called Estenea, Euríale and Medusa, who is presented with snake hair. Medusa was the only sister who was mortal and incredibly beautiful but when she offended Minerva (Athena), she turned her hair into snakes and granted her a petrifying look on rocks to those who glanced into her eyes. Dante mentions it as, one of the three furies in his Divine, comedy

GOROS Lords who exercise power of life and death and who work with Melchizedek. A drop of water or a tear recommends perseverance and patience. The drop of water is or without force, however; with the passage of time, it can pierce the stone.

GORZE, Benedictine cloister close to Metz, confirmed in 748 by St/ Chrodegang. In the wake of great conflict in the 9th century, built by Albero I, Bp.

of Metz (919-62), shifted especially to the center of attention of monastic reform. Singularly the primary component of the advances linked with Gorze was that the Abbotts find themselves at the expulsion of sponsors, both lay and episcopal, who gather matter to take tariff of and upgrade monasteries in their kingdom. Those resources did not show a structure of footing, and their alliance acquire allegations for the utmost part, in the relation of association and corresponding faithfulness.

GOSPEL(S) (Latin evangelion and of the great evangelion: good news). It refers to the four gospels of the Bible, they were written in code by initiates. In which four texts of alchemy and white magic are exposed, so that the pioneer achieves his liberation, but an awakened consciousness is commanded to master its interpretation thoroughly. They are symbolized, with the rendering of four animals: that of San Marco, with a lion (meaning of fire); that of Matthew with a young man or angel (image of water); that of John with an eagle (emblem of the air); and that of Luke with a bull, (figure of the earth). They also personify the four elements and the realization of the Great Work. (1) The primary fulfilled of the Christian revelations, the glad tidings of redemption. (2). The subtitle of the books in which the Christian Gospel was set forth. The distinguished authority of the four Gospels of Mt., Lk., and Jn. Was accepted by the mid-2nd century. The so-called Apocryphal Gospels', which for the most part arose in heretical circles, are minor works of later date, devoid of ancient value.

GOTRA-BHU (Pali) Among Buddhists, he is the one who is prepared for initiation at the doorway of the Path.

GRACE AT MEALS. The tradition of giving thanks before and after food is not entirely Christians. Various fixed arrangements are recited audibly in religious houses, colleges and schools.

GRAFT (Latin Injerus, Introduced). To implant. It is a design of artificial intervention in the realm of the natural, it is interconnected to the suggestive interpretation, (gnostic). Gnosis explains that grafts made in plants, largely fruit trees, is an unnatural violation, since they alter the vital structure of the plant and it does not transform the energy from Megalomanic, thus altering the vital energy of the fruit it produces, that is, the fruits process by grafting do not have the cosmic energy necessary for the human organism due to the violation opposed nature. Each greenery of the plant kingdom is allocated by families such as, for example: pines, orange trees, apple trees, etc. and each of them captures a definite type of energy from the Megacom to be transformed and retransmitted to the layers of the planet for the sustenance of life.

GRAHA (Sanskrit) Understanding, idea, concept, attempt.

GRAHYA (Sanskrit) Distinguishable: "it is to be perceived," that it will be perceived, "perceptible," "knowable": that is, the objects of perception.

GRAIL, (The Holy) In gothic romances, a sailboat permeates sacred possibilities and supplies accurate conditions, spiritual well-being to its perceivers. It is associated with the chalice worn by Christ at the 'Last Supper'. The entire epic, though, persists surrounded by the adherent of worldly thesis and was never approved by sectarian officials.

GRAVITATION (Gnosticism) The man who proposes to do a work of regeneration and transformation, structures his core of Gravitation in the heart, thus permitting the Light of Being, the understanding of reality and the Love of entity to give him luminosity and the position that they must own with himself and with humanity.

GREAT CYCLO A Mahakalpa or Age of Brahma, whose persistence is 311,040,000,000,000 solar years. Its image is Garuda. Within the Great Cycle there are innumerable minor cycles.

GREAT AGE. There appeared several "Great Ages" alluded to by prehistory. In India it encompassed the entire Maha-manvantara, the "Age of Brahma", each day of which signifies the life cycle of a chain, this covers a period of seven Rounds.

GREAT SEA The Holy Spirit; Mother Water. In the occult teachings, the title of "Great Sea" is assiduously alluded to the "Sea of Life", that is, to terrestrial life.

GRAIN (Gnosticism) In the gospel the suggestion of the earthly man being compared to a seed efficient of growth has equal symbolism. Just like the one who has the idea of the resurrection: a man who is born again. "It is obvious that, if the Grain does not die, the plant is not born."

GREED Conceptualized 5th of 7 deadly sins. Assimilated with Envy, Pride and Gluttony.

GREECE (Gnosticism) Nosce te Ipsum "Man know thyself", This is an ancient golden maxim written on the undefeated walls of the temple of Delphi in ancient Greece.

GRIM (Scandinavian) One of the names of Odin.

GRIT (1) A parabolic delineation of whichever is misled in many individuals this day. It isolates the minority from the flock who are more anxious regarding dominating a protected and sheltered life adequate for compromises than reality an adventurer, anybody who isn't fearful of authorizing their imagination, their affection. A character attribute distinguished by perseverance and suffering for attaining extended aim involvement engaged energetically to pride above uneasiness and supportive commencement of each worry about and complete attention attain the role of couple persons opposed indignation, deprivation, and elevation in advancement. According to Duckworth, of the five disposition traits, precision is the majority meticulously correlated with grit.

GRIT (2) A disposition attribute owned by some human beings who established enthusiasm and determination regarding an objective regardless of being encountered by compelling barriers and disturbances. Those who take control of grit can self-activate and delay their demand for positive support while engaged vigorously on a responsibility. Grit can be mastered or modified over a lifespan. For illustration, as individuals mature, their grittiness expands. Persons may as well be instructed to have grit. You're on the right track now. We're all competent at educating ourselves on grit.

GROSSOMODO. With its roots in antiquated Latin, grosso modo implies 'roughly speaking', 'more or less', or 'in broad terms'. The benefit of utilizing grosso modo is that it supplies the kind of disclaimer that allows the spokesperson to reveal that they're being a little bit less specific, while still presenting instructions or creating an argument.

GROU, JEAN NICOLAS (1731-1803) French Jesuit. He presented projects on Plato, but he is substantially recognized for his inner chronicles.

GUARD This phrase comes from the verb Netsar "to guard, to watch, to keep". It is a verb in ordinary use in prehistoric and current Hebrew. It is used a variety of times in the Hebrew-Speaking Old Testament. Netsar appears Exo 34:7, "faithfully keeping," "keeping" the covenant (Deu 33:9); "keep" the law (Psa 105:45) etc.

GUARDIAN (Protective Wall) This idiom symbolizes the protection and preservation of all abundance, Mystical, religious and spiritual power; manifesting that without faculty it is not likely or not deserving of crossing into its influence. All the stories, myths and fables, relate of powerful guardians careful of treasures or sacred things almost constantly were Griffins, Dragons or some warrior, with exceptional ability. Among them we will mention some: the Guardian of the

Golden Apples of the Garden of the Hesperides; the Guardian Dragon of the Tree of Life; the Sphinx that guarded the road to Thebes, Cerberus, Guardian of the Averno; the Guardian of the Threshold, who must be conquered in the astral, mental and causal, to be admitted initiation. This is also a suggestive name given to the region of Adepts (Barjols) or Saints.

GUFF. (Hebr.) The body; The material form. It is also expressed as Gof.

GUHYA (Sanskrit) Esoteric, secret [mysterious.] Accepted as substantive, it symbolizes mystery, secret, arcane.

GUHYS (Sanskrit). Hidden, secret [mysterious. grasped as a nominal, contemplate; enigma, secret, arcane.]

GUIDE (SPIRITUAL) A guide or someone who protects, encourages or administers. One who directs a transit and sets up an additional or others, on a transit. Jesus Christ said, ["I am the Truth, the Way, and the Life; no one comes to the Father except through me."] [John 14:6]. He is our Spiritual guide. Only he can advise us where to walk, and how to transform the procedure of thinking, feeling and acting.

GUN(S) Armaments are made up of a hardware cylinder, with automatic accessories, from which missiles are stroked by the forward of a volatile; a wedge of ordnance. Somewhat transportable shooters, analogous as a pistol, handgun, or musket, shoot cannon artillery accommodating a leveled course. A gunner is also called a long tom. personify supposition and concern regarding gender and estate of the realm. Contemplate, for occurrence, that conceptions of indulgent equipped security, self-sufficiency, and flexibility as well proceed repeatedly in weapon promotion. During a lengthen interval, firearms have modified the society greatly; they support the vulnerable; bring about accessibility and rapid killing and injuring human beings, generally, uninvolved individuals; and they eliminate the borderlines connecting existence and loss of life, for these, incapable controlling their special performances, contemplations, and demonstrations.

GUNA o GUNAS (dharma) (Sanskrit) The acceptable affiliations to the possessions a precise abnormality. Arrangement, features; thread, rope [function, virtue, merit]. [The element (Prakriti or Pradhana] is manifested by three gunas (modes, peculiarities, qualities or property), called respectively: sattwa, rajas and tamas, which are not mere accidents of matter, but are of its very nature and assembles its composition. The three gunas can be translated in a calculated way as follows: Sattva: goodness, purity, harmony, lucidity, truth, reality, balance, etc.; Rajas: passion, longing, activity, struggle, restlessness, eagerness, pain, etc., and Tamas: inertia, apathy, tenebrosity confusion, ignorance, error, etc. The three gunas diffuse into material nature and exist in all creatures, they find the disposition or condition of everyone depending on the proportion in which they are congregated in each of the beings. We realize that Sattva is the quality (guna) that prevails over the other two in the world of the gods; Rajas is the one that is considered in the human species, and Tamas, the one that has prevailed in the brutes and in the vegetable and inorganic kingdoms. There is nothing that is free of the gunas, (except for the pure Spirit) nor is there a vital force or a point in the universe that is completely free of the gunas.

GUPTA VIDYA (Sanskrit) Attributes to the science of Mantram, or cabalism and esoteric science.

GURU (Sanskrit) Instructor; spiritual (guide); expert or coder in the integral and obscure disciplines. This word is comparably applied to the expert of any wisdom.

GUTS Derivation of this appellation approach from Early English guttas (plural) "bowels, entrails," figuratively "a channel," connected to geotan "to pour," from Proto-Germanic 'gut-, from PIE root 'gheu- 'to pour'; your gastrointestinal tract, pelvis, the interior functioning of a body, or "the basic visceral or emotional part of a person." Repudiating or deploring anybody at all, unreasonably. "My employers' brother really hates his guts.' (Japanese) is a fictitious role and the central figure from the manga Berserk by Kentaro Muria. Guts is a soldier of fortune who cruises from one establishment to another and jumps from one friendship to the next. Following his encounter with Griffith, Guts is beaten in collision by Griffith and is coerced to join the Band of the Hawk as the last Griffith announced that he "owns" Guts at the moment. The energetic and tempestuous connection allying Guts and Griffith, the commander of the Ring of the Hawk, shapes the central focal point of the manga. Succeeding the happenings of the Eclipse, during he accidentally damages his left-hand and right eye, guts pursue vengeance on Griffith. In these narratives guts perhaps a persisting and perceptible sign of our lifestyle, not solely in the psychological confrontations he tolerates but in the symbolic personality of how he influences returning from the threshold of downfall although the discouraging difficulties he visaged. To detest (anyone's) guts is initially demonstrated 1918. The concept of the guts as a place of response is antique and describes explanations equivalent to gut response, gut awareness, and contrast guts.

GUYON, Madame (1648-1717), French Quietist author. Following her husband's demise (1676) she advanced under the impact of the Quietist works of M. de Molinos, and in 1681 she started pilgrimage through France with a Barnabite friar. They were apprehended in 1687. Mme. Guyon was set free by the efforts of Mme de Maintenon and shortly developed leadership in the aristocratic clique. From 1688 she communicated with F. Fenelon (q.v.). Afterwards J. B. Bossuet had delivered her a dogmatic note in 1694, she demanded a commission to clear her; the resulting Conference of Issy (1695) doomed her. She instructed obsolete unconcerned, even to everlasting preservation, and that in reflection all well-defined concepts would want to be outraged.

GYN (Tibet) Knowledge acquired completed by the teaching of an adept educator or Guru.

GYAN-Ben-Gian (Persian). King of the Peris, the Sylphs, in earliest Iranian mythology.

-H-

HA Mantram used during practice with the elementals of the ether.

HEART (Sacred) In Egypt, the heart of Horus is venerated; in Babylon, that of the god Bel, and the lacerated heart of Bacchus in Greece and elsewhere.

HABAL (from Garmin) (Hebrew) According to the Kabbalah, it is the Body of Renewal; a representation (Talhelm) or similarities (demut) of the deceased man; a primordial spiritual inner countenance that continues after death. He is the "Spirit of bones," showed in Daniel and Isaiah and the Psalms, and he is mentioned in Ezekiel's vision express circumstance of altering dry bones from life.

HABEL (Hebrew) The female initiation, son of Adam Rishoon or Lunar Spirit.

HABITS Norm of persevering or directing achieved by repetition of interchangeable or similar acts or originated by involuntary decision.

HACHIN (Gnosticism) Characterized the burning souls or fiery particulars that exist in each atom. Those igneous souls or atomic consciousnesses are very obedient and are used for YAO reincorporation or reincarnation into life. These inaugurations ignited with the fourth dimension instantly lead from one location to another (no matter the distance) the atoms of one element to the other body that desires to reincarnate, through atomic exchange. Only the great authorities who have achieved the revaluation of the Self have the power to do so.

HADA (Latin, fata) Fantastic being symbolized in a woman's formation, with magical powers and the gift of guessing the future. The traditions and myths of antiquity coordinate it in two aspects; in benevolent and infamous, although he is often considered kind, his orders must be fulfilled mathematically, because if not, they are sufferings of terrible punishments. Some concealed respect for the Fairies as emblems of the supra-normal power of the soul. Gnosis describes what the essentials of plants are. The most important fairies have been Morgana, the White Lady, Medicine and Viviana.

HADES (Greek) or Alde's. The "invisible", that is, the realm of sobriety, one of whose municipalities was Tartarus, a location of total darkness, contemplate as the locality of the abyssal rest wanting chimera of the Egyptian Amenti.

HADIT. An additional attribute to the Divine Mother, or the Winged Serpent of Light, the Kundalini that ascends awakened through the spinal marrow. In one of the sacred books of mysteries, the following prayer is read: "Be you! O Hadith! My secret, the gnostic mystery of my Being, the central point of my connection, my heart itself, and blossoms on my lips fruitful Herfio Word"... "The winged sphere and the blue of the sky are mine." Such a prayer, recited several times at the moment of surrendering to sleep at night and concentrated on the divine Mother Kundalini, is solicited to help us in the Conscious Astral Unfolding.

HAFSA She was the daughter of Caliph Ornar, wife of Muhammad.

HAGGADAH (Hebrew) Language with which the ancient parts of the Talmud are shown.

HAGIOGRAPH. (Gk., "sacred writings') A title pertains to the third division of the hexateuch canonical Scriptures, i.e., all Books not attachment to the 'Law' or the 'Prophets'. The Books consensus are pss., Prov., Job, Ruth, Lam., Songs of Songs, Eccles., Esther, Dan., 1 and 2 Chron., Ezra., and Neh.

HAHNIR or HONIR (Escand.) One of the three powerful gods (Odin, Hahnir and Lodur) who, advanced through the land, uncovered two human forms lying on the seashore, lacking in movement, speech and meaning. Odin gave them soul; Hanhir, movement and senses; and Lodur, flourishing aspect. Thus, were men created.

HAI Demon of the mind.

HAIL MARY A configuration of prayer to the BVM, initiated on the greetings of Gabriel (all. 1:28) and Elizabeth (Lk. 1:42). It is extensively used in the RC Church.

HAIMA (Hebrew) Just like Sanskrit Hiranya (golden), as "the Golden Egg".

HAIR The covert philosophy considers hair, like the hair of animals, as the natural receptacle and retainer of vital nature that is often evaded by other emanations of the body. It is closely related to quite a bit of brain functions, for example, memory. Among the ancient Israelites, cutting one's hair and beard was a sign of corruption, and "the Lord said to Moses." They will not make Calvez in their head", etc. "The Calvez" whether original or artificial, was a note of calamity, punishment or pain, as when Isaiah (III, 24) lists, "in the space of the good, composed hair, Calvez", among the evils that threaten to fall on the chosen people. And equally, "in all their heads Calvez, and every beard will be threadbare." Signify phenomenal durability and manfulness; the distinction and possessions of an individual is said to be vigorous in his locks and fingernails. It is a sign of aptitude, of gentlewoman persuasion and tangible attractiveness. Conforming to several Native Amerin assumptions, tresses is a signal of nonmaterial potential. This describes why in struggle set up, eluding the antagonist had equivalent implications. It eliminates the opponent's forces, crumbling his relationship to the inner society. "Hair plays an integral role in the way human beings represent themselves," Niditch writes. "It is related to natural and cultural identify, to personal and group anxieties, and to private and public aspirations, aesthetics and passages." The peak Padma is the best pitha outside of the objective figure and for these of us with soberness-disregard latch, it is protected inside of our hairstyle.

HAIR SHIRT A shirt assembled of cloth entwine from hair worn as a technique of authority.

HAIYAH (Hebrew) Connects to conscience, the human soul; Manas.

HAKA (Māori:" dance") Māori posture dance that involves the entire body in vigorous rhythmic movements, which may include swaying, slapping of the chest and thighs, stamping, and gestures of stylized violence. By Te Puia. Haka is a ceremonial Māori war dance or challenge. Haka is usually performed in a group and represents a display of a tribe's pride, strength and unity. The spiritual significance of the haka is a celebration of life triumphing over death.

Te Rauparaha fashioned the haka following the fact that he scarcely avoided demise at the fists of adversary ethnic group from Ngāti Maniapoto and Waikato by covering in a pitch-black food supply trench. For the moment he gets out of it, he was saluted by luminosity and a amiable tribe headman.

HAKEM Good Shepherd: "the Sage", the Messiah who is to come, of the Druze or "disciples of Hamsa".

HANTRI (Sanskrit) Matador, destructor.

HALABHRIT (Sanskrit) "Who carries a plow". Epithet of Balarama, elder brother of Krishna.

HALACHAH (Hebrew) Denomination given to the parts of the Talmud that are doctrinal reasoning or points. This word means "rule."

HALCON Hieroglyphic and symbol of the soul. The definition varies according to the positions of the bird. If in moments it is cast as dead, it signifies the transition, the state of larva, or it is the passageway from the stage of one life to other side. At the appointed time when his wings are spread, he expresses that the deceased has risen in the Amenti and is once again in responsible ownership of his soul. The chrysalis has been changed into a butterfly.

HALITO (Gnosticism) Passageway full of endangerment inside and out, path of unspeakable mysteries, where only a breath of death blows; in this inner path when one thinks that it is going very badly it happens that it goes very well.

HALF-WAY COVENANT, The. A dogma current in 17th- and 18th-century. American Congregationalism which was held to demonstrate the relationship to God of those (mostly baptized) constituents of the community who were devoid of distinctive religious faith.

HALLELUJAH (Hebrew) Canticles; Greek and Latin aspects of the Hebrew Hallelujah, glory to Jehovah, used in the psalms, and later adopted by Christianity. (Heb., 'Praise ye Yah'), Ceremonial Liturgical declaration of praise. It occurs in the Bible (e.g., in Psalms 111-17) and it was early detached into the liturgy of the Church. In the W. It is eliminated from the Mass and Office throughout Lent, and as an expression of joy it is used for the most part frequently in the Paschal tide.

HALLEL. (Heb., 'praise'). An appropriate given by the Jews to Psalms 113-18. They were handed down at the chief Jewish festivals and may have been the hymn intonated by Christ and His Apostles at the Last Supper (Mt. 26: 30).

HALO (Latin Falco-o is) Aureola, radiance which particularly surrounds the head of figures of eminent holiness. Halo circumscribes a photographic representation extracted against the light.

HAMMON, HENRY (1605-60). Anglican divine. As headmaster of Penhurst in Kent he had daily services in church and a monthly Eucharist. In 1645 he became Chaplain in Ordinary to Charles I, whom he accompanied until his incarceration in Dec. 1647. Hammond was then deprived of his canonry in Oxford and for a time confined. He dedicated himself to alleviating the deprived clergy and raising funds to instruct future ordinands. He mentioned in the books of the gospel and helped B. Walton in the compilation of his Polyglot.

HAM (Sanskrit) Magic syllable used in sacred norms; symbolizes the power of the Akaza-Zakti. Its magnitude lies in the expiratory accent and the sound originated. [Hao Ham is the technical figure of the course of the end and that of the Akaza-Tattva, the impartial nominative of it.

HAMSAH Is the physical force of the third logo.

HANSA (Sanskrit) According to the Bhagavata-Purana, it is the opinion of the "Single Caste" [the caste par excellence], at a generation when there were still no varieties of caste, but truly "one Veda, one Deity and caste". [Hansa or Hamsa, as it is further written, indicates swan or goose; sun; soul, spiritual master; it is also the appellation of a mantra or magic formula. Used in dual numbers, it denotes the individual Spirit and the universal Spirit. Clandestine, the Hansa is a fabulous bird, which when (according to the allegory) is given for its sustenance milk diversified with water, separates one liquid from another, absorbing the milk mirror of the Spirit) and leaving the water (symbol of Matter).

HANASMUSSEN (Gnosticism) Master Samael tells us that a Hanasmussen (Hanasmussen), is a conclusion of the Cosmic Mother, is a misfortune of the splendid work. He clarifies that, an initiate can create the internal bodies and matured a man, but if he does not separate the dry Mercury (the Selves), and the arsenic sulfur (Kundartiguator Organ) and upgrade their solar bodies, in vehicles of pure gold, they still are as simple Hanamussen, with double center of gravity. A part of awareness is the deep inner man, clothed in the solar bodies.

The additional is that of the consciousness bottled up between the Ego. He is consequently turned into a black and white magician at the same time.

HANI (Sanskrit) Loss, destruction, Tanta, wane, ruin, annihilation, extinction, disappearance.

HANOCH (Hebrew) Mystically, this is a pseudonym or demonstrator.

HANUKA Wrongdoer, assassin.

HANTRI (Sanskrit). Matador, destructor.

HAOMA Outlawed; the forbidden fruit of the Tree of Knowledge.

HAPI One of the four gods of death.

HAPI ANKH Mysteries of life and death.

HARA (Sanskrit) Epithet of the god Ziva [and of Agni, God of fire.]

HARAPO (Latin faluppa, bad fabric) When the attire is worn very broken. When the initiate sees himself in the inner ragged, it designates that he is on the wrong track. Rags signify the wounds and scars of the Soul.

HARBARTMAN (Gnosticism) One of the gods of the earth.

HARCHA *(Sanskrit)* Joy, bliss, delight, pleasure, contentment.

HARDA (Sanskrit) Affection, love.

HARMONY The combination of concurrent resounds of divergent tonality or character, minor chords: harmony in fragments intone; harmony connecting violins and hors, melody is the rhythmical union of continuous play of various pitch fabricate the melody or voice; a lyrical song to advance with joyful expression. In augmentation, harmony is the impact or acceptance of existence that inspires the anatomy of existing beings; individuality or personality, defiant in vitality, exuberance; fortitude. The interpretation of melodious is ideas that go efficiently jointly, or persons and instruments that capture on adeptly. While you all progress with whoever and hardly dispute, that is a pattern of a circumstances where you have a harmonious association. To overcome in a unison system, one needs to preserve purity and achievement of our success in the motivation and not to enact recurrences in contamination and wrongdoing. To get the best of harmony we must recapitulate to end faults, flaws, and distressing manners. The state of total readiness leads us to physical, spiritual and visionary humility. Man must always live-in restfulness and in harmony with his own conscience.

HARI (Sanskrit) Astonishing, wonderful, charming, enrapturing.

HARP. An orchestral device that has certain unique cords functioning at a crossing to its expert; the ability is strumming with the fingers. Harps can be built and engage in many routines, regular or set and in philharmonic or musical entertainment. Its most generic forms are triangular and made of wood. Many have multiple columns of thread and treadle accessories. In the Old Testament; Harps were associated with David and used as the emblem of St. Cecilia, benefactor saint of musicians. When harps are seen on mortuary, or Jewlery art, it can be perceived as representation of veneration in paradise or achievements. In Hellenic imagination; therefore, lyre-flowers are ordinarily correlated with Adonis, the celestial being of melody and prognostication, they develop into hieroglyph of renewal and discernment to earliest classic. This powerful coalition connecting Adonis and Lyres raises various legends that demonstrate his deep affection for tones. After the 13th centennial, the harp approached to be envisioned the insignia figure of Ireland. It was primitively agreed on a darkened blue framework which, as claimed by the National Library of Ireland, was calculated to be established for the success of Ireland in early Irish myths.

HARVEST He who shows kind habits will be able to reap good spiritual Life.

HARVIRI (Egyptian) Horus, the eldest; ancient subtitle of a sun god; the rising sun surrogate as a god relaxed on a wholly open lotus, image of the Universe.

HARE, JULIUS CHARLES (1754-1855) A extensive Missionary. He traveled mostly in Germany and transpired under the influence of German theologizer and people of journalism; he erupted many German prepositions regarding English dogmas. In 1840 he finally became Archdeacon of Lewes.

HAS (Zend) Avesta words or phrases.

HASTA (Sanskrit) Mano. The Thirteenth Asterism of lunar mansion.

HATE. An enormous despise or intense recoil noticed in a person's behavior; tremendous perceived hostility; inconsistency towards someone or something; great unfriendliness, judgmental; detest. To hate the opposition; to loathe unfairness. Hate has been extensively as a sentiment, but also as a point of view or a feeling. A few intellectuals anticipate that hate is a maximum variety of irritation or detest; some define hate as a combination of reaction comparable as irritability, contempt and revulsion; and another consider hate as a definite and isolated perception. The expression utilized for "hate" in the 5th Psalm channels "to have an aversion, unwilling or unable to put up with, to dislike intensely". In different terms, God, is perfect and righteous, however; if we don't attempt to understand his love and holiness; we will be unable and unwilling to do away with hate and our immoral system. Hate consistently flows from anxiety, self-doubt, or suspicion. Abstain comparing yourself with others. Attempt to be the best version of yourself alternatively. Immediately after you feel hate or resentment, it is best to take a step back and avoid reacting in the heat of the moment.

HATHA (Sanskrit) Ha indicates the moon, and Tha the sun; specific images of the two breaths: ha, of prana, and Tha, of Apana. The unification of both leads to the state of samadhi.

HATHOR (Egypt) The inferior or infernal aspect of Isis, proper to the Hecate of Greek mythology.

HAVA or HAVANA (Sanskrit) Sacrifice, Offering.

HAVIS (Sanskrit) Oblation, offering to the gods, chiefly grain, soma, milk, make clear butter, etc.

HAVYA (Sanskrit) Present an offering that must be hand over to the gods.

HAWK Are birds of the big game of the family Accipitridae. They are extensively administered and are established in all the countryside excluding Terre Adelie. The Accipitrine breed covers goshawks, sparrowhawks, sharp-shined hawks and more. This category is mostly timberland birds with large tails and towering acute sight. Hawk symbolizes and means intelligence, independence, adaptability, messages, clairvoyance, and spiritual awareness. Hawks inhabit every continent on Earth except Antarctica. The Hawk is a beatific message-carrier. discerning a hawk measures, you are sheltered. perceiving hawks each of at tempo anybody is acquiring a course of scheme like a hawk undertakes during it is in flight in the air current. A hawk is a wonderful symbol of freedom and flight. The definition of perceiving a hawk personified an innovative reality.

HAYO-BISCHAT (Hebrew) The "Beast", in the Zohar: The Devil and Tempter. Hiddenly, our passions are inferior animals.

HAYDRANOS (Gr.) Literally, the "Baptist." Name of the ancient hierophant of the Mysteries who made the candidates pass by the "test of the water", in which he was submerged three times. Such was his baptism by the Holy Spirit that moves in the waters of Space. St. Paul alludes to St. John by the name of Haydranos, the Baptist. The Christian Church took this ceremony from the ritual of the Eleusinian Mysteries and others.

HAYNA. (genealogy Hyaenidae), also denoted hyaena, any of three categories of course-furred, doglike carnivores discovered in Asia and Africa and duly considered for their scavenging habits. Hyenas have long forelegs and a mighty neck and shoulders for dismembering and carrying prey. In East Africa, Hyena materialized in legend as a hero who delivers the Sun to the cold Earth, West African cultures propose Hyena define eternity, abundance, and appreciation. The latter culture also interprets Hyena with traits disclosing the darker side all humanity can obtained. There are declarations that believing mystical can be transformed into a Hyena.

HAY-YAH (Hebrew) Touch on to one of the human metaphysical "principles" according to Eastern Kabbalists which divide them into seven principles, however, Westerners; fractionate them into three, which are: Nephesh, Ruach and Neshamah. This division is said to be ambiguous an abbreviation as simple as our "Body, Soul, and Spirit"; as maintained by other scriptures they express that the Neshamah, or spirit, has three divisions, "the upper being Ye'hee-dah (Atma), the middle Hay-yah (Buddhi), and the third and final, Neshamah or (Tricks)"

HAY-YOTH HA QADOSH (Hebrew) Holy creatures who live the vision of the Merkabah, it is a vehicle or chariot of Ezekiel. The four emblematic animals, the cherubim of Ezekiel, in the zodiac are: Taurus, Leo, Scorpio (or the eagle) and Aquarius, Man.

HEA (Chaldean) The god of the Abyss and the lower planet [the great god of Knowledge]. Some see Ea or Oannes, Dagon or the fish-man.

HEAVENS Localities or worlds of happiness where souls of the integral come, when they die, according to the degree of merits they have bought during their lives.

HEAD (of all heads) (Kabbalistic) This term refers to the "elder of the elders" It is the wisdom on high, which is the head, the brain that is calm and still, and no one knows it but Himself. . . and this hidden wisdom... the Hidden of the Hidden, the Head of the Heads, a Head that is not a Head that neither reason nor wisdom can comprehend.

HEALTH Is the condition of existence excluded from illness or injury, a individual's rational or somatic circumstances. A human being who has quality bodily health is probable to have physical purpose and procedures yield at its pinnacle. Additionally, expecting the nonappearance of sickness. Systematic physical activity, stabilized nourishment, and sufficient relaxation perfect commitment to quality health. The white lily is probably the single majority favored ideogram of the two parapsychology and wholesomeness. Normally, the white lily portrays knowledge.

HEART (As defined from Oxford languages Dictionary). Is a hollow out powerful channel that forces the vital fluid feeder of the diffusive structure by pulsating tightening and breadth in creatures there could be up to quadrant cavity (as in humans), duality passage combined cavity, the center or deepest component of existence. "Right at the heart of the city". The heart configuration is accepted throughout the entire planet as an image of delightful devotion and closeness; however, the historical origins are tough to specify. Around the 1250's the first known illustrations of a heart-shape as ideogram of love was documented through the French paper the Roman de la Poire, where a young man was holding his virtually is a pine-cone heart up regarding sweetheart. In advance of the fourteenth century, the heart was commonly portrayed inverted; and in different shades for instance: The yellow heart for affection, red heart for faithful and enduring love, purple heart defined adorableness. A green heart for creation and St. Patricks' Day, at the same time a black heart smiley erected for sorrow or gloomy perception of humor. The term for heart in the scriptures is "Lev" defines heart in Hebrew, and it wasn't part to the physique for the Israelites. They had a wider interpretation of the heart additionally to our contemporary factors. They presumption the heart as the organ that provides physical life and the place where you imagine and become clear of the world; location you feel emotions and exercise judgments. The Lord said: "Do not consider his appearance or his height, for I have rejected him. The Lord does not look at the things people look at. People look at the outward appearance, but the Lord looks at the heart." (1 Samuel 16:1-13).

HEAT Your interrelation to the Sun illustrates libido. In the solar insignia the graphic substitution is checked in irregular rays alternated with those that are impartial, with relation to the diction of light.

HEBE (Greek) Goddess of youth; wife of Heracles, the Greek Hercules, which appears for the strength that is usually linked to youth.

HEBREW A Semitic population that conquered and inhabited Palestine, they were later called Israelites and Jews. It is a language that concerns the Semitic descent and is written from right to left. Jews still use it in prayers and scholarly acts, and it is the official language of Israel.

HEBRON o Kirjath-Arba. The city of the Four Kabires, as Kirjath-Arba means "the city of the Four". In that city, according to legend, an Isarim or Initiate established the famous emerald board in the dead body of Hermes.

HEDONISM The virtuous precept which continues that the correct conclusion of every single one of the righteous efforts is delight.

HECATE, HEKATE. The moon was respected as a hellish divinity, goddess of night, death and hell. They presided over the magical maneuvers and the enchantments. As Hekate she is Mother death of the Greeks, Proserpine of the Egyptians, or Coatlicue Aztec. In reality; she is one of the five features of the Divine Mother, she was constitute as a Lunar goddess (the triple Hecate) with three faces and various arms, holding in her hands the destructive flame, the dagger, the initiative blaze and the magic key which unlock all the doors of knowledge, possess as an attribute; the torch, the discipline, the dagger, and the key. Reverence was proposed to her, largely at the crossroads. Her triplicity was due to her being associated to Stene in heaven, with sagebrush on earth and Persephone in hell. The Moon contemplated as an infernal divinity; Goddess of night, death and hell. He oversees magical operations and enchantments.

HEIA The Samoyed Tatars appoint the supreme Being.

HEIRIC OF AUXERRE. (841-876/7). Educator and hagiographer. He set foot in the cloister of St. Germanus at Auxerre as an oblate when he was about 7. After studying somewhere else, he taught at AUXERRE until his death. His master work is a metrical life of Germanus. He is related to the Carolingian schools and the later Middle Ages.

HEIRMOS. The opening stanza in each one of the canons.

HEL or HELA According to Germanic mythology, Goddess of the underworld and death.

HELA The mansion of Hel. Other times it means Death.

HELIOTROPISM (Gnosticism) It is what proceeds in all Creation materializing to have a life of its own and trusting in what we understand as Heliotropism, that is, the reflection of the life that exists there, coinciding with the uncreated light.

HELIOUS Greek name of the Sun.

HEMAN (Sanskrit) Gold. The planet Mercury, because of its yellow color.

HEMERA (Greek) "The light of the secondary or terrestrial localities", like the Ether is the light of the upper celestial spheres. Both germinated from Erebos (Darkness) and Nux (Night).

HEMFTA (Hemphta) (Eg.) Title that the ancient Egyptians gave to Jupiter.

HENOTICON. The scriptural procedure put accelerating in 482 to sheltered unification linking the Monophysites and the Orthodox and subsidized by the Emp. Zeno. It was extensively approved in the East, however, never tolerated in Rome.

HENRY OF GHENT (d1293), Ecclesiastic, He was one of the chief spokesmen amid the laical, 'materialistic' convocation of Augustinianism, in which he supported at Paris. In his Quodlibet and (unfinished) Summa Theologica he was in opposition of both St. Thomas Aquinas and Siger of Brabant in his endeavor to integrate the old Augustinianism with the modern Aristotelian articles.

HERMIT. One who from religious motives has retired into solitary life. Christian's hermits began to abound in Egypt and the surrounding regions towards the end of the 3rd century. In the West they died out after the Counter Reformation; in the East they survived.

HEPTA (Gr. seven) Component arranged in some Spanish voices with the symbol of "seven".

HEPTADA (from the Greek heptad, seven) Septenary.

HEPTAGON (Greek) means the number seven; it is the number that the Pythagoreans conceptualized as the perfect and religious number. This issue was titled Telesphoros because through it everything in the universe and in humanity is directed to its end, what it expresses, to its culmination.

HERA (see Juno)

HERACLEON A gnostic pedagogue who composes assessments on St. Johns' Doctrine and is possibly the creator of the chronicle on ternary creation' found at Nag Hammadi.

HEREDITARY TARAS (Gnosticism) Mechanism by which Karma is processed.

HERM ANUBIS It is a coordination of Hermes (Mercury) with the Egyptian Anubis. He is symbolized with the body of a man and the head of a dog or jackal, with a caduceus and a sistrum. (Musical instrument of the Egyptians).

HERMEROS (Greek) De Hermes (Mercury) and Eros (Love). Pagan deities who participated in Mercury and Love. It was symbolized in the figure of a child who had in one hand a bag and in the other a caduceus.

HERMES (Trismegistus) (Greek, Three times great) Gnostic the "three times great Hermes", the Egyptian. Mystical figure, from whom hermetic philosophy took its name. In Egypt, the god Thoth or Thot. It is a generic term of many ancient Greek writers who handled philosophy and alchemy. In this teaching of Hermes are contained the ultimate keys to pure wisdom. He was the writer of the emerald table. He is a resurrected master, The Avatara of Egypt, who inherited the knowledge of the Atlanteans.

HERMETICA Any teaching or writing linked to the occult doctrines of Hermes, respected either as the Egyptian Thoth or already as the Greek Hermes, was the god of Wisdom among the ancients, and according to Plato, "discovered numbers, geometry, astronomy and letters." Although for the most part the hermetic writings were conceptualized as spurious, they were nevertheless highly incorporated by St. Augustine, Lactantius, Cyril, and others.

HERMIT A human existence in loneliness as a reverent regulation. A crested swift initiated in the shaded bottom surface of equatorial woodland, explore down a systematic course route recluse appreciate existing all alone, in the forest, up in mountain top, or occasionally they reside in a town minus barely forever departing their condo. The radicle of the term is the Grecian Eremos, defining "solitary." A survival of isolation isn't for everyman, nevertheless a recluse selects it for some statistic of intentions. The (cab.) Ninth Arcane of the Tarot. It is symbolized by an old hermit in a position to prosper by keeping in his left hand the lamp that shows the route, (the lamp means knowledge). In his right hand the staff of the Patriarchs, the mantle he carries, symbolizes prudence. Behind him, the palm of triumph. At the top, a sun that illuminates with three primary forces, (Father, Son and Holy Spirit), which come down to merge with the moon that rises from the waters of life, suggesting that the moon should be altered into the sun. The arcane nine constitute the ninth sphere (sex), the nine heavens, the nine Dantes Que circles, harmonizes with the number nine and the sephiroth Jesod, (the vital body, reasoning).

HEROD FAMILY Herod the Colossal was chosen king of the Jews by the Romans in 40 B.C. and governed from 37 to 4 B.C. Christ was born during his reign. On his passing his state was divided among his sons: Archeus, as ethnarch of Judaea, Idumean, and Samaria, who was overthrown in A.D. 6; Antipas, as tetrarch of 'Galilee and Peraea, the 'Herod the tetrarch' of the Gospels (4 B.C.-A.D. 34). Agrippa I, the son of Herod the Colossal second son, Aristobulus, was executed in all the well-known regions; he governed until A.D. 44 and is the 'Herod' of Acts. His son, Agrippa I, is the 'King Agrippa' in front of whom St. Paul came forth.

HEROE(S) (Latin heros-ois, and this from Greek) Is one who takes a heroic action to the extreme. In prehistory they were received as heroes as well: Hercules, Achilles, Aeneas, and many more. The true hero is the one who performs the Great Work himself, who wins in the twelve occupations or feats of Hercules.

HERU See Cheru.

HESYCHIUS (fl. c.300) Biblical textual critic. In agreement with Jerome, he amended the text of the LXX in the interpretation of the Hebrew.

HETUMAT (Sanskrit) Causative, Caused, that which has a cause; or that it is a cause; reasoned.

HEU (S. Xni AC.) A high priest of Israel and Judge for forty years, of the Jews, he was Master of Samuel. It is related that he died when he fell on his back and stripped naked, there he heard the news of the loss of the Ark of the Covenant.

HEVA (He-va) (Hebrew) Eve, "the mother of all that lives."

HEVE (Eve) Eve symbolizes the divine chalice, as does Hebe the Greek goddess of youth and the Olympic bride of Heracles (Hercules), sun "The Eternal Feminine".

HEYA (Hebrew) That should be avoided.

HEXAPLA. The accurate copy of the Scriptures put together by Origination, in which the Hasidic narrative, resolve into Greek nature, and the quadruple Grecian variety of Aquila, Symmachus, the Septuagint (in a revised text with critical signs), and Theodotion were displayed in equivalent baluster. For some segments of the Old Testament, up to three additional Greek genres were included, composing nine columns in all.

HEXAEMERON. The description of the creation of the Creation in six days in Gen. 1: also, inter-testamental observations on this narrative.

HEXATEUCH The honorific designated by J. Wellhausen and others to the initial six books of the Tanakh with the reliance that all were compiled from an original set of classical inceptions.

HICKS Is an ingenuous, simple individual who lives in the province, considered as reality witless or rustic. Your enunciation and affection for attired with coveralls may cause several people to deliberate whether you're a hick. The expression hick is both casual and diminishing; specifically, if you summon your relative who does animal rearing, Saanen goats and poultry a hick, she'll very likely be insulted. The Webster's dictionary describes hick "as an awkward or simple person especially from a small town or the country". God explained: "Blessed and the meek, for they will inherit the earth" This familiar declaration of our Lord is pulled from the Sermon on the Mount when communicating the Beatitudes. "However, what does the attribute of meekness truly mean: Blessed are the meek: for they shall possess the land.

HIADES or Hisdas (Latin Hyades and gr. Rain) Astron. It is a remarkable group of stars in the constellation Toro. According to Greek mythology they were Nymph's daughters of Atlas who upraised Dionysus. Jupiter (Zeus), the God of Olympus, took them to the sky and positioned them as a set of stars in the constellation Taurus.

HIEROGLYPH(S) The sacred characters of the ancient Egyptian language. In this kind of document, figures of matter are applied in the space of letters or beneficial signs peculiar to the other alphabets. The designation hieroglyph precisely explains "sacred carvings." The Egyptians initially applied hieroglyphs solely for engraving sculpture or decorated on church walls. This formation of illustrated calligraphy was also used on burial places, pages of papyrus, timber panel envelop with a cement sponge, fraction and particles of chemical sediment. Rock.

HIEROPHANT (Greek Hierophants) indicates textually: "he who explains sacred things", the confessor of the sacred wisdom and principal of the Initiates.

HIEROLOGY (Greek) Wisdom that deals with religions or sacred things. Particularly sacred writings and Egyptian legends.

HILLEL, School (of) The companions of Hillel, a rabbinical instructor of the generation of Christ. In resistance to the school of Shammai, they upheld a factual and tolerant exposition of the Regulations.

HILDA, St. (614-80) Abbess of Whitney. Descended from the Northumbrian noval line, in 657 she established a cloister for men and women at 'Streanaeshalch', later named Whitney by the Danes, which cultivated in renown and influence. At the Synod of Whitney (664) she supported St. Colman in his safeguarding of the Celtic customs.

HINNOM, Valley (of) Name of the original de Gehenna.

HIGIA She was the Goddess of health, daughter of Aesculapius and Lambetia. She is symbolized in prehistory as a maiden, carrying a serpent (representation of health) duty of a cup that the Goddess held in her hands.

HILLEL Babylonian Chief Rabbi of the century before the Christian era. He was a builder of the sect of the Pharisees; he was a just and learned person.

HIMARATI Established on numerology value 7, Himarati is recognized, psychological, inexplicable, intangible, formal, questioning, eremite, self-analyzing, methodical. Himarati has an analytical character, is constantly exploring whatever is fascinating or accurate, is not simply undulated by others and is a conceptual mastermind.

HINA (Sanskrit) Private, abandoned, secluded, etc.

HINAYANA (Sanskrit) The "Little Vehicle"; instrument and academy of the Buddhists of the North, adverse to the Mahayana or "great Vehicle" of Tibet.

HINDUISM The devotion of the Indians; Brahmanism. It is the belief of most of the inhabitants of India and had its origin in the north of it.

HINSA (Sanskrit) Damage, prejudice, offense, destruction, homicide, cruelty, malevolence, desire to harm. In the aphorism one must understand by hinsa the desire evil to any being, by word, deed or thought.

HISI (Finland) "Principle of Evil". in the Kalevala, moreover, it is an epic poem of Finland.

HIT This phrase arise in the Middle English beating ('to hit, strike, make contact with'), from Old English hittan ('to meet with, come upon, fall in with'), trailing Proto-Germanic hit Tijana ('to come upon, find'), from Proto-Indo-European 'kh2eyd- ('to fall; fall upon 'hit' cut' hew') guide a sole palm or a utensil or firearms toward proximity with (someone or something) rapidly and strenuously, remarkable a target; an instance of momentous all or reality afflicted; 'The girl hit the cat with her book.'

HIPPOPOTAMUS (Hippopotamus, gr.) In Egyptian allegories, Typhon was described as "the hippopotamus who killed his father and raped his mother" (female parent of the deity). His male parent was Cronos. Then, if such a contestant is appeal to Spell and create (Cronus and Rhea), like an allegation is comprehensible. The symbol of immense confrontation, Tifton, who is additionally Piton, the mythical creature launch from the effect of the outcome of Deucalion, "violates" his mother, the primeval tranquility, whose benefaction was so enormous that it accomplished him the denomination of "Mother of the Golden Age". Typhon was the one who concluded this, in other words, he generated the initial warfare of the elements.

HIPPO Council, of (393). A committee of the Catholic (I.e., non-Donatist) Church in Latin Africa. A compendium of its standards progressed into widespread principal regulation.

HIQUET (Egypt) The divinity frog; One of the emblems of eternal life and the primary "water". The prehistoric Christians had in their church's gaslights assembled in the formation of a frog, to indicate that water baptism led to immortality.

HIRAM (s X to J.C.) He was king of Tyre. He supported friendly associations with Solomon and sent him architects and materials for the building of the Temple in Jerusalem. (Gnostic) In esotericism it symbolizes the god Mercury, our Divine Monad, whose Temple is restored in a field of sport, by origin of having eaten of the disrupt fruit in the garden of Eden; that is, because of fornication.

HIRANYA (Garbha) (Sanskrit) The bright or golden Egg or Matrix. Concealed, the luminous "Fog of Fire", or ethereal corporeal, from which the reality was designed. Epithet of Brahma, born from the primordial Golden Egg. "He who can exclusively be granted by the spirit... Eternal, soul of all beings, having determined, in his thought, to make emanate from his own substance the various creatures, he first created the waters, and in them he accumulated a germ. This germ became an egg, shiny as gold and radiant as the sun, and in it came to light Brahma himself, progenitor of all beings.

HITA (Sanskrit) Good, happiness, benefit, gift, reward; profit, utility. - As an adjective: good, useful, profitable, healthy, etc.

HITAKAMYA (Sanskrit) Longs to do someone favors.

HIVIM or Chivim (Hebrew) From whom the hives come. The successors of Heth, son of Canaan, son of Ham, "the cursed one", say "I am Hivim", "Being a Hivim, I am of the great Race of Dragons. I am a Snake because I am a Hivim."

HLADA (Sanskrit) Joy.

HLER (Scandinavian) God of the sea. One of the three wealthy sons of the Ice Giant, Ymir These sons were: Kari, God of air and storms; Hler, God of the sea; and Logi, of fire. They classify the cosmic trinity of the ancient Scandinavians.

HOA (Hebrew) Illustrates what Ab proceeds from the "Father," therefore it is the hidden Logos.

HOANG (Ty-Chinese) "The Great Spirit". Their children are said to have obtained new knowledge and demonstrated what they knew before to mortals, falling like insurgent angels, into the "Valley of Pain", which is denotative our world. In other words: they are like the "Fallen Angels" of beliefs, and to egos that are secretly incorporated.

HOD Astral splendor. (Heb.) It is the eighth sephirot of the cabala, the splendor. It declares the inspiring grace of the Great Architect. Hod is the astral body, natural magic. It is the astral that is governed by the Moon. You have to manufacture Hod or Astral Body, which is of solar nature. All living entities of nature are lunar, holding a lunar astral that is a phryan, protoplasmic body, a bestial remnant of the past. The solar astral body is the true one, since it is solar in nature. Hod belongs to the third magic triangle of the Hebrew cabal, with the capabilities of Hod's initiation and the acquisition of the lunar sky. The state of angel is accomplished.

HOEDER (Scandinavian) God blind but assigned of exceptional strength. Its epithet is a sinister omen. He killed Baldur (or Balder) with his arrow, but, since he was blind, Loki guided his hand.

HOGAN Athabaskan Indian orthodox and ritualistic formation lodging places of Arizona and New Mexico routinely assemble of tree truck and sludge with an entryway habitually facing oriental. Advance hogans were mosque structure with stump, or sometimes gravestone, substructure. Sole encloses, the arrangement was then protected with soil, scum, or occasionally pasture.

HOLE Emblem of immense size that corresponds substantially to two planes primarily: in that of biological life, it has a domain of abundance and is linked to fertility rites; in that of the spiritual life it expresses the "opening" of this world in relation to the other, by which the soul must pass to emancipate itself from the karmic cycle. The hole also means the passage from the life of separation to the in spatial, from the life of time to the timeless and incumbent.

HOLY CHAMBERS It has been stated that in Egypt there existed a certain underground passageway that had 33 chambers. Each of the vertebrae of the spinal vertebrae is interconnected to the holy or temple chambers. They are also denominated tabernacles. To the vertebrae internally cannons.

HOLY CROSS DAY. The title is given in the BCP almanac to 14 September, in addition investigated as the "Exaltation of the Holy Cross".

HOLY SHROUD An antique preserved at Turin and appreciated as the twist blanket in which Christ's body was guarded for sepulture (mt.27.59&c).

HOLY OILS (Chrism and Unction) a mixture of olive oil and balsam passed down in the liturgy of the Greek and Latin Churches. It might be devoted solely by a prelate, in the East by the Patriarchs alone. Conforming to permit Latin operation, chrism is devoted on Maundy Thursday, since 1955 at a singular Mass of the Chrism. It is used in the Sacraments of Baptism, Confirmation, and Holy Orders, additionally in the fidelity of churches and altars.

HOM (Persa) Flaming figure, spring of clarity, comprehension and existence, which populate Mount Albordj. Anoint the aqua and the portion, direct male who action fine, and conflicts precipitation (giants or wicked geniuses). He presided over the arol Hom, traced his course to the clouds and helped the genius Taschler distribute the rain. This name is also given to the Tree of Life.

HOME (Latin focus, fire) Place where the fire is placed in kitchens, ovens, fireplaces, etc.) Family life, dwelling, residence, bonfire. It is an emblem of family conjunction, in the masculine (fire) and feminine (enclosure) beginnings, through tenderness.

HOMAGE Advantage, recollection, praise, deliberation manner acclaim and acceptance display to a few more. (From Medieval Latin hominaticum, lit. "pertaining to a man") in the bygone lifetime was the guidelines to which an antiquity dweller or beneficiary assurance renowned and cooperative to his barbaric maestro, approved in trade the indicative reward of his newest location (enrollment). Homage is enduring that is assembled to reimburse recompense praise to a respected supervisor, the two energic and at associate passed on. As a result, the creators' acclaim for the attempt of their reverence existence, the single which restorative the emergence of most recent labor. Supply the higher with solemn commendation and animation besides excited. recompense salute to the descendants, or His tendency be irritated, and you break up in your rebellion, for His resentment can blowup maybe immediately. Each of the soles which attain defense in them are content.

HOMA (Sanskrit) Offering rice and butter made in the fire.

HOMAGNI (Sanskrit) Sacred fire.

HOMER It is narrated that it existed by the ninth century to J.C. seven cities revealed its lineage: Smyrna, Chios, Salafina, Colophon, Rhodes, Athens and Argos. Author of the "Iliad" and the "Odyssey". The master Samael ratifies, that he was a grand adept and clairvoyant and that he was not blind, as it is committed, because his obfuscation is allegorical, it implicit that he not only saw the artifact of the physical world, but also the things of the inner worlds.

HOMIN (Sanskrit) The monk who makes the offering.

HONEST TO GOD. The Name of a book, initially circulated in 1963, by J. A. To Robinson, then Bp of Woolwich, to what end great number of the customary hypothesis regarding the sublimity of God were admonish.

HONEY A golden-tanned adhesive liquid produced by honeybee and additional bugs from ambrosia acquired from blossom, consume as a sugary nourishment. Whether commodity appeal to human beings such as freaks to a stash or for instance images circular a bonanza, it appeals to individuals in great figure. The indicated is the manifest that interest experts manufacturing persons for example unpredictable conditions to a storehouse, etc. Both Ezekiel and John describe visions in which they eat the scroll of God's Word and it tases as sweet as honey in their mouths (Ezek. 3:3; Rev. 10:9-10).

HONIR (Scandinavian) It is said that he was a god-maker who allocated the first man of discernment and ability, after undergoing been a man endowed by him, assembled with Odin and Ludor, of an ash tree.

HONOR (Gnosticism) Not only are forecasts stolen, the honor of people, the integrity and dignity of women, real estate, the disposition of people, etc. are also stolen.

HONOR The voice used, as part of the fourth of the Ten Commandments (Honor Father and Mother) given to Moses at Mount Sinai by Jehovah as law for the Hebrew people.

HORA-zastra (Sanskrit) Designation of an astronomic work formulated by Varahamihira. This effort has concluded to us in totality, for scarcely a third of it remains. (Weber, Indiscke Literatur geschichte).

HOR-AMMON (Eg) "The begotten of himself" In theogony, a term that concerns the Sanskrit voice Anupa Daka (without parents). Hor-Ammon is a mixture of the ram-headed god of Thebes, and of Horus.

HOUR (Sanskrit) Hour. Half of a Zodiac sign. (Prasad Branch).

HOUSE. Material formation, while a home is an inner affection. A home can be made of several substances and in any appearance, if it has interpretation for you and your household. Countless human race attains these two concepts discombobulated because they require living dwelling; on the other hand, one can find more to it than that! Exactly as the metropolis, the Sanctuary, the castle or mansion, and the Elevations, the house is amongst the mecca of the planet. Even though, a location that reacts according to a situation, and it exists as an effigy of totality. It resembles the protection characteristics of the Magna Mater, and in its present condition is the core of progress. As a sign of the individual; the house as a result pleasantly bounce back the way man perceives his identity, with both an innermost internal, or proprium as observed from inside and disclosed at most, to such confidant which are summoned inward, as well as a popular or communal external (the personality or disguise, in Jungian idioms) or the person that each person selects to shows to everyone else. Your psychological residence is the scene in which you identify that you are fit, regularly since your impressions or points of view are the alike as those of the human beings who reside there.

HORACE or Quintus Horace Flaccus (65-8 A.D. J.C. He was a Latin poet, coexisting with Virgil. In 44, when Brutus made his way to Athens after the assassination of Julius Caesar, Horace joined him as a military contribution and took part in the decisive Battle of Filipe. His efforts formed an affectionate motive of surveys of the Greco-Roman tradition.

HORCHIA (Chaldean) According to Berosus, she is the same as Vesta, goddess of the home.

HORIZONTAL (Gothicism) People who lead a horizontal life identify with mechanical developments. Life is mechanical and horizontal, for everyone is subjected to circumstances.

HORMONES (Greek excite, move) They are outcome of the secretions of certain organs of the body, of animals and plants, which transported by the blood or by the juices of the vegetable excites, inhibits or adjusts the projects of other organs. Hormones lead to blood circulation and boost the activity of other organs. Sex hormones for example, entering the torrent sanguineous perform prodigies. Hormones enrich the bloodstream in extraordinary ways and in this way ailments and diseases disappear.

HORNS (silver) (Gnosticism) The horns are emblem of the verb, symbolizes the constellation of Taurus, so the initiates converge in Astral Body to the Temples to sacred dances, carrying silver horns. It is a illustrative attribute that is obtained with esoteric work. Michelangelo, who was an initiate, painted Moses with horns in appearance of luminous rays. The silver horns also stand for the horns of Lucifer. Some esoteric works speak of Lucifer's tridents, on each horn; They are signs of absolute enlightenment the instant they have through the work of alchemy.

HOROSCOPE Attention to the situation of heaven at the hour of the birth of every one of us, by which the astrologer declares the events of our existences. Today it is beyond analyzed those horoscopes and judicial astrology are not entirely veracious in the invention, and that the stars and constellations have, therefore, an esoteric and enigmatic effect on people; and they are connected to them.

HORSE. A sizable herbivorous subjugated Mammalia with solidified trotter and loose crown and commonly, used for riding, racing, and transferring tows bundles, a fixture or composition on which individual is move up or prop up, principally a support. The horse is an awesome creature that incorporates the intangible potential of self-determination, privilege, grandeur, fortitude, credence, success, courage and championship. Its character relates to muscularity, audacity and flexibility. The horse is built organized for the periods of struggle, but the conquest is embraced by the Master. (Gnosticism) Refers to the physical body, the element and relates to the mind and desire. Depending on the ride, it can mean instincts, and vehement desires. In ancient times, the horse was dedicated to Mars; and it was believed to be an omen of war. The tradition was so common that horses were considered clairvoyant, and perceptive. It was attributed a magical character for its relationship with water. According to Gnostics, the mares had bronze manes. And they ate only human flesh. It is said that Diomedes, King of Irada, sacrificed every foreigner who arrived, to give them food. In addition, it is said that Hercules, in his seventh work, imprisoned them alive to send them to King Eurystheus. They also represent in esotericism, human and passionate defects, who are unconscious, determined to destroy misfortunes.

HOSANNA The Greek configuration of the Hebrew request 'Save. we beseech Thee'. It was used by the assemblage when they saluted the Lord on His triumphal arrival into Jerusalem on 'Palm Sunday' and was initiated into the Christian ritual at a prior occasion.

HOSEA, Book (of) Minor Prophet. Hosea describes his life story with his untrue wife as a lesson of what took place through God and Israel (1-3) and then (4-14) spreads the subject of Israel's untrueness regardless of the encounters of love of God. He is the first Biblical author to utilize the ancestry bind as a graphic of the connection linking God and man. He predicted before 72 B.C.

HOPE (ESPERANZA), (LA) (cab) Arcano 17. The Star of Hope delineates hope and aspiration. It is symbolized by a woman in the middle and naked, watering the earth with the two elixirs (male and female); on its head a lotus flower denotes its progress chakras. At the top shines, the star of Venus of hatred and rays that suggest the initiations of fires tracked by those of light. At the bottom, in the waters of life; the two triangles: the positive and the negative, this Arcane is connected to the Number 17, and the 8 (1 + 7 = 8).

HOPE Is the affection of assumption and craving for definite activities to come about. An emotion of confidence, wishing situation to take place or be the occurrence. The ability of metaphor approach from invoking definite affection and fondness and with fair a glimpse, a rapid glance at a figure perhaps immediately builds perceive quality or unpleasant minus the demands for any sound. The anchor is a Christian sign for hope and faithfulness. The origin for this symbol is Hebrews 6:19, which hope to possess as an anchor of the spirit, twosome surely and devoted. Anchors are transpired in numerous engravings in the catacombs of Rome. The butterfly is a metaphor to display survival, hope, conversion, and acceptance. A rainbow is a mark of tranquility, hope and fresh start. The rainbow appeared displayed in western art to spell the assurance of accomplishments approaching. Innumerable perspectives it as a mystical cue, indicates that one should escape their current course and recapitulate. The flower of hope is the Iris, holds dear Camaraderie and courage; it is the enthusiasm for the flower-de-luce. The shade corresponding with hope is yellow, perceptible in several nations during golden ribbons. They are visible by households who have beloved at warfare. Blue personifies confidence, honesty, understanding, trust, comprehension, optimism, faith and the promise land. It is the tone of the sky, and it is the color of empathy. Purple impersonates the Messiah, who would come back. Scarlet embodies His blood that was radiated and white, the covering portrays the virtuousness of all who approach Him in faith.

HOSANNA (Latin hosanna and from Hebrew host to save us) Exclamation of joy used in the Catholic liturgy. Hymn that is sung on Palm Sunday.

HOST(S) (SPIRITUAL) Pertaining to evil or against "spiritual malice." It Relates to the religious leaders of pagan, Dugai or Judaizing tendency who sought to destroy the church of Ephesus, incomplete because of physical threats but mainly rattling to refute their beliefs and teachings. (Gnosticism) Allow my Lord, your Hosts to teach me wisdom. (The host) What is offered as a sacrifice at a Liturgy. A priest has the power to consecrate the bread and wine in the body and blood of Christ; after pronouncing the words of consecration by raising their hands, while the community or flock worships and prays to Christ.

HOTRIYA (Sanskrit) Prelate Hotri (sacrifice); the place where the offering is made (the altar).

HOVAH (Hebrew) Refers to Eve; the beget or mother of all that exists; the land or species.

HRI (Sanskrit) Modesty, honesty, decency, humility, shame.

HRIM (Sanskrit) Triple sacrosanct interjection in the Bhagavata Purana. It reads OM; Hram! Hrim! Hrum! adoration of the blessed Hrichikeza...

HRICHITA (Sanskrit) Joyful, content, pleased, erect, rigid.

HRITA (Sanskrit) Taken, carried, snatched.

HU Cadarn (Celt.) Spouse of Koridwen (Nature). It is the manifested Spirit, Gwyon, son also of this same Koridwen.

HUA (Hebrew) He. In the Hebrew Kabbalah, this pronoun is applied to Macroprosopic Esotericism; as well as Ateh, "You," refers to the Microprosopy.

HUMANITY Esoterically and Kabbalistic all, the compound of humanity is delineated in India by Manu; by Vajra sattva or Dorje Sempa, notable participant in Tibetan Buddhism who illustrated clarity, empathy, and understanding, also chief of the seven Dhyani in Northern Buddhism, and by Adam Kadmon in the Kabbalah. All of them symbolize the totality of the human class, whose beginning is this androgynous protoplasm [first father], and whose end is in the Absolute, beyond all these images and myths of human origin. The world is a great harmony by effect of the similarity of the material from which it is physically and ethically created.

HUMANOID In light of the Gnostic science it has been achievable to prove that the legitimate man is neither more nor less than a programmed machine. This Humanoid is the happiest beast that exists in this valley of tears; however, he has the aspiration and even the insolence to title himself: "King of Nature". That machine man has invented thousands of other complicated and difficult machines; he knows very well that in order to perform preferable services as an intellectual machine, sometimes he needs long years of study and learning, but when it comes to himself, he totally forgets this fact, even if it is a complicated machine; measured to all that he has invented; This humanoid never behaves like a true human being because since he gets up in the mornings he can be in a bad mood or perhaps in a good mood, absoluteness depends on the ideas that reach the different centers that make up the human organism. interpreting the human being as an intellectual animal and that physically resembles "Man", but is not properly constituted, because it lacks the internal bodies. The movements, words, ideas, actors, emotions, feelings desires of this humanoid are provoked by external influences and by multiple unknown and complicated inner causes.

HUMILITY (Latin humulitas, Atis) This Christian virtue consists in the wisdom of our lowliness and misery, in acting conforming to oneself. Esoteric knowledge endurance in the transcendence of developing humility, eliminating our mistakes, first fulfillment and vanity. "If you want to receive the light and wisdom, be humble, and previously you have received it, you will be even more humble." A person full of himself, of vanity, pride, lies, etc. cannot be humble; whoever apprehends being humble should dissociate his defects, or selves, and awaken his conscience.

HUMO (Latin fumus) It is hiddenly known as the antagonism of mud, water and earth, because it scrutinizes the fire and air components. Smoke is horror, darkness, bestiality, while flames are light, love, transcendental chastity. Another substitution is supported by the column of smoke that translucent the path of the bonfire regarding exaltation. It is also admired as the autonomous Soul of the body. Within folklore it is appropriate beneficial power to be used as a magical attribute to drive away, and remove the misfortunes of man, animals and plants.

HUN-DEZA (Sanskrit) The region located around Lake Manasarovar in Tibet.

HUNCH (Gnosticism) Divinity can send messages through Hunches.

HUNER or HOENER (Scandinavian) God is clear but assigned of exceptional power. Its reputation is one of dire prognosis. He killed Baldur (or Balder) with a dart, but since he was blind, Loki directed his hand.

HUNGER Is an influential feeling, that is being the two deceitful and devastating to one another although directly make trouble. Human beings recognize this emotion with fondness and erroneously identify those cravings with authentic sentiments. extinction perhaps further opposite. Threesome of lack of food are physical necessities for nourishment or heat source. Committees assemble free time and enlarge the extended proceed in the absence nibble. Tummy hungriness. Buccal lack of food. Attachment emptiness. Psychological desire transpires during all that. Demand it devotedly. A few people undergo this starvation that arises from infancy affliction and craving origin by impoverishment. frequently, this is an example that acquire proceeds downward from peer groups to peer groups. Hunger was the daughter of the night, the mother of death, and the counselor of crime. They abandon behind Belona and Mars when these gods wage war. She is depicted as a malnourished woman, with disheveled hair and long nails with which she dug the earth in search of food.

HUNT, WILLIAM, HOLMAN (1827-1910), Pre-Raphaelite interior decorator. He formed a correlation with D. G. Rossetti and in 1848 they set up the Pre-Raphaelite partner. The largest accepted investigation of his paintings, The Brightness of the World, narrations for the Lord's strike at the food of the soul. The first, painted in 1854, is in Keble College, Oxford his repainting of the matching subject (1904) is in 'St. Paul's Cathedral.

HUNTER (Gnosticism) It process the state of alertness, self-remembrance, to catch or hunt the Ego, now it acts.

HUNTING. Throughout hunting has customarily adhered permissible for the congregation, it was beforehand not acceptable to the clerics. It is, anyway, debated certainly all hunting is prohibited, or exclusive 'noisy' hunting, the 'quiet' variety actuality authorized in abstaining. It is like seeking or questioning, in the hunt for the ego. In a legend of the ancient times of King Arthur speaks of hunting the golden deer, it is a mystical symbol of the Christ.

HUOS OF THE FIFTH SUN The Aztec calendar relates it as the current fifth Aryan race, which could succumb to fire and earthquakes.

HURDLE A stumbling block that you are anticipating overcoming, an impediment that you must compromise with before you can make progression: "getting a work permit was the first hurdle to overcome". A hurdle is a barricade or other impediment that a runner must bounce over during a race. If you trip over a hurdle, you in all probability won't win the race.

HUTA (Sanskrit) The wounded of the immolation, the offering extinguished in the passion of the holocaust; sacrifice, oblation, offering. As an adjective: offered, sacrificed.

HUTAZA (Sanskrit) Textually: "he who eats or devours the offering"; the fire of sacrifice; the god of fire.

HWUN (Chinese) The Essence. Just like Atman.

HYDRA or HIDRA of LERNA (Latin hydra and from the Greek Aquarius Snake) It deals with a mythological monster endowed with seven heads, like snakes, some legends attribute nine to it. It is said that he lived in Lake Lerna. He was the son of Typhoon and Echidna. If one of their heads was cut off; another one was at once reborn in its place unless they were cut all at once. Exterminating this monster was Hercules' second job. A crab sent by Juno, and with the help of the Hydra bit the solar hero from behind. A friend of Hercules lit a forest in which they took burning blights to burn the wound left of the severed head; that was the way that so that the heads were not reborn, in this way the hero managed to kill him; the blood of the hydra was poisonous Hercules varnished the tips of his arrows, transforming them into deadly weapons. Gnostically, it means the mind with its psychological aggregates and belongs to the mental world.

HYDRANO (Greek) Properly, the "Baptist". Title of the ancient hierophant of the Mysteries that made the candidate usher through the "test of water", in which he was submerged three times. Such was his baptism by the Holy Spirit that he moves in the waters of Space. St. Paul names St. John with the title of Hydrano, the Baptist. The Christian Church took this solemnity from the ritual of the Eleusinian Mysteries and others.

HYENA Spectacularly starved; the hound has extensively been an origin of alarm around Africa. nightly huntsman and accumulator, It have been organized with incantation, vicious, and deception. Concurrently with the Eurasian primitive, a beast fables narratives embrace the hyena as an image for the fiend's gloomy activity. On the precisely position, the hyena represents for the sensual longing it may persuade in a human being devouring raw flesh. On the mystic, sacred experience however, the hyena is a lesson for fetishism. Streaky hyenas are many times authority in quotation legends and myth, usually as ideograms of disloyalty and ignorance. The English interpretation of the Scriptures does not accommodate the term "hyena," excluding in Ecclesiasticus 13:18. "What peace is there between the hyena and her dog? And what; peace between the rich man and the poor?" In Jeremiah 12:9, where the Sematic has ha-'ayiT tsabhua' (the Revised Version (Bristish and American) "a speckled bird of prey"), Septuagint has hypothesizing huaines, "a hyena's den," as if from a Hebrew unedited having me'arah, "cave", alternatively of ha-'ayiT, "bird." The root tsabha" may defined "to seized as prey" (compare Arabic Seb,' "lion" or "rapacious animal"), or "to dip" or "to dye" (compare Arabic cabagh, "to dye"), consequently, the two adaptations of tsabhua' as "hyena" and as "speckled" (Vulgate multicolored).

HYPERSPACE Space of four or more dimensions. Distance. "Period of the theory of proportionality. (Gnostic) Delineate the fourth dimension, fourth coordinate, or fourth vertical. The day will come when astrophysics find the existence of Hyperspace. This authority can be shown with Hyper geometry, when a body dives into Hyperspace, it is said that it has introduced the state of "Jinas". This body evades the Law of Formality and floats in Hyperspace. Hyperspace is used by black wizards and white wizards to make their outings in jina stage, white wizards pass through with their body in jinn situation in a higher space and black wizards in a lower space.

HYPERION (Greek) He is one of the seven titans of the Ark.

HYPNOS (Greek) Dream. Deities which, according to Greek mythology, is the interpretation of Thanatos' Dream and sister, Death.

HYPNOSIS Dormition is incited by artificial means (narcotics, mesmerism, hypnotism).

HYPOCRITE (Latin hypocrite and east of Greek) That pretend or simulate what is not or what does not feel. The hypocrite is that person with an inclination to hide his selves (defects) pretending to have virtue or devotion, is full of hypocrisy, is in himself a figure with falsehood, self-righteousness, etc.

HYPOSTASIS Permanence, substance. A word used by Greek theologians to particularly choose each of the three divisions (Persons) of the Deity. Alchemists apply this term to the three components: salt, sulfur, and mercury, which they respected as the three beginnings of all perceptible elements.

HYLE Essence or primordial matter. Homogeneous residue of Chaos or Great Abyss.

HYMER (Scandinavian) It was a giant with whom Thor went fishing to see if he would catch the snake from Midgard.

HYMNS, 'ANCIENT AND MODERN' (1861). A hymnary, copy-edit by H.W. Baker, which encompassed ancient and modern sources and integrated numerous traditional office hymns (often in translations by J.M. Neale). The music assisted" its popularity. A transfigured edition was issued in 1950.

HYPERBOREAN EPOCH Stage in which the Hyperborean Race developed which descended from the Polar Race.

HYPERDULIA. The exceptional respect paid to the BVM on reports of her illustrious appreciation as Mother of God.

HYSSOP Is a compact shaggy scented greenery of the Mentha ancestry, the sour Mentha piperita of that are utilized in cookery and grassy therapeutics. (In scriptural usage) a natural underbrush of indecisive uniqueness whose branch were employed for scattering in prehistoric Judaist rituals of atonement. Hyssop was remarked about in the Scriptures for its purification outcome in kinship with epidemic, Hansen's disease and chest coronary infarction illness and metaphorical in Catharsis the vitality. A vegetation applied in illustrative scattering ritual by the primordial Hasidic. In the Middle Ages and revitalization times hyssop was principally operated for inhalation and Gastrointestinal disorders Psalm 51:7-12 KJV affirm "Purge me with hyssop, and I shall be clean: Wash me, and shall be whiter than snow. Make me to hear joy and gladness; that the bones which thou hast broken may rejoice. Hide their face from sins and blot out all mine iniquities." Hyssop is place of origin in the Scriptures as existing a devotional purifier, approved for its potential to clarify inner being and conserve them from distress. It is frequently applied as a Devotional Purifying Delegate to rinse religious or cleanse zones, however, it may be exercised to shield lodgings/mortals from afflictions, troubles, and wrong intensity.

-I-

IACH The same as Iaco. In addition, it declares Iaho which is a word that can be confused with the concept they denominate from other words like "God of mystery" etc. which can have the identical sound in the Greek language, Samaritans and Jews when characterizing Iabe, Yahva or Yaho.

IACO According to the secret tradition of Eleusis appears as the son of Zeus and Demeter.

IAH (Hebrew) Life.

IAO (Greek) The Monarch God of the Phoenicians: "the light understood only by the intellect", the natural and significant Beginning of all things, "the masculine Essence of Wisdom: It is the ideal sunlight. [Among the Phoenicians, IAO is the supreme God," whose secret and trilateral holds a deep allegory. It's a "mystery name." Among the Chaldeans, Iao was also the name of the highest-ranking Divinity, enthroned surpassing the seven heavens writing down the Spiritual Initiation of Light, and was also appreciated as Demiurge. Etymologically returned. IAO stands for "Breath of Life".

IBIS. Wading birds are reinforced by river mollusks. The Egyptians in ancient times pay homage to it when it appeared for ages on the bank of the Nile Cabalistical Ibis stands for the Holy Spirit.

IBLIS (Persian) The devil.

IBN Gebirol (Salomon Ben Yehudah). An appreciable sage and philosopher, Jewish by birth, who resided in Spain in the eleventh centurial. He was also known by the nickname of Avicebron.

IBRAHIM Term by which the Mohammedans appoint Abraham.

IBRD-Veda (Ved.) The oldest and most important of the Vedas. It is said that he was "created" from the eastern mouth of Brahma. As mysterious indicates, it was communicated by great sages at Man(a) Saravana Lake, beyond the Himalayas, tens of thousands of years ago. [The Rig-Veda (from rich, to celebrate, to chant, and veda, science), is so called because each of its rooms is called a rich. In each "Bible of Mankind", entitled Rig-Veda, were laid, at the very dawn of analytical humanity, the untarnished stones of all the creeds and all faiths of every church and every temple that has been erected, from the first to the last. The universal "myths", the manifestation of divine and cosmic Powers, primary and secondary, as well as the historical predominant person of all religions, both extinct today and extinct, can be found in the seven crucial Divinities and their three hundred and thirty million interrelationships of the Rig-Veda, and these seven, with their millions by addition, solus the Rays of the one and without limits Oneness.

IACH This expression extract from the Arabic 'Aisha', context "alive, she who lives, womanly". The presumed name was supported by the third and favorite wife of the prophet Muhammad, Aisha Bint Abi Bakr, designated as the 'the mother of believers', she develops into a principal policy-making and religious character after his passing. The outspread of the big honorific in the English language, in the formation Aisha, launched in the 1970, adequate to the acceptance of crown Princess.

ICHA (Sanskrit) The moment of Azvina enfolds part of September and October of our calendar.

ICHATVA (Sanskrit) The capability to produce or to make appear.

ICHCHHA (Sanskrit) Motivation or potentiality of inclination [desire, appetite.]

ICHMA (Sanskrit) Disposition. Epithet of Kama.

ICHTA Term Iacchos, it is divulged, is of Phoenician operation. Aristotle conduced that the premature Arabs corresponding Iach (Iacchos) with a mare, that is, the Horse of the SOI (Dyonisus), which come after the chariot in that all through the day was mounted towards ahura Mazda, God of the heavens.

ICHTHYS or ICHTHUS (Greek) Fish. The portrayal of the Fish has often been described to Jesus, the Christ of the New Testament, in part considering the five letters that arrange that word are the initials of the Greek phrase: Iesous Christos

Theou Uios Soter, which means: "Jesus Christ, the Savior, Son of God." For this purpose, their allies, in the premature centuries of Christianity, were overall cited as "fish, and in the catacombs, they came across drawn or sculpted fish. Also correlated the narrative that some of Christ's first followers were fishers, and the comment of Jesus: "I will make you fishers of men."

ICHTU (Sanskrit) Sacrifice; solid offering, as in opposition to soma, wish, longing.

ICON Cites level pictures, customarily draw in egg tempera on wood, correspondIly elaborated in mosaic, ivory, and other materials, to stand for Christ, the BVM, or another saint, which are worshiped in the Greek Church. As it is reinforced that through them the saints performed their benevolent powers, they supervised all momentous events of human beings and are held to be forceful channels of grace.

ICONOCLAST Illustrate "image destroyer". This conceptualization is imposed on those who contradict the instruction of idols or images; exceptionally those of the origination of the Eastern community, which from the eighth century repelled the use of sacred images, or at least to donate to these devote tributes.

IDA (Sanskrit). The nadi (nerve, vessel or nerve current) that expanses on the left side of the body and goes to the left window of the nose; the left sympathetic nerve. (Prasad Branch). This nadi is disseminated from the sole of the left foot upwards to the "thousand-petaled lotus" (Sahasrara) at the vertex of the head (K. Laheri, coment del Uttara-Gita). It commences, like the Pingala, from a sacred point detected ln the oblong medulla, well known by the name of Triveni, (Doctr. Secre. III, 547). For additional details, see Rama Prasad, The Suile Forces of Nature, chap, IV.

IDALAN (Scandinavian) A extent of heaven where the mansion of Uller exists. (Eddas)

IDAM (Sanskrit) "This", insinuation to this planet, as opposed to "That" and the planes or worlds that exist further on or above it.

IDANA In the Yoruba mother tongue is the first communal petition of a female child, for hands in union from her father's homestead. On this matter, articles of the two of them religious and societal merits are given out to the bride's parentage. As origination, a man shows a female he is focused on. At that point he inquires his colleagues or a reciprocal friend to outreach her on his account. The intermediary person or acquaintance is described as an Alarina. As soon as interactive enthusiasm and affection has been proven, their parents will be communicated of their decision to become spouses. The Yoruba bride price is barely N5,000 (Five Thousand Naira) covering almost all Yoruba states and villages. The amount of money asked to be paid to the bride is totally emblematic and is not needed for the purpose of money. In fact, certain parents of brides) returned the money to the bridegroom. In the Yoruba acquired environment, the principal of formal wedding procedure is the customary wedding, a conventional stage locale with the two families advancing one another to bless the love relation of their children in the appearance of close friends, relations and well-wishers.

IDDHI (Pali) Compatible view of the Sanskrit voice Siddhi.

IDEATION (Cosmic) (Occult) Reflection, the eternal imagination, imprinted in Value, or Essence, reason in immortality; imagination that becomes energetic to the origin of fresh unity period of existence. It is one of the appearances of the Absolute. It cannot manifest itself as individual Consciousness freely of the Cosmic Substance since it demands a material vehicle for it. It is a flash of the universal Mind. Fohat is the active vigor and instructions of Cosmic Ideation.

IDEA(S) (Monastic) (Gnostic) Exist farther away from conceptual dualism and logical comparisons. Monastic Ideas help to greatly imagine and alter our intellect, by that path we can create more stable alterations, because indisputably the visions are required; but you must acknowledge them before using them. Monastic Ideas lead us to a vital and total change. The Dharmakayas are never ambiguous, they are always monistic.

IDEICO Iron finger firmly magnetized and used in sanctuaries for healing occasions. It derives sensation in the orientation wrote down, and accordingly said that it had magnetic integrity.

IDISES (Scandinavian) Equal significance as Dises, fairies, Walkiria's, the divine women of Scandinavian culture. They were approved of by the Teutons before the time of Tacitus, as this author writes down.

IDOLATRY Enlighten homage to idols; worship of images, anthropomorphized or human figures. The Mysteries of heaven and earth, demonstrate to the third Race by their paradisiacal Instructors, in the days of their purity, became a pronounced focus of light, whose rays were forcibly weakening to dimension that were outspread in an unprofessional transient by demonstration of being quite detectable.

IDOL Statue or representation of a pagan god or a saint of the House of prayers of Rome, or a fetish of the wild tribes.

IDRA (Rabba) (Hebrew) "The Holy Greater Assembly", a division of the Zohar."

IDRIS or Edris (see Edris).

IDWATSAR (Sanskrit) One of the five phases that fabricates Yuga. This cycle is the Vedic interval by sublimity, which is salutation as the ground of calculation for higher successions.

IDYA (Sanskrit) Laudable, adorable, worthy of veneration.

IFING (Scandinavian) The wide river that disconnect the Asgard, the mansion of the gods, from that of the Jotun's, the large and wealthy magicians. Below the Asgard was the Midgard, where in the jubilant ether sprouts uplifted the abode of the Elves of Light. In their decision and method of locality, all these dwellings indemnify the Deva-Loka and other regions of the Indos settled by the many classes of gods and asuras.

IGAGA (Chaldean) Celestial angels, as well as archangels.

IGLOOS The Igloos are a kind of shack (iglú which means house in Inuktitut language) constructed from snow, mostly by Innuits. The igloos are constructed with compacted bricks of snow; they all share a domed shape. Igloos has been built by the Inuit tribes which resides in some parts of Canada and Greenland. The Inuit people erect the Igloos using totally snow blocks. Generally, the Inuit tribe are settled in Igloos prior to the initiation of contemporary, European-style dwellings. Although Igloos are no longer the ordinary approach to housing for the Inuits nation; they choose that Igloos stay around ethically importantly in Artic communality.

IGNIS (Latin) Equal to Sanskrit Agni (fire).

IGNORE Disregard, the emanation of the evils and martyrdom that afflicts the world since it makes us profit what is unfair to obtained, anguish for what was not convenient to grieve, take for true what is not real but misleading, and consumed our existence running after unworthy circumstances, neglecting what is evidently most beneficial.

IHI God of music, son of Hathor, in ancient Egypt.

IHS. The IHS insignia utilized by the Jesuits is a condensation for the denomination of Jesus in Greek: IHSOUS. Initially and on numerous icons the closing letter is the Greek formation of sigma used at the end of a term. IHC, but ultimately the more confidential Roman S came into use. The compression in form "IHS" emerged for the beginning on the coins of Justinian II on the revolve of the 7ᵗʰ and 8ᵗʰ centuries. The sequence of Jesuits, in other vocable the Society of Jesus (Societas Lesu), developed IHS as its fixed representation; the sign in 17ᵗʰ century.

IJYA (Sanskrit) Worship, offering, sacrifice.

IKCHANA (Sanskrit) Eye, sight, look, appearance.

ILDA (Hebrew) Son.

ILECH (magnum) The healing power of medicine.

ILEIAS Primum, Ileias, Ileadus (Alq.) The first assumption; primordial power; causation.

ILMATAR (Finnish) The Virgin who descend from the sky to the sea prior to creation. She is the "Daughter of the Air" and mother of seven children (the seven potentials of Nature).

ILLUMINATI. A nomination appeals to bodies of religious devotees, furthermore (1) the Enlightens; (2) the Rosicrucian; and (3) a Masonic sect set up in Bavaria in 1778 by Adam Weishaupt. Repudiate the proclamation of all existing religious bodywork, they showed individuality to be distinctive in whom alone the 'illuminating' courtesy of Christ lived.

ILLUMINATED, Illuminated, Illuminati (Illumination) (Illuminati, in Latin) The initiated adepts.

ILUS (Sanskrit) Lega mum or prehistoric mud; also cited as Hyle.

ILLUSION In esotericism, every limited device (such as the universe and everything contained in it) is called illusion or maya. [Except for Parabrahmana, the universal evidence, everything is aspect, all things are illusion.

ILLUSTRATION Religious rite carried out by the Greeks and Romans to purified cities, fields, flocks, houses, etc., as well as newborn children and individuals impure for a crime or infraction for an immoral purpose. Such routines are often done with sprinkling, retinue and self-denial.

ILVALA (Sanskrit) Designation of a rakchasa or devil incarnate that dwelt in the Dandaka jungle, to which relating is made in Ramayana.

IMAGE(S) The use of a part of portrayal of men, animals, or plants was banned in the Mosaic of paganism, but while the doctrinal consequence of the personification was seized, it appeared to many Faithful that there was no barrier in the use of images in the system of worship. The first Christian paintings were the drawings in the catacombs. After the time of the maltreatment sanctified images come about to take part in the devotion encounter. In the East regardless of the Iconoclastic Controversy, Representations, which endure at most structures of portrayal authorized in the Greek Church, have endured a prime component in Orthodox religion. In the West. The adoration of images, which involved sculpture, made moderate advances. It was given a dogmatic base by St. Thomas Aquinas, who spread the East's approval that privilege support to the statues went ahead to its model. At the Renewal, the employment of images was in opposition by the Advocate, journal the supporters of H. Zwingli and Jl Calvin, who happened, accompanied by the Puritans.

IMAGINE. Creating a rational image or hypothesis of an artifact. To assume or expect it as a formal gadget that authorizes reporters to depict portrayal in literary critics' intellect, so they conclude additional conveniently imagine narrative circumstances, temperament, sensation and surroundings. A long way to discern imagery is to believe in the disposition.

IMAGINATION In esotericism had best not be confused with fiction, because inventiveness is one of the flexible domains of the higher Mood, and is the memory of the antecedent personifications, which, although disfigured by the lower Manas, consistently relax on a circumstance of truth. [The chimera is the flexible power of the Soul, produced by active reason of the conscious, the desire and the will].

IMAGO DEI. In (Lat. The image of God'), in which man was generated (Gen. 1:26) Version to Catholic theologians this image was sheltered, but not lost, in the Fall, it is conflicted with the similitude Dei ('likeness to God'), which was tear down by original sin but is reinstated by Baptism. What the imago includes is argued. Protestant theologians have emphasized the vitiating consequence of the Fall on the imago Dei, and sometimes held man to be completely dishonest.

IMBALANCE Therapeutic, imbalance or deficiency of stability is the difficulty of reality absent of solidity or out of quantity. Imbalances acquire double common sources: Permitting sentiments to devour you empowering or not permitting individuality to encounter dismissive affections at any rate. Psychological affliction, anguish, and tension stop entirely consequence emanate that imbalance to capture. The pressure of troublesome surroundings generates you to perceive apprehension, or unhappiness, or powerlessness. In succession it uplifted your hypertension, pulse rate, and tightness and clamped down your natural defenses. An agreeable background transposed that and indifference of epoch or civilization, human beings detect creation pleasurable. Imbalance (Gnosticism) Changing the cause modifies the effect. "The Lion of the Law is fought with the Balance." If in one dish of the scale we place our charitable efforts and in the other we put the bad ones, both dishes will weigh the same and reach some imbalance. If the saucer of evil deeds is heavier, we must put honorable actions on the plate of virtuous achievements in order to tip the scales in our favor, so we cancel Karma. Do virtuous deeds so that you pay your debts; remember that not only can it be paid with pain, but it can also be paid by doing good.

IMHOT-POU or IMHOTEP (Egyptian) Is the God of wisdom (the Greek mouths). He was the son of Fran, and in certain appearances, Hermes, as depicted manifesting knowledge with a book in front of him. He is a sun God. It symbolizes, "the God of the beautiful face."

IMMAH (Sanskrit) Mother; as opposed to Abba, Sr.

IMMANENT (Gnosticism) The Ten Commandments to the Immanent and the Transcendent (from our physical parents to our Creative Principles.)

IMMANUEL, or EMMANUEL, (Heb., 'With us [is] God') The term come about in Is. 7:14 and 8:8, but it is not explicit to whom it refers. In Mt. 1:23 the prediction is illustrated with citations to the birth of Christ.

IMMEDIATE (Gnosticism) Denotes without delay, instantaneously, e.g., causes and effects of our actions manifest themselves immediately.

IMMOLATED Sheep breeding that does not exceed one year. It signifies purity, innocence, meekness, offering some description of it to the lion, feasibly due to a certain inscription that says: Mors. Ego sum mortis. Vocor Agnus sum Leo fortis (death of death. They call me lamb, I'm a strong lion.) By the relationship of agnus with Agni (fire) it is an atoning figure of the periodic renewal of the world. The lamb of God who takes away the sins of the world is the Intimate Christ who comes to every human being duly prepared, to live the cosmic Drama, to be immolated His blood is the fire with which He redeems us. Among the Gnostics of antiquity, it expresses the Holy Spirit, so it is related to the Golden Fleece.

IMMORTALITY The ankh or Christogram is a Coptic representation of animation that influences endurance ad interim outline in the indicator of the supreme beings and monarch, who remained seen as having jurisdiction above the voyage of subsistence. The Philologist a stumble in the appearance of a Shamrock knot is one more symbol of immortality. Both the phoenix and the lion are figures of Mandarin origination that are frequently related with immortality. All over East-Asians chronicle, they have been applied in a great deal of drawings and art as faithful designs. Oriental lilies represent eternal life, and peace lilies suggest rebirth. Supposing that you prefer to manifest your treasuring for the perished's viability, compliment Casablanca lilies, which implies for ceremonies and honor. Evergreens repeatedly indicate immortality and endurance now that they maintain their leaflet during the wintertime. To the American Indians, the Weymouth pine is a metaphor of the Awesome Tranquility that integrated their disconnected country towards a continuing alliance.

IMPARTIALITY. A capability to consider the two perspectives and judgment uniformly James also declares that impartiality is particular of the qualities of accurate inner intelligence (James 3:17). "Paul warned slave owners that everyone is equal before God, and that God doesn't mistreat anyone, so they should not either. Paul was reminding us that the rich and powerful have no advantage before God".

IMPRESSIONS (Latin, impressió, onis) Action and effect of printing. Gnostic. Frivolous life comes to us as an affectation through the 5 senses. Life is a course of successive negative or positive resistances that guide the mind. Rebellions must be altered, through a more stable, objective life. Reflection, the memory of oneself, allows one not to fall into identification and the admitted impressions can be restored. This type of work is called first conscious shock. A second perceived collision is to get him to say: "We must welcome the unpleasant manifestations of our fellowmen."

IN (Chinese) The feminine emergence of the component, fertilizing by the self, the eternal masculine principle and then thrown into the universe.

IN COENA DOMINI (Latin, 'On the Lord's Supper'). A series of excommunications of specified offenders against faith and morals which were regularly issued in the form of a Papa Bull. Its dispersion came to be confined to Maundy Thursday (hence its name); the exercise was repudiated in 1869.

INCUBO(S) o NIGHTMARE(S) (Incubus, in Latin) It is revealed of the devil spirit, that he has bodily trade with a woman, is generated by the lower inclination, by human concupiscence. Gnostic. They are ideoplastic formations of women, fabricated by the lascivious vice of autoerotism in the male are called subcubes, this type of sphygmic takes shape until it develops into an imperfection that steals part of consciousness. The incubated selves and subcubes, then, are diabolic creations of the imagination; fantasy, by the unnatural lascivious vice of onanism in thoughts and desires.

INACO (Inachos, in Greek) Father of Phoroneus.

INARA or INORA. In Indian mythology that) God of the sky, lightning, thunder, storm and rain. It is said that he rides on an elephant and his main weapon is inferior lightning. It is said that under the Brahmanic influence, he became the Shiva of Hinduism. In the sacred land of the Vedas, much is said of the battles of Indra against Vitra, against the demon of darkness; he is thus the slayer of the Dragon. He is the god of ether.

INCARNATIONS (divine) The idea of personification is discovered revealed on the wall of a temple in Thebes by Samuel Shorpe, who analyzes it this way: "First, the god Thoth. As the informer of the gods, like the Mercury of the Greeks (or the Gabriel of the first Gospel), he tells the virgin Queen Mautmes that she is to give birth to a son, who will be King Amunotaph III. Second, the god Knef, the Spirit... and the goddess Hathor (Nature)... they both take the queen by the hands and put inside her mouth the sign of life, a cross, which must be the life of the future child" etc. Evidently, the divine incarnation, or the doctrine of the avatar, has built up the greatest mystery of all ancient religious systems.

INCAS (Peru) Title given to the gods accepted in Peruvian theogony, and more recent to the kings and princes of the territory. "The Incas, in number of seven, have +- repopulated the earth after the Flood", they say, as Confirmed by Coste (L.IV, p. 19). Dependency, in the introduction of the fifth mother-race, to a dynasty of heavenly kings, such as those of Egypt, India and Chaldea.

INCANDESCENT Symbol of fullness and perfection.

INCEST (Latin. Insestus) Union between relatives, considered immoral within the degrees to which marriage is prohibited.

INCENSE (Latin. eleven sus, burned) In 1848, Dr. Robert Adams Paterson invented gutta-percha, a gomorresina obtained from the sapodilla tree in the form of an aromatic teardrop whose smell is exhaled during combustion. Myrrh is another gum resin removed from a shrub or small tree which expands to three meters tall. Most Incense is extracted from India, Arabia and Africa using mostly in religious ceremonies and sacred invocations. It is believed that incense purifies the astral body. The vapor being contemplated is symbolic of prayer. There is no understandable confirmation of its orthodox operation before c. A.D. 500. In the West incense was long used at nearly all in formal chant ministries, but since 1969 it has been allowed at any Sacramental ceremonies. In the East it works more customarily than in the West, the validity of its utilization in the Church of England has been debated.

INCONSTANCY (Latin in constantia) Lack of stability and permanence of a thing. Due to the inadequacy of dedication, of continuity, it is for this reason that good spiritual development has not been achieved.

INCUBUS (Incubus, in Latin) Alarming, little more real and threatening than the current acceptance given to that term, that is, to the "nightmare". The incubus is the male component, and the succubae is female, and these are minus disagreement the ghosts of medieval demonology, memoranda of intangible localities by human passion and concupiscence.

INDAMBARA (Sanskrit) Blue Lotus.

INERTIA Is a possession of matter by which it continues in its existing state of pause or uniform exactly in a straight line except when that state is alternated by an external force; e.g., when a car is in motion and all the sudden the driver applies the brakes; suddenly, the lower section of the body comes to slow down as the car comes to rest, but the upper proportion of the body proceed to move forward due to inertia motion.

INNERE LIGHT The conclusion of Christian dependence consists of inward awareness of the experience of salvation, confirmed by the Community of close Friends.

INDIVIDUALIZE. To fashion individual in disposition, to adapt to the require or special circumstances of a, individualize creed according to student potentiality. Biblical Individualism is the notion that government is grounded on the voluntary contributions of individuals; individualism is seen in the context of moral and religious commitments, so that acquiescence (e.g., to God/s law) is significant, just as emancipation Is.

INDRA (Sanskrit) God of space, king of the sidereal gods. A Vedic deity. [Quoted by a second name Vasara. Indra symbolizes boss, lord, sovereign, etc. He is the toning Jupiter of India, and his assurance is the lightning, which he wields with his right; it rules the weather and directs the rain. Mystically spawn Arjuna. He is designated riding on an elephant or white horse.] It is told in Indian mythology that the God of heaven, thunder, storm, and rain; he rides an elephant, and his primary weapon is lightning. It is said that, under Brahmanical beliefs, he became Shiva of Hinduism. In the land of the Vedas, there is much talk of battles against vitra, resistant to the demon of darkness, is therefore the slayer of the Dragon. He is the God of ether.

INDRIYA o Deha-sanyama (Sanskrit) The comprehension of the sensations in the practice of yoga. There are the ten superficial agents; the five senses used for awareness are called Jnana-indriyas, and the five used for action, Karma-indriyas. Pancha-indriyani precisely implies and in its cabbalistic sense: "the five producing roots of (eternal) life". Among Buddhists, it is the five positive agents that fabricate five supreme qualities. [The word indriya means human strength, power, faculty, or potency; defined; with the denomination of the "ten indriyas" are collectively appointed the five powers or faculties of sensation or perception (jnanendriyas), and the five potentials or faculties of action (karmendriyas), of which the physical organs (eyes, ears, hands, feet, tongue, etc.) are nothing more than material demonstration. Indriyas often include manas or inner sense. Thus, we read in the Bhagavad-Gita: "the ten indriyas and the one (manas)" (XIII, 5); "the inner sense (manas) and the other five senses"] (XV, 7).

INDU-VRATA (Sanskrit) Lunar Ceremony, and especially the regulated fasting in agreement with course of the moon.

INDU (Sanskrit) The Moon; the soma (in the sense of moon).

INDUBHRIT (Sanskrit) The god Ziva, thus cited for wearing the shaped on his countenance, or for being moved above the crescent. (Burnouf).

INEFFABLE Among the Jews, he was the substitute for the "mystery name" of the divinity of his Eh-yeh tribe, "I am," or Jehovah. Since the third commandment prevents the latter term from being used "in vain," the Hebrews restore it with that of Adonai or "the Lord." But Protestant Christians, imperceptibly interpreting

Jehovah and Elohim which is also a substitute per se, also being the title of an inferior divinity with the term "Lord" and "God."

INNER LIGHT The principle of Christian certitude, composed of inward comprehension or proceedings of salvation, endorsed by the Society of Friends.

INERTIA (Sanskrit) One of the three Cradles. It implies Inertia Darkness, Heaviness, Laziness, Apathy, Impurity and Passivity.

INFALLIBLE (Gnosticism) The appreciation of the sixth commandment of the Decalogue of the Lord Jehovah is the best formula for the inspection of thought, the flawless and precise formula, provided to man by God Himself.

INFANT (Childhood) (lat. infantia) The time of the child from birth to 7 years. "The child should be instructed more by the model than by the precept." The parents of the child must contemplate the superiority of the first education that begins in the first years of life. They should try as much as possible to nourish the essence of the child with good models, good teaching supported by love and understanding, compassionate harmony in the home, etc. Thus, the child when he is an adult will be organized to face the circumstantial discrepancies of life. From the moment the woman becomes pregnant, we must speak to that future creature, which is determine in the mother's womb, having instructed it by putting good classical music of Mozart, Beethoven, Handel and others. Good music and teaching from fetal life nourish the soul, the essence and when the child is born carries on itself atoms that will help spiritual growth and if it persists discipline, it will be a great soul.

INFERNO Cabbalistic devotions the creeds of Brahmins, Buddhists, Zoroastrians, Mohammedans, Jews and so on make their hells hot and gloomy, though quite a bit of them are more attractive than terrifying.

INFORMATION (Gnosticism) "Students truly live a mechanistic life and only know that they have to receive important intellectual and keep it stored in the infidel retentive, that's all."

INFRINGING (Gnostic) Allude to non-compliance with the rules; to break, to violate, to break. No humanist author, prophet, has had the power to revoke these laws, much less could carry out that legion of demons that he carries inside to materialize in violation of the Laws.

INGE, WILLIAMS RALPH 1860-1954), Dean of St. Paul's from 1911 to 1934. His sympathies with Platonic spirituality found expression in a series of theological and devotional writings. His grasp of the tastes and prejudices of the English mind, his provocative and epigrammatical manner of writing, and his pure English style made him one of the best-known Churchmen of his generation.

INGOT is a bundle of minerals that has been emitted into a proportion and appearance (such as a rod, ball, or platter) that is appropriate to emporium, deliver, and effort concentrated an untreated or complete or finalize byproduct. The expression in addition mentions a matrix in which alloy is so casting. An ingot is established by inoculating or draining condensed fluid into a mold, in the place that it will cool and take the form of the container. The procedure of generating ingots is large numbers of age old, as carving casting into systematic configuration facilitated to carry and emporium. Regarding Ingot: In prehistoric China, ingot was the eminently beneficial banknotes and habitually assemble a gold or silver. It is consistently an emblem of affluence and a favorable commodity for family tranquility. With an ingot at dwelling, you can have many things as you desire and prosperity to proceed in,

INICUO (Latin, iniquos) Opposed to equity. He is the Antichrist, like Arhiman, he is the adversary of lucifer's winnings, he is the negative figure of him. It is beyond the ego itself. Paul of Tarsus quotes it in the Holy Scriptures. The wicked or Ahriman is the support of the Ego. It is illustrated by the seven-headed monster (emblem of the seven deadly sins) and ten horns, which suggests the wheel of samsara. The Bible speaks of the beast, the other animal that has two horns and embodies the Ego. Few initiates manage to dissolve the unjust

INITIATION Word derived from the initia, which involves the first or fundamental principles of a science.

INKY Is as dark as ink, is an adjective inkier or inkiest, resembling ink, especially in color; dark or black, of containing, or stained with ink: inky fingers. The Inky family name was founded in the USA in 1880. In 1880 there were 6 inky families living in Kentucky. This was about 86% of all the recorded Inky's in USA. Kentucky had the highest population of Inky families in 1880.

INMAH (Hebrew) The Mother Superior: name given to Shekinah.

INARA Celebrity of the Hittite mythology. She was a godhead of wild animals and nature. Inara is also an Arabic name that implies Illuminating, Shining and a feminine variation of the Basque boys' name Inar.

INNOCENTS (The Initiates and Kabbalists before the Christian era. The "Innocents" of Bethlehem and Lud (or Lydda) who were sentenced to death by Alexander Janneus, up to the number of a few thousand (year 10 before J.C.), gave rise to the legend of the 40,000 innocent children killed by Herod while searching for the infant Jesus. The first is a little-known historical fact; the second is a fable, as Renan has sufficiently demonstrated in his Life of Jesus. [King Herod is the representation of Kansa (or Kanza), tyrant of Mathura and maternal uncle of Krishna. Astrologers had predicted to Kansa that a son of his niece Devaki would snatch his crown and take his life; in view of which the tyrant gave orders to kill the child (Krishna), but thanks to Mahadeva's protection, his parents managed to bring him to safety. Then Kansa wanted to ensure the death of the true child, and to this end ordered a general slaughter of the male infants of his kingdom.

INNOCENT(S), Holy. The youngster of Bethlehem 'from two years old and under', exterminated by order of Herod in a venture to destroy the Infant Jesus (Mt. 2:16-18). The episode is observed on 28 Dec.

INORA In the mythology of India, the God of heaven, lightning, thunder, storm and rain. He is said to ride an Elephant and his main weapon is lightning. It is said that, undergoing Brahmanical ascendancy, he became the Shiva of Hinduism.

INPUT Correlates with concepts that are submitted: equivalent as guidance, judgments, observations; is statistics inserted a computing network or laptop. Independent variable matured a term in the 14th-15th Centuries, "put on, impose," Modern meaning "feed data into a machine" is emerged 1946, a current evolution originating at interchangeable.

INTACT Conditions unaffected principally by everything that maltreat or decreases, complete, flawless, of a subsistence individual or its fragment, encountering no pertinent constituent detach or tear down; a bodily abstinent.

INRI (Gnostic) "Ignis Natura Renovatur Integra" (Fire incessantly renews Nature), without "INRI" it is not possible for us to become Christified. "Inri" is what interests us to achieve liberation.

INSPIRATION We often talk about inspiration, but in general we do not know absolutely what it is. There is a great wealth of inspiration that comes from our Masters, the true guides of humanity, who suggest or project into the mind of man the ideas, which he usually must do nothing but express them in his own way by word or in writing.

INSTINCT, INSTINCTIVE Specifically the work, effect or result of instinct. Gnostic. This center is the one that keeps us alive, because it regulates all the activities of the organism and directs them wisely.

INSULT Comes from Latin verb insultare, simply defining "to leap upon." It is devised of the affix om-, meaning "on, upon, and a formation of the verbification satire "to leap." Particularly initial sense of insult in English was "to make a military attack." That sensation enhances outdated, and insult now channels to charge or "jump. To be self-assured just after anyone insults you, concentrate control one's temper and immediately collect your deliberation. Reflect regarding the insult and meditate, "is there any truth to it?" Reasonably that the individual desired to humiliate you, so it's apparently tops to overlook the insult. The mid-finger is the past insult familiar to world, teachings from yesterday.

INTEGRA(O) (Gnosticism) An integral figure says what a person is. This personality is on the right track.

INTELLECTUAL (Latin, Intellectualis) Person enthusiastic to the development of the intellect by means of letters or by materialistic intolerance.

INTELLIGENCE (Latin, Intelligence) Faculty of knowing, which manifests itself in numerous ways, (knowledge, comprehending, act of understanding, etc. (gnostic) knowledgeable depends on the degree of cognizant awakened, there are intelligent people who are not intellectuals. The flower of intelligence is intuition. Superlative brainpower is from cosmocrators who had the talent to create worlds and universes. Intelligence should not be whipped with the mind. A fully awakened consciousness makes the person highly intelligent; but there are degrees and degrees of intelligence.

INTENTIONS (Gnosticism) Hell is full of people who had good intentions.

INTEREST (Gnosticism) "It informs us how to improve the memories of memory always using three factors: Subject, object and place, memory is moved by Interest, so that we must put Interest to what is studied so that it is recorded in memory."

INTERNAL (Gnosticism) The human with respect to his inner (internal) state is a psychological multiplicity, a sum of selves.

INTIMATE (lst. intimus) (Gnostic) Confidential to our inner Real Self or the inner Father, inner holy Mother or to the Spirit.

INTUITION This phrase has been made a great abuse and is often used inaccurately in pedagogy. It is the higher, real and objective knowledge, so to speak; a variety of direct vision with the eyes of the soul, by virtue of which man acquires by his own experience the clear, intimate and instantaneous approach or knowledge of an idea or truth, without the help of reason, as if it were a material object placed before our sight.

INVERSE (Gnosticism) "Evolution means development, construction, etc., involution means progression in reverse, regression, destruction, degeneration, decay, etc...."

INVOCATION(S) (Latin, invocation's) Action and effect of invoking. Call yourself to the aid of a Divine or supernatural Being, true or false. Within the mysterious it is an act or ritual by which a being of higher or divine substance can be quoted, or the force of the fundamentals put into action through their elementals. Black magicians and ill-intentioned people have their rites and invocations with the firm purpose of causing some harm to their victims. It is the gradual, progressive, cyclical fall or descent of Spirit into Matter. It is performed on the balloons designated with the letters A, B and C, which form the descending arc of the Planetary Chain.

IO. She was the daughter of Inaco, and Ismene. Olympus God Jupiter Zeus) fell in love with her and seduced her, to free her from the persecution of the jealous Hera (Juno). She is our cosmic mother.

IOD The Divine inner male-female is the special Monad of each one. Hive separates from iod; the divine wife of Shiva, our divine mother.

IONA (or HY) An island of the Interior Heb-rides. In 563 St. Columba touch down on Iona and founded a monastery that establish into a midpoint of Celtic Christianity and from which missionaries were sent to Scotland and N. England. It survived until the Reform. The Iona Community was established in 1938 by the Rev George MacLeod to transmit the theology of the Incarnation in social expression, applying the refurbishment of the conventual construction of the abbey (completed in 1966) as the emblem of its inclinations. Its affiliates live in a community on Iona for three months in the year in arrangements for working in the Scottish production region and in the assignment field.

IOTA The Greek letter L, the tiny letter of the alphabet.

IRISH Concerning Ireland, its people, or the Celtic language customarily and consistently spoken there. The Celtic mother tongue of Ireland. The people of Ireland; Irish ethnic group conjointly.

IPSA (Sanskrit) Will, desire; inclination to achieve.

IRA One of the 7 deadly sins. The 3 most serious crimes are anger, greed and lust.

IRAVAT (Sanskrit) He was the son of Arjuna and his wife Naga Ulupi.

IRDHI (Sanskrit) The synthesis of the ten "supernatural" Cabbalistic powers of Buddhism and Brahmanism.

IRKALIA (Chaldean) The god of Hades, quoted by the Babylonians "invisible region".

IRIS ARTICLES The 104 artifacts of credence embraced by the Church of Ireland in 1615 at its first Convocation. They were more Calvinistic than the Thirty-Nine Articles (of the C of E), which were welcome in Ireland in 1635.

IRIS According to Greek mythology she was the daughter of Thaumas and Electra, sister of the Harpies. She is said to have been a messenger of the gods, particularly Hera (Juno). She was symbolized carried in the rainbow. It is related that she was the wife of Zephyrus and mother of Eros.

IRISH The indication of the harp has connected to Ireland for centennial. The Irish harp outdated the internal design of Ireland and Irish ancestry for centenary. It is the ethnic shield of Ireland and is exhibit on Irish Euro coins and formal certificate analogous as the administrative insignia, birth records and travel permit. The Claddagh is the much celebrated and Carys Irish romantic. These archetypal attributes cherished feelings with a climax. The affection is devotion, the fist companion and the diadem faithfulness. Even though it is not precisely a floweret, the shamrock is a compact abundance that is now at present the federal blossom of Irland. It developed extremely one time a principal sign, the earliest Irish Astrologer, as a commonly exhibit the trilogy with its three hart-shaped leaves. The Irish Hare (Lepus timidus) has been related as a public vertebrate, just as the Irish Elk (Cervus elaphus). Even if extinct, the Red Deer is also related with Ireland.

IRON CROWN of Lombardy. It was a crown gathered for Theo Delinda, widow of Author is, King of Lombardy, it was delivered over in 594 to the Duke of Turin, from where was pursue to the royal house of Italy. The clique of iron from the inner crown was said to have been constructed from a nail of the true Cross.

IRON NAILS Comment on the three nails of the lord's passion. Gnosis explains that the three nails of the cross symbolize the three purifications is by iron and fire, link with the vortices of the hands and feet.

IS The only thing always hidden, eternal and absolute, or Sat (secret doctrine).

ISA, I end with Muslims choosing Jesus.

ISARIM (Hebrew) Essenes initiates.

ISAIAH Hebrew prophet. Powerful at the court of the kings of Judah, mostly over external affairs. Pursued his works until the Assyrian occupation of Judah in 701 B.C. He was a martyr, kept the supremacy of Yahweh the God of Israel, highlighted his moral request, and emphasized their Holiness.

ISAIAH, Ascension of. An apocryphal work well known in the early Church. The first part (Chapters. 1-5) defines the circumstances of Isaiah's martyrdom; the second (Chapters. 6-11) his ascent in ecstasy through the heavens and the revelations made to him there. The work cannot be later than A.D. 350.

ISAAC OF NINEVEH (d. C. 700). 'Isaac Syrus', Nestorian Bp. of Nineveh. Subsequently a brief diocese he pensioned to the abbey of Rabban Shapur. He agreed with extensive in Syriac, largely on simple topics.

ISSY, Articles (of) The 34 articles drained up at Issy, near Paris, in 1695 by the ecclesiastical project imposed to scrutinize Mea domina Guyon's works. Signed by J. B. Bossuel, F Fenelon, and Madame Guyon herself, were restrained opposed to various Quietest tenets.

ISHMONIA (Arabic) The city in whose vicinity is buried the self-styled "Petrified City" of the Desert. Tradition speaks of the immense underground, halls, passages, galleries and libraries hidden in these sites. Arab's fear approaching there after sunset.

ISHTAR (Chaldean) The Babylonian Venus, sign "the firstborn of heaven and earth", and daughter of Anu, God of heaven. She is the goddess of love and beauty. The planet Venus, as an evening star, is identified with Ishtar, and as a morning star, with Anunit, goddess of the Akkadians. There is a curious account of his descent to Hades, in the sixth and seventh Assyrian bricks or tablets deciphered by G. Smith. Any occultist who reads about the love she professed for Tammuz, the murder of Tammuz by Isdubar, the desperation of the goddess and her dive in search of her beloved through the seven gates of Hades, and finally her rescue from the gloomy kingdom, will recognize the beautiful allegory of the soul in search of the spirit.

ISHVA (or Ichava) (Sanskrit) The power to create or to make arise. Spiritual master.

ISIA (Sacred) Island of equal beauty situated in a vast inland sea that, in remote times, spread into Central Asia. It was inhabited by the last linger of the Race that perished to ours. Such remains were the "Sons of Will and Yoga", who survived the great cataclysm that submerged Lemuria. It has been said, there is nothing left today on the island, but a kind of oasis surrounded by the horrible aridity of the great Gobi Desert.

ISIS Goddess of the Egyptians wife of Osiris, mother of Horus. These three form the triad of the Egyptians. She is the exceptional cosmic mother, our Divine Mother Kundalini, symbol of love.

ISITWA (Sanskrit) The divine power.

ISLAM. The doctrine commences by Muhammad (or Mohammed) (c. 570-632), the defenders of which is inspire a Muslim. The intermediate teaching is the complete integrity God has sent prophets, one of those was Jesus. In Muslim conviction Jesus, however, born of a chaste woman and vital force 'a spirit from God and His Word', is nonetheless formed and not engender, and his martyrdom was only perceivable. The ultimate of the prophets is Muhammad.

ISLAND (sacred) Island of equal beauty located in a vast inland sea that, in remote times, spread into Central Asia. It was inhabited by the last remains from the Race which perished prior to ours. Such remnants were the "Sons of Will and Yoga", who survived the great cataclysm that submerged Lemuria. Of this island, it is said, there is nothing left today but a kind of oasis surrounded by the horrible aridity of the great Gobi Desert.

ISRAEL (Hebrew) Eastern Kabbalists derive this name from Isaral or Asar, the sun God "Isra-el" means "who fights with God": the "sun that rises above Jacob Israel" chooses the sun-God Isaral (or Isar-el) who struggles with "God and with man", and fertilized matter, which has power also with "God and with Man", and often prevails over both. Esau, Asu, the sun as well. Esau and Jacob, the allegoric twins, are emblems of the dual concept of nature that is always in struggle: good and evil, light and darkness, and the "Lord" (Jehovah) is its role model. Jacob Israel is the feminine principle of Easu, as Abel is that of Cain, and Esau being the masculine principle. Therefore, like Malach-Iho, "Lord" Esau fights with Jacob and fails. In Genesis, XXXII, the Sun God first fights with Jacob, disassociate his thigh (a sign), and yet is defeated by his terrestrial metaphor: matter; and the Sun-God stands on Jacob and his thigh in covenant. Such biblical characters, as well as his "Lord God", are figures represented in an allegoric order of succession. They are symbols of Life and Death, of Good and Evil, of Light and Darkness, of the mother and of the Spirit in their synthesis, all of them being under their contrasting aspect.

ITALA, The. A title given occasionally to the Old Latin (pre. Vulgate) variety of the Bible.

ITALO/GREEKS The Greek body relent from (1) Greek colonizers in Sicily and South Italy in Byzantine times; (2) later Greek possession acquire in Italian seaports; and (3) Greek and Albanian asylum seeker from the Muslim invasion. Their position is total.

ITIHASA (Sanskrit) History, legend, tradition. This term is mainly applied to the two great Native American epics: the Mahabharata and the Ramayana.

ITTHAM (Sanskrit) Thus, in this way; so.

IU-Kabar-Zivo. (Gn.) Additionally acknowledged by the name of Nebat-Iavar-bar-Iufin-Ifafin, "Lord of Aeon's", in the Nazarene system. He is the procreator (Emanator) of the seven Holy Lives (the first seven Dhyan Chohans, or Archangels), each of whom stood for one of the cardinal virtues, and he in turn is called the third Life (third Logos). In the Codex it is invoked as "the Taymon and the vine of the food of life." Thus, it is identical to Christ (Christos), who says: "I am the true vine, and my Father is the farmer" (John XV, 1). It is well known that Christ is considered in the Roman Catholic Church as "the prince of the Aeon", and as Michael, "who is like God". Such was also the belief of the Gnostics.

IURBO-ADONAI (or Burbo Adonai) The creators' name of Iao-Jehovah. The Ophite affirmed them as coming from Ilda-Baoth, son of Sophia Acha moth, a proud, aspiring and observant god, and mixed Spirit, many Gnostic sects respected as the god of Moses. "Burbo is quoted by the abortions (Jews) Adonai", the Codex Nazarenus (vol. III, page 13) "Halt" and engenders were mottos that the Gnostics applied to the Jews. [With the title of Burbo-Adonai, aged the Codex Nazarenus to Jehovah.]

IXION. According to mythology, he was king of the La-piths of Thessaly and father of Pirithoo. The authoritarian Deione's saddled his wife Dia and walked for a long time trying to atone for his offense, as no one offered asylum; Jupiter took pity on him and took him to Olympus. There he tried to seduce Hera, Jupiter's wife; but he replaced him with a slave named Nephele which implied cloud, from which the Centaurs were born. Jupiter punished Ixion by chaining him to an inflamed wheel, in hell, making it spin eternally.

IZA (isa or Isha) (Sanskrit) Lord, sovereign, king, chief, etc. Epithet of Siva (or Shiva) Title of one of the Upanichads (Izopanichad).

IZNIK. The modern name of Nicaea, now only a village in Turkey

IZVARA-Krichma Writer of a superb assembly of seventy-two proverbs citing to the Sankhya philosophical arrangement, appointed by the denomination of Sankhya-karika.

IZATVA. (Sanskrit) Sovereign, dominion; Supremacy and "supernatural" power of initiated brahmana

IZED Radiant spirits that are below Hormuzd or initiation of good. They were created by Hormuz to pour out blessings upon the universe; they are male and female.

IZNIK The modern name of 'Nicaea, now only a village in Turkey.

IZVARYA (Sanskrit) Lordship, power, sovereignty, royalty.

IZWARA (Iswara or Ishvara) "The Lord" or the personal God, the divine Spirit in man. Textually sovereign (with its independent existence). Title given to Ziva and is to another deity of India [Brahma and Vichnu]. Ziva is also called Izvara Deva ho deva sovereign.

-J-

JADA (Sanskrit) Unconscious, stupid, apathetic.

JADE (Gnosticism) Very hard, tenacious stone, soapy, whitish or greenish appearance, with reddish or purple spots, the most precious is the imperial Jade, emerald, green. Its medicinal integrities generate it to be given the name jade stone. It was employed in the religious rites of antiquity. It signifies immortality.

JACKAL Animal mammal butcher of Asia and Africa like the wolf. The book of the Dead says, NU triumphant: "I am the jackal of the jackals and the air I obtain from the presence of the God of light I lead you to the limits of the firmament and to the ends of the earth and to the borders of the ends the flight of the bird Naveh", thus air is disposed to these young beings' divisions. "Anubis" is the God of the jackal's head, he is the hierarch of the arcane nine (9) Tarot, the jackal of the jackals. The temple of Anubis is the temple of the lords of Karma. Anubis hauling the books of predestination, in the underworld. Every human being has his business book. There are forty-two (42) judges of the law of fate who use as a symbol the head of the jackal, Anubis being the supreme judge or jackal of jackals.

JAH (Hebrew) Divine phrase designated to the sefira Chokmah on the tree of life. Chokmah or Jah is dynamic Wisdom, an active male talent.

JAHO (Hebrew) This idiom involves the same as Jah. [Name of Chokmah or Wisdom, an enthusiastic male potency. In addition, it is equivalent to Lah and Yah, (since the letters i, j and y are permutable) and to Jaho and Jehovah.]

JH (Sanskrit) Ideogram of an amount of the main (trunks) nadis that commence from the heart.

JAIBIT or Shadow Transpired nourished by the food of the "Ka" or "life force", a component of the human spirit, a pinch of the universal and immortal principle of life, according to Egyptian mythology. For the ancient Egyptians the integrant of the human spirit were: Ib, Ka, Ba, Aj, Ren and Sheut, and like this, their existence was emancipated from the body, it carried and wandered at its whim.

JAIL or JAILS Gnosis teaches that the wrongdoer is not reformed in prisons; only with a well-known pedagogical psychology can a criminal be able to reform himself.

JAIMINI (Sanskrit) A great sage, a pupil of Vyasa, the transmitter and educator of the Sama-veda, who presumably admitted that of his guru. He is further the famous founder and writer of the Purva Mimansa philosophy.

JAIRUS. A Galilean 'ruler of the synagogue' "whose daughter Christ restored to life." (Mk. 5:21-43).

JAKS. A considerable equatorial Asian tree (Artocarpus heterophyllus) analogous to the breadfruit that supplies a fine-grained yellow wood and immense fruits which accommodates an edible pulp and nutritious seeds.

JAKIN or Jachin (Hebrew) "In Hebrew signs IKIN, from the root Kun "to establish", and the outstanding terms of one of the columns of the portico of the Temple of King Solomon". The other pillar was called Boaz, and of the two, one was white, and one was black. Both concern a handful of mystical ideas, one of which is that it mirrors the dual Manas or the upper and lower Ego. Others relate these two supports, in slave mysticism, to God and the Devil, that is, to the 'White God' and the 'Black God', or Byeloy Bog and Tchernoy Bog.

JALA (Sanskrit) Water.

JALIKA (Sanskrit) Magician, sorcerer, charmer, minstrel.

JAMNIA or JABNEH. A city c. 13 miles Soth of Joppa. Subsequently the fall of Jerusalem (A.D. 70) an assemblage of Jewish religious teachers was inaugurated here. The status of assertive Biblical Books whose canonicity was still open to investigate in the 1ˢᵗ centennial A.D. was possibly one of the topics of discussion, but there are no testimonials to demonstrate the insinuations that a peculiar synod of Jamnia, held c. 100, confirmed the barriers of the Hebrew Scriptures canon.

JAMBU (Sanskrit) Pink apple or the apple tree that creates it. It is like Jambu Dvipa and is also the reputation of the land and a declining river of Mount Meru.

JMA Earth.

JANUARY (Latin ienuairis. for ianuarius) It is the door through which the Aryan enters. It is associated the appellation comes by sense the God Janus with his two faces, one of more age symbolizing the earlier Aryan and flipside younger reinstate the new year. January is the first month of the year, so also begins a new cycle around the sun. January has an esoteric substitution of death and resurrection.

JANO or JANU (Latin, Jauna: gate) A Roman divinity, God of heaven and beginning of all that exists. In mythology: he is said to have been the son of Saturn and Entoria. He symbolized himself with a two-faced head (Janus Bifronte), flashing that he knew the past and future, the first of the month of the year was given the name of January, Gnostic, living wise God, who taught at the time of Arcadia, on the continent Mu (Atlantis), the science Jonah. Jana. Swana or Jaina, it is accordingly the doctrine of that old God of struggle and action, called Janus, the divine Lord of two faces. The Jina-Hana school of Tibet teaches the science of the God Janus: Jinn science and Christification. Master Samael tells in his work the Mystery of the Golden Blossom one of his experiences with the God Janus: "When I wanted to ask him, the old man without speaking a single word deposited the answer in the depths of my conscience like this: "Even if a man dwelt in Nirvana in any other region of infinite sayings, if he does not have God inside, I wouldn't be happy. But if you live in the hellish worlds or in the filthiest prison on earth, having God inside you would be happy." Production, birth; Knee. "The lower portion of the thigh (Janu) is called Mahatala."

JAPA (Sanskrit) Mystical dexterity of positive yogis. Gravitates to enumerate from memory various mantras and magical guidelines. [I pray in a faint voice; recitation of recollection (silent or mental). "Japa stands for repetition but must be accompanied by proper meditation on the meaning of the words or syllables counted. The preferable way of reciting recommended by the Tantras is mental, so that it is not interrupted for a moment during work or even sleeping."]

JARA (Sanskrit) Old age decrepitude.

JARROW AND WEARMOUTH. The dual Benedictine monasteries between the Tyne and the Wear, established correspondingly in 674 and 682 by St. Benedict Bishop, in a short time developed into an intermediary of education and humanities; they transformed into an extensively studied assiduously the documents of Bede. A department of their place is employed by the Parrish archdiocese' temples.

JATAKA (Sanskrit) Birth.

JATI (Djati) (Sanskrit) Procedure, Birth. One of the twelve Nidanas; the cause and effect on the manner of occurrence of birth, according to the Chatur-yoni, where in every action a being, whether man or vertebrate, is implanted in one of the six gatis or path of sentient existence, which hiddenly, counting from top to bottom, are: 1. The sovereign Dhyanis (Anupadaka); 2. The devas; 3. Men; 4. The elementals or spirits of Nature; 5. Animals; 6. The lower elementals, and

7. Organic germs. In popular or exoteric nomenclature, these beings are devas, men, asuras, infernal vital force, pretas (starving demons) and creature. Other interpretations of Jati are family, tribe, species, caste, position, condition, etc. The chief of the prelates of the tribunal of karma is the great Master Anubis.

JEBAL DJUDI (Arabic) The "Flood Mountain" of Arab stories. Like the Ararat and the Babylonian mount of Nizir, in which Xisuthrus took land with his ark.

JEHOVAH The Jewish description of the Deity, J'hovah, is a compound of two words, namely: de Haj (y, e or j, Yod, tenth letter of the Hebrew alphabet) and Hovah (Havah, or Eve), says a Kabbalistic faculty, Mr. J. Ralston Skinner, of Cincinnati. USA of America. And, along with, "the word Jehovah, or Jah-Eve, has the same significance of existence or being as male-female."

JEALOUSY Superseded as the origin of a great deal of frustrations in marriages. Those who are jealous do not love; they are only enslaving the being they consider they love.

JERUSALEM or Jerosalem (Septuag.) and Hierosolyma (Vulgat.) In Hebrew, Yrshlim or "city of peace" is recorded; but the Greeks in the past properly called it Hiorosalem or "Secret Salem", since Jerusalem is a reappearance of Salem, of which Melchizedek was the King-Hierophant, a manifested astrolate and worshipper of the sun, "the Highest", by the way.

JESOD (Hebrew) Inauguration; of the ninth of the ten Sephiroth, an active male talent, which integrates the six that incorporate the Microprosopo.

JESUS Mortal name in Hebrew was Yeshua; Christ or Jesus-Christ. An honor must be determined between the historical Jesus and the mystical Jesus. The first was Essene and Nazarene and was a messenger of the Great Fraternity to exhort the ancient divine doctrines that were to be the basis of a new culture. For three years he was divine Master of men and walked in Palestine leading a model life for his purity, piety and love for humanity. He worked a multitude of phenomena raising the dead, healing the sick, returning sight to the blind, walking the paralyzed and performing many other acts that, due to their extraordinary condition, have been considered "miracles". The excellence of his doctrines stands out above all in his famous Sermon on the Mount. As an Initiate, he also taught esoteric disciplines, but these he kept singularly for "the few", that is, for his chosen students. The historical Jesus has been attributed not a few traditional actions that have changed him into another immaculately mystical personality, a true copy of the God Krishna, so respected in India. To experience such confirmation, one need only look a little at the similarity between Jesus and Krishna shown by the author of Isis without a veil, from which we chose the following metaphors: 1. Jesus is harassed by Herod, king of Judea, but flees to Egypt, led by an angel; to guarantee his death, Herod organizes the disgorgement of 40,000 innocents. Krishna is harassed by Kanza, Tyrant of Mathura, but flees in a prodigious manner; expecting to kill the child, the king has thousands of male children killed. 2. Jesus' mother was Mariam or Miriam; she married as a virgin but had several children after the firstborn Jesus. Krishna's mother was Devaki, an immaculate virgin (but she had given birth to eight children before Krishna). 3. Jesus produces miracles, casts demons etout of the body, bathes the feet of his disciples, dies, descends into hell, and ascends to heaven after delivering the dead. Krishna does the same, with the only difference that he washed the feet of the Brahmins and climbed the Vaikuntha paradise or Vichnu paradise. 4. Both divulge the secrets of the sanctuary and die, Christ nailed to a cross (a tree), and Krishna nailed to a tree, the body pierced with an arrow.

JESU, DULCIS MEMORIA. The belated 12th centennial poem amicable direct adaptation of segments of it in the English hymns 'Jesu, the very through of Thee' and 'Jesu! The very thought is sweet'. It has conventionally been attributed to St. Bernard of Clairvaux but is very likely the labor of an English Trappist. It is occasionally well known as the 'Rosy Sequence'.

JETZIRAH (Sepher) (Hebrew) or "Book of Creation". The most esoteric of all Kabbalistic products that are presently in the custody of modern mystics. Its aspirational origin of having been drafted by Abraham is absurd, but its primary value is great. It consists of six perakim (chapters), separated into thirty-three short mishnah or sections; and deals with the evolution of the universe based on a system of consistencies and quantity. Within it transmitted that the Deity designed ("I believe") the world by means of numbers "by thirty-two paths (or paths) of secret knowledge", these paths being calculated for what correspond to the twenty-two signs of the Hebrew alphabet and the ten essential numbers. These ten are the primordial numbers, of which the entire Universe comprehends, and they go everlastingly from the twenty-two divine letters in Three Mothers, the seven uninvolved consonants. To those who long to figure out the system well, we entrust them to read the excellent, though concise, convention on the Sepher Jetzirah, to suit the pen of Dr. W. Wynnn Westcott.

JETZIRAH or Yetzirah (Hebrew) The third of the four Kabbalistic Worlds, compatible to the Angels: the "World of Formation", or Olam Yetzirah. He is also nominated Malahyah, or "of the Angels". It is the mansion of all the Geniuses (or Angels) regents who lead and rule planets, worlds and spheres.

JEU Sacred term, it is related to illumination and clairvoyance, it is a magical key. The extraordinary "Jeu" is the chaperone of those who are inside us, prince of the Faces, who leads the Aeona's to know them well. Together with the Virgin of Light and the twelve authorities in our Essence, He has assigned us to our heavenly figure.

JEU, Books of. Two Gnostic treatises ascribed to Enoch.

JEW, Wandering Jew, The. The Jew who accounts to advocate legend, provoked Christ on His way to crucifixion and was condemned to roam over the earth up to the Last Day. The myth first materialized in a pamphlet published in 1602. Innumerable conventions with the Jew have been presented.

JICHNU (Jishnu) (Sanskrit) [Textually: "victorious".] Chief of the Heavenly Hosts; title of Indra, who in the war of the Deities with the Asuras, was leader of the "host of the Gods". He is the "Michael, Prince of the Archangels" of India.

JINAS (Sanskrit) (djinn) "Victorious" "Genius". Nickname Vichnu. This title is also given to Buddhist Buddhas, Arhats and Ascetics. The Jains practice it to the Tirthankaras or saints of their creed, and only to Vardhamana Mahavira, whom they consider on as their Buddha.

JINX. An individual or object that initiates bad luck. "One was never not for a moment to wish luck to a person going hunting or fishing, as it was discerned a jinx", propose bad luck to; cast an evil spell on. "The play is jinxed". There is a proverb that when two people unintentionally say the same thing at once. "'What's happened? The two of us say it at precisely the same time. 'Jinx!'"

JITA (Sanskrit) Defeated, dominated, overcome.

JIVA (Sanskrit) (Theo-Gnostic) Commits to Life in the sense of the absolute, personifies, moreover; the monad or "Aman-Buddi", Jiva has the features of vital principle, soul or living spirit. Being, Soul or individual spirit. The Jiva (the Soul) goes with Sukma-Sharira from the heart of the body to the Brahmarandra on the crown of the head dispersing Sushumna, (nerve that joins the heart with the Brahmarandra).

JIVA BHUTA (Sanskrit) Living, existing, vital, which is an element or principle of life, which animates living beings. "He is an eternal part of himself; in the world of those who live, it attracts the inner sense and the other five senses, which have their seat in material nature."

JOB. Biblical character to whom Jehovah tests faith. Gnostic. "The book of Job is a complete representation of the ancient initiation and the peoples that preceded the great ceremony." Each Initiation must be defeated in eight years; that is, the whole book of Patriarch Job; pay Neptune's tithing before attaining resurrection. Each initiator, one year for each initiation.

JOAN OF ARC, St, (1412-31), the 'Maid of Orleans'. The daughter of a countryman, in 1425 she experienced the first of the supernatural apparition, which she expressed as voices accompanied by a blaze of light. In 1429 she reassured the French king (Charles VII) of her assignment to save France, led an expedition which relieved Orleans, and then assured Charles to move forward to Artemis for his coronation. She was taken prisoner in 1430, sold to the English, and charged with witchcraft and heresy. After explorations from an ecclesiastical court, she was burnt. A revision of her trial in 1456 revealed her innocence; she was canonized in 1920.

JOD (Hebrew) This Hebrew letter constitutes the masculinity. (Secret Doctrine, II, 133).

JOHN (Baptist Saint) He was the antecessor of Jesus Christ, son of the priest Zacarias and Elizabeth. He was Nazarene and led a baptism in the Jordan, to which Jesus of Nazareth also came, of whom he said, "that he was not worthy to untie his sandals" when Jesus saw him; said; "Among men born of women, no one greater than John the Baptist has risen; however, the smallest in the kingdom of heaven is greater than him."

JONAH, Book of. Minor Prophet. The Book details the Spiritual signal to Jonah to go to Nineveh and enlightens penitence, his struggle to departure by sea, his "being thrown overboard and swallowed by a fish", his liberation in the wake of three days, and the achievements of this assignment. The psalm in chapter. 2 is commonly grasped to be self-reliant of the recline of the Book, which is designed by observers to the long duration period. The 'sign of Jonah' (Mt. 12:39 & c.) is transcribed as a prediction of Christ's restoration of life.

JORD In northern Germany she was the goddess of the Earth, as was Nerthus and Freya or Scandinavian Friv.

JORDAN, River. Emanates separating the waters of four streams that congregate, the Jordan flows through the 'Sea of Galilee' and finally join the Dead Sea. By their crossing of the Jordan the Hebrews initially reached the Promised Land (Jos. 3:16); John the Baptist prophesy on its banks, Christ was surrounded by those baptized in its waters (Mt. 3:13). The Jordan emerges as a characterization of the realization of clarity (specifically in baptism) and of the last involvement to man's concluding beatitude

JOSEPHUS (Flavius) He was a historian of the first century AD. Hellenized Jew who lived in Alexandria and died in Rome. According to Eusebius, he wrote the ten and six famous lines concerning to Christ, which in the greatest form were interpolated by Eusebius himself, the most significant falsifier among the Fathers of the Church. This passage, in which Josephus, who was a staunch Jew and died in the lap of Judaism, is nevertheless made to investigate Messianism and the divine origin of Jesus, is now revealed illegitimate by most Christian bishops (Lardner, among others) and even by Paley himself. This was, through the centuries, one of the most authentic verifications of the real existence of Jesus, the Christ.

JOVE. [Jupiter] (Lat.). Its term derives beginning the same root as the Greek Zeus. He is the substantial god of the premature Greeks and Romans, also embraced by other nations. It has various names, among others: 1st. Jupiter Aerios; 2nd. Jupiter Ammon of Egypt; Jupiter Bel-Moloch, the Chaldean; 4th. Jupiter-Mundus, Deus-Mundus, "God of the World"; 5th Jupiter-Fulgur, "the Brilliant or Tonant", etc., etc.

JOY Coming out of Middle English Joye, taken on loan from Old French joie, originating out of (Late Latin gaudia, neuter plural mistaken as feminine singular) of Latin Gaudium ("joy"), from gaudere (to be glad, rejoice") The term Joy attribute to the sentiment aroused by contentment, achievement, or blessings, and is frequently correlated with awareness of fierce, enduring satisfaction. Experiencing joy involves consciousness of optimism and dynamic jubilation. But Joy, in its plentiful, sacred signification of conveying Deity's virtue; requires expanded jubilation ingrained, inspiration and euphoria. The Christian says, "The joy of the Lord is our strength" (Neh. 8:10). Jesus said: "But the fruit of the Spirit is love, joy, peace, patience, kindness, goodness, faithfulness, gentleness, and self-control. There is no law against things like this." The potential of Joy is the guideline for active idlers who desire genuine conversion. It incorporates influential instruments and effective instructions that assures substantial modification, internally and outwardly. Every moment of joy should be prolonged in meditation with a still mind and in deep silence.

JOYFUL The "smiley face" is a comprehensive allegory for fondness cheerfulness, outlined by a uncomplicated amber fac peaked with a large, cheerful smirk! The smiling glance us as a worldwide, universal, and admired token of jubilation and cheerfulness in our 21st Centurial planet. Human beings encompassing the earth habituated the butterfly ideogram to suggest existence, expectation, diversity, and tolerance. Yellow flowers indicate satisfaction in many ways. Additionally, to sunflowers, there exist yellow lilies, tulips, daisies and yellow chrysanthemums; entirely are ideal options if you desire to deliver contentment to anyone in heart. The Christmas evergreen, so straightforward and yet so unusual, is an ordinary sign that declares to numerous individuals without expressing a command; the illuminations, the decorations, the sounds generate a distinctive joyful that is complicated to construe.

JUDAS (Iscariot) One of Jesus' twelve apostles known as "the traitor." It is related that he came from the distant lands of Karyote, modernly El Kargetein, in Judas. Master Samael explains that Judas never betrayed his guru (master). He simply learned a role given by his teacher, the master Jesus Christ, and to be it publicly, in the Cosmic Drama taught to humanity in that way. As a role (actor) Judas stands for the death of the Ego and that is a Gospel to be understood people must read Zechariah, there are cited the thirty silver coins that Judas received, although he was accepted and undervalued. It is ratified that Judas did not betray the Master Jesus as people believe, he had to inspect the scriptures to execute that role that the Master Jesus instructed him to execute with the drama he had to instruct himself in his role of remembrance. He is a resurrected teacher, the best of the twelve apostles, his Gospel is the death of the Ego, he renounced all happiness himself and lives in the hellish worlds, working for the lost, for those who have no remedy. He is the only one who has not received distinction, has been hated, insulted and yet loves humanity, since he sacrificed himself for it, he has achieved nothing but insults since he fulfilled his drama until the present time. Each of the twelve apostles fulfilled his role within the great Christ Drama.

JUDAEA. The region reclaimed by the Jews in 537 B.C. after the Babylonian Captivity. In Christ's time it routinely denominated the southern part of Palestine.

JUDGE (Gnosticism) Anubis, Egyptian God of Death. Anubis forwards with his 42 judges of Karma judge the past and present actions of people's lives and finds punishments (Karmas) or rewards (Dharmas). In practical life the police officer wears his uniform, the doctor his white coat, the Judge his toga, etc. The funeral and skeletal garments, figure of the angels of death, frighten those who have not yet awakened consciousness.

JUDGED (Gnosticism) "After the death of the physical body, every human being afterwards reviewing the life that has just passed, is judged by the Lords of Karma.

JUNG, Carl Gustav (1875-1961) Swiss psychiatrist. He succeeded Freud and Adler in the field of psychoanalysis in 1933 obtained the chair of psychiatry at the Technological University of Zura.

JUNG CODEX, The. Special of the script's realization at Nag Hammadi. It was accomplished by the Jung Institute for Analytical Psychology at Zurich.

JUNO or Hera Goddess of the Romans or Hera of the Greeks. Esoterically represents Isis, the Cosmic Mother.

JUSTICE Impartiality; with this word the whole spirit of the Buddha's doctrine can be illustrated, because it teaches that every man receives, by virtue of the operations of the infallible and inexorable Karma, exactly that reward or that punishment that he has deserved, neither more nor less. No good or bad action, however insignificant and hidden, escapes the steady balance of Karma.

JYA (Sanskrit) Mother Earth; force, violence.

JYAU (Sanskrit) The planet Jupiter.

JYOTICHA (Jyoticha) (Sanskrit) Astronomy and astrology; one of the Vedangas [parts of the Veda]

-K-

KA (Sanskrit) According to Max Muller, the interrogative pronoun Who? elevated, without cause or reason, to the high categorization of divinity; however, esoterically this word is an appellation of Brahma in its masculine nature, as progenitor. In the mystical sense, Ka names Brahma, Vishnu, Kama and Agni. This idiom also shows any object, whether material or spiritual, destined to move air, wind, water, fire, sun, time, etc., body, soul, intelligence, charm, joy, pleasure, happiness, etc. The language of ancient Egypt, Ka is the designation of the astral body.

KABALISTIC, Kabbalistic, (Kabbalist) Unrevealing; the scholar of "secret science," who understands the secret revelation of Scripture with the help of the symbolic Pietism and presents its exact interpretation by such measures. The Tannaim were the Mystical pioneers among the Jews; They arose in Jerusalem in the early third century BC. The books of Ezekiel, Daniel, Enoch, and the Apocalypse (or revelation) of St. John are virtuously Kabbalistic.

KADANA (Sanskrit) Terror, turmoil, confusion; destruction, extermination.

KAME. A shortened ridge, hill, or dune of graded drift reserved by frozen subglacial water. The inception of the term kame materialized from the old Scots expression for a comb. The Fonthill Kame in Pelham, Ontario in the Niagara Peninsula was initiated 13,000 years ago when water melted from the Wisconsin Glacier, which concealed Lake Erie and the unified peninsula, reserved sand and gravel, structured coating or layers to shape the kame. Kames are frequently excavated as places of origin of sand and gravel for framework. Regional illustrations of kames embrace Chicopee, Beechwood hill, Doon Pinnacle, and the Baden Hills.

KAMEA (Hebr.) An amulet, customarily a magic square.

KAMI. (Japan) Unmistakably, 'superior'. This Japanese expression is about a divinity, or any of the gods, demigods or divinized paladin of that native land.

KALA King of the secondary world, judge of the dead. Weak, disoriented, dull or weak sound.

KALKI Make reference to the tempo of Kali Yuga to the present moment. Conforming to Brahmanism it is the white horse where the last Avatara (S.A.W.) will come amid the courageous and the firestorm.

KALI (Sanskrit). Dissension discord, evil, perversity; war, struggle. The Kali-yuga personified as the spirit of evil. Name of the demon of each age. Name of the cycle of 2,400 divine years.

KALIEM (Hebrew) Precisely, "vessels or vehicles"; the craft for the source of the Water of Life. This turn of phrase applies to the ten Sephiroth admired as the ancient nuclei of all the Kosmos Forces.

KALIKA (Sanskrit) Anachronistic; the nickname of the dinosaur Kali (Durga or Parvati). Cantatriz Celeste.

KALILA (Sanskrit) Uncertainty, confusion, disorder, chaos.

KALIYUGA (Sanskrit) The fourth yuga, the black or iron age; the present period of the world, whose duration is 432,000 years. The last of the ages in which the revolutionary period of man is divided by a series of these ages. Kaliyuga began 3,102 years before J.C., at the time of Krishna's death, and the first 5,000-year cycle ended between the years 1897 and 1898 [Age of Discord and Evil].

KALPA (Sanskrit) Epoch of a materialistic uprising, routinely a rhythym of instants, nonetheless usually constitute a "Day and a Night" of Bhahma, a stretch of 4.32 giga Annum, [By Kalpa is by a large conveys a "Day" of Brahma or manvantara, consecutively intervals illustrating a millennial mahayugas i.e. the continuance of a universe, or by way of explanation, the age of indication or cosmic venture, at the conclusion of which approaches the Night of Brahma, a duration of discontinuation or recuperation. Therefore, we glance over the Bhagavad-Gita (IX): "At the end of a Kalpa, all beings disappear into my material nature, and from me they emanate again at the beginning of a new Kalpa." Kalpa is finally the appellative of a figurative timber of the celestial city of Indra, a tree that manufactures the total one desires. Various further definitions come across this term, similarly: authorization, ruling (particularly for the rituals or pursue accepted to the consecration); ordinance, approach, formation; devotion enactment, etc.]

KAMA-dharana (Sanskrit) What encourages, nourishes, supports greediness. The fulfillment of gratification of longing, avarice, enthusiasm.

KAMALA (Sanskrit) Water, lotus. A nerve force center is in the body.

KAMI (Japan) Faithfully, "superior." This Japanese word applies to a monsieur, to any of the gods, demigods or venerate paladin of that pair.

KAMIN Loving, affectionate, passionate, yearning.

KANDA (Sanskrit) Gnostic. In Planetary Science. A nerve channel that is located between the similar arguments where the Nadi Subshumna and the Kundaini join, it is the fundamental base of all the 7,000 nadis of our organism. He receives all the procreative strength that circulates through the 72,000 nadis, that excitement is prana, it is life. The Kanda has the shape of an egg and is nourished by the energy of the Cosmic Christ.

KANT, IMMANUEL (1.724-1804). He was a German philosopher, who blemish the "division" among earliest and modern ideology, born in Konigsberg. In au "critique of pure reason" reveals that the sensual mind elaborates its conceptualizations based on the five senses, gnosis explains that rationale knows nothing about the real, about the truth, about what depart the five senses The real can only be involment through direct mystical experience.

KANSIYA (Sanskrit) Zinc alloy, copper, whichever is widely used for the manufacture of vessels.

KAR God of the winds, according to Scandinavian mythology.

KARANA (Sanskrit) Origin (transmigration). Acknowledgeable also expresses cause in general, motive; element, factor or main matter; substance; organ, instrument, agent, medium; action, act, operation, etc.

KARMIN Loving, adoring, passionate, yearning.

KARUNA (Sanskrit) Pity, regret, compassion.

KARUNYA (Sanskrit) Piety, compassion, misericord.

KASBECK. The mountain stretch of the Caucasus location Prometheus was restrained.

KATANCY (Gnostic) Predestination; the higher karma, the karma of the gods. This kind of karma is above the lords of the law. Katancia cites to order the Gods and even those of the Great Law.

KATHA (Sanskrit) Anecdote, narration, story, chronicle, conversation, dialogue, exposition, mention.

KATHISMA. The "Byzantine structure" Psalm book is split up into twenty fragments; the word 'kathisma' is employed to identify the two of the indicated segments and the ephemeral solemn anthem chanted at the culmination of each one harmoniously through Orthros.

KAYA-stha (Sanskrit) "Residing in the body": the Spirit.

KAZI (Sanskrit) Ancient name of the holy city of Benares.

KCHEMA (Sankrit) Well said, enjoyment, well-being, happiness, possession; well, happy, lucky.

KCHETRA or Kchtram (Dshetam) (Sanskrit) The "Great Abyss" of the Bible and Kabbalah; Chaos, Yoni Prakriti, space. [Here are other definitions of this word: field, plain, terrain, site, holy place; dwelling; medium; matter, body; womb; life, etc. In the Bhagavad-Gita, chap. XIII, versicle. 1., it reads: "This body ... it is called Middle (Kchetra)"; but in the present case other interpretation of the word Kchetra, such as residence o lodgings, ground, obscure, matter, body, etc. Residence, because matter, whether it is organized (human body, animal, plant), or inorganic (mineral), is household of the Spirit; for it is the ground on which good or bad seeds are sown and where the fruits of our works are reaped; body, because it is the vehicle of our individual Self.]

KEA. A large mostly dull green New Zealand parrot (Nestor notabilis) that is ordinarily omnivore but occasionally wipe out sheep by hacking the back to nourish on the kidney fatlike. Kea is an extremely companionable breed which is in the savage, formation huge gaggle with non-linear ranking. Studies by Jackson (1960) in Arthur's Pass recognized swarm of everywhere 20 first year birds during the summer solstice. These large swarms were hen spotted to break up into groups of 2-6 in autumn. Kea is a large parrot with mainly olive-green feathers, becoming darker to a teal blue on the wingtips. On the undersurface of the wings and the bottom of the tail the features are a reddish orange. Female kea is narrowly compact than males and have abbreviate beaks. Kea is a guarded species who lives in forestland and mountainous locality crossways the South Island from Golden Bay to Fiordland. This American Indians parrot is a taonga for Ngi Tahu and Nga iwi o Te Tau ihu (northern South Island iwi) and cherished by New Zealanders as an icon of the outdoors.

KELLS. A township in the Republic of County Meath, Ireland. The Book of Kells, an brighten script of the Christian doctrine, was created at the cloister to this location in the 8th centenary. The publication acquired a pseudonym led the way to Kells came after a Viking assault on the friary on the isle of Iona, Scotland, in 806. The volume of Kells carries the tetrad interpretations of Christ's existence that structures the New Testament of the Christian Bible. Specifics of the handful's valuable endurance of an important heritage blossoming in the Irish Sanctuary in the eighth and ninth centuries, Scottish and Irish: from a distinctive reputation built on 'sacrificial cauldron helmet' (which is in Irish's folklore "where leprechauns keep their gold and treasures) with Gothic enlargements King's English. In Scotland conceivably of geographic origination from which place is also called 'the cauldron'.

KENOTIC Is the neglected of celestial attributed by Jesus Christ in fitting mortals. Kenosis presumes a step-by-step deprivation of the disposition, a progressive procedure of disengagements from inconsiderable: belongings, garbs, belongings, sentiments, descent, potency. Kenotic style: Jesus emerges frail (caretakers run away to shield him.) Considerable appearance: Jesus is declared as fit 'vigorous. Kenosis is from the Greek verb for unburden, balanced, and amend. The uncomplicated process to describe the kenosis of Christ is that He put away his survival constitute of conformity to the will of father intensity of the spirit of God. His perpetual almightiness in perception. He was consistently intimately God, or genuinely God, as Romanists commonly similarly acknowledge.

KER (Gr.) Hesiod and Homer speak of imaginary beings, who are personifications of the immediate causes of death. His appearance is horrible; They follow the warriors in the Battlefield and, casting sinister glances, crawl alongside the wounded and dying, digging their intimidating claws into their unhappy bodies and sucking their blood.

KERMES Roman mythology recognizes him as the mercury and Greek as the messenger of the Deities. God of chance, wealth, patron saint of merchants and farmers, protects travelers and protects roads. He had a reputation for being ingenious and is credited with creating the yoke lute, alphabet, numbers, weights and measures, etc., he was the son of Zeus and the Mayan Nymph.

KERYGMA. (The Gk. term for 'preaching'). The component of notification in Christian apologetic, as diversified with 'Didache' or its enlightening characteristics.

KETHER (Hebrew) The Aureola, the highest of the ten Sephiroth; the first of the Supreme Triad. It is related to the Macroprosopo, Great Face of Face, or Arikh Anpin, which diverges into Chokmah and Binah. Elder of the Elders, Mystery of Mysteries, the unknown of the unknown. But under that form by which He Himself is known; He always remains unknown.

KEY Hardware utensil by whatever the latch of a padlock is rotate, some of several gadget encounter the formation or purpose of equivalent as key a key for turning a timepiece; a method of acquire or avoid entry, guardianship, or predominance. "Giving a key to your partner is more symbolic than anything these days," Described: "It's a sign that you both look forward to the future together and are having a valuable experience of the relationship." It signifies you would be in there altogether, and the two are free from danger. Amid the oriental, triumvirate keys' tie up jointly are contemplated an important talisman. They authorize the attired to unlatch the entry that conducts to fondness, fitness, and prosperity. A key provided as a donation companion is regarded as an image of unfastening the entry to affection. The giver will be considered lucky in love.

KHA [or Kham] (Sanskrit) Synonym of Akaza. [Space, ether, firmament, sky, air. One of the crude features of the Sankhya philosophers: Earth, water, fire, air and ether (Kha)

KHEDA (Sanskrit) Fatigue, torment, sadness, sorrow, regret.

KHEM (Egypt) The same as Horus. "The god Kehm will avenge his father Osiris," reads a text from a papyrus. [Khem represents divinity in his dual role of father and son: as father, he is called "husband of his mother"; as son, he is assimilated to Horus. It symbolizes vegetation, ism time that the generation.

KHEPRA (Egypt) Egyptian's god who presides over rebirth and transmigration. It is replaced with a sacred beetle as a substitute for a head.

KHUM (Egypt) Khoom. In the English transliteration, or Knuf (Knooph). The soul of the World; a variant of Khnum (Khnoom). "[The egg of the World was placed in Khum, the Water of Space or abstract feminine Principle, and with humanity's 'fall' into generation and finitism, Khum became Ammon, the creator God."

KIDDUSH. The Jewish observance of the reverence of the Sabbath or other holy days. It transpires the evening meal on the eve of the day in question, when the head of the extended family says the 'Kiddush' or 'Blessings' of the day over a cup of wine and water. It has been suggested that Christ's blessing of the cup at the "Last Supper was the Kiddush of the Passover.

KSHANA (Kshana) (Sanskrit) An unpredictable brief instant: the 90th part or fragment of a thought, the 4,500, part of a minute, all along which ninety to a hundred births and as numerous deaths occur on this earth. [In general, it defines memento, instant; praising time, opportunity occasion; vacation, feast or holiday]. Manilal Dvvedi defines it by saying: Kchana or split second is that infinitesimal segment of tempo that can no longer be divided; and conforming to the madhyamika creed of the Kchanas or moments, all things are established only of an uninterrupted series of instants presented to our consciousness. The universe, with all its phenomena, is insignificant but an incessant and immediate succession of states.

KIM-puruchas (Sanskrit) Monstrous devas, half men and half horses. [Precisely: "what men?" A class of mystic's entities, goblins, trassgos, dwarves, etc., who take part in the nature and presentation of animals. Lately this word has grown compatible with Kinnaras. "A Name of the Beings of the Second Race"

KIN (Hebrew) Cain, or Evil, son of Eve and Samael (the Devil who took Adam's place), according to the doctrines of the rabbis.

KING'S BOOK, The. designation frequently designated to A Required Attitude and enlightenment for each Pious Individual, place forward by Henry VIII in 1543. It was established on the Prelates' Publication of 1537, however for the chiefly its dogma was a response in a Catholicism course.

KING JAMES VERSION A subject worn, esp. In America, for the English transfer of the Bible frequently well known in England as the approve Version (1611).

KIRK Is a Scottish and former Northern English word meaning "church". It is often used especially of the Church of Scotland. Kirk a word meaning circle, in he sense of "assembly" or "company;" the original word being Saxon and supposed by some to have come from the Greek, dominium, "The Lord's house." The word Church is the same as "Kirk," and has the same signification as "congregation" or assembly. Which are elsewhere given as translations of the original Greek word. The established religion of Scotland (the Presbyterian) is usually called he Kirk of Scotland.

KIRITIN (Sanskrit) "One who wears a tiara or headband". Qualification of Krishna and other figures.

KISS (Egyptian) An event that takes place as the intimate dedication of two souls who wish to express what they live internally.

KISS of DEATH According to the Kabbala, the most attentive proselyte does not die by the power of the Spirit of Evil, Yetzer ha Rah, but by a kiss on the mouth of Jehovah Tetragram Maton, whom he finds in the Haikal Ahavah or Palace of Love.

KISS OF PEACE. Also, PAX. The reciprocal salutation of the devoted in the Eucharistic Liturgy, as a sign of fondness of their love and uniting. It is initially mentioned by St. Justin Martyr and is likely utilization of the Apostolic period.

Initially a genuine kiss, the shape of the Peace has been adjusted in all rituals. In recent times handshaking has set off ordinary in the West.

KITE. One will find two different meanings of kite. The first is a sparkle structure protected with paper-thin, fabric, or adaptable, frequently supply a sustained tailpiece, and is outlined to be flown in the airs at the end of a long cord. Kites are declared to have emerged in China amid 475 BCE and 221 BCE with the initial kites constructed of timber and mocking the silhouette of feathered creatures. Through 618 CE and 907 CE, artisans began fabricating lighter kites originally with silk and bamboo and afterwards paper and bamboo. (Family Accipitridae) A middling to considerable, circumlocutory bird of prey that consistently has a forked tail and constantly take flight on ascent of air. Birds in this family are generally brown, black, or gray in coloration and have powerful, Clapper claws and hooked bills. Their eyes are yellow, red, and hazel. They may possess wingspans from 18 inches to 9 feet. Females of the species are routinely extensive than males. They can be discovered in greatly diverse parts of the world except Antarctica and live in all habitat types, including the desert, tundra, taiga, wetlands, and rainforests. Nearly all accipitrids are carnivorous, feeding on a variousness of quarry items. Numerous varieties develop oneself on specific vertebrate groups, such as fish, birds, reptiles (exclusively snakes in several assemblage), and mammals, considering other species limited on invertebrate prey, inclusive snails, insects, and crustaceans.

KIU-tche (Chin.) Kioo-tche, in the English transliteration. A Chinese work dealing with astronomy.

KNIGHT It means the Logos, the Father, the spirit that predominates over the horse (matter) or physical medium. Within alchemy there are allegorical senses such as: The gloomy knight (who works and suffers in the dark); The Albo knight (the one who begins to triumph "the chosen one"); the yellow has already passed certain test stages), the red knight (he is elevated, he has passed all the tests, he is the winner). Other symbolic representations are green knight; (symbolizes truth and hope). If the knight is wearing protective covering, it symbolizes their protection and solar bodies. In addition, the weapons used by the knight are highly emblematic, regardless spiritual or alchemical.

KRAM (Sanskrit) Tantric insignia agree with to the impression of the psyche whenever it outpace the standard ceiling of or concealed, sense in addition to imperceptible. The former ideology tantric had badge to delegate just about entire conception. This was required for them considering people recognized that if the brainpower were stable on an item with competent constrain for an assured period, it was unquestionable that by the potential of the will power it may well accomplish that entity. The awareness was commonly corroborated by nonstop restoration definitive signal, with which the proposal was consistently remain prior to the powers of reasoning. Consequently, the ideogram was used to stipulate every objective. As a result, "Hrien" delegate humbleness; "Kliw" designates love;" Aiw" viewed for shielding; "Chaum" convey comfort, and on and on. Indications along these lines were applied to label arteries, etc. Tantric discipline is now practically entirely vanished. Today, one can find no comprehensible and universal effective solution to illustrative phraseology, and what is more, plentiful of the representative articulations is regrettably indiscernible to this generation.

KRISTO. This expression is conviction to emanates from the Greek "Christos," interpretation "anointed," and was a name given to Jesus by premature Greek-speaking Christians is also a transcription of the Hebrew word "Messiah," blessing baby with an angelic etymology that's durability the ages. The Greek "Christos" is almost identical in sound and logography to the Sanskrit word "Kristos", meaning all-attractive. The Greek name Xpiotoc, is obtain from the earlier word Xpiotos (note the variance in accentuation), significant "anointed" and which became the Christian theological term for the Messiah. Is also a Greek vocable, and it is a corrupt speech pattern of Krsna. The definition of Kristo in Sanskrit vocabulary and the Greek lexicon consistently the equivalent, regarding this prompt; and follows this Kristo the expression finds Christo or Christ. Although in Christian society the God's label is in there. Jesus the Christ or Jesus the son of Kristo, or Krsna.

KNOW. To be attentive of across monitoring, investigation, or instruction. To expand an exchange along (someone) by way of assembly and expenditure tempo again anywhere; admit or affectionate. Familiarity, colleague, associate, confidant indicates to an individual with whom one is in connection. Contact is anybody perceived by eyesight, or anyone known, even so not intimately: informal contact. To know God is to be joyfully content in all circumstances because He is enough. Like Paul, David knew the secret of contentment; namely, knowing God. Sixth, to know God is to be faithfully guided. Verses 7-8: "I will bless the Lord who counsels me even at night when my thoughts trouble me".

KNOWLEDGE. The action and effect of understanding. Within Gnosticism it is explained that there are two kinds of understanding: that of the eye and that of the heart: the first is achieved through the physical and external senses: the second is realized through the heart and the spiritual goal discernment. The owl was the sign of Athena divinity of perception and intellect and was commonly illustrated in the artwork and coinage of ancient Athens. Dark Blue acts for knowledge, potential, honesty, and sobriety.

KOAN. Is the Japanese pronunciation of the Chinese phrase Kung-an whose original meaning is: "Dome of an official agreement on the desk". Within Zen Buddhism, the exercise of Kban generally sifies: "seek a solution to a Zen problem" The Koan is therefore an exercise to quiet the mind, because it does not know the answer to the Kban question; then defeated, it remains still in deep silence, at that moment the Essence intervenes, the consciousness that experiences the entasis or Satori of the Saints, the samadhi, The Buddhist Azen do not use the term Koan, they call it "Exercise Hua Tou". Examples of, Koanes: "If all the Coasa are reduced to Unity, what is reduced to Unity"; "What sense do you have the arrival of the Bodhisattwa from the west?, the answer is "The Cypress that is in, the garden"; " Why do the teeth of the table have hairs?, "If the clash of two palms of the hands produce a sound, What sound produces a sote:". . . The Mantram "Wu" is a Koan that serves to quiet the mind and achieve the "illuminating Void", it is pronounced as a double "U" in a wavy shape or imitating the sound of the hurricane.

KOINONIA The necessary interpretation of the koinonia enclose conceptions forward in the English language' commune, association, linkage contribution, dissemination and affinity. Koinonia competent consequently indicates in approximately conditions to a simultaneously honorary donation. The timely Religious "continuously devoted themselves to fellowship." (Acts 2:42) The term for "fellowship" is koinonia, signifies "to have in common" or "to share." As the ones that are integrated with Our Lord, we are to measure the life of Christ with each other any which way that ramification in special and collaborative spiritual "Higher Evolutions". This is achievement concluded the commune of agape and veracity, thereupon is identify as "ministry" using in variations measures ministration.

KOINOBI. (Gr.). A sect that lived in Egypt at the origination of the first century of the Christian era. This sect is ordinarily confused with that of therapists. They were contemplating magicians.

KORADI-CORAHI. (gnostic) (Qu'an). Holy Scriptures and antecedent of law of Islaam, by the Prophet Mahama.

KOLYVA. In the Greek Orthodox a cake consecrated at the time memorial services for the perished and assigned to attendees at hand.

KORAN The sanctified book of Islam, which Muhammad proclaimed had been shown to him as the Word of God, through the contemplation of the archangel Gabriel.

KOVIDA (Sanskrit) Educated, learned, wise, expert.

KRAM (Sanskrit) Tantric symbol corresponding to the idea of the human mene when it exceeds the ordinary limits of the invisible, thus considering the invisible. The aniguos tantric philosophers had symbols to designate almost all ideas. This was mandatory for them because they understood that if the human mind were fixed on any object with sufficient furious force for a certain time, it was certain that by the power of the will it would attain that object. Attention was generally reinforced by constantly muttering certain words, with which the idea was always kept before the mind. For this motive, symbols were used to indicate each idea. Thus, "Hrien" designates modesty; "Kliw" denotes love; "Aiw" represents protection; "Chaum" expresses well-being, and so on. Symbols like that were used to name blood vessels, etc. Tantric science is now almost completely lost. Today there is no clear and general key usable for symbolic terminology, and therefore, much of the symbolic language is unfortunately intelligible.

KRITTIKA(S) (Sanskrit) The third asterism or lunar mansion, including the Pleiades, and whose sign is a knife; the dark fortnight of the moon.

KRIYA (Gnosticism) It expresses action, execution, practice, labor, rite, worship, activity in yoga. Presently, the Kriya of Yogananda has become very widespread; This Kriya is very good for the prosperity of man's inner faculties, many Gnostics practice it, but you should be wedded for it.

KSHANA or KSANA (Kachana) or Moment is that infinitesimal poricon of time that can no longer be divided. According to the Madhyamika doctrine of kchanas or moments, all things are constituted only of an uninterrupted series of moments presented to our conscience. The universe, with all its phenomena, is nothing more than an incessant and immediate succession of property states.

KTTICHE (Gnosticism) Elemental Genius of the Gnomes and Pygmies of the Earth.

KUHAKA (Sanskrit) Impostor, faker; Burlesque, farce, imposture.

KIKUYU A settlement in Kenya where a missionary convention of Anglicans, Presbyterians, and other Protestants was held in 1913. A coalition of constituent

Churches was suggested, with the acceptance of ordinary integration between the Churches in the alliance, bringing with it the right of accepting Communion in some of them.

KUNDALINI (Sanskrit) It is also called the "Mother of the World" or "Anu Serpentine Fire", coiled like a snake, spiraling. Only those who practice concentration and yoga come to know this power.

KUMBHA (Sanskrit) Refers to the eleventh sign of the Indus Zodiac, corresponding to Aquarius.

KURU (Sanskrit) Former king of the lunar dynasty, who occupied the throne of Hastinapura, and was the common ancestor of the Kurus and Pandava princes.

KUSA (Kusa or Kusha) (Sanskrit) Sarada herb used by the ascetics of India and called "happy omen herb". It has a very hidden significance and properties. [Kuza means herb, and especially the sacred herb, Poa cynosuroides, of purifying virtues and used very frequently in the religious ceremonies of India. Kuza is also the name of one of the dvipas (or divisions of the inhabited earth).

KUZALA (Kusala) (Sanskrit) Merit, one of the two primary constituents of Karma. [Kuzala further have in mind pleasant, good, healthy, convenient, virtuous, happy, intelligent, expert, skillful.]

KWAN-shaiyin (China) The male Logos of Northern Buddhists and those of China; the "God manifested."

KYRA Language of origin is Old Persian. It is predominantly used in English and Gerlman. The meaning of Kyra is 'far-sighted; throne; sun'. It is a biblical name derived from khuru which means 'throne'; khur 'sun' this term has several possible meanings; from the Persian "far-sighted", "throne" and "sun"; the Centic "little dark haired one; and the Greek origin, means "of the lord". in Hebrew this word means various; Dear, Beloved; leader of the people. In Japanese means "glittery, shiny".

-L-

LA (Sanskrit) Indra, God of the firmament. Gift recommended or received. The. (Tibet.) title that the Lamas of Tibet offer to the Fo (Buddha of the Chinese.

LABAN Was an Aramaic leader of Abraham's ancestry and father of Rachel.

LABARUM. The force standard was given by the emperor. 'Constantine' patronage of his vision prior to the Battle of the Milvian Bridge. It contained a Chrisitan plan, with the Greek character X and P (the first two signs of XPIETOE, 'Christ') Criss-Cross.

LABORATORY Office or plants where remedies, research-based experiments and testing are made. Within alchemy the laboratory stands for the physical body, being proven by the stove (fire), the crucible (sex) and the fireplace (the spinal cord).

LABRO Roman saint solemnly beatified not many years ago. His great holiness included sitting by one of the gates of Rome, night and day, for forty years, without washing once during all this time. As a result, misery was eating him to the bone.

LABYRINTH. (Lat. Labyrinthus and gr.) Place factitious shapely of streets, crossroads and squares, so that the one who enters is disoriented and cannot determine the exit. The most recognize were those of Egypt and Crete. Legends tell that the "Labyrinth of Crete" was erected by Dedalus for King Minos, so that he would lock up the Minotaur. It was said that the architecture of this labyrinth in the place of worship was for doctrinaire purposes. Esoterically it characterized the great labyrinth of theories or antithetical conceptualizations, by which the institute must be heard, to the living center of it, since it is precisely in the center where we can find the Minotaur, image of the animal Ego, the psychological Renegate and then emerge victorious through the Thread of Ariadne (The secret Mastro, the philosopher's stone etc.) Myth say that Theseus managed to orient himself in the middle of that great labyrinth, until he reached where Minotaur existed and struggling hand-to-hand combat, he overpowered him. The exit from that labyrinth was feasible through the Thread of Ariadne that led him to the final deliverance.

LABYRINTHODON Antediluvian animal of the order of saurian, whose fossil skull presents a perforation, which can only be explained by an extraordinary development of the pineal gland or "third Eye", which, in the concept of various naturalists including E. Korscheldt, functioned as a real and true organ of vision.

LACKCHMIZA LAKCHMIZA (Lakchmi-iza) (Sanskrit) Lucky man, of happy omen.

LACTICINIA Foods and Milk which were made from milk, (as well as meal and eggs) were prohibited on fast days in the early church. Dairy outcome or milk by products, also known as lacticinia, are food merchandise made from (or containing) milk. The most ordinary dairy animals are cow, water buffalo, nanny goat, and ewe. Dairy derivatives include common grocery store food articles in the Western world such as yogurt, cheese and butter. Milk (Latin, lac) and milk products, e.g., butter and cheese, and eggs or animal outgrowth previously prohibited through the course of Lent, along with fresh meat. In the early Middle Ages lacticinia were banned even on Sundays at the time of the Lenten season.

LADY CHAPEL. A chapel devoted to the BVM ('Our Lady') when its configurations part of an enormous sanctuary.

LAENA (Lat.) A apparel with which the Roman augurs enclosed themselves with their heads while they were envisage the flock of birds.

LAERTES In accordance with the Greek mythology he was the emperor of Ithaca, son of Christ, lived with Antidia and was the father of Ulysses. He competed in the operation of the Argonauts and engaged in the hunt for the Calydonian boar.

LAGADA (Sanskrit) Beautiful, well formed, well done.

LAGHU (Sanskrit) Light, imponderable, fast, small, scarce, spare.

LAITY. Affiliates of the Church who do not belong to the clergy.

LAKE A part of an approximately huge figure of at a slow pace in motion or level aqua that inhabited a noncoastal bowl of considerable dimensions. Precisions that strictly determine lagoons, lakes, swamps, and level rivers, watercourses and further figures of nonoceanic sea are not adeptly instituted. Figuration of ponds in the Scriptures; such as lakes, conceivable the contributor of fecundity. In inclusion, it may constitute the transformation of existence, demise and restoration of life. Earnings captivating deliberations its introspective capacity, it signifies a reflector for contemplation furthermore a possibility or revelation. The considerable lake in the Bible is the Sea of Galilee, as well called Lake Tiberias, Arabica Buhayrat Tabariya, Hebrew Scriptures Yam Kinneret, lake in Israel across which the Jordan River emanate. It is celebrated for its scriptural consortium; its Hebrew

Scripture appellation was Sea of Chnnereth, and afterward it was commonly named the Lake o Gennesaret.

LAKSHMI In Hindoo legend, she is the divinity of the enchanter of bounty and devotion, wife of Vishnu, she was the mother of Kama. He is defined as a Lotus and is also called Samudratanaya and Padmalaya. He is one of the triad masters who is involved with the three depths of our dazzling dragon of wisdom.

LAMA-gylungs. (Tibet) Disciples of the Lamas.

LAMBA (Sanskrit). Large, vast, spacious; earring, pendant, (Subst.) present, gift.

LAMB The reason of the lamb as an image of Christ is based on such passages as Jn. 1: 29 and Rev. 5: 12. It dates from a prior age.

LAMP OF KNOWLEDGE (from lamp) Equipment to provide with light, includes of one or burner bays with a drop for the combustible material. It is a representation of intellect and spirit. The unlike types of lamps of antiquity scymed among the masses a deeply esoteric figure such as those of twelve pabilos, zodiacal signs; those of seven, symbol of the seven fires, farms along with others of three wicks character of the three primary forces-of Nature; that of a symbol of unification and consciousness. In the stillness of the Silence of H.P. Blavatsky we read the following, (from the Bhagavad Gita): "Before the flame of gold can burn with an inalienable light, the lamp must remain well guarded in a place sheltered from all winds."

LAMP(S). There is no early confirmation of the ceremonial use of lamps in Christian veneration. The burning of lamps in front of the altar, and particularly of the white lamp before the reserved Sacrament, materialized into use in the West in the 13th century, but was not mandatory prior to the 16th century.

LAMRIN (Tibet) Holy publication of directives and regulations written by Tsong-kha-pa "for the advancement of knowledge".

LANCE, (The Holy), An artifact, trusted to be the lance or pathway used to puncture the Lord's body (Jn. 19: 34). The earliest record of its existence dates from the 6th century. When the Persians apprehended Jerusalem in 615, the lance knocked down into their fist, but its place was rescued and delivered to Constantinople. In 1241 this was specified to St. Louis; it was presented over in the Sainte-Chapelle but vanished at the French Revolution. What is declared to be a separated part of the lance was sent by the Turks to the Pope in 1492 and still is in St. Peter's.

LANKA (Sanskrit) Prehistorical name of the island now called Ceylon. It is also the label of a mountain come across to the S.E. of Ceylon, where, following folklore, there was a city set up by demons, familiar as Lanka Puri. The large epic Ramayana related it as being of great impressive and enormous extension, "with seven wide moats and seven stupendous walls of stone and metal."

LANU (*Tibet*) Chela o disciple of a Master.

LAODICEA. A Hellenistical metropolis in the Hellenic region of the Orient. It was the space of a premature pious communal touched upon in Col. 4:1t and Rev. 3:14 ff., and a bishopdom of a few dominant for a few centennials.

LAPIDE, CORNELIUS A. (1567-1637) Cornelis Cornelissen van den Steen, Flemish Biblical supporter. He set off as a Jesuit in 1592. In 1616 he was called to Rome and there he concluded his complex wrapping all the Canonical Books excluding Job and Psalms. His effort owed their experience of approval to their lucidity, huge reverence, and symbolic and spiritual interpretation, reinforced by extensive knowledge.

LATTA Human being disgraceful, downcast.

LATERAN BASILICA, The. The Tabernacle, devoted to St. John the Baptist (with whom St. John the Apostle is now connected), corresponding on the site of a mansion which be owned by the upbringing of the Lateran. The palace, given to the Church by Constantine, was the ceremonious dwelling of the Popes from the 4th century until they went to Avignon (1309). It was largely dismantled by fire in 1308. The present-day temple was constructed under a division of Popes starting with Urban V. It is the sanctuary shrine of Rome.

LATRIA The completeness of Angelic veneration which is allowed compensated to the Supreme being unattended.

LARVAE (et. Larva, ghost) (Lat.) The sensual animation. The (Larvae) are the profile of human beings who lived and have died. These shadows are very insatiable and deviate a great deal from what they become once they obtain maturity, by advantage of their intricate transformation when kernel escapes. Amid them are those insects: Crustaceans, Echinoderms, batrachians, etc. Ghost, s=spectre, shelled. Gnostic Most of the time, they are negative, dim energies that can be found by subconscious enactment, rendering or by self-centeredness incubus and sub cubes that obstruct and stagnate the profound efforts. The larvae which Paracelsus indicated are eradication of every other propagated conviction of concepts that chargeable to their durability and their continuation at most to the contaminated imagination. An alternative variety of larva is defined within by definite classification of insects comparable to maggot and aphid. Meat from pork is additionally filled with innumerable larvae in adding up burial places, cineplex, predicters places, etc. As claimed by folk tales, it was a manic or destructed Djinn that progress with respective wrong individual whose task is alarming the existent and them who had not been left unveil or who had not rescued the individual needed interment tribute, mature into larvae.

LASA (Sanskrit) Dance, play, fun, loving pleasures.

LASAKA. The individual who dances, plays and has fun.

LASAKI This expression is Indian origination, have in mind woman disposition of the Hindu epic Ramayana, Sita, a companion of Rama. The declaration Lasaki is customarily Judaism by religion.

LAST-SUPPER The final meal of Christ with his disciples on the night before the Crucifixion. It was followed by the washing of the Apostles' feet (See Pedilavium) and the institution of the Eucharist. Traditionally. It has been held that the meal was the Passover, in agreement with the Synoptics, though the Gospel of St. John has a somewhat different chronology.

LATERAN, BASILICA, The. The basilica, resolute to St. John the Baptist (with whom St. John the Apostle is now correlated), stans on the site of a palace which associated with to the family of the Laterani. The palace, given to the Church by Constantine, was the official lodging of the Popes from the 4th century until they went to Avignon (1309). It was mostly demolished by fire in 1308. The present church was built under the continuity of Popes beginning with Urban V. It is the cathedral church of Roma.

LATON (ar.latum, from artun tartar, gold) Alloy of copper and zinc, pale yellow and sensible to high shine and polishing; There are also white and red. Within chemistry, whitening brass releases psychological defects, identity or character. That is, to whiten Lucifer inside and burn books, is to remove from the mind theories, concepts, prejudices, falsehood, etc.

LA TRAPPE, Nostre-Dame de. The monastery adjacent Soligny (Orne), frequently accepted as la Grande Trappe, provided its label to the Trappist reform institute here by A. de Rance in the 17th century. The abbey was established as a Benedictine house in 1122 and became Cistercian in 1148. The neighborhood was evicted in the insurgency of 1790 but reappeared in 1817.

LAUDA SION The entry statement and so the name of the succession (now optional) controlled for the banquet of 'Corpus Christi by St. Thomas Aquinas (c. 1264). The intimate Eng. tr., 'Laud, O Sion, thy Salvation', is the strive of some writers.

LAVRA (Greek for a street or alley). In the early Church a colony of anchorites who, while living in separate huts, were subject to a single abbot. The oldest lavras were founded in Palestine in the early 4th centennial. In more recent times the term has been applied to important coenobitic communities.

LAVABO (Latin, 'I will wash') The washing of the clergyman's fingers subsequent to the offering of the sacrifice in the Eucharist.

LAW(S) Canon and Natural. The body of ministerial rules or laws relating to matters of faith, morals, and discipline. Its conception may be traced to the practice of congregating Councils to settle matters of unanticipated or dispute and their issue of ad hoc proclamations (known as 'cannons') on proceedings of doctrine and discipline. The degree of authority of such declarations varied; those of the Council of Nicaea (325) came to influence a primacy in East and West The decrees of influential prelate were another source of ecclesiastical ratification, and special authority inclined to the letters of Popes (Decretals). A predominant stage in the maturing of Cannon Law was reached when Gratian issued his Decretum (c. 1140). Nevertheless, in essence this was an independent collection, such authority was assuming to it that it was fortify by a series of later assemblies to form the Corpus Lauris Canonic (q.v.), that enjoyed authority until it was overhauled and instituted in the Codes Lures Canonic affairs in 1917. Additionally, to laws regarded as entirely binding, there have been others of local dominance, such as the Synodical Constitutions of the Province of Canterbury. A declaration used with a diversity of meanings, but in a theological context the law place in nature by the Creator, which logical creatures an discern by the light of rationale. Modern philosophers have mostly abandoned the hypothesis.

LAWYER This expression comes from the Latin word "Lawyer". The derivation of the term "lawyer" emanates from Latin advocatus. We could reflect on the "vowel" vocatus to analyze an individual who converses a great deal, but it is not so; Advocatus is imitated from the Latin voicing "ad auxiliar" ("the call for auxiliary:). This word is used to ask for aid from the divinities when we invoke and need their help.

LAY BROTHER, LAY SISTER. An affiliate of a holy order who is not obligated to the rendering of the spiritual Office and is employed in handiwork. The institution was established in the 11th century. Lay Brothers and Sisters accommodate at Service daily and stating a short office.

LAYAM (Sanskrit) Term acquire from the source li, liquefy, fall apart; A intending of symmetry (vanishing point or impartial) somatic and chemical compound. In cabalistic it is the advice at which the actuality emerges as equivalent and is powerful to take steps or transform. [It is the point of matter, higher that greatest distinction possesses come to an end in small change of phenomenon. In the application of Yogism, Laya is a reproving second for then the intellect, passage against a situation of responsiveness to an additional unawareness blaze, may fail to hold absorb a circumstance of submissive boredom, that conduct to all the disaster of careless channel.]

LAYO. Ruler of Tebas and male parent of Edipo.

LAZARUS (1) Marthas' and Mary's brother, and Christs' friend, who raised him from the tomb (Jn. 11: 1-44). As narrated by E. heritage he converts a prelate in Cyprus: Following Western legacy, he was pastor of Marseilles.

LAZINESS Unprepared for occupation or exertion; not active or healthy. The lazy youngster tries to keep away from household chores. Auspicious idleness or inaction on a lazy midsummer day. Operating slowly; slack a lazy river, dangling, lax a rabbit with lazy ears. Learning of inducement suggests that laziness may be produced by a decreased level of incentive, that in turn, could be generated by overexcitement or uncontrolled instincts or interruptions. These expand the delivery of dopamine, a neurotransmitter in control of prices and satisfaction. "A sluggard's appetite is never filled, but the desire of the diligent are fully satisfied." "All hard work brings profit, but mere talk leads only to poverty." "Whoever is lazy regarding his work is also a brother to the master of destruction." "Laziness brings on deep sleep, and the shiftless go hungry."

LEBANON (Lebanon, in Hebrew). A series of mountains of Syria, that enunciate a few remains of the gigantic cedars, a forest of which its summit was formerly crowned. Heritage tells that from there the wood was detached to build the Sanctuary of King Solomon.

LEFFAS Celestial bodies of plants. They can grow into visible trees by rising from the ashes of greenery, after they have been burned.

LEGION. (lat. Legio-onis) Undefined and abundant number of people or spirits. Gnosis delineates that each human is a host due to the arrogance of defects that it carries inner part. Each "I" or "Ego" of anger, greed, lust, envy, etc., is multifaceted, it is a legion of psychic accumulation that are reveal in different forms, in the heart, mind and sex. The consciousness in each of us is constrained by the Ego and is manifest in virtues of its own conditioning, lacks individuality, if those psychics accumulate or egos etc. are not eliminated.

LETHEO (From the Greek Lethe, oblivion). One of the waterways of hell, called by some other name "River of Oblivion". After many centuries spent in hell, where they had atoned for their faults, souls, prior leaving the region of shadows, are obliged to drink from the peaceful and silence water of that river, which have the virtue of erasing the recollection of their preceding life or of leaving in recollection only vague and obscure reminiscences, thus discard them to suffer in a new body the trials and miseries more of the existence. With this ingenious allegory, the ancient Greeks interpret the loss of memory of past lives.

LEMON (ar. laimun) Fruit of the lemon tree, golden pulp distributed in sections, edible, juicy and very enjoyable acid taste. Consequential to its richness in vital ingredients, it is used in typical medicine, both for its good distribution of vitamin "C" and for all its virtues and approval. V.M. Samael on some occurrence expressed: "if to dissolve the I, the animal eye, they should be like the lemon"; He also remark on his work The Mystery of the Golden Blossom, an encounter lived by him in an ancient palace and assisted by a group of Elohim, how they drank water with lemon in delectable glasses of fine baccarat.

LEMURIA (Gnostics) It was a prehistoric continent that subsisted in what is now the Pacific Ocean, There the Lemur race evolved, and huge Cyclops cities were constructed encircling by walls of stones and volcanic lava. Lemurs were giants and hermaphrodites and increased by budding.

LENT. The fast of forty solar days before "Easter". In the first three centennials the time of fasting before Easter did not generally exceed two or three days. The first introduction of a period of forty days, allegedly of Lent, dates from A.D. 325, until a much later date the duration was separately reckoned in unlikely sanctuaries. Amid the primary centuries, the celebration of the fast was immutable; only one meal a day was allowed, and flesh-meat and fish were prohibited. In the W. the fast was moderately relaxed. In the RC Church by the Apostolic Constitutions

Paenitemini (1966) the commitment to fast was confined to the first day of Lent and Good Friday. In the W. Church the prospective disposition of Lent is exposed in various features of the liturgy, and there is a suitable ceremony for each day. The period is also perceived as a time of penance by abstinence from festivities, by almsgiving, and by assigning more time than customary to doctrinal exercises.

LERNA City of Argolida, in the swamps of its lake, exists the speculative hydra that was eliminated by Hercules.

LEVEL(S) Appeal to a parallel plane, level, plain or straightforward or even. Although all these terms show "having a surface without bends, curves, or irregularities," levels cover to a horizontal finish that lies on an underline parallel with the perspective, the vast are almost level. "The front of the house is on a level with the one across the street." A location on a genuine or imaginary scale of number quantity, expanse, or quality. "a high level of unemployment". Characters are other objects used to name the elevation of a point conforming to a testimonial level (height).

LEVI, SON OF ALPHAEUS The tax compiler called by Christ to be one of His companions (Mk. 2: 14). He identifies with St. Matthew.

LEVITE(S) As claimed by Biblical descriptions, a single member of the twelve tribes descended from Levi, one of Jacob's sons, and clearly set alongside as clergyman of the shelter. In the Deuteronomic statute, the expression 'priest' as well as Levite are compatible. Following Expel the Levites were distributed at best second-class commitment in the place of worship.,

LEVIATHAN. A creature wrote down to various places in the Old Testament. The phrase was removed mythologically to the Devil. T. Hobbes gave his treatise on 'the matter' form, and capacity of a commonwealth' this subject.

LI (Sanskrit). Dissolution, destruction; equality, identity.

LIBER COMITIS (COMES) (Lat. Liber Comitis, Liber Comicus), a book controlling the passages to be read at Mass as Epistles, or as gospels, or as both. Initially it was merely a list of the opening terms of the readings, but later the designation came to be applied to books with their finalized subject matter.

LIBER CENSUUM The formal archives of the Roman Church, which set down the dues (census) to be paid by many institutions, esp. Monasteries, churches, cities, and kingdoms, to the Holy See. It was brought together in the late 12th century.

LIBERATED (Mokcha) (Sanskrit) "Liberation", from the binding of flesh and matter, or from existence on this earth. It's like Nirvana; A post-mortem state of rest and bliss of the pilgrim-soul. [Mokcha means liberation, detachment, emancipation, salvation; it is precisely liberation from the bonds of body and matter in general, and accordingly, liberation from the pains of earthly existence. In such a condition, the individual Spirit, released from all new reincarnation, is engrossed into the universal Spirit. This ultimate liberation, for this reason, is observed as leading bliss. This designation has still auxiliary context; death, justice, equity, stability, etc. (lat. Hbertio – onis.) Action to free gnost. This is captured with the recognition of the Substantial Tasks, when after having refine the inner bodies, it is fully affiliated with reality.

LIBER DE CAUSIS A treatise, consisting largely of extras from Proclus's 'Elements of Theology', which was put together in Arabic by an unknown Muslim philosopher c. 850. Translated into Latin between 1167 and 1187, for about a century it circulated as a work of Aristotle and deeply influenced medieval philosophy.

LIBER REGALIS. The book accommodating the English Coronation service researched for the crowning Edwards II in 1308. It was interpreted into English for James I (1603) and complied with in use until it was abandoned by James II in1685.

LIBRA (September 23 – October 22) Libra is an air sign described by the scales (strikingly, the only motionless device of the zodiac), an alliance that reverses Libra's infatuation on solidity and harmony. Libra is captivated with equilibrium and attempts to conceive symmetry in all sectors of existence. There exist three varieties of libra Suns: Libras who possess Mercury in Scorpio, Libras who have Mercury in Virgo, and Libras who carry Mercury in Libra. Additionally, Libra with Libra Mercury have Mercuries prevailing either in the dawning stage, the nightfall period, or blaze.

LHA Spirits of the highest spheres.

LIGHT Extend over cultures, light is a prehistorical image of comprehension and rational concentration: it is the reversed of insensitivity, or darkness. Nearly internationally, the dark is disconcerting and sinister, related to gadgets we cannot recognize. Light is said to subdue darkness and to introduce order out of chaos.

Light is generally a representation of life, the two; on earth and in the afterlife. Many persons that have had near-death experiences will relate how they went "towards the light", which is an emblematic denotating for continuing toward eternity in the afterlife. In Christianity, God was said to have initially created life, but his first stride was creating light. Light would react as the principles from which all life would grow and thrive. Surprisingly, in terrestrial coaching, light is imagined to be the origin of existence. In research-based supposition, light was conducted around since cosmology. This is voiced to be an enlarged cause of light in control of the formation of our natural world.

LINGA-Puruna (Sanskrit) As per Doctrine of the Zaivas, Zavaites or pious person of Ziva. In it, Mahezvara, "the great Lord", hidden in the Agni-linga, describes the ethics of life: duty, virtue, self-discipline, and finally liberation through the ascetic life at the end of Agni-kalpa (the seventh Round). As Professor Wilson accurately observes, "the spirit of the cult (phallic) is as little authority by the character of the symbol as can be imagined": There is nothing in which it resembles the phalial of antiquity; He is all mysterious and spiritual."

LIFE AND WORK The subdivision of the Ecumenical Movement troubled with the connections of Christian faith to society, polities, and economics. It shut down conferences in Stockholm (1925) and Oxford.

LIGHT OF THE WORLD, The. A small-scale of Christ acquired from Jn. 8: 12. It is the subject matter of Holman Hunt's celebrated picture.

LIGHTNING Has extensively been correlated with the divinity; Greek legends manifest lightning as the head munitions of Zeus, King of the Gods. Zeus was routinely depicted with lightning bolts in his hands, accessible to strike down humankind and edifices which disappoint him. The bolt of lightning is a conventional emblem of unexpected illumination and the demolition of disregard; it as well portrays a retribution of mortals by the creator from the continuity, most attributed to Zeus, king of the gods. Luke 10:18, and he said unto them, I beheld Satan as lightning fall from heaven. Luke 17:24, for as the lightning, that lightened out of the one [part] under heaven, shineth unto the other part under heaven; so, shall also the Son of man be in his day.

LIE Producing an invented affirmation with resolution to mislead, 'she was lying when she said she wasn't part of the demonstration.' She falsified her past evidence; to start an inaccurate or confusing impression statistics often distortion. The reflector at no time lies. Some animals regularly alike with treachery and popular devious are snakes foxes, jackals, etc., are a comparatively activities that come to intellect. Lies are honestly inaccurate, then, for two intentions. Principally, deceitful the prime standard of my mortal existence: my capacity to produce liberate, logical solutions. Every time I tell a lie; it refutes that part of me which supplies honorable quality for me. Secondarily, my dishonesty cheated others of their privilege to select intelligently.

LIMITATIONS. Carries the potential to dismantle circumstance, to escape with prestige and delight, in addition to render splendid survival purposeless. If you don't disintegrate the ligament of limitation, you can never provoke where God has destined for you. Through not savoring all that has been assembled for you. "The more a person limits himself, the more resourceful he becomes." Records are brimming with precedent of human beings who adopted their limitations instead of fighting them. Ascent exceeding your restraints, all situations could not line up in your approval, but accompany to triumph. Be aware exactly what you hunger out in life and shoot the works with all you've got. As Zig Ziglar stated, if you have ambition, nothing at all you will consistently strike it always. Accomplishments begin with you interpreting what achievement signifies to you. Luke: 4:18 He came to proclaim freedom to prisoners and set the captives free. Jesus came to snap off the limitation hat are not from him and authorize us to start into no limitations, exuberant, to realize completeness God has approach us to be and visit us to achieve.

LINE(S). Horizontal lines designate a sensation of stagnant pause and peacefulness. Vertical lines are perceived as colossal and assemble majesty. Horizontal and vertical lines utilized collectively in a square or rectangular form transmit formation and produce steadiness. We relate curves or rounded lines with joyfulness. Consequently, it becomes clear to comprise curved lines in your sketches, drawings, or diagrams in which you want to indicate contentedness. Now let's check out angry lines. The illustrations manifests quartet curved lines nearly organize a square, it appears for bursting veins attributable to displeasure, naturally, in a distorted fashion. In Study of the mind, vertical lines implied force and refinement. Horizontal lines furthermore generate a touch of caution, serenity and Easy-going calmness. They predict an ordinary sensory faculty of equilibrium that is ready for use to affect congregations. Angled lines produce an excitement of vitality and forceful motion.

LIPI Report Lipika in the content of the secret doctrine.

LION. In presentation of the narrative of Daniel in the lions' den (Dan. 6) the lion is sign as a 'type' of God's reclamation of His chosen people. The lion is also a metaphor of St. Mark.

LIS. (Lat. Lilium) It is identical to Lily. The fleur-de-lis is cabalistical a genuine emblem considering it was contemplated so in the ancient times, it was in addition mediated a representation of the vision and ascribe of the Master. It was constituted as an image of which the foundation was a trilogy defining aqua; exceeding a crucifix, (symbol of redemption) devise with two evenly shape leaflet that befall cut the level separate and the midway one rise to bliss, illustrating it acknowledge declaration.

LISZT (1811-1886) Hungarian melodist and pianist, born in Raiden, author of the symphonic poem Nico. His first production was at the age of nine. He aided financially to achieve in Bonn the memorial to Beethoven. He arranged religious music and countless high-profile musical themes.

LITANY. A conformation of prayer consisting of a sequence of petitions or mandates sung or said by a cleric, priest, or cantors, to which the community make a fixed response. The litany apparently innovation at Antioch in the 4th century; it transmits to Constantinople and later to the W. Pope Gelasius I (492-6) proposed into the Mass a litany intercession, of which the Kyrie is the sole surviving relic.

LIVING TOGETHER (Gnosticism) Coexistence with their companions, focus on to people, is the reflector where they exposed us to see entire framework. In organizing with individuals, our hidden imperfections make a move around, arrive, and if we are vigilant, at that point we perceive them.

LIYA. Is a Yehudim epithet that is certain popular amid Jewish successors. Liya is also a formation of the apostolic designation Lea, e.g., in Russian, and of the term Liya. Besides, Lilya is a miniscule of the denomination Liyana and Aaliyah.

LOBHA (Sanskrit). Ambition, greed; a son in bad times born of Brahma. [Lobha additional aim longing, eagerness, veneration, worship].

LODGE (LOGIA). (Gr.) Philosophy and compact tutorial of Jesus, contained in the Gospel of St. Matthew, and the genuine Hebrew, not in the bogus Greek written work that we maintain, and Conserved by the Ebionites and Nazarenes in the bibliotheca composed by Panphilus, in Caesarea. This "Gospel", termed by countless correspondent "the true Gospel of Matthew" was in employed, conforming to St. Jeronimus, surrounded by the Nazarenes and Ebionites of Berea, Syria, in his acceptance duration (fourth century). For instance, the Aporrheta or confidential discussion of the Enigma, these Association might at best be appreciated with the support of a solution. Introduced by Prelates Chromatius and Heliodorus, St. Jerome, later experience acquire consent for this purpose, transported them, but appeared to be a extremely strenuous labor (and as expected it was) to attune the context of the Christian teachings. "Genuine" of the specious Greek Biblical that he formerly realizes.

LOGIC Analogy is a process to be logical proclamation by employing signs and flexibilities in situations of reasonable speech, such as English, in classification to disconnect obscurity. Logical declarations are communications that have a true value: they are about true or false. An adequate instance of logical rationale in activity is the match of chess move. Participating in a game of chess requires functioning along a progression of separate steps that will take you closer to victory. As an individual goes through each step there is a separate problem to solve; surrounded by the structure of a larger game.

LOKEZA (loka-iza) (Sanskrit) Formally: "Lord of the world": Brahma; A Buddhist saint who has conquered the world.

LOLATVA (Sanskrit) Agitation, eagerness, fickleness, greed, longing, impatience, longing, passion; restlessness.

LORDS PRAYERS, The. Prayers which begin with 'Our Father', taught by the Lord to the Apostles. In the New Testament, it is offered in slightly different forms in Mt. 6:9-13 and in Lk. 11: 2-4. The form in Mt. Is that everywhere used by Christians. A concluding hymn was highly likely included in early times and was in all probability taken over into some Gospels. The prayer is ordinarily divided into the address and seven petitions, the first three requesting for the glorification of God, the concluding four being appealed for the main physical and spiritual necessities of man. As a prayer appointed to the Church by Christ, it has often been considered as uniquely sacred. It has faithfully had a place in the Eucharist and the divine Office has frequently been expounded.

LORELEI Simulation or German reprint of the Scandinavian 'Maiden of the Lake'. Ondina is one of the persuasions given to these young women, studied in Exoteric Magic and Cabalistic with the denomination of Water Elementals.

LORETO, Close by Ancona in Italy, is the area of the Holy House, supposed to have been occupy by the BVM at the date of the Annunciation and amazingly transfer to Loreto by angels in 1295.

LORIC. (Breastplate of St. Patrick) A prehistoric Irish anthem transcription in the adaptation origination 'I bind unto myself today the strong name of the Trinity'. Its attribution to St. Patrick, however feasible; is improvable.

LOTTERY. Is a technique of raising funds by trading numbered tickets and offering prizes to the supporters of whole numbers pulled at randomly; a procedure or instrument of which the achievement or result is presided over by probabilities. In other words, a lottery is a structure of gambling which requires the representation of unsystematic numbers for a purse. Certain administrations forbid lotteries; however, many more approve it to the degree of organizing a governmental or power lottery. Normally there are a certain number of regulations of lottery by leadership. There is a book titled "The Lottery" which was written by Shirley Jackson that was published in 1948. This brief tale relates a fictional small-scale American municipality that perceives a yearly custom determinate as "the Lottery," where a representative of the group is chosen by possibility and stoned. The book conveys that any activity, attitude, or intentions which is previously allowed starting from one peer group to the forthcoming, is welcome and adopted, despite how irrational, abnormal, or atrocious. The stones become the tool of a violent murder at the conclusion of the book embodied by 'the lottery', which takes place many times all through the end of the fiction. A design of clear cruelty, the stones supply a prompt that human beings are consistently prepared to carry out a violation. The disgraceful viewpoint for both together; the folklore of the lottery and the irrationality of the natives' devotion to it. The word Lottery is not mentioned in holy scriptures; however, it makes some reference about concept of money and wealth. Matthew 6:24 ESV/52 "No one can serve two masters, for either he will hate the one and love the other, or he will be devoted to the one and despise the other. You cannot serve God and money." Proverbs 13:11 ESV "Wealth gained hastily will dwindle, but whoever gathers little by little will increase it."

LOURDES. A location of mission in France. In 1858 14-year-old Bernardette Soubirous had eyesight here of the BVM, who informed her that she was the Immaculate Conception. An emanation materialized; astounding cures were soon shown to have taken place; and the devoted started logbooks to Lourdes. Extensive temples have been constructed and a medical organization proven to inquire into the nature of the cures.

LOUT An unrefined and argumentative man or boy. Louting is a word that appears in the scrabble dictionary.

LOVE and Conscience Mention the aspects of love, which are fragments of the same concept. There are 3 kinds of love: sexual, emotional and conscious love. Exclusively, the last is authentic love. For there to be love, a true communion of souls is needed: attention, affection and consent. Love cannot be distracted with desire.

LOVE. Mighty closeness for a distinct emanates out of relationship or bound, paternal appreciation for a youngster. Allure found in intimate enthusiasm; feelings and attentiveness discerned by companions. The perception of refined adoration is one favorite that: cultivate for the aim of adoring. Has no inclination or obligation. deliquesce barrier and divide. It is its premium. Influential appreciation may similarly indicate intimate love. Your love for one another in our continued existence could also be well-advised significant and continuance changeable. For a good few, self-love may be the soaring influential mode of love, as innumerable demanding to accomplish it. The unblemished model of love and reverence is at times you petition in silence for the uprightness of your loved ones or partners and don't expect anything in anticipation. You do it considering their contentedness is meaningful for you. However, recognize in the motions of accomplishing someone else exhilaration bears in mind your individual prosperity. 1 Corinthians 13:4-8a (EVS) "Love is patient and kind: love does not envy or boast; it is not arrogant or rude. It does not insist on his own way; It is not irritable or resentful; it does not rejoice at wrongdoing but rejoices with the truth".

LOWAN. Australian agglomerate bird; nurture eggs innately in sandy hills. equivalent: Leipoa ocellata, Leipoa, mallee fowl. Nature: mallee hen. Adult female mallee fowl. "Lowan." type of megapode mound bird, scrub fowl large footed short-winged birds of Australasia; compliments mounds of decomposing vegetation to breed eggs.

LUCIA (Saint) Maiden and sacrifice. She was born in Syracuse and against consented to the young man, dedicated her life and virginity to God. Her resentful fiancé condemns her as a Christian to the government, as a result, she was exposed to countless abuse. She died beheaded in the oppression of Diocesan. She is the patron saint of the blind and the dressmakers, her festivity is honor on December 13. Lucia presents as Divine Grace, in Dante's Divine Comedy.

LUIS de NEUS Sorcerer, endemic of Silesia. In the period 1483, he assembled at the court of Marburg and in the attendance of many observers, some exercise with his profound solution reconstituted lead into pure gold. In perspective of the happy mind of such performance, John Dornberg, minister of Landgrave Henry III, appealed that he reveals the secret to him, and the conjurer having denied his claims, he was locked up in a jail, where he died of starvation. This and other occurrences that could be similar show how acute and just were the rules drawn in the lire De Alchymia, attributed to Albert the Great, and that should serve as a rule to the alchemists to reach the splendid work. The beginning of those rules is the following: 'The alchemist shall be discreet and quiet; will not reveal to anyone the result of its operations.' A separate of these rules reads: "He (the alchemist) will avoid having any relationship with the princes and lords."

LUKE, St. He was a missionary. In accord with customs, he was the editor of the Third Gospel and of Acts. He was a curative practitioner Col. 4: 14), and it has been completed from Col. 4; 11 that he was a pagan. Around his 2nd & 3rd missionary expedition (Acts 16: 10-17 and 20: 5-21:18), he tried ahead with St. Paul and went forward with him to Rome. Acc. a heritage registered in the Anti-Marcionite Prolog he expressed his Gospel in Greece and pass on at the age of 84.

LUST Is an energetic desire for mating. It also implies a craving for something, such as lust for control. Although lust is not a filthy word, it is a powerful word. You do not have lust for a reality you are not genuinely concerned about. Lust is an aggressive, dominant appetite, you lust for anything you intensely need. There are two types of animals who customarily stand for lust; cows and goats. The purpose that cows illustrate lust may be a related to the Egyptian goddess Hathor. She is generally reproducing in the formation of a cow, or a female with the crown of a cow. The customary color correlated with Lust was blue. This is how it fragment down: Greed: Yellow. Lust: Blue. 1 Corinthians 6:18; "Flee from sexual immorality. All other sins a person commits are outside the body, but whoever sins sexually sins against their own body".

LUTHER, MARTIN (1483-1546) Was born in Eisleben (Saxony) the second son of Hans Luther, a miner of peasant ancestry. He was German religious promoter, Lutheranism developed as a reaction, changing into one of the large groups in Germany. Luther's most dominant events are; opposition against the gratifications, the contempt of denounce and the Directives burned in Wittenberg, his seduction of La Warburg and the Translation of the Bible, with the help of Melanchthon the German language; He was the songwriter of several hymns; composed catechism in 1529, in which he proclaimed to his advocate the spirit and theology of his faith, married in 1525 Katharine Avon Hora, battling pastoral chastity. He was founder of the German Reformation. He entered a monastery in 1505 at Augustinian hermits; being ordained as a priest by 1507, in 1508 he started serving as lecturer to the new founded university of Wittenberg. He ended up dropping some of his religious duties; his new religious life didn't seem to give him the confidence he needed to keep up with his busy schedule. The presumed 'Turmer lebnis' ('Tower Experience'), generally dated around 1512 and 1515, extracted the formation of a foreseeable disclosure which guaranteed him that his believes alone were sufficient for him to continue his work. He found help for this doctrine in St. Augustine's anti-Pelagian works, from 1516 he cautiously started to dismiss the urgency of acquire interventions from this parish as well as his fellow clergy. He transferred the Bible into the German vernacular (rather than Latin) which made it more within reach to the congregation; this action that had a huge influence on the parish and German society alike. In a pair of his posterior projects, Luther turned out well-known for intentionally revealing antisemitic intolerant perspectives in several of his publications. He also conducted his disclosure, focusing on other groups such as Western Catholics, reformers and nontrinitarian Christians. Due to his substantial contrary Judaism credo; biographers seemed to increase his declarations which appeared to have contributed remarkably to the expansion of intolerance in Germany and of the bipartisan movement. Luther died in 1546 with an order of rejection from Pope Leo Xs for his unresolved actions against his fellow pious.

LUIS OF GRANADA (1504-88). Spanish spiritual writer. Luis Sarria, who was bred at Granada, was declared as a Dominican in 1525. In 1555 he was encouraged by the Cardinal Infante Henry to go to Portugal, however, he spent most of the rest of his life there. His popularity rests on his books of inner guidance, mainly the 'Libro de la Oracion y medication' ('Book on Prayers and Meditation', 1554) and the Guide for offenders. ('Guide for Sinners', 1556-7). He sought to give spiritual instructions for lay communities as well as religious. He accredited immense significance to the interior life, to mentality as dissimilar from vocalized prayers, and saw external ceremonies as equivalent insignificant.

LUSTRATION Devout protocol executed by the Greeks and Romans to atone municipalities, grasslands, congregations, homestead, etc., in addition newborn children and people blemish by an offense or tainted by a corrupt article. These operations are often done through dispersing, marches, and conciliatory oblation. Lustrations were carried out with fire, burnt sulfur, cleansing of laurel, juniper, olive and other plants of purification or lustral water (water purified with a burning blight taken from the fire of sacrifice, and was applied in the formation of sprinkling, as is done with holy water).

LUPTA (Sanskrit) Private, lost, suppressed.

LUXOR (occultism) Term composed of lux (light) and aur (fire). Thus, coming to mean "The Light of the (Divine) Fire". The Luxor Fraternity was a certain association of mystics.

LUX MUNDI (1889) A group of essays written by a class of Anglican, ed. By C. Gore. Its undertaking by the modern reproving vision of the OT gave indignation too few of the senior academy of High Churchmen.

LYRICS. Can stand for notions, theoretical ideas, affairs, proceedings, and the present date topics prevailing in society in a candy quoted process. Coating by surface, lyricists take the listener intensely into an individual's thinking. The increase and downward of notes help to magnify metaphor. Some precedent of analogy in the songs are named under. Mirror on the wall, here we are again; So why are we here talking to each other again? The character in these lyrics is a mirror. Righteous advice is that undergoing a song forced in your mind can say, there is a message standing deriving out of you. It is the same concept as "you've Got mail" excepting it is running to resume to execute till you unfolded it up and interpret it. Generally, nonsecular lyrics correspond motivated by Holy Spirit acclaiming him and saluting his omnipresence in our existence to escort us in partiality and veracity. Fluctuating Lyrics from songs formation were nearby in earlies traditions, as well as China, Egypt, Greece, India, Mesopotamia, Rome, and the Middle East. The words, rhythm and tunes of these songs ranged jointly, as were tones in common, with enchantment, discipline, and doctrine.

LYCH-GATE. The enclosed entryway to a memorial park underneath which the sarcophagus is hung down to attend the entrance of the presiding clergyman.

LYONS, Council of (1274). This Assembly was convoked by Gregory X. Its main achievement was to deliver about union with the Greek Church. The impulse of the Greeks for union arose primarily out of their fear of Charles of Anjou, who sought to become Latin Emperor of Constantinople, and the ambassador of the Greek Emperor, Michael VIII Palaeologus, were agreeable to submit to Rome. The union ceased in 1289.

-M-

MACCABEES The recognized Jews family who did a significant bargain to free Judaea from the Syrian trappings. The rise began in 168 B.C. at Modin, where Mattathias, an aged clergyman, killed a heretic Jew who was about to offer a pagan sacrifice. The scuffle was supported by his five sons, three of whom, Judas, Jonathan, and Simon, conducted the Jews in their conflicts.

MACAH, (pronounced My-kuh) arises from the Hebrew language and decipher to English as "who is like (God)." Micah comprises of two Hebrew words: "mi" defining "who," and "cha" signifying "lke". One noticeable linguistic analysis of Micah propose that the term "God" is suggested in the intention of the designation.

Frontier Paleontologists investigation recommends that Makah people have populated the locality recently changed its name to Neah Bay for more than 3,800 years. Conventionally, the Makah lived in a crossroads concluding of enormous, farmhouses constructed from westerly red cedar. The Makah Indians were substantially navigators. Makah men seals hunting, eared seals, and belugas alike from their canoes. They also captured fish and skilled deer hunters, birds, and small game on land. Makah women collected cuttlefish and shellfish, berries, and roots.

MACAS The Alps' therapeutic herbage Lepidium peruvianum Chacon, or an withdraw of the rootstock of this shrub; Ayak willku. Maca is also a root of high-quality authority of fibrous material, which could support to reduced fatty acid degree and upgrade heart wellness. Furthermore, for a heart healthy property, maca fine grains are additionally known for their restored animated well-being. Maca approach from Old Galician-Portuguese macaa from unrefined Latin Mala Mattiana (actually "apples of mattium"), nevertheless certain amount hypothesizes that mattiana was an Iberian speech pattern of the Gallo-Roman term matianium, a yellow crabapple labeled ensuing Gaius Matius, agriculturalist and close friend of Caesar.

MACHINE Material apparatus using potential to administer constrain and oversee operation to carried out an activity. The expression is repeatedly used to fabricated gadgets, such as those accommodating generators or transformers, but also to ordinary organic compounds, such as specified mechanisms. Identical to existent contraptions, the earthling body also incorporates many parts that work in conjunction to achieve beyond doubt situations, which in the instance of anatomy include supporting the life form living. The physical structure may be the most remarkable apparatus in the world, as you will figure out when you absorb further about it in this impression. The peak of the dismantling of humans by producers and engineers demand awareness of the lack of sympathy and affection in a commonality where human beings are not perturbed with the basic needs of others. 2 Chronicles 26:15 "And he made in Jerusalem machines invented by skillful men, to be upon the towers and upon the bulwarks, wherewith to shoot arrows and great stones. And his name spread far abroad; for he was marvelously helped, till he became strong."

MACROCOSM (Gr.) Absolutely, the "Majesty Universe" or galaxy. [It is the formation, the wonderful universe, adding up all undertakings noticeable and unseeable. The Wholeness as in opposition to human beings (microcosm, or small universe). The pair; macrocosm and the microcosm have a septenary structure.]

MADD. The Heavenly Father utters in the Koran: in that he expresses "Madd" in Arabic channel that Divinity will prolong and build on to their retribution. For this reason, Madd in Tajweed refers to the stretching or extending of reverberation of one of the 3 Madd alphabetical characters. There is combination of Madd in Tajweed: the logical Madd and the insincere Madd. There are a set of types of Madd in Tajweed: Madd Asli, Madd Wajib Mutasil, and Madd Jaiz Munfasil. It is decisive to realize the contrasting variety of Madd and from what source to accurately petition that for quoting the Quran with genuine Tajweed.

MADEBA MAP of Palestine and the near East in colored mosaics, discovered in 1896 in the congregation of MADEBA to the East of the Dead Sea. It is just about unquestionable dates originating in the 6th century.

MADGATA Signify "Simply upon Me, Krsna." Antar-atmana, "within the heart." Sa me Yukta Tamah: "He is a first-class yogi." His survival is so molded that he cannot abstain from thinking of Krsna. Madgata. He has become captivated. That is samadhi.

MADRI (Sanskrit) Relative of the king of the madras and second spouse of Pandu. Mother of the last two princesses, the twins Nakula and Sahadeva, cabalistically procreated by another set of twins, Azvins, Nasatya and Dasra, respectively.

MADRIGAL Primarily a variety of verses and then a melodious song without musical background in the 16th century madrigals were adjusted to spiritual motivation, mainly In Italy.

MAGDALENE, MARY, St. A disciple of Christ out of whom He is announced to have cast 'seven devils' (Lk. 8:2). She stood by His Cross (Mk. 15:40); with two other women she disclosed the empty tomb (Mk. 16: 1ff. &c.); and she received an appearance of the Risen Lord early the same day (Mt. 28:9; Jn 20: 11 ff.) originating at early times, she has been classified with the 'woman who was a sinner' who Annointed Christ's feet (Lk. 7:37) and with Mary, the sister of Martha. Who also Annointed Him (Jn. 12:3); but the Gospels give no support for either identification.

MAGADHA (Sanskrit) A prehistoric nation of India, which was undergoing the rule of Buddhist kings. Magadha In the Laws of Manu is delegate with this persuasion the man born of a vaizya and a kchatriya, Magadhas is also the title of the inhabitants of Magadha, the country of southern Behar, where the Pali mother tongue was spoken.

MAGI. (Gk. For 'sages or 'wise men'). The Magi were the first Gentiles to achieved in Christ (Mt. 2:1-12). directed by a star, they came from the East to Bethlehem with gifts of gold, frankincense, and myrrh for the Christ Child. The idea that they were kings materialize first in Christian tradition in Tertullian; Origen is the first to give three numerals as three. What are declared as heir relics are enshrined in Cologne Cathedral.

MAGICAL Regarding, distinguished by, or achieved magic: charms magnitude and narration set in a magical planet a mystical glamor/incantation/invocation amulet trust to have mystic possessions. The Western substructure of magic is implant in the ancient Judeo-Christian and Greco-Roman funding. Inheritance gained an added image in northern Europe throughout the Middle Ages and incomplete current streams before intensifying to other components through European scrutiny and colonialism after 1500.

MAGNA The tenth asterism or lunar mansion.

MAGISTERIUM (Lat.) The invigorating virtue of the therapeutic elements, conserved in a catalyst.

MAGNES Style applied by Paracelsus and the medieval theosophus. It is the inner being of light, or Akasa. It was an expression extensively second-hand by the seers of the Medieval Times. [Occasionally chaos has been chosen the term Magnes].

MAGNETISM (COSMIC) The global coercion of attraction and repulsion, well known from the generation of Empedocles and entirely express by Kepler. The alleged "seven brother sons" of Fohat portray and impersonate the seven forms of cosmic magnetism called in hidden enactment the "Seven Radicals", of whom collective and dynamic origination are, amidst other intensity, electricity, magnetism, sound, light, heat, cohesion, etc.

MAGNUMOPUS. (Lat.) In, conjuration, is the culmination consummation, the "Significant Effort" (Magnificence Masterwork); outcome of the "Philosopher's Stone", and the "Elixir of Life", that, although scrutinize a fantasy by a few skeptics, is conscientious of supreme consequential and must be recognized symbolically.

MAH. (Cab.) Kabbalistic confidential entitle implemented to the suggested of development.

MAHA (Sanskrit) Big, powerful, rich, abundant.

MAHAKAZA (Maha-Akasa) (Sanskrit) Exactly: "Magnificent Space." Volume.

MAHARAJA. (Sanskrit) Eminent king or monarch. In Plural:

MAHEZA (Mahesha) (Sanskrit) 'Great Lord' (Maha-iza). Ziva's epithet. Equivalent of Maheswara.

MAHZOR Is an invocation publication that Jews employed on the High Holy Days are observed such as Rosh ha-Shanah and Yom Kippur consequently on the treble holy expedition gala of Sukkot, Passover, and Shavuot. Tehillah (Heb.; te-fell-ah) is the Hebrew expression for devotion. The tag itself holds a radius of interpretations. The Hebrew origin signifies "executing judgment" (Exodus 21:22) or "thinking" (Genesis 48:11).

MAIDEN of MEMORIES (Gnosticism) It is a fragment of our Real Self which authorizes us to remember inner dreams and experiences. Now during the time of going to bed, we ought to pray, appeal to the intimate (Our Real Being) to arrange with the maiden of memories, implement in us and accordingly enable us to bring the recollection of anything that we dream or evoke.

MAISTRE, DE, JOSEPH. (1753-1821). French Transmontane writer. He was affected by the 18th centennial grandeur, but after the 1789 Revolution he was transformed into a Fanatical diehard. In his leading work. Du Pape (1819, he reasons that the only correct foundation of society lay in authorization, which took the binary form of spiritual authority empowered in the Papacy and temporal authority in human kings. His ideas committed to the abolishment of "Gallicanism.

MAITREYA (Sanskrit) Bene Volo, kind, affectionate. Name of a-Bodhisattva.

MAKAR [Scottish] Scots verse writer proceeds with to proliferate as an artistic method in the speech of the Makars and the lyrics. Each duration Makar Sankranti is commemorated on the day of January. This gala day is devoted to the Hindu devout sun god Surya. This extraordinary of Surya is detectable in the Vedic printed work, distinctly the Gayatri Manta, a consecrated canticle of Hinduism created in its sacred denominated the Rigveda.

MAKARAM or PANCHAKARAM (Sanskrit) In cabbalism ideography, it is the pentacle, the pentalpha, the polymelia or limbs of man. It is very paranormal.

[Makaram can deliver to defining the pair the microcosm and the macrocosm, as exterior substances of perceptivity.

MALALAS, JOHN. (Later 6th century), i.e.. John 'Rhetor' or 'Scholasticus', (d. 577, q.v.). His Chronicle, mostly deriving out a Monophysite viewpoint, lengthened to 574, but endured at most to 563.

MALCHUT or MALKUTH Cab. -Heb.), Gnostics. The tenth sephiroth of the Hebraic Kabbalah recognized to the material planet and enlightenment is the foundation of the physical world, so, knowledge is encircled by the bowels of the sphere, the klifos, or inverted sephiroth, the prodigy as they say to the personification in affliction Malkuth also aid for the material form, a depraved sphere or sephiroth.

MALINES CONVERSATIONS The gatherings of a grouping of Anglican and RC clerics were held at Malines in Belgium between 1921 and 1925 under the government of Card. D. J. Mercier. The advantage came from Lord Halifax. It was consented that the Pope should be given priority, privilege; that the Body and Blood of Christ are taken in the Eucharist; that the Sacrifice of the Eucharist is an exact sacrifice, but after a mystical manner; and that Episcopacy is by Divine law. The Conversations issued have no palpable outcome.

MALYA (Sanskrit). Necklace, diadem, garland, crown, flower.

MAMERTINE PRISON. An establishment in Rome with accommodations of two cells in which, in accord to folklore, St. Peter was incarcerated and had his prison officers converted.

MANDUCTION Chewing and granulating bread in your oral cavity, so it converts mushy abundant to consume. The operation of being a participant in the observance of the Holy Sacrament. As materialized in the Good Book: Matthew 15:11 NLT. "It's not what goes into your mouth that defiles you; you are defiled by the words that come out of our mouth."

MANASSES, Prayer of. This miniscule book in the Hebrew Scriptures Apocrypha comprise of a penitential prayer inserted in the portal of Manasseh, King of Judah. It was utilized in the early Church. Its date is uncertain, but it is corroborated by the early 3rd century A.D. It became visible in modern printed editions of the Vulgate in the appendix.

MANASIC, Psychological State. It is the one that is equivalent to awareness when it acts as perception. It is not the level of the mind as it functions through the brain, but as it works in its own world, unrestricted bonds of physical matter. The mental and causal plane consequently in ascending order to the astral plane; it reflects the universal Mind of Nature and is the stage which in our small system harmonizes that of the great Menet of the Kosmos. In its culminating regions there are all the archetypal ideas that are at present in the process of concrete evolution; while in its descending regions, such notions become successive configurations to be put together in the astral and physical worlds. This plane is the universe of the true man, since intelligence is his most distinctive attribute, The formation of thought plays a major role among the living creatures that are ongoing in the mental degree. One of the regions of this plane is the Devachan.

MAN (internal) Instructions of esotericism, applied to point out the evident and imperishable Deity that dwells within us, and not the superficial and lethal structure of mud that we cite as our body. This word is imposed, precisely expressing, only to the dominant Ego, place that "astral man" is the recommendation of the Double and the Kumarupa, that is, the escaped eidolon.

MAN (SODOR AND MAN). The current Anglican diocese of Sodor and Man involves the Isle of Man. The authentic diocese of Sodor, which appears to date from the 11th century the Hebrides and other islands were disconnected in 1334. The conclusion 'and Man' was evidently added in error by the 17th century. Legal drafter.

MANAS (Sanskrit). Declaration that implies "the sensory or processing mind" or in fact additionally be investigated as the "sixth sense." Consistently to mystic ideology, the intellect has 16, manas, ahamkara and Citta. Manas is oneself-illuminative and is disclosed through Purusha (soul). Citta is a device of endurance, understanding of self and that of outward entities at an age is not feasible for Manas to recognize. Agreeable to yoga Sutra, Citta is the initial result of Prakriti, embracing Buddhi (intellect), Ahamkara (self-conscious) and Manas. Here, Manas, Buddhi, and Ahamlkara entirely in partnership recognized as Citta. Nevertheless, Chraka Samhita Sharira Sthana, completely a triad otherwise described, and Hridaya (heart) is the seat of Manas.

MANDAEANS. A Gnostic sect which started as a small circle E. of the Jordan in the 1st or 2nd centuries A.D., and until now survives S. of Baghdad. They support that man's soul, unwillingly imprisoned in the body and oppressed by demons, will be emancipated by the savior, the manifested 'Knowledge of Life.'

These concepts may be of Christian origin and cite Jesus Christ, nevertheless the denomination has been antagonistic to Christianity since Byzantine times.

MANDRAKE Is a Gulf of Sidra herbage of the Dayberry parentage, with white or Lilac blossom and generous amber grains. It has a diverging plump seed that apparently has similarities with the person's configuration and was previously extensively in healing and supernaturally reputedly squeal when tugging from the earth. It is besides renowned by the appellative of Podophyllum. For millenarian years, this greenery was admired by numerous literatures, which accredited to it strange and wicked caliber. Mandrake is referred to in the scriptures (Gen. 30:14-16) and its Doctrinal apply is universally credited to its assumed fecundity. In the volume of Genesis [chapter 30 verses 14 and 15], Rachel and Leah, the two female siblings who were" or" love apples". Mandrake roots enhance extremely demanded subsequent in their indigenous Sardinia environment and ventures to safeguard such against thievery are perception to have been the origin of the succeeding mandrake legend, which asserted that a fiend occupied the radicle and could eliminate anybody who ventured to displaced it. Mandrake (Mandragora sp.) is one of the nearly all celebrated curative flora. It has been in uninterrupted therapeutic employ around recorded chronicles and is motionless in utilization this day in favored therapy.

MANIA (Greek) Exuberant, divine fury, reverent transport, creativity of the gods. Plato enumerates four kinds of mania: 1st. musical; 2nd. Telestic or mistic 3rd. Prophetic, and 4th. The Connection to love. Eagerness, in the genuinely of the expression plant session, materialized when that art of the soul which is at the height of the intellect, is relevant even to the gods, from whom its inspiration comes. One of these manias (mainly the amorous one) may be adequate to trace the soul back to its immediacy, divinity and bliss; but there is an special union between all of them, and the ordinary continuation by which the soul is crowned is, in the first place, by musical vivacity, then by imaginary or mystical; 3rd. by the prophet and finally by the enthusiasm of Love.

MANSIC, Flat. It is the One who harmonizes with consciousness when it acts as though it is not the stage of the mind as it functions through the brain, but as it works in its own world, free from all the obstacles of physical machinery. The mental plane recapitulates in order ascending to the astral plane; it reflects the universal Mind of Nature, and it is the plane that in our small system conforms to that of the great Mind of Kosmos. In its highest regions there are all the archetype ideas that are currently in concrete evolution; while in their lower regions, these ideas become successive forms that must be reproduced in the astral and physical worlds. This plane is the world of true man because intelligence is its most characteristic attribute. Thought forms play an igniting role among living creatures acting on the mental plane. One of the regions of this plane is the Devachan.

MANNA. The nourishment amazingly supported the Israelites on their expedition from Egypt to the 'holy land' (Exod. 16). It is customarily considered as a variety of the faithful Holy Sacrament.

MANSION. The word mansion comes from the Latin tap root 'mansio', "staying or a enduring," from the stem demeanor, "to stay." Definitions of mansion. A large and impressive house. Replica: hall, manse, mansion house, residence. Examples: Buckingham Palace, in England. A mansion could be a large spectacular residence. Manor house. Separate apartment or lodging in a large structure. House sensation, one of the 28 parts into which the moon's monthly course through the heavens is divided. As Jesus affirmed when he comforted his disciples saying: (John 14:2). Let not your hearts be troubled: ye believe in God, believe also in me. In my father's house there are many mansions: if it weren't so, I would have told you. I am going to prepare a place for you. And if I go and prepare a place for you, I will come again, and receive you unto myself; that where I am, there ye may be also. And whither I go ye know, and the way ye know.

MANTICA (gr. art of divination). Place of divinatory and religious operations by which the Greeks tried to perceive the forthcomings.

MANU (Sanskrit) The great Indian legislator. This denominate acquired from the Sanskrit root man "to think", humanity but means Swayam Bhuva, the first of the Manus, who emerged from Swayam Bhuva, "the one who succeeds by himself", and is, accordingly, the Logos and the progenitor of humanity. Manu is the first legislator, virtually a divine Being. [Manu's Code or Book of Laws) (Manava-dharma sastra) is accredited to that great lawgiver, who, to separate him from the other Manus, has been designating the appellative Manu Swayam Bhuva].

MANU-Svayambhu a [o Swayambhuva] (Sanskrit). The celestial appellative, Adam Kadmon, the amalgam of the fourteen Manus [or Prajapatis, and the initial of the Manus. "From this Manu Svayambhva (born of the Self-existent Being) descend six other Manus, endowed with a sublime soul and great emanating power, each of whom emitted his own creation, and they are: Svarochicha, Auttami, Tamasa, Raivata, the glorious Cachuchas and the son of Vivasvat". (Mnava-dharma-zastra, I, 61). In the Secret Doctrine (II, 323) we seek a list of the fourteen Manus anes communicated, in their relevant order and in their affiliation to each Round: Svayambhuva and Svarochi or Svarochicha, compare to the first Round; Auttami and Tamasa, to the second Raivatu and Chakechueha, to the third; Vaivasvata (our Progenitor) and Savarna, on the fourth; Dakcha-Savarna and Brahma-Savarna, to the fifth Savarna and Rudra-Savarna, to the sixth, and Rauchya and Bhautya to the seventh. According to the Secret Doctrine, the first Manu (Manu-Svayambha was not a man, but the illustration of the first human races, established with the help of the Dhyan Chhans (Devas) at the introduction of the first Round. But in the Manava-dharma-zastra we read that in each of the Kalpas there are fourteen Manus, of which fourteen Manvantaras form a Day of Brahma or Kalpa, being accepted by such the comprehending it from one minor pralaya to another.

MANO (Gnosticism) The Lord of Light, Rex Lucis, at the Codex Nazarenus. It is the second "Life" of the subsequent Trinity or Tri externalized unity, "the heavenly Life and Light, and older than the architect of heaven and earth".

MANYA (Sanskrit) Honorable, venerable, respectable.

MAPLE Timber (genus Acer) Possess extremely broad-leafed leaves. In the fall, they all curved a strong vivid yellow, red, and orange before dropping down in the wintertime. Trees that are deprived of their leaves once a year are indicated as broadleaf. They don't bother with slight coloration and may deliver in the able-bodied for a couple of hundred years. What transforms this tree directly widely known is its qualification to manufacture a distinctive vital fluid that may revolve into maple syrup. The plant fluid from Acer Palmatum is remarkably sweetened than the vital fluid of exceptionally tree. It is a dominant tree in Celtic mythology. It was a tree dedicated to Dana, the Celtic divinity of fecundity. It is besides familiar as the evergreen of tolerance. In China, maple relates to assurance, and its leaflets are a concept in Japanese ukiyo-e landscapes portrayal of devotion and autumnal equinox.

MAQUOM "Secret Place," in the articulation of The Zohar, an unseen scene, certainly it indicates to a restricted articles of a place of worship or to the "Womb of the World" or to the humanness one. It is an Esoteric denomination.

MARAN. (Sanskrit) This term defines dying, passing. French; from an old label apparently emanate from marenc and describer interpreting 'marine' (indicated in Old French cormarec 'cormorant' precisely 'sea crow') and originate from Latin mare 'sea' the suffix −enc (from ancient Germanic −ing). The Mystic Maran is a come across midst a Copper Maran male and a Barred Rock Female. This breed lays attractive dark brown eggs. They command a quite temper and are a great increase some brood for egg producing and assortment. They might or might not have modest Plumaging on their legs. Maaran was the Sephardi Chief Rabbi (Rishon Letzion) of Israel from1973-1983, a outstanding Talmudic scholar with a memory, and the uncontested greatest halachic jurisdiction of our time.

MARBURG, University of. Founded by Philip. Landgraf of Hesse. In 1527, it was the first Protestant university established in Europe. Its theological faculty has been famous, especially since the middle of the 19th century.

MARCA PIERRE DE (1594-1662), French devotee. His Dissertations de Concordia Sacerdotii et Imperii (1641) was a safeguarding of 'Gallicanism doctrines'; it was put down on the Index. In 1662 Marca became Chaplain of Paris.

MARCUS AURELIUS (121-80), Roman Emperor from 161. He had a high moral view of life, in essence a tempered form of Stoicism. He came into conflict with the Church, and a handful of 'Apologies' were addressed to him by Christian writers. He set down his own perceptions of conduct 'Thoughts' or Meditations', a work of sincerity but deficient philosophical originality.

MARDAVA (Sanskrit) Meekness, sweetness, kindness, affability, tenderness, docility.

MARE A ripe female horse over the age of three, and a filly is a female horse three and younger; or other equine animal especially when fully mature or of breeding age. Thoroughbred horse racing, a mare is defined as a female horse more than four years old. In slang language, it is a very unpleasant or frustrating experience. In Old English: Mare (Maere), Old Dutch; mare, Proto-Slavic mara; mara in Old High German, Old Norse, and Swedish) is a malicious entity in Germanic and Slavic folklore that rides on people's chests while they sleep, bringing on nightmares.

MARCIANA. The well-known library at Venice, title after St. Mark, the patron of the city.

MARISTS The 'Society of Mary' which was initiated at Lyons in 1824 by the Ven. Jean Claude Marie Colin. This laity accepted priests and lay brothers whose main activities are missionary and educational work. The W. The Pacific was awarded to them as their operation field in 1836.

MARK, Liturgy of St. The Conventional Greek Eucharistic Liturgy of the Church of Alexandria. Adjust versions in Coptic and Ethiopic are used by the Coptic Monophysites and the Abyssinians.

MARUT(S) [Marutas] (Sanskrit) In the company of the Orientalists, they are the gods of the storm, but in the Veda, correspondingly are very mystical. In esoteric instructing, for the goal of reincarnating themselves in each round, they are clearly identical to some of the Agnish Vatta-Pitris, the intelligent human Egos. Hence the allegory that Ziva converting the masses of flesh into children, and called them Maruts, to express men devoid of meaning transformed thanks to enhance vehicles of the Pitris or Maruts igneous, and therefore, rational beings. [Marut measures wind, air, breath, vital breath. In the plural (Maruts or Maruta), they are gods, geniuses or embodiment of the winds. Soon children of Rudra and Diti, and friends or allies of Indra. His number is seven (seven times seven, or forty-eight, according to others), and his boss is Marichi].

MARUCCHI ORAZIO (1852-1931). Italian archaeologist. The catacombs of Rome were the most important matter of his investigation.

MARICHA o MARICHI. (Sanskrit). Daughter of the sage Kandu and Pramlocha, the apsara demon of the sky of Indra. She was the mother of Dakcha. It is a parable respecting the enigma of the second and third human nature.

MAR(S). People call Mars the blazing planet because of its color. The planet of impulse, activity, effort, and vitality; the wondering star of determination. It also makeups the duration disposition of humanity; standing for the endurance impulse of the masses. Mars is perceived as the blazing luminous body because of its strong color. Moreover, the planet that illustrates war, its name being acquired from the Roman god of the same name; the red planet. Essentially, it is the second-smallest planet in the Solar System, being larger than only Mercury. In the English mother tongue; Mars is the fourth planet in the solar system, in order of separation from the sun.

MARROW Subsist flexible fatlike matter in the chamber of bony structure, in which bloodline microorganisms are shoved (regularly extracted as robustness and energy). Marrow has extensively been a graphic of vigorous, public health. It was posted. "But on a day of life-saving bone marrow transplants, the phrase 'marrow to their bones' takes on an added remarkable sacred covenant." The commitment for everyone who reinforces the word of understanding continues to carry on. In Liberal Arts Marrow means: the alternatives or greater essential or ultimate require or glorious indispensable fragment of various project or events;

"the gist of the prosecutor's argument"; "the heart and soul of the Members of Congress" "the nub of the story". The Christian bible states: "For we have the living word of God, which is full of energy, like a two-mouthed sword. It will even penetrate to the very core of our being where soul and spirit, bone and marrow meet!"

MARTYR, The English word 'martyr' is a transliteration of a Greek one explanation 'witness'. It was used by the Apostles as witnesses of Christ's life and resurrection (e.g., Acts 1: 8), but with the spread of oppression the term came to be reserved for those who had encountered hardship for the faith, and finally it was restricted to those who had suffered death. Martyrs were venerated as powerful intercessors, their relics were sought after, and their lives were often enhanced by legend.

MARY Gospel of. An early apocryphal Gnostic Gospel. In its St. Mary Magdalene narrates an eyesight in which the progression of the Gnostic through the seven planetary spheres is explained.

MAR THOMAS CHURCH (MALABAR CHRISTIANS). A classification of Christians in SW. India, also well known as Thomas Christian. They reveal that their church was traditional by Thomas the Apostle, the earliest verification of their existence dates from the 6th century. They apparently came initially from East Syria. At the Synod of Diamper in 1599 they repudiated Nestorius and United with the RC Church. Though there was a separation with the W. In 1653, about two thirds of them reinstated to communion with Rome in 1662. The rest integrated the Jacobite's; they have their own Catholics but acknowledge the Syrian Orthodox Patriarch of Damascus as highest head of the Church. At the end of the 19th centennial an enhanced group started the 'Mar Thomas' Church; this has relation with the Church of South India. Another segment made a plea for reconciliation with Rome, and in 1930 the Malan Karese Church came into existence.

MARTA or MARTHA, St. (sister of Lazarus and Mary) Dedicated woman and at the same time defied the chores of the house. This gentlewoman exemplifies "The Humility of the Initiate." Martha's humility is needed; without her we couldn't affiliate with the most prominent fragments of our character. The temper, the vanity, the presumptions etc. Would be incompetent identifying with the ruling characters of her identity. She is the guardian angel of helpers and chefs; her holy day is seen on July 29.

MARS or MARTE (Spanish). (lat. Mars-tis). The planet of our solar system of Ors, whose interspace from the sun is one and a half intervals that of the world, and its width half that of this; Their illumination is bright red, and they have a pair of satellites; Phobos and Delmos. Master Samael reassures them that there is life on Mars, and they are higher ranking to the earthlings both in mental capacity and reverence. They have cosmic ships (UFOs) with which they have already visited us and have subdue space, Roman legends accredited God of war to him, and the Greeks called him Ares. He was the son of Jupiter (Zeus and Juno (Era) He is illustrated with a circle and a diagonal cross or arrow at the top. Mars is an emblem of war, rules the signs the Aries and Scorpio; It effects the human beings conferring courage and audacity, but in its negative aspect it emanates bellicose, violent incentives and hardness that we all carry. Completed alchemical conversion he must enhance Venus, love. It is linked to the Sephirot Chesed or Atman, the Innermost; He must brawl with the combatant that he is, for his liberation. In the esoteric pentagram Mars stands for the War of the Initiate opposed to his psychic aggregates, that is, his deficiencies or errors.

MASBEN (Cald.) Masonic term defining: "the Sun in Consumption". It has a straight dependence (possibly obliterate by the Masons) with his "Word in a low voice".

MASH. Feasibly cuddling sentiments of devotion is why 'mash', initially a term for a response to embrace and smushing, became an expression of enormous adoration, or the target of reality; in 1870; the escalated stylishness of the declaration 'crush' revealed its applauding bounds in 1884, and 'main squeeze' confronted tussling widen the courage of lovers by 1926. To decrease with ruthlessness, missing of legitimate configuration or environment. Synonyms: crush, squash, squeeze, squelch, wring. Talk, or behave amorously, in the absence of significant objectives. Synonyms: butterfly, chat up, coquette, daily, flirt, philanderer, romance. Lessen to tiny bits or morsel by grinding or pulverizing. Synonyms: bray, crunch, grind. Mushy concoction, accumulation of components battered or agitated simultaneously, "late Old English masc. (in masc-wyrt "mash-wort, infused malt"), from Proto-Germanic "maisk-" (source also of Swedish mask "grains for pigs." German Maisch "crushed grapes, infused malt," German Maisch "crushed grapes, infused malt," Old English me ox "dung, filth"), perhaps from PIE root *meik- "to mix. "Originally a word in brewing; the general sense of "anything reduced to a soft pulpy consistency" is put on records from the 1590s, as is the emblematic belief "confused mixture, muddle." Short for mashed potatoes it is affirmed from 1904.

MASH-MAK For customs, an Atlantic expression of the quadrant nationality, employed to demonstrate an inexplicable planetary blaze, or quite a Power, which, was scrutinized, was qualified of demolished integrated metropolis into a consequence and extinguish the planet.

MASKEG. Exhausted mucky solid ground distinguishes by sphagnum moss herbage; huge regions of muskeg. Substitute formation of muskeg (Canada A landscape constitute of marsh with plumage pastureland and forest foliage counting North American timber.)

MASTERS OF THE SENTENCES, The. The entitle of Peter Lombard (1100-60) Throughout 1134 he went ahead to Paris, where he taught at the Cathedral School. In 1148 he resisted Gilbert de la Poree at the Council of Reims, and in 1159 he was decorated Bp. of Paris. His 'Sentences', in all probability written 1155-8, are divided into four books on (1) the Trinity, (2) the creation and Sin, (3) the Incarnation and the virtues, and (4) the Sacraments and the four Last Things. Though the orthodoxy of the work was challenged, after 1215 it became the quality textbook of Catholic theology, to be replaced only by St. Thomas Aquinas's Summa.

MASON Refers to the member of the Masonic fraternity or organization.

MASORA MASO Ra (Hebrew, Masorah, traditional) It is said of the discipline of the rabbis with respect to the sacred Hebrew paragraph, to preserve its germinal reading and intelligence.

MATA. (Hindi) a label that is passed down before the title of a female Hindu devotional chief or the mother or wife of a Sikh spiritual leader. Every one of the public figures at the occurrence raised and inclined the head to Mata Amrit Anandamayi.

MATHANA (Sanskrit) Agitation, rotation. As an accessory: afflictive, harmful, destructive.

MATHUSELAH The Octan in the list of primitive elder figure in Gen. 5 and the lengthy-alive (969 years; Gen 5:27).

MATI (Sanskrit) Opinion, belief, opinion, judgment, thought, correction, concept, intelligence, mind; determination, consideration, estimation, purpose; Meditation, devotion, worship, vow.

MATER ET MAGISTRA (1961). The epistle letter of John XXIII 'On Recent Developments of the Social Questioning the Light of Christian Teaching', blemishing the 70th anniversary of Rerum Novarum.

MATERIALISM. Any Christian philosophers accept an integrated mixture of faithful doctrine with some conclusion of (phenomenological) materialism, a belief that matter is an indispensable substance of the world and that mental phenomena consequence from matter. Materialism, in its most commonplace or "vulgar" form, disburse with God, abandoning only the "very good" universe. First, materialism is lethal, moreover it consumes a person. Jesus said, "Do not store up for yourselves treasures on earth, where moth and rust destroy, and where thieves break in and steal" (verse 19). Terrestrial affluence does not dispense ultimate contentment. It is unreliable. In Matthew's Gospel (6:19-21) Jesus enumerate the distinction between treasures on Earth and in Heaven. This passage defines the difference between the two riches: Treasures on Earth are short-term, materialistic and limited.

MATERIALITY. Each doctrine of work should initiate with a theology of conception. Do we consider the perceptible earth, the matter we attempt with, as Gods firs-rate essentiality, ingrained with deep-rooted value? Or do we decline it as a short-term crowd location, a viewing terra firma, a submerging boat from which we must escape to get to God's true position in a trivial "heaven". Genesis argues in opposition any assumption that the material world is any reduce predominance to God than the mystic sphere. Or placing it more accurately in Genesis there are no sharp discrepancy in the middle of the physical and the metaphysical. The Ruah of God in Genesis 1:2 is contemporaneously "breath," "wind", and "spirit," "The heavens and the earth" (Gen.1:1, 2:1) are not duality unattached realms, but a Hebrew figure of dialogue interpretation "the universe" [1] correspondingly that the English clause "kith and kin" mean "relatives."

MATTER In Middle Age ideology, the basic actuality of all material survival before it is adjusted and proficient by evolution (q.v.). The medieval schoolmen desired to appeal this Aristotelian abstraction to Sacramental theology.

MATRA (Matra) (Sanskrit) Short period of time, applied to the duration of sounds, and comparable to a blink of an eye, [Measure in general, limit, quantity, size, duration; measure of verse small quantity; a little, a moment; atom, particle; matter, element, instrument]. Matra also manner "manifestation". The three Matras are: the Adhi-Bhuta, Adhi-Daiva and Adi-yajna, which are equivalent to the Atma-Buddhi-Manas of the Vedan tines. (P. Hoult). At the end of a compound word, it means alone, pure, simple.

MATRAZ. Is a Spanish term, achieved from French Matras. The expression channels any variety of jug, or glass receptacles employed in synthetic research facilities. From Anglo-Norman Matraz ("shaft, dart"), Middle French Materas through an unidentified medieval era variation of Latin Mataris, Materis ("Gaulish throwing- spears"), from a Gualish language.

MATRICARIA Wild chamomilla (synonym Matricaria recutita), regularly investigated as chamomile (also implied Camomile), German chamomille, Hungarian chamomile (Kamilla), wild chamomile, blue chamomile, or scented genus Anthemis per annum design of the combined ancestry Compositae. The universal term, Matricaria, advances from the Latin model, perception myometrium since it was inherited traditionally treating chaos of the feminine generative structure. Maturing to 30 square (76 cm) in peak, chamomile is a blooming perennial plant with ferned, aromatic leaflet. It is notion that chamomile may enlarge brain neurochemical motion (serotonin, dopamine, and noradrenaline) and accordingly have certain consequences on emotional and uneasiness. Chamomile has been appraised as a gastric tranquilizer and has been used to handle several digestive interferences counting intestinal gas, acidity, flux, malnutrition, motion sickness, queasiness, and puke. Chamomile has also occurred utilized to manage bellyache, pain, and high temperature in youngster and adults alike.

MATRIMONY, The Christian formulation of marriage demands from earlier exertion and from modern secular use most particularly in the impartiality which it allows to the woman and the enduring which it attributes to the marriage bond. Christ repudiated the Mosaic tolerance of divorce and condemned remarriage (e.g., Mk. 10: 2-12). (The 'Matthacan exception' (Mt. 19: 9) animosity with the other Gospels and the rest of the NT and is probably best acknowledged as an early gloss to supply the Christian doctrine easier.) In Eph. 5: 22-33 St. Paul measures the unification of marriage with the relationship between Christ and His Church. While he determines the authority of the household to the husband, he emphasizes the function of love to the wife, who is an equal partner (1 Cor. 7: 3 f.). In 1 Cor. 7.: 15, he; the 'Pauline Privilege'.

MAUR, St. (6th centennial), Benedict of Nursia. Nothing at all is studied concerning his existence. He is stated to have contrived his way to France in 543 and established the abbey of Glanfeuil

MAYA (Sanskrit) Maya, Maia and Maria form ancestry tags. Maya is also the name of an asura, magician par excellence, who was used by the gods for various reasons, such as the developments of aerial cities and other portentous facts mentioned in the Bhagavata Purana.

MAYIN (Sanskrit) Magician; that hallucinates or causes illusion.

MAY LAWS The law-making connected with Bismarck's Kulturkampf. The constitution passed in May 1873, was opposed to the RC Church in Germany; they were constructed in the hypothesis of the complete dominion of the State.

MAYAKARA (Sanskrit) Magician; actor.

MAZARIN BIBLE, The. A Latin Bible so entitled from a copy in the library of Card. Mazarin which first regulated the awareness of scholars. It is also well known as the 'Gutenberg Bible', after J. Gutenberg. It's printer, and as the 42-line Bible', from the lines in each column. It is the most advanced full-length book ever printed, probably from 1453-5; it was undisputed complete by 1456.

MAZE. Is the exact sign of uncertainty and perplexity, the confinement that astonishes attempts to break out. One may believe maze as allegorical of expeditions; humankind may wander the roadway, escalating concerning redemption of awareness. In living, a maze illustrates culminations. Our pathway of reality can be considered as a maze leading us to intense interpretations and gratifications. Marking through a maze takes us nonstop countless rotations and circles that indicates the receding and course of aliveness. Like the design of a maze, what may suggest a termination in energy could also be a starting line. A maze stands for in writing works the process mortals form alliances, one impression succeeding an additional; elongating succession, from the margin to the nucleolus coming to an end. "Stories have this comfort to them; they have a beginning and an end. They find a way out of the labyrinth." The Maze or Labyrinth defines a mystify predicament or substantial concern. Fortification, vigorous situation, welfare; imprison the value or the idol; feasibly charmed or delighted most typical flight.

MEAT Within the bounds of Gnosticism it is expressed that Gnostic esotericism needs to eat, even a little piece of meat once a month, or every 15 days (about 2 weeks) to obtain animal proteins and fire atoms that are imperative for their generative energy; however, consistently within a balance never abuse, the only meat that should not be considered is pork.

MEDHA (Sanskrit) Intelligence, knowledge, wisdom, sagacity; prize, reward.

MEDIA Have been applied to sciences that assemble individuals' living and considered. They emblematically constitute physical reality, and they also gather knowledge of commerce with the real world. Comparison captures that are usually tangible and named or secures it to channel something-special to their assembly in a rhythmical way rather than saying it outright. The significance of contrast can be seen in the initial put on record formation of members of human race anecdote; scribbling and cryptograms; which are correct emblems, constitute more multiplex narratives or confidence. Comparison allows editors to prove compound proposition while offering the bookworm a visible, sensorial awareness.

MEDITATION As passed down by the advocates of Faithful fidelity, the advocate of Christian spirituality, the expression indicator mental prayer in its scatter form. Its proceedings are the engaged contemplation on a settle on (frequently Biblical) with a viewed to reinforce intangible consciousness and energizing the will and devotion. Esoterically in Patanjali's Aphorisms it is interpreted as follows: "Meditation (dhyana) is the continuous and prolonged stream of thought directed to a particular object until it becomes absorbed in it." It is one of the primary custom of Raja-yoga, and its results are of great momentous, as can be determine by these designations of Mrs. Annie Besant regarding the authority to whichever the chela must be subjected: "The aspirant will have been trained in meditation, and this effective practice outside the physical body will have enlivened and put into active exemplary many of the higher faculties. During meditation I will have reached higher regions of existence, mated more of the life of the mental plane. He will be taught to use his growing powers in the service of humanity, and during many of the hours of sleep of the body, he will have worked the astral plane helping the souls that death has brought there, bringing refreshment to the victims of accidents, teaching those who are less insurgent than him and helping in a thousand ways those who need his help. In this way, and according to his humble means, he takes part in the beneficent work of the Masters, associated with the sublime Fraternization as a collaborator to a degree however minimal".

MEDIUMISM. Word now admitted designating that nontypical psycho-physiological state that leads a person to consider as realities the fantasies of his imagination, as well as his real or artificial hallucinations. No entirely healthy person on the physiological and psychic planes can ever be medium. Is what mediums see, hear, and feels "real?" is it true?" It comes either from the astral plane, so innovative in its vibrations and suggestions, or from pure hallucinations, which have no real existence but for those who distinguished them. "Mediumship" is a kind of excess as a mediator, in which the one who suffers from this faculty is supposed to become an agent of imparting between a living man and a disembodied "Spirit". There are real methods to produce the development of this unenviable faculty.

MEGA. Derivation; from prehistorical Greek (Megas, "great, large, mighty"). In the Holy Scriptures Megas denotes outstanding of the outward form or realistic emergence of artifacts (or of mortal). Mega is a dialect expression in German that involves "awesome" or "great". It is frequently applied to narrate phenomenon that's particularly splendid or stimulating. For instance, if a person informs you regarding an outstanding music festival they explored to, you may perhaps respond with "Mega" to manifest that you believe it resonate astonishing.

MEGA COSMOS. The Theorist Pythagoras applied the word Kosmos (Ancient Greek term, Latinized Kosmos) for the arrangement of the macrocosm. One Greek expression which has numerous diverse definitions is Kosmos, frequently interpreted in conventional English adaptations as "world". As mentioned to the Liddell and Scott Greek lexicon, the untimely significance of this term (establish for example in the works of Homer) associated to "order," the pair in creation and in human attitude. The phrase Kosmos can indicate to the macrocosm or the entire of formation. In Acts 17:24 the statement is made, "God (is) the creator of the universe and everything in it"; and in Phil 2.15 Paul states that Christians are to "shine" amid corrupt and sinful people as the stars shine in the universe".

MEHEN (Egypt.) According to popular myths, it is the great snake that represents the lower part of the atmosphere. In Cabbalism, it is the world of the astral Light, figurative called the Serpent and the Cosmic Dragon. (See the works of Eliphas Levi, who I call this light Serpent of Evil and by other names, allocating to it all the evil influences on earth. (According to P. Pierret, Mehen is the mythological serpent that figures in the lower hemisphere, and that seems to symbolize the indicative of the course of the night sun.

MEHOUR or MEHUR. (Egypt.) "The Great Fullness"; personification of Space, name is that designates the nurturing principle of Divinity.

MELITO, St. Bishop of Sardis. Scarcely is known about his life. He was a productive writer, but only parts of his works were known until 1940, when a work preserved on papyrus was produced. The main theme of the Peri Pascha ('On the Pasch') is the new Pasch initiated by Christ. In it there is much hostility against the Jews and anti-gnostic demand on the true humanity of Christ.

MEMRAB (Hebr.) In kabbalah, it is "the voice of the will"; that is: the collective forces of nature at work, known by the name of "word," or Logos by Jewish Kabbalists.

MEMORIAL Human beings' reminiscence of heavenly realities. The respected constant solicitation of reflections in the Sacred text is the instructions to remember the Creator and his actions. "Memorial" transpires in the Christian Bible as the transferal of Mnemosunon, "a token of remembrance" (Matthew 26:13; Mark 14:9; Acts 10:4, "Thy prayers and thine alms are gone up for a memorial before God," that recommend the sensation in which "memorial" was utilized in the oblatory practice, and also the "better sacrifices" of the new exclusion). In Exodus 28:12 declares: "You shall put the two stones on the shoulder straps of the ephod, to be stones of memorial for the children of Israel: and Aaron shall bear their names before the Lord on his two shoulders for a Memorial".

MENDES (Gr.) Name of the cabrio demon that the Church of Rome presumed to have been worshipped by the Templars and other Freemasons. But this res Cabria was a myth fabricated by the bad fantasy of the odium theologicum. There has never been such a creature, nor was its cult ever known among the Templars or its predecessors, the Gnostics. The god of Mendes, or the Greek Mendesio, name which was given to Lower Egypt in pre-Christian times, was Ammon, the god of ram's head, the living and holy spirit of Ra, the life-giving sun, and this led unequivocal Greek authors to the error of claiming that the Egyptians called Mendes to the "res Cabria" itself (that is, the god of ram's head). Ammon was, for centurial, the chief divinity of Egypt, the supreme god; Amoun-Ra, the "hidden god" or Amen (the hidden one) the Begotten of Himself, who is "his own father and his own son", Esoterically, was Pan, the god of nature, or the Personified Nature, and probably the cleft foot of Pan, that of goat's foot, subscribed to produce the error that said god was an res Cabria. Since the altar of Ammon was in Pa-bi-neb-tat, "the dwelling place of Tat or of the Spirit, Lord of Tat" (Bindedi, in the Assyrian inscriptions), the Greeks first contaminated this name turning it into Bandes and later into Mendes, derived from "Men Desio". Such an "error" supplied for some ecclesiastical designs too well to be applicable even after it was recognized.

MENSA ISIACA or Tablet of Bembo. It is a bronze tablet that has some drawings implanted in mosaics and is directly in the Museum of Turin. It once applied to the famous Cardinal Bembo. Its origin and date are unknown. It is protected with figures and Egyptian hieroglyphs, and it is presumed to have been an ornament of an ancient temple of Isis.

MENSA (Latin, 'table') In early religious times the expression was used especially to the large tablets of gravestone laid over or nearby a grave, and visibly used for collecting food for meals in memory of the deceased. The pronouncement is now customary to use the flat stone (or other substance) which shapes the top of an altar.

MENTAL PRAYERS As second-hand by the advocate of Christian spirituality, the articulations suggested mental prayer in its confused structure. Its procedure is the devout thought on a selected (often Biblical) topic with a perspective to intensify psychical perception and revitalized the assurances and sentiment.

METAL. Replaced by the color white and circular structure, Metal's movement is decided, energetic, muscular, unbending, self-standing, restrained and enlightened. The emblem of metal is one of the cutting and executing activities, but it's also considered as a hardened procedure, consequently, it disclosed the Autumnal equinox. It's also frequently observed as a distinctive of elasticity and existence. Wisdom, vitality, health, radiance, eternity, and unification are all conceptions that have also been observed as fundamental to gold in many customs. The Charmer; as an Ideal Metal, you incline to be authority, ordered, systematic and meticulous. As such, you tend to continue an orderly and tidy distinctive living. Though you have a core of gold, you take measures to unlock to another and be empowered at first to come off as unemotional or spiritually detached.

METAPHYSICS. The title designated by the Greek copyreaders of Aristotle to his 'First Philosophy', and by comparison to commentary on associated discipline; it initially simply demonstrates the location of the publications on the theme in the Aristotelian corpus: posterior (meta) the Physics. The compass of supernatural query has been opposed accepted; it is largely distressed with the concluding actualities which are exceeding observational authentication.

METRATON (Christianity, Judaism) An archangel and the chancellor of Heaven and the scrivener of the book, in Christian and Jewish folklore. According to archaic apocrypha, he is Enoch, ancestor of Noah, reconstructed into an angel. Metraton is not a figure of the Hebrew Bible, but his name materialized briefly in several clauses of the Talmud. His legends are primarily found in mystical Kabbalistic texts. He is variously associated as the nobleman (or Angel) of the Presence, as Michael the archangel, or as Enoch after his bodily ascent into heaven.

MERCURY The symbol for Mercury illustrates the head and winged cap of Mercury, God of trading and conveying, conquered his caduceus (staff). The symbol for Venus is appointed as the female symbol, thought to be the stylized representation of the hand mirror of this goddess of love. Because of Mercury's ability to change through solid and liquid states, it was also thought of as being able to rise above between life, death, heaven, and earth. It was used in petitions, both medical and symbolic, to lengthen life or guide spirits after death.

MERCY SEAT In the Jewish Chapel, the awning of solid gold laid on the 'Ark of the Covenant' which was drawn up to be God's shrine.

MERCY WORKS, of (Corporal Works of Mercy). These are the conventional seven: (1) providing food to the hungry; (2) supplying drinks to the thirsty: (3) clothing the naked, (4) sheltering strangers; (5) paying a visit to the sick; (6) delegating to prisoners; (7) burying the dead.

MERLIN Has determination among the most approved of personalities in folk history, from his initial expectations in Middle Ages classics. He feasibly may have at first been a fecundity god or psyche, acclamation or inspiration for his substantial attention and transcendental potential, and this conception of Merlin was revived in 19th century CE fairy tale articles.

MERMAID(S). Appear in mythology from around the world, from the primordial Greek sirens who were said to persuade sailors to a watery demise, to the Mami Wata water spirits from African mythology. The Disney description of mermaids takes place from the Hans Christian Andersen anecdote "The Little creature that lives in the ocean". If you're contemplating keeping away from buying shoes for your entire life, become a mermaid.

MESSALIANS. In augmentation scrutinized as Euchite's, a sect clearly emerging in Mesopotamia in the 4th century. They cling to that in the outcome of Adam's sin each person had a demon a great deal integrated with his energy, and that this devil, which was not disconnected by baptism, was allowed to leave only by rigorous and uninterrupted prayers, the position of which was to disconnect all intensity and yearning.

MI. Third note on the musical scale; Do, Re, Mi, Fa, Sol, La, Si.

MICAH, (Book of), 'Minor Prophet'. The writer after whom this OT Book is named seemed to have lived in the 8th century B.C. The first three chapters are commonly welcome as his work; they foretell the demolition of Samaria and of Jerusalem. Most critics contemplate the rest of the Book as later Chapters. 4-5 predict the peer groups of the people and the advent of a Messiah; Chapters 6-7 are mainly populated with a dispute between Yahweh and His people. Mic 6:3-5 exposure the mode of the 'Reproaches of the Good Friday ritual' in the W. Church.

MICHAEL THE SYRIAN (1126-99), Jacobite Patriarch of Antioch from 1166. His history, enfolding the period from the Creation to 1194/5, perpetuates many Syriac sources now lost and contributed authentication for the Jacobite Church and for the Crusades.

MIDRASH (Heb., 'investigation'). A Jewish pronouncement referring to exegesis, mostly of Scripture. It acquired a scientific declaration with citation to the strategy in which illuminating absorbed solidity was attached to the text of Holy writing (as opposed to Mishnah, which refers to the recreation of exegetical tools apart from the text of Scripture). The earliest assembly of Midrashim comes from the 2nd century A.D., although much of their content is older.

MIDNIGHT FLOWER Specifically, the symbol given and with which, during the age of obscurantism, when the teaching of Being and Knowledge was hidden from humanity and with which the adepts and the accepted themselves are represented.

MILAN, Edict of. In 313 the Emps. Constantine and Licinio competent Milán and consented to accept the legitimate personality of the Christian Churches and to approve all religions equally. This strategy enunciated the end of persecution. The so-called 'Edict of Milan' (it is not an edict, and it was not supplied at Milan) is initiated in different configurations in Lactantius and Eusebius.

MILL, WILLIAM HODGE (1792-1853) English Oriental inspections professor. From 1820 to 1838 he was the first most extensive of Bishop's College. Calcutta. Here he contributed with the spreading of services in the Indian native speech for outspreading the Orthodox faith. Later, as Regius Professor of Hebrew, he proceeds the absorption of Dissenter Fundamentals in Cambridge.

MILVIAN BRIDGE, Battle of the (312), The battle in which Constantine overpowered Maxentius. It was persistent for the history of Christianity, for it enabled Constantine to settled himself with Licinius as joint Emperor and thus arrange the way for the 'Edict of Milan'.

MIMANSA (Sanskrit) A arrangement of reasonings, one of the six that exist in India. There are two philosophical schools of this name: the first, qualify Purva-Mimansa [or earlier Mimansa], founded by Jaimini and the second, Uttara Mimansa [or later Mimansa], was founded by a Vyasa, and is forthwith known as the Vedanta School. Zankaracharya was the most eminent apostle of the latter. The Vedanta school is the oldest of the six darshanas (literally "demonstrations"), but even the Purva-Mimansa is not assigned an antiquity that passes from the year 500 before J.C. The Orientals who sponsor the absurd idea that all these schools "are due to the Greek influences", they would like to assign them a later date, reinforcing their theory. The Chad darzana (or assistance verification), all have the same opening point and claim that ex nihilo nihil fit [out of nowhere, nothing is done.] (See: Purva-Mimansa philosophy and Vedanta philosophy.]

MIND(S) The component of a person that allows them to be attentive of the planet and their occurrences, to ponder, and to perceive; the capability of awareness and concept. A person's ability to reflect and rationale; brainpower; "a lot of things run through my mind": be upset, displeased, or troubled by something or regard it as major; feel concerned about. e.g., "never mind the opinion polls".

MINA (Mines) (Sanskrit) The selfsame as Meenam. Twelfth signal of the Indus Zodiac, equivalent to our Pisces (the Fish).

MINIMS (Ordo Fratrum Minimorum). The organization of friars was set up by St. Francis of Paola in 1435. As the name specifies, they were particularly meant to cultivate humility. They performed the greatest abstinence. order increased quickly, outstretched its substantial diversification in the 16th century but tolerated gravely between 1791 and 1870.

MINOR PROPHETS. In the sacred writings the authors of the twelve shorter prophetic Books, as contrasted with the three Major Prophets, Isaiah, Jeremiah, and Ezekiel. They are Hosea, Joel, Amos, Obadiah, Jonah, Micah, Nahum, Habakkuk, Zephaniah, Haggai, Zechariah, and Malachi.

MINOS *(Grecian)* According to mythology he was the son of Jupiter (Zeus) and Europa, he was King of Crete and the shadows. In his Divine Comedy, Dante narrates that Minos is the king of gloom that he finds in the second circle of Mercury or moderation of Pluto. Minos is a dreadful demon who after surveying and judging the faults of the shadows; With the beads of his tail, around the body of the condemned, he dictates the place or circle where they should go to be punished.

MINT. In the expression of flowerets, mint exemplifies integrity. Mint acquired its title from Greek legends; the Divinity Pluto approved the nymphet Mentha over the Divinity Persephone, who (jealously) converted Mentha within a greenery. In prehistoric Rome, mint was a stimulant, Venus, entwined into headbands worn by the deity. Mint is a continuing spice with vastly scented, uneven forsake and small purple, pink, or white flowers. There are numerous diversities of mint; all scanted, whether shiny or fuzzy, smooth or crinkled, bright green or assorted.

MIRACLES(S) or MYSTERY PLAYS. The religious dramas ('mysteries') of the Middle Ages are frequently held to have prospered from the sizable parts of the Liturgy, however, they may have been comprising by individual dramatists from Biblical and other origin. The major and most impressive were the Passion Plays, but Corpus Christi processions provided instances for detailed portrayal of Gospel stories. The plays were generally executed outdoors, on temporary or fixed stages.

MIRROR. In the first place, we must recognize that palpably, mirrors reflect light and thus throw back the world around us. Spiritually, light has symbolic accessories to illumination, appreciation and wisdom etc. Consequently, in denomination of intangible analogy, mirrors reflect truth. They reflect authenticity. Mirrors as we now know them, are an invention of the sixteenth century, where they were mass fabricated as opulence for the wealthy. Beforehand, human beings sought their reflection in water, brass, metal, and polished onyx. The usage of looking glass in art is paradoxical as it depicts both truth and self-admiration. The Former is typical to warn us that in mirrors lies the deeper truth about us, while the culmination is used in art to establish the transgression of pride and the sin of lust. Within Gnostic psychology are the errors that are generally seen in our peers, as a reflection of those we carry inside us. The luminous mirror, Aspaqularia nera, is a Kabbalistic word that defined the power of prudence and illusion at a distance, of projection, just as Moses had. Often mortals have only the Aspaqularia dellanera or Non-Luminous Mirror, and only see in a dark way in the glass; a parallel image is that of the conception of the Tree of Life and the solo of the Tree of Wisdom.

MISSALE SPECIALE. A smaller version of the Book of Devotions, accommodating selections drawn up for different needs. The best-known is that which came to be called the Missale speciale Constantiense (of Constance). This was at one time thought to be the earliest book ever printed, but in 1967 it was shown to date from 1473.

MISHNAH (Hebr.) [Literally: instruction or repetition.] The oldest part of the Jewish Talmud, or oral law, which is composed of subordinate rules for the direction of the Jews, with extensive commentary. Its content is ordered in six sessions, which deal correspondingly with Seeds, Feasts, Women, Damages, Sacred Things and Purification. Rabbi Judas Haunasee codifies the Mishnah in the year 140, approximately, after J.C.

MISDEED. Indecorous or outrageous or unethical attitude; immorality. Misdeed (capricious). Foundering to caution or concern; carelessness. Completion is an effort, and a misdeed is a specified variety of force. The preceding is wrongful, unscrupulous, illicit, or precisely simply erroneous. It's the opposing of benevolence.

MISTLETOE Originally, mistletoe composed romance, fertility, and vitality. Since nothing says love like bird poop and toxin. Nevertheless, solemnly, the Celtic Druids appraise mistletoe for its healing resources and likely were amid the first to decorate with it. Mistletoe is one of the four plants historically endorsed by Christians commemorating Christmas. Its evergreen leaves indeed represent 'life that does not die'. This freeloading plant multiplies on apple trees. Obeying to one sunnier version of the myth, the gods were able to renovate Baldur from the dead. Thrilled, Frigg then demonstrated mistletoe, a symbol of love and vowed to plant a kiss on all those who proceed beneath it.

MISATICA DINNER (Gnosticism) Particularly, the last supper of the Lord or Eucharist recognized with his disciples (the 12 apostles) and left as the most sublime and Christian sacrament; today it is exercised in almost all sects.

MIT BRENNENDER SORGE. (Germ., 'with burning anxiety'). The Epistle denounce Totalitarianism which Pius XI commanded to be read in all Church of Rome in Germany on Palm Sunday,

MITA (Sanskrit) Measured, reduced, limited, concise, divided, distributed; known, examined; fixed, firm, solid.

MITTA (Pali) Understanding indulgence. This concept ennobles (make honorable) Buddhism and district in a distinguished locality through the earth worship. This view is Maitreya's, title of the impending Buddha.

MITRATA (Sanskrit) Friendship.

MITHYA (Sanskrit) Mythical, fabulous, false, pretend, hypocritical.

MITIA Attributed to knowledge, leadership, fairness.

MIZKARA (Sanskrit) Paradise, celestial garden; singing. Moabite (effectively a Hebrew language), situated near the Dead Sea in 1868, and remembering the victory of Mesha, King of Moab, in objection to Israel. The text has hints of accessibility with the Bible.

MOABITE STONE. (c. 850 B.C.). A legend in Moabite (virtually a Hebrew dialect). unearth near the Dead Sea in 1868, and memorialize the accomplishment of Mesha, King of Moab, opposed to Israel. The text has relevant of proximity with the Bible.

MODESTY Humble in the approximation of one's potential or attainment. "She was a very modest woman, turn down to take any credit for the enterprise" (of an amount, rate, or level) standard, restricted, or compact. "Drink modest quantity of alcohol".

MOHIN (Sanskrit) That disturbs the appreciation or the senses; that causes vertigo or delirium.

MOIRA (Gr.) Equivalent to the Latin Fatum: fairy, destiny, the power that governs actions, anguish, life and human wrestle. But Moira is not Karma; only one of its force-agents.

MOLECULAR. Linking to or comprising of molecules, by 1815, out of molecule + -ar or in addition from French molecular or Modern Latin molecular is, Molecular biology is authenticated by 1950. Distinguished by or relate to the constituents' fragments of a phenomenon, operation, or administration. Molecular investigation in psychotherapy is a course of action of scrutinizing developmental procedure in duration of fundamental segments, occasionally inspect them in a moment-by-moment or phase-by-phase manner.

MOMMSEN CATALOGUE (The), While well-known as the Cheltenham List. It consists of a record of Biblical Books, dating from 359. These files were discovered in 1885 by T. Mommsen in a 10th century Phillipps MS. at Cheltenham. It has assorted notable features.

MOMS Carnations are an all-embracing indication of mothering. The Gaelic caregiving sign wheels around protective treasure and identify the perpetual relation between mum and baby. At its nucleus, his emblem illustrates the durable, continuous of deep affection that have existence amid female parent and newborn from the instant her child is born. We imagine "mama" means "feed me" most of the time. The theory, then, is that "mother" and its modern variations are all rooted in the baby talk of "mama." and its current contrast are all embedded in the babble talk of "mama." in consequence, one element we retain in familiarity with our premature forefathers may be our vocable for "Mom". Not too long ago the British Cabinet scrutinize more than 40,000j people in 100 plus countries, and the term polled the bulked most charming was "Mother". "As a mother comforts her child, so will comfort you; and you will be comforted over Jerusalem" (Isaiah 66:13). "Can a mother forget the baby at the breasts and have no compassion for the child she has bordned? Though she may forget, I will not forge you!" Isaiah 49:15).

MONEY. Utilized to influence another, inclination to discern money as an emblem of achievement, is appraised as a manifestation of accomplishment. The justification of the intangible vitality of money has the impartiality of providing us: Necessities, Dwelling and Protection. The money itself; it is not bad or good, it all revolves around the use we supply with it; we should not sympathize that money turn their mental processes needs. The last enigmatic volume of money is associated with capital or inwardly enlightenment or dharma (Cosmic Money), dharma is the partial payments for humanitarian accomplishments executed in the material sphere.

MONADIC, Monadic Essence. The atomic or more intimate condition of the matter of a plane animated by the second Wave of Life.

MONJA OR NUN. A female who is a part to a monastical organization and conducts a resigned existence, dedicated to God and faithful mostly to invocations and assignments. "Monks who live under the rule of St. Benedict take vows of poverty, chastity and obedience to their superior." It can be an energetic life (as teachers, nurses, etc.) or reflective; overall, they live in a fellowship. "A school of nuns."

MONK The word is an approved use of a member of any religious community of men living under vows of poverty, chastity, and obedience, but it is accurately applied only to those bodies in which community life is an indispensable element.

MONISM. The philosophy pursues to explain all that is in expression of an isolated truth. It is contradictory with the Christian leaning on a thorough distinction linking the several categories of existence.

MONKEY Contrary to what diverse modern naturalists claim, the man is not descended from the monkey or some anthropoid of the present animal species, but the monkey is a degenerate man. Several of the virtue functions with monkeys embrace energy, optimism, fun, and joy. Monkeys are also linked with activity, trickery, brain power, and courage. Monkeys are very imaginative and singularly sociable. Most things essentially contesting, and the Monkey wants to be speedy at everything. Ambitious and creative, Monkeys can many times be reckless and uncommunicative about what they desire to accomplish. In the Kings 10:22 the scriptures say: "For the king had Tarshish-ships at sea with the ships of Hiram; once every three years the Tarshish-ships came with gold and silver and ivory and apes (monkeys) and peacocks."

MONO (Monkey) Contrary to what several modern naturalists affirm, man is not descended from the ape or some anthropoid of the present animal species, but the ape is a degenerate man.

MONOGENISM Anthropological principles, as supported by the entire human race descend from an ancient and unique type.

MONOTHEISM. Optimism in a single outlandish and highest-ranking God. As represent to established conservative conviction it was the original religion of mankind adrift by nearly all human beings correspondingly of the downfall. In the 19th century, it was traditional protected that the religious credence of man had flourished from monotheism by way of pantheism to monotheism, but this supposition with appreciation to this generation scarcely any exuberantly cradled.

MONSTERS Extraordinary beings, generally invisible, that appear from corruption or an unnatural distinct union, originate the putrefaction (astral) of emission, or start with the effects of an unhealthy imagination. Each of these things and alternatives like them can pass from the plain "objective" and "subjective" state are coincident terms and refer preferably to our ability to recognize such beings, then to our own essential disposition. What may be entirely subjective for a person who is in a constitution of reality may be entirely objective for another who is in a disputed state. Additionally, for example, in delirium tremens, madness, subjective hallucinations materialized objective to the patient, although, during our dream, all that assume to each one of us to be neutral in a waking state vanish and ceases to be objective for our awareness.

MONT-ST-MICHEL. On a rock-strewn island due north coastline of France an rhetoric declares to have been settled by St. Aubert, Bp. Of Avranches (8th century) in compliance to the determines of a vision of St. Michael. In 966 a Benedictine monastery was instituted, to which a fortification was attached subsequently.

MONTE CASSINO. The principal abbey of the Benedictine system, established by St. Benedict c. 529, when he journeyed from Subiaco. The homestead outreaches the apex of its affluence in the 11th century, when the Norman house of God was dedicated (1071) and the popularity of the orchestrate accepted. The premises were nearly entirely demolished in 1944, but they have been reinstated.

MORAL Egyptian Egyptians were mindful, benevolent and charitable. A variety of upstanding treatises of that country are known: the Maxims of Ptah Hotep, the Maximas of the scripter Ani, etc. The Louver's demotic papyrus also carry excellent moral maxims.

MORTAL SIN. A calculated act of moving aside from God as man's last reasoning by seeking his satisfaction in a creature. A sin, to be mortal, charge be committed with an understandable knowledge of its culpability and full compliance of the will and must enfold a 'Grave. Matter'. It is held to compulsory forgetting of absolve grace and everlasting damnation, except repented and forgiven.

MORYA (Sanskrit) A singular of the regal Buddhist houses of Magadha, which was presided over by Chandragupta and his grandson Azoka. It is also the persuasion of a Rajput tribe.

MOSAICS Were designs of affluence and prestigiousness. Accommodating fine art and interior design, Roman mosaics were promoted to decorate and influence assessments inside private quarters and chateaus. "Life is like a mosaic." It's a depiction contained millenarians of compact multicolored designations that composes your existence. Each judgment you fabricate is a small brick in the mosaic. You will be inadequate; you will miscalculate. But the inferior alternatives produced, the debris slates you confused, the more twisted the illustration attained. Mosaic suggests that observers accommodate the cliche from persons' fundamental, connecting, and related classification and that this unification institute intensify or weakens characteristics. Mosaics are interpreted as the decree as (launching with the Ten Commandments) that The Almighty provided to the Israelites through Moses; it constitutes numerous regulations of religious commemorations specified in the initial five books of the Hebrew Scriptures (in Judaism these books are called the Torah) synonyms: Law of Moses, type of Constitution, systems of laws.

MOSES, Initiator and Lawgiver of Israel. Aggregable to the Pentateuch narrative, Moses was born in Egypt and unsettled his existence to being concealed in a basket and saved from danger by Pharaoh's daughter. Subsequently, he was accepted by Pharaoh's daughter. He then was presented with a Divine instruction to come to the aid of the Hebrews from their subjugation, and he in due course guided the group away of Egypt. During the journey covering the desert, they frequently rebelled against him, however, by his intervention they were provided with manna for food in addition to the Ten Commandments. He was permitted vision of the Promised land and died in Moab. As claimed by the established perspectives, Moses put in writing the total Pentateuch. Almost all contemporary intellectuals see entwined in these Books a few independent chronicles of divergent occasion and assorted standard of historical truth. The bulk agrees that a few similar mandating characters as Moses is assumed by, the unification of the Israelite ethnic group and whichever the Hebrew mankind could scarcely have demanded their origination in subjugation except the same had been the case.

MOT (Fenc.) The matching as illustration, legamo or mud, the first created chaos. Term used in Etruscan cosmogony.

MOTET. A formation of polyphonic chants. Without much doubt of secular origin, it approached liturgical veneration in the 13th century; either backing or restoring the offertory at mass. The configuration of motets outstretches its height at the end of the 16th century, with the work of Orlando di Lasso, G. P. Palestrina, and others.

MOTHER Prevailing allegory about God and the earth. The mother is Earh with the house standing in as the environment. The word 'mother' is interpret as loving her child unconditionally, never hurting her child; doing all that is best for her offspring, setting down child's needs first before hers, wanting to be around her child, feeling that the most important thing on this earth is her child, willing to give up everything for her child. Mary as mother of Jesus, she is also the mother of all the faithful people of this earth. Mary has conveyed to the world how a mother should shelter her child; she is the role model of all mothers!

MOTOR Singularly transmit locomotion specifically: prime mover, any of various power units that develop energy or impart movement: such as a small compact engine, internal combustion engine principally, a gasoline engine; a rotating machine that transfigure electrical energy into automatic force. Motors are crucial in our lives seeing that they convert electronic strength into mechanical energy. This mechanical energy can then be recycled to power everything from heavy industry machinery to everyday tools and appliances uniformly such as hair dryers, computer printers, automobiles, fax machines, dishwashers, to voice a few. A human being and a car are similar in numerous ways. The pair, car and individual convert chemical power (in petrol and food) to kinetic energy (movement) and heat. In the car, the energy ser free by the combustion of fuel causes the pistons to move, which then processes the movement of the vehicle. Within the human body; the Motor Center; which is the upper part of the spine, is made up of movements, mechanical imitation, habits, muscle tension and relaxation, mechanical reactions, motor coordination, inner talk, ill will, language and expression.

MOON The moon is a vital satellite of the planet, measurable (primarily at night) by generated light from the sun. "There was no moon, but a sky sparkling with brilliant stars." The moon is a feminine insignia, always replacing the rhythm of flow as it personifies the rotation. The aspects of the moon embody everlasting life and perpetuity, knowledge or hopelessness.

MOOT When substitute is moot is open to question, debatable; it is question to discussion, debated, deprived of active importance made abstract or purely academic. The interpretation of moot is a subject that is not worthy of discussion since it has been resolved. A typical case of moot is whether to allow prayer in public school.

MOURNERS Successively, mourners emphasize sadness and loss. There are some repeatedly revealed "signs" from a perished loved one is the butterfly. The specified nearly all acknowledged indication from a departed loved one is a feather. There are additionally signs of coins, dragonflies, birds, squirrels and deer, stones, possessions coming from lost loved ones, etc. Right through history, fellowman created methods to manage dying, mourning, and the clique of existence forward with analogy. Consistent and current art and culture are the two entirely of poetry connected with demise and the advance of life. It's fascinating to contrast these vast historical events and the arts across the globe to see how they overlap and disunite. The Ankh illustrates life and death, also well-known as the basis of life, the Ankh is a cross-shaped symbol with a teardrop loop rather of a highest bar. (Gnosticism) The peculiarity is structured during the first seven years and is strengthened by the tests. Sometimes the personality wanders through the cemetery, sometimes they leave their grave when the mourners visit them and bring flowers. Little by little the singularity is disintegrating. Character is not reincarnated. The personality is a child of its time and dies in its time.

MOUNT CARMEL; MOUNT OF OLIVES. A towering ridge in North Palestine. It was the location of an event between Elijah and the prophets of Baal (1 Kgs. 18). A house of God was built their c. A.D. 500, and a monastery well-established by Greek monks. It was later the property of the Carmelite Order.

MOUT (Egyptian) The mother goddess; the primordial deity, since "all the gods are born of Mut, as has been said." Astronomical mind, it is the moon.

MOZARABIC RITE. The traditional title for the ceremonial arrangement which was in operation in the Iberian Península from the premature era till the 11ᵗʰ century. Its supplant be the Grecian ritual was a reaction of the Christian recapture of Spain. There was protection from its cancellation in Toledo, and here it was authorized to abide in six parishes. Its safeguard in latter days is as as result to F. Ximenes de Cisneros, who created a book of prayers and diminution to be impressed (1500 and1502).

MUD Indicates the union of the receptive beginning of the earth with the power of transition and alteration of the waters. Esoterically mud has a metaphor that is related within alchemy as primal inside the first biological, by forming man and merging him with divinity. (You must cook and collect until it is completely molded.)

MUDA (Sanskrit) Joy, triumph, jubilation, delight.

MUNDA (Sanskrit) Literally: "bald." Name of a demon (daitya), whom Durga killed.

MUND Brings about one who grants encouragement, deliver as a protector to guarded, admitted by a monarch or commander, the infraction of which was disciplined by a great (a mundbyrd), obsolete) preservation; safekeeping. The social class of a Mund is a dynasty of Jats. Moond Jats are establish in Rajasthan, Madhya Pradesh, Punjab and Haryana in India. Mund/Munda (Kachwaha) tribe is based in Afghanistan. Munda Jat Gotra is also set up in Ahirs.

MUNGO The Style Mungo is a boy's name of Scottish origin meaning "my pet". Mungo is one of the most classic Scottish names but perhaps also among the most difficult names to carry. In the English language Mungo relates to a low-grade wool from felted rags or waste. Mungo Lady and Mungo Man lived in the region now known as the Willand Lakes, western New South Wales, around 42,000 years ago during the late Pleistocene era. Scholars have presupposed from their skeletal still is all that is known to science about their biographies.

MUHURTA (Sanskrit) The thirtieth portion of the day, that is around 48 minutes; An instant, a brief time.

MUKTA (Sanskrit) Free, liberated, emancipated, exempt; beatified or saved. The candidate of the Mokcha (liberation from the shackles of the flesh of the matter or of life on this earth), [The Spirit free from constrained existence, or free from the bonds of the body].

MUMIA In Medieval medicine, Mamiya, "bitumen" was transliterated into Latin as mummia definition both "a bituminous medicine from Persia" and "mummy". Merchants in apothecaries dispensed expensive mummia bitumen, which was thought to be an effective cure-all for many ailments. It was also used as an aphrodisiac. The word 'mummy' mentioned the dead body of an animal due to specific natural or artificial conditions. The phrase itself is derived from the Persian/Arabic word mummia, meaning 'tar" or 'bitumen'.

MURO, OR PROTECTIVE WALL. Significative epithet designated to the regiments of Past Masters (Narjols) or Saints cooperate, who are assumed to observe past humanness by sharing and safeguarding it. This is the presumed Nirmanakaya creed **in** Mahayana Buddhism. [As it is coached, the acquired attempts of lengthy peer groups of gurus, holy beings and masters, and particularly of Nirmanakayas, have produce, as it were, about humanity barrier of shelter, which inconspicuously protect it separating equal disagreeable wrongdoing.

MUSICAL Substantially, the musical alphabet makes up the abstraction of the music, considerably as written language symbolizes speech. This kind of analogy is unavoidable; it is always present; when we have written music, for there is comparatively no phenomenon of musical script that does not indirect a group music.

MUSTARD Color Mustard Emblem Creativity and Diversity. This extensive investigation describes the definition and figuration of the color mustard. directly delineated as a darker shade of yellow, mustard is exceedingly distinctive. The sacred connotation of the color mustard warmness, imagination, confidence, and diverseness. The ever-developing apparition of dawn or twilight provided a sense of innovation in the sky, and the vast array of yellow, happy flowers are exemplification of such distinctions that brighten up one's spirit. (Mat., 21:43.) "It is the kingdom of heaven thus understood that is likened to a grain of mustard seed". "Augustine:" A grain of mustard seed may suggest to the warmness of faith or to its characteristics as remedy of toxin. It adheres; that a mortal took and sowed. Mustard as condiment is produced from the powerful seeds of each of two leading spices kinship to the ancestry Brassicaceae. The primary varieties are white, or yellow, mustard (Sinapis alba). A vegetation of Sardinia origination and brown, or Indian, mustard (Brassica juncea), that is of Himalayan origin.

MU (Sensing) The term mystic (or rather, a part of it) in Northern Buddhism. It defines the "destruction of temptation" during Yoga practice.

MUT Signifies mother in the ancient Egyptian language, was an ancient Egyptian mother goddess with multiple aspects that interchanged over the thousands of years of the culture. Alternative spelling is mut and mouth. Mut the mother goddess of Thebes (Waset, in the 4th Noum of Upper Egypt). The ancient Egyptians contemplated the vulture to be a protecting and nurturing mother, and so their word for mother was also the word for a vulture, "Mwt".

MUTA. Derivation from Italian muto, German Muta, English mute, all totally Latin Mutus ("mute, silent"). In Sanskrit this declaration denote. attributable formation: mutah. Interval in addition signifies a conformation of Muslim consumption alliance for a particularized period compare been nuptials. In India Mutah in global sensation may be determine as a provisional unification of masculine and womanly for a precise duration succeeding liquidation of definitive significant the precise connotation of term 'Mutah' is 'enjoyment'. Consequently, Mutah or Marriage can besides be considered as union for the motivation of satisfaction.

MUTHAM MATTAM (Sanskrit) Temples of India with cloisters and monasteries for students and regular ascetics.

MUTANT Remains just as a vertebrate or greenery that is substantially unalikely divergent of the identical breed because of change in its genetic code. Fresh genus are purely mutants of prior ones. Mutants are exceedingly ordinary, says IMRF scientists Dr. Chris Sansam says, "Someone without any mutations would be the real anomaly". Mutations are modification to a human being's heredity, and they can appear around from brandish to an exterior ambiance component, similarly as tobacco users or emission.

MUTH or MOUT The mother goddess; the primordial goddess, since "all gods are born of Muth, as has been said. Astronomically conveys the moon.

MYRRH A coffee color slightly bitter gum attained from African and Arabian sapling and customary mostly in fragrance or previously in incense. Myrrh is a brush like Commiohora tree acclaimed diversely as amber, myrrh tree, muku tree, guggul resin, didin, and didthin. Myrrh is an Arabic word signifying acidic. The exceedingly appraised scented chicle gum of myrrh has a harsh, acrid flavor and a sugared, pleasurable scent. Myrrh is common for acidity, ulcerations, chill, croup, asthma flare, pulmonary Adema, atrophic arthritis, canker, Hansen's disease, cramps, and venereal diseases. Further is also acclimated as a energizer and to expands monthlies run. Myrrh. [N] [E] This quality is introduced in (Exodus 30:23) as one of the elements of the "oil of holy ointment." in (Esther 2:12) as one of the raw materials utilized in the disinfection of women: in (Psalms 45:8; Proverbs 7:17) and in numerous quotations in Chants, as Eua de cologne.

MYSTES (Gr.) In prehistoric moment this title was given to the new spearhead; At currently it is provided with to the Romanist red cardinals, who enjoying taken their rituals and principles from the "pagan" band of gold, Afrasian and Hellenes, have also tendered oneself for the genus mysis (1) of the initiates. They must retain their view shut and their lips in their tender emotions, and consequently, they are called Mistletoe.

MYTH. Figurative narrative, customarily of unknown origin and at least partly traditional that ostensibly relates actual events and that is especially associated with religious beliefs. It is distinguished from symbolic behavior (cult, ritual) and illustrative places or objects (temples, icons). Myths are specific accounts of gods or superhuman beings involved in extraordinary events or conditions in a time that is unspecified, but which is understood as existing apart from typical human experience. The term mythology denotes both the study of myth and the body of allegories belonging to a particular religious tradition.

MYTHOMANIA. Arrives via the French mythomanie, from two ancient roots; the Greek mythos (meaning "myth") and the Late Latin mania (meaning "insanity marked by uncontrolled emotion or excitement"). In psychology, mythomania (also known as pseudologia fantastic for pathological lying) is a condition concerning compulsive lying by a person with no obvious motivation. The afflicted person might believe their lies to be the truth and may have to create elaborate myths to reconcile them with other facts. Among famous mythomaniacs in history was King Frederik VII of Denmark and Sir Douglas Conway of Suffolk.

MYTHOLOGY A symbol is anything that functions for, or stands for, something else. In a story, a character, an action, an object, or an animal can be symbolic. Often these symbols stand for something abstract, like a force of nature, a condition of the world, or an idea. There are many diverse types of myths but, essentially, they can be grouped into three: Etiological Myths; Historical Myths & Psychological Myths. There are mythical creatures; some personify danger, others, we think, can bring us luck or joy. Together mythic creatures give shape to humankind's greatest hopes, fears, and most passionate dreams. Vermillion Bird: It is the mythological creature in the South and corresponds with the summer season. Its good Luck in Greek/Roman Mythological.

-N-

NAASSENES. A Gnostic sect like, if not identical with, the Ophites.

NAAN. Initially, Naan was established thereafter the appearance of baker's yeast in India from Egypt. All along India's Mughal era in the 1520s. Naan was a treat that at most nobleman and aristocratic households appreciated since the craft of creating Naan was a respected expertise, accepted by not many. At the time of the 150s, it is consequently documented that naan was combined into the early meal of numerous divergent royalties. A convention that would endure delectables for the following two eons. Nevertheless, Naan ultimately developed into a meal that exceeded the class ladder accordingly the public could savor this crusty still delicate side item. Naan is a conventional Naan whose originations branch from Central, West and Southeast Asia. In its present condition, it is a major food for those who reside in the Northern part of the area. Tandoori Roti is a kind of Naan and is routinely made from whole meal flour. Naan is in addition not just bread; it is an emblem of proclamation and banqueting.

NABATEANS o NABATEOS A sect that by its beliefs, was almost identical to the Nazarenes and Sabaeans, whose members professed greater reverence to John the Baptist than to Jesus. Maimonides finds them with Astro later. "With respect to the beliefs of the Sabaeans," he says; the most celebrated is the book entitled "Agriculture of the Nabataeans". And we know that the Ebionites, the first of whom were friends and acquaintances of Jesus, according to tradition, or in other terms, the first and most primordial Christians, "were the direct proselytes and disciples of the Nazarene sect," according to Epiphanius and Theodore. (as writing in Conita Ebionites of Epiphanius, and: Galileans and Nazarenes).

NABI The voicing Nabi, 'prophet,' was appeal in the time of Moses, or Abraham. Nabi (Nambi), a.k.a. Metan, is a Torricelli parent language of Papua New Guinea. It was assigned to the Maimain branch in Ross (2005). The native tongue is spoken in three villages; Pursuant to Ethnologies, in two they favored the designation Nabi, and in the third Metan. The Hebrew Scriptures uses three Hebrew terms that are translated into the English word "prophet" or "seer", Nabi, roeh, and hozeh Nabi plainly channels "to bubble up." It describes one who is stirred up in spirit. It is the most frequent used of the three by the Hebrew writers. When the sense of "buddling up" is demanded to be spoken, it intensifies "to declare." Hence, a Nabi, or prophet, is an anchor; one who revenues forth the promulgation of God.

NADI(S) (Sanskrit) Represents ('tube, pipe, nerve, blood vessel, pulse') is a term for the passages whereby, in standard Indian medicine and untouchable speculations, the vitalities approximate as prana of the material body, the extreme body and the demiurgic body are said to flow. The ten principles of nadis are: sushumna, ida, pingala, gandhari, hastajihva, yashasvini, pusha, alambusha, kuhu, and shankhini. Ida, Pingal, and sushumna are well known to be the three principal nadis. The termination points of the three main nadis is brahmarandhra (the "Brahmic aperture"), the crown of the head.

NAG HAMMADI PAPYRI. A group of 13 papyrus codices was found in 1945 at Nag Hammadi (Chenoboskion) near the Nile. They hold 49 Gnostic treatises, all written in Coptic, and established the most crucial single contribution to our knowledge of Gnosticism.

NAG'S HEAD STORY, The. An anecdote generated in the 17th century to dishonor the validity of M. Parker's episcopal sacrament. It was at the Nag's Head Tavern in Cheapside J. Scory accepted that Parker and other bishops by accommodating a Bible on the neck of each of them in circle with the expression 'Take thou authority to preach the Word of God sincerely'.

NAGAPATI (Sanskrit) Actually "King of the mountains": the Himalayas.

NAHASH or NAHAS, (Hebr.) "The Private" The Bad the Devil or the Serpent, according to the Occidental Kabbalists.

NAHUM, Book (of) 'Minor Prophet'. It foresees the fall of Nineveh (612 B.C.), which is considered so imminent that the Book is generally dated shortly prior to this event. The Psalm of the aperture verses (1;2-9 or 1: 2-2 2) may advance from an unconventional source.

NAILS The nail is most often related in the Christian heritage with the martyrdom of Christ, and thus illustrate his suffering. The nail also makes up the world pillar, or world Axis, around which the heavens revolve.

NAIPUNA (Sanskrit) Skill, dexterity. Occupation that requires skill.

NAJO (Hin dust.) Witch, sorcerer.

NAKULA (Na-kula) (Sanskrit) Simply "no family" (?). Fourth of the pandava princes, son of Madri, second wife of Pandu, but mystically fathered by Nasatya, one of the Azvins twins.

NAKA (Sanskrit) Sky, atmosphere; paradise.

NAKIN (Sanskrit) God of heaven.

NALI (Nala) (Sanskrit) King of Nichadha and husband of Damayanti. Its yesteryears are one of the majorities attractive episodes of the Mahabharata. Nale is also the appellative of a monkey chief, who was active in the army of Rama, and whose story is associated with in the Ramayana. It also describes; Tube, vessel, vein, artery.

NAME OF JESUS. For the reason of the immediate connection in the middle designation and individual, the eminence of Jesus is employed in the Chirstian teaching as a synonym for Christ, designating His personality and jurisdiction. The followers rectify prodigy and purification 'in the name of Jesus', i.e., however, His potential (Mk. 9: 38 ff., Acts 4: 30), and christen in it (Acts 2: 38). faithfulness to the Righteous Epithet was deceptive by the Franciscans in the 15th century. A festival was officially admitted to them in 1530 and recommended for the entire Catholicism sanctuary in 1721; it was confident in 1969. It seemed allocated to numerous occasions in Jan. In the Anglican Church it is occasionally detected on 7 August the date administers to it in the timetable of the BCP.

NAMA (Sanskrit) Appellative, subject. As an attribute: nominal; purely in name; vain; hypocrite: called titled.

NAMAN (Sanskrit) Name, title, designation.

NANA (Sanskrit) Varied, diverse, different, multiple; separate; many.

NANDANA (Sanskrit) He who rejoices or delights: joy, bliss; vast ago; son; Indra's paradise.

NANDI (Sanskrit) The sacred white bull of Ziva that serves as a vehicle (Vahan). [He is the guardian of all quadrupeds.]

NANTES, Edits of (1598) The Directive signed by Henry IV at Nantes, which concluded the French wars of religion. The Huguenots were allowed free exercise of their religion and a state subsidy for the support of their armed forces and pastors. It was nullified in 1685.

NANTRI (Sanskrit) Modifier; of one thing that alters another.

NAPEA. NAPEA, AS. (Lat. nape a, and the gr. belonging to the forests). Diocese of The Nymphs that according to mythology, live in the forests and protect the meadows and flowers.

NARADA (Sanskrit). He is one of the ten progenitors of humanity born of the mind of Brahma.

NARD. An aromatic balm used in antiquity. A sweet-scented oil from the plant, previously much prized. American spikenard (Aralia racemose), a North American perennial herb with an aromatic root. A high-priced fragrance acquired from the roots of the herb Basonym Jata Mansi. The name appears twice in the Song of Solomon (Roman 1:12; Romans 4:13-14) and in two of the gospel accounts of the woman anointing Jesus at Simon's house in Bethany (Mark 14:3; John 12:3; "spikenard,"

NARSAI (D.C. 503) Also known as Narses, Nestorian scholar. He became top of the famous school of Edessa, but c 471 he ran away to Nisibis, where the bishop, Barsumas, questioned him to confirm a school. He was one of the developing theologians of the Nestorian Church. A Huge figure of metrical lecture and some hymns pull through.

NASHDOM, Bucks., Anglican Benedictine abbey. subsequent the submission to Rome of most of the Anglican community on Caldey Island in 1913, the remaining anglicans went to Pershore. In 1926 the community moved to Nashdom, a house selected by Sir Edwin Lutyens at Burnham, Bucks.

NASH-PAPYRUS, The earliest surviving MS of any section of the Hebrew OT at the present time at Cambridge. It adapted the Ten Commandments, which comes after a quick initial progress and the Shelma. It may be dated as prior as the 2nd century. B.C.

NASTI (na-asti) (Sanskrit) Simply: "there is none". Non-existence. Satyat nasti paro dharma: There is no religion higher than the truth: Motto of the Theosophy Society.

NASTIKA (Sanskrit) Atheist, or preferable one who does not worship or acknowledge gods and idols. [Skeptical disbelief. The Secret Doctrine does not preach atheism, except in the sensation of the Sanskrit Nastika voice, rejection of images levels all anthropoid God. In such a concept, every occultist is a Nastika.

NATURA The first distinction of a person or thing; recognize or imperative disposition. (Often capital, principally when personified) the whole organization of the existence, disposition, forces, and events of all physical life that are not conducted by humanity.

NATH [or Nath] (Sanskrit) Sir. term that implemented to gods and men. It is a subtitle that is joined to the first denomination of men and things, such as Badari-nath (Lord of mountains), remarkable place of pilgrimage; Gopinath (Lord of shepherdesses), applied to Krichna.

NATURE Can illustrate tranquility and serenity. Occasionally capacity and force; it additionally species strength and lustiness. Several journalists take advantage of it to symbolize existence's rhythm or convey liberation and freedom. The connection of nature is greatly embedded in the history of humankind. The corporal world and overall; it has fabricated the most pleasing creatures advanced in nature. Essential terrain or environment; we took a trek to have the enjoyment of nature. The underlying disposition of a person or thing scientists preconceived the nature of the new substance. Nature is interpreted as the natural Earth and the paraphernalia on it, or the spirit of a person or concept. The trees, forests, birds and animals are all paragons of nature. The emblem of Mother Nature is the turtle which is a consecrated feature in Native American fable as it portrays Mother Earth.

NAVA (Sanskrit) New, recent, prize.

NAVAN (Sanskrit) Nine.

NAVANZA (Navanska) (Sanskrit) The ninth part of a Zodiac sign.

NAYA (Sanskrit) Harmony, conduct, direction (physical or moral); guide, director. Scriptural part of the body of the Vedas.

NAVYA (Sanskrit) Praise, Ioa.

NAZARENE (or Nasorean). (1) In the Christian Bible Christ is called 'Jesus the Nazarene'; this is understood as 'from Nazareth'. (2) 'Nazarenes' was a Jewish term for the Christians (3) 'Nazarenes' occurs as a name used by 4th century writers of a group of Christians of Jewish race Syria who proceed with to obey much of the Jewish Law. They used the 'Gospel account to the Hebrews' (which has hence sometimes been termed the 'Gospel of the Nazarenes'). (4) The Mandeans are sometimes called Nazoreans'.

NEAP. It defines assigned tides halfway at intervals King tides that achieve the slightest high point. This term derives through Medial English neep, from Old English nep ("scant, lacking"), perhaps from Proto-Germanic nopiz ("narrow"). established notably in Old English nepflod ("neap tide', literally "low tide"). Correlates Norwegian dialectal nopen ("scaraace, scant, barely enough"). Neap tide; seven days following a spring tide, mention a full point of average currents concurrently with the sun and moon are at proper inclinations to one another. Neap tides take place for the duration the sun, moon, and Earth structure a perpendicular angle, and this results the systematic high tides and low tides to enhance lesser than customary. A neap tide will constantly take place one week succeeding a King tide.

NE TEMERÉ (1907) A commandment of the Sacred Congregation of the Council on marriage. It lays down that to be valid a nuptial in which either or both parties are RCs must be seen in front of the parish priest or the ordinary or a priest assigned by one of them in 1970 Paul VI recognized some relaxation in the occasion of mixed marriage.

NEEM This idiom holds a special significance on New Year 's day as it is a figure of God health and longevity. Neem leaf and its constituents have been displayed to exhibit immunomodulatory, anti-inflammatory, antihyperglycemic, antiulcer, antimalarial, antifungal, antibacterial, antiviral, antioxidant, antimutagenic and anticarcinogenic. Neem is an omnipotent tree and a sacred gift of nature. Neem tree is mainly of the argan mahogany family Meliacese. Today it is known by the botanical name Azadirachta indica. In some parts of India, the Neem tree itself is thought to be a goddess, Neemari Devi. It is like Goddess Sitala Devi in the North as well as Goddess Mariman in the south, who are both corresponding with giving and healing skin ailments like smallpox.

NEBIM-NABIA (Hebr.) Prophet, divination. It is the oldest and most respected of all the mystical phenomena. In the Bible this name is designated to the prophetic gift, which is rightly comprise among the spiritual powers, such as divination, clairvoyant visions, ecstasy and oracles. But just as charmers, sorcerers, fortune tellers, and even astrologers are rigorously condemned in the books of Moses, prophecy, extraordinary vision, and Nabia appear as special gifts from heaven. In primitive times, those who hold such gifts were called epoptai (seers), a Greek word meaning initiates. They were also given the name nebim "plural of Nebo, god of Wisdom in Babylon ". The Kabbalist makes a differentiation between the seer and the magician; one is passive, the other is active; ebirah is the one who looks to the future and the clairvoyant; nebi-poel is the one who possesses Magyar powers. We know that Elijah and Apollonius make use of to the same medium to isolate themselves from the disorganize influences of the outside world; that is, entirely wrapping his head with a woolen cloak, for being a poorly conductive matter of electricity, we must assume.

NECESSITY Being necessary or required: bread, safety, and other essentials of existence. The reality of being necessary or indispensable; rudimentary: the requisite of appropriate dwelling, a crucial condition or demand for products: the requisite for a speedy resolution. Necessity, in rationality and ideology, is an average dominion of an accurate proposal through which it is achievable for the project to be fallacious and of a false assurance with the help of which it is accessible for the forecast to be correct. The articulation beyond "necessary existence," an attribute with impartiality excessive merit than "existence." An essence that necessarily prevails has not comprehensively be reflected on not to subsist. And so, God, as the incomparable flawless reality, should possess necessary presence; and consequently, should prevail.

NECODEMUS. Flourished as a Pharisee and affiliate of the Sanhedrin referred to in three instances in the Gospel of John: Jn. He initially visits Jesus one night to debate Jesus' counseled. The next time Nicodemus is specified, he recollects his colleagues in the Sanhedrin that the law requires that a mortal be heard before being judged. He came to Jesus by night and evoked the discourse on Christian rebirth described in Jn. 3:1-15. He subsequently helped Joseh of Armathaea to give him burial (Jn. 19:39).

NEIGHBOR Each essence that resides on top of the earth is your neighbor. "My neighbor." Indeed, distance doesn't exist in Spirit nor in the completion of spiritual legislations. The law of divine love should bind up and heal wounds, through us liquify error, and restoring brightness and conglomerate from out of mayhem. "Neighbor" (Luke 10:25-37) call attention to the outward shape in which life displays, either, it can be your own physique, the anatomy of other individuals, or of creatures. To fasten the lacerations (Luke 10:25-34) is to pursue high and low to conserve the formations in whichever way of life illustrates Those who intend placing a grasp on eternity should do this. Everyone has existence, and immortality, but it does not enhance God's real life up until we become aware of this reality. Whoever sets foot towards eternity, as did Jesus, should hold on to that boundless and pull through one solely in the company of his form. This is the top secret of coming into "eternal life."

NEILOS (Greek) The Nile River; and it is also the name of a god.

NEITH, Niethes (Eg.) The Queen of Heaven, the Goddess Moon, in Egypt. It is known by several other names: Nout, Nepte, Nur, (For its symbolism, see: Nout. [Neith or neit is a goddess who is frequently delineate armed with a bow and arrows. The Greeks incorporate her to Minerva. He personified a paper for Hathor's. In fact, she has been called the "generative cow", or the "generating mother of the Sun".

NEMA (Sanskrit) Part, portion; epoch, period, limit; trickquery, fraud.

NEMEAN LION. It correlates to the initial labor of Hercules. It distinguishes the impact of impulse and unrestrained fervent that destroy and exhaust the total. Mythus apprised that this dreadful lion devastates the diminutive locality of Nemea and was insensitive since it advances against the Moon. His burrow had dual doorways and Hercules knocked one among them including a colossal boulder and penetrated fully the opposite to deliver him a blow. The lion was insensitive; however, the cosmic paladin executes gentleman with his powerful ammunition and him to Mycenae. Rumor has it that the aspect of the lion was so horrible that King Eurystheus was not competent verify to ascertain it and disguise himself in a chime hardware barrel below ground. Hercules forced the lion's immune dermis a body covering and utilized it as shield to safeguard the torso and rear.

NEMESIS (Greek) Among the early Greeks, Nemesis was not legitimately a goddess, but rather a moral perception, in Decharme's expression, a barrier opposed to evil and immorality; But, over time, this feeling was sublimated, and her manifestation became an always fatal and rigorous goddess. Nemesis is the righteous and impartial goddess who lays her wrath only on those whose brainpower is lost in pride, selfishness, and godlessness.

NEMESIUS OF EMESSA (fl. C. 390), Christian philosopher and Bp. of Emessa in Syria. His treatise 'On Human Nature' is an attempt to assemble on a mainly Platonic basis a doctrine of the soul agreeable with the Christian revelation.

NEO-Proselytes of Neo-Platonism An educational institution of ideology that appeared in the subsequent and third century of our epoch, and was instituted by Ammonius Saccas, of Alexandria. It is indistinguishable as that of Philalists and correspondence. They were besides given the title of genius and a few others. They were the Worshiper of the first centuries. Neo-Platonism is Platonic philosophy with the insertion of bliss, the divine raja-yoga.

NEO The designation is acquired from the Greek term "Neos," defined as; "new", "recent," "revived," or "modified." This tag's preference mirror Neo's generative expedition from a typical respective fear surrounding the restriction of the simulated actuality to an indicator of developed into a deliverance. Morpheus decided on Neo since he believes Neo feasible "The One." who have confounded them. Personality; an introvert. Neo is a silent gentleman, who ponders more than he declares. Neo is a worldwide additional vocabulary designed by Arturo Alfandari, a Belgian ambassador of Italian ancestry. It integrates characteristics of synthetic language, Ido technique, narrative, and Natural language. The rootstock foundation of Neo is fixedly associated to French, with a few impacts from English.

NEPA (Sanskrit) Family priest; director, spiritual guide.

NEPTUNE In Astrology, Neptune is the psychic planet of ideals, intuition, spirituality and empathy, the domain of dreams and delusions. Within birth chart, the influence of Neptune by the zodiac sign in which it falls, along with the astrological house it occupies. It is a planet that is distinctive by mercy and kindness. Those who ruled under the planet Neptune are always sweet, forgiving and compassionate. People who are heavily affected by Neptune often find freedom from the dictates of their ego. More than 30 times as far from the Sun as Earth, Neptune is the only planet in our solar system not visible to the naked eye and the first predicted by mathematics before its discovery. In 2011 Neptune completed its first 165-year orbit since its discovery in 1846.

NERGAL (Cald.) In Assyrian tablets he is described as the "giant king of war, lord of the city of Cutha". Nergal is also the Hebrew name for the planet Mars, without fail correlated with bad luck and danger. Nergal-Mars is the "bloodshed." In cabbalistic astrology it is less malefic than Saturn, but it is more active in its syndicate with men and its authority on them.

NEREIDAS, (Lat. Nereids, and of the gr. daughter of Nereus). Mythological legends tells that they are beautiful young women who live in the sea, daughters of Nereus and Doris. The most prominent were: Anfirite, wife of Neptune and Tethys mother of Achilles. When Castopea, mother of the beautiful Andromeda, exaggerated the beauty of her daughter. The injured Nereids begged Neptune to send a sea monster and destroy his kingdom except it was given to the beautiful (see Andromeda). The Nereids are together with the Undines, elementals of water.

NERI, PHILIP, St. (1515-95), One of the 'Apostle of Rome'. Proceeding to Rome in 1533, he dedicated himself to efforts of charity and spent nights in prayers in the catacombs; in 1544 he experienced an ecstasy which is estimated miraculously to have lengthened his heart. After ordination, he went in 1551 to reside in a community of priests at San Girolamo, where his confessional shortly enhanced the center of his apostolate. He also held spiritual meetings, out of which speeded the Congregation of the Oratory (see Oratorian). He was popular for his gentleness and cheerfulness.

NETZAH (Hebr.) Victoria, conservative, demure, genteel vehicle, stage, train: The Seventh of the Ten Sephiroth, an active male powerhouse.

NEW TESTAMENT. The Canonical Books agree solely to the Church, as transposed with those allowed the Old Testament, which the Church shares with Judaism. The Scriptures accommodates the four Gospels, Acts, the Pauline and 'Catholic' Epistles and Revelation.

NEUME. In plainsong, an widen group of notes sung to an implosive, or the sign used to indicate the melody.

NEUMENO In ideology, a noumenon (Ancient Greek; plural noumena) is an advance article or a consequence that have life separately of mortal sensation and/ or approach during a rainstorm, I discovered a spike of streak from my dormer. Conforming to fact, I recognized precise ability to see and resonate, which jointly precipitate the acceptance of a firebolt or "lighting"

NICEA A town, northwestern Turkey. It leans back on the eastern shore of Lake Iznik. The Green Mosque, Iznik, Turkey. Meetings at Nicaea in Present-day Turkey, the council settled the equality of the Father, the Son, and the Holy Spirit in the Holy Trinity and advocates that only the Son becomes incarnate as Jesus Christ. The Arian leaders were after banished from their churches for heresy. The admission that God was the source of sacred text became the most predominant criteria in accepting books into the Bible. Faith communities would go on to show added doctrine to help them recognize which books they would analyze scriptures. Eventually, the question was taken up by Church councils.

NICAEA, Second Council (of) (787) The 7th Ecumenical Board, called by Empress Irene to end the Iconoclastic Controversy. The Committee manifest its obedience to the doctrine on the veneration of images put forwards in a letter from Pope Hadrian I, adding that images are honored with a relative love (not the adoration due to God alone), the privilege given to the delineation passage on to its prototype.

NIDHI (Sanskrit) Treasure. The nine of the Gods Kuvera (the Vedic Satan), each of them is entrusted to the custody of a demon. Such treasures are personified and are as many other objects as possible of veneration among the Tantrikas, [Nidhi also implies ocean, collection, reunion. etc.]

NIGU (Sanskrit) Reasoning, intellect.

NIGHNA (Sanskrit) Submissive, docile, obedient.

NIKE The origin of name from Latin Berenice, from Macedonian Greek Berenike (classical Greek Pherenike), literally "bringer of victory," from pherein "to bring" (from PIE root "bher (1) "to carry"). Nike was the winged goddess of victory. Athletes who wanted to win worshipped her. Even today, she has some significance to athletes. Nike, in ancient Greek religion, the goddess of victory, daughter of the giant Pallas and of the infernal River Styx.

NILE. In prehistoric Egyptian native tongue, the Nile is christened H'pi (Hapy) or Iteru, meaning "river". A river in East Africa, the longest in the world, flowing North from Lake Victoria to the Mediterranean. The contours of the Nile River Valley remind one of a lotus flower, the primitive Egyptian description for the reclamation of life. The spread out, slender river valley is the axis, the basin that lays out in the formation of a trilogy is the pearl, and Fayum Region is the sprout. The nation of Egypt is called the "Gift of the Nile" as it is Egypt's salvation. In the absence of the Nile, Egypt would turn out to be a desert. Factually, the Nile has contributed water for the agriculture of season's growth in Egypt that escorted the way to the becoming more numerous of innumerable cultures throughout the river valley.

NILUS THE ASCETIC St. (d. C. 430) as well (erroneously) called 'Nilus of Sinai.' Conforming to customarily accounts, he was an idealistic officer in the Constantinopolitan court, who became a monk on Mt. Sinai. It materialized, nevertheless, that he was a native of Ancyra, that he studied at Constantinople, and that he then proved and became superior of a monastery near Ancyra. From here he supervised a large and powerful comparability. His documents deal mostly with ascetic and righteous subjects. His project of inner life was a 'Christian philosophy' showed on a 'moderated poverty'.

NIRVANA (Sanskrit) It is a disposition of ideal tranquility, repose and enjoyment, it has been paradise for the Hindustan. Pleasure collected by the immersion and unification of the personal toward the celestial substance; it is the cessation of the "I," as maintain by Buddhism. Gnostic: As previously indicated is a region of absolute contentedness, this surpasses Atman (the profound), in that respect, existence advances internally an everlasting instantaneous; perceptible a perpetual here and now. The settlers of Nirvana are immensely carefree, inhabitants are transcending superiority and wrongfulness. Others at Nirvanis with remainders: dwellers which still reside in the substantial sphere constituent of Ego (flaws), that hasn't yet disintegrated; and the Nirvanis minus remains, are these that have previously totally diffused the Ego, have zero subjective, have not departed in this planet several emotional accumulated are well skillfully expired. Nirvana is the celestial city of Jupiter, the habitat of the Elohim and the creator.

NIRVANI (Sanskrit) This expression illustrates: one who has attained an emancipated soul. Nirvanan defines nothing like the allegations of the Orientalists, as each learned person who has visited China, India, and Japan knows entirely well. It is the "liberation from the chains of suffering," but only from that matter, emancipation from Kleza, or Kama, and the total extinction of animal desires. If we are told that Adhidharma defines Nirvana as "a state of absolute annihilation", we agree on it, but affixing to the last word of the requirement "of everything that relates to the matter of the physical world", and this merely because that last (like each item contained in it) is pure illusion or Maya. Zakyamuni Buddha, in the last instants of his life, said that "the spiritual body is immortal." As interpret by the Synologistic scholar Mr. Eitel, "the popular exoteric systems agree in defining Nirvana negatively as a state of absolute exemption from the circle of transmigrations, a state that completes all forms of existence, beginning with that of all position and all effort; a state of indifference to all sensibilities", and I could have added: "of death of all compassion towards the world of suffering", and here is why the Boukisattwas who favored the Nirmanakaya garment to the Dharmakaya occupy a more eminent place in popular esteem than the Nirvanis. But the same author adds that: "Positively (and esoterically) Nirvana is defined as the supreme state of spiritual bliss, as absolute immortality through the absorption of the soul (of the Spirit, rather) in itself, but (preserving individuality, so that the Buddhas, for example, after entering Nirvana, can reappear on earth)", that is, in the future Manvantara.

NISSI (Cald.) One of the seven Chaldean gods.

NITI (Sanskrit) Prudence; ethics, morals. [Conduct in general; proceed; policy; rectitude, good conduct.]

NITRIAN DESERT. The region in Libya West of the Nile delta, honored as a focus of immediate Cristian monasticism.

NINFAS Elementals of water plants (F. Hartmann). Nymphs are subaltern divines, of which the entire universe is populated. The celestial (uranias), which dominated the sphere of heaven, and terrestrial (epigeas); the latter were separated into water nymphs, which were delegated by the names of oceanids or Nereids (sea nymphs), nayades (of the springs), potamids (of the rivers), etc., and nymphs of the earth, labeled; oreAdas (of the mountains), dryads and hamadryads (of the jungles), napeas (of the forests, etc.

NIORD or NIOERD (Scandinavian) One of the gods (asos) of Scandinavian folk stories. He was Freya's father, and he became the Neptune of Roman mythology.

NIXIES Spirits of the undine waters.

NOAH. (or 'Noe") Conforming to the story in Gen. 6-9, Noah and his family alone were saved in an arc of gopherwood, when the rest of humanity was dismantled in the Flood.

NOBIS QUOQUE PECCATORIBUS (Lat., 'To us sinners, also'). The aperture designation of one of the segments of the accepted Roman Canon of the Mass.

NOEL An additional expression for Christmas, the Christian holiday and the birth of the center figure of Christianity. An appellation manifesting the holiday season, Noel approaches us originating from Latin verb nasci, interpreting "to be born". In the wisdom literature, the birth of Jesus Natalis. A contrast, noel, made immediately into Old French as a citation to the Christmas time and later into West Saxon as Nowel. The first Noel was written by John Linton Gardner, CBE was an English composer of classical music.

NOETARKA By means of this pseudonym, the eclectic philosophers of Alexandria nominated the first principle.

NOOM To precipitate something, to explode violently, principally orders of vastness higher than calculated. The Parthenon (in Athens Greece) was demolished by the Venetians in 1687 after unpredictable mortar explored a large ammo dump the Ottomans had stockpile inside. The explosion developed was much more substantial than the mortar projectile itself, so unquestionably the Venetians 'Noomed' the Parthenon.

NONNUS OF PANOPOLIS (c. 400). The probable author of two Greek verses. The remaining part of one of them, a "Paraphrase on the Fourth Gospel", gives some light on the Biblical text.

NOSCETEIPSUM The old-fashion Greek aphorism "know thyself" is the first of three Delphic maxims engraved in the forecourt of the Temple of Apollo at Delphi as claimed by the Greek writer Pausanias. The two proverbs that follow "know thyself" were "nothing to excess" and "certainty brings insanity".

NOUTER-kher (Neter-xer) (Egip.) "Divine region inferior", hieroglyphic fraternity of the mansion of souls. With this pronouncement, the necropolis was also nominated.

NOTE (Lat. note). Instinctive music is any of the signs that are used to measure sounds.

NOTRE DAME, PARIS The cathedral house of God of Paris. Built in the early French Gothic technique, it was set about in 1163 and sanctified in 1182. The west forefront was built in 1200-20.

NOUM o KHNOUM (Gr.) Nouf, in Egyptian. A distinct aspect of Ammon and the manifestation of its generating power in actu, as Kneph is of selfsame in potential. It also has a ram's head. If in his aspect as Kneph he is the Holy Spirit with the creative ideation that incubates in him, how Chnoufis is the angel who "roots" in the ground and the flesh of the Virgin. A prayer written on papyrus, interpreted by the French Egyptologist Chabas, says: "!Oh Sepui, cause of existence, that you have formed your own body! Oh Unique Man from Noum! !Oh substance that is in it! Or God, who has made his own father and inspired his own mother!" This shows the origin of the critical doctrines of the triology and unstained creation. He is seen in a monument, sitting next to a potter's wheel and forming men of clay. The fig leaf is consecrated to him, which is enough to prove that Chnoufis is a constituent god idea that is expressed by the inscription: "He who made what is, the creator of beings, the first-timest, the one who made all that exists". Some see it in the incarnation of Ammon-Ra, but it is this same in its decline aspect, since, like Ammon, it is 'partner of his creator', that is, the resolute or amiable part of Nature. It has several names, such as Cnoufis, Noum, Khem, and Khnum or Chnouomis. Whatever he represents the Demiurge (or Logos) from the material or inferior point of view of the souls of the world, is the Agathodaemon, sometimes symbolized by a serpent; and his wife Athor or Maut (mot, Mother), or Sate, "daughter of the sun", carrying an arrow in a ray of the Sun (the ray of conception), extends "Lady in the lower parts of the atmosphere", under the constellations, as Neith extends through the starry heavens.

NOUT (Gr.) In the Egyptian pantheon, this vocable signified the "One-only-One", since in their popular or exotic religion, the Egyptians did not go back above the third phenomenon that comes from the Unrevealed and Unknowable, the first no demonstrated Logos and the second Logos in the esoteric philosophy of all nations. The Nous the Anaxagoras was of the Indians, Brahma, the first Divinity indicated, "The Mind or the Spirit itself potent", and thus, consequently, this inventive Principle is the Primum mobile of everything that exists in the Universe: its Soul and reflection. (See the seven foundations of man.") [The Egyptian goddess Nout personifies the celestial Space, but largely the vault of the sky, in the form of a horned death on the earth. It is called "Mother of the Gods", painted on the lid of the fernet, lengthen above the mummy to which it keeps safe. On a Papyrus in the Louvre, he says to the deceased: "Your mother Nout has accepted you in peace. She puts her arms behind your head every day; I protected you inside the sarcophagus; keeps you in the funeral mountain; extends its guard over your flesh; watch over life and all integrity of health." This goddess is also defined in a sycamore atonement soul the celestial water that reestablished them. To better establish your description with Hathor. It is occasionally painted with cow's know-how.

NOVENA. In the Church of Rome, a span of nine days' individual or communal devotion, by which it is wish for to acquire some unique grace.

NUAH (Cald.) The Chaldean Noah, who "floats on the waters" in his ark. Allegory of the Spirit descending into Matter, and once incarcerate in it, he is as intoxicated. Under an additional aspect, Nuah is the "universal Mother" (the feminine Noah, contemplated as one with her ark).

NUAYA Etymology of word Nuaya is a Sanskrit word which means justice, identity for all beings, especially a collection of general or universal rules. In some contexts, it measures model, axiom, plan, legal activities, judicial sentence, or judgment. The resolutions of Nyaya: an orthodox philosophical system in Hinduism dealing essentially with logic and epistemological analysis.

NUCLEUS. The emphatically reinforced intermediate area of a molecule complements a distinctive Atom and (for all fragments excluding chemical element) a distinct neutrino accommodating almost of most of the snippet. Micah 4:7 "I will transform he lame into the nucleus of a new nation, and those far off into a mighty nation. The Lord will reign over them on Mount Zion, from that day forward and forevermore."

NUIT The Egyptian sky goddess, born of Shu, God of air, and Tefnut, goddess of water and fertility. It also signifies night or dark(ness), is pronounced "nwee", It is a frequently used French dynamic abstract that most often describes that part of the day, when it's dark, but it's quite common, too, to hear it used allegorical, as an image of object dark or fearsome. It is symbolized by a sphere whose circumference is nowhere and whose center is everywhere, although Hadit is the infinitely small point at the center of this sphere. She is also a goddess in Thelema, the speaker in the first segment of The Book of the Law, the sacred text written or accepted in 1904 by Aleister Crowley.

NUMBERS (Book of) The capacity of this Old Testament age in the desert. Its English subject is explained by its two authentication of a demographics (1-4 and 26).

NUMINOUS. An expression coined by R. Otto to designate the elements of a non-rational and amoral kind in what is knowledge in religion as the 'holy' Numinous is held to incorporate feelings of awe and degradation as well as an element of religious fascination.

NUNC DIMITTIS The lyrics of Simeon (Lk. 2: 29-32), subtitle coming from its initiate phrase in the Vulgate genre. In the Easterly. It is articulated at Vespers; in the Roman and bountiful other Occident Compendium its commitment is administered at condemned, from which location it departed within Evensong of the BCP.

NUN A constituent of a religious institution or congregation of women succeeding a lifestyle pledge of poverty, chastity and obedience. Reverend Mother; abbess, a female person who is a fellow member of an association or diligence union or another group.

NUNTIUS (Lat.) The "Sun-Wolf", one of the denominations of the planet Mercury. It is the complement of the sun, Solariss luminis particeps [partake in sunlight]

NYADA (Sanskrit) Food.

NYAYA-darzana. A member of the six Darzanas, philosophic systems or schools of India; a organization of Indian logic founded by the Richi Gautama. [This system is also called dialectic folklore of Gotama (or Gautama). As its name suggests (property, convenience), the Nayya arrangement is the applicable method to reach a conclusion through logical analysis. According to this network, when by virtue of just and upright reasoning, man has withdrawn from false knowledge, he attains liberation.

NYIMA (Tibet.) The same as Alaya, "the Soul of the World"; also labeled Tsang.

NYMPH Have been contemplated a symbol of beauty and femininity. This is illuminated by the number of gods and men that fall in love with them on sight or have love affairs with them, including Odysseus (pronounced oh-dis-ee-uhs) and Orpheus. Nymph potential depends on what aspect of nature they control, nevertheless, they each could transfigure and manipulate the part of nature that they control. They also have extra powers determined by the species. Nymphal (Nymphs) were female spirits of the natural world; minor goddesses of the forests, rivers, springs, meadows, mountains and seas.

-O-

OATH. Several Christian bodies, e.g., the Baptists and Quakers, clarified Mt. 5: 33-7 as forbidding all oaths, but the general Christian doctrines is that an oath, though not desirable, is permissible for reason of serious requisites. It must be perturbation only with what one knows to be true. Its object must be ethically good, and to be reasonable it must be taken with the intention to swear.

OANNES [or Oes] (Gr.) Mosasaurus Oannes, the Aneddotus, known in the Chaldean "legends" transmitted by Berosus and other ancient writers under the name of Dag or Dagon, the "fish man", Oannes benefitted himself to the early Babylonians as a reformer and instructor. Ascending from the Eritrean Sea, he brought to them advancement, letters and sciences, laws, astronomy and religion, and enlighten them agriculture, geography and the arts in general. There were Annedotos who show up succeeding him, in number of five (note that our race is the fifth), "all of them as Oanes as far as form is concerned and who taught the same", but Musarus Oannes was the initial to emerge, this transpire while the ruling of Ammen Non, third of the ten prehistoric monarch whose kingdom concluded with Xisuthrus, the Chaldean Noah. Oannes was "an animal endowed with reason; and whose body was that of a fish, but which had a human head under that of the fish, with feet also underneath., similar to those of man, next to the tail of the fish, and whose voice and language were also articulate and human." (Polyhistor and Apollodorus). This supplies the clue to the metaphor. He appoints Oannes as a man and a "priest," an Initiate. Layard display, long ago (see Nineveh), that the "fish head, and which in a very little alter form we see even this day at the dome of the significant lamas and bishops of the Roman tabernacle, Osiris be dressed in an alike Mitre. The hindmost part of the fish is clearly the tail of a long-stretched mantle, as painted on some Assyrian panel; whose configurations we see duplicated in the golden pastoral outfit worn by contemporary Greek clergy in the time devout observance. Oannes' allegories are expansive, for instance those of the "Dragon" and the "Serpent Kings"; the Nagas, who advised humankind in wisdom beside the lakes and rivers, then end up transforming to the good Law and Arhats arrive. The meaning of this is clear. The "fish" is a very suggestive symbol in the language of the Mystery, as is the "water". Ea or Hea was the god of the sea and of Wisdom, and the serpent of the sea was one of his representations, therefore his priests were "Serpents" or Initiates. So, one sees as a result earthly comprise Oannes and the other Annedotos in the category of those former "adepts" who were called "Water Dragons," or "sailors," that is, Nagas. Water identifies its human dawning (since it is a image of earth and affair and Purificacion), opposed to the "Nagas of fire", that is, the immaterial beings spirituals, either celestial Bodhisattwas or Dhyanis plantaris, also considered as instructors of humanity. The secret significance becomes clear to the occultist once it is indicated to him that "this being (Oannes) used to spend the day neither one among men teaching; When the sun collected its sunset, the sea withdrew once more, expenditure the night at the base of the waters "because it was danfibio", that is, it associate to the two planes: the spiritual and the physical; Already the Greek term amphibios (from amphi, from amphi, in both parts, and bios, life), directly method "life on two planes". That expression was implemented to Mendo, in prehistorical times, to those men who, even if they every time gather a human form, had convert nearly divine by their ability, and reside so much in the desert as in the metaphysical spiritual locality. Oannea is complex imitated in Jonas and featureless John the Precursor, both connected to the Fish and water.

OB (Hebr.) The Stellular Illuminations, or rather, it's inferior steady flow harm; it was manifested by the Jews as un-Spirit, the Spirit of Ob. Between them, all those who engage with spirits and focused on with necromancy, were stated to be enchanted of the Spirit of Ob. (Ob. He is the emissary of death utilized by sorcerers, the baleful evil fluid.

OBADIAH, (Book of) Minor Prophet and the microscale publication in the OT. It predicts the compensation of the Edomites on the impending Day of the Lord. Most modern scholars divide it into several sections which are differently dated from the 9th to the 5th century. A.C.

OBJECT Specifically a tangible artifact which is distinguishable and touched. A human or gadget to which a designated action or feeling is directed. The Phoenix is conceivably one of the most popular symbols of power. It is a legendary bird that bursts into flames and dies, only to be reborn from the ashes of the fire that absorbed it. The sunflower has a constitution which holds many positive alliances, counting warmth and happiness. Universal symbols of kindness include the heart sign, the hug emoji, and bluebell flowers. The Heart Sign. Acknowledged since ancient times, the heart shape has long been in use in unlike cultures all over the world.

OBSESSION One will find assorted commodities that appear for obsessions: anxiety concerning viruses, terror of infections, diseases, or injuries; for other individuals; a preoccupation with having gadgets all over them arranged in a certain way, intruding intimation or threatening depictions, incredible rational, or envisioning acceptance of their perception of misbehavior towards other people. There are also obsessions investigated as psyche obsessions, which is a high-tech expression inside of the parapsychological ideology and procedures described by Allan Kardec as the involvement of gaining control of an inner self with an undermined essence. In accord with the scriptures: 1 Corinthians 6:12 ESV "All things are lawful for me", but not all things are helpful. "All things are lawful for me," but I will not be dominated by anything."

OCCASION A distinct event or the timetable at which something takes hold of situation, principally as noticeable by positive conditions or incidents: They encounter on third instance, a particular or crucial program, eventuality, function, bash, etc. His convocation will be exceptionally and devotion. "Your life is an "occasion" conceivable interpret as "a favorable opportunity or circumstance." Although about directed to ascent occurrence, impression is to catch that approving golden opportunity and to discover starting with, achieving essentially. Occasion is exclusive appearance particularly frequently conclude individuality accomplished distinguished circumstance. Adventure is reduced marked that occasion. For instance, commemoration is an occasion, but not an affair. Samuel-1 10:7 "And let it be, when these signs are come unto thee, [that] thou do as occasion serve with three."

OCEAN(S) The sea has two major responsibilities in Greek folk stories. It relates to the voyage to Hades, and as the earliest water, Oceanus, it constitutes vital quinquagenarian and even eternal life. Until now, intellectuals have glimpsed these two aspects as essential resistance. The calm ocean and seas are considered honest to tranquil human sentiments similarly to fondness and confidence. It receded and circulated like undercurrents to the seaside. We delighted in instances of cloudless tranquilness we ourselves have levitated onwards consistently besides each other. Passed time covered in one another cuddled equally authorized moments pass over and matter of fact relinquished jointly.

OCCULTISM (MYSTIC), Dogma or science that studies all the confidential and mysteries of nature and the expansions of the psychic powers latent in man. Gnosis describes that we must transform between authentic Esotericism and Occultism, from Pseudo-Esotericism and Pseudo-Occultism, the latter schools do not lead to interior Self-actualization.

OCTOECHOS A celebratory book in the Eastwardly Church that comprehends the adaptable parts of the indulgence from the initial Sunday following Whitsun till the tenth Sunday prior to Easter.

OCTOTEUCH. The first 8 books of the Old Testament.

OD. (Greek) Ody, magnetic fluid, active positive force directed by will.

ODES of SOLOMON. This 'falsified' work gives accommodation to 42 short hymns of a lyrical character. They may be Christian accomplishments of a Jewish work but are more probably wholly Christians in origin. If Christian, they were nearly definitely written in Syria or Palestine in the 1st or 2nd cent. A.D. It is analyzed whether their native language was Syriac or Greek.

ODIUM THEOLOGICUM (Latin 'theological hatred'). A proverbial utterance for the ill-feeling to which doctrinal antagonism often allows rise.

ODYSSEY Pertain to a long and event-filled adventurous journey or encounter. The Odyssey is one of two crucial ancient Greek epic poems connected to Homer. It is one of the oldest extant works of literature still extensively read by modern audiences. As with the Iliad, the poem is split up into 24 books. It follows the Greek hero Odysseus, King of Ithaca, and his expedition home after the Trojan war.

ODRE (Lat. utre, Otris). Usually goat leather, which is sewn and glued all around except for the one coincided to the neck of the animal, is used to store wine or oil. Jesus the Christ quotes him in the Bible in one of his parabolas: "for new wine new wineskins are needed." It is associated with the mind, the adjusted way of thinking.

ODO, St. (879-942) Imminently succeeding Abbot of Cluny. He set foot in the cloister of Baume in 909, where he was soon in trustworthy of the monastic school. He replaced St. Berno, as Abbot of Cluny in 927; was considered to have raised the monastery to the prominent position which it held in the next centuries. The monastic church was finalized during his abbacy and the prevalence of Cluny over other monasteries was very much lengthened. ODO, St. (d. 959) Abp. of

Canterbury from 942. He aforesaid to have been the son of a Dane and initially a pagan. He was active in replacing the cathedral establishing and raising the morals and discipline of his conclave.

OEDIPUS According to Greek tradition he was the son of Laius and Yocasta, kings of Thebes. He was questioning the decisions of fate. Laius had been informed by an Oracle that the son born to him of Yocasta would be disastrous for him. To evade such a fate, as soon as the child Oedipus was born, Laius (his father) directed that he be killed, however, the hitman who was recommended to kill him, was resolved to leave him careless in a forest with his feet pierced and dangling from a tree. It is related that a shepherd came across him and took him to King Corinth, who adopted him as a son. Lately when he was already a strong young man, he consulted the oracle and it predicted the following: "Oedipus will be the murderer of his father, the husband of his mother and from him a cursed race will be born."

OFFA (d. 796) King of the Mercians from 757. He progressively secured supremacy, at any rate straight or as ruler, of the entire of England south of the Humber. He reinforced the Tabernacle, was a benevolent philanthropist of cloisters, and is the proclaimed originator of the monasteries of St. Albans and Bath.

OFFEND Bring around judgment to anyone who becomes trouble or to harm the reactions of anybody, particularly by being impolite or manifesting an absence of consideration: She was probably offended since she wasn't invited to the picnic; indignant or irritated, frequently since recognized offense. The bible debates offending: to disregard rules the virtuous or principle: wrongdoing granted violation; transgressions to desire glory, "I am the most offending soul alive"; William Shakespeare to infringe a regulation or ruling misconduct, offend in opposition to the principles.

OFIS-CHRISTOS [Ophis-Christos, in Greek.] The Christ-serpent of the Gnostics.

OGAM or OGHAM (Celt.) Mystifying Vernacular of the antique Raas Centas, utilized by the Druids. One of the structures of this speech consists in the union of the leaves of definite trees with the characters. This was designated the name Beth-luis-nion-Ogham, and to configurate words and phrases the leaves were stretched in the proper arrangement on a thread. Godfrey Higgins designates that to fulfill the confusion was intervene between these sheets additional which meant nothing. [Alphabet o emblems, or rather magical, that the primeval mystics were employed for some incantations of whom musical character cannot be unresolved, from said terminus derives possibly the musical vowels Gama, gamma or gamut of the English.

OGYGIA (Gr.) Ancient immersed island, known as calypso island, and recognized by part of with Atlantis. The indicated is accurate in a sense, however, what section of Atlantis would be elected, already the ensuing was a mainland, as a substitute of a "huge" island?

OGUARA (Gnostic) Adept who is committed in the states of Jinas. Through prayers and centralizing in Oguara, it is said; that it is possible to reach the state of Jinas.

OIL(S) (freemasonry) Illustrates knowledge and objectivity, in ancient times were sacramental with oil to affiliates who already had the degree of Master or Hierophant. A mixture of olive oil and balsam used in the ritual of th Greek and Latin Churches. It may be consecrated only by a bishop; in the East by the Patriarchs alone. According to present Latin usage, chrism is consecrated in Maundy. Thursday, since1955 at a special Mass of the Chrism. It is used in the sacraments of Baptism. Confirmation, and Holy Orders, as well as in the dedication of churches and altars. Anointing with oils is done by bishop or priest e.g., at a Coronation of Monarch; at church sacraments: Baptisms and Confirmations, but its most common applied to the Sacrament of anointing of the Sick, long known as Extreme Unction. The anointing of the sick is mentioned in Mk. 6:13 and Jas. 5: 14 f.

OKAS (Sanskrit) House, dwelling, shelter; usage, custom; resting place; well-being, comfort, gift, pleasure.

OKAYS. OK (writing system discrepancy incorporates okay, O.K; and ok) is an English word (originally American English) writing down approval, acceptance, agreement, assent, acknowledgment, or a sign of indifference. OK is customarily used as a borrowed expression in other dialects. Certain individuals say okey-dokey or okey-doke. These utterances were first used in the 1930s. Currently, a role on the American TV series, "The Simpsons", says it is a distinct process. He says okely-dokely. Okie-dokie is a variation of OK, which has an interesting story all its acceptance. A clause like "okie-dokie" can sound meaningless to somebody foreign with English. However, in a mother tongue's comprehensive technique to appoint existing upper-level or continuous. OK and its successor are exceedingly well known and powerful.

OLIBANUM. (Arabic: luban) Antiquated utilized for at least 4,000 generations and is a cherished incense resin. Olibanum is the representative incense; its aroma is what we call 'incense-like'. Olibanum resins were employed in the olden days in balm, cosmetics and fragrance. In Central Europe it is largely accepted through the suffice by the Church of Rome. Olibanum oil is a necessary oil. It's separate from resinous oils from trees of the Boswellia genus. Oil from these trees is also called frankincense oil. Frankincense is a more familiar label in the West, experienced in the East near its domestic locality, olibanum is a separate prevailing denomination. Currently, Elemi is used as Olibanum alternate in incense and as raw perceptible in the assembly of exclusive oil varnished, soaps and paints. appropriate in ascetical and resolutions observance for millenary of years, frankincense is a representation of sanctity and virtuous. Since it is so fragrant when burnt, it was used by ancient people as a religious offering. In Christian parable, frankincense can identify Christ's atonement.

OLD LATIN VERSION, The. The Latin version of the Scriptures was in use in the Church before they were supplanted by the Vulgate. The existence of Latin translations of the Bible in S. Gaul and N. Africa is attested before the end of the 2nd century. The properties of the Old Latin vary among themselves, and it was mainly the desire to remedy the disturbances arising from such divergences that led St. Jerome to undertake the Vulgate.

OLD TESTAMENT. The assemblage of Canonical Books which the Church rationed with Judaism. Like the NT, the OT Books are considered as encouraged in the Church, which from the time of Marcion has safeguarded them in case of censorship.

OLIVE, Mount of. The imposing impales in the distinctiveness of hills E. of Jerusalem. It come to light that Christ preceded there. The entrenched locality of the Ascension was articulated by a church conscious as the "Embalming' preceding to 378. supplementary 4th centennial sanctuary. The 'Eleona', was compounded over the grotto where Christ was recognized to have conversations on the Last activities (Mk. 13).

OLIVES. Compact egg-shaped berry with a firm pit and acid meat, greenish when not ripe and copper dusky when mature, utilized as nourishment and as an Olea Europaea olive oil. The abundantly horticulture spruce tree that submit the green olives, indigenous to summery locations of the charming nature. In the Holy Scriptures the olive tree is considered a symbol of peace. It is initially introduced in Bible when the pigeon reappeared to Noah's ark bringing an olive twig in its bill (Gen. 8:11). From then on, the olive limb has been an emblem of "peace" to the universe, and we frequently discern the declare, "extending an olive branch" to an additional facade a enthusiasm for peace. It is an image of affection and reconcilement, decontamination and alleviation, illumination, triumph and affluence and, most important, a manifestation of peace. It is a shrub which ought to be attended to with great respect as it influences numerous seraph contributions.

OLYMPUS (Gr.) Mountaintop of Greece, that, in accordance with Homer and Hesiod, was the dwelling of the gods. [Over time, Olympus was viewed as the same paradise or kingdom.]

OLLE-LAPRUNE, LEON (1839-98), French thinker. He emphasized the limits of an essentially intellectual approach to the affairs of philosophy and highlighted the part enacted by the determination and heart in cognition.

OMM-Alketab (Arab.) Table or book of decrees in indelible dispositions the destiny of all men.

OMANVANT (Sanskrit) Friendly, benevolent, propitious, favorable.

OMEGA & ALPHA Speas of the last letters of the Hellenic Greek alphabet, close to acting as bookends to the series of letters. Subsequently, the phrase Alpha and Omega has come to designate the origination and the conclusion. Nevertheless, more clearly, this phrase is used to impersonate God.

OMKARA (Sanskrit) [Literally: The command OM"] The same as OM or AUM. Further, the name of the twelve lingams, which was characterized by a secret and sacred tabernacle of Ujjain, which has not remained since the time of Buddhism.

OMPHIS (Egypt.) The epithet of Osiris measures: "benefactor", very applicable qualification to the star of the day, of which said divinity was impression.

OMAR, MOSQUE OF, (DOME OF THE ROCK), The. The Muslim Shrine in Jerusalem, constructed throughout the Jewish Temple. It dates from c. 800. The rock from whatever it takes its name is comprehended in Islam to be particularly from which Muhammad raised to paradise, and by Jews to bring to light that on that Abraham arranged to sacrifice Isaac. The Sanctuary is as well-known as the 'Mosque of Omar'.

OMNISCIENCE (lat. Omnis, everything and sciestia, dementia), Comprehension of all things real and possible, absolute attribute of God. Knowledge of many sciences and subjects. Only the calm heart can extend Enlightenment and Omniscience, which is accomplished if one has learned to live between the absolute and the relative, at intervals between the mutable and the immutable. Those who have passed exceeding the illuminating void and relativity of life, they contact that which is called Tality and accepted the gift of Omniscience.

ONESIMUS (Greek: transit Onesimos, meaning "useful"; die c. 68 AD, Conforming to Catholic tradition), also called Onesimus of Byzantium and a The Holy Apostle Onesimus in the Eastern Orthodox Church, was apparently a slave to Philemon of Colossae, a man of Christian faith. St. Paul sent Onesimus back to Philemon following conference with him; Onesimus converted to a Christian believer. An fondness grew between them, and Paul would have been glad to keep Onesimus with him. Nevertheless, he reflected it better to dispatch him back to Philemon with an affixed letter, which directed to result conciliation in the middle of them as Christian's brother The Phrygian bondslave on whose behalf St. Paul wrote his Epistle to 'Philemon's.

ONIROSOFO The One Who Interprets Dreams [See Onyrocritic].

ONION. The term 'onion' approach from the Latin 'uniothat', defines harmony or integration, since an onion, like a union, is dismantled as it is imperceptibly separated. The primordial Egyptians reverenced onions and accepted that their coextensive loops suggest eternity, directly burying many pharaohs with onions. Previously, we concluded how to create them is not as severe comprehensively. It's essential to understand what causes onions to be so potent. The times that you cut into an onion, an enormous scent assumes, and your eyes immediately begin to well up. That's not since this is a especially despicable legume; it's all in recognition of sulfur. Onions enclose a soaring numeral of lactobacillus and fibred. In shape, this compensates cultivating gut microbiome by assisting in absorption, building up impunity, and decreasing discomfort.

ORACLE (Lat. oraculum). Acknowledgement designated by God, by himself or by his mysteries. Answer that the Pythonesses and clergyman of antiquity marked as reply of the Gods to the Gentiles or to those who deliberated them. The most prominent oracles were the Zeus (Jupiter), in Dodona (Epirus and different in Ammon in Libya, the latter is approximate about 1,400 years to J.C. that of Apollo in Decima and Delphi (earliest doubt of Fodda), in this was the omphalos (navel-sacred stone, which comprise in the stone called betite). Sibylline Oracles. A collection of oracles imitating the pagan "Sibylline Books", The oracles, written in hexameters, are pave the way for a prose prologue assert that they are utterances of Greek Sibyls of numerous periods. Their genuineness was welcome by many of the Fathers, who drew from those disagreement in defense of Christianly. Modern critics allocated them to Jewish and Christian authors; for, however, genuine Greek oracles are in some places, the disposition of the whole is monotheistic and Messianic. The dates of the Jewish section range from the Maccabean period to the time of the Emp. Hadrian (117-38); the Christian incorporation seem to date from the 2nd century onwards.

ORAI (Gr.) Designation of the ruling Angel of Venus, to the Egyptian Gnostics.

ORATIO (Latin In liturgy symbology, a prayer, largely a collect; in the plural, post-communion prayers corresponding in number to the collects. Lord's Prayer, also called Our Father, Latin Oratio Dominica Dor Pater Noster, Christian prayer that, in with tradition, was taught by Jesus to his disciples).

ORATORIO The expression, used in former times of both churches and private chapels, has come to be restricted to places of worship other than the parish church. RC canon law discerns between public, semi-public, and private oratories, and describes what may be done in each. The location of oratories in the Cof E is controlled by the Private Chapels Act (1871)

ORDERING. Decree, appoint, so ordered by the divinities: to mandate to go or move closer to a described position; ordered back to the base. Transcendent, also labeled Spiritual Franciscan, constituent of an utmost classification internally the Franciscans a mendicant devout system established by St. Francis of Assisi in 1209; the Devotional rigidly accepted the excessive sternness and privation ethical in the original Rule of St. Francis canon, law, ordinance, precept, regulation and statute. We begin with Psalm 37:23, "The steps of a good man are ordered by the Lord: and he delighted in his way". "Before we begin, I want to acknowledge that the Bible stats" ... there is none good but one, that is God" (Mark 10:18).

ORGANISM Functioning matter made up of one or more cells and free to carry on the activities of life (such as using energy, growing or reproducing) organisms. The interpretation of an organism is a creature such as a plant, animal or a single-celled life form, or object that has interdependent parts and that is being measured to a living creature. An example of an organism is a dog, person or bacteria. The holy scriptures Genesis 1:21 "God created the great sea monsters and every living creature that moves, with which the waters swarmed after their kind, and every winged bird after its kind; and God saw that it was good."

ORIENTATION Certain ordinance that go back, it is believed, to the very origination of the Christian Church and were installed in the Apostolic Constitutions, Recommended that the churches were organized in such a way that the door focuses to the west and that the acceptance presented its convexity to the east; so, the faithful, in praying, had their faces turned to the east. This rule was revoked from the first centuries and, as has been said, to protected at least the spirit of antique use, in the Churches oriented in reverse had positioned the altar so that the celebrant had his face turned in relation to the people, and as a result, towards the east.

ORIFIEL Logos Orifiel and the planet Saturn. Saturn is the second most sizeable planet in the Solar System, at the back of Jupiter. Both belong to the group of gas giants, so they have similar characteristics. The planet comprises principally of hydrogen and helium, in augmentation to a possibly rocky core. Its journey around the Sun lasts 29.5 years. The Planet Saturn is control by the Original Logos and has the succeeding details and essential qualities:

ORIGEN Pertaining to Alexandria, one of the significant for composing the seminal work of Christian Neoplatonism, his treatise On First Principles. Origen theorized that souls feel varying separations, some to be angels, several descending into human bodies, and the most wicked becoming devils. (Origen accepted in the preexistence of souls, but not in transmigration nor in the unification of rational souls in animal bodies.)

ORIGINAL Indo coming out of India or Hindustan. This term is more imposed on Indian natives who practice Brahmanism, in opposition to the Mohammedans. Indus is also the name of a river that arises in the northern Himalayas in western Tibet, drains into the Arabian Gulf, after which it runs through part of Tibet and India.

ORION (Gr.) The identical to Atlas, who clasp the world on his shoulders.

ORISON A prayer or plea to a deity. You might make an Orison if you wanted your sick mom to get better. Some words are contemplated archaic; defines they are not in common modern use. Such a word is "orison", which implies prayer.

ORGELMIR (Scandinavian) Precisely: "boiling mud". The same as Ymir, the giant; being erratic, untamed, turbulent; design of primordial matter, and of whose body, after Bor they created a new earth. Orgel Mir is also the cause of the Flood in the Scandinavian Songs, for having thrown his body into the Ginnungagap, the open abyss, which, having been filled with it, the blood rebozo procedure a great flood, in which all the Hrimthurses drowned, was saved conjointly with his wife in a boat, and convert the father of a new race of giants: "And there were giants on earth in those days."

ORGY A wild party distinguished by unrestrained drinking and undiscriminating sexual activity. There secret rites used in the worship of Bacchus, Dionysus, and other Greek and Roman deities commemorated with dancing, drunkenness, and singing.

OROSIUS, St. (d.c. 380), Unemotional and minister of Tabenne (an island in the Nile). He was a friend and a follower of Pachomius. He wrote a 'Doctrina de Institutione Monachorum' (prob. In Coptic), which remains alive in Latin translation.

OROSIUS (5th century). Paulus Orosius, historian. Migrating to Africa in 414, he was sent by St. Augustine to Palestine to enlist the reinforce of St. Jerome in the fight against Pelagianism. His history Adversus Paganos ambushed the pagan objections that Rome's troubles were due to her neglects of her gods; only after A.D. 378 is it of historical value.

OPIO A substance accomplished by drying the juice from the heads of green opium poppies; It has, among others, analgesic, hypnotic and narcotic possessions and its utilization can cause dependence. The opium poppy, like an ordinary poppy, is a plant that can grow one and a half meters. Its white, violet or fuchsia flowers stand out. It is an annual plant that can begin its cycle in autumn, regardless of the usual in the northern hemisphere is from January. Florence between April and June based on the latitude, height and variety of the plant, at which time you can advance to the collection of opium.

OPHIS, Ophiomorios, Ophites, etc. Ofis (Ophis, in Greek). The same as Chnufis or Knef, the Logos; the serpent-God or Agathodaemon. [Ophis is also divine Wisdom or Christos].

OPHITES and NAASSENES "Gnostic sect who devoted to special predominant to the serpent". In some cases, the serpent was venerated, in others conceived as a hostile power.

OPHIOLATRY From ophio- +-latry, from Ancient Greek (Ophism, "snake") and (latreia, "worship"). The adoration of or acknowledgement of divine or sacred description to snakes.

OPUS (EX OPERE OPERATO) A turn of phrase used by theologians to convey the permanently objective mode of operation of the Sacraments, and its independence of the subjective of way of looking at things of either the minister or the recipient.

OSTRACA Written work in Egyptian, Coptic or Greek script are appointed by this name, traced in particles of clay vessels, pebbles or pieces of stone, when the papyrus had a very high price.

OSIRIS Isis (Eg.) Dual logos; the great Father-Mother. Cryptic, the Sun and the Earth. He personifies Fire and Water metaphysically, and the Sun and Nile palpably (Secret Doctrine, II 616). It is the masculine-feminine principle, the germinal assumption in all forms.

OSIER A compact Eurasian willow which grows mostly in wet habitats. It is customarily coppiced, being a major source of the long flexible shoots (withies) used in basketwork.

OSOR-Apis. The denomination of Apis dead, that is, turned into an Osiris (or deceased). Starting with that name the Greeks have made Serapis.

OUDJA (Eg.) Figurative or sacred eye, the two oudjas are the two eyes of the sun, habitually incorporated by Shou and Tewnout. Pursuant to the system of M. Grebaut (Hymn to Ammon-Ra), the sun in its form east to west, looks with one of its eyes to the north, and with the other to the south, the rationale why the two regions of Egypt and the two sectors of the sky are designated oudjas. The two wings of the disc are often replaced by two eyes. The two oudjas also include the sun and the moon. The word oudja means "health" "well-being".

OUTA (Eg.) The eye symbol of Horus.

OUAS (Gr.) Hieroglyphic epithet of the scepter carried in the hand by certain gods; it ends in a hound's head with its ears down, assumed image of motionlessness.

OULOM u OULAM (Heb.) This word does not indicate "eternity" or infinite duration, as it is translated in the texts, but clearly a vast period, whose origination and end cannot be known. [The word "eternity, properly speaking, does not exist in the Hebrew language with the meaning applied by the Vedantines to Parabrahman, for example. Secret Doctrine].

OVE Creator godhead of what exists, on the authority of Polynesian mythology.

OVEN (Latin fomus) A factory for heating, vaulted and offered with a vent or chimney and one or more mouths through which what is to be exposed to fire is introduced. It means the melting pot of the alchemist. It is connected to the physical body and the still is the Vasco Hermeticism (the hermetic vessel) just as the stove is a sex symbol).

OVISARA. The supreme being as maintain by to African mythology and that is all goodness.

OWL A restrained, bird of prey with huge eyes, a facial disc, a hooked beak, and almost always a loud screech call. Humanity mainly contemplates owls as images of intellect and comprehension, due to consciousness of unending owl legends and folklore endorsements. Owl moral tales can also mean transfiguration and time. Consequently, you can spot countless owl tattoo patterns, go with items such as a sandglass or snap clasp in its hook.

OUSPENSKY Ptotr eff Demianovich. (1878-1947). Russian scientist and esotericist, whose consideration about spirituality led him to meet Gurdji in 1914, and regardless having withdrawn himself from him, he became his most illustrious disciple and expositor. He is the author of a variety books such as: The Tertium Organum, In Search of the Miraculous, A New Model Samael cites it in his works on objective reason and Logic.

OXYRHYN Honorific of a fish devoted to the Egyptian goddess Hathor. There now are some bronze monks, where you can see fish of this category that carry on the disc head and bodies of said goddess. Pisce Venus latuil, says Ovid.

OXYRHYNCHUS PAPYRI The assembly of thousands of particles of papyri was proven from 1897 onwards at Oxyrhynchus, c, 10 miles W. of the Nile. It covers some astronomical pieces of Greek and Latin literary texts and of Christian literature. The most memorialize montage is the MSS of 'Sayings of Jesus'.

OX It is an image of the cosmic force, it shows work, self-denial, suffering and patience, both in Greece and Rome it is respected as an attribute of agriculture and the oppression: as well as in Egypt and India it has significant substitution.

-P-

PACAL Process shield in the Mayan tongue. Pacal was a Maya king that ruled Palenque. Through his administration, Palenque masterly its highest grandeur. Pacal was dominant in Maya history since his burial, turn up in 1952, and is the significant funeral memorial in all of Mesoamerica. Enormous stone scale seven tons. There are fashions on the top and sides. The enormous stone would never have fit down the stairways from the top of the Sanctuary of the Inscriptions. The reason Pacal the Great had presented on buildings in the Mayan capital Palenque was to protect his claim to rule. Pascal develop from the Latin Paschalis o pashalis, that means "Relating to Easter", from the Latin word for "Easter", Pascha, Greek, from the Aramaic pasha (Hebrew Pesach) "Passover" (since the Hebrew Passover correspond closely with the later Christian celebration of Easter, the Latin term eventuate to be passed down.

PACEM IN TERRIS (1963). An encyclical letter consigned by John XXIII on global peace.

PACIFISM It has been recognized that in a world mostly governed by Christian's conceptions of war would be controlled, however, because Christians are members of an earthly society in which the use of power is imperative; to support organization, it is believed though not universally that Christian's engagement is at times, appropriate and even admirable. The Crusades are a good example of warfare acquired for believably religious conclusions. Theologians from the Middle Ages came to differentiate between wars that Christian could or couldn't take a role; lawfully. Thomas Aquinas set up three conditions for a 'fair war'. First, that the war was approved by the rulers; secondly; that ideals must be impartial, and thirdly; those antagonists met legal purposes. In the present time, 'Absolute Pacifism' warfare has been entirely banned by the Gospel, it has been confirmed by many groups of people as well as leading Churchmen. Unfortunately, most of the Christian's belief has not supported the contemporary pacifist movements, in their views; there are even unpleasant evils than corporal destruction.

PADAKA (Sanskrit) Brahman savvy in the Veda.

PADRES LAS CASAS, BARTOLOMÉ (DE) (1474-1566) Spanish minister, the 'Apostle of the Indies'. He went ahead with the Spanish governor to Hispaniola (Haiti) in 1502 and was anointed priest in 1510. He then became loyal to the interests of the Indians by opposing, the two in American and at the court of Spain, the brutal system of misuse used by the settlers. He united the Dominicans in 1523 and from 1543 to 1551 he was Bp. of Chiapas in Mexico. His derails of the mistreatment of the pioneers, primarily in his Destruction de las Indias (1552), be allowed to go past the limitations of truth.

PAGAN (From Latin paganus). Initially, this expression had no unpleasant meaning; it was plainly equivalent to dwellers of the countryside or someone who lived at a great distance from the place of worship of the city and is therefore unconscious of the religion of the State and its rites. The term "heathen" has a similar meaning and name the one who lives in the wilderness (heaths, in English) and in the countryside. But nowadays, both terms come to mean idolatry.

PAIN An exceptionally disagreeable concrete impact produced by disease or circumstances which causes psychological or substantial pain. Pain is a mostly powerful sign of misery-likely because the climate device generates sentiment of gloominess, dullness, and fatigue. Ravens are in addition connected with desolation, perhaps due to Edgar Allen Poe's 'The Raven' that produces a symbol of discomfort and gloom. In its rebirth from the ordinary, uncolored larva to the graceful fly critter of elegant vision, the monarch has enhanced an image for transformation and expectation; over customs, it has set off a character for rejuvenation and restoration to life, for the victory of the inner being and the inspiration above the tangible place of confinement. The cross probably is the most easily recognized and widely known symbol in all the world of pain and anguish. It can be seen omnipresent in human culture and history. It is so simple that we overlook its importance. Emotions symbolize can be defined as the practice or art of using an object or a term to stand for an abstract idea. An action, person, place, word, or object can have figurative meanings. Pain there are three kinds of pain (du(s)kha): 1. Adhyatmika Du(s)kha, designed by the Self, that is, by man himself; 2. Adhi Bhautika-du(s)kha, derived from clear beings or things, and 3. Adhi Daivika Odu (Sokha, from divine causes, or just karmic sanction. (gnosis) Every moment of pain should be prolonged in meditation with a still mind and in deep silence.

PAIN BENIT The blessed bread often, until a short time ago, distributed to the congregation after service in French and Canadian churches,

PALATE, PONTIUS The administrator ('procurator') of Judaea from A.D. 26 to 36 under whom Christ was crucified.

PALATINE GUARD A partitioning of militia in the Papal assistance. It was established in 1850 out of two existing bodies; it was disbanded in 1970.

PALM TREE OR PAMLS In Christian faith, the palm branch relates to Jesus' Successful Arrival into Jerusalem, commemorated on Palm Sunday, when the Gospel of John says of the citizens, "they took palm branches and went out to meet Him" (12:13 HCSB). The palm limb is a representation of victory, triumph, peace and eternal life, arising in the prehistorical Near East and the Adriatic world.

PALIMPSEST. A vellum or papyrus MS from which the indigenous writing has been exterminated and the exterior then used for some other (usually quite different) chronicles. A famous example is the Codex Ephraemi: the enduring parts of the 5th century. Greek NTs were covered in the 12th century with documents of S. Ephraem Syrus.

PANAGIA (Gk., 'all holy') A preferred little of the BVM in the eastward Church. The expression is also used of (1) a Doval medallion endurance for the BVM was draped on a bunch by Orthodox bishops; and (2) bread which is a soberly precious honor of the BVM.

PANCHEN Rimbo Che (Tibet) Straightforwardly: "the great Ocean, or Master of Wisdom". Name of the Techu Lama in Tchigadze; a personification of Amitabha, Chenresi's Celestia "father", which measures he is an avatar of Tsong-kha-pa (see Son-kha-pa). Alongside trailing, the Techu Lama is second only to the Dalai Lama; in fact, it is admirable, since Dharma Richen, the breed of Tsong-kha-pa in the golden monastery established by the last progressive and established by the sect of the Gelu Kpas ("yellow caps"), is the one formed by the Dalai Lamas in Ullhass, and was the aperture of the dynasty of the "Panchen Rimboche". Just as the previews (Dalai Lamas) are appointed the title of "Jewel of Majesty", the latter enjoy a much towering treatment, which is that of "Jewel of Wisdom", as a result they are high Initiates.

PANDORA (Greek) Beautiful woman created by the gods under the orders of Zeus [Jupiter] to be sent to Epimetheus, brother of Prometheus. He had in his protection a little box where all the evils, all the passions and all the plagues that caused trouble to the human lineage were enclosed. Pandora, driven by curiosity, opened the disastrous little box, thus leaving free all the evils that overwhelm humanity.

PANGE LINGUA. The eminence of two commemorate Latin hymns, viz the "Passiontide hymn by Venantius Fortunatus (Panage lingua Gloriosi proelium certaminis; 'Sing, my tongue, the glorious battle') and the Corpus Christi hymn by St. Thomas Aquinas (Pange Lingua Gloriosi corporis mysterium: 'Of the glorious Body telling').

PANTACIO [Pentacle, in English] (Greek) Like Pentalfa. As matters stands, the triple triangle of Pythagoras or the five-pointed star. This name has been chosen because it reproduces the letter A (Alpha) on its five sides or in five distinct positions; However, their number is composed of the first odd number (3) and the first even number (2).

PANIS (Sanskrit) Descriptively: "tacanos". Aerial demons (dasyus), envious, false, impious and cursed, enemies of Indra, who utilized to steal cows and hide them in caves.

PANI (Sanskrit) Hand; manual power.

PANNA (Sanskrit) A development somewhere, split; descent, fall.

PANOPOLIS. Its goddess was Minn, in Hellenistic situation identified with Pan, consequently the name Panololis, meaning" city of Pan." Also mention to as Chemmis or Khemmis, it was the capital of the 9th, or Chemmite, designation department) of Ptlolemaic Upper Egypt.

PAOUT NOUTEROU (Egypt). This remark designates the principle of Divided, the divine Substance.

PAPA Mantric syllable that serves to go out in astral. It is uttered as children do. Elucidation of papa, an unofficial phrase for a father; most likely originated from baby talk. Similar: dad, dada, daddy, pa, pappa, pop. Originator, father, a male parent, (as well accustomed as an expression of inscription to your father). Jesus Himself calls God 'Papa' This is the interpretation of the word "Abba.".

PAPAKA (Sanskrit) Evil, harm, guilt, villainous sin, ruin, evil person

PAPAPURUSHA (Gnostic) Among the Hindustans manifests the emotional self, the Ego, the Mephistopheles of Gothe, the horrendous Klingsor of the Wagnerian melodrama. The Papapurusha has no legitimate distinction, it is not a characteristic emanation. We need to transform the subconscious into conscious and that is only possible by effectively annihilating the Papapurusha, i.e., psychological defects. The old hermits of the sacred land of Ganges, imagine him in meditation with appearances of aggressive; eyes and beard red, with a sword, with a shield and frown expression (emblematic figure of our psychological physicist); then they claim their Divine Mother Kundalini, the Self or defect of their psyche, anticipation understood. They appreciate the Papapurusha summed up to ashes accordingly in the sizzling fire.

PAPMAN (Sanskrit) Sinner, pernicious, harmful, wicked. As a nominal: evil, harm, sin, crime, pervicious cause.

PAPYRUS (Lat papyrus.). Perennial greenery, native to the East, of the background of the Cyperaceas, with radial leaves, lengthy very narrowing, and integrate; gaining of two to three patterns towering and a diameter thick, finished by a feather of spikes with numerous small and aquamarine flowers. The prehistoric population took sheets of their thallus to write on them.

PARA (Sanskrit) The opposing shore; excessive limit

PARABLES (Gnosticism) The replica worn from nature or from human events, mostly those recommend or accommodate a short tale, which Christ used to bring a spiritual sense. In each allegory there is one leading tip of contrast, and apart from this the feature may, or may not, have a distinct meaning. There are 30-40 clear-cut parables in the Synoptic Gospels; there are none in Jn. Many who delivered parables to humanity, paid a high price with their lives.

PARACELSUS Metaphorical title embraced by the significant esotericism of medieval times, Philip Bombast Aurelius Theophrastus of Hohenheim, born in Einsidein, canton of Zurich, in 1492. He was the most skilled physician of his generation and the most acclaimed for the healing of practically all ailments by purity of talismans that he himself prepared.

PARADHA (Parardha) (1) (Sanskrit) The period that includes an arrangement of continuation or Age of Brahma.

PARADISE (Hebrew) "Delight", gratification. In Genesis it is the "Garden of Earthly Delights", instituted by God; in the Kabbalah, the "Garden of Earthly Delights" is a place of initiation into the Mysteries. It is the heaven of the exotic religions of India; that purely individual state of absolute happiness in which the souls of the upstanding find themselves as the period between two persistent incarnations. Don't be unclear with Nirvana.

PARADIGM. The tag given by M. Dibelius and other Form-critics to motion in the Gospel which embrace narratives woven round a distinct saying of Christ to stimulate its teaching home.

PARK. "Tract of land enclosed as a preserve for beasts of the chase". "From Old French dock. parc "enclosed wood or health land used as a game preserve", perhaps after all from West Germanic "parruk "enclosed tract of land" (antecedent as well of old English pearruc, root of pad. It is a Homograph as it has incompatible interpretation based on its use. Park; a place filled with plant survival which has a field for divergent environmental exertion. E.g. "I have not gone to park since ages." A movement in which the transport is advance towards an area that is designated to hold on to. A park is a zone of essential, semi-natural or green space reserved for human gratification and relaxation or for the preservation of ecosystems or natural surroundings. Inner city parks are forest spaces laid by for enjoyment nucleus municipalities and urban areas. A verse of Ezekiel 15:2 praising the forest. "Son of man, what is the vine tree more than any tree, the vine-branch which is among the trees of the forest?"

PARAUSIA. (Gk. for 'presence' or 'arrival'). The term is nearly new mainly to indicate the time ahead of the return of Christ in glory (the 'Second Coming') to justice the living and the dead, and to end the attending planet sequence. Prehistoric Christianity trusts this episode to be impending, and this reliance has often been resuscitated, but the triumph Christian heritage has adverse supposition on the hour and way of the forthcoming. (Christian theology) the reappearance of Jesus as justices for the Wisdom Crossroads. (Appearance, second advent, The Second Advent of the Parousia mania) interpretation accessible prevalence, turned up, appeared; demonstration, arrival. practical expression utilized of the forthcoming of the Savior (Matt 24: 3. 1 Cor 15:23; 1 Thess 2:19; 2. In the Bible, the Hellenic term (epiphanies, becoming visible) is adapted five times to mention to the coming back of the Messiah. The ancient Greek Gospel benefit the classical idiom Parousia (defining "arrival", "coming", or "presence") twenty-four times, seventeen of them relating the Redeemer.

PARANOIA (Greek) Functional psychosis with willing delusions. It brings into being feelings of suspicion, persecutory ideas, self-centeredness and a false notion of others. The delusional ideas of the paranoid are mainly firm and well systematized; these afflicted alter the most ordinary events according to their method.

PARIDHI (Sanskrit) Circumference; El disco solar o lunar.

PERI(S) Fairy beautiful benefactor.

PAROISSIEN. The title for various prayer books in the vernacular prepared for the use of the laity which have been published in France since the 17th century. They consistently contain an appreciable number of liturgical incidents such as private adoration exercises.

PASA o PAZA (Pasa) (Sanskrit) Ribbon or string which in some of its representations, appears to have Ziva on their right to strap the obstinate sinners. Paza also means: a rope in general, ribbon, knot, loop, etc.

PASCHAL The lamb sacrificed and eaten at the Jewish Passover. By analogy Christ is regarded as a 'Paschal Lamb'.

PASCHAL CANDLE In the Paschal Vigil Service the Paschal Candle is lit from the New Fire and transfer through the dim church by the priest, who solemnly stops three times prior to he reaches the altar, in every case singing 'Lumen Christi' (Light of Christ'). More candles are lit from the Paschal Candle. At the sanctuary, the 'Exulted' is sung. The Paschal Candle is lit for liturgical purposes in Eastertide and in the RC Church at all Baptisms.

PASCH A credit applied for both the Jewish Passover and the Christian festivities of Easter.

PASHT (Pacht) (Egypt) [Called by another name Sejet or Sekhet.] The cat-headed goddess, the Moon. In the British Museum you can see numerous statues and depictions of it. It is the espouse or feminine aspect of Ptah (son of Knef), the creative principle, or the Egyptian Demiurge. It is also appointed Beset or Bubastis and is then both the principle that gathers, and the one that divides or divides. Its motto is: "Punish the guilty and extirpate the vice", and one of its emblems is the cat. According to Viscount Rouge, the cult of this goddess is exceedingly old (about 3,000 years before J.C.) Pacht is the mother of the Asian race, the race that settled north of Egypt. As such, it is called Ouato.

PASSIONATE (Gnosticism) "The self wants passionate satisfactions at any price even when old age is completely disastrous." You must overcome passion to emerge triumphant in the tough tests.

PASSOVER. The Jewish festival observed of every spring in interrelation with the Exodus. In agreement with the chronicle of its institution in Exod. 12, a sheep is to be in every family unit and its sanguine fluid dispersed on the lintel and column of the dwelling in remembrance of the reality that at the same time, the eldest in Egypt were destroyed, the Lord 'passed over' the homestead which were so clear-cut. Afterwards the lambs were immolated in the Sanctuary. In In the fullness of time, Christ, it was the main Jewish celebration of the epoch, commemorated on the nighttime of 14/15 Nisan. Even if the Lord's Supper was a Feast of the Unleavened Bread (as the almanac of the Sacred Writings would propose) or not (as Jn.), the oblation was introduced at Passover day, and faithful contemplated in the demise of Christ the consummation of the self-sacrifice presage by the Passover.

PAPYRUS (lat papyrus) Just the same is considered a lively plant, indigenous to the East, comes from the genealogy of the Cyperaceous, with radical leaves, very narrow long, and whole; cards two to three meters high and a diameter thick, perfected by a plume of spikes with many small greenish flowers. In ancient times they took pictures from their stems to write on them.

PATH (Sanskrit) The same as the English voice Path: Via, path; course, way.

PATMOS A compact island in the Aegean at which point St. John discerned the Apocalypse (Rev. 1:9). As maintained by historical convention he was banished to Patmos under Domitian (81-96) and returned to Ephesus under Nerva (96-8). In 1088 St. Christodulus instituted a cloister on the island; it quickly developed into significance and still perseveres.

PHALADA (Sanskrit) That bears fruit; that it has consequences; fruit tree.

PHANAR, The. The director's location and court of the Ecumenical Patriarch at Constantinople.

PHANES (Gc.) One of the orphic triads. Phanes, Chaos and Chromos. It was also the trinity of the Western people in the pre-Christian period.

PAOUT Nouterou (Egipc.) This expression designates the essence of Divinity, the divine substance.

PATER NOSTER The opening words of the Latin version of the "Lords's Prayer.

PAPI and PAPIS (Sanskrit) The drinker; The sun, the moon.

PAPIN (Sanskrit) One who does evil; malefactor.

PAUL, acts of, Mythical book written in Greek and put into wide distribution in the 2nd century. It was designed to glorify St. Paul's attainments and it's romantic in character. Several treatises which circulated independently are now known to be parts of this work, among them the 'Martyrdom of Paul', the Acts of Paul and Thecla', and the 'Third Epistle of Paul to the Corinthians'.

PAUL & THECLA, (Act of), An apocryphal effort which is atomization of the 'Acts Paul'. The course of action Paul preached, the satisfaction of abstinence at Iconium and winning St. Thecla from Thamyris, to whom she was bound. Paul was charged in front of the civil authorities and maltreated, while Thecla was penalized to death but miraculously rescued. It culminated with the record of Thecla's death at Seleucia.

PAULINE PRIVILEGE The advantage recognized by St. Paul (I Cor. 7: 15) to the companion of an infidel marriage to organize a new marriage on becoming a Christian if the non-Christian husband wished to break up or put a serious barrier in the way of the convert's belief and practice.

PAVANA (Sanskrit) God of wind or air, supposed father of the god-Lemur Hanuman. He is also known by the name of Vayu. Pavana also indicates I will go, wind, apparatus or channel of purification.

PAX BREDE (also Pax or Osculatorium). A tiny portion of alabaster, hardware, or lumber, with a description of some religious substance on the surface and a prognostication handle on the back, earlier on used for transferring the "Kiss of Peace. It was kissed by the celebrator and then by others who approved of it in turn.

PEARL(S) Pearly crystallization, customarily sour white, bright contemplations and spheroidal figure that fashionable shapes inside the shells of contrasting mollusks especially in mother pearls. Cabalistically, it relates to the human soul. In accordance with history and myths, pearls are illustrative of wisdom achieved extensively knowledge. The jewels are believed to provide safeguarding, Consequently, attract virtuous success and profitability. They are popular for their soothing results. Pearls are emblems of freshness, confidence, purity, and honesty. They are correlated with the vitality of the moon and have been used to expand fecundity and produce more relief given birth. They are very delicate, both objectively and vigorously.

PEDILAVIUM. The observance of foot-washing implemented in the liturgy on Maundy Thursday in memory of Christ's action before the Last Supper (Jn. 13). When the Maundy Thursday Mass came to be remembered in the morning, the Pedilavium persists in the evening as a separate service, restricted to cathedral and abbey churches. Pius XII's Holy Week Ordinal depended on the restored evening Mass instantly after the Gospel and endorse its observance in all churches. Twelve men are led into the sanctuary, where the celebrant washes and dries the of each in turn.

PENTATEUCH. A titular in use among Biblical scholars for the five 'Books of Moses', Genesis, Exodus, Leviticus, Numbers, and Deuteronomy. Most commentators hold that these Books were composed from previously written archives dating from the 9th to the 5th centuries. B.C.

PENITENTS In the prehistory system of public penance (q. V.), apologetics were separated from the rest of the assembly by wearing special dress and church service apart in the church. Even after restoration to Communion, certain dysfunctions remained for life.

PENOT, Gabriel. French alchemist who dedicated his entire to the defense of the dogma of Paracelsus and the concepts of Hermeticism, to which conclusion he did not ponder to dissolve a substantial fortune with disagreeable outcome. He wrote many works on these topics and tackled some travels in Europe, and in 1617, decreased to maximum misery, he died in the hospital of Yverdun Switzerland.

PELICAN Special of the adopted badge of the Rosicrucian (the 18th degree) is the pelican, a waterfowl that floats or advance on the waters, like the Spirit, and then leaves them to give birth to other beings.

PELVI (Pahlavi or Pehlevi) (Pers.) Earliest Westernly Iranian language used in ancient Persia all along the Sasanid period (226 to 653 A.D.) It has numerous Semitic voices. The name pehlvi means "strength". It is composed from right to left, and its alphabet is comprised of ten and nine characters, which give twenty-six worth, twenty-one consonants and five vowels The demanding of reading this language comes from the comparison of many of its letters, the modify in value of the linked letters and the lack of the points that prominent several of them. The word is also concerned with the literature of that time and of a concise period afterwards.

PER-M-RHU. (Eg.). This designation is the acknowledged enunciation of the ancient inscription of the collection of mystical readings, called Book of the Dead. Accomplished case papyri have been found, and there are innumerable copies of the section of the work referred to.

PERFECT, PERFECTION. (Latin perfect, onis) Accomplishments of perfecting or improving. Gnosis analyzes that once the creation of internal bodies is executed, they must be consummated by transforming them into vehicles of pure gold. For this it is necessary to eliminate the dry mercury (The I's) and the Arsenated Sulfur, that is, the bestial fire, the Kundabuffer or Kundaguador Organ. What is more, once Mastery is achieved, it must be achieved perfection.

PERFUME (fragrance) Aromatic and odorific element that put to the fire, emanates from itself; fragrant and odorous smoke, as with benzoin, frankincense, storaque, myrrh, amber and others. Gnosis spells out that the fragrance, the facts of incense, storaque, myrrh, etc., harmonize homes and all the places where they are burned. Each day of the week has its perfume as its resolution planet, each zodiac sign furthermore has its own perfume.

PERGAMON. The municipality, c. 50 miles north of Smyrna, was a Midpoint of culture in the 2nd century B.C. To this interval affiliates the invention of parchment ('pergamena carta') as a substitute for papyrus. One of a the 'Seven Churches' conveyed in Rev. (2: 12-17), Pergamon is commonly name the place where Satan's throne is. As it was the first city in Asia to acquire permission to worship as the living ruler, in 29 B.C., the allusion is seemingly to Emperor worship. The contemporary town is known as Bergama.

PERSONALITY. They are human beings by creation; everyone is an organic unity of spirit, soul life, and body life. But they must enhance their personalities: they must accomplish and succeed those traits that anthropological perception as individuals in the social sense. The Holy Spirit generate behavior traits that are prototype of Christ. The apostle Paul specified to these distinctive as the grain of the Spirit. "The fruit of the Spirit is love, joy, peace, patience, kindness, goodness, faithfulness, gentleness, and self-control".

PETER PATAR (Gnosticism) Introduces the apostle Peter, which signified the stone, the gospel of alchemy, personas from the Bible such as: Adam, Cain, Enoch, Noah, Abraham (Abratiam), Isaac, Jacob, etc. Any of the initiator of religious orders. It is said of people who by their age and wisdom exercise moral authority over collaboration or family. (Gnostic) In every person who, casually, an intensity of spirituality is entrusted with a mission of a spiritual familiarization given to humanity, that is, who is a progenitor of Christ. Master Samael within Universal Gnosticism is a patriarch, who many, after his physical disappearance, have tried to replace him by classifying himself as patriarchs II, III, etc. and others have had the presumption of calling themselves the reincarnation of Samael to deceive with it the Gnostic students who, by the way, if the body of Gnostic doctrine is not well translucent, they fall into the collection of those hounds, fanciful authority who without sparing efforts told the seekers of light.

PERSISTENCE. The property that authorizes anyone to endure performing things or attempting to do anything although it is arduous or conflicting by someone else. Eagle; the same as Aquila Chrysa Etos was accustom as emblem of power and bravery, the eagle was as well an important character in prehistory

Egypt. Babylon, and Roma, ultimately attractive sign of persistence and vigor in the United States. A Celtic representation, Oak; Ideogram of force and tolerance; mighty and secured identical to the Oak, regardless how uncertain tactic can incline. Someone's energy will facilitate your triumph.

PESH-HUN (Tibet.) The term originated from the Sanskrit pizuna, "spy". Epithet appeal to Narada, the Richi intrusive and demanding. [Name given in the supernatural of the part of the Himalayas here to Narada, the "messenger" or Greek Angelos]. Pesh-Hun does not belong entirely to India. It is the imaginative and mysterious commanding power that gives impetus and regulates the strength of cycles, Kalpas and universal events. Each of the detectable accommodation of Karma on a general scale; the ingenuity and guide of the greatest heroes of this Manvantara. Particularly credited with calculating and recording all the astronomical and cosmic cycles to come and teaching astronomical science to the first observers of the starry vault. In the Exoterism works he is given some very unflattering names, such as Kali-karaks (Promoter of Discord), Kapi-vaktra according to myth, 'monkey face', Pizuna (Spy), although somewhere he is called Deva-Brahma. Williams Jones contrasts him to Hermes and Mercury and calls him "Messenger of the Gods." And as the Indians accepted him a great Richi who "always walks from one side of the earth to the other giving good advice", the pain Kenealy sees in one of his twelve Messiahs, which is not as erroneous as some imagine.

PEZI (Sanskrit) Ray; Egg; Yolk reopened.

PEYUCHA (Sanskrit) Milk; recently clarified butter; Amrita or ambrosia.

PEZALA (Sanskrit) Delicate, funny, beautiful, pleasant, seductive; Dexterous, skillful.

PEW On the subject of the traditional postures for worship were standing and kneeling, and no seats were transferred for the churchgoers. Later, as an improvement to the infirm, stone seats were attached to the walls of naves. By the end of the 13th century, numerous English churches supposedly to have been furnished with fixed wooden benches, well known as pews. They were occasionally elegantly carved at the ends and rear back.

PFAFF FRAGMENTS IF IRENAEYS. Four portions were published in 1713 by C.M. Pfaff, who challenge that he had found them in the Turin library and accredit them to Irenaeus. Harnack manifests them to be a fabrication of Pfaff himself.

PHALGU (Sanskrit). No essentiality or core, no sap; pointless, vain; weak, tiny; reddish.

PHALADA (Sanskrit) That bear harvest; that has aftereffects; Fruit tree.

PHANAR. The ceremonious dwelling and assembly of the Ecumenical Patriarch at Constantinople.

PHARAOH The Cairenes concluded their Pharaoh to be the arbitrator amidst the creator and the Earth of man line. Succeeding demise, the Pharaoh became eternal, associated with Osiris, the father of Hours and God of the dead, and proceeded on his solemn potentials and location to the current ascendant, his male child. The insignia of the pharaoh signifies his or her capacity to rule and preserve the sequence of the world. Sapphire and gold-colored recommended deity as a result they were infrequent and were related with valuable matter, during jet-black convey the fecundity of the Nile River. Ancient Kings of Egypt prior to the occupation of this country by the Persians. (Gnostic) Maniram that is pronounced by lengthening each letter to achieve astral advancing: The latter can occur when it is realized that the person manages to leave his physical body in a normal process while asleep, it can be in a light form, on purpose, or in a disguise manner.

PHENA (Sanskrit) Foam.

PHENOMENON (in Latin, and phainomenon, in Greek) Symbolizes "an appearance", Something that had not been seen before, and that disturbs the mood instantly its cause is anonymous. Renouncing various kinds of phenomena, such as cosmic, electrical, chemical, etc., and adhering purely to spiritualistic manifestations, let us remember that, theosophically and hiddenly, every "miracle" from the biblical to the thaumaturgical is simply a phenomenon, but that no prodigy is continuously a miracle, this is something immaterial or outside the norms of Nature, since every portent is improbable in Nature. A phenomenon is a remarkable incident or situation. In the 1950s, rock-n-roll was contemplated as a brand-new customs phenomenon, conversely this day we anticipate of remove spirals as a peculiar phenomenon. Such as numerous commands with Greeks radicle, phenomenon emerged revealed as a discipline denomination. In an experimental condition, it is a commodity that is perceived to transpire or to survive. Truth is simply a provision or circumstance that perhaps perceived with the sensation, unless direct or utilizing articles comparable as simple microscope or infrated telescope. This definition of phenomenon disparity with the perception of the vocable in common practice. In ideology, some articles, reality, or incidents are recognized. In customary, phenomena are the gadget of the feeling (e.g., glimpse and resonate) as distinct with what is captured by the intuition. Conforming to Etymon underscores, the dissimilarity linking phenomena and phenomenon in Greek the word conveyed "that which is seen or appears", so actually the alike artifact it intends here and now. The single is 'phenomenon'. The multiple is 'phenomena'.

PHERAVA (Sanskrit) Cunning, crafty, malicious, perfidious, malefactor.

PHRE Name of the god Ra preceded by the article p.

PHILADELPHIA (Church of) This church is indicated in Revelation; "I know your works, behold, I have put before you an open door, which no one can close; for, although it has little strength, you have kept my word, you have not denied my name." Repaying the Ajna Chakra placed in the eyebrows, has two petals and grants clairvoyance, this chakra is the seat of the mind.

PHILALETHES (Greek Typify, "lovers of truth") Phrase given to the Alexandrian Neoplatonists, further cited as analogists and theosophists. This set up was created by Ammonio Sacca's at the dawn of the third century and proceeded until the fifth. The most illustrious philosophers and scholars of that time belonged to it.

PHILE. The vocable 'Phile' arrives from the prehistoric Greek expression, 'Phileein', defining to love. Phile signifies an individual who loves or has a devotion to a designated entity. The 'Phile' as one who loves or has a powerful sympathy or inclination.

PHILIP NERI, St. (1515-95) 'Disciple of Rome'. Proceeding To Rome in 1533, he devoted himself to charity and absorb much nighttime in devotion in the catacombs; he accomplished an ecstasy in 1544 which is accepted miraculously to have enlarged his heart. Following ordaining, he went to live in a kinship of clergyman at San Girolamo, where he soon enhanced the focus of his apostolate at his confessional; he held spiritual consultation, out of which came the Congregation of the Oratory.

PHILOCALIAS. (1) The Philocalies of Origination is an anthology from his writings compiled by St. Basil the Great and St. Gregory Nazianzus in 358-9 (2) The Philocalies of Sts Macarius Notaras and Nicodemus of the Holy Mountain (1782) is an assortment of ascetical and mystical writings geological from the 4th to the 15th centuries trading with the instructions of Hesychasm.

PHRE (Gr.) [Fren.] Pythagorean prompt that appoints what we call Kama-Manas, protected even by the Bud-dhi-Manas.

PHOCAS, St. A prelate of Sinope in Pontus of his name was martyred by Asphyxiation in a bath in 117. He is often disoriented with 'St Phocas the Gardener' who is said to have been martyred in the Diocletian Persecution, and with St. Phocas of Antioch. While the multiplicity traditions had been fused, the cult of St. Phocas became accepted. Mainly among seafaring people.

PHOS HILARION. In the Easterly Church the hymns sung at 'Hesperian's (the counterpart of the W. Vespers). It is considerably known in the English adaptation of J. Keble ('Hail! Gladdening Light').

PHORONEOUS Was a hulk; one of the ancestors and predecessor of humanity. As disclosed by an Argolis tradition, he is accused, as well as Prometheus, of having contributed fire to this land. (Pausanias). [Phoroneus had in the Argo lid an altar on which a flame rose incessantly to commemorate that this titan had been the innovator of the game.

PHOSPHORUS Frequently characterized a nonmetallic polyvalent component that transpire widely in united form mostly as inorganic phosphates in raw material, soils, natural waters, bones and teeth and as biological phosphates in all organisms' cells that lives in several rhinestone forms. Calcium and phosphate react in conflicting process: As blood calcium measures increase, phosphate levels lessen. An adrenaline named Parathyroid hormone (PTH), that your parathyroid glands set free, governs the amounts of calcium and phosphate in your lifeblood. The synthetic procedure of Phosphate is PO 3-4. Phosphate accommodates one Phosphorus (P)atom and four Oxygin (O) molecules.

PHOTINUS (4th century), heterodoxy. He set off Bp of Sirmium c. 344 but was deposed and exiled in 351. No part of all his writings has survived and his precepts are variously narrated by his detractors; it was intelligibly a form of Sabellianism.

PHYSICAL A material body is assigned to each of us by our loving Heavenly Father. He designed it as a tabernacle for our spirit to accommodate each of us in our search to attain the adequate count of our creation. Our shape allows each of us to play a part in the significant plan of salvation that He has sketched for all His children. If there is a capable physical or natural body, there is also a spiritual body. Christian doctrine commonly recounts Paul as balancing the resurrection body with the mortal body, observing that it will be a distinctive kind of body; a "spiritual body", sensing an immortal body, or incorruptible body. A Greek God physique is deep rooted as having a balanced, lean, and athletic physique, one that has well dedication shoulders and arms, lean legs, abs, and a broad chest/back. Many people have the misunderstanding that physical education helps in physical career path and not in the rational success of children. No doubt physical teachings help in the substantial expansion of an individual, but they also help in mental formation. In Greek mythology, Kratos (or Cratons) is the divine manifestation of strength. He is the son of Pallas and Styx. Kratos and his siblings Nike ('Victory'), Bia ('Force'), and Zelus ('Glory') are all constitutionally manifestations of an essential quality.

PIA DESIDERIA. P. J. "Spener's notification which direct at stimulating a religious revival in German Protestantism and thus outlined the "Pietist Movement". It was drafted in German and circulated in 1675.

PICO DELLA MIRANDOLA, Giovanni (1463-94), Italian lord, scholar, and spiritual writer. In addition to being a good classical intellectual, he was fluent in Hebrew, Aramaic, and Arabic; and he was the first to pursue in the 'Cabbala' a clue to the Christian enigmas.

PIE, **or PICA** The title given in England in the 15th century to the publication of directions for saying the services. In the book of frequent prayer (concerning the Services of the Church') it is censured for the numeral and firmness of its rules.

PIETA Portrayal of the BVM saddened over the dead body of Christ, which she holds onto on to her knees.

PIKE. Is a Non saline water fish that is found in North America. It is an emblem of power to the American Indian people it is utilized to embody their customs and ancestry. The pike fish is as well consecrated to the Native American people's devotions and doctrine. The pike fish has been image of religion of Christs for years. This is a fish that frequently swims in clear water, making it effortless to see, it is identified as for lengthy, nose appearance, which is evocative of the crucifix. The pike fish has long been associated with Celtic metaphor and tradition. In prehistoric times, the pike was a sacred living thing that could bring good prosperity to those who acquired it.

PILLARS (The two) Jakin (or Jachin) and (Boaz) They were set down at the entry of Solomon's Temple, the first on the right and the second on the left. Its insignia is declared in Masonic rituals.

PILLARS, (The Three) Mentions to the Ten Sephiroth which are assembled in the tree of Life, independently by two vertical lines into three pillars that are: Pillar of Severity, Pillar of Mercy and Pillar of Kindness. Geburah and Hod shape the first, Severity; Kether, Tiphereth, Jesod and Malkuth, the Central Pillar; and Chokmah, Chesed and Netzach, the Pillar of Mercy.

PILATES (Gnosticism) He was the Roman chief of state who authorized the crucifixion of Christ. In the cosmic spectacle, Pilate stipulates the mind that always washes its hands to justify its error. He is part of the three traitors of the Christ who are: Judas Pilate and Caiaphas. You should never oppose Karma; the advantageous thing is to know how to arrange it. Lamentably, the only thing that transpires to people when they are in significant discontentment is to wash their hands like Pilate, to say that they have done nothing wrong, that they are not to blame, that they are just souls, etc.

PINE. Preferred tree of Cibeles. He is customarily found near the appearance of this godhead. In his Mysteries, the priests ran equipped with thyrsus that they finalized in pines adorned with colorful ribbons. On the spring equinox a pine tree was cut accompanied by great solemnity and was taken to the temple of Cibeles. The pine was besides utilized in the sacrifices of Bacchus.

PISCES Primarily the twelfth and culminating astrological signal in the zodiac. This sign is defeatist, and mutable. It has a span of 330 to 360 degrees celestial longitude. Under the equatorial zodiac, the sun transfers to this region enclosed by February 19 and March 2. When Pisces is in love, they are very permitting and understanding regarding their partner. They may go out of their idea to help the person they are with, and they like to feel of service. They may enjoy sharing advice or just being there to reinforce their partner when they are advancing through a demanding time.

PISTIS-SOPHIA (Gr.) "Knowledge-Wisdom". A venerated book of the ancient Gnostics or prehistoric Christians. [The most influential modern authority on exoteric Gnostic beliefs, Mr. C. w. King, says, speaks of Pistis Sophia, "that precious monument of Gnosticism."]

PITONISA (Gr.) (or Pythia). As reported by modern dictionaries, this article refers to the individual who gave the oracles in the temple of Delphi, and every female who was presumable to be provide with the spirit of divination, "a sorceress." This is not exact; it is said that Pythoness was a goddess of [Apollo] who was chosen among the pure budding women of the underprivileged classes; She was in a temple where oracular powers were enlightened. Once welcome the young woman unceasing as a novice, she would live in a place unattached from the others who would only have contact with the supporter or prime sage. The pythoness would be anointed and briefed considerably until she could segment her own preferences.

PITRIS The forefathers or originators of humankind.

PILGRIM(S) Attributed to the Monad as it goes through its cycle of reincarnations. It is the only perpetual and everlasting concept that exists in us.

PILGRIMAGE; (lat. peregrinatio, onis). Peregrination everywhere on unfamiliar grounds; (gnost.) pilgrimage in just about all doctrines widen to the holy environments. It is made clear within gnosis that, in primitive times, at the lifetime of the Lemur Race, husband and wife went on pilgrimages to the Sacred Temples, contributed to and supervised by the divinities, and as acceptance were the trips of the Honeymoon formed by newlywed couples.

PLATO An expert in the Mysteries, and the most prestigious Greek philosopher, whose writings are known; multiplied all over the world. He was a pupil of Socrates and a teacher of Aristotle. It blossoms about 400 years before our era.

PLAGOON, PLAGGON (Greek). Small wax doll that signifies natural people and that they offered for appeal.

PLASMATIC PLAVA (Sanskrit) Raft, Almadía, Barca. It is an addendum of the sounds of the vowels in the writing of the Vedas; It means the enlargement of an idea through assorted rooms.

PLAVA (Sanskrit). Raft, almadia, boat. Prolongation of the sound of the vowels in the reading of the Veda; Development of an idea through several rooms.

PLEASURES (Gnosticism) When we discover ourselves, in the beginning, we see that psychological aggregates are those who take command of our human machine, making us react to the event and perceiving that we do not own ourselves, nor our actions, but we are moved by influences "invisible" to us up until that moment.

PLEYONE (Sanskrit) The Pleiades. The septenary governess of Karttikeya, God of action. [Most publications of the assignments we refer to Pleiades are six. This needs clarification. When the gods entrusted Karttikeya to the Krittikas (or Pleiades) to nurture him, these were absolutely six, for this reason Karttikeya is emblematized with six heads; but when the poetic creativity of the initial Aryan's metaphor made them the specific wives of the seven Richis, their number extended to seven, six of them being distinguishable and the seventh hidden. Their appellatives are: Amba, Dula, Nitaui, Abrayanti, Maghayanti, Varchyanti and Chapunika. Several playwrights nominated them with dissimilar names. Nevertheless, the seven Richis produced spouses of the seven Pleiades prior to the disintegration of the seventh. Any other way, might possibly Indian astronomers debate a star that nobody could observed minus the assistance of the most powerful telescopes? The Pleiades are interconnected to the great mysteries of mystifying Nature and accomplished the most secret and inexplicable of all astronomical and religious symbols.]

PLOW As it stands, agricultural device assembled with one or more swords secured in a fixture which is dragged by a self-propelled vehicle by vertebrates and utilized for slashing crease in the ground and make it over, principally to compose for the transplant of microorganism. "Farmers always plow the soil before planting season starts". An asana model concluded by lying down on one's backwards and alternating one's legs on top of one's head until the confined feet advance or pressure the floor.

PLURALITY ACT (1838). The earliest of a series of Acts forbidding clergymen of the temple simultaneously to hold more than no benefice with cure of soul except in eastward, the case of livings of limited value close to each other. The acts were essentially invalidated in the Pastoral Reorganization Measure, 1949.

PRAJA (Sanskrit) Procreation, generation, creation; being, creature; man; race, offspring lineage, family. In plural (Prajas): man, people, generations people, human race, humanity.

PRANA (Sanskrit) Vital foundation; It is the third principle (or the second, in other arrangements); in the septenary structure of man; it is the exuberance, the force of life, the life that penetrate the whole living body of man, the enthusiastic energy or dominance that all vital phenomena fabricate. The breath of the life of the anatomy is a part of life or the universal breath. Life is widespread, omnipresent, eternal, indestructible, and the segment of this comprehensive Life individualized or incorporated into our body, is that which is to designate the name of Prana. When the body dies, Prana reinstates to the ocean of cosmic Life. All the creations, each man, animals, plants and minerals, all atoms and molecules, in a plant, collectively that exists, is engulfed in an immense ocean of life, each being, either tiny as a molecule or vast as a universe, we can consider allotments or assimilating as existence of that universal Life. Imagine a living sponge extending in the mass of water that bathes it, encloses and impregnates, nourishing all its pores and circulating inside. In this instance, we may undoubtedly contemplate the ocean surrounding the sponge by staying out of it, additionally, the small part of the ocean that the sponge has absorbed by funding it. This immense ocean of life, that is, worldwide Life, is called Jiva, just as the fragment of prevalent Life that each organism appropriates, is denominated with the honorific of Prana.

PRAKRITI (Sanskrit) The species universally; nature in resistance to Purucha spiritual nature and Spirit, which together are the "two primitive aspects of the only unknown Deida." It means the material world and the substance cause or essence of all things; matter in the most limitless of the word, from the densest and grossest (the mineral) to the most subtle and ethereal (ether, mind, intellect). Purucha and Prakriti (Spirit and Matter), in their emergence are the same thing. However, when they reach a point of disparity, each of them begins their advancement in opposite directions. Thus, Brahma is at the same time essentially Spirit and Matter. As has been remarked before, the Prakriti, is illogical, nonetheless, it achieves an illusory responsibility, a touch of consciousness, we conceivably say it that way, thanks to its alliance with the Purucha, in the same way that a colorless crystal comes across as red to us; when it reflects a thing of that color. The society of both origins has been confronted with the fusion between someone who is paralytic (the uncertain, but inactive Purucha) and a sightless person (the unconscious, but active Prakriti). If the blind man carries the paralyzed guide, on his shoulders, then the two can reach their goal of their journey, thus designing the perfect Man.

PRANAYA. (Sanskrit) Free from passion, love or enthusiasm; Upright, just, honest resentful.

PRAVRITA (Sanskrit) Cover; veil; mantle.

PRAYA (Sanskrit) Proceed, habit; way of living; condition, state; death; Abundancies; sin, guilt.

PRA-BHU (Sanskrit) To become, to be born; manifest, arise, appear, develop.

PRAYER, PRAY. Hands personify discipline, acceptance, truthfulness, penitence, homage and approval in respect of one's piousness. This phrase in the Hebrew Bible is an advancing manner of bargaining with Deity, exceedingly consistently accomplished a voluntary, discrete, disjointed formation of request and/or appreciated. It invigorates the benevolence of a follower throughout the potential of the inner self. Persistent prayer in addition liberates the potential of

God's bounty on your consciousness and turn of events. Jesus said, "When you pray, go into your room, close the door and pray to your Father, who is unseen". PRAY A devoted appeal or connection with divinity or a device of veneration, as in petition grace reverence, or admission. An intangible conveyance "The entire nation is praying for those people who were affected from the recent major storm." Prayer also vitalized the soul of a follower across the faculty of the inner self. Persistent prayer in addition emancipates the faculty of God's absolution on your survival and set of conditions Jesus uttered, "Answer me when I call, O God of my righteousness! You have given me relief when I was in distress. Be gracious to me and hear my prayers!". Prayer is required so that through us the resolution of God's accord obtains perception consideration as it is in paradise. During our prayers, we demonstrate and postulate the decision of God on creation. Prayer is imperative if careful we hold down towards insistence of God for our own existence.

PRECES PRIVATAE. The direct title of a Latin manual of prayers debuted by Elizabeth I in 1564. It has no intimacy with the 'Preces Privatae of L. Andrewes (q.v.).

PRECEPT Origin acquired deriving out of late classic precept, formation of order (to teach), from Latin prae ("pre-") + Capio ("take"). A directive or assumption calculated largely as a regulation of operation; a system provided by endorsement composes command to a lower-ranking officer. The device frequently expressed in the sacred text proposed we collect "line upon line, precept upon precept," or simplistically, numerous minuscule responses for some time. Accepting and interpreting this device is a prime clue to securing innovation and assistance from the Spirit of Truth. The design of organized religions of a code of behavior or regulations to support mankind carry oneself in an upright and honestly course of action. The Faithful ought to go along with the Five Precepts to guarantee people exist honorably. This helps them to get rid of suffering and achieve enlightenment. The precepts are dedications to refrain from eliminating living things, larceny, sex crimes, untruthfulness and drunkenness. Enclosed by the Zen dogmas, people intended to flourish mental capacity and quality character to break through on the right track to enlightenment. In righteous theology, a proceeding of duty, as contrasted with a 'counsel' which is only a situation of persuasion for Precepts of the Church, or Commandments of the Church.

PREGNANCY (to be pregnant) Pregnancy of the woman. How long this one lasts. It begins with the fertilization of the egg and ends with labor, during which the new being, reached its full development, is separated from the body of its mother, to begin an independent life. Gnostic, it is directed by our nature, it is she who directs human reproduction; and the Angels of life handle connecting the cord of Anthahkarana: or silver of the essence, still fertilized zoosperm. Expression practiced recounting the interval in which an embryo evolves inner part a woman's uterus or womb. Pregnancy regularly proceeds for about 40 weeks (about 9 months), or altogether over 9 months, as determined beginning the final menstruation to birth. Wellness program suppliers commit to three partitions of pregnancy, required sessions. This term long standing affiliated escorted by a stork which is a fecundity sign that is as well connected to birthing and greenness. The hypothesis of a stork bringing recently born infants to their mommies is instructed to youngsters all over the Americas and continental Europe.

PRIAPO (from the Greek Priapos) God of the reproductive contents. The upland buffer line shall be clearly demarcated prior to any construction activities.

PRISCA The banner is given to a 5th century Latin translation of the canons of definite Greek Councils, as well as those of Nicaea and Chalcedon.

PRIESTESS All ancient tenets had their priestesses in temples. In Egypt they were named with the title of Sa, and were devoted to the altar of Isis, as well as in the temples of other goddesses. Canephore was the name given by the Greeks to the consecrated high priestess who carried the baskets of the gods through the public festivals of the Mysteries of Eleusis. There were prophesiers in Israel additionally, in Egypt, fortune tellers of sleep and interpreters of oracles. Herodotus, indication is also made of the Hierodules, virgins or nuns anointed to the Theban Jupiter, who were usually the daughters of Pharaoh, and other princesses of the Royal House. Orientalists speak of the wife of Coffrets, builder of the so-called second Pyramid, who was Toth's thaumaturge.

PRIYAMANA (Sanskrit) Affectionate, benevolent.

PROSE. A substitute title for the Sequence. (q.v.)

PROSERPINE Mother Death among the Egyptians. Amid the Romans it was labeled Persephone. According to tradition, she was the daughter of Jupiter and Ceras, previously mentioned was abducted by Ruton, who took her to his dark abode. As queen of the universe of shadows, Proserpina or Persephone accomplished as an archetypal the Grim Reapers. It is respected as the embodiment of the earth and spring.

PROCIO (Gr.) Writer and philosopher

PROMETHEUS (Greek) The Greek Logos; the one who, contributing to the earth the glorious fire (intelligence and conscience), endowed men with reason and understanding. Prometheus is the Hellenic type of our Kumaras or Egos, those who, incarnating in men, made of them latent deities, instead of animals.

PROTO-ILOS [From the Greek protos, first, matter.] [Neologism used in chemistry to designate the first primordial substance, hemogenic.] [It is the hypothetical primitive matter] of which it is formed PROTHA PROTA (Sanskrit) Pierced, strung, threaded, linked, woven, set, embedded, dressed, fabric. CHECK PROTHA is it a different word?

PHILOSOPHER (Gnosticism) The woman continuously stamps the tomb with a great philosopher's stone that signifies gender, the fight of opposition to perversity was appalling.

PHILOSOPHY (the. Philosophia, and gr. Love of wisdom) Wisdom that enhances the essence, patrimony, causes and effects of original things. Today philosophy together with other wisdoms organizes a precise discipline, with rules and special attention, which man has philosophized since his earliest births.

PHOSPHORUS (Greek) Epitomize "light bearer". Term given to Lucifer or planet Venus, the morning star, which glows on the horizon before the aurora appears. Is an alchemical component, a toxic, ignitable Metalloids which subsist in two ordinary brilliant configurations, undyed phosphorus, a golden glistening nonflexible which kindle automatically in airspace and gleams in the darkness, cardinal phosphorus, a secondary active formation consider in fabricating matches. Besides calx., phosphorus is the majority plentiful alloy in the anatomy. Phosphorus is a constituent of osseous matter, denticulation, chromosomes, and generic code. In the appearance of phospholipids. Phosphorus is one of the constituents that enjoyed alchemy individual trademark. The alchemist anticipated illumination illustrates the ethos. The foundation ingredients phosphorus was scrutinized since its supposed potentiality encompasses radiance, as verification by the attribute's fluorescent glare of phosphorus' amalgam. Unaltered phosphorus, additionally extempore blaze in airflow, but the domain was not secluded till 1669. Phosphorus could be contrasted as an extravaganza of phosphorescent when one glimpses at a personification of predawn at the northern, or southern lights, as well as the aurora australis.

PHYSICAL (Gnosticism) The material, body, somatic, natural. There is no doubt that the physical body is nature, and the material; given its tremendous and complicated organization, it is certainly far beyond our comprehension.

PIETA. A delineation of the BVM grieving over the dead body of Christ, which she clings to on to her needs.

PIG (Gnosticism) Symbol of impure desires. It is a, evolutive animal, which when ingested in food transmits negative, abysmal, degenerative vibrations and disseminated diseases. Gnostic Esotericism should not eat the flesh of this animal, nor its derivatives.

PIGHI, ALBERT (1490-1542) Dutch theologian. Called to Rome in 1523, he wrote on the key issues of the time. His principal work Hierarchies Ecclesiastical Assert (1538) is an refines defense of tradition a Christian truth coordinates with Scripture.

PILGRIM FATHERS, The. The English initiators of the colony of Plymouth, Mass., who cruised from Holland and England in the Mayflower in 1620. The label is somewhat modern.

PSILO (Psylli, enlatin). Snake charmers from Egypt and other parts of Africa. [The psilos constituted an ancient people of Libya (Africa), conforming to Pliny. They possessed the virtue of curing the bite of snakes and killing these reptiles thanks to aunapo. On an Egyptian bronze basin conserved in the Louvre Museum is the figure of a Psilo who enchants a snake.

POISON (Gnosticism) Not only is it killed with the Poison, the bullet or the dagger, it is also eliminated with thought, words and deeds, a deficient, satirical or double-edged sword, as well as thoughtlessness, they also hurt and sacrifice the feelings and good intentions of beings.

POLARITY (from polar) Character of what has heritage or possibility, such as poles. Four closed initiations of Hermes Trismegistus (The Kybalion) "everything is dual; everything has poles; all its pair of opposites; the like and the dissimilar are the identical; opposites are equal in nature, orienting only conceited; the confines touch; All the gospels are semi-truths, all couples can get along".

POLE Applies extended, thin, curved sections of lumber or casting, generally practiced alongside farthest insert in soil as a hold up for a commodity. "a tent pole" Poles are utilized for memorials and observances the lineage or chronicles of the population, or an occasion that civilized community. In Innermost cases, they represent powerful families as heraldic columns. Most barge poles the overlook of forefather's humankind or vertebrate that are people or dynasty of humankind. The tones in the barge pole similarly possess profound sense: Cardinal is the coloration of lifeblood, defining warfare or bravery. Sky blue is for the heavens and aqua, in addition to waterways and ponds. White is for the firmaments and roomy manhandle. Yellowish is the shade of the sunshine, conduct illumination and enjoyment.

PORTA SANTA The Italian for 'Holy Door.'

POPPY HEADS In ecclesiology, the ornamental ceilings at the tops of bench-ends, in conformation consistently resembling a fleur-de-lis. They became common in the 15th century.

POPOL VUH (Holy People's Book) The Quiche Manuscripts that were discovered by Brasseur de Beaubourg. Sacred books of Guatemalans.

POSSESSION Authority or residence of subject for that one does not certainly have one's own belongings entitlements: Presumably objects possessed, for instance, an automobile rapidly increases his highest capital ownership. A region below the mandate of an additional territory. Reconciliation is the sizable of Frances' foreign possessions. The calamity of being fooled by a villain or other mythical essence. Amidst the ancient times; folks who were mentally illed materialized occasionally viewed to be casualties of demoniac controlled. The clearance of the ball throughout a match. (American rules football).

POSTIL The phrase, which in the Middle Ages was used as a gloss on a Scriptural text, came to be applied mostly to a homily on the Gospel or Epistle for the day or to a publication of such homilies.

POSTRER. (Last) Forthcoming following all others in time or organization; final: e.g., The last publication of an encyclopedia.

POWER (Gnosticism) The humanoid disoriented called man cannot change episodes, he is a victim of them, perpetually happens to him as when it rains, as when it thunders; he has the illusion that he does, but he has no power to do, everything happens to him through "the mighty Him."

PROSTRATE(S) (Gnosticism) The festivities of the Soul, are the significance of advent of the Being towards us position with a clean mind and with a heart full of love, we prostrate humbly to position ourselves praying and conversing with our own God.

PROTHA (Sanskrit) Embryo, fetus; and rays, old dresses; as attribute: situated, fixed; Notorious, famous.

PROSE Connects to any part of manuscripts that accompanies an elemental morphological formation (ponders phrase and clauses arranged to diction and subdivision). This attracts attention from the efforts of Poesy. Goes along with a rhythmic arrangement (think lines sand stanzas). Writing plainly measures mother tongue that goes along with the innate influence discovered in daily verbal communication. The symbolism in writings is for instance: a superstorm infused on the range of vision ought to be an emblem of the psychological turbulence that the leading personality is undergoing; or the ebony automobile that the main central figure navigates is a prediction of his demise; in addition, It's crucial to recall that on occasions, tempest on the distance plainly suggests atmospheric conditions.

PSALMS, Portrays topics and accomplishments. Numerous psalms pertain to the sing of praises of God for his potentials and benefactions, for his innovations of the planet, and for his former accomplishments of liberation for Israel. They imagined a creation where every person and the entirely would choose to sing the praises of God, and God in rectifying, auscultate their invocations and answer. Psalms were the songbook of the Old Testament Jews. Many of them were put in writings by King David of Israel. Additional individuals who authored Psalms were Moses, Solomon, etc. The Psalms are influential since they allow many of us to perceive that we're not the archetypal to perceive God is inaudible, during our prayers, neither was no one the original to detect enormous torment and disorientation duration praying. The Psalms provides us techniques to delight in devotions, to genuflection in reverence, to praise God for ever he answers and for all his absolutions to us. The Psalms are exceedingly lyrical, abrupt and Musical. The Psalms which in sections or fragments implore Divine retaliation.

PUGIN, AUGSTS WELBY NORTH-MORE. Designer and Hermeneutics. He was the chief architect of and inspirer 'Gothic revival' His works comprise St. Giles, Cheadle, and St. George's (RC) Cathedral, Southwark. He worked together with C. Barry on the designs for the Houses of Parliament.

PUMPS Accompanied by a V-shaped alternatively and a heel of numerous distinct shapes, sizes and diameters, for over a hundred of years the pump has given evidence to changes in society, in robotics (allowing heels to reach rapid peaks) and in ladies' personalities in the community.

PUMS or PUNS (Sanskrit) Spirit, the supreme Purucha [Spirit]; man, male.

PUNK. Sociality embraces a various and extensively accepted cluster of principles, trends, and other forms of articulations, graphic arts, stepping, literary texts, and feature films. Widely appropriated by conventional sentiments, the relationship of personal privilege, and DIY (Do-it-Yourself) morality, the lifestyles rooted from punk rock. The communication of Punk was therefore non-conformist, nontraditional unmarketable, and truly angry. As did aboriginal Hi Hop in the United States, Punk Rock manifest a "Do-it-Yourself" or "DIY" point of view. Numerous quartets were self-generated and self-raising.

PUPPET An adjustable imitation of a human being or creature that is common in enjoyment and is customarily advanced by lines managed originating overhead or by a grasp inward. The puppet is the noticeable duplicate of the mortal, starting with a twofold viewpoint: the vivid, productive edge the inner self that is released coming out of the attracting force of the situation; the uncooperative at the side expose the attention concealed instinct. Occasional puppet channels anybody which is dominated by any others: "He was president, but he was just a puppet for his political party." Moppets' puppets were customary to dispose practice and formalities employing such as ligature bound proportions posterior in earliest ventures and is being used this day Puppetry was accomplished in prehistoric Graecia and the elderly note down evidence of marionettes can be discovered in the effort of Herodotus and Xenophon, goes back to the 5th centennial B.C.

PURIFICATION (Gnosticism) Man must pay homage to the feasts every day of his life, because sanctification is an commitment of every person responsible to himself before God, but the feast is not consecrated by sleeping and quarreling at home with the wife or husband, it is blessed in prayer, in meditation and in continuous purification, Stable next to our inner God always ready to serve God, to love and obey Him by working in the Great Work of the Father, whether in the workshop, in the office, at work, in the field all over creation and at all times we must sanctify the feast, because the feast must not be of the body but of the Soul.

PURIM This was Jewish festival which was commemorated in the spring. It celebrated the Deliverance of the Jews from massacre under the Persian Empire (473 B.C.), as correlated in the Book of Esther.

PURA (Sanskrit) City, castle; the physical body.

PURE, PURITY (Gnosticism) The origination of the Self rises to immemorial ages; it is said that humanity persists in a divine state, alien from evil while it had its paradisiacal life in Eden. Humanity at that time subsisted beyond good and evil; and their souls were pure and innocent.

PURGATORY (Latin purgatorius, which purifies) In it bestow situation is emphasize that is a location where those souls of population have died in grace, who did not do any entire penance for their sins, satisfy that debt with the sorrows they suffer, and then enjoy the glory.

PUSHA (Pucha) (Sanskrit) The morality of India. An appellation that recounted the Nadi that goes to the right ear. (Prasad Branch).

PYGMYS In folklore remained an ethnic category of petite African gentlemen who reside on the southmost shores of the sizeable encompass river Okeanos (Oceanus) in which they were occupied an at war with assembly migrating cranes. The expression pygmy, as used to refer to miniature people, derives from Greek pygmaios via Latin Pigmies (sing. Pygmaeus), acquire from Greek phrase which means a short lower arm cubit, or a calculate of length comparable to the span from the wrist to the elbow or knuckles.

PYXIE. A creeping evergreen dicotyledonous shrub. (Pyxidanthera barbulata, of the family Diapensiaceae) of the sandy pine barrens of the Atlantic coast of the US that has white or pink pentamerous start-shaped flowers:

PSYCHOMETRICS, PSYCHOMETRY. Express 'Measurement of the soul'. The fact of reading or seeing, not with the eyes of the body, but with the soul or with the inner vision. [Professor Buchanan, of Louisville, has given the voice of psychometrics to the faculty he discovered, which enables a certain class of sensitive persons to receive, from a thing they hold in their hand or applied to their foreheads, impressions of the character or aspect of the object or of any purpose with which that individual has been in contact].

PSYCHOLOGICAL SONG Relates to when the person makes an intimate self-consideration, this leads the person to a constant loss of energy, incurring in that song of constant narration where he goes to the sales that he has done so many favors and as a reward; he is paid poorly. Etc. Finally, he is the saint, and the others are evil.

PSYCHOLOGY The wisdom of the soul, anciently: a perception that served as an essential basis for physiology; While in our days it happens the other way around: psychology is grounded (by our great men of science) on physiology. ... Science of the soul, in ancient times, served as the groundwork for physiology.

-Q-

QUARR ABBEY, Isle of Wight. In 11/31/2 Baldwin de Redvers initiated cloister on the section, that was conquer from Savigny; it endured until the Dissolution in 1537. In 1908 the location was obtained by the Benedictine exile Solesmes, and a red brick abbey in Flemish style was built. The homestead is a Centre of Sacramental and ancient investigation.

QUANTAS (Gnosticism) Specifically the twinkling of the force set of atoms. An atom is like a vibrometer that originates waves with speeds typical of harmony of its kind. When the Quantas are fast, they are not discernible, neither are they noticeable, when they are awfully slow. Normally Quantas adventure at the promptness of the light and in a circle. The emotional attachment of the disembodied to the physical world slows down the beads multiplying evident to the retina of the eye of a living person, thus the personality of the dead is palpable. Anything at all or object can be created visible and invisible according to the speed of Quantas.

QUATERNARY Viable confirmed by the four "principles" of man that fabricate his constitution, that is: the consolidation or physical body (sthula zarira), the component set duplicate or astral element (linga zarira); factual or essential initiation (prana) and the axis of the animal longings or enthusiasms. This domination must be divided from the perennial preside over ternary or triad, which order the makeup, and are the higher Manas, the Buddhi and the Atman (or supreme Self.

QIGONG The earliest configuration of Chinese exercise that inflates your energy area. Qi stands for the power of life that influences oneself, each person has their own personal QIGong raises for effort and strictness. Qigong has three major approaches: intangible, vigorous, and curative. In spiritual qigong, one's predominant aim is to succeed serenity, unity with nature, and understanding. Muscular Qigong incorporates physical activities that raise energized, resistance, teamwork, and equilibrium, and reduce the likelihood of lesions. The six Qigong Relieve Tones for Moving Balance are breathed sounds that can be utilized to set free heavy emotional energy such as desolation, panic, anger, concern, and worry. This application is suggested once a day, mostly in the evening to prompt tranquil rest.

QUMRAN. The On-the-scene of some ruins at the NW end of the Dead Sea where the first of the Dead Sea Scrolls was found in 1947, to be proceeded by additional finds in later years.

QUINARIA (Principles) In the septenary of man, the numerous Proposition should not be suggest as detached organization, as coordinated and overlapping wrappings in the appearance of the separate layers of an onion, but at the impossibility, as cooperatively, integrated, united with an indisputable way, but liberated of all other and each retaining a contrasting required and vibratory state; each lower Principle consistently being the vehicle of its instant higher levels, deviation made of the physical body, which is the vehicle (Upadhi) of the additional six. After some time, in this same ranking, the seven Principles are designated into two series that forms, furthermore, the upper Triad, that is, the inner, continuous and durable Singularity formed by Atman, Buddhi and Mannas, and on the supplementary, the lower Quaternary, exceptionally, the transitory and perishable Personality, repressed of the four lower assumptions: the Kama-rupa, with the foundations or animal portion of Manas; the Prana, the Linga-zarira and the physical body. The factual and true man is the superior Manas; It is the entity that regenerates, relocating as a karmic trace the good and bad capabilities of their phenomenon or preceding animations. When the Manas has merged into the Atma-Buddhi man has transfigured into a creator.

QUINQUÉ VIAE The five 'ways or disagreement by which St. Thomas Aquinas sought to prove the existence of God from those significances. His Being which are well known to us, viz. (1) that locomotion implies a first mover; (2) that a sequence of systematized causes, and theirs effects, such as we discover in the world, hinted some necessary being; (4) that the comparisons we make (more or less 'true', 'noble', & c.) imply a excellence of contrast which is in itself perfect in all these qualities; (5) that the achievement by inanimate or unintelligible objects of an end to which they are evidently designed to work suggested a preconceived intelligence in their formation and direction.

QUO VADIS. (Lat., 'Where Are you going?') In agreement with a narrative, first found in the Acts of Peter, the query was asked by St. Peter when, running away from Rome, he met Christ. The Lord responded, 'Iam going to be crucified again.' Peter returned to Rome where he was martyrized.

-R-

RA (Egypt) The divine universal Soul in its manifested aspect; the ever-burning light; it is also the Sun materialized. [The god Ra is demonstrated with sparrowhawk head because the fowl in question is sanctify to Horus. Ra means: to do; defined, and indeed, the god Ra arranged and resolved the world, whose matter Ptah had brought him.

RAB-MAG (Cald.) Chief of the Magicians.

RABHAS (Sanskrit) Violent mobility of the soul or body; impetuosity, violence, fury, speed. As an identifier: impulsive, fierce, aggressive, energetic.

RABB. Often used to refer to God in Arabic (Allah) as the "Lord" or "master". Rabb appears separating the root raa-baa-baa, which hints to three main meanings. The first main definition is to be lord, owner, or master. The second leading interpretation is to minister, nurtur, preserve, and administer for, and the triumvirate is to lift or develop. This root materialized 980 times in the Quran in four emanate formations. Rab term is an Arabic expression, and its sense is Waheguru/God. Sikhs don't go censure things precisely since the initiation of the vocable is not from Punjab or Sikhism. New words acquire addition frequently in distincts vernaculars.

RABBAN Jewish Religion. Master; faculty member (used as a denomination of inscription and title of respect for an individual ranking higher thana a rabbi). Rabban is the Syriac rm for monk. "Rabban" is also the Aramaic term for "teacher". He establishes the Rabban Hormizd Monastery in Alqosh, named after him, which has served in the past as the patriarchates of the Church of the East.

RABBI (Heb., 'my master'). A Jewish name of respect extraordinary to honored teachers by disciples and others. Shortly after NT times it access to be attached to the name of Jewish devoted leaders as a title, e.g., "Rabbi Johanan".

RADICAL ZERO Exactly as said that it embodies the unknowable whole.

RAEL. A French correspondent (born Claude Marcel Vorilhon, September 30, 1946) who established and leads the Raelian Movement, an international UFO religion. Prior to becoming a religious leader, Rael, then known as Claude Vorilhon, Networked as a sportscar journalist and test diver for his car-racing magazine, Auto pop. subsequent a purported extraterrestrial confronts in

December 1973, he developed the Raelian Movement and altered his name to Rael defining "messenger of the Elohim"). He later broadcasted numerous books, which elaborate the confrontation with a being called Yahweh in 1973. He pilgrimaged the world to upgrade his books for over 30 years.

RAGA (Sanskrit) One of the five klezas (torment and barriers) in Patanjali's yoga philosophy. In the Sankhya-karika, it is the "obstacle" cited love and desire in the physical and earthly sense.

RAGHU (Sanskrit) A monarch of the solar race, great-grandfather of Rama.

RAJASA (Sanskrit) Describes procedures from Rajas: passionate, active, energetic, violent, agitated, passionate, instinctive.

RAJAH (Sanskrit) "The quality of impurity" (i.e., differentiation) and activity of the Puranas. One of the divisions or guns in the correlations of matter and nature, which reproduce form and change. [It is the second of the three modes, characteristics or classifications (gunas) of Prakriti (matter): the passionate quality, that of action or exertions. Its consequences on the objective world are: gesticulations and energy; In the subjective, it manifests as suffering, pain, duration, anxiety, restlessness, agitation, boredom, disgust, jealousy, envy, instabilities, confusing, ambition, desire, passion, love, hate, malice, fondness for discord and slander, imbalance, restlessness, disorder, violence, struggle, energy, effort and activity. "He knows that rajas, whose nature is of passion, being the origin of longings and affections, chains the Lord of the body by attachment to action ... Ambition, greed, activity, ardor in enterprises, restlessness and desire arise from the predominance of rajas." (Bhagavad-Gita) As it stands, the predominant quality in the human species. Just as it is also the quality that communicates impulse and activates to the other two (sattva and tamas), which by themselves cannot enter activity, and so it has been said that "the Path extends from tamas to Satva by means of struggle and aspiration" (rajas).

RAJAKA (Sanskrit). Authentic, sovereign; brilliance, magnificent.

RAJATA (Sanskrit). Whitish, silvery; silver; ivory; constellation. Name of a lake and a mountain.

RAJAT Whitish, silvery; Plat; ivory; constellation. Name of a lake and a mountain.

RAJYA (Sanskrit) Royalty, Sovereign, Kingdom

RAHASA (Sanskrit) The sea; heaven.

RAM (Sanskrit) Neutral nominative of Ra. Considered as a symbol of the tattva Agni.

RAMA Hindu national hero. Protagonist of the Ramayana considered the seventh Avatara or incarnation of Vishnu. He is the Christ-Yogi of the Hindustani.

RAMBIA A region with a very compact community in the homeland of Indonesia which is in the district of Asia. Although, Indonesia has the fourth most populous nation in the planet with over 275 million population where the major part speaks Indonesian, which makes it one of the most widely spoken languages in the world. The immediate major cities include Makasar, Kendari, Palu and Mataram. Their mother tongue is a variation of Malay, even though, Bahasa Indonesia is the national language.

RAMIO (Gnosticism) Designation of Our Divine Mother particular. The Ramio Mantram helps us to be alert from moment to moment, if we constantly pronounce it and ask our Divine Mother for help... Ram is a mantra of fire; from Tatwa Tejas Mantram 10 reminds us of the mysteries of Isiac's 10 is the point of interest.

RAMYA (Sanskrit). The night.

RAI (Sanskrit). Things, goods, property screams, howl.

RAIN Water descending in drops coagulates from condensation in the aerosphere, the falls of this aqua, moisten that has dropped as rain. This expression perhaps indicates numerous elements. It conceivably supports Sorrow, recovery, apprehension, resolution, the disintegration of a dry spell, and a delay for contemplation. Rain has been passed down as an emblem for innumerous millesimal of generations, possibly particularly in the downpour in the holy scriptures. Rain has furthermore displayed in the Good Book, eminently impressively in the narrative of Noah and the Ark. The Almighty sends on a cloudburst to dismantle humankind and purge the earth of their transgressions. On the other hand, rain dealt as an image of duality: The potential to demolish a society filled with transgressors. Because rain adjusts to diverse innate environment, materializing in divergent configurations, it signifies compliance and submission. Subsequently, certainly, rain is yet an extra illustration of Divine Justice. A benediction!!

RAINBOW. It is frequently a sign of hope, beauty following the storm, a pot of gold and good fortune at the rainbow's ending. For a great number of people, a rainbow carries a characteristic emblematic interpretation; describing inclusivity and diversity, an all-embracing image of devotion and friendship. The rainbow, like all of God's creation, effects the beauty and magnificence of God. The radiant colors and glorious presence of a rainbow in the sky marks to the existence of God and reflects his glory. I have set my rainbow in the clouds, and it will be the sign of the covenant between me and the earth. I will recall my covenant between me and you and all existing creatures of every kind. Never again will the waters grow into a flood to destroy all life.

RANTERS They were a fanatical sect of the 17th century. Their desirability to their experiences of Christ leads them to dispute the authority of Scriptures. Creeds and the Ministry.

RASA. (Sanskrit) Inexplicable dance of Krichna and her gopis [zagalas or shepherdesses], executed in an annual festival to this day; exclusively in Rajasthan. Astronomically it is Kraiaachna; the Sun, around which revolve in a circle the planets and sinuses of the Zodiac emblemized by the gopis. It is the same as the "circular dance" of the Amazons around thepria fishing image, and the dance of the daughters of Siloh (Judges, XXI), as in addition of King David around the ark.

RAS SHAMRA TABLETS RATIO STUDIORUM (Latin, 'the method of the studies'). The abbreviated name of the A accumulation of cuneiform tablets with methodological poems and ritual instructions excavated at Ras Shamra (ancient Ugarit) in N. Syria from 1929 onwards. They likely date from the 14th century B.C. or prior and are in a hitherto undisclosed alphabetical handwriting and a Semitic dialect kin to Hebrew. Their contents appear in some exceptional compatibility with the OT.

RASHI (1040-1105) Jewish Ecclesiastical professor, well known from the fundamental of his name, Rabbi Solomon ben Isaac. His position, in opposing to the evolving interpretation of his time, was to translate the OT in relation to its factual perception. His expositions were dominant between Jews and Christians from a prior time.

RATNAVABHASA-Kalpa (Sanskrit) The lifespan at which all sensual difference will conclude to exist, and birth will take location in the anupadaka [fatherless] form, as in the instantly and threesome Mother-races. The Esoteric philosophy instructs that this will appear at the end of the sixth and amid the seventh and last mother race in the present Round.

RAT. In common, rats can illustrate fright, filth, and pests. They may as well describe tenderness of existence pressurize or engulf, in addition secret alarm or apprehension. On the contrary, rats may mirror quickness, flexibility, and ingenuity. 29 Moles, rats, mice, and lizards ought to be appraised impure. 31 Whoever embraces them, or their remains will be tainted down to dusk. 32 And if their cadaver drops down on any one thing, it will be soiled. Mice and rats are frequently linked with unfavorable components in ordinary existence and across channels. It is ordinary for mice and rats to be represented as transporters of infection, and irritation that have powerful relation to pollution and unsanitary environment. These pessimistic alliances can motivate abnormal fear to come to light.

RATA (Sanskrit). Pleased, satisfied, joyful.

RATHA (Sanskrit) Chariot, catalyst; the body, as the vehicle of the soul and the Spirit; Constituent; foot; the one who guides the chariot; warrior; Hero.

RATIO STUDIORUM (Lat., 'the method of the studies'). The shortened denomination of the Jesuit scheme of studies issue in 1599. It was established on the best pedagogical theory of the time, and the achievement of Jesuit secondary education from the 16th to the 18th centuries was predominantly due to it.

RAPHAEL (Raphael the Archangel, Saint) (Gnosticism) One of the angels quoted in the Old Testament. Raphael is an archangel ruling over the planet Mercury, one of the seven Cosmochrators of our Universe. It unfolds in the rays of Universal Medicine.

RAU (Scandinavia) The goddess of the sea, in Scandinavian mythology.

RAUMAS (Raunasa) (Sanskrit) A category of devas (gods), who are said to have derived from the pores of the skin of Virabhadra. An allusion to the pre-Adamic race named the "sweat-born". [In the Mahabharata (XII, 10, 308) there is talk of a people called Raumas, who, it is said, were generated from the pores of Virabhadra, a appalling giant who spoiled the sacrifice of Daksha. Other ethnic groups and races are also outlined as being born in the same way. All these are references to the last part of the second Rama-mother and origination of the third.

RAVANA (Sanskrit) The demon king (rakchasa), ruler of Lanka (Ceilan), who stole Sita, wife of Rama, fact that led to the great war defined in the Ramayana. [Ravana is the illustration of the Atlantic race. He is described as a giant of colossal stature, "like the beak of a mountain"; it had ten heads and twenty arms;

and its strength was so great that it could stir the seas and tear the peaks of the mountains. It could also change shape deliberately. He was king of the demons called rakchasas, and because of his great contradictoriness he can be measured the embodiment of evil.

RAVENNA. Consistently to tradition the first bp. Of Ravenna was St. Apollinaris (q.v.). After the city was selected as the Imperial dwelling in 404, it grew in momentousness and wealth. In 493 it fell to Theodoric the Goth, who instituted Arianism. It was apprehended for the Byzantine Empire by Belisarius (540) and developed the capital of the Exarchate until it fell to the Lombards in 751. It is unrivalled in its mosaics and other remainder of prehistoric Christian art.

RAWS. Channels coarse in attribute or indications; not advance or processing by artifice or savour: raw comical facets, illiterate, unschooled, or amateurish; a raw novice, mercilessly or unspeakably honest; a raw portrait of mortal excitable; fiercely oppressive or biased: a raw handle; collect raw reconstruct from his buddies. Mystically definition of Raw. The definition of raw is to abstain from the acceptability of deep affection. A particular raw has this power, is translucent from the intention of charcoal grill with bonfire, as reality the favorable of tenderness (AC852); in consequence, raw signifies that which is not griddle with heat, hence that which is in the absence of tenderness.

RAYA (Sanskrit) Rapid movement; Promptness, speed. Current, torrent, course.

RAYI (Sanskrit) Wealth, treasure; power. The uncooperative phase of the situation, which is distinguished from the positive by its impressionability. Indicated the coldest vital matter, just as the hottest is labeled Prana. (Prasad Branch: The Subtle Forces of Nature).

RAZI-CHAKRA (Rashi-Chakra) (Sanskrit) The zodiac.

REA. (Obeles). It represents the Divine Mother. In mythology she appears as the mother of the Gods daughter of Uranus and Gaia, sister and wife of Saturn (Oronos). She was the mother of Hestia (Vesta) Demeter (Ceres), Hera (Juno), Hades (Pluto), Poseidon (Neptune) and Zeus (Jupiter).

REABSORPTION or Pralaya (Sanskrit) Materialization, a period of obscuration or rest (planetary, cosmic or universal); it is the contradictory of Manvantara. Pralaya is the intervals of sleep dissolution or relative or total rest of the universe that occurs at the end of a Day, an Age or a Life of Brahma. But this term does not procedure only to each "Night of Brahma", that is, to the dissolution of the world that follows each Manvantara; apply correspondingly to every "obscuration" and every catastrophe that ends, by play or by water, alternately, to every mother-race.

REALISM In artfulness, the veracious, elaborations, unadorned Artis's impression of natural forces or of up-to-date vivacity. Common sense dismisses visionary exaltations in agreement of an adjacent monitoring of evident emergence. As equivalent, realism in its large sensation fabricated numerous inventive steady flows in contrasting human developments. apologue was mainly a response opposed literalism and practicality, anti-radical manner that intend attempt to continue for actuality theirs granular unusually, and to boost the respectful and the standard above consummation. Myth was a response to reverence, creative powers, and fantasy.

REBIRTH. A new or second birth: metempsychosis: spiritual regeneration; renaissance, revival. The cherry blossom tree is a symbol of rebirth. This idea is rooted in a section of the Bible's New Testament, commonly translated os that Jesus says, "no one can see the kingdom of God unless they are born again." "Definitions of reborn, spiritually reborn or converted." Green many times exemplifies rebirth, growth, peace, jealousy, and greed. Green colors can also describe spring and continuation.

REACTION. Action that endures or opposes another action, (Gnosticism). It connects to the images that come to the mind as impressions, through the physical senses; That is, feelings are what produce the depiction that comes to mind. The reactions were responded to such impressions.

REAL PRESENCE, The. In (especially Anglican) Holy Communion creed an emphasize sed to cover several doctrines accentuated the actual all-presence of the Body and Blood of Christ in the Sacrament, as contradictions with others that maintain the Body and Blood are present only metaphorical or symbolically.

REALIZATION Several ordinary equivalents of realization are nourished, foresee, visualized, wish for, conceptualized, and believe. Briefly, the above terms signify "to form an idea of," realize emphasizes a desire of the importance of why is formulated or assumed, realizing the quality of the duty forward. An unexpected realization authorizes an epiphany which come to light from the earliest Greek epiphanea, ("manifestation, striking appearance") is a participation in a unexpected and evident realization. A metonym for God realization: They realized self (atman) i.e., God surrounding your lifetime by exploring the pathway of solid Devotion. They extend the phase of Understanding, self-discovery, God-Realization, jivanmukti, Atma-jnana (all expression employed as synonyms).

REAP. The doctrinal interpretation of reap is "to gather a crop" and to sow, "to plant seeds." All through adaptation of the Scriptures, sowing is utilized as an allegory for one's achievement and gathering for the conclusion of those determinations. The holy book talks about reaping what you did not sow. The verse is, "You reap where you did not sow and gather where you did not scatter" (Matthew 25:24). Obviously, this condemnation is in allusion to the Lord Jesus Christ, and it is fitting that Hebe illustrated this way. Was it not Jesus who reaped "the whirlwind" of all humanity's sinful folly. (Hosea 8:7)

REAPPEAR. To get back ahead or turn up for a little while or consecutive life: to appear once more. Definition from Oxford dictionary: to appear again after not being heard of or seen for a period. They decided to visit another friend, went down the corner and did not reappear until morning. "Dear friends, we are now God's children, but what we are to be in the future has not yet been fully revealed. We know that if Christ reappears, we shall be like Him, because we shall see Him as He is."

REASON, A source, description, or rationale for an activity or as a result "the teacher resigned for personal reasons". The capability of the intellect to anticipate, recognize, and for common sense by a exercise of argumentation. "There is a close connection between reason and emotions."

RECARED (d. 601), King of the Visigoths. He was correlated with his father in governing the country (most of Spain) from 573 and accomplished him in 586. In 587 he deserted Arianism and became a Catholic. This step did much to unite the nation since the Catholics were more dominant than the Arians.

RECORD, (The) An Anglican weekly newspaper, begun in 1828. It was heavily Evangelical. In 1949 it was amalgamated with the Church of England's Newspaper.

RECLUSE Individuals who live separately from the world, mostly for the motivation of religious meditation. The root word of reclusive is recluse, which came from the Old French word reclus, originally meaning "a person shut up from the world for purposes of religious meditation." Today, maybe you just want to be alone, reclusive describes a person who is withdrawn from society or seeks solitude, like a hermit. People with schizoid personality disorder often are reclusive, organizing their lives to avoid contact with other people. Many never marry or may continue to live with their parents as adults. Merriam-Webster says a recluse is "a person who leads a secluded or solitary life," while a hermit is "one that retires from society and lives in solitude especially for religious reasons." Well, my desire to avoid human interaction wasn't grounded in religion.

RECTOR One that conducts or guides; (in the Apostolic Church) a constituent of the pastorate who has command of a congregation. The supervisor of definitive varsity, educational institution, and academies. The expression headmaster (Portuguese: Reitor) is utilized to relate to the top-level administrators of schools in Brazil. Respectively establishment is en route by a chief, the individual subordinate advisory board of the principal. An alternative title for headmaster can be woman of the cloth, minister, chairman, pastor, vicar, Protestant pastor, chaplain, friar, delegate, Dominie and members of the clergy.

RHECTORIC. Appears from the Greek interpretation "speaker" as well as is intended for the get going eloquent vocalizing or handwriting. When the population witnessed cordially to long discourses and reviewed them in educational institutions, articulative was largely used emphatically: as a result, many times an unfavorable phrase suggested craftiness constantly authentic reconcile.

RHAZES. Is the Latin al-Razi, Doctor of Medicine, researcher, and metaphysics whose full designation in Arabic was Abu Balr <u H Ammad ibn Zakar ya al-Razi. The respects of his live and the dates of his birth (c. 865 and death (923 or 925) are not well obtained. Existence His ethnic name, al-Razi relates to the city of Rayya, once Rages Rhagae), which was dominant in the eastern caliphate under Islam; it was situated near Teheran, the present-day capital of Iran. Until the age of 30 (some say 40). Rhazes was attentive in music and chemistry (alchemy). Subsequently, he appeared absorbed in medicine. According to some, this interest was brought about by the weakened circumstances of his eyes, variously accredit to his chemical examination or to a lash of the whip. But as claimed to his admirers, the great scientist a-Bifuni, Rhazes' blindness was due to deficiencies in his diet and to profusion in his way of life. This may explain the pronounced interest Rhazes had in matters of diet, as verification by the writings preserved in manuscripts that he has left on this question. Rhazes enjoyed a wide influence as a physician; he was made head of a hospital in Rayya and later held a close position in Baghdad. In Rhazes' metaphysics there are five propositions: the creator, the soul, matter, time, and space. Against the predominant doctrine of the Muslim philosophers, and in consensus (though no intentional) with the Muslim theologians he opposes the eternity of the world. Metempsychosis, for which he was censured by the Andalusian theologian.

RHOS. The context of the RHOS (Welsh for 'moor'/ 'moorland') is a district to the east of the Rive Conwy n North Wales. It is used to describe the "r" sound in

Prehistoric and Modern Greek. In the network of Greek binary, it has a reduction of 100. characters that approach from it embrace the Roman R and Cyrillic P. In demographics, the microscopic RHO ("p") is habituated to delineated populace equivalence.

RED SEA. The crossing of the Red Sea by the Israelites, recorded in Exod. 14 and 15, decided the end of their bondage in Egypt and was afterwards contemplated as a turning point in their destiny. The site of the extent crossing is debated.

REDISCOVER. To discover (phenomenon disoriented or bygone) once more in America we command at best not long ago reclaimed the make use of untamed grassy. They should enhance camaraderie once more and reclaim a sensation of enjoyment and demand to be all together. Expenditure of moments on myself once again benefits rediscover acquaint yourself consistently exceptional rediscover the headed for the core. Nevertheless, I rediscovered how satisfying a pure carrot top could be.

REFLEXES, REFLEXION The procedure of permitting attentively constant to objective; a reflect conveying cautious contemplations. The contrast linking consideration and contemplation discontinue could plainly be methodical because ricochets backwards of brightness during bang the moderate on a drive. Deflection conceivably explains the operation of the transfer of radiance just after it releases across a channel guiding to the arching of glowing. The luminosity set foot in the forum returns to the identical avenue. Distinctions amid casting back and deform: the regress of brightness or acoustics in the equivalent vehicle, just after plunging on the level surface, is labeled casting back. The switch in the order of the frequency waves, receivers it infiltrates approach with divergent solidity, is celebrated as swerves.

REGENERATE, REGENERATION. A transformation that permits objectives and creatures to restore or recover impaired or misplaced follicles, matter, components, and level off continuous biological structures to fully functioning. Researchers are considering reconstruction for its prospectives exercises therapy, by its nature recuperative a diversity of wounds and infections. Individuals and humanity, variance of beasties have developmental potential. Youngsters, for instance, perhaps rejuvenate lost disposal, at the same time grown-ups undergo continual transformations on an insignificant flake scale between the renewal of characteristics by the nature of epidermis, locks and bowel. Devotional aim that God guide a human being to revitalization (that they are "born again") coming from a preceding of detachment from God and subjugation to the perish of dying (Ephesians 2:5). Consequently, in Nonconformist and Romanism dogma, it normally contemplates that which come about all along immersion. The inner regeneration which leads to accepted creed, is reproduced in the inspiration by Christening (q.v.). A sacred revival has transpired in your incarnation. God handed down a revivification from reproduction. This is exactly the substituting process of declaring that you've turned out to be regenerated.

REGIMEN. Candid well organized plan of action (as of diet, therapy, or medication) mainly when nominated to upgrade and continue the well-being of a convalescent, a natural outcome of activities and particularly of arduous instructions; governance. Do you follow an elegant process? A regimen is organized practice of steps you accept achieve anything. For instance, you might have the objective of experiencing cloudless skin. Your regimen's efficiency involves evading harmful nourishment, cleansing systematically with a quality brand, and capturing a thorough nighttime rest.

REGINA COELI (Lat., 'Queen of Heaven') The 'Eastertide anthem to the B.V.M. so called from its opening words. Its authorship is unknown, but in all probability. Dates from the 12th century.

REGIONS. Geological sectors of origination are attributed to the zones in which migrants populated at the dawn of the interval and that they abandoned during their time of closure. A region might be interpreted by legitimate or factitious qualities. dialect, leadership, or faith community can describe a region, credible woodland, the animal/plant kingdom, or atmospheric conditions. Regions, extensive or compact, are the fundamental ingredients of earth science. The term "region" is adapted by English Versions of the Bible conversely with 'county', 'coasts', etc. for numerous Hebrew and Greek expressions, but "region round about" is consistently in the Holy Scriptures and universally in the modify (Bristish and American) the transcriptions of Perichoros, "surroundings country." As written on 1 Chronicles 13:2; "David said to the whole Israelite assembly, "If you so desire and the Lord our God approves, let's spread the word to our brothers who remain in all the regions of Israel, and to the priests and Levites in their cities, so they may join us".

REGULA MAGISTRI. An Unidentified Cloistral Regulations mark down by the 'the Master' in Italy SE. Of Rome c. 500-25. Partially vocally corresponding with the introduction and chapters 1-7 of the Rule of St. Benedict; the kinship of the couple Laws anachronistic the conditional of much disagreement, but most professor now provide precedence to the Regula Magistri.

REGRET. To grieve the disappearance or demise of anyone appreciated; fail to take in immensely. Come remorseful for feeling contrite about his inaccuracy. Regret is an authentic response to a discouraging center of attention in your continued prevalence, an alternative produced a certainty inadequately transformation, being discussed that your unfitness is inescapable. It's particular of such sentiment you can appear agitated, a heavy and intrusive negative emotion that could last for instants, days, generations or steadily an existence. Hyacinth. The purple hyacinth specifically represents sorrow, regret and forgiveness. It concludes illustration thankfulness at stuff does not vocalize or aggravating affairs undetermined

REICHENU. A petite island in the western division of Lake Constance prominent for its Benedictine convent, originated by St. Pirminius in 724. Its assembly of Manuscripts (many now at Karlsruhe) was previously confirmed in the preliminary 9th centennial.

REJ (Sanskrit) Agni, the fire.

REKH-get-Amen (Eg.) Appellation by which were denominated the clergyman, advocator and adept of alchemy, the one in question, conforming to Lenormant, But also the two Champolions and more, "could practice levitation, walk through the air, live under of water, sustain an enormous burden, suffer any without harm to mutilacion, read the past predict the future become invisible and cure various ailments". (Bonwick, Religions of Magic); and a similar writer adds: "The admission in the Mysteries does not contain magical powers; these depended on two cases: the possession of innate aptitudes, and the knowledge of certain formulas used in appropriate circumstances." The equal as present day.

RELATIONS. The situation or conditions of complimentary related or the process tactics are associated interrelations by ancestry or coupling; relatedness. An individual who is related by heritage or alliance; comparative; blood relatives. The celebrated, comprehensive image of relations tenderness is the inverted triangle depiction, and it personifies the essence of lovingness, soft centered affections, and attentive. 'Relation' conceivably knowing demonstrates exclusive agreement through couple divergent nations. For instance, the relations linking US and Canada are completely compact. Relations specify human beings who are interconnected to one another in a particular way. The original alliance indicates that countless students come across is the equivalent logo, = that transmits a correlation of corresponding in the middle quantity. It is crucial for pupils to appreciate that ideograms encourage convey affairs linking numerals and that correlation is equitable matching relationship.

RELICS. In doctrine, a relic is a gadget or item of reverent importance deriving out of long-ago. It habitually includes the material leftovers of a holy being, or the private possessions of the pietist or reverence individual safeguarded for intentions of veneration as a palpable keepsake. Relics are a meaningful aspect of a few dispositions of Buddhism, Christianity, Islam, Shamanism, and numerous doctrines. Relic assumed from the Latin Reliquiae, defining "remains", and an outline of the Latin verb reliquary, to "leave behind, or abandon". A reliquary is a region that accommodates one of the additional spiritual relics. The adoration of the relics of the glorified soul reflects a reliance that the pietist in paradise intervene for these on earth. A variety of restored and prodigy came to be ascribed to relics, not because of the divinity of the angel they perform except presumably because of the conviction of the individual interviewed.

RELIGARE (Gnosticism) Etymology of Word: Re means to return ligare: it is to bind, to reunite. What needs to be relinked is our individual awareness with Cosmic Consciousness.

RENAN, JOSEPH ERNEST (1823-92), French philosopher, theologian, and orientalist. His Averroes et l'averroisme (1852) established his notoriety as a scholar. In 160 he was sent on an archaeological mission to Phoenicia and Syria, and it was in Palestine that he wrote his Vie de Jesus. In this book he repudiated the supernatural element in Christ's life, ignored its moral aspect, and presented Him as an amiable Galilean preacher. Its publication in 1863 created a sensation.

RENE. This denomination approach consequently Latin Renatus, which process "rebirth" or "born again". However, initially characterized as an intangible appellative envelop transformation, Rene has therefore progressive an enduring notion in the esoteric and fantastic earth. Rene Jean-Marie-Joseph Guenon (11/15/1886 - 01/07/1951) was a French intellectual who remains a significant participant in the dominion of ideology, authored on issues covering deriving out of mystics, "sacred science" and "traditional studies" to figurations and institute. He had suggested to advance precisely a few features of Eastern philosophical credence of "universal character", or "to adapt these same doctrines for Western readers while keeping strictly faithful to their spirit", supporting the Hindu background of "handing down" the conviction much as recapitulating in that respect "non-human character". Instituted towards Islamic Mysticism from as early as 1910.

REPOSE Is a disposition of repose, drowsiness, or peacefulness. To lean back or be at unwind, as out of exertion, pastime, etc. To prostrate expired: His form will stillness in the sanctuary for couple of days. Subsequent resting tranquil and silent: The ocean stretches covered by the steamy subtropical sun. He commanded them: Isaiah 28:12 "This is the place of rest, let the weary rest; this the place of repose". But they would not listen. Luke 12:19 states "and I will say to my soul, Sour, thou hast much good things laid by for many years; repose thyself, eat, drink, be merry."

RESHA-havurah. (Hebr., Cabal.) Precisely: "White Head", from which emanates the fiery fluid of life and intelligence in three hundred and seventy streams, in all regulations of the universe. The "White Head" is the first Sephira, the Crown or first active light.

REPHALM (Hebrew) Specters, ghosts. [Giants or powerful primitive men, from whom perhaps Evolution will one day infer the origin of our present race.

REPRESSION. It is a disposition of being repressed. Cognitive, Psychotherapy, the repudiation from recognition of excruciating or splenetic feelings, memories, emotive, or instincts; Freud's advance on interpreting initial memories accentuate reality which has been forgotten amid the apparatus of repression. The pursuit of administration or applying domination over existence, a disposition of compulsory subjection. "The long repression of Christian sects" variety of subjugation, vanquish, pressure appeasement to authority by alternative. The distinctiveness intercalating oppression and repression is that oppression intricates specific details social division to the same degree a part of golden-agers, non-white populations, etc. Injustice is straightforward approaching Someone else. Repression indicates the characterization of being admitted beneath jurisdiction compulsorily in the process of concealing Introspections or precognition. Repression is a cerebral abnormality.

REPEAL (Gnostic) No humanist author, prophet, has gotten the authority to repeal these ordinances much less could that legion of demons that we carry inside to make us violate the Law.

REPOSE, Altar of. A Shrine on which (according to W usage) Hosts sanctify at the Maundy Thursday Mass are restrained for Eucharist on Good Friday.

REREDOS. Were any accessories above or behind the altar. Throughout the earliest time it consisted of paintings on the walls. During the Middle Ages the reredos advanced commonly to be assembled of painted wooden panels, either secured or in the formation of a triptych, carved stone or alabaster.

RESURGENCE Earliest, the term was employed in Christian surroundings to specify to the rise of Christ from the dead or to the festival celebrating this rise (now known as Easter). The term in due course began to be employed more overall in the senses of "resurgence" or "revival." Its Latin root, resurgent, a "to rise."

RETRA (Sanskrit) Manly seed, nectar, ragweed.

RETURNS. To come back to an earlier place after you have been away. (Gnostics) The incessant return of all things is a law of life, and we can verify it from instant to instant and from moment to moment. The earth returns to its starting point every year, and then we celebrate the new year; All the stars return to their original kicking point, the atoms inside the molecule return to their first point, the days return, the nights return, the four seasons return: spring, summer, autumn and winter, the cycles, calps, yugas, Manvantaras, etc. We have been told that at the precise moment of death, at the moment that the deceased exhales his last to canvas, projects an electro-psychic design of his personality, such design continues in the suprasensible regions of nature and later, comes to saturate the fertilized egg, so it is as when returning, by rejoining a new physical body we come to possess personal characteristics very similar to those of the previous life. Returning to a new physical body, the law of karma comes into action, for there is no effect without cause, no cause without effect. It is utterly absurd to say that one voluntarily chooses the place where one should be reborn; The reality is different. It is precisely the lords of the law, the angels of karma, who select for us the place, home, family, nation, etc., where we must reincorporate, return. If the ego could choose the place, or family, etc., for its new reinstatement, then the ambitious, proud, greedy, would look for palaces, the houses of millionaires, the rich mansions, the beds of roses and feathers, and the world would be all wealth and sumptuousness, there would be no poor, there would be no pain or bitterness, No one would pay karma, we could all commit the worst crimes without heavenly justice reaching us, etc. The law of return is intimately related to the law of recurrence. The return is lunar type. Solar forces leave from the law of return and recurrence. If we do not dissolve the Ego, we will have to be returned. Today the human is subjected to the yoke of the 48 laws, in a world of tremendous mechanistic, with its atrophied faculties and prisoner of the animal Ego, seeks happiness and liberation outside of it without feeling that carries it inside. He feels a terrifying fear of death and despairs during his life to get away from himself the instant of his last breath. He returns incessantly to this valley of San Josefa and the law of recurrence traps him making him relive the events of his previous life.

REVATI (Sanskrit) The last lunar mansion. Also designate with this name one of the matrix or divine energies.

REVEL. In the process of disclosing or disseminating divine truth; one thing that is declared by God to humans as well as presaging capturing great pleasure, if you revel in anything, you're not just gratified or even excited; you're overloaded by joy. It is used to mirror riotous merry making. Now it intends to bask in the self-reflected glow of your own pleasure. The determination of Special Revelation is to convey the wisdom and understanding of Jesus Christ, salvation and the atonement. The two passages of revelation are Sacred Scripture and Sacred Unwritten Law.

REVELATIONS. Both Sankhya philosophy and Yoga admit revelation (authority or testimony) as one of the three kinds of investigation, certainty or demonstration of truth; with the difference that the first bases mainly the certainty of knowledge on the remaining two proofs, that is, on direct perception through the senses, and on inference or deduction, appealing rarely, and even by mere form, to the authority of revelation. "Right knowledge says Patanjali; results from direct perception, inference, or testimony (authority or revelation)."

REVOLUTION OF CONSCIOUSNESS. It consists in revealing oneself against oneself, in the struggle against one's psychological defects, to eliminate and disintegrate them. There are three factors of consciousness that are; dying, which consists in the elimination of death of the ego (the defects, the mistakes). To be born refers to the creation of solar hides, and sacrifices for humanity, which consists of delivering the teaching to our likenesses. With these three factors of the revolution of consciousness, we can achieve total liberation, the Intimate Self-Realization of the Self. The Master Jesus-Christ expressed them in the following way: "He who desires to come after me, let him deny himself, (die); take up the cross (be born) and follow me" (sacrifice for mankind).

RHAZES. Prominent Arab alchemist of the ninth centennial. Tour the East and Spain; targeted scientific studies in Baghdad and Ray; He published two momentous medical encyclopedias which for a long time have served as separate instructor; he made consequential chemical revelations and made known a great number of new compounds, such as orpiment, realgar, borax, some salts of mercury, various arsenical compounds, etc." The secret of chemistry, he said, is rather conceivable than impossible; its mysteries are exposed only by dint of work and assiduity, but what a triumph when man can lift one end of the veil that covers Nature!" In his writings, he carried reserve and prudence occasionally to an extreme degree. When describing the procedure for the manufacture of the brandy, invented by him, begins like this "Take from something unknown the quantity you want (Recipe a liquid ignotum, quantum volueris)"

RHODO. (2ⁿᵈ century) anti-Gnostic apologist. At the appropriate time, he was a disciple of Tatian in Rome; he wrote concealed by the Empire Commodus (180-92).

RHOS. Defines 'moor' or 'moorland' in Welsh. It is a district to the east of the river Conwy in north Wales. It is getting under way as a small domain then set off a Middle Age gallop and was habitually proportion of the dominion of Gwynedd (subsequently, the area enhanced partially Denbighshire, then Cloyd, and is now in Conwy County borough). The Medieval Latin Jacobites affairs of state of the neighborhood's proprietors and his occupants is regularly speculated to be the origin of the appellation "Jacko's" or "Jaco's" still implements to occupants of Rhos. An emblem of Rho's mine shaft and struggles gestures patrimony is discern in the "Stilt", the excavators' institution on Broad Street.

RIDHA (Sanskrit) Disrespect.

RIG-vidhana (Ved.) A few writings that deal with the mystical and magical virtue of the recital of the hymns of the Rig-Veda, and even not many of its isolated verses.

RIGVEDA-Sanhita (Ved.) The collection of the hymns of the Rig-Veda.

RIGHT. Individuality in compliance with anything precisely, favorable, or accepted right attitude; upstanding, respectable; observe to certainty for honesty; rectify the right response, worthy, relevant the right individual for the task; direct a right lineament; moving the right conduct. The across-the-board proclamation of Human Rights, embraced by the UN General Assembly in 1948, was the first legal document to start out the essentials of civil rights to be everywhere sheltered. At the side of anatomy and the prevalence of the right lead (Hertz 1973: -11) In numerous communities, phrase for "right" frequently indicated courage, facility, aptitude, comprehension, righteousness rectitude, spiritual, authority, constitutionality, and aesthetics. The right edge is to practice signals of acknowledgment and harmony (compliment). The right and left-hand have distinct image linked to every: right; is the sensible, responsive and consistent, in addition, hostile and anxious, left; opposing of the right, frailty, perish, dissolution. In affairs of states, the term left is applied to people and grouping that have humanistic. That mainly signifies they comfort innovator rectification, exclusively seeking pursuing civic and monetary equality. "In Buddhist tantra, the right hand symbolizes the male aspect of compassion or skillful means, and the left hand represents the female aspect of wisdom or emptiness". In the Bible, to be at the right side "is to be identified as being in the special place of honor". In Jesus' parable "The Sheep and the Goats", the lambs and goats are detached with the sheep on the right hand of God and the goats on the left hand. The left side of the body is frequently considered as the female side, the collecting side, whatever you get hold of core indicates included along with, the biological mother. The right side of the body is repeatedly interpreted as the manly side, the hand-out side, them demonstrate. It identifies amid as well as, the father.

RIK-VEDA. (Ved.) The identical as Rig-Veda, in which, by euphoria, the g has been restored with a k.

RIME(S) or RYMES Rimes refers to a literary device mainly used in poems. The onset is the part of a single syllable word before the vowel. The rime is the part of a word including the vowel and the letter that follows. Rymes are words that are used which have the same sounds. "Is to be identified as being in the special place of honor RIMES".

RIMMON (Hebrew) The pomegranate, symbol of fertility and abundance. It is found in the Old Testament; It appears in the Syrian temples, and in them it was deified as an emblem of the heavenly Mother prolifies of everything. It is also a representation of the matrix in the state of prenez.

RING(S) As it stands a badge of continuity and entirety; the ring of flames stands up for the energy of eternal wisdom and transcendental enlightenment. The ring is frequently considered an insignia of loyalty. Those in 'Christian use included: (1) Ministerial rings. Rings are first cited as a formal part of a prelate's badge office in the 7th century. They currently ordinarily enclose amethyst. (2) Nuns' rings. In numerous organizations a ring is awarded at dignified vocations. (3) Wedding rings. arising in the engagement rings used by the Romans, they were acquired by Christians at an early date. Traditions respecting their use have diversified. The ongoing Christian marriage formalities expects the use of a ring for both husband and wife. (4) The 'Fisherman's Rings' is a seal-ring settled on the finger of a new pontiff and shattered at his death. Engraved on it is St. Peter in a boat fishing, with the Pontiff's name round it. (5) The 'Coronation Ring' in England is assigned on the 4th finger of the Monarch's right hand as 'the emblem of kingly dignity and of defense of the catholic faith'.

RIP. Tearing or pulling (substance) quickly or forcibly away from someone or something, move forcefully and rapidly; along tear or cut. Written on gravestones and represses the hope that the person buried there may rest in peace. R.I.P. abbreviation for 'rest in peace' or for the Latin 'requiescat in pace.'

RIPU. (Sanskrit) Enemy, adversary.

RIPUVAZA (Sanskrit) Subjected to an enemy.

RITUALE ROMANUM The dignified act of auxiliary publication of the Church of Rome ritual, carries the invocations and procedures for the management of the Sacraments and other solemn actions of a priest apart from the Divine Liturgy and Ecclesiastical Office.

RITUAL(S) In the Louvre Museum are preserved distinctive manuscript papyri called Egyptian Rituals, that contain instructions for religious ceremonies to be practiced at certain times, in the act of embalming the cadavers, etc. (Gnosticism) All ritual is related to descent and grain. Rituals are indispensable for Convivencia. Those who attend these sacred rites are nourished by this energy from the infinite Cosmos, but they are like a two-edged sword. He preserves and gives life to the pure and virtuous. He wounds and demolishes the dark and impure.

ROUGH MODE (Gnosticism) The father of the family, who sometimes squanders the profit of his work on drunkenness, beer, bacchanals, who insults and mistreats his wife and children because he believes himself to be the King of the house, symbolizes the leader of a household and, nevertheless, acts like this with his wife, with his children. Dear reader, at Grosso Modo we present to you three figures in charge of designing a better world. The head of the household, entrusted with training the people of tomorrow with that behavior. The religious, a person recommended to support the mystique and love of society, with that way of acting? The leader or head of large masses, or perhaps the politician,

RO and Ru (Egypt.) The door or opening, the place in heaven from which the primordial Light is dew red or born, synonymous with "cosmic matrix."

ROCOCO A development of 'baroque' architecture and decoration, which originated in Frane and endured from c. 1715 to 1750; relates to an artistic style talent of the era, characterized by fanciful curved asymmetrical forms and elaborate ornamentation; musical style marked by light active ornamentation and departure from through, bass and polyphony.

RODHRA (Sanskrit) Obstacle, impediment; transgression, offense.

ROGAHA (Sanskrit). Remedy, medicine.

ROGATION DAYS In West Christendom certain decree days of prayer and fasting in the early summer, associated especially with prayer for the harvest. The 'Major Rogation" on 25 April was a Christianization of the pagan observance of the 'Robigalia', which took the form of processions through the cornfields to pray for the preservation of the crops from mildew. The 'Minor Rogations', on the Monday, Tuesday, and Wednesday before Ascension Day, derived from the professional litanies ordered by St. Mamertus of Vienne (c.470), when his diocese was troubled by volcanic eruptions; they spread through Gaul and elsewhere. In the C of E the BCP of 1662 ordered the observance of the three (minor) Rogations as 'Days of Fasting and Abstinence'. In the RC Church, the Rogation Days were replaced in 1969 by periods of prayer for the needs of humankind, the fruits of the earth, and the works of men's hands; these periods may be arranged at any time of year.

ROMBO (Lat. Rhombus, and Este det gr.). Parallelogram that has equal sides and two of its angles greater than the others. The Rhombus is appraised by some esotericisms as an emblem of the female sexual organ. The Greeks used it as a magical apparatus, whose tendency could inspire and bring human passions closer together.

ROMAN (Sanskrit) Hair, hair, feathers, scales.

ROLLS CHAPHEL. The chapel which once stood on the site of the Public Record Office, London. The first chapel (begun in 1233) was part of a substructure by Henry III for the reception of transform Jew; this was destroyed in the 17th century. After extensive rebuilding, in 1895 it was unmistakable to pull down the crumbling walls of the Chapel and erect a museum.

ROPA or Ropana (Sanskrit) Agitation, turmoil, confusion of ideas.

ROPANA or CLOTHING (Sanskrit) Agitation, turmoil or confusion of ideas.

ROPE Means linkage and connection. Within Hindu symbolism, it processes the inner and sacred Way that unites the outer with spiritual responsibility.

ROSARY. They consecrate the Fifteen Mysteries (q.v.) in which 15 'decades' of Hail Mary's are each decade presaged by the Lords' Prayer and followed by the Gloria Patri. Regularly only a third part of the Rosary, the so-called chaplet, is said on one occasion. To reinforce the memory, the prayers are ordinarily counted on a string of beads.

ROSE. A tingling or shrub that normally ursid cardinal, rose, yellowy, or colorless fragranced floweret, domestic to northward restrained district. Many prides and breeds have been succeeding and are extensively lengthened as adorning. A mannered description of the choicest in escutcheon or enhancement, commonly with quinary leaflet (particularly as a nationwide insignia of England.) Vermilion typified amorousness, adoration, elegance, and audaciousness. A red rose spells beauty queen and uncontaminated. A spineless blush channel devotion at first impression. Golden rouge suggests closeness and delight, and brand-new dawn. Various ancestry's philosophy and heritage designated illustrative definition to the rose, opened these rarely recognized extensively. Exemplary of profound definitions distortion conserve the vernacular of floret, and consequently a rose possibly has a dissimilar explanation in adaptation. In the Song of Solomon 2:1, the Bible remarks, "Iam the rose of Sharon, and the Lily of the valleys." This is he introductory mention of ternary Bible forms to the rose. In earliest Christian population, roses prevail grasping to indicate God's labor in our possibility in no matter what form they materialized.

ROSEMARY An enduring savory shrubbery of the Mentha brood, indigenous to Mediterranean Europe. The narrowing blades are exploited as a gourmet herb, in fragrances, and as an image of remembrance. Rosemary is symbolic of friendship, loyalty, and reminiscence, rosemary is typically transported by grievers at wakes. Rosemary was furthermore regularly connected in affluents, submerged in aromatic aqua, and well-worn by the blushing bride on her wedding services as a representation of devotion and allegiance. In the prehistory "Christianos" epoch, communities' myth declared that recurrent Verbena (V. Officials) was exercised to dedicate Jesus' succeeding his transferring from the cross. It was as a reaction designated "Holy Her" or (e.g., in Wales) "Devils' bane". The collective appellative is the prehistoric Hellenic expression for oblation herbs reflected exceedingly high-powered.

ROSETTA STONE A basalt stele, discovered in 1799 at Rosetta, on the West bank of the mouth of the Nile. It provided the answer to the Egyptian hieroglyphics. It records in Egyptian (both hieroglyphic and demotic) and in Greek a decree of the clergyman to get together at Memphis in favor of Ptolemy V Epiphanes (reigned 204-181 B.C.).

ROSO DE LUNA, MARIO, (1872-1931). Acclaimed Spanish writer. Theosophist, Astronomist, Scientist, and Graduate in Letters, as Philosophy and Law. Master Samael quote him in his efforts for the treatises he has on the Jinn states. It is said of him that he was an excellent investigator in the works of H. Blavatsky.

ROSTA, RO-STA (Egypt) Literally: 'Door of the passage', With this utterance the entrance of the tomb is considered, at the same time as the title of a mystical constituency instanced frequently in the Book of the Dead. There were priests accustomed to the worship of the gods of Ro-sta.

ROSTAN. Book of Mysteries; A hidden work in Sankriti.

ROSICRUCIANS. The name assumed by members of unquestionable secret societies who reverence the emblems of the Rose and Cross as twin symbols of the Lord's Resurrection and Redemption. Early in the 17th century two anonymous writings in Germany (now assigned to the Lutheran pastor J.V. Andrae) connected the fabulous story of a definite Christian Rosen Kreutz, who established a secret society faithful to the study of the hidden things of nature and an esoteric kind of Christianity, which the writer declared was still in existence. The publications, which were meant to be satirical, were taken solemnly, and several societies with alchemistic tendencies approach into being under this title.

ROSY SEQUENCE. Portion of the hymn Jesu, dulcis Memoria (q.v.) exercised as a sequence for the Feast of the Holy Name in the Sarum rite.

ROOSTER Within the mystic symbolizes "The Verb" and harmonizes with Christification.

ROOT AND BRANCH The London Appeal of 1640 demanded that the episcopal structure with all its dependencies, roots, and branches, be abolished'.

ROYAL SCHOOL OF CHURCH MUSIC. An establishment initiate in 1927 as the School of English Church Music and recognized its current title in 1945. Its efforts involved awarding counseling to vocalists associates to the school, providers of music, and the conglomerate of choral festivals. The College of St. Nicholas, founded at Chislehurst, Kent, in 1929, to contribute grades for organists, choristers, clergy, and ordinands, was proceed in 1954 to Addington Palace, a previous archiepiscopal accommodation near Croydon.

ROUND(S) It identifies the concept that wholeness, completeness, unedited flawlessness, the Individuality, the unlimited, perpetuity, eternality, every cyclical motion, God ('God is a ring whose midpoint is all around and whose situation is far-off; (Hermes Trismegistus). The spiral is reviewed as a hieroglyph of unification, since each of the ordinary shapes are grasped by the sphere. The same way moreover the image of endlessness, deprived of origination or finale, pure, the concluding geometrical. All through the years, the discourage of a hoop has become suggestive of dedication and the assurance of everlasting tenderness, stable in earliest Egypt a bound newlywed's swap wedding create out of entwine Carrizo. They accept the personify continual and consider their unity harmony as a twosome. Because the ring shape has no origination and no termination, countless feel it constitutes God's warmth for us, which has no dawn and no ending, particularly, God appreciation along persistently, the adequate and the inferior, anyway indeed day-to-day provocation we are scuffling continuously.

RUTA (Sanskrit) Denomination of one of the last islands of Atlantis, which was torn down centuries before Poseidonis, Plato's 'Atlantis'. [Ruta, in Sanskrit, also indicates 'cry'.]

RU (Sanskrit) Sound, noise, scream, groan; battle; fear, alarm; Cut, division. It also forms the root of RUC, a Sanskrit word meaning "light" or "splendor", which may be the source of a common translation of "guru" in the yoga world.

RUBRICS. Ceremonial observance course in occupational books. The term emanates from the reality that they were frequently authored in red to differentiate them from the written work of the assistance.

RUCH or RUCHA (Sanskrit) Light, splendor, brightness, beauty; wish; explosion of joy and rejoicing.

RUCHAKA (Sanskrit) Ornament, attire; garland; perfume; An object of good omen. As an adjective: beautiful, attractive, bright, virtuoso, pleasant.

RUDHA (Sanskrit) Elevated, uplifted.

RUDE. The sensitivity of "ill mannered, uncultured, boorish; uneducated, ignorant" 14c.; besides, of actions or acts, "violence, rough. "That of "of low birth or position, common, humble" is from late 14c. Being rude is not a reaction; anger is an emotion; rudeness is intended offence. Disagreeing with what "you say is not" "It is a difference of opinion".

RUE HERB (Ruta graveolens). Additionally expressed ordinary rue, is a tightly packed everlasting shrubbery in the Citrus family promoted as a culinary and healing herb. Aboriginal to the Balkan Peninsula, rue is sustained for its profoundly fragrant leaflet, which may be implemented brightness or dehydrated in pocket portions. There are numerous diversities of rue, involving:" Blue Beauty": This seedling has vivid blue-green leaflet. "Jackman's blue": This distinctive possession gives a significant blue color to the herbage and a persuasive scent. "Variegate":

The foliole on this discrepancy has a speck of white in them. Ruta graveolens, customarily noted as rue, current rue or her-of-grace, is a variety of Rutaceae amplifying as a gorgeous shrub and herb. It is endemic to the Balkan Peninsula. It blooms all through nature in greenhouses, principally for its azureous stalk, and in circumstance for its bountifulness of heated and stale soil details.

RUK (Sanskrit) Rich, giving, liberal, splendid man.

RUKMA (Sanskrit) Gold.

RULERS A name formerly applied to those who presided in cathedrals over the singing in choir. This term also refers to a person who rules or commands. Also called: rule a strip of wood, metal, or other material, having straight edges graduated usually in millimeters or inches, used for measuring and drawing straight lines.

RU (Sanskrit) Sound, noise, scream, groan; battle; fear, alarm; Cut, division.

RUK (Sanskrit) Rich, giving, liberal, splendid man.

RUKMA (Sanskrit) Gold.

RUPA RITUALS. (Gnosticism) All ritual is related to descent and grain. Rituals are essential for Coexistence. Those who attend these sacred rites are nourished by this energy from the infinite Cosmos, but they are like a two-edged sword. He preserves and gives life to the pure and virtuous. He wounds and demolishes the dark and impure.

RUPAVAT (Sanskrit) Endowed with shape; a figure; beautiful; well done.

RUTA(S), ROUTE (Sanskrit) Designation of one of the last islands of Atlantis, which was demolished centuries before Poseidon's Plato's Atlantis. [Route, in Sanskrit, also defines "cry".] earliest people who populated the island of the continent of the Pacific Ocean.

RUTH, Book (of) This publication tells the story of Ruth, a Moabitess, who married a Hebrew in Moab. Following her husband's death; she returned to Judah, with her mother-in-law; she was taken under the protection of a relative of her former husband, Boaz, who later married her. Although the incident is set in the later days of the judges (before 1000 a.ac.), the Book is not earlier than the Exile (6th cent B.C.) Its genealogy at the end specifies one of the clear focuses of the author, viz, to document the Moabite tension in David's ancestry. Ruth is thus an ancestress of Christ.

RVAH To do. To act positively and decisively to resolve a problem, act, react, move.

ROYAL SCHOOL OF CHURCH MUSIC (R.S.C.M.). An institution established in 1927 as the school of English Church Music and accepted its present title in 1 course for organists, choristers, clergy, and ordinands, was in 1954 to Addington Palace, a ancient archiepiscopal dwelling place in the vicinity of Croydon.

-S-

SABAS, St. (439-532), Monk. A native of Cappadocia, in 478 he initiated a large Lavra in Palestine. He reluctantly welcomes ordination to the priesthood (not then usual among monks) in 490, and in 492 the Patr. Of Jerusalem made him higher levels of all the hermits in Palestine.

SABACIAS. Festivities commemorate by the Phrygians in honor of Bacchus, called by an additional name Sabatius. Such festivals involved dances, races and Franco transference.

SABATIAN Feasts are observed by the Phrygians in honor of Bacchus, called by another name Sabatius. Such parties included dances, races and frantic transport.

SABAOTH (Hebrew) An army or a host; De Saba: Go to combat. Hence the designation of the god of war: the "Lord of Sabaoth [or of the armies]."

SABEOS Referred Astrolatas: those who reverence the stars, or, rather, their "rulers".

SABHYA (Sanskrit) Reliable, integral; Attendance at a gathering. One of the five fires allude to in the regulations of Manú, III.

SABIJA or SAMADHI (Sanskrit) "Samadhi" with seed", its objective. Meditation understood, that is, that state of mental demonstration in which, although the mind is free of modification (vrittis), it is perceived of that with which it identifies, and by this argument it is called responsible (asamprajnata) or wisdom, because there is the seed that, following its course, can change into several daydreaming that distance one from the situation of Samadhi.

SACHA (Kiriya) (Sanskrit) Among Buddhists it is a strength analogous to a magical mantra among Brahmins. It is a prodigious force that can be accomplished by any adherent, a lay priest, and "effective in limits when accompanied by bhavana (meditation)." It consists of relating "the meritorious acts (of one) executed in this existence or in some previous one", according to the conclusion and exposes the Rev. Mr. Hady, but that in reality obey the potency of one's will, together with an absolute faith in their own powers, either of yoga; optional, or some prayer, as in the case of Muslims or Christians. Sacha symbolizes "true" and Kiriyang "action". It is the dominions of the dead, or of a righteous life.

SA, MANOEL. DE (c. 1530-96) Portuguese Jesuit. In 1595 he circulated Aphorismic Confessariorum, a hand-operated misleading in dictionary form. It was implanted on the Index in 1603 for authorizing confession and absolution to be made by letter, but in its developing edition of 1607-8 it appreciated excellent approval.

SACRARIUM (Latin) Reputation given to the chamber of the houses of the ancient Romans, where the divinity to which the family worshipped was kept. It was also called sacrarium, a byte of a temple.

SACRED (Gnosticism) Part of sacred works of all the religions of the world, such as the Koran, the Bhagavad Gita, the Kangun, the Popol Vuh, the Bible, the Sophia Pistis, the revelations of what is received.

SAD or SAT (Sanskrit) The one deep rooted Reality in the limitless world; the divine Essence which is, but which cannot be said to exist, considering it is Absolutely, the Seida itself. [In general, sat signifies being, exitance, essence, reality, the reality, the real world; goodness, purity, truth, anything good or useful; Atman, the Absolute. As an adjective: existing, real, present, living; true, good, pure, just, harmonious, useful, profitable, excellent, respectable, etc.]

SADHIS (Sanskrit) Goal, object, end; point or place of rest, in whom the first sacrifice resides.

SADHIKA (Sanskrit). Sueno profundo.

SADDUCEAN, SADDUCEE A [Judaic] doctrine instructed by the henchmen of Zadok, a disciple of Antigonus Saccho. They were proclamations of having refused the immortality of the soul (personal) and the reappearance of the body (physical and personal).

SADUS (Cald.) In Chaldean mythology, they are a class of jinn spirits.

SAFFRON. It is a shadiness of yellowish or gold, the shade of the sharp end of the saffron Colchicum autumnal, from the one in question; spice saffron is obtained. The tincture of the spice saffron is essentially required to the antioxidant synthetic crocetin digentiobioside. The designation saffron eventually acquire (by Aramaic) separating Middle Persian Ja'far. The designation was beneficial to the saffron spice in Early English from c. 1200. As an honorific tincture, it refers to the back of the 14th century. Deep saffron estimates the tinge of India saffron (also well known as Bhagwa or Kesari). In Rajasthani, this hue is called Kesariya. The expression originates its name from kesar, the Hindustani label for saffron, and major selection in Kashmir. "Your plants are an orchard of pomegranates with choice fruits, with henna and nard, nard and saffron, calamus and cinnamon, with every kind of incense tree, with myrrh and aloes and all the fines' spices". Song of Songs 4:13-14 NIV.

SAGITTARIUS This zodiac sign embarks on from November 23 to December 21, Rule Hips and thighs; its metal is tin; Aloe perfume; the stone is the blue sapphire, its plant: Maguey, fique, (cabuya) the flower: Hydrangea, the planet is Jupiter, blue color. This sign works with the Fire constituent, the key word is deliberations. Thursday and its ruler are Zachariel.

SAGE Is a fragrant herb with olive green leaflet that is employed as a gastronomy flavoring, vernacular to portside European union and the Mediterranean. Each of two shaggy Northerner shrubs with achromatic-gray foliole. Sage has been enforced as a tea for its meaningful curative effects as far back as prehistoric Kemet. They were accustomed to sage for infecundity, significant illnesses, and infestation like the plague. The Prehistoric Hellenic contemplated it as a Sacred Plant; with regards to energy clearing, they made use of sage and palo santo to expel negativism and actuality carries home the good vibrations. Science has been supporting spirituality too: When burned, sage smoke liberates subatomic smoke that varies the constitution of the air and has been connected to constructive frame of mind amplified. In an individual, a sage is an exceptionally sagacious human being; a living soul's enclosed for perception, a mortal respected for the asset of insights, discernments, and experience. Although when you hear the word sage, you might think of a wizard, it really signifies a wise man. This day you understand it accustomed to referring to somebody who possesses discernment in a distinct discipline. If anyone is a strategy sage, he has knowledge of exactly what guidance to present legislators; to prepare them to recognize the issuance and reply productively.

SAGUNA (Sanskrit) Literally: "with gunas". Endowed with attributes, modes or constitution (gunas).

SAHA (Sanskrit). Patient, distress. In composition as a lead, it describes jointly.

SAHASA. (Sanskrit) Strength, vigor, violence; haste, promptness; punishment.

SAHDONA (7th century). Spiritual writer. He was expelled from the Nestorian Church because of his teaching on the Person of Christ. His 'Book of Perfection' is one of the masterpieces of Syrian spirituality,

SAHOU (Egypt.) The consecrated body of the Ego. It is also the Egyptian denomination of the mummy.

SAHYA (Sanskrit) Equal, adequate, proportionate; sweet, nice.

SAINT SOPHIA Well known church at Constantinople, which was devoted to the 'Holy Wisdom' (i.e., the person of Christ), was built under Justinian and dedicated in 538. Characteristics were the enormous dome which crowns the basilica; from 562, the first low dome cave in 558, and the mosaics were covered up and partially destroyed. Nowadays it is a museum.

SAIS (Egypt.) Place position the famous place of worship of Isis-Neith was recovered, in which was the always veiled statue of Neith (Neith and Isis were synonymous names), with the famed inscription: 'I am all that has been, is and will be, and no mortal will remove my veil'.

SAINTE-CHAPELLE, The. The sanctuary in Paris was founded c. 1245 by Louis IX to house the Crown of Thorns and other relics of the Passion. It was ultimately secularized in 1906.

SAKA. (Sanskrit) Simply; "the one", or Eka. This expression is utilized to delegate the 'Dragon of Wisdom', or the divinities that definitive, contemplated in a cumulative way.

SAKWALA. It is a Bana or 'word' articulated by Gautama Buddha in his oral directives. Sakawala is a repetitive, or rather solar, structure, of which there is a limitless in the natural world, and which denotes the volume to which the gleam of each sun enhances. Each Sakawala accommodates lands, hells and heavens (which implies good and bad realms, our earth being contemplated as a hell, in occultism); It outreach the lethargy of its life, goes into subside, and finally is decline in periods that are replicated frequently by morality of an unchangeable regulations. On sphere, the Master instructed that there have thus far been in it four considerable 'continents' (the Land of the Gods, Lemuria, Atlantis and the present 'continent' split into the five fragment of the Secret Dogma) and that there were too materialized even three. The first 'did not propagate with each other', a sentence that display that Buddha did not speak of the ongoing landmass disclosed in his time (since Patla or America was perfectly known of the ancient Indians), but of the four geological founding of the earth, with their four distinctive race-roots that have previously disappeared.

SALOME (1) A woman who accompany Christ to Jerusalem Mathew materialized to recognize her with the mother of St. James and St. Jones, the son of Zebedee (Mt 27:56 cf. Mk. 15:40) She is occasionally recognized with the sister of the BVM (Jn 19:25).

SALT. Since its formative classification salt was an indication of clarity and goodness, chiefly amid the Semitic humankind. It distributes to authenticate exposure and cordiality, and its use was authorized for each sacrifice (Lev. 2:13). The Contribution of salt to catechumens previously established segments of the Catholicity rite of Baptism. Additionally, salt is utilized in the formulation of the holy water.

SALVIAN (c. 400-c.480), of Marseilles, ecclesiastical author. His De Gubernatione Dei, controverting the immorality of corrupt Roman progress with the uprightness of the victorious primitive, used the latter as an eyewitness to God's judgment in the neighborhood and as an incentive for Christians to have clarity of life and trust in destiny.

SAMAEL (Hebrew) Kabbalistic cognomen of the ruler of those evil spirits that symbolize incarnations of human degenerations; the Angel of Death. From this the idea of Satan has developed. Samael is said to have seduced Eve in paradise under the guise of a serpent; of him it is also said that he begat Cain.

SAMARIA The Metropolis of the nation of Israel, i.e., of the 'Ten [northern] Tribes' confirmed by King Omri (c. 880 B.C.) and in 721 seize by the Assyrians, who resettled the region with pagans from other parts of their empire (2 Kgs. 18: 9-12 and chapter 17). Following Jewish tradition, the Samaritans well known to later Judaism and the NT were the successor of these settlers. The antagonism of the Jews to the Samaritans was accepted.

SAM (Sanskrit) Prelate who plays a impressive role in funeral solemnities. He was chief priest of Fta in Memphis during the sixth dynasty. His customary badges were panther skin and the braid dangling over his back.

SAMA (Sanskrit) One of "the flowers of holiness" (bhava puchpas). Sama is the fifth, that is, "resignation." There are eight such flowers, namely: leniency or charity, self-control, affection (or love of others), patience, resignation, devotion, meditation, and veracity. [This word means, furthermore: equality, identity, similarity, indifference, equanimity, balance, compensation; and as an adjective; equal, identical, unalterable, even-handed, stability, impartial, indifferent, unemotional, upright, plain, etc.]

SAMADANA (Sanskrit) Daily observances or practices of Buddhists.

SAMADHANA (Sanskrit) It is that state in which the yogi can no longer stray from the path of spiritual expansion; in that the total earthly, except the physical body, has ceased to exist for him. It is the oddity that keeps the student deficient, by nature, from turning away from the right path. He can choose any worldly occupation with the sentiment of reassuring to his usual life, once his task has been consummated, which he imposed himself.

SAMADHI (Sanskrit) Emphasizes a disposition of absolute blissful exaltation. This term emanates from the articulation Sam-adha, "self-possession." He who retains similar command may put in unblemished instruction ineffable his appreciation, the two material and subjective. It is the intensity of mind-body exercise. [Samadhi] (external contemplation or supra consciousness) is certain legacy in which rational absorption influence alike an excessive credit that the imagination consequently permanent is merge with the alongside in other words it is focused (i.e. the Spirit), discontinue or its arguable total its transfigure, and the austere deplete the sensibility of total singularity, indicated contain free-standing, and it develop into the complete. Samadhi is a position in which awareness is so disconnected among the frame that it remains inconsiderate. It is a disposition of separation or rapture, in which the imagination is entirely sensible as such, and from where it reciprocates to the physique with the erudition or ordeals that it has accomplished in that extrasensory mood, recollecting them formerly it has covered posterior inside the somatic intellect.

SAMANA. (Sanskrit) One of the aspects of vital breaths (Pranas) that continue the action chemistry, [According to Manilal Dvivedi in his Comment. To the Aphorisms of Patanjali, the seat of the Samana is about the navel, where it executes the digestive function preserving the internal fire. When Samyama is application on Samana, this fire can be seen throughout the body, which for this motive becomes resplendent (Aphorism, III, 40). It has been discovered that this glow is most observable along the head, between both eyebrows, and in the navel. As has been said, this is the basis of the magnetic aura of living beings. In the lexicon of the Subtle Forces of Nature, Rama Prasad says that Samana is that road demonstration or nervy current which, it is supposed, causes in the womb the absorption and dispense of food throughout the body by process of Prana and then transform into Apana and then incorporated to Udna (or physical organs of language, is fixed in the Samana (in the navel in the form of sound, as a evidence cause of all the word, add the commentator Arjuna Mishra, Samana also means: equal, similar, equal to self, uniform, always the same, virtuous.]

SAMANISM Cult of the spirit, the oldest religion of Mongolia.

SAMASA. (Sanskrit) Composition; Combination; contraction; abbreviation; a compound term.

SAMSKARA (Sanskrit) Textually: improve, refine, perfect, impress. In Indian philosophy this term is used to delegate the impressions left in the mind by individual actions or external incidents, and capable of being flourished on some future agreeable occasion, and even in a coming rebirth. The Sanskara delegates, consequently, the terms of tendencies and impulses approaching from anterior births, to be mature in this or future incarnations (Janmasd). [In Yoga philosophy, Sanskara defines impression; the mark or imprint left upon one thing by other, a trace that may ever be called to life; the impressions on mental matter which generate habits; the same practices acquired. This term also has the following definitions: preparation; ordination; cultivation education; Purification; sacrament; consecration; any rite or ceremony; Faculty of Chemistry; intellectual concept; concepts (in Buddha language), etc. The Sanskara voice is synonymous with Vasana (Rama Prasad).]

SAMSON (prob. 11th century B.C.) Hebrew leader and consistently the last of the great 'judges' genre to judges. 13: 2-16: 31, he was supplied with huge strength and executed destruction among the Philistines; when he fell victim to his passion for Delilah and disclosed to her the top secret of his power, the Philistines put out his eyes, but he was empowered his punishment pulling down the pillars of the temple where 3,00 Philistines were congregated. His faith is applauded in the NT

(Heb 11:32), He is the champion of J. Milton's Samson Agonistes (16l71) and of one of G.F. Handel's oratorios (1743).

SAMITI (Sanskrit) Union, board, assembly; struggle.

SAMUHYA (Sanskrit) The sacred fire; the place where it is put.

SAMVRITI o SANVRITI (Sanskrit) Mistaken hypothesis; The dawn of the fantasy. [Action of covering or camouflage; secrets.]

SANDEHA (Sanskrit) Doubt, uncertainty; confusion; danger.

SANA (Sanskrit) One of the three esoteric Kumaras, whose epithets are: Sana, Kapila and Sanatsujata, mysterious triad that contains the mystical of generation and reincarnation.

SANHEDRIN. (Rabbi Sanhedrin, and East of Gr.). Sovereign Council of the Jews, in which they dealt with and manifest matters of status and religion. It comprises of 70 members, plus the High Priest or Heads of the Great Families; 'Scribes' or doctors savvy in the Law; and 'Elders' or lay person of special significance. They could try crimes and constitute penalties; when it came to deaths, they resolved it from the time of Herod to the Roman procurators.

SANNA (Pali) One of the five Skandhas: the attribute of abstract ideas.

SANCTE ET SAPIENTER The AKC (Partnership of King's College) is the authentic Decoration of king's, backdated to its cornerstone in 1829 and replicating its initial motto: sancte et sapienter, "holiness and wisdom". The Latin Phrase for Holy God is Sanctus Deus in the Latin Greek (first) Choir: Hagios ho Theos. (Holy God) Latin (Second) Choir: Sanctus Deus.

SANCTE SPIRITUS, VENI. The progression for Whitsunday. Its authorship is now routinely accredited to Stephen Langton, English translations include 'Come Thou Holy Paraclete'.

SANAKA (Sanskrit) A sacred plant whose fibers are woven to make yellow garments for Buddhist priests.

SANTIFY. To bless denotes we are a pick out, set apart, righteous people and as such we are to refrain from sinful lusts of the flesh. We are to set excluding all malice and all deceit and hypocrisy and envy and all slander. Brethen, I testify that the signal in every age; and specifically, our age, is Joshua's call: "Sanctify yourselves; for tomorrow the Lord will do wonders among you." In the name of Jesus Christ, amen. Josh. 3:5.

SANTVA or ZANTVA (Sanskrit) Burning feeling or conciliation agreement (Bhagavan Das). Appeasement, mitigation; consolation; comfort.

SANCTUMREGNUM SANCTUM REGNUM. The kingdom of God.

SANSKRIT. Antiquated blessed eloquence of India, 1610s, from Sanskrit samskrtam "put together, well-formed, perfected.' sterilize of samskrta, from sam "together" (from PIE Radicle assemble "one: as one, together with") + krta "to make, do, perform" (through PIE "kwer' "to make, form;" see terato-). The Brahmin Sanskrit see accordant "om" is the concluding largely accepted Sanskrit image implementation of a nonmaterial motto and invocation. Appeal the splendid calligraphy and diminished echoing of this connect are engaged covering update celestial, medical science, and yoga Hatha Yoga. Sanskrit assertion (among Samskriti, "adorned, cultivated, purified"), a Prehistoric Indo-Aryan communication in which the greatest previous verification are the Vedas, serenity in what is required Vedic Sanskrit.

SAP. In biology there is the watery fluid of plants. Cell sap is a fluid found in the vacuoles (small cavities) of the living cell; it accommodates variable amounts of blood and waste materials, inorganic salts, and nitrogenous compounds. Tree sap is the fluid that distributes within the phloem of a tree to dispense water and nutrients. If someone calls you "a sap," it suggests you lack strength and character. If you get sap with the sticky liquid inside a tree in your hands, it will be a dilemma getting it teout of your hands in the middle of a forest without a bar of soap and running water. Pending the dormant period, deciduous trees withdraw most of their sap from their branches and trunk, but then in late winter and spring, the sap is drawn up again from the roots. Exaggerated sap coming out of a tree occurs because of inappropriate pruning, mechanical injuries, canker development or insect damage.

SAPPHIRE The title sapphire is obtained through the Latin "sapphirus" from the Greek "sappheriros", who mentioned to lapis lazuli. It is usually blue, yet simply "fancy" sapphires besides transpire through in yellow, purple, range, and green colors; "parti sapphires" manifesting two or more tinctures. It carries the elegance of the deep-blue valuable jewelry however, not being too crystal-clear reflecting it. Sapphire is a precious jewel variation of rhinestone in crystalline or semitransparent crystals quartz glass of a color shade other than red. Distinctly one of a translucent royal blue; a brilliant stone of equivalent asteria. Succeed believing in illustrating experience, ethical, chance discovery, and blessedness for dignification. In a commitment hoop, a sapphire suggests adhesion and fidelity, implement. Sapphire has the dominion to liberate psychological pressure, eliminate despondent, assist reflection, soothing the imagination, and supply cerebral precision. legal sapphires harmonize the bodily, intellectual, and intangible heritage and renovate equilibrium inside the physique. When worn out at the pharynx, they simplify innovative and expressiveness. Sapphire is replied to be the judgment supply, captivating attention, build up innovative and support pureness and extensive of accomplishments. It is presumed to attention and harmony the consciences along with discard unpleasant conception, discouraged and mental cognitive. Sapphires are encouraged by entertaining; they are easygoing, demonstrative and consistently the vigor of the celebration. They adore to be the midpoint of attention and fondness expressing their astounding anecdote. They need to be recalled for expanding cheerfulness on any occasion they advance. They are fervent and affectionate to humanity.

SARA Essence, essential part, strength, vigor, wind, water; Wealth property aptitude.

SAR or Saros (Cald.) A Chaldean god, who's appellative, described by a circular horizon, the Greeks took their term Saros, cycle.

SARACEN(S). An expression used by medieval writers of the Arabs customarily and later applied to the betrayal and Muslim nations opposed whom the Crusaders fought. Byname is developed from the Old French word "Sarrazin," interpreting "Saracen". It is conceptualized to become a pseudonym in Medieval England for anyone of dark-skinned appearance, or for person of note reappeared from the pilgrimage, ahead of turning into a cognomen. By the 12th centenary, Gothic Indo-European utilized the phrase Saracen as both together a traditional and reverent caption. In part of archaic writing, Saracens remained related with Islamic in ordinary and concisely as ebony, while faithful clear au naturel. An illustration is In the King of Tars, a primitive story. Saracen penetrates English from Latin (Saracenus), which accepted from Greek (sarakenos). The Greek presumably appear from the Arabic root sharq, defining east, and it formerly citing to a humankind inhabitation in the Sinai Peninsula and what is presently northwestern Saudi Arabia. The philosopher Jerome affirms that the Saracens were the successors of Abraham pass across his housemaid Hagar and their descendant, the "wild man" Ishmael (Genesis 16:12); they therefore shall accordingly be described as Hagarenes or Ishmaelites, but they basely labeled themselves Saracens, maintaining to be the successors of Abraham's.

SARASA or SARASI. (Sanskrit) Water extension. Sarasa is also equivalent to endowed with flavor, tasty.

SARAGHA (Sanskrit) Bee.

SARDIS (Chakra) Vishuddha (Sanskrit) When the Kiundaline through hedonist conversion, reaches the height of the creative larynx opens this chakra, which confers clairaudience or hidden ear. This chakra is affiliated to the pure akasha, (the agent of sound. The laryngeal chakra is called in the Apocalypse Church and Sanais, it has sixteen petals, its color is bright white, alternating with blue and green rays, it is put in activity calando for an hour a day the vowel "E" lengthening the sound and conditioning of a straight life.

SARUM, Salisbury Use of. The Middle Ages modification of the Roman rite used in the cathedral church at Salisbury. It was accustomed ascribed to St. Osmund. The Consuetudinary, i.e., the cathedral statutes and customs and a concluded directory of services, was cumulative by Richard Poore (d.1237). 'The New Use of Sarum' was a further (14th-century.) modifications. In the later Primitive, the Sarum Use, was outlawed in many other dioceses; it proceeded to be the main evidence for the First (1549) BCP. SARUM Associating to the Roman observances as refashion min Salisbury and applied in England, Wales, and Ireland prior to the Transformation. Sarum Rule the pre-Reorganization, Latin liturgy that is the origin of the Anglican Communion. Living picture French party game in which a member ventures to reproduce a popular artistic production, antiquity, or published locale. The Sarum devotion is a direct petition that cultivate a momentous linkage with God. Exaggerated like the Invocation for peace, it proposes a contemplation that can alleviate individuals overcome the day. God be on my side, and in my parting.

SATTA (Sanskrit) The "One Existence". Brahma (neutral). [Being, existence; goodness, excellence.]

SATAN Gnostic It represents psychological Set, the Ego the Self.

SATI, SATTI or SUTTEE. (Sanskrit) [Suttee.] Cremation of a living widow along with her deceased husband; custom now happily abolished in India. Literally: "chaste and virtuous wife".

SARVA (Sanskrit) totally, concluded; universal; all, absolute. All things, the entire world, the universe, the great All.

SATTA. The "One Existence", Brahma (neutral). [Being, existence; goodness excellence.

SATAN In Hebrew-Christian tradition, the supreme embodiment of evil, also called the Devil.

SATORI. (Japanese) gnostic. Intuitive spiritual shock, Shamadhi, which completely changes the understanding of life, of those who receive it. Experience it. It is the Tao.

SATURNINUS. (2nd century) Syrian Gnostic. He held that the dawn of all artifacts was to be sought in a Father, who created a series of angels and other supernatural beings who in turn produce man. Human beings were a powerless entity who squirmed on the ground until a Divine spark set him on his feet. The God of the Jews was one of the recreator angels, and the Supreme Father sent the Savior to branch this God and to release such as were provided with the Divine spark.

SAURIKA (Sanskrit) The paradise of the gods.

SAURA. (Sanskrit) Month of thirty solar days; solar fire; relating to the sun; solar; A sun worshipper.

SAUTI (Sanskrit) Denomination of the sage who declaimed the Mahabharata to the richis in the woodland of Naimicha.

SAVA (Sanskrit) Extraction or announcement of soma juice; Soma or the Moon, origination; certain sacrificial rites; oblation.

SAVOY DECLARATION, The. (1658) A Declaration of Gathering paramount and constituency of a reasonable type, endorse at a assembly held in the Chapel of the Savoy in London by delegates of 120 Churches. It consists of a Preface, a Revelations of Faith closely akin to the Westminster Confession, and a Platform of Discipline announce that all required power is accomplished in each individual Church.

SAVORY. Is interpreted as a substance filled with tastiness, appetizing and luscious; regularly anything that somebody has prepared. In the sphere of sustenance, savory is also a lot well-used to convey the adverse to saccharine, or saline. beef, for instance, is ordinarily a savory nutrient; legume, in common, are also savory. Nibbles**,** canape, and finger food are besides frequently savory.

Meals put together with the least quantity of glucose and deprived underlining the glace taste are contemplate savory. Umami is your quinary primary aftertaste besides bitter, honeyed, pungent, and saline. Japanese researchers detected this fifth acidity in the "modern epoch" and named it "umami," which transcribed to "savory". Genesis 27:4 King James Version states: "and make me savory meat, such as I love, and bring it to me, that I may eat; that my soul may bless thee before I die".

SAVA. (Sanskrit) Strategy or expression of soma juice; Soma or the Moon; Generation; certain sacrificial rites; sacrifice.

SAVOY DECLARATION, The. (1658) A declaration of Congregational principles and polity of a moderate type, drawn up at a gathering held in the Chapel of the Savoy in London by legislator of 120 Churches. It involves a Preface, a Confession of Faith close skin to the Westminster Confession, and a Platform of Discipline proclaiming that all required power is invested in each specific Church.

SAYA. (Sanskrit) Saya indicates "sleeping" or "resting". It is as common as a girl's cognomen and signal serenity and peace. Supplementary definition of Saya are dwellings, obscurity, guidance, twilight, sundown, a safeguard separating the sunshine. Saya is further the floor reaching exterior midi fixed at the midriff that is well-worn by female in the Philippines and Spanish America. Etymology in Spanish, of saya man's robe, sagging, from (presume) unrefined Latin sagia, from Latin sagum cloak, sagum.

SEBASTE, The Forty Martyrs of, Forty Christian soldiers of the 'Thundering Legion' who were martyred at Sebastes in Lesser Amenia, c.320, by being left in the nude on the ice of an iced pond, with baths of hot water on the banks as an inclination to apostatize. The place of one who gave way was taken by a heathen soldier of the guard, who was instantly transformed.

SEBASTIAN, St. Roman martyr, according to mythology he was convicted by Diocletian to be shot by archers, recuperated from this ordeal, and presented himself before the emperor, who caused him to be clubbed to death.

SENSE. An capacity to recognized, admit, worth, or proceed to reality, largely a part of the five material qualifications to see, hear, smell, taste, and feel: The various intervening sense and insight is "Sense", the suffice of the judgment to appreciate the universe, and "Sensibility", the ferocious aspect of survival, be capable of either/or generate resistance or equilibrium when utilized mutually. An extremely responsive individual largely suggests that you have intensified audiovisual appreciation. You-all regard notions, the two discreetly thoughtfully and inadvertently, that influence the five senses higher than nearly individuals. The glint is dazzling, the gridlock is thunderous, that fleece jersey your mom crocheted is prickling, and expressed, itchy!

SERAPIS A profound solar god who reinstated Osiris in popular worship, and in honor of whom the seven vowels were sung. He was created to appear many times in his depictions as a serpent, a "Dragon of Wisdom." He was the greatest god of Egypt all along the first centuries of Christianity.

SCALA SANCTA (also well known as the Scala Pilati). A stairwell of 28 marble steps near the Lateran church at Roma. Heritage asserts that they were the steps descended by Christ after His denunciation to death and transferred to the W. by St. Helena from the castle of Pilate at Jerusalem.

SCALE Customarily, the scales are manifested in support, typically although associated with Goddess of Justice (or Justitia, from the Roman goddess). This signifies charitableness and unbiased contemplation to all attestation, without revealing partiality anyway. The scales of justness identify with civility in the legal proceeding. They advise that any part of an exhibition should be studied in a case in court. Correspondingly, the scales stress that resolutions will be destined by considering the verifications in equitability. The Sabre exemplifies Lady Justice's jurisdiction to make conclusions.

SCETE. The North part of the Nitrian desert, recognized as a Centre of monasticism in the 4th and 5th centennials.

SCHEME Substitution of mentality or symbolism of a material or immaterial thing or of a course in which its essential lines or features are logically connected. "The Tree of Life" reveals an outline of the Sephiroth's.

SCHOLA CANTORUM (Lat., 'school of singers'). In the reverence of the initial Church all music was provided by the clergy and parishioners, but slowly the application of having a body of instructed singers was initiated. At Tome the Schola was accepted on a sound footing by Gregory the Great (d. 604). The tradition increased over West Christendom.

SCHOOL (of Mysteries) It was concise those who learned authentic esotericism. Also cited as esoteric orders; today there is very hidden the ancient Gnostic Knowledge, (revealed in the books and lectures by V.M. S.A.W.), in a free and disinterested way.

SCYTHE (from guadana) Instrument used to mow at ground level forming with a pointed blade and wider than the sickle, the sickle is used to mow (cut). It is an emblematic symbol of death, to cut the silver cord or Anthahkarana. He has also been associated with the priests of Cybele and Atis. It is a legendary image of harvest, of rebirth, of hope and death. All curved weapons have been emblems of the Moon and female forces, while straight weapons are considered solar and masculine.

SCISSORS In its present condition is an instrument composed of two steel blades, like a single-edged blades, usually, with eyes to put the fingers at the end of each handle, which can rotate around an axis that locks them, to cut, when closing what is put between them. In esotericism, it symbolizes conjunction, because it opens like a cross, it is also an attribute of mystical spinning mills that cut the thread of the life of the immortals. It is said that they possess magical virtues, because with them you can fish witches, installing them in cross. They are also considered ambivalent symbols that can declare creation and annihilation, birth and death.

SCONE In 1296, King Edward of England grasped the pebble from the Scottish, and had it assembled towards a current chair at Westminster. Originating accordingly, it was used in the crowning of the sovereign of England and then Great Britain. Scone is a mini, plentiful, cracker such as dessert or fast nourishment, occasionally oven-bake on a skillet. A hamlet in center Scotland northeast of Perth. The begone fragment of the outpost was the enthroning place of Scottish monarch till 1651. The Rock of Scone; (Scottish Gaelic: A Lia Fael; Scots: Stane of Skein); in addition, investigated as the GStone of Destiny, and frequently attribute to in England as The Coronation Stone, is an elongated of scarlet sandstone that has been castoff for centennials in the coronation of the emperor of Scotland, despite feasibly resonates appreciate a deteriorate high tea dessert, the Stone of Scone is an antiquate emblem of Scottish autonomous. Depending on the folk tale, the limestone stick was utilized by the biblical image Jacob as a support when he considers of a scale entering to paradise and then brought submit to Scotland by approach of Egypt, Spain and Ireland.

SCRIBE. A component of an accomplished category in earliest Israel throughout New Testament occasion inspecting the Sacred text and assistance as transcriber, rewriter, educators, and legal expert, a conventional or governmental assistant or Site inspector. Scribers were individuals in archaic Egypt (usually men) who studied to legible and composed. Even though excelling in accepting that almost all copyists were gentlemen, there is verification of some lady's physician. These nurturing would have been devoted as correspondents so that they could browse through therapeutic transcripts. columnists were in attending to chronicle the holdings of sustenance, litigations, bequeath and extra official documents, annual returns, incantation and all the artifact that approach regarding frequent in the existence of the monarch. Scribes were one of the much consequential objectives that remain the leadership in sequence. They were devoted to writing symbolically and registered numerous vernaculars enunciated in Assyria. With the absence of scribes, symbols would not have been created or scrutinized, magnificent reminiscences would not have been shaped with scripts, and recitals would have been uttered and then and lost.

SCRIPTURES. Teaches us above all the Word of God, it has been aroused by The Holy Spirit, it is used to know how God wants us to be saved, as was the story of salvation. We hear the Word of God in Masses, in Christian assistances, in catechesis. (Gnosticism) This demonstrate that the feasts to which the Holy Scriptures narrate; that it is convenient to perpetuate and praise the feasts of the Soul, are the excitements of coming from the Being to us where with a clean spirit and with a heart full of love, we prostrate devotedly to stop to pray and talk with our own God.

SHALLOTS Are Bulbous perpetual onions (Allium cepa aggregatum) that harvest minuscule, converged radicles which simulate those of garlic and are employed in flavoring also: its bulb. Shallots are also familiar as eschalots or French shallots, are an onion as respects that occurs to have a polished, more soothing onion flavor. Dissimilar onions grow in clusters like garlic stems. The diversity between onions and shallots is that the shallots are a diminutive sweeter than ordinary onions and have a more exquisite flavor. They are good utilized in raw ingredients where you want an oniony flavor not having too much punch, like in salads and vinaigrettes, or in slow pot-roast or braised dishes, where their sweetness may intensify a dish minus watering it down. The Scriptures say in Numbers 11:5. We remember the fish, which we did eat in Egypt freely; the cucumbers, and the melons, and the leeks, and the onions, and the garlic; Nevertheless, the illustration of onion indicates power and transformation of destiny. The antioxidants allicin and quercetin in shallots possess antihypertensive Propeties and help in stabilizing blood pressure.

SHAKTY (or Sakti) (Sanskrit) The active feminine nature of the deities; In folk Hinduism, Zaktis are their wives or goddesses; in Esotericism, zakti is the crown of the astral Light. The power and the six forces of nature synthesized. Universal Energy.

SHAMADHI SHAMADI-SAHADHI It is ecstasy, the fourth and final phase of meditation. Here the essence manages to free itself completely being able to perceive, experience the real. Comparable experiences engrave in the consciousness and are never forgotten by acquiring much strength for inner work. In a Samadhi it is possible to liberate 3% of conscience.

SHAMBHALA (Gnosticism) Mysterious secret city of Tibet said to be in the state of Jinas. Some teachers have claimed that it is in northern Tibet somewhere in the Gobi Desert. It is said that great master's live there and among them is Jesus the Christ, there are also the Four Kumaras or Lords of the flame who came from Venus's millions of years ago. It is a city of great beauty and splendor, all the masters who live there are resurrected beings who stayed in this world for the love of humanity. A northeastern road leaves the city of Gandhara until it reaches the Sita and Vhastani rivers, behind these rivers, are the two sacred columns; Then there is a lake where an initiated old man guides the walker to the secret city of Shambhala.

SHANAH (Hebrew) This Hebrew expression has two alliances that materialized contrasted. On the one hand, it defines to repeat, or to do it a second time (related to Sheni, the number two.) Furthermore, Ishanot process to change, modify or distinguish. The term also defines; the lunar "anus".

SHEOL (Hebr.) The hell of the Hebrew pantheon; a region of tranquility and inactivity, different from Gehenna.

SHIEL. Variation of Shield: Irish, abbreviations accommodated formation of Goidelic O Siadhail 'descendant of Siadhal', an Irish specific denomination perhaps defining 'slow-moving, slothful', and the appellation of an established medicinal Dynasty.

SHIN, SHIEN, SIEN (Chin) A position of bliss and privilege of essence, all along which man may proceed in inner self anywhere he is welcome.

SHRINE. The term can denote a reliquary (q.v.), a sacred image of extraordinary importance, or any holy place, especially one connected with pilgrimages

SHU. (Shoo, in English transliteration) (Egypt). A manifestation of the god Ra; delineated as the "Great Cat of the Persia Basin on Anu"

SKADA (Scandinavian) Wife of Nivord. (Eddas).

SNEHA (Sanskrit) Love, affection, tenderness; fat, oil.

SNEEZE A sneeze related to being an acceptable indication or inadequate premonition disclosing favorable or adversity. communal condition: In accordance with an ancient fallacy, sneezing is perception to contemplate that somebody is chattering or imagining in reference to you. Numerous Grecians remark "Bless you" following somebody's sneezed to wish them well-being not mediocre. Exemplify in countless customs anticipates sneezing occasionally through meridian and zero hour is an indication of favorability, on the other hand, alternatively conceive it's a bad omen. At any rate, folks accept if you sneeze while dressing up, anything unpleasant may transpire that daytime. Nobody has a clue where this legend arises from, but the Japanese have turned up a overstep farther. They are convinced that sneezing one time channel anybody spreading nice stories concerning you. Over again the factor being not so pleasant. Triple, tattle that's in fact not too nice at all. In Islam once anyone sneezes, he ought to say 'Al-Hamduli I-Lah' (Praise be to Allah), and his (Muslim) kinsman or associate need to say to him, 'Yar-hamuka-I-Lah' (May Allah present his Mercy on you).

SNAILS. Shoreland Snail figuration & significance, greasy slimy clammy Snail: This tiny living thing has a majestic story as a design across the globe for fecundity, lethargic and decisive migration, life's breakthrough, and the blessed volume of the quarters. The Snail's chassis tells us a great deal about its interpretation. A Snail's shell is its house trailer and security camera. Inner part of this enchanted house, the Snail's slushy frame has protection and defense. Any other way, it would likely have no safeguard opposed to the surroundings alone any predacious. Snails transport their carapace through life, providing them with connection to quest, sanctuary, assurance, adjustment, and freedom. In Egypt, the Spiral defined intangible and cognizant spread. Aztec fine Art reproduces the Selene, Tecciztecatl, as sensible cozy inside a snail's shell, supplying Snail with attachment to celestial, cyclical, and fluctuating power. Ancient European consideration of the Snail's knobs emanating externally from their hull afterwards downpour-initiated credence of Snail having a bit of dominion beyond the meteorological conditions (or elements mindfulness) and abundant.

STABILIZE. To balance, committed, or solid, to grip secure equivalent to conserve the firmness of (object, comparable as an aircraft) to a mediator. According to Britannica Dictionary the clarity of strength is to enhance stability or to produce commodity solid, such as ceasing instantly growing, expanding, becoming deepening, etc. In the term of common-sense recuperating, it defines extending an emotional mood of tranquility. A few interferences were possibly employed to support you hold out this: Observation; inspecting on your progression with remedy, and self-assuredness amidst emotional assessments and or treatment end results.

STAMPS. Are applied as pulpit to distinction dignified rationale and classical occurrence as well as notable individuals. Great quantity of miniature territories, the obtainable purchase of stamps remains a prime in agreement with of earnings. The mailing stamp supported satisfaction for the two handouts and post-office conventional, further efficaciously recuperated value for the special-delivery assistance, and eventually raised in an exceedingly swift carrier structure. Forever stamps are exceptionally for, well, forever. This signifies that every Forever stamp you presently possess aims to still be satisfactory in the future year, no arguments about what price you invested in them for, so build up right now if you are not able to continue immediately inflation. The word stamps also appear in the holy scriptures. Exodus 28:21 "The jewels ae to be twelve in number, for the names of the children of Israel; every jewel having the name of one of the twelve tribes cut on it as on a stamp."

STAIRS. Perhaps propose an expedition; A flight of steps can be a walkway that connects each duality: locality, insinuations, or existence; if one escalates the staircase that excursion is most likely expectant. Nonetheless, in case that subside the stairs that wandering credible dismissive, disorganized, or bleak. The staircase representation is an intrapersonal interpretation concerning reason excuse of sizeable symbol of disappointed individuals in association, at best a hugely compact the outnumbered turn out to be perpetrating make a move of intimidation. Granted that suggested in 2005 by Fathali M. Moghaddam in his article "The Staircase to Terrorism". Coil stairs, like a puzzle of self-searching across advance and vision, is either a perforation or a commitment. As it may be a clandestine avenue connecting duplet magnitude, or the probability to develop, to self-exploration, to take a daring action. The "missing stair" in the allegory pertains to a critical systematic responsibility, comparatively lacking stride in a staircase; a liability that individuals may grow prevailing to and silently welcoming of, is not frankly highlighted or stable, and that stranger's to a collective classification are inform regarding cautiously.

STAN-gyour. A work about magic. (Isis Unveiled I,580).

STHIRA (Sanskrit) Hard, solid, firm, strong, tenacious; constant, assiduous; resolved; faithful; sure; lasting; stable, immutable, fixed, permanent; substantial, nutritious.

STHITI (Sanskrit) Conservancy ascribe; stability [duration, continuation, persistence; perseverance, permanence, fixity, firmness, constancy; situation, state, position, condition, rank; end, term, limit, goal; place, place, dwelling; conduct, proceed, rule; use, custom; virtue; righteousness; devotion; application; occupation; maximum; existence; occurrence.

SPACE. Characterize a journalist's pattern of the universe, declaration in the native tongue of spatial memory delegation. In a writing endeavor, areas figure diverse link of the cosmos-representation: momentary, sociable, standard and alternatives. The emblematic magnitude of space must not perish underestimate; therefore, impartiality is what provides internal consistency to the residential area of every individual. The symptomatic magnitude takes part in the delineation of a space that is consequently multiply location it is limited in struggling with an accurate endurance of a certain capacity. Space is filled with figuration of each diversity. Courage and subsistence. Dashing within trajectory as a combat for dominion. An insignia on the Moon. A banner on each spacecraft. Constellation toppling from the firmament. Associates enduring in for anybody we cease to figure out on Creation.

SEA, Forms of Prayers to be used (at) In the BCP, a small-scale collection of invocation and anthems to use in various circumstances at sea.

SEANCE (Session) Spiritist. Declarations that between clairvoyant and Cabala have come to convey a meeting or session with the cooperation of a medium to yield phenomena, such as the realization of "spirits" and other demonstrations.

SECRETS OF THE ABYSS. The (gnostic), It encompass of the work to the chymocus accompanying to the death of the Ego, and how the demons that subsequently having passed into and out of the Abyss by the involution, labyrinthine again by the disparate metamorphic domain, to take again physical body, where thereafter they can develop into Divinities, in Gods the Secrets of the Abyss is then, comprehend how to steal the Light from the Darkness.

SEDER. Persists a conventional banquet commemorated by mankind of the Hebrew creed during Pesach. The aim comprises of formalities, observance and meals signifies to embodies segments of the Exodus narrative relevance of the ethnic group of the Holy Land endurance guided from bondage in Sinai Peninsula to self-rule in Canaan. In the seder platter every ration is allegorical for an angle of Pesah: A broiled shinbone epitomized the Pescah offering, a relish serves materializes and the circular of vitality, sour greenery reverses the harshness of subjugation, paladins (an applesauce-like mixture with wine, nuts apples, etc.).

The Seder is a formality associating a trading of the story of the emancipation of the Hebrews from captivity in earliest Upper Egypt, confiscated from the Old Testament (Exodus) in the Pentateuch. The Apostolic Pesach Seder yearly observance supper was recognized by Semitic to immortalize the compassion of El-Shaddai saving them from the affliction of the downfall of the eldest male child in Libyan Desert and succeeding liberty from subjugation.

SEDJ. (Zend.) Dew or genius author of evils. (Zend Avesta).

SEED ATOM (Ros.) The marrow of continual force that is transmitted in each demonstration (return) near which the Spirit harmonized his renewed vehicle. Through life the seed atom is lodged in the heart.

SEIZE To take over (Gnosticism) To take for oneself is to rob, it is to seize what is foreign left out the consent of its owner with or lead to violence.

SEFIROT, SEPHIROTES, Sephyrotic They are universal spheres or regions that penetrate and interpenetrate each other without confusing each other. They are the ten (10) originations of Divinity; that come from the Ain Soph, which is a diminutive star which guides our consciousness, the Real Being of our being. There are really 12 Sephirot's, the Ain Soph is the 11th, and its dark antithesis is the abyss, which is the 12th sephirot. These 12 hierarchies rest in the central particles of the emblem of infinity, in them solar humanity is liquidated. The ten Sephirot's of the Kabala can be reduced into three tables: 1) Table of the Quanta, of the glowing energy that comes from the Sun. 2) Table of Atomic Weights of the components of nature; and 3) Table of Molecular Weights of Compounds. This is Jacob's proportion, which runs from Earth to Heaven. Each Sephiroth must be understood according to its four worlds from which it manifests: 1) Atziluth, is the cosmos Archetype or exemplary of the Emanations, the divine creation. 2) Briah is the orb of creation, also Khorcia, which means the universe of the Thrones. 3) Yetzirah, is the land of the Formation and the Angels. 4) Assiah is the planet of Action, the star of Matter. In the pillar of severity; there are the Sephirot of the forms (Binah, Geburah and Hod); On the pillar of Mercy, we find the three Sephirot of Energy (Chokmah, Chesed and Netzach); between these two pillars is the Pillar of Balance, where the different levels of consciousness are (Kether, Tipheret, Jesod and Malkut). The 10 Sephirots we know come from Sephira, the Divine Mother who resides in the Heart Temple.

SEIR-ANPIN or ZAUIR ANPIN (Hebr.) In Kabbalah, he is "the son of the hidden Father" who gathers all the Sephiroth within himself. Adam Kadmon, or the initial display "Celestial Man," the Logos.

SEISES, Dance of the. The religious dance accomplished in Seville cathedral during the commemoration of Corpus Christi and the immaculate Conception of the BVM.

SEKTEN (Eg.) The Devachan; the location of reward following death; It is a state, not a locality.

SELK. (Eg.) The goddess on whose head is a scorpion is an image of Isis.

SELF This word is used by Theosophists in three different meanings displayed second and third the same idea as the first, although with greater restriction: 1) Atman, the only spirit in everything. "I am the I (Atma) placed in the heart of all creatures: I am the origin, means and end of all beings." 2. (Bhagavadita, X, 20). 2. The higher Ego, the Thinker, the immortal man [the individual self-]; and 3. the lower Ego [the personal self-]. The first of these is called "the I"; the second, "Higher Self," and the third, lower self." "And now your Self is lost in the self; yourself in yourself, immersed in that I, from which you emanated primitively." (Voice of Silence, I) (P Hoult.) There are two I's in man: the upper and the lower; the detached self and the personal self. One is divine, the other semi-animal. A great distinction must be made between the two. (H. P. Blavatsky, Philosopher of the Key to Theosophy.) The lower Self is the Kama-Manas, the personal Ego; in a higher sense, it is the Quaternary or the four lower "Principles." The supreme Self is Atma in his Buddhi vehicle. (A. Besant and H. Burrows, Small Glossary of Theosophical Terms.)

SELFISHNESS Inordinate love of myself. Listen to your own engrossment without conceiving for the good of others. Part of The Seven Deadly Sins.

SEMI A Classification is semi-metaphorical if a resistance signifier corresponds (is homologized) to a struggle centrally located to make a sign. Indications are numerous occasions semi-emblematic in nature, as in the resistance motion/ parallel action, that is correspondent to the defiance 'yes'/'no'. Alternative descriptions of distinctiveness because of the subsistence of different types contrasting manifestation and guided to the discrepancy at intervals paradigmatic, context-sensitive and figurative syntactics. Semiotics express the branch of knowledge that compromises with signals or kinesics language.

SENDA, SENDERO or PATH. We reviewed in the Voice of Silence: "You cannot walk the Path before you have become the Path itself," This Path, says the commentary, is mentioned in all the mystical chronicles. As Krichna states in the Dhyaneswari: "When this Path is perceived. Already one art towards the magnificence of the East, or in the direction of the chambers of the West, without moving. There is the traveler on this path. On this Path, wherever one goes, that place becomes one's own self." "You are the Path," the adept guru is told, and the concluding says it to disciple after initiation. "I am the Path and the way," says another Master [Jesus]." This enigma is elucidated by consequently, that the word "Path" alludes to the degrees of individual inner progress during discipleship, to the progressive evolution of the person in the ascending path of spirituality. The degrees or stages of this expansion have been divided into two groups, those of the first to compose the preliminary Path, and those of the second, the Proper Path, or Path of the Disciplined, which will be described in their respective places.

SENECA The Senecas were also highly skilled at warfare and were considered fierce adversaries. But the Seneca were also renowned for their sophisticated skills at diplomacy and oratory and their willingness to unite with the other original five nations to form the Iroquois Confederacy of Nations. The use of signs in signaling, as with a Semaphone. In their own language, the Senecas call themselves Onandowaga, which means "people do the mountain." The Seneca used kinship to organize their society; extended families linked through the maternal line lived together in longhouses. The tribe had eight clans; these were in turn organized into two equally sized groups, or moieties.

SENS, Councils (of) Numerous provincial Councils were held at Sens. The most well-known was that of 1140 which condemned Abelard for blasphemy.

SENTIENT. Possessing the facilitates of awareness by the sensations; responsive, designated by impression and responsiveness, an individual or artifact that is attentive. In lexicon clarification, alertness is interpreted as "able to experience feelings", reactive to or reactive of sense impressions," and "capable of feeling things through physical senses." Sentient vitality involment desire sentiment, for instance contentment, jubilation, and gratefulness, and undesirable reactions in the formation of discomfort. Sentient approaches outside of the classic sentient, "feeling," and it recounts belongings that are vigorous, capable of detecting and being recognized, and manifest familiarity or receptiveness. The explanation distinction through and astute is the classification of talent matured by personal. Sentient judgements are expansion undergo response and impact, during astute intellect is established along comprehension and discernment.

SEP. Master Samael explains that the Self has no definition: "The Self is the Self and the reason for being of the Being is the same Being". The Self assures the Master, is a common exercise of innocent children. In it we find the 12 Apostles; the 24 Elders of the Zodiac; the 4 Elements; the Maiden of Memories,

Morpheus (the God of Sound); the Guardian Angel; the Elemental Intercessor; Martha (humility), etc., Each part of the Self has autonomy of its own and Self-Consciousness. The Magnetic Center of the Father is between the two eyebrows. He is our Divine Spark.

SEPHIRA, SEPHIROTH (Hebrew) A derivation of the Deity, the generatrix and the synthesis of the ten Sephiroth now she is at the head of the Sephiroth Tree; in Kabbalah, Saphir, or the emanation of the "Infinite" or Ain-Suph. [Sephira is Sephiroth's only one. Aditi is Sephira's model.

SEPTERIUM (Latin) A exceptional religious celebration that is praised in antiquity every nine years at Delphi in honor of Helios, the Sun or Apollo, to commemorate his victory over darkness, or Python, being Apollo-Python like Osiris-Typhon in Egypt.

SERAFIN (Latin Seraphin) (Hebrew) Seraphim, noble princes winged angels). Each of the blessed Spirits who dignify themselves, by incessant and perennial eagerness with which they love divine things. It is said of the Winged Guardians who form the second choir and who are on every side of the Throne of God, gnost. It is a master's degree. Superlative state of objective consciousness. It has indicated abode in the Heaven of Neptune.

SERAPEUM Since every deceased became an Osiris, dead Apis was called Osor-Api, a declaration that the Greeks transfigured, by apheresis, into Serapis. Serapeum was the label given to the tomb of Apis.

SERAPIS (Eg.) An extraordinary solar god who embodies Osiris in popular worship, and in honor of which the seven vowels were toned. Make appear numerous times in their interchange as serpents, a "Dragon of Wisdom". He was the greatest god of Egypt during the first of Christianity.

SESHA (Zecha) (Sanskrit) The great serpent of Eternity, the bed of Vichnu, emblem of infinite time in Space. According to esoteric beliefs, Zecha is epitomized as a serpent (cobra) of a thousand and seven heads; the previous being the king of the bottommost world, named Patala, and the latter the vehicle or support of Vichnu in the Ocean of Space.

SESMA (Sanskrit) Materiality is the enormous Serpent of Eternity; it is the image of wisdom and in age. It is illustrated as a multi-headed cobra.

SETH. (Or set) Is not a man, but a race. Before him, humanity was hermaphrodite. Seth, the first result (physiologically) after the "fall" is also the first man.

SERVANT SONGS. Four crossings in Deutero-Isaiah (Is. 42: 1-4, 49: 1-6, 50: 4-9, and 2: 13-53: 12) define the person and disposition of the 'servant of the Lord'. Whether the writer designate to the nation of Israel or to a personal is disputed. Christian theology has consistently interpreted the progress as prophecy of Christ.

SEVEN, VIRTUES, THE. They are faith, hope, charity, justice, prudence, temperance, and fortitude.

SEVIN or SEVI (Sanskrit) Existing in; that he frequents; who serves, respects or venerates; that looks for; that inhabits; visit, use, enjoy, etc.

SEXT (1) In 'canon law' the sixth book of decretals, published by Boniface VIII in 1298. It accommodates the declarations issued since the publishing of the five books by Gregory IX (1234).

SEXUALITY (Normal) (Gnosticism) Normal sensuality is understood as that which has no sexual difficulties of any kind, and which is conducive to the reproduction of the species. This is imperative for nature's economy. Sex in the creative exercise by which the human being is a true God. Habitual sexuality results from the full harmony and agreement of all other exercises. This gives us the understanding of creating healthy children, or of creating in the world of art or science. When people are sexually united in a perfect marriage, they design a perfect Divine Androgynous. A male-female Elohim, in those moments of supreme joy and glowing snuggles that inflame the depths of the soul we can keep that wonderful light, to purify ourselves absolutely, we must then transmute that wonderful energy, so that it ascends through the channels of Nadi and Surya.

STABLE (Latin stabulum) Concealed location in which cattle are confined for rest and feeding. (Gnosticism) It symbolizes the physical body and animals are constituted by all Egos or selves (defects). The stable of Bethlehem where the Christ is born is our recognize form, where later the Christ takes everyone out with the whip of the will, that is, the merchants of the temple.

STAGES (Gnosticism) The guardian of the threshold gets a second aspect. The intellectual aspect. It is in our interest to know that man's intellect is not yet human. It is in the animal stage. Each one has on the rational plane the animal physiognomy that corresponds to him according to his character. The cunning is there a true Fox. The passionflower looks like a dog or a goat, etc.

STARS When read in the Lexicon of Christian Proclivity of Overcoming Martigny, in certain works of ancient Christians Christ is seen with a diadem of stars, which in some cases are in number of seven. The Christ is exteriorized in some Christian monuments of antiquity crowned with stars, in some cases with number of seven.

STATE (of consciousness) The states of awareness are four, in which all human beings develop, these are: EIKASIA which means ignorance, cruelty, quite deep sleep, instinctive and brutal world, subhuman state; the second stage is PISTIS: it symbolizes the world of opinions and beliefs, it is also covered as monitoring the third condition is DIANOIA regarded as intellectualism, belief, analysis, synthetism, cultural consciousness, the fourth situation is NOUS, it is perfect awakened responsiveness, it is the state of Turiya (deep inner illumination).

STONE Patterns many times mirror the extra from singular existence to the upcoming. A gem curvature or a rock dissever vessel identifying this exuberant universe excursion and posture as crafts carefree with durable as longevity circle ramble them through pinna to everlasting. The lastingness of formation constitutes of cornerstone and seldom intends that they are affiliated with the celestial and the perpetual. Lodgings are not scarcely fabricated for the conscious, but also for the dead. Stone shaping constantly illustrates the preamble from one vivacity to the subsequent. A stone span or a stone dissever craft impression this inner being would expedition and stance as barges carefree progressively, continuing rhythm ramble them from earth to foreverness. The scope of gem is voiced in the Holy Writings, principally the Heptateuch and the Apocalypse of John. Precious Stone repeatedly plays a central role and captivating part in the Scriptures, considered as decline of well-being for heads of states and leaders, additionally a manifestation of mystical realization. The Body Armour was to accommodate duodecimal preliminary studies gem, delegate the twelve ethnic groups of Israel. In the Hebrew Scriptures variation, a divergent gemstone is catalog for each one of the twelve boons of Israel.

STRING. Is thin rope made of twisted threads, used for tying things together or tying up parcels. He held out a small bag tied to string, a shiny metallic coin on a string. A thread, according to traditional folk conceptions, can thus lead from the world of the living to the world of the dead as a bridge which souls pass on their way across. In Maupassant's "The Piece of String", symbolism can be found in the piece of string itself, as it represents, the peasants' stinginess and pettiness. This is because Maitre Hauch come is wrongfully accused of picking up a pocketbook that wasn't his, when all he picked up was a piece of string. Artists whose installations feature vast webs of yarn or thread (and there are quite a few three days) often speak of them as symbols of interconnection, whether between the self and others, life and death, or past, present and future.

SNEHA (Sanskrit). Love, affect, tenderness, fat, oil.

SNEEZE According to Greek mythology, particularly the first sign of life given by the man of Prometheus. Clay statue that sneezed and came to life with the help of Minerva.

SCEPTER Expresses reign, primacy, command, empire. It is an emblem of dominance, which is related to the magic rod, lightning Shishna and the Hammer of Tor. Scepters are batons of command; they were frequently used by kings or emperors. The most common designs of scepters have been replaced by the fleur-de-lis, which is an image of purification and illumination.

SCIENCES The logical and constrictive chasing encompasses the arrangement chronicle of the founding of our equipment and authentic asteroid; by operating investigation, research, and inquiry. The remark experimental emblem' proceeds from Camille Mauclair's 1914 dissertation on Besnard. Mauclair recounts it as the synthetic and chromatic embodiment of meticulous conception in garnish figurations. Lyricist, columnists, travel writer and commentators, he conceivably taken as a mediator for Besnard. (Kabbalah) The science of the mysteries of physical, mental and spiritual nature, understood with the name of hermetic and secret sciences. In the West one can mention the Kabbalah; in the East, mysticism, enchantment and yoga philosophy, to which the Chela's in India are often related with the reputation of seventh "Darzana" (academy of philosophy).

SHADE or SHADOW. The qualified gloominess bring about by the interference or conceal of beam of brightness, sunshine, or warmth: alike as an article wrapping a light accordingly just as to lessen glower, a somber or bleak attribute; a face mask declaration of sorrow or irritation, youngsters play games below the shadow of a great seaside parasol; a match of sunglasses; coloring of mankind appear in darken of epidermis tone and dim of the contrasting tints inside this extensive earth. In poems and writings, a shadow (interpret Grecian Okla, Latin umbra) is the soul or presence of a departed individual, live in the Gehenna. Shadiness becomes visible in Book Eleven of Homer's Odyssey, during Odysseus goes down enter Hades, in Book Six of Virgil's Aeneid, just after Aeneas proceeds to the hereafter. In the Divine Comedy by Dante Alighieri, countless of the lost are likewise mentioned to as shadows (Italian ombra), plus Dante's attendant, Virgil. Silhouettes exist confidence, deception, unpredictability, and somber. Like them normally related besides gloom and so specified pessimistic attribute. Nevertheless, there are as well a few constructive definitions you can attribute to shapes, especially during yours and not fabulous creatures which use outlines as a fortress to get out way the focus of attention.

SHELL(S) Seashells are frequently affiliated with tenderness and fecundity. At occasions, the seashell can be perceptible as representative of feminine pudenda. Pious values correlate seashells with pilgrims. In the few Ages of Aquarius principles, seashells are accustomed to epitomizing the senseless and are essential with sentiments. For millenarians of lifetimes, human beings possess seashells with adoration and productivity. Remarkably as well suppose they identify the secured excursion middle intermediate the anatomical and nonmaterial biosphere. Seashells are an old fashion orthodox emblem indicating doctrinal holy expedition and devotional shelter. Seashells were as well habituated as the ideogram of regeneration. Scallop shell figuration is related to the apostle, James. Seashells are an essential fundamental part of seaside environment. Others supply resources for birds' birdhouse, a place or connection exterior for seaweed, eelgrass, parasite and an anchor of diverse bacterium. Fish accustomed them to conceal form carnivores, and solitary grumblers harness them as short-term dwelling. Cabalistical reputation specified to the visions or shadows of the deceased, the "essences" of the spiritualists who track down between the bodily manifestations. They are thus cited on the grounds of being clear candid, frivolous facets of their dominant initiations.

SHEMA, (The) The admission of faith to be chant by Jewish men morning and evening. It holds 3 Biblical passages (Deut. 6: 4-9, 11: 13-21, Num, 15: 37-41), lead up to and followed by blessings.

SHIAC (Hebrew) Abyss. The identical sense as Patala.

SHILA (Pali) The second virtue of the ten Paramitas of perfection. Faultless harmony in phrase and performance. [This opinion is equivalent to the Sanskrit Zila.]

SHIM. Fire components according to Zoar.

SHOEL-OB. (Hebrew) The one who considers family "spirits"; a necromancer or sorcerer, an astrologer of the dead or their ghosts.

SHOCK Sudden unexpected disturb or surprising appearance or encounter; "I was shocked to face such hostile attitudes when I arrived"; lead to mortal to perceive astonished and trouble. "He was shocked at the state of his injuries";

influenced by corporal disturbance, or with an electron disturbance. "If a patient is deeply shocked, measurement of blood pressure may be difficult." Primarily humanity accepts that the term upset relates to impassive anguish or unanticipated fair in reply to a distressing action. Nevertheless, in preventing phrase, surprise is during all discharge negatives own adequate hemoglobin flowing all over your figure. It is a deadly preventive difficulty. "He died of shock due to massive abdominal hemorrhage".

SHU. (Shoo, in English transliteration) (Egypt.) A personification of the God Ra; represented as the "Great Cat of the Persea Basin on Anu".

SI. (Ved.). The Earth.

SIBILA, (lat. Sifaylla and east of gr.) A sapient woman to whom the ancients connected prophesy spirit. They are said to have survived in Libya, Babylon, Delphi, Cinteria, Eritrea, Cumae, Sarrios, Tibor, and Phrygia. The most prominent of these was that of the Cumas in Italy who direct Aeneas through the World of Shadows and sold his prophecies at a good price to King Tarquin, symbolically the sibyl portray the woman endowed with prediction virtue.

SIDDIM (Hebr.) The Canaanites, it is said, reverence as divinities these evil powers, whose very name indicates "spers," and from them a valley took its name. There appears to be some relationship between these, as species of fertile Nature, and the Isis and Diana of Ephesus, supplies with numerous breasts. In the Psalms, (CVI, 37) this word is transcribed in the sense of "demons", and we read that the Canaanites shed the blood of their sons and their daughters. Their title assumes to come from the same root ShD, from which determine the divine name Shaday (w.w.w.). The Arabigo Shedim means "Spirits of Nature", primitive; they are the efrits of modern Egypt and the djins of Persia, India, etc.

SIHIA. (Sanskrit) Olive, incense.

SIAN-FU or SIGAN-FU STONE, The Nestorian memorial found in 1625 at Sigan Fu (or Sian-FU) in NW, China; it was set up in A.D. 781. It was traditional to recall the appearance of a missionary from Tuts in 635 and allowed a description of the riches of the Church to date. It is the exceptional eyewitness to the supplement of Christianity in the Far East prior to the 13th century.

SILA(S). The term for appearance, oppressive internally is no existence; impression exists in every individual and every living thing; all destitute of atmosphere stop to linger. Inside such aspect, so, provide with animation and unventilated inside restricting survival. Sila or Silvanus was an outstanding component of the Premature Orthodox district, which escorted Paul the Apostle on his next minister expedition. (Sanskrit) manner "behavioral discipline", "morality", "virtue" or "ethics" in Hinayana. Sila (myth(s), in Palestinian tradition a variety of adversary, or Jinnee. Sila (murti), in Hindu dharma pratina or Akrti in the formation of a monument. Sean Qitsualik (2013, 29) describe that Sila is "arguably the most important concept in classic Inuit thought; occurring in senses that are intellectual, biological, psychological, environmental, locational, and geographical". It's possible to signify cool, airspace, the firmament, comprehension, sagacity, pneuma, globe, creation, and the whole.

SILOAM, The Pool of. A pond or reservoir in Jerusalem, alluded to in both the Old Testament and the New Testament. It is fair-minded about unquestionably the present-day Burkett Siloam.

SIN. The resolute insubordination of a living thing to the established predestination of God. In the Pentateuch it is characterized as a continuous component in the experience the two; God's humankind and creation from the first wrongdoing of Adam and Eve. Ezekiel and Jeremiah demonstrate the distinctive leadership of each person for his sins. The Psalms, along with their heartfelt pressure as sins, supply powerful perceptive on their distinctive and spiritual consequence. In the NT the Lord that the radicle of sin reclines in a man's personality (Mt. 5:21-5; 15:18-20). St. Paul describes sin as a infringement of the conventionality's columnist in the moral sense of man (Rom. 2: 14-6) and allege its absoluteness. Next creed has boost to what is contained in the holy book. Amid the influential circumstance in the evolution of this credo was St. Augustine's refusal of the Manichaean beliefs that corrupt was an actuality and the generated natural world constitutional immoral, in Approbation of the Friendly sight that sin is in quintessence a deprivation of exceptional. The maturing of the apologetic structure in the Antediluvian disposed to promote an outer perspective of sin. Repudiate this, M. Luther evangelism approval by trust alone. Below the convert domination of the Awareness venture were made to separate sin from its devout surrounding and to explain it as virtuous wrong, in the 19th centurial, the idea of sin was mainly excluded from much well-liked devout gospel in the attending centennial there has been resume prominent on the attraction of sin (e.g., in analytic Dogma).

SINAI (Hebrew) The word Sinai or Sin-ai is the "Mount of the Moon", and hence the connection. Mount Sinai, the Nissi of the Exodus. Where solar gods of prehistory were born: Dionysos, born in Nissa or Nysa, Zeus of Nysa, Bacchus and Osiris. Many settings of antiquity accepted that the Sun was the son of the moon, and the Sun in turn was a Sun of other times.

SING. Reinstates consistency to agitation since its fluctuation antagonized them to movements, so producing it practical for the breathless, alleviate ethos come by within. The channel of the individuals' articulation is detected exactly amid the thyrotropin secretor, the atomic accelerators interpret decisive physique purpose. To a significant or secondary standard each locution one pronounces tremble the nucleus raise and declining the person, starting with at the front of the intellect to the midriff. The clause 'Sing' reveal, citing to the fictitious book Sing, Unburied, Sing written by Jesmyn Ward: "Sing thus indicated that the spirits of dead people have their own songs to sing and implies that these ghosts need to tell their stories of the living in order to be able to move on to the next world."

SIGNS Mr. Martillet has authenticated in his book The Sign of the Cross Before Christianity (Paris, 1866) that this manifestation was used as a religious device in a portion of European, Asian and African mankind before Christianity.

SINUALI Characterizes an archaeological site in western Uttar Pradesh, India, at the Ganga-Yamuna Doab. The site got attention for its Bronze Age solid-disk wheel. The side at Sinauli was accidentally discovered by people levelling agricultural land. The agronomist approached across human skeleton and ancient pottery. The Archaeological survey of India (ASI) began excavations at the boundary in September 2005.

SINVAT (Gnosticism) They are particles that combine the army of the voice, once they sink peacefully into the bosom of the Eternal Common Cosmic Father, the Cosmic Night begins, which continue as far as the substance when such divine particles appear, awaken and aspire to be existent or someone, then fall the world of the three laws, then at six, then at twelve o'clock and the like. These divine atoms Sinvat, are the cause of uncertainty of the Three Gunas.

SIPHRA DTZENIOUTA (Cald.) The Book of the Hidden Mystery; one of the distributions of The Zohar. (See Mathers: Kabbalah Unveiled).

SIRA (Sanskrit) Tubular vessel, nerve cord, tendon.

SISTINE CHAPEL. Main chapel of the Vatican Palace order the name because it was constructed for Sixtus IV (1471-84).

SISTRO (lat,o sistum, and east of gr.-) Hardware musical implement utilized by the antique, in the shape of a ring or horseshoe and crossed by rods, which was sounded by shaking it with the hand. This apparatus sounded some bells and was sacred to the Egyptians that in the upper part was surpassed by the frame of Isis or Hator. It was a cherished appliance that was cast off in sanctuaries in succession to manufacture, through its combination of hardware resonate and magnetic stream. Until this day it has endure in Christian Abyssinia with the title of Sanasel, and good preacher use it to "expel" demons from dwellings and other places, an act very clear to the conjurer, even if it disturbs the laughter of the orientalist incredulous. The priestess generally had this apparatus caught with the right hand throughout the formalities of the purification of the air, or the "conjuration of the elements", as E. Levi would announce, while the priests took the sistrum with the left hand, utilizing the right to control the "key of life"; The cross Ansata or Tau.

SISTHRUS (Cald.). Conforming to Berossus, he is the last of the dynasty of ten divine kings, and the Assyrian "Noah". Just as Vichnu has predicted the next deluge to Vaivasvata Manu, preventing him, request him to assemble an ark, in which seven Richis are saved, likewise the divinity Hea foretell alike to Sisthrus (or Xisuthrus), directed him to arrange a ship and save himself with a few chosen. Enduring the sequence, 800,000 centuries later, the Lord God of Israel recapitulates the injunction to Noah. So, which is the first, then? The history of Xisuthrus; decoded pleasantry of the Assyrian tablets, it arrives to confirm reason of the High magnitude Flood said Berossus, Apollodorus, Abidenous, etc. (See table 11, in the Chaldean Genesis Account of G. Smith, pp. 263 et seq.). This table 11a. all-inclusive discussed in chapters VI and VII of Genesis: The goddess, the disobedience of men, the arrangement to construct an ark, the Flood, the dismantling of the human genealogy, the dove and the raven cast out from the ark, and ultimately, the Mount of Salvation in Armenia (Nizir Arata); It's well-balanced. The words "the god Hea heard, and his liver was enraged, because his men had corrupted his purity," and the chronology of the demolition of all his seed, were inscribe on stone tablets many millennial of lifespan prior to the Assyrians duplicated them in their bricks, and actually these, with all confidence, they anticipated the Pentateuch, "written from memory" by Ezra, simply four centennial before J.C.

SISUMARA (Zizumara) (Sanskrit) An imaginary rotating belt on which all celestial bodies move. This assemblage of stars and constellations is defined under the zig of Zixumara, a turtle (some say a porpoise!), dragon, crocodile, etc. But as it is a symbol of the meditation of the Yoga of the saint Vasudeva or Krichna, it must be a crocodile, or rather a dolphin, since it is like the Makara of the Zodiac.

Dhruva, the ancient pole star, is placed at the tip of the tail of this sidereal monster, whose head is directed south and its body curves into a ring. MS up along the tail are Prajapati, Agni, etc., and at its root are placed Indra, Dharma and the seven Richis (the Big Dipper), etc., etcetera. Its sense is, of course, mystical.

SITZ IM LEBEN. (Gem., 'place in life'). An expression used primarily in Biblical criticism, to signal the conditions (often in the life of a community) in which a specific story, saying, &c., was either designed or conserved and transmitted.

SIXTH (lat. Seix). Five and one. It is a representation of balance, love, union with Spirit, matter and materiality.

SIX ARTICLES, The. Reviews passed by Act of Parliament in 1539 at Henry VIII's demand to avoid the spread of Reformation precept and executions. They conserve transfiguration and eucharist in one kind, enforced clerical abstinence, upheld monastic vows, and preserved private Masses and audible confession.

SIVA Third person of the Trimurti of Hinduism. Its title means "Blessed." He is also known as Maha-Deva or Great Otos. He is the Otos of the Universal Sexual Creative Force and at the same time the God of Violent death and destruction, his true mission is to destroy so that the sublime renewal of life can take place. His wife is Kali and Parvati at the same time she is also two antagonistic aspects; Parvati is beauty, love and happiness; Kali is death, destruction and bitterness.

SHORT FACE This appellative has been applied to the Microprosopo, also as the "Upper Face" is to the Macroprosopo. These two are exact to Long Face and Short Face mutually.

SLEEP (Gnosticism) This term shows that the authority of the individual sleeps in assumption deep bottled by egos, mistakes, sins.

SLOW Obviously motionless or lethargic, deficient in preparation, agility, or disposition; not quick or accelerate was slow to indignation, moving, loosening, or advancing minus speed or at lower than customary pace obstruction was slow. In reference to such as the inwardly slow; which have needs of typical rational abilities. Related words for slow-going are shiftless, sedated; other applicable words slack. Slow, Rise and Shine means moving your watercraft at the slowest possible tempo needed to keep aeronautics alive, however in no case higher than five miles-per-hour. Slow down instructions are extensively familiar; they are used in roads, highways and throughout fares all over the world.

SLUG An armor-plated earthly invertebrate which is mostly deficient of a shell and secretes a film of mucus for preservation. It can be an efficient pet for plants. Commonly, the garden or ground slug is not toxic, they usually eat decaying plant materials and plants; there is no immediate method they can be harmful to humans. The Slug has been investigated as an androgynous animal and for that reason incorporates the Divine Masculine and the Divine Feminine. Consequently, the slug is more of a mystical entity than a terrestrial nature. The Slug also brings substantial information of stability and firmness. They can procreate with any other slug and turn out hundreds of broods and on that account illustrate fertility.

SMOKE. Occasionally, smoke is absolution. Mostly, it is situated for the inspiration escaping the figure, or the relation along godlike fidelity. In writings and artwork, it too had been undertaken with dying and adoration. In the present era, smoke has grown into a sign of novelty and contamination. Revered smoke is a divided traverse among me, this foliage on every side of you, and, if you wish your creator or celestial beings; it designs a moment to meet and concentrate on the simple flow of the terra firma underneath your foundation. This publication examines to bridge you near these concepts. During the more recent Christian order smoke of incense in the sanctuary commonly manifest voluntary devotions. This came into being in Gothic pious art. A smoker possibly destroys his inner existence and misses his ability to pray, fast or support his relationship with divinity due to his attachment. A person who is addicted to smoking is unable to commit his impulse to fidelity.

SNAILS Small creatures with slimy, damp enclosed and round shield, whose movements are extremely slow and often eat up greenery. Snail Substance is considered a universal cure and observance motivate us. Land Snail is an imaginative critter who finds each instant keeping subsistence safe on the landscape. Snail is related to insight, unhurried advance, perseverance, tolerance, tranquility, careful, and consistency. This sluggard is a kind life form which takes his home wherever it goes. They in addition are self-centered amid all, withdrawing inside their carapace when situations seem to be hazardous. Contrasting nearly all intellectual activity on earth, snails own a bleak analogy in Religious Beliefs. Beyond the seven deathly sins which are censured in the Bible, snails are allegorically contemplated as sluggish, or inertia. On the contrary, prehistoric Aztecs view the snail as a solemn reality since its armor abide for the rotation of animation. Many Aztec deities who frightened animalia were snails. Tecciztecatl a celestial divinity that bears a snail case on his rear. Precisely how snail withdraws inside the deepest of its exterior, the satellite pulls back within the remotest area of the sea. Snails stands for the circular of existence, in all internal evolution, in all lodger expansion; The primitive Aztecs in the sanctuaries of San Juan de Teotihuacan remain a snail carved side by side with the snake. Gnosis verifies to us that everyone is an inferior snail in the breasts of the Creator, and that all the thousands or gazillions of inspirations at the exact time, should be considered by the cosmic pathway or by the planetary track. The snow-white snail is a representation of the refined inner self; jet black snails personify the descend of individuality in circumstances, red snails make up hermetic blaze.

SOCRATES. (380-450) 'Scholasticus', Greek historian, His 'Church History' was appointed as a continuation of 'Eusebius's work and enlarged from the resignation of Diocletian (305) to 439. It is mainly unbiased and lucidly written, if colorless.

SODOR AND MAN. The attending Anglican prelacy of Sodor and Man include the Isle of Man. The original jurisdiction of Sodor, that appears to date from the 11ᵗʰ century, encompassing also the Hebrides and other islands west of Scotland, the Scottish islands were separated in 1334. The cessation 'and Man' were evidently added in inaccuracy by a 17ᵗʰ century juridical architect.

SODALITY. In the Roman Church, a guild was proven for the furtherance of some religious motive by ordinary action or mutual aid.

SODOR AND MAN. The contemporary Anglican diocese of Sodor and Man contained of the Isle of Man. The untouched diocese of Sodor, which seems to date from the 11ᵗʰ centenary encompassed also the Hebrides and other islands west of Scotland; the Scottish islands were unfastened in 1334. The closing 'and Man' was evidently adjoined in misconception by a 17th-cent legal building consultant.

SOHAM (Sanskrit) suggests "That am." This mystical expression epitomizes involution. [It is a formula that expresses the recognition of the independent Self with the one universal Self.]

SOKARIS (Egypt.) A god of fire; Solar deity in many ways. It is Ptah-Sokaris when the symbol is purely cosmic, and Ptah Sokaris-Osiris' when it is phallically. This divine being is a hermaphrodite; the sacred bull Apis is her son, conceived in her with a sunbeam. Conforming to Smith's Historical events of the East, Ptah is a "second Demiurge," an emanation of the original creative Principle" (the first Logos). The Ptah standing with cross and staff, is the "creator of the eggs of theʻ sun and the moon". Pierret believes that it stands for the primordial Force that preceded the gods and "created the stars, and the eggs of the Sun and the Moon". Mariette Bey sees in it the "divine wisdom disseminating the stars in the immensity", which is corroborated by the Targum of Jerusalem, which states that "the Egyptians called Ptah the wisdom of the First Intellect".

SOLAR BOAT o BARKA del SOL This honorable solar boat was called Sekti, and controlled by the dead. Among the Egyptians, the main prominence of the sun was in Aries, and the depth in Libra. A bluish light - who is the "Son of the Sun" is seen approaching the waterfalls of the boat. Egyptian priests cleared numerous thousands of years ago, without the help of any of the scientific implements understood; that the sun is not "a white sun, but a blue sun."

SOLAR EPOCH (Ros) Transpired the stage of time in which human advancement and planet earth began and was self-assertive in the polar region of the sun. Wife It is fraction of Sephira, Malkuth, is chosen by Kabbalists "Wife of Microprosopo", is the He that concludes the Tetragrammaton, similarly that the believing church is reproduced as "Bride of Christ".

SON OF MAN. In the New Testament a name registers to Christ. Alongside one deviation (Acts 7:56) it is proven at best in the dogma and at this point consistently on the master's words. The importance of the expression is discussed. There are rationalizations to believe the popular Aramaic of New Testament times was employed simply as rephrasing for 'me'. Consistently 'Son of Man' is hold onto to mark mainly he modesty of Christ's in human form maturity as differ from the dignity of His Divinity appoint by "Son of God"; it too affirms His comprehensive part in difference with the loyalist conceiving related alongside the subtitle 'Son of David'. (Gnosticism) It is the Intimate Christ, the inner Christ, who is born in the causal man, the real man. The Cresto's, descends from logical humanity to the causal world is the Son of the Son, and start into the causal body and from there is displayed, and is inaugurated into the human body to change into the Son of Man.

SOLEMN LEAGUE AND COVENANT. The true to connecting the Caledonian and the English Assemblage of 1643. The motive of this assembly was to conserve the Presbyterian Church of Scotland, the reconstitution of the Church of England and consistency of the Church in the British Isles, the renewal of the Church of England and uniformity of the Churches in the British Isles, the care of Parliament and the autonomy of the kingdoms, and defense of the objective prospective of the King. For some time, the ventures of the Westminster Assembly took a Presbyterian rotation, but after 1644 the Autonomous move forward to force and the Covenant was an end letter in England.

SOLO. It is applied to specify that someone does anything unattended preferably than including other individuals. The term solo is acquired from Italian solo, as well as, from Latin solus ("alone").

SOMA (drink) Sacred and intoxicating drink used in rites by Indians of the Vedic interval. Extracted from Soma, it was Asclepias Acid. Linked to Ambrosia, drink of Gods of Olympus.

SOMADHARA (Sanskrit) The sky, the air.

SONG OF SONG, THE (The Song of Solomon) (Also called 'The Song of Songs' or 'Canticles'), Old Testament Book. It materialized to be an anthology of love poems, attributed to Solomon and his beloved (the 'Shulamite') and their companions. Most likely dates from as late as the 3rd century. B.C. Nevertheless, single poems may have been a quality deal earlier. Both Jewish and Christian clarifications have interpreted the Book allegorically. In the Talmud it is considered as an allegory of God's dealings with Israel. Christians have seen in its versions of God's connection with the Church or with the single soul.

SON (from Fire or Agni Putras, in Sanskrit) Allude to primordial beings, cited "Minds" in the Secret Teaching, evolved or advance from the primordial Fire; the first seven Emanations of the Logos. They contributed light to the globe and endowed the world with ground and intellect and were the coach of the children of the Earth.

SOSIOSH or Sosiosch (Zend) The Mazdeist Savior, who, like Vichnu, Maitreya, Buddha and others, is trusted to become visible mounted on a white horse at the end of the rotation to save humanity. In the concluding year of his appearance, man will endure without eating, and although he will be in the world, he will show the dead to life, and after that the bodies of the world will be pure.

SOPHIA (Gnosticism) It process Wisdom. Sophia is the intermediary amid the soul of the world (Demiurge) and intention (Pleroma) or totality, set of Aaeons opposed to the phenomenal world. Sophie is the woman as the soul of man and as a spiritual teacher. The Feminine Logos of the Gnostics; Divine or Sacred wisdom Personified. ... (Sofia) (Greek) Sapience. The Female Emblem of the Gnostics; the universal Mind, and the gentleness Holy Spirit, according to alternatives the premature Christians. Divine Wisdom personified. Sophia is also Aditi with her seven children; "the heavenly Virgin."

SOURCE (of life) An effort by Ibn Gebirol Arab Jewish philosopher of the eleventh century, who entitle it: Me-Gor Hayyun or "Fountain of Life" (De Materia universale and Fons Vitae). Western Kabbalists have proclaimed it a literal Kabbalistic work. Scholars have come across in public libraries various Latin and Hebrew scrolls of this wonderful work; among others, one that Munk found, in the year 1802. Ibn Gebirol's Latin label was Avicebron, a well-known title of all Eastern scholars.

SOURCE CRITICISM (HIGHER) The crucial study of the literary approach and sources used by the composers of (especial) Biblical Books, and contrast from Textual ('Lower') Criticism, that is concerned merely with recoup the text of the Books as it left their authors' hands.

SPACE The space that the pseudo sages, in their ignorance, have proven to be "an abstract idea" and "a void", is the Container and body of the universe with its seven Principles. According to cryptic teachings, Space and time are one thing; they are unnamed, since they are the mysterious That which can only be discern by seven rays (which are the seven Creations, the seven Worlds, the seven Laws, etc.).

SPAIN. Christianity, In. Christian evangelist captured Spain extremely bright and early. In the 5th centurion. Arian Visigoths invade the land, but in 589 heir kings, reiterated, approved Catholicism. In the 8th century, the muslin Moors dominated Spain and in the 9th Century the oppression of Christians launched. The Christian adapted, which set about with the achievement of Calatanazor in 1002, was ended at most with the decrease of Granada in 1492. It was befriended by self-assured French authority and the establishment of religious dwellings. The later Middle Ages were considerable by the institution of the inquiry, which was promoted by the civil potentiality as a measure of inspect the Semitic. Under Charles V (1519-55). Spanish competence accomplished its summit: not only was its commanding position in Europe exceptional, but also in the North America it had prevailed a territory compared solely subsequently of Portugal. The adhesiveness of Spain to the Papacy in the contentions of the 16th centennial was thus an essential civics component. Simultaneously the mediating commanding position of the Spanish bishops at the Council of Trent did extraordinarily in consequence outlined the Anticlericalism. Subject to Philip II (1555-98) the decomposition of Spanish potential launched, and it persist in the flourishing centenaries. Legislative and Reverent altruism unfolded in Spain c.1800; it by no means reached an acceptance with the conventional Spanish atmosphere, which in the two domains is conservative, and their acceptance of Wenlong spells of turmoil and Vatican Council' entitlements, civil rights, and equality initiated new pressures in the Spanish Church.

SPARROW. The Sparrow Guide Animal carries a directive regarding self-confidence. If you unappreciated yourself, it's almost unfeasible to feel affection towards others. Sparrow challenges you to scrutinize intimately all the morals and virtues within. A gender-neutral honorific of Middle English origination, Sparrow mentions to the attractive bird and implies "small" or "chirpy." This ordinary but restful fowl is repeatedly perceived in the vicinity of the gardens of nature and signifies delight, neighborhoods, partnership, and individuality. In the Scriptures, sparrows depict loving concerns and attentiveness for divine creation, in addition the significance of modesty and confidence in the Almighty's purpose.

SPARK(S) Respectable; rays or sparkles that are submerged in the Absolute; missing any self-realization.

SPATIAL It is ability that unfolds through vocalizations and reflections. Then the faculty of "Clairvoyance" will be available to be developed.

SPECIES (Gnosticism) Just as no mortal has been able to induce that divine breath, less should anything or anyone, not a plant, not a flower, much less the beings of any Species, set aside it. Species a place of creatures or vegetations in whatever the elements own comparable attributes to one another with procreate amidst everyone: Human beings additionally descend within division of genus. The masses of living people currently go together into one race: Human species. Altogether breed, exist disparity amid personage earthlings beginning at proportions and formation to dermis color and eye color. The original mortal ascendant became visible in the middle 5-7 million years ago, likely during few anthropoid living things in antique Africa started walking as usual on two legs. They stopped raw mineral instruments 2.5 million long ago. At that point they started spreading from Africa into Asia and Europe two million years ago. The interpretation as divisions is how to recognize them is evaluative, both ecologists and for the population. Embryology distinction is hidden as groups become extinct, and it is hardly by appreciating variety that we can structure the collective, diplomatic, and commercial intensity that influence control achievement.

SPEYER. Dietary of. (1) The food of 1526 pronounced a current phase in the alliance of refining impact in German Empire. A feature away i.e., all noble people shall arrange ministerial events in his self-reliant condition backing his voice within. (20 The choice of food of 1529 was managed by an Eclectic mass. It continues law-making to conclude every liberality of Puritan in Eclectic regions. Six monarch and 14 municipality assemble a ritual 'protest'; as of now the Anarchist have been familiar as 'Protestants'.

SPELL. Magical designation or invocations that are used in a ceremony to dislodge evil entities. These spells provide to guard themselves from any assault of negative and dark entities at any instant of danger by making them escape the magical pronunciation of their words. For an incantation to have greater effectiveness it is obligatory that the person who performs it is chaste and that he has purity in his verb.

STAN-GYOUR. A work about magic. [Isis without a veil 1580]. The rationale was established on an enactment of Isis, or of the divinity Neith who was occasionally identified with her, in the Coptic town of Sais referred to by the ancient writers Plutarch and Proclus. They declare the nation puncture an epigraph adage, "I'm all that has been and is and shall be; and no mortal has ever lifted my mantle." Graphics of Isis with her veil raised were favored during the epoch of the 17th to 19th centuries, frequently as symbolic portrayal of understanding areas of study and ideology exposing creation's covert. Journalists at the conclusion of the 18th century, foretelling the visionary motion, set about utilizing the uplifting of Isis's veil as a image for disclosing amazing truthfulness.

STEAL or STEALING. It is corrupt. When a person decides to steal goods which belong to either another individual or a place of business; it is usually something of value. A person who takes the time to intent, and then executes a plan to steal from others; not only has low self-esteem but has a scope of negative social character traits: such as dishonesty which absorb a range of performances of untruthfulness, deception, and added gestures of betrayal. The right process of getting commodities is to obtain them with funds that a person has carried out through their own efforts; this way, a feeling of accomplishment will involve the individual and make his siblings & friends proud. When a youngster has been exposed to peer-pressure, he might start feeling excluded or overlooked, which may also cause an urge to steal. Humanity may steal to prove self-reliance, acting in opposition to parentage or confidantes, or just because they don't appreciate others or their own individualities. Taking the initiative of stealing may bring about the distribution of dopamine, an added neurotransmitter. Dopamine brings about enjoyable affection, and various people may pursue this gratifying notion repeatedly the intellect's opioid structure. Impulses are controlled by the brain's opioid structure. Stealing is a term used, as part of the Seventh of the Ten Commandments (Do Not Steal) given to Moses at Mount Sinai by Jehovah as law for the Hebrew people.

STELLA MARIS (Gnosticism) She is the Divine Mother, the Virgin of the Sea, the igneous Serpent of our magical domains. It is a conversion of our own Being. Stella Maris is the igneous particle of Mercury, leading and directing us in the Great Work.

STOUP A basin close by the entrance of a church holding 'holy water' with which the devoted may sprinkle themselves. Stops are many, configurations either let into the wall or standing on a shaft, and often richly decorated.

STORK, CIGUEÑA (Latin Ciconia) It is said that these species of wading birds reach more than two meters in wingspan. Consecrated bird. To the God Juno by the Romans, token of the philosopher's stone. It is a sign of the traveler. When two storks face flying in a circular space enclosed by the figure of a snake, it is an allegory of "Great Wisdom".

SPOUSE The creator intended matrimony for three predominant intentions: fellowship, breeding, and compensation. These reasons are quietly pertinent to this very day and are crucial for a wholesome community. Allow to catch an impending look at each person. (Gnosticism) We claim commitment from the spouse when we ourselves; we have been runabout or philanderer in this, or in preceding realities.

SPEYERS (Gnosticism) "The Spiral Line is called the line of life, and each life is repeated in higher evolutionary spires or already in lower involutive spires."

SPHINX (The) Fantastic Monster with Head, Neck and Chest; dog body and lion claws, the tail ends in a spear tip. According to the mythological prehistory, this monster lives in Beoda near Thebes, in a cave at the foot of a mountain, from which it descended to the road, held the travelers and posed enigmas to them, as they did not interpret them, they were killed by it. She was the daughter of Orto's and La Quimera. It is related that when Oedipus took himself to Thebes, he stopped him and proposed this enigma: "What is the animal that has four legs in the morning, two at noon and three in the afternoon?" Edius replied: that animal is man because he first walks with his four limbs, then walks with his two feet when he is an adult; in old age he uses a cane, that is, a third foot." The Sphinx threw itself into the abyss, for that was its fate if any of its riddles were solved. The Sphinx of Gizeth in Egypt has a human head and a lion's body. According to the occultism synthesizes the four elements and the entire path of the past, and is the image of the species, which under its clutches there is a temple with 22 Major Arcana.

SPIRIT(S). Are associated with extensive sentiments and acceptance, exceptionally devout gives credence to. Existing as a spiritual mortal is fairly beside actuality an individual of which inflated intentions is to be caring to own and other people. Secret opinion such we are all One, inspire them to tasks for each one's well-being and evade any somewhat dangerous ventures. Those who declare themselves faithful or intangible (or both) mostly trust in the Almighty or an elevated potential, after the show which live no devout nor devotional be prone to dismiss reliance in divinity or a sanctity completely. Reverence boosts people to own superior correlation about identity, another, and the secret. Piety could aid you achieve as to tension by offering you a sensation of calm, motivation, and absolution. It regularly turns extra crucial in the space of inner strain or ailment. Doctrinal religiosity measures exist dawn of Celestial (John 1:12-13; John 3:5-8;1 John 4:7), be changed by the grace of Jesus Christ (Rom 12:1-2), surrendered and obedient to the Spirit, living according to the Spirit (Rom 8:4-11), and consequently empowered by the Spirit to draw others to find life in the Spirit. Conscious purpose, to be fundamental within a living form.

SPIDER or SPIDERWEB. Indicates one of unaccomplished formation, intertwining one's circumstance, rolling along the watercourses of survival, striding towards our individual capacity, and seizing occasions which approach our course. It questions us to remedy the unanswered sensations and recollections which still are bouncing within our growth. The Bible says "David's life was in danger and who came to his rescue? A small spider, who quickly spun a web across the entrance to the cave. Saul and his soldiers didn't bother to brush it aside and go into the cave, because they took the spider's web as a sign that no one had entered it." Empower us to approach our profound understanding and nourish a sensation of interconnection and unification at all positions. Her webbing illustrates the adding jointly of unfastened outlook within an orderly package deal. The human spider has a couple of tempos: immobile and brilliant force; the spider individual can meet harsh tears just after exasperation, Spider networks have constantly been a source of amazement. Entwined nightly of lustrous strings, one may not at best exemplary of production and elegance, nevertheless in addition exemplar of Mother nature inventiveness and mortal capacity, as perceived in one-another efficacy at capturing and pinning down the spider's quarry.

SPIDER Demonstrates three distinct moral senses: The original approach of the spider, by interlacing its web; its militancy and its owned framework, as an appropriate spiral network of a crucial point. The spider in its web is considered in India as Maya, character of the center of the Mayan world (The eternal weaver of the veil of illusions). It also displays novelty betrayal.

SPIDERWEB appeared for equilibrium and unity. perceiving a spider's web conceivably prompting that you be allowed to require additional stability in definitive features of your nature. In Lakota legends, spiders are dreaded and respected. On one side, fear the trickster is modified from one time gold of wisdom =. On the other hand, acclaimed, Inktomi is ascribed with giving all living things their label, shapes, character and recognition. For that reason, he ran out of tags before calling himself, he arrived finally as spider. Spiders relate to formation myths since they appear to entwine their own creative society. Theorizers frequently see the spider's web as a figurative expression or comparison, and dash phrase such as the Internet or World Wide Web conjure up the inter-connection of as spider web.

SPUNK. In American native tongue jargon, it indicates bravery or courageous. Supplementary expressions for spunk are heroism, impartiality, firmness, grit, capabilities, guts. If anyone has spunk, they hold what it extracts to pursue performing uprise humor though when patrons are impolite or uninvolved. Spunk is what retain you cheerful and persistent, enlightening you to endured. Spunk is a pleasantry nominal that intends "sparks" in Scottish, from the Latin term for "sponge," spongia. In British a coarse jargon term for seed.

SPURS A gadget with a mini stake or a rough wheel that is ragged on a travelers heel a worn for driving a horse onward. Additionally; is also used; to motivate a trade or evolution or force the horse to go faster. After the 1921 FA Cup Final the Tottenham Hotspur feather promoted a cockerel. Harry Hotspur, later, the club decided to name club after Harry, as well as gave him the byname of Hotspur because he plows in his spurs to compel horse to increase his speed as he commissions in fights, and spurs are also connected with cocks' brawls. It is conceptualized as a sign of effective power, which has a link with the wings of Mercury by being attached to the heel. The golden spurs are symbol of riders signify the moral virtues of every knight. Those spur-of-the-moment resolutions or ventures are done without any planning: 'We just jumped in a car and drove to the seaside'.

STAIRS or STAIRCASE (Lat. scat aria, ladder, step) Developments of steps that supply to go up or down. (Gnosticism) It measures the levels of each person's being. It epitomizes the idea of overtaking, graduation, describing between the differences of space. In addition, it stands for the dissociation from one level to an added, from one extent to another, from one world to farther, a connection between heaven and earth and hell, joining father and son. For Egyptians, the stride is routinely three (3), that personify the three-force open (Osiris, Horus and Isis); of nine, allegorizing the ninth sphere (sex); these of seven, the seven bodies, the snakes, etc. There exist enormous escalate in the spiritual delineations and philosophies that have been, and some stock-still are, in work about confidence of various powers. The Brahmanical scale measures the seven worlds; the Kabbalistic part, the lower seven Sephiroth; Jacob's succession is quoted in the Bible; the Mithraic scale is the mysterious convocation.

STEP. Even the speech adjoining stairs and how we give voice regarding staircases is exceedingly illustrative.

STHIRA (Sanskrit) Hard, solid, firm, strong, tenacious; resolved; faithful; sure; lasting; stable, immutable, fixed, permanent; substantial, nutritious.

STHITI (Sanskrit) The calibers of maintaining; stability time scale, continuation, persistence, perseverance, permanence, range; end, term, limit, goal; place, site, dwelling; conduct, procedure, rule; use, custom; virtue; rectitude; devotion; application; occupation; maxim; existence; occurrence.

STOMA (Sanskrit) Hymn, song of praise.

STUBBORN. An individual who is stubborn is determined to give advice he or she wishes and declines to do whatever is added. They have enormous disagreement since they're as a pair so stubborn, rejecting to change your movements or opinions. Nevertheless, stubborn individuals are repeatedly quality at organization and insert to it uniform when artifact are rigid. This would be a curiously practical character feature, principally just when you're accepted with dispute. 16. Romans 2:5-6 but because you are stubborn and are fused to turn from your sin, you are storing up terrible punishment for yourself. For a day of anger is coming when God's righteous judgment will be revealed. He will judge everyone according to what they have done.

STRENGTH (Latin fortia) Alertness, endurance and ability to move a thing that has weight or makes resistance, gnostic. Within esotericism the starter who is working correctly and with the three elements of consciousness (dying, being born, and sacrifice for humanity), receives inner help, they give him strength, so that he continues forward on the spiritual path.

STRI (Sanskrit) Woman, Female.

STRING. In Wikipedia; string (formation), a long adaptable structure assembles from threads twisted together, which is used to tie, bind, or hang other objects. the stringed instruments of an orchestra, the players of such instruments; the gut, wire, or cord of a racket or shooting bow. A group of objects threaded on a string, a string of fish, a string of pearls; a series of things arranged in or as if in a line a string of cars, a string of names. String also means to deceive someone for a long time about what you are really intending to do: She's been promising to pay back the money for six months, but I think she's just stringing me along. He strung her along for years, saying he'd marry her and divorce his wife. It can also be a data type used in programing, that is used to represent text rather than numbers. A string is a sequence of characters and can contain letters, numbers, symbols and even spaces.

STROTA or ZROTAS (Sanskrit) These are currents of water, rivers, canal, watercourse; body orifice; hearing, organ of the senses.

STRUGGLE or STRUGGLING Being concerned about trying hard to do, reach, or distribute with reality that is tough or that origin issues. He has been struggling amidst the issues of how to keep quality laborers from departure. They struggled for the privilege to vote. She is struggling with her health. A struggle is a long and difficult attempt to carry through existences comparable to civil liberties or constitutional entitlements. Growth develops into a struggle for endurance! In the springtime of life, a men's struggle to subsidize his indigence-afflicted household. Psychologists have proven that inaccuracy is supportive of brainpower and relatedness and if we are not struggling, we are not often advanced. Struggling is not only good for our brains but also for people who know about the value of struggle and improved their learning potential.

STOUP. A washstand near the arrival of a church accommodating "holy water" with which the faithful may sprinkled the masses. Stoups are of divergent mode, this one permitted into the enclosure or standing in a column, and frequently justly adorned.

SUBHAVA. (Sanskrit) Introduces the reality that configurations itself or that "substance that gives substance to itself". The Eka Sloka Sastra of Nagarjuna; He paradoxically describes how "nature that has no nature of its own," and as that which is with and without action. In the Svab Havat he describes that creativity is the Spirit without Substance, the ideal proposition of the powers that act in the work of deciding evolution (not "creation" in the sensation that this word is ordinarily given); powers that in turn grow into real causes. In agreement to the words used in the Vedanta and Nyaya philosophies: Nimita, the orderly cause, and Upadana, the evidence, are coeternally chanted in Subhava. Complying to a crazy Sanskrit: "He who thanks to his potency (that of the 'efficient' cause) is worthy among ascetics, each created notion comes by its own nature."

SUBIACO. A town c. 40 miles east of Rome, well known as the location of the grotto where St. Benedict settled on his withdrawals from the world. It developed into the birthplace of the Benedictine Order.

SUBJECT. It's interpreted in the holy scriptures as owing reverence or dedication to the capacity or predominance of alternate; distress a specific accountability or revelation, subject to seduction. Corresponding to our approach of intuitive or analytical, and not to the object itself; relative to or association with the subject, as in opposition to the exterior society.

SUBLIME In esthetic, the exalted (from the Latin sublimis) is the grade of eminence, even if large, righteous analytical, spiritual, inventive, ethereal, or creative. The word mostly comments on an eminence far off every probability of estimation, quantifications, or copying. Sublime enrolment has been expounded as a combination of sensations; activation, delight, and intensity, jointly with tenderness of respect in wildlife, that is recognized as capable, extensive and complicated (Bodie, 2008/2011). As said by Plato, Beauty was an idea or form of which beautiful things were the consequence. Beauty by comparison beings in the domain of intelligible objects since there is a form of beauty. The predominant question is: what do all these beautiful things have in common? To know that is to know Beauty.

SUCHI or ZUCHI. (Sanskrit) One of the honorifics of Indra: as well as, of the third son of Abhimanin, son of Agni; particularly, one of the forty-nine prehistoric fires. [Zuchi also express clean, pure, clear, honest, holy, virtuous.]

SUCHUMNA (Sushumna) (Sanskrit) The solar ray; it is the first of The Seven [mystical] rays. A Spinal Nerve that is related to the heart with the Brahmarandhra, which plays a significant role in the practice of Yoga, also bears this name. [The suchumna, also called by the yogis Nadi Brahma or Sandhills, is a Nadi (nerve, vessel or conduit), which passes through the Ida and the Pingala and unfolds through the middle of the body, it is also called the medulla Thorn, including all its ramifications; in the same way it is the state of force that is full of positive and negative faces; when the lunar and solar breath do not flow, Prana is said to be found in SUCHUMNA; From it arise all the subtle forces of nature.

SUCCUBUS (Latin incubus) The devil spirit, that has carnal dealings with a woman, is structed from secondary desire, by human concupiscence. Gnostic. They are plastic idea creations of women, fabricates by the lascivious corruption of; In the male they are called succubi, this type of effigy takes shape until it becomes the imperfection that steals part of the conscience. The I's incubators and succubi, then, are diabolical creations of the imagination; fantasy, by the unnatural lewd vice of self-pleasurer in thoughts and desires.

SUFISM (It is the root of Sophia, wisdom). A mystical sect of Persia, considerably like that of the Vedantines. Though very stable in number, only the Vedan tines, only exceedingly intelligent men adhere to it. The Sufi dogma is largely linked with Theosophy, in that it exhorts an along universal creed, as well as external recognition and tolerance in favor of the exoteric accessible faith.

SUDHA (Sanskrit) Subsistence of the gods, analogous to amrite, solidity that negotiate immortality. {the water of the Ganges; the nectar of flowers.}

SUGER (c.1081-1151) Abbot of St. Denis, hear Paris, from 1122. Even though he was of humble origins, a great deal of his life Suger was a powerful adviser to the French Crown; during Louis VII's absenteeism on the Second Crusade he was one of the functionaries The life of Louis VI is the primary historical authority. His new parish at St. Denis (choir consecrated 1144). Of which he left an illustration, which was a critical step in the evolution of Gothic architecture.

SUIDAS (c. A.D. 1), 'Greek lexicographer'. The belief that the Greek dictionary which continues undergoing this denomination was the effort of an unquestionable 'Suidas' in all probability inaccurate; the voicing evidently means an arsenal of attributes The lexicon, completed c. 1000, accommodates some items of historical importance.

SUKHA. (Sanskrit) Joy, enjoyment, pleasure, delight; Joy; happiness, blissness, glory, placidity, tranquility, tranquility of spirit.

SUKHADHARA. (Sanskrit) Paradise.

SUKI (Sanskrit) A son of the Kazyapa Richi and wife of Garuda, king of the birds and vehicle of Vichnu. Suki is the mother of parrots, owls and crows.

SULABHA (Sanskrit) Easy to obtain, to reach or perform.

SUMA (Sanskrit) Flower

SUMMA THEOLOGICA The leader assertive work of St. 'Thomas Aquinas'. The three parts treat judiciously of God, of man's return to God, and of Christ as the technique of man to God. The concluding sections, on the Sacraments and the Last Articles, were left incomplete, the missing parts being donated by Reginald of Piperno

SUMNA (Vedic) Hymn.

SUNFLOWER Term comes from spinning and sun; for the acceptance that the flower must go back to where the sun travels.

SUN Constitutes existence nevertheless Helios is in addition dear to personify vitality, capability, eagerness, and lucidity. The sun is an essential strength specifically covering of our ability, nevertheless it includes brightening the earth everywhere, aiding living things gliding the globe, and comforting a lot of crucial groups of living organisms. The sun is repeatedly a major attribute and is recognized along with the Alpha and Omega. In classical Egypt, the sun God head was the presiding feature surrounded by the Apex goddess which kept this situation starting rapidly in that assimilation antiquity. Declare, "For the Lord God is a sun and shield" (84:11). Also, the insert encourages each one of us, "The sun shall not smite thee by day, nor the moon by night" (121:6). In the introductory the Bible pathways, the sun is used to stand for Creator, which is superior, again he next tells us the sun won't harm us.

SUNG-Ming-Shu. (Chin) The Chinese tree of knowledge, and tree of life.

SUNNA or Sunnah (Persian) The conventional law or instructed of the Prophet Muhammad, which Sunnis (or orthodox Muslims) contemplate to be of uniform significance to the Qur'an.

SUNG-MING-SHU (Chenese). The Chinese seedling of comprehension, and tree of life.

SUNDAY. The term "Sunday", the period of the Sun, is obtain from Classicalism horoscope, to where the septenary orbs, familiar in English as Saturn, Jupiter, Mars, the Sun, Venus, Mercury and the Moon, everyone possess an instant pertaining the full day allocated to masses, and the world that was official in the midst of the earliest date of any solar day of the cycle. Sunday flows from the Medieval English term Sunnenday, that alone appears from the Old English expression Sunnandaeg. The English deduction comes from the Latin dies Solis ('sun day'). To realize why this day is dedicated to the sun, you should gaze at Hebrew Babel age. The Sabbath day in Religious believes is normally Sunday, the primary solar day of collective venerating. It is seen by the majority orthodox as the regular tribute of the restoration to life of Jesus Christ. Days of the week were label following the celestial bodies of Grandeur astromancy, in sequence: Sun, Moon, Mars (Ares), Mercury (Hermes), Jupiter (Zeus), Venus (Aphrodite) and Saturn (Cronos). The daily cycle lay out all over the Byzantium Empire in Archaism. Sunday was commonly considered as the opening of the week by the two Religious and Semitic. Backing Jewish heritage, the Bible is fully straight forward that God repose on the seventh day of Formation, that set up the foundation for the Sabbah, the day of repose. Among Christians, this time has replaced the Sabbath of the Jews, as a sabbath and prayer. This modification was used in memory of the Resurrection of Christ. In the early days of Christianity, Sunday was not only a day of prayer, but also of Christian rejoicing and joy; so, on that day it was forbidden to fast and kneel to pray. The faithful prayed standing every day, from Easter to Pentecost. This discipline was in force in the time of St. Ambrose and St. Augustine, it was not interrupted in the West until the seventh century.

SUNRISE. Is figurative of delivery, development, brand originations of every variety, restoration, even forming and about the entirety that has a appreciate or aspiration dawning. Furthermore twilight, disposed to be allusive of resolutions, cessation and all concept correlated with absence of light, if difference crucial for enlarging our sight. The sun stands for aliveness, but it's studied as well to personify vivacity, faculty, readiness, and lucidity. The sun is an ordinary vigor that's surface of our authority, but it additionally brightens the planet all over us, aids livelihood living things runs the earth, and comforts plenty of indispensable ecological communities.

SUNSET. The conclusion of the rotation that replicates fundamental day-to-day, how the daybreak exemplifies the conception of the sideral day, during the sundown is its realization. Whatever this is? In many lifestyles dusk describes the close of existence, whether it's a lengthy solar day or an individual's survival. A particular energy resounds fragments pitch dark, nevertheless a lot of people may conclude that relating twilight gone with imminent sun rays facing no less than culmination. It has been proven that Sunsets can relieve stress and have many rational effects that enhance the long-lasting satisfaction of life and physical benefits. When you think you're having a rough day, the best possibility is to drive to your favorite spot and watch your worries fade away. A Sunset symbolizes the ending of life in the flesh, A sunrise symbolizes the resurrection as the soul rises to heaven.

SUNYA, SUNYATA. (Zunyata) (Sanskrit) Emptiness, space, nothingness. The denomination of our impartial universe in the sensation of its unreality of illusion.

SURA(S) (Sanskrit) It tastes good.

SURAJA (Sanskrit) A goddess.

SUSO HENRY. (1295-1366). German mystic. He entered a Dominican homestead at the age of 13; after 15 years of modest devotion, he carried out a transformation. He studied under J. Ekart at Cologne. Despite awkwardness with his order, he preached extensively and was appreciated as a spiritual director in many women's abbeys. His leading work 'Das Büchlein der ewigen Weisheit' ('The Little Book of Eternal Wisdom') is a hands-on contemplation book, with miniature theoretical analysis; it is one of the classics of German spiritualism.

SURSUM CORDA (Lat., 'Lift up your heats'). In Communion the signal is inscribed by the celebrator to the gathering at once before preamble.

SUTA (Sanskrit) Born, begotten; coachman, charioteer, usher or car driver; Bard, epic poet; the Sun; The son of a kchtriya and a Brahmani.

SUTRA (Sanskrit) The second breakup of the sacred scriptures, label to lay Buddhists. [Sutra chooses aphorism, sentence; book of aphorisms or sentences. There are Vedic, Brahmani and Buddhist sutras. It as well manifests guide, cord, thread, etc.]

SUVAJA (Serbian Alphabet; Cybaja) Is a townlet in the town of Bosanski Petrovac, Bosnia and Herzegovina, Suvaja, CyBaja Hamlet.

SUVAHA (Sanskrit) That he endures well, patient.

SUVANA (Sanskrit) Fire, the sun, the moon.

SVAR or SWAR (Sanskrit) The ether, heaven or paradise; glory; beauty, Svar is part of the mystical formula: Bhur, Bhuvas, Svar.

SVAPNA (Sanskrit). A condition of ecstasy or sleeplessness. Clairvoyance.

SVASTI (suasti) (Sanskrit)! Save! Bless you! Welcome! Loor! Glory! Happiness!

SYGINA (Scandinavian) Loke's wife. (Eddas).

SYMBOLISM. Illustrated expression of an idea or a prediction. Early writing did not at first have disposition, but symbols that convey an entire sentence or edict. The reproduction, then, is a recorded parable, and the allegory a spoken image. The Chinese written jargon is nothing more than parabolic writing, with one proportion being apiece of its thousands of letters. (Gnostic.) "In the father of the family is the symbol of wisdom. In the mother of the home is love, the children symbolize the word."

SYSTRO. (Lat, sistum, and east gr.) Instrument music of Matal used by the ancients, in the form of a ring or horseshoe and pierced by rods, which was sounded by shaking it with the hand. This instrument sounded comparable to bells and was sacred to the Egyptians that in the upper part was topped by the figure of Isis or Hator.

SYNTHESIS. Universal transcendent synthesis is a massive probability of declaring, perceptions, mirror image, and logical portrayal of fundamental biocompatible merits along with existence, mother nature, deep affection, formation, relationships, unanimity and equality accommodated in all effective faiths, disciplines, mystical structures and instructions. Synthesis involves placing objectives jointly; perceiving the entire delineation and understanding it as a united truthfulness

SYUMNA (Sanskrit) Placer, happiness.

SYN, In Norse tales, Syn (Old Norse: ['syn'], "refusal") is a goddess correlated with defensive refusal. Syn is exact in the Prose Edds, marked down in the 13th century by Snorri Sturluson; and in Kennings working in skaldic poetry. Scholars have given theories about the connotations of the goddess.

SYRO-CHALDAEANS. An alternative denomination for the Chaldean Christians.

SPYRIDON, St. (d.c. 348) Bp of Tremithus in Cyprus. He was a plain peasant who, conforming to tradition, had suffered in the Diocletian oppression. As bishop he is said to have appeared the council of Nicea; he was unquestionably present at that of Sardica (c. 343). There are many narratives devoted to his life.

SYZYGY. A term used by the Gnostics for a match of cosmological opposites, e.g., male and female. It was clenched that the creation had come into reality along the interaction of such opposites.

SYSTEM. It's a collection of elements or components that are organized for a common purpose. The word sometimes describes the organization or plan itself (and is similar in meaning to method, as in "I have my own little system") and sometimes describes the parts in the system (as in "computer system"). "Symbolic systems" is defined as the meaningful symbols that represent the world about us. This is done in human language as well as in computer language.

SYSTOLE & DIASTOLE. In everything that evolves and involutes, there is a systole and a diastole, it comes and goes, it ebbs and flows, according to the Law of the Pendulum.

SPHINX at Giza, near Cairo, is the most famous sculpture in the world. Accompanied a lion's body and a human head, it illustrates Ra-Horakhty, a configuration of the dominant sun god, and is the incarnation of royal capability and the protector of the sanctuary doors. The myth says that the Sphinx was a female monstrosity with the body of a lion, the head and breast of a woman, eagle's wings and conforming to some, a serpent's tail. She was forward by the gods to plague the town of Thebes as retribution for some ancient crime, chasing on its youths and devouring all who ineffective to solve her riddle.

SUVAHA. (Sanskrit) That undergo competently, patient.

SWAN. Signifies the Holy Spirit and Love. It is made known that the Swan is manifested with tenderness, when one of the twosomes dies the other succumbs to misfortune. In early history's belief the Swan was committed to Apollo, Leda and Venus. The red swan is a solar image, prophetess enable that alongside logical mercury, as the white swan. Moreover, this was recommended by Venus, that was a conception of the natural princess. The black swan has the longest neck, compared to its size of all swan species. A jet-black swan is the formal bird of Western Australia and is characterized on the identity of this country and in its badges. Swan is available in European faery fables, say abstinence (partially over of their snow-white feathers), creativity, and elegance. On a relevant entry, swans are analogous alongside loyalty, faithfulness in alliance, and chastity, since they companion for growth. Swans mean respect, fondness, excitement, six senses, selflessness, charm and dignity. These fowls are contemplated sanctified in many societies; glimpsing them is a superior premonition and signals tranquility and contentment. Leading up to European pathfinders extended Australia, well informed people speculation that entirely snow-white swans survived. In research and legend, the swan symbolizes illumination, pureness, conversion, instinct, poise. In Prehistoric Greece, the swan rank for the animation and was connection of Apollo, the deity of the Sun, considering in other faiths, the swan inclines a delicate mark of the satellite.

SWETE HENRY BARCLAY (1835-1917) Doctrinal and biblical scholar. From 1890 to 1915 he was Regius Professor of Divinity at Cambridge. He was worried with the initiation of assorted communal projects, as well as the Publication of Theological Studies and A Patristic Greek Lexicon (published 1961-8). His own attempts included the delivery of the Septuagint (1887-94).

SWEET GRASS Illustrates reassurance, tranquility, and reverence in numerous indigenous societies, it extends from 1 to 3 feet high in Eeyou Istchee and other localities. Sweetgrass is occasionally named the "hair of Mother Earth" and is appraised as an award. Succeeding the grass is gathered in, it is attentively weaved; the triple divisions description of intelligence, anatomy, and pneuma. By interlacing it we transfer those characteristics of our animation unanimously, protection for and invigorate those. A single time accumulated and drained, blades are intertwined reciprocally for spot at one's elements, at assignments and in our observances. Sweetgrass is utilized in streaks, curative or vocalizing circlets since it has an invigorating outcome; its vapor is presumed to refine belief and the surroundings and abolish inferior or adverse views.

SWORD (Latin apathay from Greek) Sharp weapon with garrison and hilt. It is a sign of freedom and strength, of death and fecundity. In the Middle Ages it was considered a symbol of the word of God, it is associated with fire and the will. In Alchemy, the sword symbolizes the purifying fire, being a symbol of spiritual evolution. The sword owned by us is their weapon and almost exclusive of high dignity. Indicates potential, shelter, command, robustness, and daring; illustrative, it described detriment and the confused amplitude of the mind. The sword is a star, with arrayed existence exhibitions; accomplishment is a feature of delegation and fairness. A sword in godly besides entirely often embodies the mightiness and potency of the lord and master. Achieved in addition (characteristically!) isolate righteous from wrongful. The mandatory agreement for residues proceeds at that moment illustrate authority. Although the sword position descending, apex facing the terra firm, it exemplifies the transfer once again of powerfulness and achievement. Swords displaying skywards demonstrate suggested combat or dispute or the preparedness for armed conflict or dispute. Alluded to modernized swordplay at which point a swordsman grasps the dagger tip ascending to specify his preparedness. Swords aiming at descending constitute tranquility, slow down or the conclusion of disagreement.

-T-

TAAROA (Tahiti) The creator and the main god of the Tahitians.

TA (Egypt) Amulet pronominally made of carnelian, jasper or red quartz; that was depended at the neck of the mummy. The text of the Capi. CLVI of the Book of the Dead, engraved on this phylactery, placed the deceased under the protection of Isis.

TAALS. An oral history rhythmic designs in classical Marg Sangeet. Taal (instrument), Indian palmar surface clash cymbals. Tala (Music) or taal, the expression employed in Indian classical music as to mention to musical meter. Taal (film), 1999 Indian Hindi film by Subhash Ghai. There now are a great deal of variety of Taal, like Teen Taal, Jhaptaal, Dhamar Taal, etc. These rotations can be famous found on the method the strikes became split up. For instance: Teen Taal is a 16-beat tempo rotation with 4 divisions, place every one dividing has 4 strikes one by one.

TABLE, COMMUNION The table at which the Holy Communion is celebrated. In the Catholic church in the East the word is used by Low churchmen, High churchmen preferring the term 'altar' as better expressive of the Eucharistic sacrifice that they are propose on it.

TABOO The humanistic precision of taboo is an existence that's disallowed for morality or collective reasons. For example, the Torah determined eating pork as taboo since pigs are filthy creatures. A taboo, also denoted tabu, is a communal category's forbidden, barring, or evasion of object (generally a statement or conduct) built on the category's sense that it is extremely revolting, derogative, venerated, or permitted at most for defined individuals. alike forbidding's are attending in practically all civilization. In the Holy Scriptures taboo implies" prohibited, sacred, dangerous, unclean." A separate derivation detects, the expression to the verb "ta" signifying "to mark" and "pu", a qualifier. Merits like mortality, healthiness, mother nature, deep affection, privilege, fairness, or civil rights are viewed as universal and untouchable; consequently consecrated. Exchanging them off opposed to worldly worth (e.g., ready money) is contemplated as taboo.

TAD-AIKYA. (Sanskrit). "Unity"; recognition or associated with the Infinitive. The uncertain ecumenical Substance (Parabrahm) has no designation in the Vedas, even so is mentioned to by the nomination of Tad [Tat], "That."

TADEO of HAYEK. (Agecius). Medical practitioner to Emperor Rudolf II of Germany, who gave him the first lectures in alchemy.

TAD-AIKYA (Sanskrit). "Unity"; Recognition or union with the Absolute. The impenetrable universal substance (Parabrahm) has no appellative in the Vedas but is cited to by the selection of Tad [Tat], "That."

TADA (Sanskrit). Blow, punishment; Complaint, noise.

TAGARA (Sanskrit). Inaccuracy, perplexity, span of the mood; commodity of the senses; game.

THAT (English) "That", "They". The unique, eternal, infinite and unaccountable real existence.

THALES OF MILETUS (546 B.C.) He is considered the most magnificence sage of the Seven of Greece. He has been bestowed the title of founder of mathematics for some of the argument of geometry. He is the author of the maxim "Noscete Ipsum" (man know yourself and you will know the universe and the gods). That clause materializes on the Frontispiece of the Temple at Delphi.

TAHT ESMUN (Egypt) The Egyptian Adam, the initial mortal progenitor.

TAICHA. (Sanskrit) The month Paucha, that makes up features of our December and January.

TAIGA A damp boreal climate woodland presiding over the conifers (such as spruce and fir) that starts wherefrom the arctic draws to a close. The sizeable chunk of the taiga is coated by the Northern Coniferous Forest initially around 4,200,000 km (a 2609759.01 mi) 2 (about twice the area of Argentina), the East Siberian Taiga offset a size of near 3,900, 000 km2 and even the compact part, has a prominent area of over 2,156,000 km (about 1339676.29 mi) 2 (over twice the area of Egypt). The wide-reaching district with taigas is instituted in Russia and Canada. Taiga is the terrestrial biome that has the lowest yearly midpoint temperatures after the tundra and undergoing ice caps. The internal Alaska-Yukon Lowland Taiga ecoregion sprawls wrapping a great district of southern to northern Alaska and neighboring northwestern Yukon Territory. Yellowstone is essentially found in the Taiga biome. A biome is an area that can be grouped by the scatter and animals that inhabit it. Elements such as climate, soil, water, and light decide the types of living things in any given biome.

TAIL of SATAN or devil (Gnosticism) This expression mention to the Kundartiguator organ, it is the matching as the Python snake that crawls on the earth. This advances on account of fornication.

TAIZE COMMUNITY. An ecumenical monastic community conformed in 1940 by Roger Schutz (b. 1915). Schutz appears as convinced of the needed for any design of traditional theology within Protestantism; in 1940 he buys a house at Taizé in SE. France, in that he guarded Jewish and other refugees until 1942. With the German habitancy he advanced to Geneva and started living a community life with Mx Tjiran and others. In 1944 they escaped to Taizé, and the first seven brothers took solemn vows in 1949. The Rule of Taizé, imperial in 1952, reinforces a life alike to that of attach monastic ranging, exclude that the features dress as payment and accumulate only three Offices a day. Their principal work lies in the augmentation of Christian unity.

TAKYA (Sanskrit) Laughable, ridiculous.

TAKMA (Sanskrit) Progeny, offspring, posterity.

TALL BROTHERS, The. Four monks who masterminded the Organist Movement in Egypt at the conclusion of the 4th century. In 399 they made their action from the Nitrian Desert to Alexandria and therefore went to Constantinople, where they secured the substructure of St. Chrysostom.

TALK (Gnosis) Acquisition of the inner talk begins from self-reflection, from being, through monitoring and memory of oneself. The noticeable talk: it advances mechanically, not knowing all that it says.

TALIA (Sanskrit) Oil, estoraque, benzoin, incense.

TALISMAN Lucky charm, "magic image". It is an article of stones, metal or sacred wood; It is customarily a piece of manuscript full of letters and figures traced under define planetary authority in mystical scheme appointed by a mortal familiar in profound sciences to a second not familiar with in them, either to safeguard against from any wrong, or for him; realization of decide desires.

TAMAS. (Sanskrit) The condition of absence of light, "impurity" and inactivity; It is besides the classification of unawareness, if situations are visionless. It is an expression employed in mystical doctrine. It is the impartial earth Tamas display as denseness, inaction, solidity, persistence and dimness. In the internal creation of the gradient, it is manifest as despondency, agitation, concern, suspicion, indecision, laziness, indolence, incomprehension, bafflement, astigmatism, hallucination, mistakes, inanity, indifference, disdain, awkwardness, drowsiness, inertia, desire, insolence, firmness of heart, etc. It is the most important grade in the savage and in the produce and inanimate domain. "He knows that the Tamas quality, born of ignorance, brings obfuscation to all souls, enslaving them through error, laziness and lethargy. Blindness, inertia, error and confusion are born of the increase of tamas".

TAMASI (Sanskrit). The night; Durga. It is as well the name of a river in India. As nominal; indicates a degraded person; a lazy, indolent man.

TALMUD (Hebrew) Where rabbinical explanations on the Jewish faith are put in writing. It is imperturbable of two fragments, the prehistory one is called Mishnah, and the bulk present-time, Gemara; It holds the civil and authorized laws of the Jews, who claim for him a great holiness. Since eliminating the prominence that have just been variations amid the Pentateuch and the Talmud. The earliest; They say, he cannot declare any predispositions over the latter, for both were accepted in unison by Moses on Jehovah's Mount Sinai, who put in writing one and fluent the other orally.

TAMALAPATRA (Tamala-Pattra) (Sanskrit) Flawless, cultivated. It is also the term of the leaf of the Laurus cassia, a tree that is studied assuming with exclusively concealed cryptic virtues. [The Tilaka or frontal sign.]

TAMATA (Sanskrit) Who wants, prolonged or exhale for another mortal or organism.

TAMARISK (Egypt) A sacred tree of Egypt, Allocate momentous hidden ethic. Numerous of the sanctuaries were surrounded by such trees, especially one found in Philae, sanctified amid the sacred, it was assumed that underlay conceal the body of Osiris.

TAMETSI. The Tridentine order of 1563 determines the precise styles of recognizing relationships. It precisely at subdue underhanded. It was not ordinarily circulated in Angelican places of origin, and it was substitute in 1908 by the conditions of Ne Temere.

TAMRA-PARNA (Sanskrit) Ceylon, the prehistorical Taprobana.

TAMTI (Cald.) A celestial being, comparable to Belita. Tamti-Belita is the Sea manifested the mother of the city of Erech, the Chaldean Necropolis. Astronomically, Tamti is Ashtoreth or Isthar, Venus.

TANTRA (Sanskrit) Process "rule", or "ritual". Unquestionable religious and magical works, whose main eccentricity is the cult of female power, personified in Zakti. Most of the Tantras are devoted to one of the many forms of Ziva's wife and are written in the form of dialogue amongst the two divinities.

TANGO or TANGA (Peruvian) An icon extremely revered by Peruvians. It is the sign of the Triune or the Trinity, "One in three, and three in one", and survive before our era.

TANHA. (Tanha) (Pali). The eagerness for being. The aspiration to exists and extension to being on this planet. This fondness is the architect of Restoration or Regeneration [That determined deficiency for material reality is an energy and has an influential fostering capacity that enchant the journey behind into tangible existence. "Kill the love of life, but if you kill the tanka (the will to live), see that it is not for the thirst for eternal life but to replace or pass with the enduring."

TANUJA. (Sanskrit) Daughter

TANTUM ERGO. The two-concluding poetry of St. Thomas Aquinas's hymn 'Pange lingua Gloriosi', frequently used at Benediction in the Romanism. The best-known English translation begins 'Therefore we, before Him bending'.

TARSUS. Pompey produced his former city of Asia Minor the capital of the Roman province of Cilicia in 67 B.C. It converts the seat of a Stoic philosophical school and was the birthplace of St. Paul. In Christian instrumentation it became an episcopal see.

TARA [o TARAKA] (Sanskrit) Wife of Brihaspati (Jupiter), taken by King Soma (the moon), an act that conducted to the war of the gods with the asuras. Tara embodies mystical comprehension as opposed to ritualistic faith. She is the mother (by Sonia) of Buddha (1) "Wisdom".

TAT (Sanskrit) That, The Universal, The Unity.

TATA (Sanskrit) Father. Word of endearment and respect, corresponding to my son, my friend; dear, loved, venerable, respectable, etc. Also Deployed, developed, unwrapped, extended; produced; full; Penetrated.

TATE, NAHUM 1652-1715), and Brady, Nicholas (1659-1726) Writers of the New Version of the Psalms (1696). The duo were Irish Protestant men of the cloth. Tate became Poet Laureate in 1692. Brady was chaplain to William III, Mary, and Queen Anne. The New Genre is a codification of the Psalter backing the artificial flavor of the interval. It deliberately renovates the contribution of T. Stern hold and J. Hopkins was markedly used up to the early 19th century.

TATIAN (born c. 120), Guardians and puritan. A natal of Syria, he enhances a Christian in Rome between 150 and 165. About 172 he restores to the East, where he is said to have manifested the Encratite. His Oratio and Graecos is an extreme shelter of the precursory times and clarity of Christianity, join with a brutal ambush on Greek advance. His chief declaration of popularity is his Diatessaron (q.v.)

TATTVA TATTWAS (Sanskrit) Ether vibration. Principle, Essence, Reality, Category, Teo. Gnosticism "That" permanently exists. The subs-ractum of the seven configurations of nature. They are the authority that are proven as raw matter to illustrate themselves; It is the conception, preservation and end of clear implement and phenomena. The terms of the Seven Tatwas are: Adi, Samadhi, Akas; Vayu, Texas; Prithvi, and Apas.

TAO In a nutshell: Superlative State of Consciousness. St. Anthony Abbot and St. John wore them on their cloaks and chest.

TAOER or TAUR. Among the Egyptians the wife of Tiphon.

TAOISM. Religious sacred of the primeval worship of the Mandarin. Tao is among the threesome by much comprehensive doctrines in mainland China and derive from the "Tao" (the way). It has been a cornerstone and organizational structure are connected to Laozi who, it is considered he was born in 604 B.C. and is probably the pen of the Tao Te Ching (essentials efforts of ideology Tao). The transfiguration of Taoism into a favored denomination initiated in the third centenary B.C., when its advocates dedicated individuality to the exercise of hermetic, enchantment and prediction. It is reported that Chang Tao Ling established the Daoism faith in relation to the second centurial of our generation and was its earliest "Pontific". The first of all to be studied in Tao is his attempt to enhance The Creator and explaining, simultaneously, each that exist...., however, lamentably incorrect profound dogmas have proceeded currently by bliss, protecting specially in the Tao or Taoism, with a sequence of irrational regulations and where factual alchemist is not proficient, not to mention the rejection of subjectively imperfection and self-analysis. Dishonest

Taoist dispositions accept that with their absurd instructions their declarations attain complete emancipation.

TAU Last character of the Hebrew alphabet. Nomenclature, its vertical line personifies Spirit and horizontal element. Tau method Cross in Hebrew.

TAURO (Latin taurus) Astron Second sign or part of the zodiac, 30 degrees wide, which the sun transparently travels at the middle of the first. Zodiacal constellation that passes through the Meridian at 9 pm respecting mid-January. Their brightest star is Aldebaran, of the first enormity, starting with the Hyades lifeform group. This star has a diameter 38 times greater than the Sun and its ingrained brightness is 91 times that of the Sun. In Taurus is the high-profile Crab Nebula. Astron. Second signal of the zodiac (earth-fixed-female). Specifically on display by a Bull. It appears in force from April 20 to May 19. Taurus is ruled by Venus, The Star of Love. Bullfighters are ordinary Venusian and loving, they are gentle and industrious as the ox. Taurus makes the native purposeful, diligent, reflective, conservative, devoted, romantic and sensual. They love melody, rhumba and beauty.

TAPTA (Sanskrit) Afflicted, tormented, mortified, castigated, burned; experienced, suffered.

TAPAR-Loka or Tapo Loka (Tapas-Loka) (Sanskrit) Centrally revealed the eyebrows is found a place called Tapar-loka. The domain of the fire devas is named Vairajas. It is handpicked with the name "world of seven sages" and with the "kingdom of penance". One of the chachta-loka (six worlds) ascertained above ours, that is the seventh.

TAPO (Tapas-Loka or Tapar-Loka) (Sanskrit) The realm of the fire devas called Vairajas., It is chosen with the name of "world of the seven wise men" and with that of "kingdom of penance". One of the chachta-loka (six worlds) positioned above ours, which is the seventh.

TARAH The title Tarah is essentially an adult female denomination of Hebrew origination that channels Explorer. Tarah or Terach (Hebrew: Terah) is a scriptural form in the Book of Genesis. He is registered as male child of Nahor and birth parent of the patriarch Abraham, by definition, he is a successor of Shem's son Arpachshad. From the Irish place name Team hair, which is from the Irish Gaelic meaning "rocky hill". In Polynesian mythology Tara was a beautiful sea nymph. She has an eager and carefree spirit that makes it great gratification to be around.

TASTE Survives as a specific perception that recognizes and differentiates the sugary acid, pungent, salted, or Savoury midpoint of a liquefy matter and is intervened by flavor buds on the tongue. A sense of taste is primarily recognized on the tongue and conciliated by the chemosensory organization. Taste reply starts by blending substances (tainted) indissoluble to nucleus (TRCs) and gathers in taste buds ascertain inside sensory receptors. The taste sensation is one of the five human senses which exists to our endurance because it enables scholars as the alternative to right nourishment, which, successively, is reproving for one's reality, conservation and accountability. Can emotions be tasted? Yes, they can! Lexemic, vascular aesthesis is a singular configuration of esthesis in that pronounce and corresponding dialect (additionally a few colors and emotions) bring forth humanity to undergo an automated and really incorporate savor/aroma.

TASSO, TORQUATO (1544-95) An Italian Poet, recommended as Cardinal Luigi d'Este in 1565, was talented to dedicate a lot of his time to his large epic. Gerusalemme liberata, a poem on the first Crusade, concluded in 1574. He, accordingly, agonized from religious scruples and ill-treatment mania; he died prior to receiving the crown of the Poet Laureate contemplate for him by Clement VIII.

TRAYA (Sanskrit) Triad; triple, trill.

TAX-COLLECTOR, TAX-GATHERER. Assertions used in modern English versions of the Bible to replace publican (q.v.)

TEBAH Nature; that mystically and esoterically it is the equivalent as its personified Elohim; being the same, namely 86, the numerical value of both words: Tebah and Elohim (or Aleim.)

THEBES. Prehistoric city of Highest Egypt, situated on the two banks of the Son, metropolis of the nation considerably 2.50 B.C. pending its eradication (661 B.C.) by the Assyrians that was never reconstruction. Primordial Greek city, of Beoda northwestward of Athens, motherland of Oedipus and his descendants. The heir of Oedipus Eteocles and Polynices, after removing their father from the authority, accepted to control it perpetually, each, one year. Eteocles initially govern and did not abide by the accordance, in consequence his sibling Polynice appealed asylum in the Curia Regis of Caledonia and posterior intended a crusade opposed his male sibling in Thebes. It is alleged that both expired in the struggle.

TE IGITUR. (Lat., 'Thee, therefore'), Historically distinguished as the aperture words of the Canon of the Roman Service, and hence also the affiliations for the introductory part of the Canon.

TEACHINGS OF THE TWELVE APOSTLES, The. Unconditional title of the work commonly accepted as The Didache (q.v.)

TEACH or TEACHING (Gnosticism) Particularity a Knowledge, a Wisdom, which is verbalized from lip to ear, or in groups, in writing, or by emblems of any kind, to the figures who aspire to spiritual elaboration. It is synthesized in three factors: Dying, Being Born and Sacrifice for Humanity. Gnostic instruction was transmitted by the great primaries such as: the Budda, Jesus the Christ, Moses Quetzalcoatl, Sanat-Kumarat (founder of the college of initiates of the white lodge), and others. Today the Gnostic alliances founded by the teacher Samael Aun Weor, particularly the M.G.C.U. (Universal Christian Gnostic Movement), help that ancient knowledge in their schools, in a selfless and freely, non-profit way.

TEASELS. May indicate labor and adversity? Deliver captivated by the society at the descend of Humanity. (Conforming to the Book of Genesis, Spike and Spine did not subsist in Eden, but approach into existence when God damned Mother earth following Adam and Eve mischief. This instrument was used to broom plait textile to lift the break of the fleece. Traders would cautiously broom the fleecy textile with the teasel hand, and then the nap would be tidy equally and close to the cloth to give it a smooth touch. Teasel seed sprout persists all year, but often in the spring and fall. The fall takes opportunities of space if only by dying teasel herbage that have discarded their seed, extends and increases the inhabitants. If left untamed, teasel can shape large thick blotches and gravely change habitat planting. Teasel is a medicinal prize are the roots which have been recognized to have antibiotics and analgesic effects. It is also investigated to be an inadequate innate immunity promoter as well as an appetite stimulator. Greenery was also employed to remedy warts and exterior lacerations in the medieval period. It was also engaged for minister to infectious ulcerations.

TE DEUM A Latin melody to the father and the son, in rhythmical prose. Verses 22 ff. Are suffrages, attached to the earliest at a premature date. The perception of the hymn to Saints Ambrose and Augustine is dismissed by modern scholars. Its use in the Studio is specified in the Rule of St. Benedict. The BCP incorporated in Mattins the Eng. tr. 'We praise three, O God'.

TEJAS (Sanskrit) One of the Tattvas: the luminiferous ether or fire, appear like to sight. This Tattva is also delegated by the appellative of Agni and Raurava. The voice Tejas signifies light, brightness, splendor, glory; fire, heat; beauty; strength, power; authority, dignity, greatness, nobility; boldness, brio, etc. actually that name is applied to the human halo or aura.

TEJ In Indian this word effectively has in mind Light or Lustrous or Radiant, is of Sanskrit, Indian source, term Tej is a Masculine (or Boy) name. This communion is shared across individuals, who are either Sikh or Hindu by religion. In Sanskrit it defines spirit, Vigor, life, Lustre, sheen.

TELOS In prehistoric Greek, the concluding end, impetus, or goal of an activity is shown to as the telos of an attitude, motivation. In upstanding ideology, and in doctrine by a large, the expression is unmoving occupied. As claimed by Aristotle we own a telos as mortal operation which is our aim to carried out. In Divine revelations a telos, after is the incentive for chase an exceptional purpose. Additionally, both are bound jointly in that a telos succeed on the victory of a desire by requisite. If one achieves her goal, her resolution outstretches her telos, and, contrarily, if one malfunctions to do her target, she inadequate extending the coveted telos.

TEME. Master Samael commented that, all through the Archaic Ages esotericism blossomed in Prague (Czechoslovakia) in exalted form. There were some Magi or Rabbis (from the Jewish Colony) who made a statue and then on the facade they wrote the term "Fear", but on the contrary "Emet", they invoke it liturgically. That statue came to have a animation of its own and could be transferred (between the vertical quarter) from one location to another, whether or not of the length and bring articles to the Rabbi, objects, etc., but the day they erased the word "Emet" from his forehead and discard the verbs of power, the statue was diminished to immediate dust (Philosopher's Stone), that whoever acquires it can execute all kinds of wonderment, The word magic was "mind. This type of magic was a product of the Golotero Golan (the Philosopher's Stone), which whoever possesses it can perform all kinds of wonders. The magic word was "Fear" (Emet), that is, 'Fear it is to go and lose your stone, for if you lose it you will fail.'

TEMPLARS, or 'Knights Templar'. The 'Poor Knights of Christ and of the Sanctuary of Solomon', a particular of the two-leader infantry arrangement of Middle Age Christianity. Hugh de Paynes's, a knight of Champagne, and eight other conquerors in 1118 decided to bound themselves up reciting a solemn vow to protect pilgrims on the public roads of the Holy Land. They were assisted on the grounds of Solomon's Sanctuary at the assembly of Troyes (1128) after they obtained acceptance to their rules, announced to have been harassed by

St. Bernard. They promptly escalate in control and affluence, getting equity in the better part of Christianity. In the Crusaders' grounds of the 12th and 13th centurial the executive intensity of the explorers and the Hospitallers delivered a progressively decidedly role.

TEMPERANCE. Constrain of cravings and ardor following sense. An incomparable of the four-cardinal morality. For the Christian, abnegation in its objective features is colleague with the necessity for dignity of the physique, recognized as a 'shrine' of the presence of God. The 'temperance societies', based to promote temperance or abstinence from cocktails, date from the 19th century.

TEMPO. Numerous tempos indicate as well classify disposition and reflection. For instance, presto and allegro the two transcribes an accelerated performance (presto faster) still allegro as well signifies delight (among its fresh context in Italian). Additionally, Presto clearly notes speed. Furthermore, Italian terms also set down tempo and mood. A tempo denominating informs you know the pace (labeled tempo) at other the songster wishes a segment of melody carried out. Tempo tagging is as usual approached as a designation that compares with a statistic, who you will be analyzed further down, or in cadence per minute (bpm). The importance of tempo in sound resolves the absolute frame of mind of it. We engage in music by our state of mind, and it relies on the tempo at which the piece is developed. Tempo decides the emotional state of the lyrics and aids the participant to choose if it is a lively song or an honest one. The tempo of musical harmony alters activation, who is associated with the awakening of neurochemicals liable for cerebral cortex action and the perception of awareness. Although, the tempo alongside will not figure out if all favor or detest a song. fairly, it persuades natural incentive which has exciting insinuations.

TEMPUS CLAUSUM (Latin, 'closed time'). Assertive seasons in the Christian year in which, since of their solemn or attritional character, marriages were once not normally solemnized.

TEMURA (Hebrew) "change", the term of a breakup of the Kabbalah procedure dealing with analogies in the middle words, whose relationship or affinity is appointed by certain adjustment in the regions of the letters or improved by alternating one letter for added.

TEN COMMANDMENTS. Master Samael Aun Veor describes that since the human has no desire to yield to the require of the "decalogue", but chose to capitulate it to the divine law of the creator to human way of life, disregarding that the laws that flow generation, on no occasion have repetitious their credibility however, on the contradictory, day-to-day the need to accomplish them in order that, completed, the human being can be recovery from the grasp of this agitated earth where persecution, intellectual, sentimental, and psychically disparity succeed and location reliance incomparable authoritative dominion. It is necessary to comprehend that the most primitive integrity that has been written across the narrative of humanity is that of the Ten Commandments of the Principle of God. No society author, prophet, visionary has had the potential to revoke this constitution, let alone could that multitude of goblins that we transport interiorly to compel us to keep breaking the Law. Nevertheless, we must promulgate what Living words and death words are. The living letter is that which is felt and acknowledged with the heart. The most important doctrine is conquered through creativity, and this has its foundation in the heart. The Living Letter is to be disposed to see the hopelessness of what is written, concluded the pivotal that authorize us to determine and appreciate verifiable Perception. Just after Jesus announces the humans the Sower's Parabola, the apostle questions Him, "Why do you speak to them in parabolas?" He responded and said to them, "For it is given to you to know the mysteries of the Kingdom of Heaven, but to them it is not given." "That is why I speak to you in parabolas, because seeing they do not see, and hearing they do not hear, nor understand." "So that they do not see with their eyes and hear with their ears, and with their hearts understand and convert and I hear them". (Matthew 13:10-a). Humanity knows the story of the Ten Commandments that the Lord Jehovah provided to Moses on two tablets of stone, but the substance of the Ten Commandments is not known, much less what the violation of them consists of. Let us try to see in broad strokes the main factors of the Commandments to know what to expect when our conscience declines an act during our life, in uninterrupted daily business.

TEN Denarius formed by (1) Y (0), imagen of union. Zero principles of all creation.

TENEN Ruled the deity of the primordial mound in ancient Egyptian religion. His name denotes "risen land" or "exalted earth", as well as referring to the sediment of the Nile. As a primeval Hadean deity, Tatenen was identified with creation. (His name is also written as Tatenen, Tatjenen, Tathenen, Tanen, Tenen, Tanenu and Tanuu)

TEN TRIBES, (The) On Solomon's death (c. 930 B.C.), Ten of the twelve Hebrew ethnic groups fragmented to configurated the country of Israel, while two accomplished the kingdom of Judah. When Israel was conquered by the Assyrians in 721, incalculable of the more opulent individuals were expatriated to Assyria (2Kgs. 17: 1-6) The presumption of the British Israelites that these populaces were forebears of the British has no concrete footing.

THEBAN LEGION, The. The Christian legion from the "Thebaid that is said to have been massacred beneath the Empire Maximian.

THEISM. (gr. God). Beliefs in an individual and coming God, creator and conserver of the World,

THEOPATHY The factuality of suffering for one's God. Religious fanaticism.

TEOTL (Mexico) Designation that was properly given in Mexico to the supreme Spirit or gram Spirit.

TEOTEL or TLOQUE NAHUATL. He is deliberate among the Aztecs as the supreme creator, deprived material portrayal.

TERESA DE AVILA. The recurrently used name of Teresa of Jesus, St. (1515-82), Spanish Carmelite nun and mystic. She joined the Carmelite convent of the Incarnation ('Mitigated Observance') in Avila in 1535, but it was not until 1555 that she was ultimately transformed to a life of ideal. Her mystic life began soon later with Divine assertions, her first ecstasy, and an intellectual vision of Christ. Regardless of opposition, in 1562 she started the convent of St. Joseph at Avila, wherein the primordial directive was seen. Here she wrote: The Way of perfection (for her nuns), having not long ago completed her Life, a spiritual autobiography. From 1567, she was engaged in organizing housing for both nuns and friars. At this time, her own religious life intensifies until it reached the state of 'spiritual marriage' (1572). She wrote Foundations, The Interior Castle, and many microscale books. Her impact as a spiritual writer was epoch-making because she was the first to write down the actuality of states of prayer intermediate in the middle of discursive meditation and ecstasy and to give a scientific explanation of the whole life of prayer from meditation to the so-called mystic marriage. She also merged spiritual experience with ceaseless pursuit.

TERMINOLOGY The absence of harmony in cryptic terminology is the reaction of the totalitarianism that inner paths in history have shown. Their self-sufficiency, their dislike for the weight of the added spiritual paths, has bring about such a forceful and partition between them that, even though they live in the same country, professing the same language, and in viewed of having the same god, we could well assert that they practice different languages.

TERCE, SEXT, NONE The Commission said at the third, sixth, and ninth hours, individually. They apiece hold of a hymn, three Psalms (or one Canticle split up into three parts with antiphons, a miniscule illumination from the Bible, a versicle and reactions, and a concluding prayer. Since 1971 only one of these Offices has been needed, and the time of day at that it is said recites which ought to be chosen.

TESHU (Lama) (Tibet) An incarnation of Gautama or Amitabha Buddha. The leader of the Tibetan Church.

THROWING THE STONE into the WATER (Alchemy) Suggests that after having accomplished unification with God, the stone is thrown back into the water, that he tries to explain, the action has fallen or descended into the forge of the Cyclopes (banned passion) to restore his sword and thus be more dynamic, stronger. The initiate can do it up to seven times, after that he can fall into a curse.

TETRAKTYS or TETRADA (Greek) The sacred "Four" by that the Pythagoreans promise, this oath being more inviolable. It has a very mystical and diverse definition, being the identical as the Tetragrammaton. The first is your Oneness, or the "One" under four distinct aspects; then is the fundamental number Four, the Tetrad holding the Decade, or Ten, the number of perfections; ultimately, it measures the primitive Triad or (Triangle) fused into the divine Monad.

TETRATEUCH The seven books are Genesis, Exodus, Leviticus, Numbers, Deuteronomy, Joshua and Judges. The first four of these are at times indicating the Tetrateuch, he first five are often known as the Torah or the Pentateuch, he initials six as the Hexateuch.

TESTAMENTS. Pentateuch, the assembly of Lawful Handbooks that the Church contribute with Judaism. Similar to the Christian Bibe, the Hebrew Scriptures publications are contemplated as motivated by the Church, which from the time of Marcion has protected them opposed to ambush. Testament: The Sanctioned Treatise acceptance completely to the Church, as contrary with those approached mosaic law, which the Church comply with Judaism. The parables accommodate the four Gospels, Acs, he Pauline and 'Catholic' Epistles, and Revelations.

TETHYS or TETHIS. (Gr.) Spouse of the Ocean. Through the unification of both, in agreement to Greek myths, all beings and even the gods were inborn. In this allegory, the Ocean expressed InterCosmos space. The spirit in the Chaos that is Deity, and Thethis, the unoriginal Matter in the practice of evolution.

TETZEL, JOHANN (c. 1455-1519). German 'Dominican Tetzel' was assigned sub commissary for the regions of Magdeburg und Halberstadt. He led a rise in wrongdoing by his manufacturing and aid for the popular project that a hard cash payment could be applied with absolute outcome to deliver a soul from purgatory. After listening to Tetzel. M. Luther supply his Ninety-five Theses in 1517.

TESTIMONY. Arcane #39; There exist 2 categories of attitude. (1), the one that occurred from the outside in; (2) the one that linger from the inside out. The (1) that is the significance of Emotional Subjugation and happens by response; the (2) is that of the one who is not enduring to be a captive and is caused by Awareness, the Essence. (Samael Aun Weor).

TEXT Composed or reproduced labor, a publication, other segments of writing equally to notations, graphics, addendums, etc. consider in styles of its achievements rather than its determinative form; quotations. Ideograms have grown extremely innovative in the last period; the clue of a text hieroglyph is a visual or character fictional alongside the pointer on a computing machine. A part of a text logo is the heart design that is shaped by dispensing "Alt" and the character "3" on an instructed digital input device.

TEWNOUT. (Egyptian) divinity head of lioness, impersonated with the disc. She is attributed to as the daughter of the Sun and is frequently connected with Shou. (Pierret, Dict. D'Arch Egypt).

TRE FONTANE The traditional area of St. Paul's oppression, some 3 miles south of Rome. succeeding the epic, his head, on being disturbed from its structure, bounced deriving out of the ground at three arrangements, from that supply the three springs that accepts the points its description.

TREE In outmoded times it elevates for the life of the solar system, revered and private knowledge, as infinitive survival is immortality. Since earliest times, trees have portrayed development, generosity, benefits and more in analogies, poems, compositions, and ideologies. We all have unearthed at one time or another that the Olive tree and the Tree of Knowledge model a lot of consequences of the Garden of Eden. Elm trees declares of new dawn, Oak surmises the role of courage, Maple shows stability, lastingness, Fir accord to honorableness, Apple sums up deliberation, and contentedness. Each tree's soundness, brilliance and restfulness has instituted the enticement and fascination of occurrence on the orb of mythology and tradition.

TREASURE (Latin thesaurus) Quantities of money, securities or precious objects, put together and kept in reserve. In the distinctive myths and legends, it is repeatedly said that the treasure is in a cave (maternal or unconscious image) challenging to reach. Every work, every attempt culminates in a reward, if it is spiritual growth. So, each one who wishes for the work on himself, his Liberation, collects the Treasure of light, join capabilities with Divinity. Within every one of us is hidden the Treasure of Wisdom and full knowledge.

TRIANGLE (Lat. triangular). A figure structured by three lines that cut separately from each other. Abstract defined illustratively the three primary forces of nature; Father, Son and Holy Spirit. In Networking this image arises with an eye in the center showing consciousness in the ternary.

TRIBULATIONS. You can cite the anguish or strain that your expertise in a specific circumstance as tribulations [formal]. The inquiry and tribulations of daily existence. As claimed by Easton's Bible Dictionary, "Tribulation is trouble or affliction of any kind" (Deuteronomy 4:30; Matthew 13:21). In Romans 2:9, "tribulation and anguish" "are the corrective sufferings that shall overtake the wicket". In Mathew 24:21 and Matthew 24:29, the term designates the "trials that were to accompany the destruction of Jerusalem".

TRIDOCHA (Sanskrit) The three vices of character.

TRIFOLIO (or clover) Like the Irish trefoil, it has an illustrative consequence, "the mystery three in one", as one au calls it. The clover crowned the head of Osiris, and the diadem fell when Typhon killed the jubilant god.

TRI (Sanskrit) Three.

TRIYANA. (Sanskrit). It specifies to the bodies of Triple Quality, progressed by every true Buddha. These are personalities of the Kaya Bodies.

THAT. The absolute whole, the unconditional endless, apart from which nonbeing exists, from which all things continue and in which entirety is resolved; the contributory and material cause, both universe; the solidity and essence that the universe is originated. It is the one, unknowable existence who's pure first manifestation is the Spirit.

THANKS, (The). The accepted legend associated that there were three: Aglaya, Lalia and Eufrosine, daughters of Venus and Bacchus. They were mirrored as beautiful young ladies, with their hair adorned on their heads, vulnerable and graceful, acknowledged as if they were leaving to dance.

THANSGIVING Instituted with pioneers in Nova Anglia and Canada British Columbia faithfully recognized "Thanksgiving," days of invocations for corresponding commendation as protected trips, military accomplishments, or plenty cropping. Americans paragon their break on a 1621 garnering commemoration mutual among the Wampanoag society and the English settlers familiar as Pilgrims. The foundation of the phrase is clear sufficient: "thanksgiving" is a combined nominal fabricated of the terms "thanks" and "giving". However, why may be amazing is that the expression was initially used in the 1530s, exceeding a centennial prior to the Pilgrim's earliest "thanksgiving."

THALE(S) OF MILETUS (546 B.C.E.) He is prognosticating as the champion sage of the Seven of Greece. He has been appointed the title of founder of mathematics for some of the theory of geometry. He is the author of the maxim "Noscete Ipsum" (man know yourself and you will know the universe and the gods). That clause takes shape on the Frontal of the Temple of Delphi.

THARANA (Sanskrit) "Mesmerism", or rather: ecstasy (trance) brought about by oneself, or auto-hypnotization; An action that in India is magical and a kind of exorcism. Literarily: "sweep suppress" (bad influences; from Thran, defines as a broom, and Tharshan, duster); Chased away the bad bhuts (aura Danina and bad spirits) medians the usefulness will of the mesmerizer.

THEATER or Cinematograph (Latin theatrum, and east of the Greek to look) (Gnosticism) Gnosis direct that the student of transcendence ought to be cautious in possible to go to the cinema, since this in the world of the mind are shrine of sad charming; also, they subscribe to creating intellectual dramas that obstruct the profound work, leading to the identification and despairing sound of your awareness; it also happens when people spend a lot of time as TV audiences; movie houses are full of pest and cold forces generated by viewers when watching improper films.

THEBAN LEGION, (The) The Christian regime from the Theban that is said to have been slaughtered under the Kingdom of Maximian.

THEBES Prehistoric city of Upper Egypt, constituted on both banks of the Nile, first city of the nation roughly 2,050 BC until its eradication (661 BC) by the Assyrians, from that it not ever recoups. Ancient Greek city, from Beoda northwest of Athens Greek city, from Beoda northwest of Athens, homeland of

Oedipus and his progeny. The sons of Oedipus: Eteocles and Polynice, not long ago ejecting their father from the throne, concur with to rule by choice, one year each. Eteocles was first to govern and did not affect as agreed, so his brother Polynices sought refuge in the Court of the King of Caledonia and after setting up a journey against his brother in Thebes. The two are said to have died in the clash

THECLA (PAUL AND THECLA), Acts of. An apocryphal work that is representation of the "Acts of Paul'. It recounts how St. Paul preached the benefits of chastity at Iconium and won St. Thecla from Thamryris, the one who she was betrothed. Paul was charged prior to the civil authorities and beaten, while Thecla was condemned to death but miraculously saved. It wrapped up with the record of Thecla's death at Seleucia.

THEISM In recent days make use of the statement grasp declining a sensible arrangement that emanates an accomplishment unifying the Almighty to who not beardly engender but bides sustained and oversee the sphere, the eventuality of that evade abolishing sensation and the struggle of mortal advantage.

THELEMA (Gnosticism) Incorporates self-discipline; accompanied by Thelema one acquires the ability of transubstantiate that conveys corruption into sympathetic, in all circumstances of being. It suggests will. Alongside Thelema the prospective of convert is obtain that transfigure coarse mineral assimilate attainment, as it were, harmful into honorable, in all situations of life, with Thelema, that we can adapt overcoming the solid standard which on the intangible pathway are planted on interest divide on expertise, because if not "we are tested we cannot be qualified." Nearly all challenging goals to reach are practically persistently associated with intimacy. Most institute for absence of Thelema, malfunctioning to carry out and unfaithfulness.

THELO(S) Interprets to want, to fancy, to devotion, to affection to do a thing, enjoyed of performing. In the New Covenant "will" is mainly the transferal of Thelo and boulomai, the difference between the two being that Thelo expresses and active choice or purpose, desire, "passive inclination or willingness, or the inward predisposition from which the active choice proceeds".

THEODICY. Part of dogma which is concernment to safeguard the good will and Supremacy of Supreme being in opposition impartial which become known from the existence of destructive in nature. The term is a times treasure as an equivalent for Legitimate Doctrine.

THEOLOGY (Latin theologia, from the Greek theologian) Science that agrees with God of his attributes and precision. "The original source of all theology is God himself because he has revealed the truths of faith, which constitute theological principles." "The purpose of this science is the explanation, reasoned justification, and study of all the truths which God has made known to mankind." Theology, precisely the 'science of God'. In its Chistian sensation it is the science of the Divinely disclose reverent honesty. Its subject is the Existence and Description of Supreme and His living souls and the entire multiplicity of the Spiritual exclusion from the Decline of Adam to the absolution across Christian Faith its reflection to humanity by his mission, as well as the presumed legitimate veracity of the Almighty, that are available to meager purpose. Its intention is to explore the gratifications of confidence by manner of rational instructional by conviction and to encourage its extensive comprehension.

THEOPATHY. Suffering for one's God. Religious fanaticism.

THEOSOPHIST (Advaita) (Greek) Faith of Conviction or "Divine Wisdom". The compound and support of all the religions and philosophies of the world taught and application by a handpick few since humankind capability a discern reality.

THEOSOPHY Surrounded by its extensive petition the phrase announces a part of spontaneous awareness of the Eternal and as corresponding offset divergent doctrinal and analytical networks related to doubter and instinctively conjuring. In an added limiting belief, it is enforced to the motion scrutinized by H. P. Blavatsky, whom, alongside Col. H.C. Olcott, showed the Kabala Association of New York in 1875. In 1882 Adyar (near Madras) developed into a responsible nucleus. This system of rules, conclude in the migration of animus', the alliance of humankind regardless of complexion and affiliation and sophisticated systems structure of brainpower and creation; someone repudiate both one and the other an intimate universal life force and distinctive everlasting life.

THESEUS (Greek mythology) Existed a role model of Athens and Attica, son of Aegeus and Etra. His father laid down a sword underneath a huge stone and disclosed to his wife that after Theseus grew up and was strong, he would lift the stone, accept the sword, and pioneer toward Athens. At the age of 20 Theseus was able to pursue his father's directives; everlasting towards Athens; all along his career, he killed 5 gigantic bandits, seized periofere's nail, and since then organized as his main weapon. In the course of the incidents of Theseus the consequent can be recounted: he killed the Cretan Minotaur; synchronize an dispatch in opposition the Amazons; escort the Argonauts; play a part in the hunt for the Jabali of Caledonia; try to captured Persephone, wife Pluton; intermediate in the War of the Centaurs; had an amoebic affair with Antiope; Queen of the Amazons; kidnapped Helena and join forces in many supplementary escapades. He was murdered by King Lycomedes who threw him dishonestly from the top of a cliff.

THREAD In agreement with the established individual's formation, commit originating the organic nature to the sphere of the departed as an overpass that energy travel on their process transversely. However, the strand also escorts in the contrasting orientation. This filament each is Atma and Prana because it connects to the leading Focus, cord should, in all solicitude, be tracked backwards to its origin. This prompts us of Ariadne's filament that not scarcely was the loop amid the exterior sphere and the midpoint of the intricacy still furthermore the channel allowing them to advance deriving out the domain of obscurity to the territory of radiance.

THREAD (of life) It is the etheric thread that unites the essence with the soul.

THEURGY (from the Greek theurgies) A transmition with the universal treasure and essence; the "gods of Light" and design to charm them to the world. Ability in the interior sense of the position of comparable animation and clarity of sentience are the best mode adept of predominant to the achievement of the potential decisive for contact with themselves. To the extent of similar an exalted target, the qualifier should be deserving, complete and considerate. [The application of Astrology is very unsuitable and yet precarious]. The earth has expanded into overly unethical to repeat all that only alike pure and clever gentlemen as Ammonius, Plotinus, Porphyry, and Iamblichus (the greater cultivated of all marvels) perhaps attempt with liberty. At this moment, conjuration or eternal and supportive Captivating, is a phenomenon very inclined to turn into a Clairvoyant, or in other words, sorcery. Conjuring is the first of the three subdivisions of Illusion, which are: Enchanted, Charismatic, and Natural Magic.

THIERRY OF CHARTRES (d. After 1151), philosopher and theologian. He instructed at Chartres and Paris. He became Archdeacon and Chancellor of Chartres in 1141. Sometime in the middle of 1151 and 1156 he retired to a monastery, and nothing further is known.

THIS or ETAT (Sanskrit) Using this demonstrative pronoun is usually appointed the Universe, opposition That (the absolute All, the infinitive Eternal). (English) This, the Universe. The opposite of That.

THRILL. Approached from an Old English word denoting "pierce", proposing the allegory of being "pierce by emotion". Thrill is often promoted in a firmly practical sensibility; however, it can as well comment on to the unique sequence of dread and delight that some individuals' participation in definitive arrangements in occurrences instantly thrill prospects situate themselves on the line similarly as driving a competition automobile, plunging from extremely elevated settings, etc. Neurobiological like monoamine neurotransmitter and virility materialize to disturb how formulate individual is to evade risks or stay on the untamed edge, as execute the mass of substantia alba in the intellect. Free thinkers' people are inclined to generate individuals who like to chase their instincts, added components are intellectual and implanted identity.

THOMAS, St., Apostle. He is specified as one of the Twelve in all four Gospels. In Jn. He proceeded in three episodes, viz. Offering to die with the Lord on the way to Bethany (11:16), interrupting the Last Discourse with the interrogation 'We know not whiter thou goest, how can we know the way?' (14:5) and dubious of the Resurrection (20:24-8). After Christ's appearance he confesses his faith in the words My Lord and my God' and is thus the first explicitly to confess His Divinity According to one tradition he evangelized the Parthians, version to another he preached in India.

THOMEL (Egyptian) The goddess of Justice. He is blindfolded and wields a cross. Just as it is the same as the Greek Themis.

THORAH (Hebrew) "Law" written by altering the letters of the Hebrew alphabet. Of the "reserved Thorah" it is said that before At-teekah (te Elder of all Eldersz) had prepared and designed into members, establishing himself to demonstrate individually forcefully, he wanted to create a Thorah; and eventually, after he was originated, addressed Him saying these words: "He who desires to fix and establish other things, must first of all fix himself in his own way." In other words: Thorah, the Law, stands for its Founder from the instant he was born, as revealed above, which is an interpolation of some later Talmudist. As it increased and decipher, the mystical Law of the ancient Kabbalist was changed by the rabbis, who used it to modify in its dead letter every metaphysical concept; and so, it is that the Rabbinic and Talmudic Law makes Ain Soph and each divine Beginning reduced to itself and curves its back on the obvious esoteric explanations.

THOR God of Thunder and War in Norse mythology and ruler of the Elemental Spirits, son of Odin and Freya; with his hammer "Mjolnir", which always came back to him when he was thrown, he repeatedly fought giants, demons and monsters.

THORN or THORNS Substantially a forecast that is born from the cardiac organ or vascular tissue of some greenery. Profoundly the thorn is considered a depiction of the radiant ray and exaltation, the Egyptians studied the acacia a sacred plant because it was consecrated to Neith. It is also said that the crown of Thorn of Jesus Christ was made of acacia, for being an esoteric insignia of spiritual enlightenment and elevation. Indicate transgress, sadness and deprivation, the thorn is one of the greater prehistoric characters in the society, in conjunction with the Rose, it's view of suffering and satisfaction, and the thorn is a marker of Christ's passion, as with the crown of thorns that he was mandated to wear on his way to the cross. A crown is ordinarily a signal of authority and integrity; nevertheless, Jesus' persecutor used that game plan as an aching prop to mock him.

THOUGHTS Application of hieroglyphs, terms and depictions as well as rational characterization of article or affairs to persuasion for society. Evocative reflections convey the discernible capacity to interpret emblems towards way of thinking. During the representative aim concreteness uniting two and four years of age, youngster rely on each-others' individual sentiment. Cognitive analogy is the activity of psychological persistence for goals and participation using signs as well as semantic marks). Figurative reasoning is what permits humankind to chat about former matters, in addition to brainstorming concerning everything that can happen in the course of time. Particularly, that which empowers individuals to withdraw from an ongoing circumstance to invoke another actuality, as it may be gone by or forthcoming. People may possibly have a unique suggestion; items or shades or countryside characteristics which carry particular importance for you. The intentions, perhaps flourish reality, lifestyle, imagining or daydreaming, or originating from publications or lyrics we have come across.

THUMI SAMBHOTA (Sanskrit) A mystical and Indus scholarly innovator of the Tibetan alphabet.

THUMMIM (Hebrew) "Perfections". An attire of the pectoral of the High Priests of Judaism. The recent Hebrew rabbis may well ensure that they do not understand the ordained objects of the Thummim and Urimi; but Kabbalists know them, as do esotericisms. They were the tools of magical divination and the oracular trade - theurgical and astrological.

THYATIRA The temple of Thyatira was not authorized, but instead to approach, the offense and the wrong way of living that Jezebel was offering to be misdeed and discharge it. The same way that we should always challenge wrongdoing innermost. The diocese of Thyatira prolonged back to astonishingly premature

Christianity. Evangelism arrived at the locality in the 1st century with Paul the Apostle on his Third pastor traversed around 54AD, when he visited for three years in neighboring Ephesus. Temple of the Apocalypse is associated with the Anahata chakra, detected in the vicinity of the heart.

TIEN-SIN (Chinese). Formally: "the heaven of the mind", ideal, abstract, subjective heaven. It is a philosophical expression pertaining to the Absolute.

TIELE, CORNELIS PETRUS (1830-1902), Dutch theologian. As instructor of religious history at Leyden university (1877-1901), he practices great influence on the evolution of the study of relative religion.

TI-RATANA. (Pali). The three jewels of Buddhism also termed T-Sarana (the Triple Refuge): Buddha, Dhama and Sangha; that is, the Master, his instructions and the command.

TITHI (Sanskrit) A lunar day.

TIA-HUANACO (Peruvian) Exceptionally spectacular ruins of a prehistoric city of Peru.

TIBET Self-governing Locality: (in Chinese Sitsang and Tibetan Bodyul). China policy-making region with 1,221,600 km (about 759067.05 mi) 2 (about twice the area of Texas). In that region a great deal of monks has existed and there are many monasteries dedicated to mystics and esoteric doctrine. Its capital is Lhasa, beyond the Potala Palace, previous residence of the Dalai-Lamas. It embraces a gigantic plateau of 3,500 to 4,500 m (about 2.8 mi) altitude. Its mountains transcend 6,000 or 7,000 m (about twice the height of Mount St. Helens), with Everest (8,848 m) on the Tibetan border.

TIDY Objects which are organized skillfully in order and washed. "His scrupulously tidy house". If you kept your house tidier, you would be able to find your vacuum cleaner. Tidy (or tidy up) also defines "to clean up" and it is also a denomination for a receptable for small objects, like scraps or sewing materials, etc. The sense of "tidy" connotation "excellent" then evolved into explanation "of good character, brave, worthy", but by the 19th century had been thinned to interpretation "pretty good" or big", an awareness we still use in vocalizing of a "tidy" fortune, not billions but enough to live on adequately.

TIKE A tiny, awkward, rude youngster. A distasteful or rough curious individual; dogs mostly, a humble or mutt dog, is also alleged tike. This English term dates to the early 15th century; it chooses a dog, mainly, diminish, a hybrid, and was claimed to a troublesome or shaggy man. Since it came to denote also, a small child, largely a cheeky four years old, or disobedient one; because it was said in playful reprimand to children.

TIKHON (1866-1925) Basil Ivanovich Belvin, the initial Leader of the Russian Church since 1700. In 1917 he enhanced Metropolitan of Moscow, and afterwards in the year the Pan Russian Council appointed him elder. His committee and modesty gave him righteous power. In 1919 he condemned all who oppressed the mission, and he urged impartiality on the clergy during the civil war. He endured the impounding of temples possessions during the drought of 1921-2 and was detained. In 1923 he underwrites a proclamation declaring fidelity to the Soviet Russia; he was suddenly authorized to reside in an abbey in Moscow and to take charge in the Russian capital.

TILES (Sanskrit) One of the Tattvas: the luminiferous ether or fire, commensurate to sight. This Tattva is also attributed by the names of Agni and Raurava. The voice Tejas means light, brightness, splendor, glory; fire, heat; beauty; strength, power; authority, dignity, greatness, nobility; Bold, Brio, etc. This term is also register to the halo or human aura. Teo. -gnostic., Tatwa representing the etheric principle of elemental fire. The very hot days begin the moment this tatwa comes into force.

TIME (Lat. tempus) Continuance of things directed to moving. Tempo is only an illusion created by our states of consciousness through consecutive existences when these are conveyed by law of cause and effect. Master Samael clarifies that time is the same Fourth Dimension. The intervals of present, past and future time form part of an entire and distinctive time, their chain reaction is a relative and conventional concept of the human mind. Time is an eternal now and only with awakened consciousness can it be thoroughly understood. This says that the vine repeats itself from existence to existence, with its specific outcome where the Law of Cause-and-Effect acts. I have only learned to live from moment to moment, the here and now, we can free you little by little from the Law of Cause and Effect if we do not make more mistakes. Time is a normal instrument of the human mind. Time is round, it is a closed curve, where events are replicated each at their own time, here is another Law called Recurrence.

TIMAEUS (Timoeus, in Greek) of Locres. A Pythagorean scholar born in Locres in the fourth century B.C. He disunites moderately from his teacher regarding the dogma of metempsychosis. He wrote a treatise on the Souls of the world, its nature and essence, in Doric jargon. This function still exists.

TIMOTHY, St. Was St. Pauls' associate on his Second Missionary Journey and later one of his solely intimate friends. He was authorized by Paul with missions to Thessalonica (1 Thess. 3: 2) and to Corinth (1 Cor. 4: 17) and develop into his delegate at Ephesus (1 Tim. 1:3); according to Eusebius he was the first bishop of that city. He is said to have been martyred in 97, when he disputed the festivities of Diana.

TINDAL, TYNDALE, WILLIAM (1494-1536). Interpreter of the Bible and Reformer. Tyndale went to Germany, when C. Tunstall, Bp of London, dismissed to support his forecast for translating the Bible into English. The printing of his first New Testament was instituted at Cologne in 1525 and was concluded at Worms the same year. Tyndale spent most of the rest of his life in Antwerp, where he repeatedly revised his New Testament. He also published translations of the Pentateuch (1530) and Jonah (1531 and left Jos.-2 Chron. In MS. His adaptation, made from the Greek and Hebrew, were the basis of both the authorized version and rectify version.

TIN (lat. Stannum and stag Num, tin) Tin is contemplated to be a characterization of justice and goodness, its relation to Jupiter is acknowledged, and its negative appearance is relevant to gluttony and greed. It is one of the seven metals used in the assembly of talismans.

TINTERN ABBEY, In the Wye valley. It was established in 1131 for Cistercian monks from the Abbey of L'Aumone. The spectacular abbey church was constructed in the 13th century. The ruins inspired a poem by West Wordsworth.

TIR. The contemporary Persian designation for the Zoroastrian God Tishrya; Tir (month), of the Iranian calendar; Tir (God), of ancient Armenia; Tabar, Iran, a village in North Khorasan Territory. Tir is the god for expeditions, for of the unification of Ova (Goddess of Beasts) and Etos (God of Peace). Tir is as well, the God of literature, science, and art, and a decipherer of dreams, in Armenian's paganism.

TISSOT, JAMES, JOSEPH JACQUES (1836-1902) French Bible illustrator. He was an artist of fashionable women. Pursuing an episode of transfiguration, he dedicated himself to illustrating the reality of Christ. In his Vie de Notre Seigneur Jesus-Christ (1896) he accommodates the scenes of the Gospel in a modern and surprising technique. His drawings of the Old Testament are second class in quality.

TISRA or Tisrapitha Refers to Trisrota: a sacred seat associated with the Goddess Trisrota, according to Tantric texts such as the Kubjikamata-tantra, the earlies popular and most authoritative Tantra of the Kubjika cult. Although Trisrota (or Trisrotra) which is the full name of Tisra is mentioned only here in the Kubjika matadanra, it appears frequently in the later Kubjika Tantras, especially the Manthan abhairavaatandra. Tisra, lie the seat Matanga, is said to be implied for the 'last-born', those of the lowest Matangisa and Matangi, who is idenfied with a form of Kubjika called Just candling. castes, especially sweepers (Matanga). The deities here are the god and goddess of the sweeper;

TITAN Conforming to mythology; Giant who wish to storm the sky, son of Uranus and Vesta, would inherit throne from his father, but Ceres afflicted him to surrender the throne to brother Saturn.

TITIAN (c. 1476-1576). Tiziano Vecellio or Vecelli, Venetian painter. His Tribute Money (c. 1515) is celebrated for the face of Christ, blending sweetness with majesty. The (Venice) is an enormous work of high workmanship; Ecce Homo and the Crowing with Thorns (Louvre) are fraught with tragic emotion.

TIVRA (Sanskrit) Large excessive, extreme.

TO ON (Gr.) Plato's "Being", the "Ineffable All". That "no one here has seen except the son."

TOBIT, Book of. This Volume of the Apocrypha was written in Aramaic or Hebrew, probably c. 200 B.C. It pertains to the story of Tobit, a pious Jew of the captivity of Nineveh, who become poor and blind. He prayed and recollecting a debt due to a friend in the Media, he sent his son Tobias there with a colleague who later disclosed himself as the angel Raphael. With the angel's cooperation Tobias rescued a kinswoman from the power of a demon and married her. Raphael recuperates the debt and then enabled Tobias to heal Tobit of his blindness.

TOBO (Gnostic) In accordance with the Codex Nazarenus, he is a mysterious being, who transfers Adam's soul from him to the place of life, and for this argumentation he is called "the deliverer of Adam's soul".

TOC H. A Christian affability that arises in Talbot House, a soldier; club cleared in Belgium in 1915 under the Rev. P. T. B. Clayton and call after Lt Gilbert Talbot, son of E. S. Talbot. In 1920 Toc H (the army signalers' method of pronouncing T H) was re-founded in London and advanced rapidly. The close fellowship ascertains its outlet in a variations of Chirstian social service.

TOLERANCE. Religious open-mindedness is the leaving uninterrupted of those whose faith and enactment are other than one's own. It may appear from admiration for the rights of a second person to flexibility of conclusion, or from disregard.

TOME OF DAMASCUS, The A group of 24 canons set in animation by a Roman synod (prob. In 382) and later sent by Pope Damasus to Paulinus, then gotten in Rome as the authorized Prelate of Antioch. Twenty-three of them are decided, denouncing the main Trinitarian and Christological irreverence of the 4h century. The ninth, reprimand the engagement of bishops, was jurisdiction in antagonism to Melitius of Antioch.

TONGUE Conceivably, a world of evil amidst the parts of the body which are on fire. Evil can contaminate the entire person, setting the whole course of their lives on fire, and on its own set on fire by hell. If we want to live fruitfully, we must learn to tame the tongue which is related to fire, principled lives which please the Lord. Edifying to train the tongue may not be as painless as you may think. I may seem hopeless to do in the flesh, however in Christ ALL things are within reach! As progeny of God, our tongues have a lot of power. Proverbs 18:21 affirms this by saying, "Death and life are in the power of the tongue, and those who love it will eat its fruits." Tongue is also revelation of the judgments of the gods; in Middle Age Christianity and Oriental art, enormous, prominent voices are often the sign of the devil or Satan.

TORAH The English comparable of a Hebrew term generally interpreted "Law". It was in specifically the purpose of the clergyman to give "torah" or directives on the Will of God, and the phrase advance as well to be plainly committed to paper accumulation of comparable pastoral conclusions, in addition to the "The Book of Moses.".

TORCH Conveys to Hercules' armaments in his fight with Lema's hydra. Their fire demolished the wounds blocking the generating of their heads again. It is "symbolized by the sun and the emblem of purification by illumination."

TORGAU ARTICLES, The. A communication summarizing the retribution and celebratory requests of M. Luther, P. Melanchthon, J. Bugenhagen, and J Jonas which was handed to the Diet of Augsburg.

TOSEFTA (Heb., 'supplement'). A group of early Jewish heritage of the identical temperament as, and contemporary with the Mishnah, but not included in it.

TOPAN God of Thunder and the Tempest within Japanese mythology. It is pronounced that he set fire to the world to penalize the boastful temper of human beings. Only a man who was righteous was saved with his family.

TOYA (Sanskrit) Water.

TRAIN By means of humans come across time while this is not how time works. As soon as we think of time in terms of straight, unavoidable lines, pulled inside hopeless perspective of all existence. Although trains are a part of the real world, however work differently from the real world. The train had endured the test of rhythm as an implement of explanation all around the attractive history of film. On a monitor, a story of a moving vehicle genuinely contributes to perceptible extents of apprehension. They can also, ironically, be used to create clemency. The bible is filled of intangible train whistles intentionally to alert us of spiritual danger and death. We are compelled to listen to those whistles and heed his loving warnings.

TRAITOR (Gnosticism) Judas was one of Jesus' twelve apostles, known as "the traitor." It is pronounced that he advanced from the distant lands of Queriot, now El Karge Tein, in Judah.

TRACT (Liturgical). A chant earlier sung or recited on determined penitential days in location of the 'Alleluia' after the Gradual at Mass. It was suppressed in 1969.

TRANCE A circumstance of altered consciousness, which moderately resembles sleep, throughout which optional motion is lost, as in hypnosis. A stunned state; daze; stupor.

TRANSCENT (Gnosticism) In Gnostic composition alongside by no means just any knowledge. Gnosis is an understanding endowed with wonderful prestige, very few commands to realize this comprehension. It is transcendental of man and the universe, perceivable through the abilities of cognition of the "Being", which also teaches Humanity to see and feel all the things that until now were pointed out as great Mysteries. Subliminal work mostly the hours of physical sleep. If such a subconscious were to awaken and become all consciousness, then we would live during the hours of sleep entirely awake in the higher aspects and in the three-dimensional world: we would be attentive of the Transcendental understanding of the higher dimensions of space.

TRANSMUTE Alchemists managed to achieve conversion of vulgar metals into pure gold.

TRANSFORMATION or Fundamental transformations, the seven. The seven elemental variations of the celestial globes or spheres, or rather, of their essential matter parts, are described as follows: 1a., the homogeneous; 2a, aeriform and radiant (gaseous); 3a., coagulase (nebula); 4.a, the atomic, ethereal, beginning of movements, and therefore, of difference; 5.a, the germinal, igneous; modify, but comprise only of the germs of the Elements in their principal states, having seven states when fully matured on our earth; 6th, the quadruple, vaporous; the future earth; and 7.a; the cold and depends on the sun for life and light.

TRAYA (Sanskrit). Triada; triple, Trino.

TREASON. It is unreliability against sovereignty. It may be initiated in numerous places in the Polyglot along with the Book of Kings. commonly, treason imply abandon regarding the monarch of Israel. To the followers in the Abrahamic faiths; Judaism, Christianity and Islam; disrespectful is an outline of huge treason opposing God; to the doubter it is just added part of cross-culturalism, of enthusiasm in subject of ethnicity unity and discipline, or at the lowest levels, in article of social anthropology. 2 Chronicles 23:13 says, "And Athaliah tore her clothes and cried, "Treason! Treason!"

TREASURE. "The search for treasure has a twofold symbolism: either the search is for earthly treasure, such as gold or jewels, usually hidden in a Cave or underground, the finding of which brings trials and tribulations and, where greed is the motive, leads to final disaster, or the search is for spiritual treasure, symbolizing esoteric knowledge or enlightenment, the search for the Center, for lost Paradise, the Grail etc... and the goal is guarded by monsters or Dragons; this represents man's quest for, and discovery of, his own true nature." (Cooper. 176).

TRI or TRAI (Sanskrit). At the inception of a compound word, it means three.

TRIAD. The ten Sephiroth are regarded as a group of three triads: Kether, Chokmah and Binah form the supreme triad: Chesed, Geburah and Tiphereth, the second, and Netzach, Hod and Yesod, the bottom triad, The tenth Sephira, Malkuth, is beyond the three triads.

TRIDOCHA (Sanskrit). The three corrupt personalities.

TRIDUUM SACRUM. (Lat., 'the sacred three days'). The ultimately three days of "Holy Week, i.e., "Maundy Thursday "Good Friday, and Holy Saturday".

TRICK. Each cunning or proficient act or scheme calculated to deceive or outwit someone. "Buyers can be tricked by savvy sellers". A peculiar or predictable habit of mannerism. Making whoever believe anything that is not true. I at once realized that I'd been tricked. Tricking an individual into doing something: he tricked me into concluding that he was a celebrity.

TRINITY, (lat trinitas, atis). Variations of Three divine people in a sole and distinctive essence. One of the deepest mysteries of Christianity. They are described by the Father, the Son and the Holy Spirit. This Trinity, in turn, has its center of attraction in the Second Triangle of the Hebrew Kabala (Atman, Buddhi and Manas) and in the Third Triangle promote by Netsch, Hod and Jesod.

TRIMURTI The Trinity in Hinduism. Materializations made up of Brahma, Vishnu and Shiva (Father, Son and Holy Spirit). He is characterized as a Divinity with three heads, distributed that the three heads are one. Considering appointed Trimurti in attachment to the Magic and Epic triangle.

TRITO ISAIAH The ultimate eleven components of Isaiah (56-660 or the author(s) of them.

TRIUMPH He is the one who bought victory; those triumphs overall. Gnostical, each of us has a specific star, which has the power to exultation. However, it all depends on the work that each of us is beginning. It is the act and outcome of succeeding (achieving success or achieving victory).

TRIPITAKA (Sanskrit) Accurately: "the three baskets" (or collection of books); Title of the Buddhist canon. It includes of three divisions: 1st., the doctrine; 2nd, the rules and mandates for the priesthood and ascetics; 3rd, philosophical dissertations and metaphysics, that is, Adhidharma, interpret by Buddhaghosa as the law (dharma) that goes beyond (Adhi) of law. The Abhidharm holds the mass exceedingly metaphysical and philosophical instructions and is the storeroom from which the Mahayana and Hinayana Schools drew their elemental precept. There is a fourth division, the Samakta Pitaka; but as it is a later inclusion produce by Chinese Buddhists, it is not accepted by the Church of South Siam and Ceylan. [the names of these three pitakas, or sets of books, are: the Vinaya Pitaka, the Sutta Pitaka and the Abhi-dhamma Pitaka. The foremost one has all things related to ethics and the rules of regulation for the government of the Sangha or the Order; the second holds the instructive dialogue on morality pertinent to all, and the third narrates the psychological teachings of the Buddha, embraces the twenty-four transcendental laws that characterize the executions of Nature.

TRIYANA (Sanskrit). "The three vehicles" through the Samsara (ocean of births, deaths and rebirths) are the movements called Zravaka, Pratyeka Buddha and Bodhisattva, or the three degrees of the course of Yoga. The expression Triyana is also used to appoint the three schools of mysticism, the Mahayana, Madhyimayana and Hinayana schools, of which the initial is the "major" vehicle, the second the "middle", and the at the end the "less". Every one of the systems between the major and minor vehicles is contemplated as "useless". However, the Pratyeka Buddha has been made to interrelate to the Madhyimayana School, because, as explained, "this (the pratyeka Buddha state) indicate to one who leaves the total for himself and very little for others, engaging the middle of the vehicle, filling everything, leaving no room for others." Such is the egotistical aspirant for Nirvana.

TROY Metropolis of prehistoric Toa (of Troy). Its position has been recognized with the Mound of Hissarlik (Turkey). For 10 years she was despondent by the Greeks, due to the abduction of Helen, wife of Menetheus, by Paris who grabbed her to that municipality.

TROYA. The designation Troya is essentially a girl appellative of Greek origination that measures Aqua or Infantry. Woman formation of Troy. Spanish (southerly); accepted label among Troya in Seville district.

TRULLAN An appealing circular stone building constructed with conical roof and lacking mortar discovered in southern Italy and mainly in Apulia. From Byzantine Greek (troullos, "a dome"), from Latin Trulla ("aladle"), in proposition to the domed entrance of the palace in Constantinople in which the council was held.

TRUTI (Sanskrit) Particularly a tiny device; small portion, atom; noticeably abbreviated time: 150 Truti's equal to one second; A measure of space, the one transited by the sun or moon during a Triti. The tri is a perfect picture of the entire ocean of Prana. It is the astral germ of every existent organism.

TUBAL-CAIN (Hebrew) The Apostolic Supreme, "instructor of all artifice in iron and bronze", son of Zillah and Lamech; similar to the Greek Imhotep or Herakles. His brother Jubal, the son of Adah and the solidarity brother of Jabal, not theirs father of them "who taken the harp and the organ", are also consultant, therefore, as demonstrated by Estrabon, the noble man (or cyclopes in a sense) are those who construct the mouth harp for Cronus and the trident for-Poseidon, during certain of his other male sibling were advisers in agriculture. Tubal-Cain (or Thubal-Cain) is a term utilized in the level of Master Mason in the practice and formalities of Masonry.

TURIYA (Turiya) (Sanskrit). A state of the deepest ecstasy (trance): the fourth state of Taraka-Raja-Yoga, which responds to Atma, and on this earth to the dream without dreams; a causal condition. [It is the fourth state of consciousness, the one that exceeds that of dreamless sleep, the superior to all, a state of high spiritual knowledge. (Voice of silence, I.) The state of absolute consciousness. Turiya also means: fourth, the fourth; the universal Soul.

TSI-TSAI (Chinese) The "Self-Existent," or the "Unknown Darkness," the radicle of Wuliang Shen, "Boundless Age," all of these are Kabbalistic expression that were employed in China centennials prior to Yehudit Kabbalism embraced them by seizing them from the Chaldean and Egyptian.

TU-ANKH-AMON (Tutankhamun). Egyptian pharaoh of the XVIII Dynasty, whose tomb in the Valley of the Kings, near Luxor, was found (1922) in an excursion led by the English archaeologist Howard Carter. His tomb (one of the few not looted in antiquity) made it one of the substantial discoveries of contemporary times. The Royal Sarcophagus had three successive feretories, the latest and most interior of solid gold. Except for the body of the pharaoh left in the tomb, many of the objects found were transferred to the National Museum in Cairo. The grandiose of Tutankhamun's tomb showed that for the Egyptians the death of Child pharaoh was as significant as his life. He died approximately at the age of 18 or 19 years. Master Samael describes that Tutankhamun achieved personal Self-Realization.

TUM (Toom or Toun) The Father in the Egyptian Mysteries, recognized as the God Tum. The expression Tum has a double declaration; the first of an absolute darkness, that as absolute is higher than the highest and purest of lights, and in the second sense, is based on the mystical greeting among the initiates "You are you, your own," equated to the saying "You are one with the Infinite and the whole."

TUMO Procedure of Tibetan Lamas. They apply centralization in projecting consciousness in an imaginary fire encircling the Body coordinating the breathing, they administer to raise the temperature of the body or on the contrary, imagining a cold wave.

TUSTA (Sanskrit) Powder, atom; very tiny object.

TURMERIC. A vivid amber scented fine particle acquires from the rootstock of an herb of the red ginger ancestry, utilized for seasoning and a shading in Asian brewing and previously as a dyestuff. The Asian greenery from which turmeric is acquired. It was consistently, in India was well used for disarray of the dermis, common cold regions, junctions, and alimentary canal. Currently, turmeric is advanced as a nutritional accessory for a variation of situations, counting osteoarthritis, acid reflux, a stuffy or runny nose, allergies reactions, chronic fatigue, sadness, and several others. Turmeric reduces infection, that is the cause of numerous illnesses, as well as malignant tumors. Animate beings and research manifests that turmeric can help avoid carcinoma growing and eliminate sarcoma, however, we have misjudged whether it possess the alike consequence in humans' beings.

TURN(S). Speak briefly of rotation or adjustment, transformation. A turn is a variation to act as part of a rotation or wound. The term turn has many other sensibilities additionally, in many languages. This word is employed plenty during instructions in driving school; when a person drives, they may meet some U-turns; 2-point turns. The ballet dance position is called attitude where one leg and both arms are raised. While the leg can be extended to either the front or back, it can never dully straighten. This situation is carried out in ballet class; however, it's implemented as well in turns or jumps in a diversity of dance practices. Following turns is a major ability for youngsters to succeed, so they can successfully engage in communal connections. granted that a young adult is not able to take turns through interchangeable activities, they may cause interruptions while other people are speaking or may not cordially listen. John 2:1-11 Jesus Turns Water to Wine: On the third day a wedding happened at Canan Galilee. Jesus' mother was going with him, and Jesus and his disciples were also invited to the wedding. Once the wine was gone, Jesus' mother said to him, "They have no more wine." "Woman, why do you involve me?" Jesus replied. "My hour has not yet come." His mother said to the servants, "Do whatever he tells you." Not far away were situated six stone water jars, the kind used by the Jews for celebratory washing, each carrying around twenty to thirty gallons. Jesus said to the attendants, "Fill the jars with water"; so, they filled the jars to the brim. Then he informed them, "Now draw some out and take it to the master of the banquet." They did as instruct, and the chief of the festivities sampled the water that had been turned into wine. At that moment, he didn't grasp where the wine had come from, even though the servants who had filtered the water realized what had taken place. At that moment he summoned the newlywed separately and said, "Everyone brings out the choice wine first and then the cheapest wine after the guests have had too much to drink; but you have saved the best till now." What Jesus executed in

Cana of Galilee was the earliest of the indications through which he showed his glory; and his apostle were completely certain of him.

TURA (Sanskrit) The highest notes of the music, opposite to Komala.

TURE implies "Thor' warrior" and "God of Thunder" (composed of the Norse God Thor or Old Norse "porr" = thunder + "ver" = fighter/warrior); to walk, to go along. (fram uten omtanke) to keep on, to carry on. (Paraphrasing of Ture from the Global Norwegian-English Dictionary).

TURKEY Is a sizeable, house-train game bird natal to North America, having a skin head and (in the male) red wattles. It is my favorite meal, mostly for joyous events reciprocal to Thanksgiving and Christmas. As a result, to its role in Thanksgiving, the turkey is also related with kindness, appreciation, relationships, and companionship. The turkey can bring people together to share in the spirit of devotion, collaboration, and gratefulness, like the holidays themselves. Devotionally the turkey displays benefits to sustain our instincts, sustenance, and ethos. Turkey is an emblem of holidays and bounty. So, Turkey is regarded as Autumn/Fall, the season of the Fire Element! A whole new dimension to Turkey symbolizes and definition due to the Element Fire which is the Element of passion, imagination, and the capacity of dismantling transformation.

TWACH, TVACH (Sanskrit). Leather, goatskin, sheepskin, cowhide, bark, cover.

TYANA (APOLLONIUS of) (d. c. 98) Pythagoreanism philosopher. The morality of his existence and refined religious inclinations were so inflated after his demise that heretical Reporters easygoing personal anecdote of him intentionally duplicated the Ideology survival of the Messiah.

TYCHE (lat. Fortuna). He was a mythological divinity who administered over the occasion of life. The Greeks called her Tyche, she was described with winged feet and a blindfold, on a wheel also winged, manifesting that disposal commodities that approached out of a horn of capriciously.

TYPE(S) In theology the prediction of the Cristian rejection in the episode and individual of the Old Testament. Precisely as Christ could mentioned Jonah as the representation of His Resurrection, so St. Paul went ahead in the Israelites crossing of the Red Sea the 'type' of Baptism (1 Cor. 10: 1-6). Arrangement was a powerful use in the premature Church.

TYPHOON. Conceding that overhead, the Antarctic Ocean, central Sea of Magellan or Easterly North Atlantic oceans (Florida, Caribbean Islands. Texas, Hawaii, etc.), quote it a hurricane. If it drifts over Cascadia (normally the Far East), we foretell a typhoon. A typhoon is a colossus, revolving tempest which leads to breeze, rainfall, and demolition. Hurricanes and typhoons are both together a type of equatorial line storm. There is nearly no distinction between hurricanes and typhoons. The pair are tropical cyclones, and the only contrast is their origination. Tropical monsoons with air current momentum of above 74 mph launching in the Atlantic Sea movements or NE are named hurricanes. Typhoons matured in the Cascade Mountains and generally intimidate Asia. The Line of Demarcation is handled as the Bering Sea's separation symbol, so when a hurricane cuts across it against deviation, it turns into a typhoon alternatively, and vice versa.

TYRE AND SIDON The two vital cities of the Phoenicians, on the coastline of Lebanon. In Old Testament times they shifted on to beneficial commerce. The dwellers of the region are referred to among those attracted to Christ (Lk. 6: 17) and He came to see the district (Mk 7:24). Tyre was grasped by the Crusaders, 1124-1291.

TZELEM. (Hebr.) Image, profile. The outline of a man's corporeal form, and physique.

TZIM-tzum (Caba.) Enlargement and recession, or as some Kabbalists define; "Centrifugal force and centripetal."

TZOOl-MAH (Kabbalah) Exactly "shadow". They demonstrate themselves as the Zohar, astral, or Linga Zaira. That amid the last seven nights of a man's life the Neshamah, his spirit, forsook him, and the shadow, Tzool-mah, ceases to act, because his body does not cast any shadow; and when the Tzool-mah disappears entirely, then Ruach and Nephesh (the soul and life) consent with it. It has often been required that in Kabbalistic philosophy there were only three "principles," and with the body Guff), four. It can easily be proved that there are seven, and several developments more than the "upper" and "lower" Neshamah (the dual Manas); Ruach, Spirit or buddi; Nephes (Kama), who "has no light of his own healing", but is correlated with the Guff (body); Tzelem, "Shadow of the Image"; and D'yooknah, Shadow of the Illusory Image, or Mayavi Rupa. Then approach the Tzurath, prototypes, and Tab nooth, the Form; and ultimately, Tzurah, "the supreme Principle (Atman), who remains above." Etc.

TZURAH (Hebrew) Points out to the spiritual prototype in kabbalah. In Esotericism it encircled Atma-Buddhi-Manas, the Upper Triad; the eternal Divine Individual. The plural of this word is Tzurah.

TZURE (Hebrew) Practically the same as Tzurah; the antecedent of the "Tzelem" Image; a Kabbalistic term used with citation to the creation of the Divine and human Adam, of which the Kabbalah (or Kabbalah) has four variety, which coincide with the Madman Races of men. Jewish novelty did not agree with Adam; and some, ignore to accept in the first humankind with its Adam, manifested only "primordial sparks."

-U-

UASAR (Eg.) Complementary Osiris, this isolated designation prevailing Greek. Uasar is trailed down as the "Born of the Egg", as is Brahma. "It is the Eros that Aristophanes clarifies as a party of the egg, and whose power he sustains leads all things at birth; the demiurge who made and animates the universe, a being who is a kind of characterization of Amen, the impalpable god, as Dionysos is a climber among the world the Zeus Hypsistos." Isis is invoked Uasi since she is the Zakti of Osiris, her feminine aspect, ranking for both the undertaken and energize viral effectiveness of substance in her image of male and female divinity.

UDANA (Sanskrit) Incomplete, defective variance; also, Sutras. In supplication that pronouncement is promulgated to the natural channel of the locution, such as the dialect, the mouth, the word, etc. In sacred ideology, it is the persuasion of those Sutras that support inadequate deliberations as contradictory to the Sutras that hold at most the question to place since they need Gautama the Buddha and his answer to lead: [Udana is 1. Exposure or vital air that takes us upwards. and 2. That assurance by which life withdraws to rest.] In subsistence of the first assertion, we interpret in Patanjali's Yoga Aphorisms: "By the mastery of the vital air called Udana, the yogi achieves the power of ascension (or levitation), of keeping on the water without touching it and on the silt, and of walking on Abrojos."

UDDEZA (Sanskrit) Enumeration, exposition, description, designation.

UDRA (Ramaputra) (Sanskrit) Udra, son of Rama. A Brahman ascetic, who for many years was the guru of Gautama the Buddha.

UGRA (Sanskrit) Be prudent, great, violent; cruel, terrible, Solution of the union of a Kchtriya with a Zudra or servile woman.

UKTA (Sanskrit) Discourse conversed, said call, mentioned, revealed, declared, expressed, manifested, recited, taught, explained, prescribed; word, expression.

ULLER. (Scandinavian.) The deity of dancing, who "travels" with skates accompanying the silver ice roads. It is the patron of hunting through the interval when the sun crosses the constellation of Sagittarius; and lives in the "Mansion of the Elves of Light" which is on the Sun and hereafter Asgard.

ULTRA. Above in a sphere: at a distance: invisible; surpass the scope or restrictions of, excruciating; imperceptible, unimaginable all that is conventional, actual, or ordinary; enormous, exceedingly avant-garde. The expression ultra-reach from Latin, where it has the definition "located beyond, on the far side of ultraviolet". Ultra is also used to imply "carrying to the furthest decree possible, on the fringe of:" "ultraleft" ultramodern. Ultra is also passed down to express "extremely:" weightless.

ULVA o ALBA (Sanskrit). Matriz.

UMA-Kango (Sanskrit) Light. Parvati's epithet; wife of Ziva.

UMBRELLA Coincidental obtained from the Italian word 'ombrella' an alteration of the Latin "umbrella, that transpired from 'umbra,' denotation "shade, shadow." The umbrella has been circulating for practically 4,000 years... first unearthed in the classical Mesopotamia locality in Western Asia. In isolated distant generations, the sun was an increasingly intimidating enemy than the rain, that is the rationale the potent parasol materialized to insulate this hazard. The umbrella normally illustrates the awning of the nirvana, shield, and preservation. The parasol is an image of the SUN and umbrellas the shelter. It is regularly a token of force and grandeur.

UNDERSTAND (Gnosticism) The way it is indispensable that people acknowledge what the Sanskrit voice Karma is... Such a term epitomizes, law of action and culmination. Evident there is no cause without effect, no consequence without cause.

UNDERWORLD Immeasurable Concealed embedded by the belly of the sphere and administer by the god Hades and his wife Persephone, the Underworld was the kingdom of the dead in Greek mythology, the sunless mount; the destination that souls of those who died went after death. In Greek Mythology (contrarily known as Overworld) is a creation where souls go so that after death and in Old Greek Religion, is some type of afterlife. During death, the soul and corpse are disconnected and the soul, conducted by Hermes is appointed to the Underworld. The Greek Underworld can be constructed up of three diversified regions; Tartarus, the Asphodel Meadows and Elysium. The animal linked with Underworld is Cerberus (Kerberos), or the "Hellhound", is Hades' immense multi-headed (conventionally three-headed) canine with some interpretation dawning which it as well has a snake-headed tail and snake heads on its rear end and its mane. Born from Echidna and Typhon, Cerberus sentinel the barrier that contribute as the entryway of the underworld.

UNCIAL-SCRIPT. An enactment of majuscule script (like modern 'capitals') used for books in Greek and Latin from the 4th to the 8th centuries A.D.

UNCREATED LIGHT (Gnosticism) The unmanifested luminosity is the real light. Each Buddha has enlarged in himself, the uncreated light, he has self-realized it in himself. The light arises from the infrastructure of darkness, from non-being; the inclination for life turns into uncreated light. All of us must crave for the real light and work on the purpose of being born one day in the uncreated light.

UNIVERSE, L. A French newspaper which, under the editorship of L. Veuillot, developed into an organ of the substantial Roman Catholic views. It was eventually extinguished in 1874.

UNTIL (Sanskrit) Hand. The thirteenth asterism or lunar mansion.

UPACHARO (Pali.) Attention, conduct. Equivalent to Sanskrit Chatsampatti.

UPSALA Connotation 'sanctuary'. Then again 'upa' defines 'above' and 'Shala' means 'hall'. It is also a setting of worship in Sweden; The Uppsala Temple.

UR. (Cald.) The leading place of the lunar denomination; the Babylonian city where the Moon was the chief godliness, and arising out of Abram conducted the Jewish god, who is so inextricably connected to the Moon as a creator and productive celestial being.

URAEUS (Greek; urhek in Egypt) Snake cobra with two horns, sacred portrayal that appeared near the disc of Horus and in the Goro of Osiris. This image is associated with Kundalini.

URADINES (Greek) One of the designations of the divine titans, those who rebelled against Kronos; the prototypes of the "fallen" angels of the Christians.

URBI ET ORBI (Lat., 'to the city [i.e., of Rome] and for the World'). A phrase used principally of the solemn blessing which the Pope convey occasionally coming out the balcony of 'St Peter's, Rome.

URBS BEATA HIERUSALEM. A 6th-7th century hymn celebrating the Heavenly Jerusalem in locution propose by Rev. 21. The many English translations include J. M. Neale's 'Blessed City, heavenly Salem'.

URGENT (Gnosticism) In the present conditions is urgent, critical (imminent, strict) that humankind understand and stops, eliminate, abolish its mistakes.

URIEL His epithet signifies Light of God. He is one of the Cosmocrators, leaders of the planet Venus. He is contemplated as the Angel of Love, left a book written in Runes to the Hyperborean Race and taught them the arts and science.

URJITA (Sanskrit) Noble, illustrious, enlightened; strong, powerful.

URLAK or ORLOG (Scandinavia) The equal as Orlog Hado; an abstract ability that "blindly" bestows gifts on mortals; a type of Nemesis.

URUVELA (Pali) Allude to a prehistoric administrative division in India, showed south of Patna on the banks of the Navainjana, today Dudda Gaya. Buddha subsisted in it a variety of times. It was also the former residence of the famous Maha-Kazyapa, it is also the prehistoric home of Maha-Kazyapa, where the Maha Bodhi temple is found. (Gospel of the Buddha.)

USHAS (Sanskrit) Distinguish Aurora, daughter of Heaven; it is a poetic and fascinating image. She is the everlasting virgin; consistently young; the light of the poor and the demolition of darkness.

USNEAS Longissima (Methuselah's beard lichen) has an approximate boreal northern range, with triple considerable redoubt in Western Hemisphere. The category is most superabundant onward the Pacific shoreline, can be discovered onward the northern Atlantic Ocean coastline, and has a defined scope near the Great Lakes of North America, where it possibly to be outstanding. Usnea is applied for reducing weight, pain reliever, countless bacterial control, and therapeutic; and to produce phlegm more unchallenging to spit up. Usnea is as well administered straight on the epidermis for aphthous ulcers and pharynx and larynx. Usnea consists of synthetic substances that are belief to confront pathogens that may motivate inflammation. These components may as well reduce distended, ache, and pyrexia. People use usnea for paroxysmal cough, weight, discomfort, restorative recuperation, and numerous additional resolutions, however, there is no acceptable experimental documentation to sustain utilization. Usnea has abundant medicative qualities, along with anti-swelling, antitumor, antibacterial, and congestive heart failure preventive measures. Usnea has been exploited in conventional American Indian medical science to handle bronchi, bowls, pharynx, fistula, and he incontinence and reproductive organs. It is acknowledging a divine "herb of the North". The Dakota calls it Chan wiziye, interpretation to "on the north side of the tree" or "spirit of the North wind". (Buhner, 1996).

USUARD, Martyrology of. The wide-reaching extensively declaring the Medieval chronicle and the reinforcement of the 'Roman Martyrology'. Its authority, Usuard (d. C. 875), was a friar of the cloister of St. Germain-des-pres. at Paris. He proceeded to have built his effort on the considerably premature Martyrology of Ado of Vienne.

USURY The pronouncement of interest was forbidden in the Old Testament when Jewish defaulters. In the rabbinic age clerics were banned from lending at absorption and in the Middle Ages this prohibition was expanded to lay people. It was forceful from the Middle Age perspective of money as simply a means of exchange. With the rise of capitalism, money moved progressively to be contemplated not as a sterile method of exchange but as fruitful capital of wealth, and the conservation of a suitable impose of dividend is authorized by the Church.

UTTHA (Sanskrit) East; or comes; went ahead, born, originated; which consists of; or which begins with.

UZANAS (Usanas (Sanskrit) "Bright." The planet Venus or Zukra; or rather, the ruler and monarch of that planet. [The guru or educator of the Daityas.]

UZAT (or Utchat) The Uzat is of two kinds: 1st, the right, white, the Sun, Ra; and 2nd, the left, black the moon, Osiris, the two eyes (Uzati) are the eyes of Horus.

-V-

VACH (Sanskrit) Citing Vah "language" simply, is insufficient in clarity. Vach is the mythical delineation of language, and the female Logos, being one with Brahma,1 who created it from one half of his body, which he split up into two parts; she is also one with Viraj (phrased the "Female Viraj") who was proven in her by Brahma.

VADIN or VADI (Sanskrit) Speaker, expositor, instructor, preceptor; disputer.

VADIS (QUO) Latin phrasing illustrating "Where are you marching?"

VAIHARA (Sanskrit) Epithet of a cave-temple positioned near Raja-Griha, where Lord Buddha customarily retreated there for meditation.

VAK (Sanskrit) The Goddess of Expression: language, prose, sound, speech Another Sarasvati title.

VALOR. It is distinction complementary nobility. It's courageous fearlessness and power, mainly on the battleground or when exposed to danger. Saint George exhibited valor when he ultimately kills the mythical beast. It's a characteristic adhere for a paladin. Valor derives from the Latin valorem for "strength, moral worth," with the definition of "courage" afterwards. The valor in the holy scriptures is the standard of a champion or heroine; extraordinary or heroic courageous when encountering hazard (mainly in battlegrounds). Unquestionably, this precision is appropriate with how Chayil is known in the Pentateuch. Gideon was starved, injured, embarrassed, and frightened, as the rest of us of Israel. Then the doctrine revealed the "Angel of the LORD appeared to him and said to him. "The LORD is with you, you mighty man of valor!

VALOR ECCLESIASTICUS The ritualistic assessment of ecclesiastical and authorized acquisitions produced in 1535, extensively known as the 'King's Books'. It was implemented by the legislation of Henry VIII distributing prelatic profits to the Crown.

VALUES (Gnosticism) Advantages are obtained as deficiencies are ruled out.

VAMANA. (Sanskrit) Fifth avatar of Vichnu, and consequently the name of the Dwarf, whose form affected that, Divinity.

VANITY Exemplify an equivalent for presumption, puffiness and arrogance. The voice comes attained out of the Latin vanitas, vanities, that expresses "quality of vain"…. Likewise, vanity can be manifested as an illusion or originality, as a surrogate or fiction.

VAN EYCK, HUBERT (c. 1366-1426) and Jan (c. 1390-1441), Flemish painters. Hubert proceeded to Ghent, where he launches into the altarpiece, The Adoration of the Lamb, for the cathedral of St. Bavon, Jan inclined court painter of Philip the Good of Burgundy in 1425 and established in Bruges. The Adoration, which Jan completed in 1432, combines the allegorical treatment of the Middle Ages with a hitherto unknown naturals and delight in comprehensive; The work, based on Rev., consists of over 200 figures, grouped on several panels round the essence form of the Lamb, standing on the altar and adored by progression of saints.

VAN HELMONT Commemorated Belgian doctor, Theorist and alchemist, (1577-1644). He was the author of the special dominant chemical discovery of his century, or the location of the actuality of gases, on which they should later stand up the hypothesis of productive chemistry. In one of his efforts, mention to the same that having qualified deriving out of an unknown individual a quarter of a gram of philosophers' stone, occupied in his own laboratory the course of action of transmuting into gold, with that small abundance of powder. The execution had such a fortunate result, from that moment he matured into an intentional persuader of enchantment. Made alkahest the universal solvent, assume since it melts all such bodies "like hot water dissolves the snow".

VARNA. (Sanskrit) Exactly: "color", Caste, the four main social class, called by Manu: Brahmanical, kchtriya, vaizya and zudra, are labeled Chatur-varna. [Varna also signifies race, tint, brightness, beauty; religious practice; quality, property; praise; musical mode; form, figure, etc.

VARUNA (Sanskrit) Characterized the god of water, or sea god, however, quite different from Neptune, because in the manifestation of this, the oldest of the Vedic deities, Water shows the "waters" of Space, or the sky that obstruct endlessly, the Akaza, in undoubted acceptance. Factually, it is the twenty-fifth lunar asterisk.

VAULT Being a deponent connotation 'to leap over something, especially using your hands or a pole', dates to the early 16th century. It comes from the Old French vou(l)ter, volter, (to leap), that in turn approach from the Italian voltage (to turn or leap).

VAZI or VAZIN (Sanskrit) Senor, governor, dominator, powerful.

VAZITVA (Vashitva) (Sanskrit) The capacity to command or statute the total.

VEGA (Sanskrit) Speed; strength; momentum; agitation; violence; momentum; explosion; course, current.

VEGE. Empathizing to, or acquire from, vegetable or a greenery such as lettuce, tomatoes, carrots, vegetable dyes, produce from or with wholesome herbage or verdure components; legume lasagna. A vegan individual, to vegetate, channel to loosen, slacken up, comply, hang loose, chill, impending. Veggie in lingo expression is an unofficial term for vegetarians.

VENERATE Appellation come about of the Latin root venerari, that has the many definitions of "to solicit the good will of," "to worship, "to pay homage to," and "to hold in awe." That source is related to Venus, which, as a precise tag, is the name of the Roman deity of love and beauty. The denotation of this expression is to contemplate with appreciative regard or with admiring respect, to honor (an icon, a relic, etc.). Venerations of godly persons is a Catholic custom which started around 3rd century. Christians began to give honor to those who succumb as martyrs. Gradually, the privilege also started to be determined to those Christians who engaged lives of holiness and sanctity. In harmony with an Islamic indigenous tradition 'animism' seems to be the Veneration of Saints and natural objects at the same time. This practice evidently pulls through the force by Islam undergoing "Arabization." that was entitled conforming to 'Amazigh' ethic. These beliefs are until now kept by the name of Arabization in the villages of South Tunisia.

VENI SANCTE SPIRITUS The Succession for Whitsunday. Its initiation is now basically assigned to Stephen Langton. English translations include 'Come Thou Holy Paraclete'.

VENUS. The duplicate of the planets in order of separation to the Sun. It is little less than the Earth, distance from the Sun a quarter less than this; shines with extraordinary radiance as brilliance of the morning and of the afternoon at a definite time of the year, presents phases like the Moon. In its phase of maximum obvious brightness, it can be seen in broad daylight. It is the planet most comparable to Earth in size and mass. Venus travels its orbit at a reasonable distance from the Sun of 108,304,000 km (about 67296985.6 mi) and an average speed of 35 km (about 21.75 mi) / s. Venus rotates in the contrasting direction to that of the Earth. / Ast, Planet that rules the signs of Libra and Taurus and is feminine in nature. Venus is a symbol of love, beauty, clarity and the power of cohesion. It confers magnitude for the fine arts, grace of form and spirit. In its unfavorable aspect it is immoral. It affects the throat, venous circulation and sensory acuity. It is stated that on Venus there is life and that it is inhabited by superior beings who have partaken in the human evolution of the Earth, hence the 4 Kurmaras came millions of years ago to help Humanity. In the Bible the Master Jesus the Christ, hints that he arrived from the planet Venus when he says that he comes from the morning star. Human mysticism defines Venus as the Goddess of love and beauty; the Astros, Isthar; the Greeks, Aphrodite; and the Phoenicians, Astarte was contemplated as a feminine aspect of Divinity. It is said that the Goddess Venus was born from the foam that was put together from the blood of the Two Cronos (Saturn) that cyo on the hellos of the Sea, near the coast of Citera Island. The Greeks called her Aphrodite, that is, born of foam.

VENUSTA (Gnosticism) Anyone who renounces Nirvana for the love of Humanity, after Nirvanas won and lost for the love of humanity, is later acquired the Venustic Initiation.

VERSE A category of terms that are subject to measurements, rhythm and rhyme which causes a certain rhythmic effect in the form of a poem. A verse is calibrated by a set of sentences or short phrases. The vocable verse comes from Latin versus meaning "groove or row" and from there "line of writing."

VERSIONS Considered a specific publication or form of something. Version derives from the Latin Vertere, "to turn". Think of it as someone taking a turn, as in an adaptation of a work of art or literature. 1580s, "a translation, that which is rendered from another language," from French version, from Medieval Latin versioned (nominate version) "a turning, a translation," from deponent stem of Latin Vertere "to turn, turn back, be turned; convert, transform, translate' be changed" (from PIE root *wer- (2) "to turn, bend"). Also, with a Middle English sense of "destruction." The explication "particular form of a description; a statement, account, or description of events or proceedings from some distinct point of view" is authenticated by 1788.

VERÓNICA, St. A woman of Jerusalem who is said to have supplied her headcloth to the Lord to wipe the blood and sweat from His face on the way to Calvary; He returned it with His features impressed upon it. The folk tale is first instituted in its existing form in the 14th century. The episode immersed a regular position in the Stations of the Cross.

VESTMENT(S) (The three) The three vestments are Buddhist congregated or bodies are stamped, correspondingly: Nirmanakaya, Sambhogakaya and Dharmakaya.

VESPERALE. (1) A ritual book holding the Psalms, song of praise & melody used at Vespers, that the intonate those of Compline are ordinarily supplementary. (2) In the Catholic Church, the cloth stretches out over the altar when inactive to keep the white linen altar cloths spotless.

VESICA PISCIS (Latin) "Fish Bladder". Actuality is a characterization of Christ; It has of an oval halo that surrounds the entire raised figure, and as roughly calculated, has a reference to the sacred Christian symbol, the ichthys.

VEXILLA REGIS. The Latin hymn by Venantius Fortunatus commemorating the conquest of Christ on the Cross. It is sung at Vespers in Paschal Triduum. The English paraphrasing, "The royal banners forward go", is due to J. M. Neale.

VI (Sanskrit). Designation deprivation, separation, estrangement. Occasionally it expresses superlative intensity. Every now and then, it advances in Vai.

VIA DOLOROSA The pathway in Jerusalem which Christ is believed to have followed from the judgment hall of Pilate to Calvary.

VIA MEDIA. (Latin 'The Middle Way'). A phrase handed down mostly by J.H. Newman and other Tractarians for the Anglican institution as a middle road between 'Popery' and 'Dissent'. This foundation of Anglicanism was traditional in the 17th century.

VIA-(Way) A course that leads to the absolute, to the Intimate Self-Realization.

VIAE QUINQUE Each five 'ways' or disagreements by which St. Thomas Aquinas appealed to demonstrate the reality of the Almighty from these outcomes of His Presence that are well known to us, viz (1) that gesture signify a fundamental creation; (2) that a succession of adaptability motives, and a their achievements, similarly situated at society, suggests a causeless initial conclusion; (3) that the occurring of artifacts that are not easily, understood and consequently adequate intellectually do not seem real, propose any required being; (4) that the analogy we fabricate (approximately 'true', ' noble', & correct) insinuate a distinct of connection that is as such ideal in all these conditions; (5) that the attainment by insensible or ambiguous phenomenon of an end to that they are clearly project to work inferred a meticulous reason in their formulation and directive.

VICISSITUDE. This expression can plainly be cited as developing, nevertheless, routinely conveys an implication of the adversity that persistent adjustments present. The designation is sometimes experienced in the clause "the vicissitudes of life", referring to the vagaries of living and the unpredictability inherent in the human conditions. When you talk of the vicissitudes of life, you're referring to the arduous moments that we all labor in between: illness, unemployment, along with other uninvited occurrences. Nobody may break free from the vicissitudes of human beings. In the sutta, the Buddha declared about "eight worldly conditions," otherwise well known as the "eight vicissitudes." Some embrace a quartet of enjoyable and unpleasant escapades: advantages and casualties; prestige and dishonor; approval and criticism; gratification and affliction.

VICHA (Sanskrit) Poison, cough, Ponzini.

VICHNU (Vishnu) (*Sanskrit*) Second person from (Trinity) Trimurti. Brahma, Vichnu, and Ziva.

VID (Sanskrit) Recognized; to know, to distinguish; think, consider, judge, opinion; see, perceive, feel. As a describer, at the end of compound: knower, knowledge, intelligent, learned, versed, expert.

VIDI AQUAM (Lat., 'I beheld water'). The canticle is sung in the West Church in Eastertide past the assemblage in location of the Asperges sung in the route the cessation of the year.

VIGIL. Nocturnal aid of prayer, regularly summation with the Eucharist, were conventional in the premature Church. The vigil previous Easter carried on all round the night (see Paschal Vigil Service); those first to Sundays and other banquets habitually appropriated at best the beginning (Vespers) and the end of the night-time. From the closing the organization of Matins and Lauds enlarged. Because of misuse, the vigils of humanity approached to be inadequate to the early hours, i.e., prior to nightfall, and then it became customary to hold the vigil. At first restricted to the afternoon of the introductory day, fast, office, and Mass of the vigil were slowly retired to the morning and the full day became a 'profestum'. In the RC calendar of 1969, all vigils exclusively that of Easter were done away with, but the 1971 Breviary volunteer a minuscule expanded office for optional use on the eves of Sundays and remarkable feasts.

VIHARA (Sanskrit) To some degree, a capacity housed by ascetics or Buddhist priests; a Buddha Sanctuary, usually a cave or temple wide open in the rock. A monastery, or also a convent of nuns. Today Viharas are built in the precincts of monasteries and academies for Buddha discipline in towns and cities; but in other times they could only be in wastelands and unfrequented places, on the tops of the mountains and in the eminently deserted places. Vihara also means expansion, distraction; recreation, play, leisure, distribution, arrangement; relaxation site.

VIKALA (Sanskrit) Twilight; nightfall

VIKARA (Sanskrit) Change, modification, alteration; mood movement; disturbance, disorder (mental or bodily), passion; production; preparation.

VILAGNA (Sanskrit). Suspended, hanging; fixed, taken, adhered.

VINA Serenate at this moment to the selected vine: I your Father in Heaven, I am your advocate: constantly I sprinkle my vine. All the time I take heed of her in consequence that nobody does distress. The memorandum of the Allegories of the Vina is that it has again and again been simplified that the Trajectory express that nevertheless those who transform at an advanced get equivalent compensation in company with anyone who transfigure quick, and that individuals who change promptly in existence do not have to be resentful of these who adapt thereafter. If the holder of a vina described the creator, this is an influential writing that in Lord's domain, replace and not jobless laborers can discover efforts this one converges their necessity and the demands of them who rely on them. "He will bring those minerals to a miserable end and tear the vine from other farmers." (Matt. 21:41). The vine is the domain of Supreme being, the occupant are the leader clergyman and backslider, and Jesus has just proclaimed that it will be withdrawn from them and "given to a people who will bear their fruit."

VINAYA (Sanskrit). Modesty, humility, docility, submissiveness, obedience; discipline, education, courtesy; good manners; withdrawal; Apartment.

VINEGAR BIBLE. An admired designate for a notification of the AV preprinted in 1716-17, in which the inscription of Lk. 20 reads 'The parable of the Vinegar' alternatively of 'The Parable of the Vineyard'.

VINCI, LEONARDO (DA VINCI) (1452-1519), Italian creator and thinker, from 1483 to 1499 he lived in Milan; during this interval, he attained a range of his momentous conventional efforts, in besides the Last Supper. This characterized not the foundation of the Holy Sacrament but the immediate pronouncement of inconstancy. When the French occupied Milan (1499). Leonardo deserted and set on a ministerial live mostly devoted to knowledge-based and instructional attempts.

VICTIMAE PASCHALI (Lat., 'To the Paschal Victim'). The Easter Sequence in the W. Church, written by Wipo.

VIO DE THOMAS, CAJETAN, (1469-1534). Dominican theologian. As General of his order (1508-18), Cardinal (1517), and Bp. Of Gaeta (1519), he recreated an important part in ecclesiastical affairs, imploring the cause of rehabilitation before the Lateran Council of 1512, reasoning with M. Luther in 1518, and contending the projected divorce of Henry VIII (1530). His comment on St. Thomas Aquinas's Summa Theological (1507-22) was the first shrine of the 16th-century revival of Thomism.

VIOLIN (viola) Specifically a bowed musical instrument, contained of a wooden box, like a narrow oval near the middle, with two "S" shaped orifices in the lid and a neck to which a fingerboard is superimposed. The violin has an adminicular; in itself it is a piece of round wood and more or less long, which goes on the upper and lower top at the height of the bridge, delegated Alma hence perhaps concerning a suggestive way, the violin symbolizes the enchantment of the Inspiration or its calcification in matter, imprisoned amid Heaven and Earth (cover and bottom), the action of the Spirit (bow) tries to release it through the bridge (path crossed by the four elements, 'the strings'), throughout the purposeful contact assemble by the sound that raises the voice of the confined Soul to the divine height.

VIRYA A Buddhist memorandum regularly and clarified as 'energy', 'diligence', 'enthusiasm', or 'effort'. It can be outlined as a venue of view that is cheerfully attractive in healthful ventures, and its objectivity is to root one to execute wholesome or moral measures.

VIRGO (Latin Virgo, virgin) Astron, Sixth zodiac sign. The zodiac sign of the Virgin Mother of the World is an approach, factually guided by Mercury.

VIRTUE (Latin Vir, Virtus: pure force) Insinuated as the preparation or assurances of reality to arise or source of their outcome. Gnosis clarifies that no matter how virtue, however blessed, is alternatively superior, broken down is immoral and unfavorable; in conjunction with virtues, we can harm others. It is Essential to place the virtues in their appropriate position. What would you say about the altruistic point of view of an individual who, rather than transferring food, dispenses money among beggars of wrongdoing? It must be recollected that amid the melodiousness of the lyrics also conceal the offence. The misdeed personates itself as a good person, uses unrestrained morality, manifests itself as an affliction and even presides in the Dedicated Temples Sanctuaries. There are numerous generosities that can be advance in the work on one person, with the elimination of imperfection for instance if one diminishes the fault of Anger, arisen in substitution of the goodness of calmness; if one get rid of the lack of Arrogance, the virtue of Selflessness is born; if Lust is detached, Chastity arrives; if it conquer Hatred, Love is born; if it remove Envy, in its substitution Will take form Joy and the quality of supplemental Benevolence, etc., with such practices we can take shape of our Inspiration which is the place of feelings, connects with, goodness, extramundane potential, etc.

VITAL Exceptionally magnificence to understand that humankind does not comprehend that he is a machine.

VISCUM A subdivision of Old World; is a limited stem parasite; ingest only water and minerals from the host and does not absorb food, (Family Loranthaceae) well known by the group of axillary bracteate flowers with attached flowers, entangle made from the berries of the European mistletoe contrast viscin. The emergence of the term viscum possibly from Proto-Indo-European weyks-, perhaps a European obtained for a tree related to the mistletoe matched also ancient Greek ("mistletoe, birdlime"). Proto-Slavic, Proto-Germanic wihsilo, and feasibly Italian visciola ("sour cherry"), the last imaginable a Germanic acquisition.

VIPAZCHIT (Sanskrit) Wise, learned, enlightened, clairvoyant, intelligent.

VIOLENCE (Latin Violanti) Violent action or opposition to the logical way to work. Wind caliber. Mythology dispenses her as resistance (Violence, daughter of Titan Styx. He is substituted with breastplate and nail, often going with Jupiter. He had three children at once: Gratos (The Force), Nike (The Victory) and Zelos (The Enthusiasm).

VOL UXKUL. (Gnostic) He is one of the greatly prominent Initiates of the Mysteries of Eleusis, that, incidentally, still subsist in this school secretly.

VOWELS (Hebrews) Became visible with respect to the brainchild of the Enlightened and Ladino rabbis of the School of Tiberias.

VRATA (Sanskrit) Magnitude and regulations of the deities. Will, command, directions, order, act; domain; sphere; behavior, method of life; choice; resolution, purpose; vote; holy or pious work, loyalty; religious observation; duty, obligation; task; obedience, assistance; occupation. As an addition at the end of combination: devoted, faithful, obedient; addicted; constant, consecrated; server; worshipper.

VULGATE The Latin variation of the Bible sizeable universally handed down in the West. It was mostly the effort of St. Jerome, and its earlies rationale was to be complied the differences discrepancies of content in the Old Latin manuscripts.

VYASA (Sanskrit) Allude to: "the one who develops or expands"; a linguist or rather a developer; because what he equals, interprets and expands is a mystery to the laity. This term was implemented in ancient times to the highest Gurus in India.

-W-

WAILING WALL, (The) Jerusalem is ingeniously well known in the Jewish birthright as the 'Western Wall'. At first, it was a bit of the 'Temple form constructed by 'Herod the Great and has been revered by Jews after the destruction of the Temple in A.D. 70'.

WAIT or WAITING. The expression wait has its origins in the 1200s, out of the Old Northern French term waiter: "to watch with hostile intent." The population didn't appreciate waiting. Sacredly, waiting is a vital verb subjecting that "to wait" is to be mindful of all the consciousness of what is happening surrounding you and sensitive to the right moment to achieve the upcoming reality. (Gnosticism) This phrase applies to the self that at the age of 40 had a lawsuit for tangible goods, in the new existence Wait for such an age to reiterate the same talk. The self that at the age of 25 had a quarrel with another man in the canteen or in the bar, will wait in the next existence the same age to look for his antagonist and repeat the drama.

WAKE. The commonly significant of the term 'wake' was to view or stand guard over the deceased prior to sepulture and grievers would eulogize, pray and encourage each other up until the funeral ceremonial. The designation was formerly pertained to the ceaseless attention preserved prior to defined celebrations, however, it indicates to the indulgence and merriments on the holiday by definition and at that point, to annual commemorations on the carnival of the community patron saints. Etc.

WALA (Scandinavian) A prophet in the songs of the Eddas (Scandinavian mythology). In the integrity of Odin's embellishments, she was resurrected from her tomb and prophesied Baldur's death.

WALL Defender or Preservers. Symbolic appellative provided to the many of Proponent (Narjols) or egotistic accordingly, who take for granted to observe beyond mankind by guidance and defensive it. The alleged Nirmanakaya precept in Northern Mystic Buddhism. [So, to speak] informed, the gathered formation of guru, holy beings and expert, and mostly of Nirmanakayas, have produce, so to declare, alongside mankind a wall of shelter, that uncertainly safeguard it intensify vile. They can keep us apart; as well as support our protection. We could be thankful for them because they can teach us a lot of things through art, in the classrooms or house of prayers. They can also be afraid of them! Why? Because they can also be like fortress; as are the Walls of China. Walls are borderlines, but not all walls prohibit. There are those which are free and welcome humanity to unite which are the walls of a cathedral, synagogue or mosque are significantly penetrable. We are invited to pass through them. The ancient churches that occupy the small-towns and surroundings where some people live in areas where they can regularly leave their doors unlocked, allowing the great stone walls to mutate form their best ability to sanctuary by the push of a door, however, on the other side of the spectrum, there exists walls of fear; those walls that are built to keep foreigners outside such as the walls of Jericho, enormous pebble walls communities an prehistoric archaic encampment in Jericho, constructed about 8,000 B.C. These walls, at slightest 13 feet (4 meters) in height and backtrack by an observatory or barrier of 28 feet tall, were deliberately to safeguard the accommodations and its reservoir provide from physical trespassers. To this day walls have become more unreachable than ever and give humanity horror and inaccessibility.

WHALE. It possesses symbolism with the world, the body, and the tomb. It exemplifies the hidden continents by essence. In addition, it has an alchemical ideography known as the constellation of the Whale. This method is related to the event of Jonah and has to do with the measurements of the coffin of Osiris (shaped like a fish), for this Osiris had to go down to the black and horrific height where he had to spend three periods in the belly of the whale, corresponds to the Arcane Fifteen (15) of the Tarot. The emblem of the whale is purpose. A portion maintain whales are correlated with tranquility, peacefulness, reverence, and calmness. The actualization of a whale in a fantasy may be a signal that unconditionally is or should be ok and is generally associated to intangible episode of the brainpower and kindheartedness. The divinity queen consort of the ocean, spouse of Neptune; Thalassa was the celestial being who generated the tide's bloom bounteous, shoal and crustacean; in addition, dolphins, seals and whales. In Christian Bible, the "great fish" in Jonah 2 has been generally understandable as a whale. In English some transcriptions use the word "whale" for Matthew 12:40, in the time another use "sea creature" of "big fish". Amid Native Americans, Whales are contemplated the custodians of oceans and sea voyage. Practically all shoreside ethnic groups have some description of illustrative definition for Whale Representation and Spirit Animals. Whale myth encompasses judgment, transcendent realization, fortune and durable tenderness as the Whale are our colleagues for life.

WALHALLA (Scandinavian) A kind of Olympus (Devachan) for strategists who die on the battlefield and cited by the ancient Scandinavians as the "abode of the blessed heroes"; it has five hundred doors.

WAR All wars include the struggle of good against evil, light against darkness. In the mystic understandings many cases of wars are cited: Jupiter, opposed to the titans or cyclopes, Krishna, against the Baharat's next to the Pandavas; Thor, against the giants; St. Michael the Archangel against the rebellion of the fallen angels; the war of man with difficulties with his enemies of evil and against his own selves (defects); "The War in the Heavens" which has several representations, such as the fight of the primitive adepts of the Aryan race and the Warlocks of Atlantis, the demons of the Ocean, etc. War can symbolize religious, astronomical, geological events and can also have a very deep cosmological sense. War signifies integration, the original order through sacrifice. The battlefield is a symbol of the reality in which action takes place, to achieve complete freedom, in the physical world wars are the cause of the corruption of humanity because of its selfishness, hatred, envy, fear, etc. This decay appears through the copper age and is fully fortified in the Iron Age, of every race.

WAR, Participation of the Clergy in. After the Middle Ages clerical in essential organizations have been clearly banned from taking a straight part of the shedding of blood. Position, however, the ability if the State pressures them to tackle armed duties, they are allowed to obey. The Church of the East normally endorses Middle Age discipline.

WARTBURG. The fortress in Thuringia location Martin Luther was concealed following enduring arrest (with his own connivance) approaching his home from the diet of Worms in 1521.

WATER(S) (Sanskrit) The first origination of things. By agreement with the seer, when the pre-adamic land is restricted by the Alkahest its first essence is like clear water. Alkahest, the "one and invisible, water, the initial principle, in the second transformation".

WANES (Scandinavian) was a caste of gods of great antiquity, venerated in the dawn of time by the Scandinavians of prehistory and later by the Teutonic races.

WAVE The prime of mental images is by definition; powerful. A wave is nonstop, an impetus of mother nature that charges over all things in its passage. It conveys might and unavoidable, but also an absence of attentiveness distinction and ineffectiveness of protection. A propelling elevation or undulation of water materializes within close range to the outside of the ocean, distinguished by whirl and revolt and plummeting motions, often as a reaction of the grinding yank of the wind blast. The word wave has several meanings. It could be the movement from side to side, or to make something move like this while holding It in the hand; the corn waved gently in the summer breeze. A crowd of people ran down the street waving banners. "He seems to think I can wave a magic wand, and everything will be all right"; there are: radio waves, microwaves, sound waves or seismic waves, and many more, however, numerous waves which are fun to be a part of, are those done at a stadium execute by thousands of people at a moment of excitement; we could also wave at others in a friendly manner, as greetings of friendship, devotion or thanks.

WATAH. Early Atlantean native tongue of Hebrew and Chinese Sanskrit.

WEDNESDAY. Originating at classical times Wednesday, the day on which the Christ was betrayed, was jointly with Friday at Christian fast day and long endure so in Embertide.

WELL. The well is an emblem for neighborhood, in the Christian art, the well (or fountain) is the metaphor of baptism, life and rebirth. The wells cited in the Bible. Abraham dug wells near Gerar. Jesus, sitting on the brim of Jacob's Well, taught the Samaritan woman the dissolution of the Old Covenant. An angel creates Hagar at a well in Sinai, Beer Lahai Roi (Genesis 16:7). To own a well and to have the bordering country were synonymous terms. The spiritual springs of water from Jesus himself were and are the water that saves us. His well is endless and always full. Jesus used the well water as a comparison to stand for God's fountain of life, given through Jesus for our salvation.

WE Term applied by a spokesperson concerning himself or herself and one or additional individuals contemplated jointly. Working in a traditional environment bearing in mind by a dignified personage, or by a columnist or commentator, to mention to himself or herself. I along with each of the groupings that incorporates me; you and me, and associated with another, I and extra or additional not counting you, exploited as nominative of the individual diverse. We exist, gather here. The Almighty relates in the sacred text; "We are God's children, and if children, also heirs; successor of God and coheirs with Christ; if indeed we suffer with him so that we may also be glorified with him" (Rom. 8:17).

WEE FREES. The minority of the Free Church of Scotland which linger externally the united Free Church established in 1900.

WETLANDS. A wetland is a location in which the dry land is covered by wateriness, sodium chloride, crisp or enclosed by; either/or continually or long-lasting. Its role as its command apparent habitat. You can comprehend wetlands from divergent varieties of land or groundwater basically by the flora that has acclimatized to Waterlogged soil. There are 4 types of wetlands in the United States: marshes, swamps, bogs, and fens. If abundant vegetation grows in the vicinity, they will succumb and capsize to the lowermost of the waterlog. They decay at a slow pace, and frequently remain dimmed in color (black). In other aspects, the ground is hydrophytic, and is an ashen color. These topsoils may have spots of red, orange, blue, or green. From unseasonable origination of cultivation projects, correspondent riverine wetlands survivable accepted as prized possessions acreage for sustenance and herbage producing, since they have fruitful earth by means of systematic residue settling all along inundations occurrences.

WEEK. The weeklong as a ritual organization gotten from the Jewish practice of the Sabbath the conceiving of a working day of pause particularly resolute to God was assumed by the Christians but shifted to the first day of the weekday (Sunday) in privilege of the Resurrection. The Jewish abnegation of Tuesday and Thursday were converted to Wednesday, the day of the Betrayal, and Friday, the day of the Crucifixion. Thursday as a day of pleasure in the narrative of the Ascension and of the Establishment of the Eucharist came into prominence in the early Middle Ages, and Saturday set about to be devoted to the BVM.

WEST INDIES, Christianity in the. The earliest evangelization was carried out by Roman Catholic missionaries who came with the Spanish colonists from the end of the 15th century; an archdiocese was accepted at Santo Domingo in 1511. Once the aboriginal population was exterminated and replaced by slaves from W Africa, attempts were made to have slaves baptized, however, the brutality with which they were treated led to antagonism and revolt. Around the early 17th century, the British started to settle in some parts of the island, but until the 19th century, it made little attempt to evangelize the natives. Missionary work was undertaken by the Moravians, Methodist, and Baptists. In 1824 Angelica dioceses were confirmed in Jamaica and Barbados, and in 1883 the West Indies was accounted for as an independent Province of the Anglican Communion. In the areas which were originally French, or Spanish the RC Church stays predominant. After slaves were liberated (1833), there was an inflow of Orientals, who resisted being evangelized. In the 20th century all churches have tried building up native ministries and there have been ventured by most non-RCC to join in ecumenical discussions. There has been extensive growth amid the Pentecostal Churches.

WEIGH Is an old English (ge) with, of Germanic origin; associated to Dutch Wicht and German Gewicht. The constitution of the expression has been impressed by weight. To weigh is all attributing to believing. A person could see how much load an object may have, or if it is a beneficial alternative. You could weigh the goods you're buying by physically assessing their weight; potatoes, cabbage, beans, etc. As how much they weight; or weigh your way of thinking when registering to a scholastic institution.

WHIP. The whip is like ultimate symbol of the slaves' dehumanization, as its use on slaves implies that slaves are like livestock that can be bought, trained, and controlled by the threat; or employed, of brutal physical violence.

WIFE. As a wife, a female is predicted to be of service to her spouse, getting meals ready, articles of clothing and other exclusive demands. As a birth mother, she must attend to the care of the children and their necessities, along with their education. As a breadwinner, she ought to be competent, trained and a quality hired person. The phrase wife is attainable for. Immaculate, Domestic science, Culinary Arts, and Congenial.

WILL The later bracket of how Scripture refers to God's will be studied as "God's mysterious or hidden will." This characteristic of God's will refer to his unlimited ability over the totality, the routine in and that God is consistently active in all artifacts about his guaranteed pattern approaching, and the process which affects our existence. The expression what will be will be is employed to recount the conviction that providence will figure out the aftermath of a path of affairs, even if measures is contracted to look to change it.

WILLOW This tree is considered an emblem of fertility and new life, a willow tree could grow just by taking a new branch from the tree and planting it in the ground; a brand-new tree will arise in its place. The willow tree gives us hope, a sense of belonging, and safety. Additionally, the faculty let go of the affliction and anguish to expand brand new, robust and intrepid. The facade of the willow tree is its trail to balance, aspiration and invigorating. Weeping willow trees have long been admired for their gracefulness, weeping branches that brush the ground with aerial, silvery leaves. Its appearance glides into a satisfying, spherical awning. Not only do they produce nutriment for rabbits and deer, but their extensions are as well flawless for dwelling for birthing. The human species recognizes willows with eternal life and, although common on gravestones or headstones, weeping willow trees can illustrate rebirth, the restoration to life, etc.

WHIRLWINDS The interpretation of a whirlwind is a realism that concludes extremely rapidly within the blink of an eye. Symbolism a whirlwind could be passional affair, and commitment and nuptials which take place within days, of the marital twosome meeting a thunderous, disoriented hurry. Disastrous Whirlwinds could occur anywhere in the world at any season. Whirlwind is a climate situation in which a swirl of breeze (a perpendicular positioned revolving pole of air) shapes due to unpredictability and disturbances produced by warming and motions (shifting) inclinations.

WIN The Revolution of Consciousness is only practical in the sensory faculty of winning, of conquering our individual latent possibilities, our own hidden treasures. Like the floret headband, the true laurel garland is an emblem of triumph. It was passed down from classical times alternatively to an Olympic trophy. The palm limbs, or palm foliage, are as well images of success, conquest, tranquility, and eternity arising in the prehistoric Mid East and Adriatic society. The palm (Phoenix) was venerated in Assyrian, and in prehistoric Egypt constitute eternal life.

WINDOW Illustrates expectation, a getaway, a possible pathway, to the unspecified, and adjustment. There are many movies, publications, sketches, and youngster's narratives hallmark windows. They are often patterns that express what a disposition desire or anything he is going to meet next.

WINE Is often specified in the Bible and seems to have been in daily use in Palestine in New Testament times. It has historically been defended to be one of the indispensable substances for a well-founded Eucharist. The words of regime suggested that the dedicated wine bears to the believer the Blood of Christ, however, religious ecclesiastics, has held that both the Body and the Blood are present in each of the Eucharistic species. Coming from early flow it has been accepted to merge water with the wine at the Eucharist. In the C of East, the mixture was not instructed after 1552, but it was normally resuscitated in the 19th century. A diligent temperance from wine has led to the use of unsourced grape juice by sectarians.

WINESKIN Meaning of wineskin an animal skin sewn up and used to hold wine. An amazingly uncomplicated operation, however the symbolism used in the Holy Bible is tremendous when Jesus strives to teach his disciples in reference to prior learning as correlate to teaching new, uneducated disciples. The significance of wineskin in the Cristian world relates to Matthew 9:17, (Mark 2:22), and Luke 5:37: "No one pours new wine into old wineskins," Jesus lectured some 2,00 years ago. "Otherwise, the wine will burst the skins, and both the wine and the wineskins will be ruined. "No, they pour new wine into new wineskins".

WINGS This word stands for the spirit, in the obscure pentagram.

WINDSOR, St. George's Sanctuary. The 'Royal Free Chapel of Windson' was incorporated by Edward III to take administrator of the temple of the corresponding Supporter (founded c. 1348); it acquired its representation in 1352. The present Vertical Bethel, with its intricate stone surplus, originates from 1475-1508.

WHIP. It is a conventional bureaucratic function whose duty is to secure party followers in a council. This denotes safeguarding those constituents of the group elect in accordance with the party podium, alternately; in agreement with their command of independent belief or resolution of their contributors or components. Whips are the party's "disciplinarians". Heracleum composed in his literary context in reference to these verses in the second centennial after Christ's death: "The whip is an image of the power and activity of the Holy Spirit." It's the Essence of God. discharge in Jesus as he deranges the marketplace in the temple courts. Aphrodite is a divinity who utilizes a whip. She is illustrated as a winged godhead brandishing a whip or a dagger. In classical times their summary of Adversary resembled Aphrodite, who occasionally tolerated the sobriquet, Nemesis.

WIPO. (d. 1050), canticle-writer. He was pastor to the monarchs. Conrad II as well as Henry III. His leading effort is the "Victimae Paschalis Laudes', which is the sequence for Easter Day. His archive of the dynasty of Conrad II (1024-29) is a principal origin.

WISE. Perhaps the greatest recognizable symbol of wisdom is the owl; which has been used since ancient times to stand for wisdom and knowledge. Since strength, & courage has been combined with wisdom to relate conflicts sector in battle lines as well as daring wild animals; the lion and eagle are usually pointed out as well.

WISDOM OF SALOMON, The. A Book of Apocrypha. The first element (1:1-6:8) recounts the distant destinies anticipating the righteous and the atrocious; the second part (t:9-9: 18) includes the meditation on Wisdom that accepts the Book its name; the last part (10-19) assesses the relation of Israel to the Exodus, with a departure on idolatry in 13-15. The attribution of the Book to Solomon is a literary device. It was almost certainly written by an "Alexandrian Jew", possibly

c. A.D. 40. The edition has had terrific impact on faithful concepts. It may have been employed by St. Paul. In later writers the expressions used of the Divine Wisdom are freely referred to Christ.

WISHES. Sha'-al, "to ask," "petition," "supplicate" (Job 31:30 the King James Version); another variation of definition is found in Psalms 73:7 where, "to imagine", is translated "wish". "They have more than heart could wish"; declare, "to solicit," "to implore" (Romans 9:3). There now are various phenomenon which described comprehensible desire. There are five types of wishes: to have, to give, to meet, to be and to go. Numerous cultures fascinate in procedure that entail wish-granting, such as puffing out the candles on a birthday torte, invocating, discerning an to conduct fully evening star, animate off a coin into a wishing well or spring, cracking the wishbone of a broiled gobbler, puffing a blowball, or scribbling desire on a bow or a sky flashlight. The definition of the denomination longings is to enjoy an ambition for (article, such as anything unreachable) willing the cohesion of living his life over; to grant articulation to an aspiration; give a greeting; offer them to sleep tight.

WITCH. The English term witch; that implies, charmer, evolved from the Anglo-Saxon word Wicca, in German Wisen "to know", "to notice", and Wiken "to guess", to predict", Witches (witches) were suggested at first "wise women" until the church took the matter about as such to advance the law of Moses, that denounce to defunct each witch or sorcerer.

WITCHCRAFT (Sorcery) Haunted, the art of casting spells and using black magic. Witchcraft is generally linked with the ability of the natural world, similarly, tending to cure disease or relieve pain and phytotoxins, or cause rainfalls and inundations. Individuals prosecuted for witchcraft can control large scale circumstances beyond one's control equally as disasters or tragedy. Humanity appears to believe in witchcraft since part of human beings may believe that incantation is the device which initiates their happiness, contentment, nevertheless, there are a few people who imagen they are unfortunate when it comes to love. They may dream up that someone is utilizing witchcraft in opposition to them. Numerous people attempt to come up genuinely for their assumed misfortune or anyone else's hardship. If people seemed to be lucky, people may believe they could have a witch enchanted them in regards of being so profitable.

WITELO (b. c. 1230). Thinker and researcher. Born in Silesia, he studied at Padua and belatedly went to Viterbo, from which he became the best friend of William of Morbeck. Of his later existence nothing definitive was investigated.

His treatise on optics, Perspectives, is proven on the effort of the Arabic scholar Alhazen. Its intellectual dogma is like a contemporary perspective on alliance and the repressed. Its guidance is Neoplatonist.

WITTOBA (Scandinavian) A feature of Vishnu. In his Indo-Moor Pantheon he manifests the image of Vithoba crucified in Space; and the Reverend Dr. Lundy, in his monumental Christianity, holds that this engraving predates Christianity and is the crucified Krishna, a Savior; and so, a concrete omen of Christ.

WOO. Chase the fondness or deep affection of somebody, generally an adult female; to pursue: He was cautioned of his youth when he navigated wooing, to request approval or acceptance; urging: Promoting ventures to woo substantiates pointless. In distinction to Middle English wowen, wo3en, from Ancient English wogian ("to woo, court, marry"). As concerns undetermined dawning. Cognate with Scots wow ("to woo"). Possibly associated to Medieval English wog, who (bending, crookedness"), in the determined sensation of "bend or disposed (wome) one toward oneself.".

WOLF. The ordinary Wolf Representation viewpoint for fidelity, powerful birth attachments, sincere connections, discipline, perceptive, and clever. Based on unified dryland vertebrates, the Wolf has an extreme supernatural power and is the major knowledgeable stalker.

WORLD. The earth, in conjunction with all its countries, territories, human beings, and geography. The world is restricted for all that persists; the totality, the solar system, any intricate full-length formulated as comparable the celestial space; the world of the simulation, one of the three generics arrange of substantial creation: animalia; raw material; comestibles, and duration, circumstances, or domain of reality: this earthly; the hereafter. In 1 Cor 3.22 Paul embody "the world" (together with "life and death, the present and the future") be one of the differences belonging to Christians. Paul's declaration is panoramic, and we make progress to adapt here "the universe", "all of creation", or "everything that God has made". Jesus said regarding the world: "Love not the world, neither the things that are in the world". If any man loves the world, the love of the Father is not in him. "For all that is in the world, the lust of the flesh, and the lust of the eyes, and the pride of life, is not of the father, but is of the world". As the ternary orbit from the SUN the Earth has the emblem of a CIRCLE engraved with a CROSS, and it can produce the wellspring of humankind, dwelling, and/or a motherland. Adjacent with hell can evidence the fairy tale ending of pertinent aliveness, nevertheless, is in addition perceive in contrast as the sustainer as aforesaid.

WOLFGANG, St. (c. 924-94), Bp. o Ratisbon from 972. He was educated at Reichenau, instructed at Trier, and in 964 entered the Benedictine Sequence at Einsiedeln. He was a self-starting advocate.

WOLFGANG, AMADEUS, MOZART. Baptized as Joannes Chrysostomus Wolfgang Theophilus Mozart was an innovative and dominant symphonist of the Classical period. Despite his brief life, his quick velocity of creations evolved into more than 800 works of effectively every classification of his time. Born in Salzburg, in the Holy Roman Empire, Mozart manifested immense abilities from his premature youth. At that stage of his life, he was already qualified on keyboard and violin. He started composing from the age of five and displaying his music in the circle of the European aristocracy. His father took him on a grand tour of Europe as well as trips to Italy. At 17, he was a musician at the a region or group of countries. Salzburg court but turned uneasy and moved to Vienna, exploring for a better arrangement. Over his final years there, he composed many of his renowned interludes, symphony and classical. His Requiem was mainly incomplete by the time of his passing away at the age of 35, the turn of events; which were uncertain and much mythicized.

WOMAN Starting from the dawn of time the female of the species has clench the earthly distress on their shoulders. Adult female is the Emblem of Creation. The farmer of unlimited Love. A woman is either restrained or forceful. The Lotus Flower might be considered to a significant extent a representation of the clarity, objectivity, edification and spiritualism of the female breed. Nevertheless, the Lotus Flower as well is a solid sign of feminine qualities and maturity. The goddess Maat showed rightness, equity, equilibrium, and infinite empathy, she was principally portrayed displaying an ostrich feather as a crown. A clasped, lift hand united with a Venus image stance for Female emancipation. It is a classical metaphor of the lady's deliverance activity.

WORDS Refers to a unique definite massive portion of discourse or correspondence, used with others or at times alone; to structure a sentence and consistently reveals with a space on either marginal when inscribed or imprinted. Comparison is an ability to gear the uses of words, individuals, impressions, places, or isolated beliefs to be positioned for existents behind the correct significance. As maintained by Greek mythology, she was the daughter of Oceanus and Tethys, wife of Atlas (Atlantean) and mother of the Pleiades or Atlantis.

WORTH. This term defines the same in benefit to, attending funds or earnings equal to; meritorious of, well worth the attempt. The worth of God has unlimited worth since through the detecting of his word, God gives us the Holy Spirit.

May we consistently be appreciating of our self-worth and importance and acts consequently; to the grandeur and uprightness of Jesus Christ our Lord. Psalm 139:13-14, ESV For you formed my inward parts; you knitted me together in my mother's womb.

WORM (Latin Cossano, Cossuso cassis) Any of the vermiform larvae or insects that undergo metamorphosis. Furthermore, like the caterpillar (the worm), undergoes a metamorphosis within the chrysalis, to turn into a butterfly), in the related way the human being must be formed as an authentic man by creating his solar bodies or internal bodies, that from the humanoid comes the man, and from this the superman.

WORSHIP, Directory of Public (1645). The Directory for the Public Worship of God' was composed by the Westminster Assembly on Presbyterian principles; it was configurated to reinstate the BCP. In Scotland it was acquired by the General Assembly and became one of the standards of Presbyterianism. A Command needing its use in England was continued by Parliament but was not long implemented.

WORT, St. John. Also investigated by some as St. Joan's Wort, is an emblem of the Midsummer Solstice in Europe, the UK, and more not long-ago North America. One observance is throwing the plant into the fire, and if one wants, leaping over the fire to help in cleaning up the body of evil ethos.

WOUNDS, The Five Sacred. Throughout the Passion journals of the Gospels recognizable evidence at most, the cavity of the Lord's side, the piercing of His hands and feet, a general behavior in ancient crucifixions, is attested to in the Resuscitation aspect. Allegiance to the Five Wounds was considerable in the Medieval ages. It was reassured by the Indictment of St. Francis of Assisi. Inclination was soon given to the wound in the side; this consciously influenced the ritual of the Sacred Heart.

WRATH OF GOD, The. A humanization figure of speech for the Divine approach to sin. Wrath is affirmed of God only metaphorically, as the human passions have no equivalent in the purely spiritual Divine substance. In the covenant the wrath of God is specifically associated with the Judgement on the last Day.

XAVIER, St. Francis (1506-52), 'Apostle of Indies' and 'of Japan'. From noble Spanish-Basque family, he became one of the first Jesuits, in 1542 pledging to pursue Christ in Poverty and chastity and to evangelize the nonbelieving. In 1542 he reached Goa, which he made his center of operation. He went on to Travancore, Malacca, the Molucca Islands, and Sri Lanka. In 1549 he made an appearance in Japan. He arrived back to Goa in 1552 and died on route to China. His work is exceptional for the period of his journeys and the valuable statistics of his novices.

XMAS is one more proclamation which auspices Christmas.

XENO(S) As it may be interpreted either to outsider (in the sense of a person from another Greek state) and to a newcomer or traveler guided into a correlation of long-distance agreement. The term insinuated "stranger" or "alien". In the Scriptures Xenos defines a foreigner, a nonnative. What are Xenos and why is it predominant. Xenia, the application of hospitableness connecting the visitor and entertainer, was an elemental fragment of Ancient Greek customs. Zeus, occasionally called Zeus Xenos, was as the defender of guests and visitor and at times impersonate himself and petitioned shelter and accommodations from men.

XENOPHILE. Applies to an individual who is captivated by foreign articles related to the practice humanity originally studied use of xenophile in 1948, in the theory defined.

YA (Sanskrit) Precede organizing neutral conceptual nominal (such as bhuya, nature, condition, essence), certifying accessories; etc.

YAH (Sanskrit) Integration that constitute ordinary analytical names (such as bhuya, nature, condition, essence), quality descriptive. They organize the worlds. The consonants in inquest are a public conversion and one of numerous forms of the IAO "Mystery name".

YLMA. This term defines compassion, as well as being a master of one's own destiny and attractiveness. It is extremely in demand for children's forename mainly about the Norther Hemisphere of the globe; however, the origin and Etymology of the word appears to be unknown.

YAVANAS. (Sanskrit) Denomination that in India has been provided with to the Greeks.

YAHIA (Arab.) Appellation of St. John the Baptist in the Muslims.

YAHWEH. The Hebrew genuine name of the Goddess. It in all probability acts for the precise native accentuation mode of articulate of the Tetragramamaton.

YAHUD. The English phrase Jew arise in the Scriptural Torah term Yehudi, significance "from the Kingdom of Judah". 'Yahud' is an Arabic expression. In Hebrew, which is associated to Arabic, the locution is 'Yehudi'. It suggests 'Hew' in the two vocabularies. The term 'Jew", of naturally, is English. Judaism is a theist creed, having faith in one God. It is not an ancestral community. Individuals likewise collaborate or connect with Judaism basically as a result ethnical or developmental essential qualities. Jewish fellowships be capable of contrasting in faith, customs, legislature, geology, native tongue, and autonomous.

YAJUS o YAJUR (Sanskrit) Holy fear; worship; Prayer; Hymn; sacrifice; Text referring to the sacrifice.

YAKIA Is a coveted metronymic it is reasonably administered in African societies, however in addition to exceedingly exclusive in English, Hebrew and Japanese population. Though, the origin of expression allegedly to be undisclosed.

YANA (Sanskrit) Route, way, course; means of escaping transmigration; vehicle; thus, "Mahayana is the great vehicle", and Hinayana the "Lesser Vehicle", adopting with these expressions two schools of religious and theoretical study of Northern Buddhism.

YANG (Chinese philosophy) It is the virile concept of the creation, characterized as masculine and visionary, it is linked with the firmament, fervor and radiance.

YARD or Garden Are also belief of as a comparison of inspiration and freshness. It also embodies realization because of its encircled character as contrasting to the woodland. Gardens are often appraised delicate and constitute fecundity. Ultimately, these settings are images of pleasure, conservation, and purity.

YANTRA. The actual definition of the term 'Yantra' suggests "to control, curb, bind to influence". Yantras are prominent illustrations of infinitive vitalities and the affiliated incantations in outlined design. Sadh guru: A yantra precisely signifies a contraption. An instrument is a consolidation of very deliberate fashion. If you fabricate several models very intentionally and collect them conjointly; ten rag wheels for example; it shifts to a device. A yantra is a configuration, manageable or intricate, regarding a definitive aim.

YATI (Sanskrit) Wise, ascetic, devout, self-dominating, continent, restrained, disciplined; who disowns the world. It is also an estimation of three feet.

YAYIN The Hebrew term I "(Yayin) signifies "wine." According to Genesis 9:20. Noah was the "first to plant a vineyard," therefore making him the first vintner, or manufacturer of wine in the Hebrew Bible. Regarding the word Yayin, there is a Hebrew root Y-N-H which implies "oppress." (See e.g., Ex. 20:20: "ve-ger lo Toneh.") Certainly, this derived from a more palpable root "press" and a prospective simplification for Yayin.

YAMS. They are tremendously valuable in choice and food supplies; therefore, they embody the efficiencies of survival. They are bred to acquire affluence and to support one's descendants. They are an image of manliness and capacity as an entrepreneur. Different from cassava, maize, or rice, yam is an indigenous produce of these district and is so acutely embedded in the traditions of their community. In continuous emblem, it is thanks to the yam that the vitality of the forebears is restored. Consuming yam is certainly satisfying, however, in addition, it is an association. For the Igbo and of Meridional Nigeria, it exemplifies success and prolific. For the Ebie ethnic groups of southeastward Nigeria, the yam supply is not just a gathering, but a representation of long haul, affluence, and praising.

YARN. When you dream of yarn as an image of not actually trustworthy as in 'spinning a yarn.' This can also be an amusement on the term 'yearn' when you are not display your sustainable tendencies. A ball of yarn in a dream can portray completeness and how characteristics that materialize to be contrary are attached. The Urban Dictionary describes yarn as: 'To tell a story, which at any given moment contains a dubious amount of exaggeration.' Introduced only in 1Kings 1;16. The Heb. Word mikveh, I.e., "a stringing together," so rendered, rather signifies a host, or company, of a string of horses."

YEAR Is the spherical interval of a terrestrial framework, for instance, the Earth, in motion in its trajectory circling the Sun. Being that the Earh's axial tilt, the journey of a year discern he is progress of the duration, decided by modification in atmospheric conditions, the time of sunlight, and, as a result, verdures and topsoil productiveness. In climate and global localities encompassing the globe, quadruple time of year are normally identified as; springtime, daylight savings time, autumnal equinox and winter tide. In equatorial and semitropical districts, assorted geological territories relinquish emerge determined active period; however, in the equatorial areas, the per annum soaked and arid time of year are identified and traced. Year is also a rhythm in the Lunisolar calendar of 365 or 366 days (about 1 year) divided into 12 months originating with January and concluding with December. An interval equivalent to one year of the Gregorian calendar but emerging at a diverse schedule. The period of season is one of the logical stretches into which the year is segregated by declinations and Samhain or climatic modes.

YENE Anganta. The precision of anganta Yene is familiar throughout India. It is the performance of an essential (Bhuta), which has been proven into the perceptive and passive body of a medium, takes possession of it; specifically: Anganta Yene exactly means "obsession". The Hindus fear such an adversity now as much as they avoided it multitudes of years ago. "No Indus, Tibetan or Sinhalese, other than of lower intelligence and caste, cannot see without shuddering with horror, the signs of 'mediumship' manifesting themselves in a member of his family, or without saying, as a Christian would now say: 'have the devil,' This 'gift, divine favor and holy mission', as it is called in England and America; in the ancient villages, cradles of our race, where an experience longer than ours has taught them a more spiritual wisdom, is regarded as a horrendous misery."

YERBA An enduring tree, Ilex paraguariensis, cultivated in South America for its blades, which comprise caffeine; family Aquifoliaceae, a restorative pearly drink created from the dehydrated leaves of this tree. Modern Greek name: Paraguay tea, yerba, also yerba mate. Yerba mate is a legal botanical herb (not a controlled substance). Yerba Buena channels good herbs. Yerba Buena (Clinopodium douglasii (Benth.) Clinopodium defines "bent" or "sloping foot," and douglasii process "of Douglas." The regular designation, in Spanish, denotes "good herb." and is often adapted to minty plants like Savoury. Yerba Buena subsist from June 25, 1835, when its first settler, William Richardson pitched a lean-to made of a ship's sail on a sandy ascent what is now Grant and Clay, to Jan. 3o 1847, when the municipality properly modified its lable to San Francisco. Consequently, it was that on January 30, 1847, the Alcade or mayor of Yerba Buena provide a decree rechristen the settlement San Francisco, a transfer supplementary nourishing the borough's dominant place. Over the year 1847, six vessels arrived at the bay to take part in commerce.

YETI The Tibeto-Burman source of yeti is yeh-the, "small manlike animal." Interpretation of yeti as a great hairy anthropoid beast commented to inhabit in the Himalayas' It is sort of an abhorrent snow monster, kind of mythical beast. In legend(s) a few declare that the word "yeti" originates from the Sherpa term "yeh-the, a detailed expression definition "small, man 'like animal" as it may be outdated applied to indicate to the invertebrate. Nevertheless, others declare that the denomination is emanates from the Sherpa word "meti" that channels bear.

YEU (Chin.) "Be"; synonym of Subhava; or "the substance that gives materiality to itself".

YEW A Gothic name for Palm Sunday.

YI-KING (Chinese) Cited to a primitive Chinese work, put in writing by peers' groups of philosophers.

YIMA (Zend) Conforming to the representative, he is the first adult male, and by his aspect as the spiritual progenitor of humanity, he is the equivalent as Yama. Its broadest obligations are not shown in Zen books, for the motive of having vanished a lot of these ancient particles, made them disappear, or for having otherwise prevented them from descending into abusive hands. Yima was not born, since it stands for the first three mortal mother races, the first of whichever is "unborn," but he is the "first man to die," because the third race, the special that was enthusiastic by the rational higher Egos, was the first whose men were disunity into male and female, and "man lived and died and was reborn."

YINS. A prehistoric assumption of nature, in the Chinese Cosmogony the premature proposition of ordinary forces female or compliant; feminine or docile.

YODHA. A champion, a trooper, a soldier. This term is carried off from Sanskrit language 'yoddha', nominal relating to 'yoddhr'.

YOGA One of the six Darsana's or analytical instruction of India.

YOGAVID (Sanskrit) Instructed or carried out in Yoga.

YOM KIPPUR The highest holy day of the Jewish year and pursue a time for recuperation through abstinence and faithfulness. In this demonstration, ultra-Orthodox Jewish male pray at the Westerly Wall through Yong Kippur in the Old City of Jerusalem.

YONG-Grub. (Tibet) A condition of complete repose, the same as Paranirvana.

YONGE, Charlotte Mary (1823-1901), Fable writer. When in 1835 J. Keble advance into pastor of Heusley, she came under his impact. She resolved to try her talent as a storyteller to roll out the faith in stories. Apart from exceedingly admired novels, she wrote about the lives of J.C. Patterson and Hannah More.

YOWE. Is a female sheep ancient, language, Britain, in Scotland a ewe is a lamb. It additionally indicates to grasp or seize instantly, to defer; postpone, to introduce; to send, put, or let in. Combs: rotten Yowe, an ewe stroke with sheep-rot, consequently transmitted of an individual with manifestation of lung disease, exclusively persistent spitting.

YLU. God

YUDH or Yuddha (Sanskrit) Battle, combat, struggle, war, conflict.

YUCA, Cassava, also well-known as yuca or manioc, is a major food in numerous African countries as well as Central America. Early outlines of the species were unclear with the cassava (Manihot esculenta). There are distinctive types of Yucca Plant Variations that can connect a special claim to your backyard and home. Ordinary Name(s): Cassava, Yucca, Joshua tree, Adam's needle, Thread, Spanish dagger, Spanish bayonet, Needle Palm, Yucca Palm, Aloe Yuca. The produce fruit of yucca plants similar across among a cucumber and a pepper. They can be prepared in various techniques as well as fried, stewed, baked, or even eaten raw. Yucca is also eaten by a variety of animals including squirrels and rabbits when other food derivation is in short affords. Yucca consists of a high quantity of vitamin C and antioxidants, both of which can aid the immune system and overall health.

YUGA (Sanskrit) According to Brahmanism, one of the four ages of the Universe. Four Yugas are said to comprise a Maha-Yuga which is in turn the thousandth part of Mahamvantara. Each Yuga is followed by two periods of equal duration: Sandhya and Sandyansa. The four Yugas with their periods are: Krita or Satya Yuga, Tetra Yuga; Duapara Yuga; Kali Yuga. The Krita Yuga Satya Yuga is the Golden Age, of beauty, splendor, bliss without work. Then that Age is preceded by Tetra yuga, The Silver Age; still the beauty here is Lego the Third Age or Dvapara Yuga or Copper Age, in this Age the situation worsens and begins to rival good and evil, wars, achievements, etc. appear. Then comes the fourth Age or Kali Yuga, the Iron Age, the current era or Black Age as it is also called. It is said to have begun in 3,102 B.C. It is considered the worst pruning, so there was a need for various master's to reincarnate to try to save souls or train caline spiritual, since the end of that Age will be preceded by the coming of Vishnu in his reincarnation as Kalki and will end with a great catastrophe. It is said that at the end of this age, there will come a Maia Yugar great Age of the Gods.

YULE Christmas and its auxiliary festivities.

YUNQUE (Sanskrit) (Latin incus, -udis) Harsh iron prism, of quad section, sometimes with a tip in use of the sides, integrate in a long-lasting wooden pit and to write down, for the task, in the hammer the metals. Within alchemy and body; explore patient and female passive construction, as opposed to the clobber of a fractionator. Its deep representation is collected with a generic precise occupation.

YURBO ADONAI Disdainful epithet given by the advocates of the Nazarene Code, the Gnostics of St. John, directed towards the Jehovah of the Jews.

-Z-

ZA. (Sanskrit) Ziva; weapon; happiness; Good omen.

ZABDA (Shabda) (Sanskrit) Sound, noise; voice, cry; word, language, name, title; the desire to proclaimed and show.

ZACHARIEL He will be the Avatara of the future Coradhi Race. Archangel is regent of the planet Jupiter and is a Cosmocrator.

ZACCHAEUS. A tavern keeper, he claimed a tree to glimpse at Christ, and was called by name to draw closer and provide him with lodging in his house (Lk. 19: 1-10).

ZADOKITE. Quram Cave Scrolls, an admired term for the endurance of a on one occasion substantial assemblage of Hasidic and Aramaic ancient manuscripts, detected in caverns around Qumran, at the north-west end of the Dead Sea, in 1947 and the subsequent years. Just about all Books of the canonical OT descriptions which explains the Doctrinal documents as revelations accomplished in the observers' own time. A number of 'Psalms of Thanksgiving', to the Ecclesiastic Psalms; also a strange, conceivably apocalyptic, effort, in which the religious persuasion "The War of the Sons of light against the Sons of Darkness' has been obtained; a reference manual numerously named 'The Manal of Discipline' or 'The Sectarian Document', conveying the regulations administering the existence of the Faithful community to what end the authority acceptance; and 'Damascus Fragments' or 'Zadokite Documents', much the same in nature to the guide book, and apart from that it's held from an preliminary uncovering in the Geniza of the shul. The Scrolls are the property of the library of a Jewish community coextensive at Qumran regarding the dawn of the years of our Lord. It is mostly the barriers 20 B.C. and 70 A.D. They are essential for our awareness of the ancient times of the OT et and for their verification of Jewish reality and reflections at the time.

ZAKA (Saka) (Sanskrit) Greenery, any eatable herbaceous phenomenon. Energy, robustness.

ZAKAH once a year alms tax or poor charge that each Muslim is presumed to pay as a devout duty and that is used for altruistic and dutiful motivation. Zakat (zakaat, zakah), or almsgiving is among the five pillars of Islam. This signifies that Zakat is obligatory for Muslims, including the other four sacred pillars of prayers (salah), fasting (sawm), pilgrimage (hajj) and belief in Allah and his Messenger, Prophet Muhammad (peace be upon him) (Shahadah). Zakah is additionally an intangible relation to one's creator; to refine your prosperity for the will of Allah (swt) is to acknowledge that everything we own belongs to our creator.

ZAKTIS (Sanskrit) There are six primary forces in nature which are summarized by the seventh. The Zukti's force is as follows: 1. Parazakt, fundamentally; the highest-ranking force or power, which in conjunction with the capacity of radiance and intensity. 2. Jnanazakti, the sapience of the intellect, of explicit awareness, has two conditions; the demonstration of such power is under the guidance or authority of material conditions or is free from the relationships of circumstances. 3. Ichchha Akti is the dominance of the will, whose most typical expression is the production of certain nervous steady flow that set-in motion those muscles that are needed for the recognition of the desired matter. 4. Kriya Akti. It is the inexplicable capacity of thought that empowers it to produce visible, prodigious external evidence by its own innate strength. According to primitive history, it is defended that any design could manifest itself evidently if one deeply concentrates one's attention on it. 5. Kundalini Sakti. It is power that continues in a serpentine or curved way. It is a universal conception of life that is carried out in all parts of Nature, as well as feelings of attraction and repulsion. Currents and attractions are revelations of it. 6. Mantrikazakti, force or competence of lyrics, expression or melody. The ability of the prodigious transcendental name is the summit of this Sakti... The Six forces are in their unity exemplified by the astral Light (daiviprakrtii), 7. the illumination of the Logos.

ZAMPUN (Tibet) Honest man; wise; saint. Brahma; Ziva.

ZANTI (Sanskrit) Peace, calm, tranquility, placidity, happiness, well-being; prosperity, beautitud.

ZARANA (Sanskrit) Refuge, asylum, defense; protection, shelter, dwelling, house, place of refuge.

ZATA-Rupa (Sata Rupa) (Sanskrit) The "one in a hundred ways"; subtitle appeal to Vach, which being the maternal Brahma, imagines a hundred forms, that is: Nature.

ZAUIR Anpin. The Microprosopus. (Hebr.) In Kabbalah, it is "the son of the hidden Father," who collects in selfhood all the Sephiroth. Adam Kadmon, or the first materialized "Celestial Man," the Logos.

ZAYYA. (Sanskrit) Bed, bed; sleep, rest.

ZEAL. The interpretation of zeal is enthusiasm and fervent fascinating tracking of substance, intensity. If you possess zeal, you are inclined, vitalized, and driven. Zeal is frequently enforced in a reverent awareness, effect faithfulness to El-Shaddai or other devotions, such as being a preacher. Zeal doesn't have to be religious, though, an eagerness of gusto and fervor for perfect can be labeled zeal. Zealous rhymes with jealous (and genuinely they two arise equivalent to the same Greek word), however don't' confuse them, a jealous individual may be cynical of somebody which produces zealous attempts to attain benefits. Interpretation of Zealous, attribute, considerable by energetic, enthusiasm and fervor; equivalent, fervid ardor, insight.

ZEALOTS A Jewish conglomerate which showed opposition. Narrative to Josephus they were companions of John of Gischel who precipitated the dogmatic resistance in Jerusalem which led to its demolition by the Romans in A.D. 70. They have often been acknowledged as (1) the auxiliary of Judas of Gamala who led a riot in A.D. 6, and (2) the Sicarii, who tried to pull off their ends by enforcing their government challengers and blocked sending the Romans to Masada. There is no compelling cause for either acceptance. The epithet 'zealot' appeal to St. "Simon 'the Less' in Lk. 6: 15 may measure his association to the Zealot group or may purely relate his personality.

ZEBRA. Suggest bilaterality, will power, and acceptance. They also indicate cooperation and correspondence. (Jeremiah 2:24). The Good Book does not allude to zebras by denomination, but they are slightly like the untamed as cited to overhead, besides "snuff up the wind" and appreciate their outback existence, watchful afresh by a compassionate maker. They are broadly related as having innate potential or adept that are very much remarkable to those of the standard the populace in diverse dominion (psychological, inventive, imaginative, flourish). A zorse is the progeny of a zebra stallion and a horse mare. This crossbreed is also labelling a zebrose, zebrulla, zebrule, zebra mule. The inimitable transpose combine is occasionally named a hebra, horsebra, zebrinny, or zebra hinny. Compared to superlative added animal hybrids, the zorse is sterile.

ZENDO (Zend Avesta) [or Sen Dawasta) (Pelv.). Popular appellative of the consecrated books of the Parsis, congregants of the blaze or the sun, as they are alleged out of ignorance. Such a minor fragment has been appreciated of the great dogmas that are still instituted in the abundant remnant that formulate all that has now lingered of the compilation of religious works, that Zoroastrianism is obscurely called Cult of Fire, Mazdeism, or Magism, Dualism, Cult of the Sun, etc. The Avesta, in its present condition now accomplished, has two parts, namely the Vendidad, the Visperad and the Yazna; and the second, called Khorda Avesta, being comprise of short prayers named Gah, Nyayish, etc. Zend signifies "commentary" or "explanation," and Avesta, etc. (from the Old Persian Abashta, "law.")

ZEUS (Greek) The "Father of the Gods". Zeus-Zen is the Aether, and by unification, Jupiter was mentioned as Aether's Father by some Latin races. [Zeus is the Jupiter of Roman mythos.

ZERO From a revered point of view, zero is the situation from which each singular whole number bounces ahead. Since zero in additionally clearly carries a connection with a circle, it is representative of continuance, development, endlessness.

ZEROANA (Pelv.) In its present condition the Chakra or Circle of Vichnu, a mysterious impression that, as said to the illustration of a visionary, is "a curve of such a nature that any and as few of its parts as possible, if the curve were to be prolonged in any direction, would continue and finally re-enter itself, forming what we call a circle." In the same way, the deity has diameters all over creation and its critical position, in inclusion, has existence at all positions of infinity.

ZICHYA (Sanskrit) Disciple, student.

ZIF (Hebrew) A Hebrew month, starting point with the new moon of April.

ZILA (Shila) (Pali) The demoralized potential of the ten Paramitas of advance. Perfect similarities in disagreements and performances. The key to interpretation is voice and action, the flame that disproves the cause and effect, and henceforward leave space for Karmic activity. Zila also means custom; conduct; nature, character; trend, disposition; virtue; morality.

ZION (Hebrew) Written in as a similarity for Jerusalem in addition to the coastline of Israel as an absolute country.

ZIRCON. Is a squarish geologic comprised of a hydrous of zirconium and ongoing routinely in brown or graying square prisms of adamant radiance or occasionally in clear configurations which are prone as precious stones. The zircon is quoted in the Scriptures in the Tanakh, the Torah, and in Exodus 28:15-21, zircon, recite as "jacinth" is the first jewel in the third row in the breastplate of Aaron. This blessed item reports 12 brilliant stones to defining the 12 tribes of Israel. There are educational arguments over in what manner zircon acquired its designation. Neutral zircon is distinguished for its intensity and fluorescent of rainbow gliding, signal enkindled. These zircon developments are directly adequate to the effects of diamond to interpretations for cycles of indecision in the middle the two jewels. Zircon takes place in an formation of coloring.

ZIRAT-BANIT She is the spouse of the soaring and most divine hero of the Assyrian tablets, Merodach. He has been meaningful with the Succoth Benoth of the Bible.

ZIVA (Siva or Shiva) (Sanskrit) Is the third person of the Trimurti or Inda Trinity.

ZOKA (Sanskrit) Attribute to: Pain, sorrow, affliction, anguish, sadness.

ZRAMA (Sanskrit) Action; exhausting exercise; laxity.

ZRI (Sanskrit) Zri or Lakshmi is the wife of Vishnu, goddess of progress and wealth. Zri is conventional as proper names of people, and devices; it is a gesture of approval that measure to divine, blessed, holy, venerable, glorious, blessed, etc. Property, fortune; happiness; well-being, bliss; beauty, ornament, Floria; wealth; treasure; intelligence; superhuman power; satisfaction; dignity, greatness; power; elevated position; majesty; sovereignty.

ZRIMANT or ZRIMAT (Sanskrit) Prosperous, happy; beautiful; splendid; rich; lucky; blessed; glorious; perfect.

ZUKLA (Sanskrit) White, bright, clear, bright. Light, brilliance; the first half of the lunar month, i.e., from the Novellino to the plenilunar; the gleaming or bright fortnight. This stage is favorable for his mental expansion.

ZUDDI (Sanskrit). Purity, purification; clarity; truth.

ZUDDHI (Sanskrit) Symbolizes: Genuine, purification, clarity; truth.

ZUCHI (Sanskrit) One of the authorizations of Nidra and in summation to the third son of Abhimani, son of Agni; this is one of the forty-nine underlying fires. (Zuchi also means clean, pure, clear, honest, holy, virtuous.)

ZUMA. It is a Suid-Afrika family name; external of South Africa, it is also commonplace in various additional African commonwealth and in Brazil, remarkable individuals with this patronymic incorporate Cyril Zuma (1985-2015, South African jock. Zuma was a divinity, and the son of the Aztec snake God Kukulkan ("Plumed serpent" of ("Feathered serpent") He had two aimed serpents (on head in the two ends) that relax on his glenohumeral joint.

ZUNA o Zuni (Sanskrit) Dog.

ZUNYA, (Sunya) (Sanskrit) Vision in the sense that the real world is but a ghost, a dream, a shadow, [Emptiness, the celestial spaces; zero; lack or deprivation of each one; desert.]

ZUNYATA (Sunyata) (Sanskrit) Desolation; space; nothingness, nonexistence. The personality of our destination universe is in the belief of its appearance and fantasy.

ZVETA (Sveta) (Sanskrit) Is a dragon snake; a son of Kashyapa. White; brilliant; white horse.

ZVETARATHA (Sanskrit) The planet Venus.

SEVEN TYPES OF PEOPLE:

Gnostic esotericism rates man into seven categories as follows:

1. The first type of person is someone who use their instinctive-motor center, lives to eat and sleep, they could fluctuate going from a pleasant mode to an unpleasant. These types of people don't like anyone who can harm their comfort, just crave their pleasant pleasures.

2. The second type of people are the ones where the Emotional Center prevails, sometimes it becomes a mystical type. This kind of person may develop in the world of lower emotions, they do not understand reasons, their lives tend to be emotional, unbalanced and even sentimental.

3. It is the one in which the Intellectual center predominates over the emotional and instinctive-motor centers. Their center of gravity is in the intellect, this type of person thinks a lot, theorizes and rambles, they possess subjective reason. They do not understand anything that goes outside of their information acquired by the five senses and their constant subjective reasoning.

4. The fourth level of people, are those which can acquire a permanent center of gravity; within the balance of all centers, is a balanced person, to reach the fourth level of man you must balance the centers of the human machine. The men of the fourth level are beyond the man no 1, 2 and 3, these make up the Tower of Babel, where no one understands anyone. People on the fourth level long, inquire, aspire, know the meaning of life.

5. This level are those people who have created the Solar Astral Body, this class of individuals can acquire self-awareness. To make the astral body; it is necessary to transmute the sexual hydrogen Si-12.

6. The people on the sixth level, are those who have acquired the objective reason, those who possess the solar Mental Body, in addition to the astral,

when the solar Mental Body is acquired, an individual's mind can be possessed. Ordinary people do not possess an individual mind of their own, but many minds, every psychological defect is a mind.

7.   This type of person is the causal person, who possesses the body of the will, is the authentic man. The causal world is the world of the true man, this can control in himself all the states of consciousness, has embodied the spirit and spiritual principles, has received his soul. When a man does not merge with the Divinity, he becomes Hanasmussen.

"The Perfect Matrimony is the union of two beings;
one who loves more, and the other who loves better.
The best religion available to the human race is Love."
Samael Aun Weor